Autodesk CFD 2027 Black Book

By
Gaurav Verma
Matt Weber
(CADCAMCAE Works)

ISBN # 978-1-77459-212-0

NOTICE TO THE READER

Publisher does not warrant or guarantee any of the products described in the text or perform any independent analysis in connection with any of the product information contained in the text. Publisher does not assume, and expressly disclaims, any obligation to obtain and include information other than that provided to it by the manufacturer.

The reader is expressly warned to consider and adopt all safety precautions that might be indicated by the activities herein and to avoid all potential hazards. By following the instructions contained herein, the reader willingly assumes all risks in connection with such instructions.

The Publisher makes no representation or warranties of any kind, including but not limited to, the warranties of fitness for a particular purpose or merchantability, nor are any such representations implied with respect to the material set forth herein, and the publisher takes no responsibility with respect to such material. The publisher shall not be liable for any special, consequential, or exemplary damages resulting, in whole or part, from the reader's use of, or reliance upon, this material.

DEDICATION

To teachers, who make it possible to disseminate knowledge
to enlighten the young and curious minds
of our future generations

To students, who are the future of the world

THANKS

To my friends and colleagues

To my family for their love and support

Training and Consultant Services

At CADCAMCAE WORKS, we provide effective and affordable one to one online training on various software packages in Computer Aided Design(CAD), Computer Aided Manufacturing(CAM), Computer Aided Engineering (CAE), and Computer programming languages(C/C++, Java, .NET, Android, Javascript, HTML and so on). The training is delivered through remote access to your system and voice chat via Internet at any time, any place, and at required pace to individuals, groups, students of colleges/universities, and CAD/CAM/CAE training centers. The main features of this program are:

Training as per your need

Highly experienced Engineers and Technician conduct the classes on the software applications used in the industries. The methodology adopted to teach the software is totally practical based, so that the learner can adapt to the design and development industries in almost no time. The efforts are to make the training process cost effective and time saving while you have the comfort of your time and place, thereby relieving you from the hassles of traveling to training centers or rearranging your time table.

Software Packages on which we provide basic and advanced training are:

CAD/CAM/CAE: CATIA, Creo Parametric, Creo Direct, SolidWorks, Autodesk Inventor, Solid Edge, UG NX, AutoCAD, AutoCAD LT, EdgeCAM, MasterCAM, SolidCAM, DelCAM, BOBCAM, UG NX Manufacturing, UG Mold Wizard, UG Progressive Die, UG Die Design, SolidWorks Mold, Creo Manufacturing, Creo Expert Machinist, NX Nastran, Hypermesh, **SolidWorks Simulation**, Autodesk Simulation Mechanical, Creo Simulate, Gambit, ANSYS and many others.

Computer Programming Languages: C++, VB.NET, HTML, Android, Javascript and so on.

Game Designing: Unity.

Civil Engineering: AutoCAD MEP, Revit Structure, Revit Architecture, AutoCAD Map 3D and so on.

We also provide consultant services for design and development on the above mentioned software packages

For more information you can mail us at:
cadcamcaeworks@gmail.com or info@cadcamcaeworks.com

Table of Contents

Chapter 2 : Model Setup in Autodesk CFD

Chapter 3 : Creating Analysis Model

Chapter 4 : Solving Analysis

Chapter 5 : Analyzing Results

Chapter 6 : Comparing and Visualization

Chapter 7 : Practical

Chapter 8 : Practical and Practice

Preface

Autodesk® CFD is a software developed by Autodesk Inc. to perform computational dynamic study and thermal simulation on the model. There are various areas where CFD is implemented in Design industry. Some examples of CFD applications are finding: Wind resistance of a car or motorcycle, Pressure drop through a valve, Component temperatures in an electronics enclosure, Comfort of people in a crowded meeting hall, and so on.

The **Autodesk CFD 2027 Black Book**, is the 6th edition of our series on Autodesk CFD. The book is targeted for beginners of Autodesk CFD. This book covers the basic equations and terms of Fluid Dynamics theory. The book covers all the major tools of Flow Simulation modules like Fluid Flow, Thermal Fluid Flow, and Electronic Cooling modules. This book can be used as supplement to Fluid Dynamics course if your subject requires the application of Software for solving CFD problems. Some of the salient features of this book are:

In-Depth explanation of concepts

Every new topic of this book starts with the explanation of the basic concepts. In this way, the user becomes capable of relating the things with real world.

Topics Covered

Every chapter starts with a list of topics being covered in that chapter. In this way, the user can easy find the topic of his/her interest easily.

Instruction through illustration

The instructions to perform any action are provided by maximum number of illustrations so that the user can perform the actions discussed in the book easily and effectively. There are about 520 illustrations that make the learning process effective.

Tutorial point of view

The book explains the concepts through the tutorial to make the understanding of users firm and long lasting. Practical of the book are based on real world projects.

For Faculty

If you are a faculty member, then you can ask for video tutorials on any of the topic, exercise, tutorial, or concept. As faculty, you can register on our website to get electronic desk copies of our latest books, self-assessment, and solution of practical. Faculty resources are available in the **Faculty Member** page of our website (**www.cadcamcaeworks.com**) once you login. Note that faculty registration approval is manual and it may take two days for approval before you can access the faculty website.

Formatting Conventions Used in the Text

All the key terms like name of button, tool, drop-down etc. are kept bold.

Free Resources

Link to the resources used in this book are provided to the users via email. To get the resources, mail us at ***cadcamcaeworks@gmail.com*** or ***info@cadcamcaeworks.com*** with your contact information. With your contact record with us, you will be provided latest updates and informations regarding various technologies. The format to write us e-mail for resources is as follows:

Subject of E-mail as ***Application for resources of ....Book***.
You can give your information below to get updates on the book.
Name:
Course pursuing/Profession:
Contact Address:
E-mail ID:

For Any query or suggestion

If you have any query or suggestion please let us know by mailing us on ***cadcamcaeworks@gmail.com***. Your valuable constructive suggestions will be incorporated in our books and your name will be addressed in special thanks area of our books.

About Author

Gaurav Verma is a Mechanical Design Engineer with deep knowledge of CAD, CAM and CAE field. He has an experience of more than 12 years on CAD/CAM/CAE packages. He has delivered presentations in Autodesk University Events on AutoCAD Electrical and Autodesk Inventor. He is an active member of Autodesk Knowledge Share Network. He has provided content for Autodesk Design Academy. He is also working as technical consultant for many Indian Government organizations for Skill Development sector. He has authored books on SolidWorks, Mastercam, Creo Parametric, Autodesk Inventor, Autodesk Fusion, and many other CAD-CAM-CAE packages. He has developed content for many modular skill courses like Automotive Service Technician, Welding Technician, Lathe Operator, CNC Operator, Telecom Tower Technician, TV Repair Technician, Casting Operator, Maintenance Technician and about 50 more courses. He has his books published in English, Russian, Spanish, and Hindi worldwide.

He has trained many students on mechanical, electrical, and civil areas of CAD-CAM-CAE. He has trained students online as well as offline. He has a small workshop of 20 CNC and VMC machines where he challenges his CAM skills on different Automotive components. He is providing consultant services to more than 15 companies worldwide. You can contact the author directly at cadcamcaeworks@gmail.com

Chapter 1

Introduction to Autodesk CFD

Topics Covered

The major topics covered in this chapter are:

- ***Introduction to Fluid Mechanics***
- ***Introduction to CFD***
- ***Introduction to Autodesk CFD***
- ***Downloading Autodesk CFD***

INTRODUCTION OF FLUID MECHANICS

During the course, you will know various aspects of Autodesk CFD for various practical problems. But, keep in mind that all computer software work on same concept of GIGO which means Garbage In - Garbage Out. So, if you have specified any wrong parameter while defining properties of analysis then you will not get the correct results. This problem demands a good knowledge of Fluid Mechanics so that you are well conversant with the terms of classical fluid mechanics and can relate the results to the theoretical concepts. In this chapter, we will discuss the basics of Fluid Mechanics and we will try to relate them with analysis wherever possible.

BASIC PROPERTIES OF FLUIDS

There are various basic properties required while performing analysis on fluid. These properties are collected by performing experiments in labs. Most of these properties are available in the form of tables in Steam Tables or Design Data books. These properties are explained next.

Mass Density, Weight Density, and Specific Gravity

- Density or Mass Density is the mass of fluid per unit volume. In SI units, mass is measured in kg and volume is measured in m^3. So, mathematically we can say,

$$\text{Density (or Mass Density) } \rho = \frac{Mass\ of Fluid}{Volume\ Occupied\ by\ Fluid}\ \text{kg/m}^3$$

- If you are asked for weight density then multiply mass by gravity coefficient. Mathematically it can be expressed as:

$$\text{Weight Density w} = \frac{Mass\ of Fluid \times Gravity\ Coefficient}{Volume\ Occupied\ by\ Fluid}\ \text{N/m}^3$$

- Most of the time, fluid density is available as **Specific Gravity**. Specific gravity is the ratio of weight density of fluid to weight density of water in case of liquid. In case of gases, it is the ratio of weight density of fluid to weight density of air. Note that weight density of water is 1000 kg/m^3 at 4 °C and weight density of air is 1.225 kg/m^3 at 15 °C.

Note that as the temperature of liquid rises, its density is reduced and vice-versa. But as the temperature of gas rises, its density is increased and vice-versa.

Viscosity

Viscosity is the coefficient of friction between different layers of fluid. In other terms, it is the shear stress required to produce unit rate of shear strain in one layer of fluid. Mathematically it can be expressed as:

$$\mu = \frac{\tau}{(\frac{dx}{dy})}\ \text{N.s/m}^2 \text{ or Pa.s}$$

Where, μ is viscosity, τ is shear stress (or force applied tangentially to the layer of fluid) and (dx/dy) is the shear strain.

As the density of fluid changes with temperature so does the viscosity. The formula for viscosity of fluid at different temperature is given next.

For Liquids, $\mu = \mu_0 \frac{1}{1 + \alpha t + \beta t^2}$

For Gases, $\mu = \mu_0 + \alpha t - \beta t^2$

here, μ_0 is viscosity at 0 °C

α and β are constants for fluid (for water α is 0.03368 and β is 0.000221)

(for air α is 5.6×10^{-8} and β is 1.189×10^{-10})

t is the temperature

PROBLEM ON VISCOSITY

Dynamic viscosity of lubricant oil used between shaft and sleeve is 8 poise. The shaft has a diameter of 0.4 m and rotates at 250 r.p.m. Find out the power lost due to viscosity of fluid if length of sleeve is 100 mm and thickness of oil film is 1.5 mm; refer to below figure.

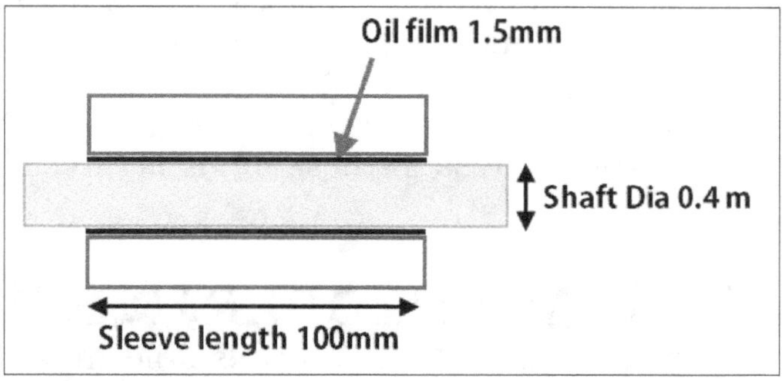

Solution:

Viscosity μ = 8 poise = 8/10 N.s/m² =0.8 N.s/m²

Tangential velocity of shaft $u = \frac{\pi \times D \times N}{60} = \frac{\pi \times 0.4 \times 250}{60}$ = 5.236 m/s

Using the relation, $\tau = \mu \frac{dx}{dy}$

where dx is 5.236

and dy is 1.5×10^{-3}

$\tau = 0.8 \times \frac{5.236}{1.5 \times 10^{-3}}$ = 2792.53 N/m²

Shear force F = τ x Area

$F = \tau \times \pi D \times L = 2792.53 \times \pi \times 0.4 \times 100 \times 10^{-3} = 350.92$ N

Torque (T) = Force x Radius = 350.92 x 0.2 = 70.184 N.m

Power = 2 π.N.T/60 = (2 π x 250 x 70.184)/60=1837.41 W Ans.

Now, you may ask how this problem relates with CFD. As discussed earlier, the viscosity changes with temperature and as fluid flows through pipe or comes in contact with rolling shaft, its temperature rises. In such cases, CFD gives the approximate viscosity and temperature of fluids in the system at different locations. This data later can be used to find solution for other engineering problems.

TYPES OF FLUIDS

There are mainly 5 types of fluids:

Ideal Fluids: These fluids are incompressible and have no viscosity which means they flow freely without any resistance. This category of fluid is imaginary and used in some cases of calculations.

Real Fluids: These are the fluids found in real world. These fluids have viscosity values as per their nature and can be compressible in some cases.

Newtonian Fluids: Newtonian fluids are those in which shear stress is directly proportional to shear strain. In a specific temperature range, water, gasoline, alcohol etc. can be Newtonian fluids.

Non-Newtonian Fluids: Those fluids in which shear stress is not directly proportional to shear strain. Most of the time Real Fluids fall in this category.

Ideal Plastic Fluids: Those fluids in which shear stress is more than yield value and so fluid deforms plastically. The shear stress in these fluids is directly proportional to shear strain.

THERMODYNAMIC PROPERTIES OF FLUID

Most of the liquids are not considered as compressible in general applications as their molecules are already bound closely to each other. But, Gas have large gap between their molecules and can be compressed easily relative to liquids. As we pick pressure to compress the gas, other thermodynamic properties also come into play. The relationship between Pressure, Temperature, and specific Volume is given by;

$$P.\forall = RT$$

P = Absolute pressure of a gas in N/m^2
$\forall$ = Specific Volume = $1/\rho$
R = Gas Constant (for Air is 287 J/Kg-K
T = Absolute Temperature
ρ = Density of gas

If the density of gas changes with constant temperature then the process is called Isothermal process and if density changes with no heat transfer then the process is called Adiabatic process.

For Isothermal process, p/ρ = Constant
For Adiabatic process, p/ρ^k = Constant

Here, k is Ratio of specific heat of a gas at constant pressure and constant volume (1.4 for air).

Universal Gas Constant

By Pressure, Temperature, volume equation,

$$p.\forall = nMRT$$

Here,

p = Absolute pressure of a gas in N/m^2
∀ = Specific Volume = 1/ ρ
n = Number of moles in a Volume of gas
M = Mass of gas molecules/ Mass of Hydrogen atom = n x m (m is mass gas in kg)
R = Gas Constant (for Air is 287 J/Kg-K
T = Absolute Temperature

MxR is called Universal Gas constant and is equal to 8314 J/kg-mole K for water.

Compressibility of Gases

Compressibility is reciprocal of bulk modulus of elasticity K, which is defined as ratio of Compressive stress to volumetric strain.

Bulk Modulus = Increase in pressure/ Volumetric strain

K = -(dp/d∀)x∀

Vapour Pressure and Cavitation

When a liquid converts into vapour due to high temperature in a vessel then vapours exert pressure on the walls of vessel. This pressure is called **Vapour pressure**.

When a liquid flows through pipe, sometimes bubbles are formed in the flow. When these bubbles collapse at the adjoining boundaries then they erode the surface of tube due to high pressure burst of bubble. This erosion is in the form of cavities at the surface of tube and the phenomena is called **Cavitation**.

PASCAL'S LAW

Pascal's Law states that pressure at a point in static fluid is same in all directions. In mathematical form $p_x=p_y=p_z$ in case of static fluids.

FLUID DYNAMICS

Up to this point, the rules stated in this chapter were for static fluid that is fluid at rest. Now, we will discuss the rules for flowing fluid.

Bernoulli's Incompressible Fluid Equation

Bernoulli's equation states that the total energy stored in fluid is always same in a closed system. In the language of mathematics,

$$p + \frac{1}{2}\rho V^2 + \rho g h = constant$$

Here, p is pressure
ρ is density
V is velocity of fluid
h is height of fluid
g is gravitational acceleration

Eulerian and Lagrangian Method of Analysis

There are two different points of view in analyzing problems in fluid mechanics. The first view, appropriate to fluid mechanics, is concerned with the field of flow and is called the eulerian method of description. In the eulerian method, we compute the pressure field p(x, y, z, t) of the flow pattern, not the pressure changes p(t) that a particle experiences as it moves through the field.

The second method, which follows an individual particle moving through the flow, is called the lagrangian description. The lagrangian approach, which is more appropriate to solid mechanics, will not be treated in this book. However, certain numerical analyses of sharply bounded fluid flows, such as the motion of isolated fluid droplets, are very conveniently computed in lagrangian coordinates.

Fluid dynamic measurements are also suited to the eulerian system. For example, when a pressure probe is introduced into a laboratory flow, it is fixed at a specific position (x, y, z). Its output thus contributes to the description of the eulerian pressure field p(x, y, z, t). To simulate a lagrangian measurement, the probe would have to move downstream at the fluid particle speeds; this is sometimes done in oceanographic measurements, where flow meters drift along with the prevailing currents.

Now, we know the two methods of analyzing fluid mechanics problem. But, there are further three approaches for these two methods by which problems are derived to solution. These approaches are:

1. Control Volume
2. Differential
3. Experimental

Control volume analysis, is accurate for any flow distribution but is often based on average or "one dimensional" property values at the boundaries. It always gives useful "engineering" estimates. In principle, the differential equation approach can be applied to any problem. Only a few problems, such as straight pipe flow, yield to exact analytical solutions. But the differential equations can be modeled numerically, and the flourishing field of computational fluid dynamics (CFD) can now be used to give good estimates for almost any geometry. Finally, the dimensional analysis applies to any problem, whether analytical, numerical, or experimental. It is particularly useful to reduce the cost of experimentation.

Since the Differential Equation approach is more concerned to CFD so we will discuss this approach a little deeper.

DIFFERENTIAL APPROACH OF FLUID FLOW ANALYSIS

As discussed earlier, in this approach, the fluid is divided in to very small finite number of elements via a computer process called meshing. Various equations for different properties of a fluid are given next.

Acceleration

Acceleration **a** can be given as:

$$\mathbf{a} = \frac{d\mathbf{V}}{dt} = \mathbf{i}\frac{du}{dt} + \mathbf{j}\frac{dv}{dt} + \mathbf{k}\frac{dw}{dt}$$

Various components of acceleration **a** are:

$$a_x = \frac{du}{dt} = \frac{\partial u}{\partial t} + u\frac{\partial u}{\partial x} + v\frac{\partial u}{\partial y} + w\frac{\partial u}{\partial z} = \frac{\partial u}{\partial t} + (\mathbf{V} \cdot \nabla)u$$

$$a_y = \frac{dv}{dt} = \frac{\partial v}{\partial t} + u\frac{\partial v}{\partial x} + v\frac{\partial v}{\partial y} + w\frac{\partial v}{\partial z} = \frac{\partial v}{\partial t} + (\mathbf{V} \cdot \nabla)v$$

$$a_z = \frac{dw}{dt} = \frac{\partial w}{\partial t} + u\frac{\partial w}{\partial x} + v\frac{\partial w}{\partial y} + w\frac{\partial w}{\partial z} = \frac{\partial w}{\partial t} + (\mathbf{V} \cdot \nabla)w$$

Summing these into a vector, we obtain the total acceleration as

$$a = \frac{dV}{dt} = \frac{\partial V}{\partial t} + \left(u\frac{\partial V}{\partial x} + v\frac{\partial V}{\partial y} + w\frac{\partial V}{\partial z}\right) = \frac{\partial V}{\partial t} + (V.\nabla)V$$

Similarly, you can divide other parameters as vector like Force, Pressure, Temperature, and so on.

INTRODUCTION TO CFD

The CFD stands for Computational Fluid Dynamics. It uses computations based on theory and experimental data to derive solutions for fluid dynamics problems. In the seventeenth century, the foundations for experimental fluid dynamics were laid in France and England. The eighteenth and nineteenth centuries saw the gradual development of theoretical fluid dynamics, again primarily in Europe. As a result, throughout most of the twentieth century the study and practice of fluid dynamics involved the use of theory on the one hand and pure experiment on the other hand.

Computational Fluid Dynamics constitutes a new "third approach" in the philosophical study and development of the whole discipline of fluid dynamics. It nicely and synergistically complements the other two approaches of pure theory and pure experiment, but it will never replace either of these approaches. There will always be a need for theory and experiment. The future advancement of fluid dynamics will rest upon a balance of all three approaches, with computational fluid dynamics helping to interpret and understand the results of theory, experiment and vice-versa; refer to Figure-1.

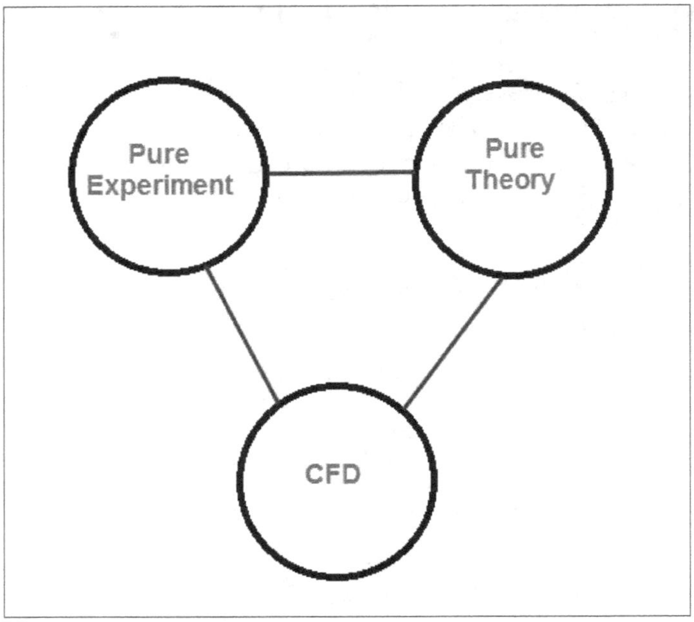

Figure-1. The three dimensions of fluid dynamics

Note that computational fluid dynamics is commonplace enough today that the composition CFD is universally accepted for the phrase "Computational Fluid Dynamics". We will use this composition throughout the book.

Computational fluid dynamics (CFD) is the use of applied math, physics, and computational software package to examine how a gas or liquid flows, also as how the gas or liquid affects objects as it flows past. Computational fluid dynamics software function based on the Navier-Stokes equations. These equations describe how the velocity, pressure, temperature, and density of a moving fluid are related.

Navier-Stokes equation

The Navier-Stokes equations are the elemental partial differentials equations that describe the flow of incompressible fluids. Using the rate of stress and rate of strain, it can be shown that the parts of a viscous force F during a non rotating frame are given by-

$$\begin{aligned}\frac{F_i}{V} &= \frac{\partial}{\partial x_j}\left[\eta\left(\frac{\partial u_i}{\partial x_j}+\frac{\partial u_j}{\partial x_i}\right)+\lambda\delta_{ij}\nabla\cdot\mathbf{u}\right] \\ &= \frac{\partial}{\partial x_j}\left[\eta\left(\frac{\partial u_i}{\partial x_j}+\frac{\partial u_j}{\partial x_i}-\tfrac{2}{3}\delta_{ij}\nabla\cdot\mathbf{u}\right)+\mu_B\delta_{ij}\nabla\cdot\mathbf{u}\right],\end{aligned}$$

Where η is the dynamic viscosity, λ is the second viscosity coefficient, δ_{ij} is the Kronecker delta, $\nabla.\mathrm{u}$ is the divergence, μ_B is the bulk viscosity and Einstein summation has been used to sum over j=1, 2, and 3.

- **Dynamic Viscosity**

Dynamic viscosity is the force required by a fluid to overcome its own internal molecular friction so the fluid can flow. In other words, dynamic viscosity is defined as the tangential force per unit area required to move the fluid in one horizontal plane with reference to other plane with a unit velocity whereas the fluid's molecules maintain a unit distance apart.

A parameter η is defined as

[Shear Stress] = η [Strain Rate]

Written explicitly.

$$\sigma = \eta \dot{e} = \eta \frac{1}{l} \frac{dl}{dt} = \eta \frac{u}{l},$$

Where l is the length scale and u is the velocity scale. In cgs η has units of g cm^{-1} s^{-1}. Dynamic viscocity is related to kinematic viscocity ν by

$$\eta = \rho \nu$$

Where ρ is the density.

- **Second Viscosity Coefficient**

For a compressible fluid, i.e. one for which ∇.u=0, where ∇.u is the divergence Σ of the velocity field, the stress tensor of the fluid can be written

$$S_{ij} = \eta \left(\frac{\partial u_i}{\partial x_j} + \frac{\partial u_j}{\partial x_i} \right) + \lambda \delta_{ij} \nabla \cdot \mathbf{u},$$

Where δ_{ij} is the Kronecker delta, η is the dynamic viscosity, and λ is the second coefficient of viscosity. λ is analogous to the first Lame constant. For an incompressible fluid, the term involving λ drops out from the equation, so λ can be ignored.

- **Kronecker Delta**

The simplest interpretation of the Kronecker delta is as the discrete version of the delta function defined by

$$\delta_{ij} = \begin{cases} 1 & i = j \\ 0 & i \neq j \end{cases}$$

The Kronecker delta is implemented in the Wolfram language as KroneckerDelta[i, j], as well as in a generalized form KroneckerDelta[i, j, ...] that returns 1 if all arguments are equal and 0 otherwise. It has the contour integral representation

$$\delta_{mn} = \frac{1}{2\pi i} \oint_{\gamma} z^{m-n-1} \, dz,$$

Where γ is a contour corresponding to the unit circle and m and n are integers.

In three space, the Kronecker delta satisfies the identities

$$\delta_{ii} = 3$$
$$\delta_{ij} \epsilon_{ijk} = 0$$
$$\epsilon_{ipq} \epsilon_{jpq} = 2\delta_{ij}$$
$$\epsilon_{ijk} \epsilon_{pqk} = \delta_{ip}\delta_{jq} - \delta_{iq}\delta_{jp},$$

where Einstein summation is implicitly assumed. i,j=1,2,3,and ϵ_{ijk} is the permutation symbol.

Technically, the Kronecker delta is a tensor defined by the relationship

$$\delta_l^k \frac{\partial x_i'}{\partial x_k} \frac{\partial x_l}{\partial x_j'} = \frac{\partial x_i'}{\partial x_k} \frac{\partial x_k}{\partial x_j'} = \frac{\partial x_i'}{\partial x_j'}.$$

Since, by definition, the coordinates x_i and x_j are independent for i=j,

$$\frac{\partial x_i'}{\partial x_j'} = \delta'^i_j,$$

So

$$\delta'^i_j = \frac{\partial x_i'}{\partial x_k} \frac{\partial x_l}{\partial x_j'} \delta_l^k,$$

and δ'^i_j is really a mixed second-rank tensor. It satisfies

$$\delta_{ab}{}^{jk} = \epsilon_{abi}\epsilon^{jki}$$
$$= \delta_a^j \delta_b^k - \delta_a^k \delta_b^j$$
$$\delta_{abjk} = g_{aj} g_{bk} - g_{ak} g_{bj}$$
$$\epsilon_{aij}\epsilon^{bij} = \delta_{ai}{}^{bi}$$
$$= 2\delta_a^b.$$

- **Divergence**

The divergence of a vector field **F**, denoted div(**F**) or ∇.**F** (the notation used in this work), is defined by a limit of the surface integral

$$\nabla \cdot \mathbf{F} \equiv \lim_{V \to 0} \frac{\oint_S \mathbf{F} \cdot d\mathbf{a}}{V}$$

Where the surface integral provides the value of **F** integrated over a closed small boundary surface $S=\partial V$ surrounding a volume component V that is taken to size zero using a limiting method. The divergence of vector field is thus a scalar field. If ∇.**F**=0, then the filed is alleged to be a divergence less field. The symbol ∇ is referred to as nabla or del.

- **Bulk Viscosity**

The Bulk viscosity μ_B of a fluid is defined as

$$\mu_B = \lambda + \tfrac{2}{3}\mu,$$

Where λ is the second viscosity coefficient and μ is the shear viscosity.

- **Reynolds Number**

The Reynolds number for a flow through a pipe is defined as

$$\mathrm{Re} \equiv \frac{\rho \bar{u} d}{h} = \frac{\bar{u} d}{\nu},$$

Where ρ is the density of the fluid, **u** is the velocity scale, d is the pipe diameter and v is the kinematic viscosity of the fluid. Poiseuille (laminar) flow is experimentally found to occur for **Re<30**. At larger
Reynolds numbers flow become turbulent.

- **Density**

A measure of a substance's mass per unit of volume. For a substance with mass **m** and volume **V**,

$$\rho \equiv \frac{m}{V}.$$

For a body weight w_a placed in a fluid of weight $w_{w,}$

$$\rho = G_s \rho_w = \frac{w_a}{w_a - w_w} \rho_w,$$

Where G_s is the specific gravity for an ideal gas,

$$\rho = \frac{mP}{kT}.$$

- **Kinematic Viscosity**

A coefficient which describes the diffusion of momentum. Let η be the dynamic viscosity, then

$$\nu \equiv \frac{\eta}{\rho}.$$

The unit of kinematic viscosity is Stoke, equal to 1 $cm^2 s^{-1}$
V_{water} = 1.0 X 10^{-6} $m^2 s^{-1}$ =0.010 $cm^2 s^{-1}$
V_{air} = 1.5 X 10^{-5} $m^2 s^{-1}$ = 0.15 $cm^2 s^{-1}$

The story of CFD starts with Navier-Strokes equation. This equation is based on conservation laws of mass, momentum, and energy. These law's can be defined as:

CONSERVATION OF MASS

The conservation of mass law states that the mass in the control volume can be neither created nor destroyed in accordance with physical laws. The conservation of mass, also expressed as Continuity Equation, states that the mass flow difference throughout system between inlet- and outlet-section is zero. In equation terms, we can write as:

$$\frac{D_\rho}{D_t} + \rho\left(\nabla \cdot \vec{V}\right) = 0$$

Where, ρ is density, V is velocity and gradient operator ∇

$$\vec{\nabla} = \vec{i}\frac{\partial}{\partial x} + \vec{j}\frac{\partial}{\partial y} + \vec{k}\frac{\partial}{\partial z}$$

When density of fluid is constant, the flow is assumed as incompressible and then this equation represents a steady state process:

$$\frac{D_\rho}{D_t} = 0 \quad \text{so,} \quad \nabla \cdot \vec{V} = \frac{\partial u}{\partial x} + \frac{\partial v}{\partial y} + \frac{\partial w}{\partial z} = 0$$

here, u, v, and w are components of velocity at point (x,y,z) at time t.

Note that incompressible fluid is also called Newtonian fluid when stress/strain curve is linear.

CONSERVATION OF MOMENTUM

The momentum in a control volume is kept constant, which implies conservation of momentum that we call 'The Navier-Stokes Equations'. The description is set up in accordance with the expression of Newton's Second Law of Motion:

F=m.a

where, F is the net force applied to any particle, a is the acceleration, and m is the mass. In case the particle is a fluid, it is convenient to divide the equation to volume of particle to generate a derivation in terms of density as follows:

$$\rho\frac{DV}{D_t} = f = f_{body} + f_{surface}$$

in which f is the force exerted on the fluid particle per unit volume, and f_{body} is the applied force on the whole mass of fluid particles as below:

$$f_{body} = \rho \cdot g$$

Where, ρ is density, g is gravitational acceleration. External forces which are deployed through the surface of fluid particles, $f_{surface}$ is expressed by pressure and viscous forces as shown below:

$$f_{surface} = \nabla \cdot \tau_{ij} = \frac{\partial \tau_{ij}}{\partial x_i} = f_{pressure} + f_{viscous}$$

where τ_{ij} is expressed as stress tensor. According to the general deformation law of Newtonian viscous fluid given by Stokes, τ_{ij} is expressed as

$$\tau_{ij} = -p\delta_{ij} + \mu\left(\frac{\partial u_i}{\partial x_j} + \frac{\partial u_j}{\partial x_i}\right) + \delta_{ij}\lambda\nabla \cdot V$$

Hence, Newton's equation of motion can be specified in the form as follows:

$$\rho\frac{DV}{D_t} = \rho \cdot g + \nabla \cdot \tau_{ij}$$

Navier-Stokes equations of Newtonian viscous fluid in one equation gives:

$$\underbrace{\rho\frac{DV}{D_t}}_{I} = \underbrace{\rho \cdot g}_{II} - \underbrace{\nabla p}_{III} + \underbrace{\frac{\partial}{\partial x_i}\left[\mu\left(\frac{\partial v_i}{\partial x_j} + \frac{\partial v_j}{\partial x_i}\right) + \delta_{ij}\lambda\nabla \cdot V\right]}_{IV}$$

I : Momentum convection

II: Mass force

III: Surface force

IV: Viscous force

where, static pressure ρ and gravitational force ρ.g. The equation is convenient for fluid and flow fields both transient and compressible. D/D_t indicates the substantial derivative as follows:

$$\frac{D()}{D_t} = \frac{\partial()}{\partial t} + u\frac{\partial()}{\partial x} + v\frac{\partial()}{\partial y} + w\frac{\partial()}{\partial z} = \frac{\partial()}{\partial t} + V \cdot \nabla()$$

If the density of fluid is accepted to be constant, the equations are greatly simplified in which the viscosity coefficient μ is assumed constant and ∇·V=0 in equation. Thus, the Navier-Stokes equations for an incompressible three-dimensional flow can be expressed as follows:

$$\rho\frac{DV}{Dt} = \rho g - \nabla p + \mu\nabla^2 V$$

For each dimension when the velocity is V(u,v,w):

$$\rho\left(\frac{\partial u}{\partial t} + u\frac{\partial u}{\partial x} + v\frac{\partial u}{\partial y} + w\frac{\partial u}{\partial z}\right) = \rho g_x - \frac{\partial p}{\partial x} + \mu\left(\frac{\partial^2 u}{\partial x^2} + \frac{\partial^2 u}{\partial y^2} + \frac{\partial^2 u}{\partial z^2}\right)$$

$$\rho\left(\frac{\partial v}{\partial t} + u\frac{\partial v}{\partial x} + v\frac{\partial v}{\partial y} + w\frac{\partial v}{\partial z}\right) = \rho g_y - \frac{\partial p}{\partial y} + \mu\left(\frac{\partial^2 v}{\partial x^2} + \frac{\partial^2 v}{\partial y^2} + \frac{\partial^2 v}{\partial z^2}\right)$$

$$\rho\left(\frac{\partial w}{\partial t} + u\frac{\partial w}{\partial x} + v\frac{\partial w}{\partial y} + w\frac{\partial w}{\partial z}\right) = \rho g_z - \frac{\partial p}{\partial z} + \mu\left(\frac{\partial^2 w}{\partial x^2} + \frac{\partial^2 w}{\partial y^2} + \frac{\partial^2 w}{\partial z^2}\right)$$

p , u, v, and w are unknowns where a solution is sought by application of both continuity equation and boundary conditions. Besides, the energy equation has to be considered if any thermal interaction is available in the problem.

CONSERVATION OF ENERGY

The Conservation of Energy is the first law of thermodynamics which states that the sum of the work and heat added to the system will result in the increase of energy of the system:

$$dE_t = dQ + dW$$

where dQ is the heat added to the system, dW is the work done on the system, and dE_t is the increment in the total energy of the system. One of the common types of energy equation is :

$$\rho\left[\underbrace{\frac{\partial h}{\partial t}}_{I} + \underbrace{\nabla\cdot(hV)}_{II}\right] = \underbrace{-\frac{\partial p}{\partial t}}_{III} + \underbrace{\nabla\cdot(k\nabla T)}_{IV} + \underbrace{\phi}_{V}$$

I : Local change with time

II: Convective term

III: Pressure work

IV: Heat flux

V: Heat dissipation term

The Navier-Stokes equations have a non-linear structure and various complexities so it is hardly possible to conduct an exact solution of those equations. Thus, with regard to the physical domain, both approaches and assumptions are partially applied to simplify the equations. Some assumptions also need to be applied to provide a reliable model in which the equation is carried out to further step in terms of complexity such as turbulence.

VARIATIONS OF NAVIER-STROKES EQUATION

The solution of the Navier-Stokes equations can be realized with either analytical or numerical methods. The analytical method is the process that only compensates solutions in which non-linear and complex structures of the Navier-Stokes equations are ignored within several assumptions. It is only valid for simple / fundamental cases such as Couette flow, Poisellie flow, etc. Almost every case in fluid dynamics comprises non-linear and complex structures in the mathematical model which cannot be ignored to sustain reliability. Hence, the solution of the Navier-Stokes equations are carried out with several numerical methods. Various parameters based on which Navier-Strokes equation can vary are given next.

Time Domain

The analysis of fluid flow can be conducted in either steady (time-independent) or unsteady (time-dependent) condition depending on the physical incident. In case the fluid flow is steady, it means the motion of fluid and parameters do not rely on change in time, the term $\partial()/\partial\tau=0$ where the continuity and momentum equations are re-derived as follows:

Continuity equation:

$$\frac{\partial(\rho u)}{\partial x}+\frac{\partial(\rho v)}{\partial y}+\frac{\partial(\rho w)}{\partial z}=0$$

The Navier-Stokes equation in x direction:

$$\rho\left(u\frac{\partial u}{\partial x}+v\frac{\partial u}{\partial y}+w\frac{\partial u}{\partial z}\right)=\rho g_x-\frac{\partial p}{\partial x}+\mu\left(\frac{\partial^2 u}{\partial x^2}+\frac{\partial^2 u}{\partial y^2}+\frac{\partial^2 u}{\partial z^2}\right)$$

While the steady flow assumption negates the effect of some non-linear terms and provides a convenient solution, variation of density is a hurdle that keeps the equation in a complex formation.

Compressibility

Due to the flexible structure of fluids, the compressibility of particles is a significant issue. Despite the fact that all types of fluid flow are compressible in a various range regarding molecular structure, most of them can be assumed to be incompressible in which the density changes are negligible. Thus, the term $\partial\rho/\partial t = 0$ is thrown away regardless of whether the flow is steady or not, as below:

Continuity equation:

$$\frac{\partial u}{\partial x} + \frac{\partial v}{\partial y} + \frac{\partial w}{\partial z} = 0$$

The Navier-Stokes equation in x direction:

$$\rho\left(\frac{\partial u}{\partial t} + u\frac{\partial u}{\partial x} + v\frac{\partial u}{\partial y} + w\frac{\partial u}{\partial z}\right) = \rho g_x - \frac{\partial p}{\partial x} + \mu\left(\frac{\partial^2 u}{\partial x^2} + \frac{\partial^2 u}{\partial y^2} + \frac{\partial^2 u}{\partial z^2}\right)$$

As incompressible flow assumption provides reasonable equations, the application of steady flow assumption concurrently enables us to ignore non-linear terms where $\partial()/\partial t=0$. Moreover, the density of fluid in high speed cannot be accepted as incompressible in which the density changes are important. "The Mach Number" is a dimensionless number that is convenient to investigate fluid flow, whether incompressible or compressible.

$$Ma = \frac{V}{a} \leq 0.3$$

where, Ma is the Mach number, V is the velocity of flow, and a is the speed of sound at 340.29 m/s at sea level.

As in above equation, when the Mach number is lower than 0.3, the assumption of incompressibility is acceptable. On the contrary, the change in density cannot be negligible in which density should be considered as a significant parameter. For instance, if the velocity of a car is higher than 100 m/s, the suitable approach to conduct credible numerical analysis is the compressible flow. Apart from velocity, the effect of thermal properties on the density changes has to be considered in geophysical flows.

Low and High Reynolds Numbers

The Reynolds number, the ratio of inertial and viscous effects, is also effective on Navier-Stokes equations to truncate the mathematical model. While Re -> ∞, the viscous effects are presumed negligible and viscous terms in Navier-Stokes equations are removed. The simplified form of Navier-Stokes equation, described as Euler equation, can be specified as follows.

The Navier-Stokes equation in x direction:

$$\rho\left(\frac{\partial u}{\partial t} + u\frac{\partial u}{\partial x} + v\frac{\partial u}{\partial y} + w\frac{\partial u}{\partial z}\right) = \rho g_x - \frac{\partial p}{\partial x}$$

Even though viscous effects are relatively important for fluids, the inviscid flow model partially provides a reliable mathematical model as to predict real process for some specific cases. For instance, high-speed external flow over bodies is a broadly used approximation where inviscid approach reasonably fits. While Re<<1, the inertial effects are assumed negligible where related terms in Navier-Stokes equations drop out. The simplified form of Navier-Stokes equations is called either creeping flow or Stokes flow.

The Navier-Stokes equation in x direction:

$$\rho g_x - \frac{\partial p}{\partial x} + \mu\left(\frac{\partial^2 u}{\partial x^2} + \frac{\partial^2 u}{\partial y^2} + \frac{\partial^2 u}{\partial z^2} +\right) = 0$$

Having tangible viscous effects, creeping flow is a suitable approach to investigate the flow of lava, swimming of microorganisms, flow of polymers, lubrication, etc.

Turbulence

The behavior of the fluid under dynamic conditions is a challenging issue that is compartmentalized as laminar and turbulent. The laminar flow is orderly at which motion of fluid can be predicted precisely. Except that, the turbulent flow has various hindrances, therefore it is hard to predict the fluid flow which shows a chaotic behavior. The Reynolds number, the ratio of inertial forces to viscous forces, predicts the behavior of fluid flow whether laminar or turbulent regarding several properties such as velocity, length, viscosity, and also type of flow. Whilst the flow is turbulent, a proper mathematical model is selected to carry out numerical solutions. Various turbulent models are available in literature and each of them has a slightly different structure to examine chaotic fluid flow.

Turbulent flow can be applied to the Navier-Stokes equations in order to conduct solutions to chaotic behavior of fluid flow. Apart from the laminar, transport quantities of the turbulent flow, it is driven by instantaneous values. Direct numerical simulation (DNS) is the approach to solving the Navier-Stokes equation with instantaneous values. Having district fluctuations varies in a broad range, DNS needs enormous effort and expensive computational facilities. To avoid those hurdles, the instantaneous quantities are reinstated by the sum of their mean and fluctuating parts as follows:

$$instantaneous\,value = \overline{mean\,value} + fluctuating\,value'$$

$$u = \overline{u} + u'$$

$$v = \overline{v} + v'$$

$$w = \overline{w} + w'$$

$$T = \overline{T} + T'$$

where u, v, and w are velocity components and T is temperature.

Instead of instantaneous values which cause non-linearity, carrying out a numerical solution with mean values provides an appropriate mathematical model which is named "The Reynolds-averaged Navier-Stokes (RANS) equation". The fluctuations can be negligible for most engineering cases which cause a complex mathematical model. Thus, RANS turbulence model is a procedure to close the system of mean flow equations. The general form of The Reynolds-averaged Navier-Stokes (RANS) equation can be specified as follows:

Continuity equation:

$$\frac{\partial \overline{u}}{\partial x} + \frac{\partial \overline{v}}{\partial y} + \frac{\partial \overline{w}}{\partial z} = 0$$

The Navier-Stokes equation in x direction:

$$\rho\left(\frac{\partial \overline{u}}{\partial t} + \overline{u}\frac{\partial \overline{u}}{\partial x} + \overline{v}\frac{\partial \overline{u}}{\partial y} + \overline{w}\frac{\partial \overline{u}}{\partial z}\right) = \rho g_x - \frac{\partial \overline{p}}{\partial x} + \mu\left(\frac{\partial^2 u}{\partial x^2} + \frac{\partial^2 u}{\partial y^2} + \frac{\partial^2 u}{\partial z^2}\right)$$

The turbulence model of RANS can also vary regarding methods such as k-omega, k-epsilon, k-omega-SST, and Spalart-Allmaras which have been used to seek a solution for different types of turbulent flow.

Likewise, large eddy simulation (LES) is another mathematical method for turbulent flow which is also comprehensively applied for several cases. Tough LES ensures more accurate results than RANS, it requires much more time and computer memory. As in DNS, LES considers to solve the instantaneous Navier-Stokes equations in time and three-dimensional space.

Favre Time Averaging

In Favre-averaging, the time averaged equations can be simplified significantly by using the density weighted averaging procedure suggested by Favre. If Reynolds time averaging is applied to the compressible form of the Navier-Stokes equations, some difficulties arise. In particular, the original form of the equations is significantly altered. To see this, consider Reynolds averaging applied to the continuity equation for compressible flow.

Favre time averaging can be defined as follows. The instantaneous solution variable, ϕ, is decomposed into a mean quantity, $\tilde{\phi}$, and fluctuating component, ϕ'', as follows:

$$\phi = \tilde{\phi} + \phi''$$

The Favre time-averaging is then

$$\overline{\rho\phi(x_i, t)} = \frac{1}{T}\int_{t-T/2}^{t+T/2} \rho(x_i, t')\phi(x_i, t')\, dt' = \overline{\rho\tilde{\phi}} + \overline{\rho\phi''} = \bar{\rho}\tilde{\phi}$$

Where,

$$\tilde{\phi}(x_i, t) \equiv \frac{1}{\bar{\rho}T}\int_{t-T/2}^{t+T/2} \rho(x_i, t')\phi(x_i, t')\,\mathrm{d}t', \qquad \overline{\rho\phi''} \equiv 0$$

Favre-Averaged Navier-Stokes (FANS) Equations can be given as:

Continuity Equation:

$$\frac{\partial}{\partial t}(\bar{\rho}) + \frac{\partial}{\partial x_i}(\bar{\rho}\tilde{u}_i) = 0$$

Momentum Equation:

$$\frac{\partial}{\partial t}(\bar{\rho}\tilde{u}_i) + \frac{\partial}{\partial x_j}(\bar{\rho}\tilde{u}_i\tilde{u}_j + \bar{p}\delta_{ij}) = \frac{\partial}{\partial x_j}\left(\bar{\tau}_{ij} - \overline{\rho u_i'' u_j''}\right)$$

Favre-Averaged Reynolds Stress Tensor:

$$\lambda = -\overline{\rho u_i'' u_j''}$$

Turbulent Kinetic Energy:

$$\frac{1}{2}\overline{\rho u_i'' u_i''} = -\frac{1}{2}\lambda_{ii} = \bar{\rho}\tilde{k}$$

STEPS OF COMPUTATIONAL FLUID DYNAMICS

The process of solving Computational Fluid Dynamics can be defined in 5 stages which are: Creating Mathematical Model, Discretization of model, Analyzing with Numerical Scheme, Getting solution, and Post Processing (Visualization). These steps are discussed next.

Creating Mathematical Model

In this stage, various equations are defined based on physical properties, boundary conditions, and other real-world parameters of the problem. The mathematical model generally consists of partial differential equations, integral equations, and combinations of both. In this case, it will be Navier-Stokes equation with other mathematical equations to define boundary conditions and thermodynamic properties. Note that at this step there will be some assumptions which converting real problem into mathematical model like material might be assumed isotropic, heat conditions might be considered adiabatic and so on. These assumptions should generate permissible level of error in the solution and as a designer you should be aware of the quantum of those errors.

Discretization of Model

While studying the behavior of fluid, you will find that there are infinite number of particles with different physical properties in the fluid stream. These infinite particles will generate infinite equations to solve if mathematical model is to be solved directly which is not possible. So, we convert the mathematical model into finite number of elements and then we can solve equations for each of the element. In case of CFD, elements are called cells. The process of converting a mathematical model into finite element equations is called discretization. In simple words, the partial differential and integral equations are converted into algebraic equations of **A.x = B**.

There are many methods to perform discretization of mathematical model like Finite Difference Method, Finite Volume Method, and Finite Element Method which use mesh type structuring of the model. There are also methods which do not use mesh like Smooth Particle Hydrodynamics (SPH) and Finite Pointset Method (FPM). Note that there is again loss of information at the stage of discretization.

Analyzing with Numerical Schemes

Numerical scheme is the complete setup of equations with all the parameters and boundary conditions defined as needed. The scheme also includes numerical methods by which these equations will be solved and limiting points upto which the equations will be solved. When you start analyzing the problem with specified numerical scheme, there is no input required from your side in system; everything is automatic by computer. Every numerical scheme need to satisfy some basic requirements which are consistency, stability, convergence, and accuracy.

Solution

At this stage, we get the solution of equations as different basic variables like pressure, speed, volume, and so on. The resulting flow variables are obtained at each grid point/mesh point whether the scheme is time dependent (transient) or steady.

Visualization (Post-processing)

At this stage, everything is based on interpretation of designer. Various desired parameters are derived from basic calculated parameters at this stage. You also need to check whether results of CFD analysis are realistic or not.

Now, one question left here to understand in more detail is discretization. Discretization can be performed by various methods like FDM, FVM, FEM, and so on as discussed earlier. Out of these methods, Finite Difference Method and Finite Volume Methods are the most used methods for CFD. Here, we will discuss FDM in detail.

FINITE DIFFERENCE METHOD

At discretization stage, the model need to be converted into numerical grid with different cells defined by nodes; refer to Figure-2. For a 2D problem, i and j will be used for direction in horizontal and vertical directions.

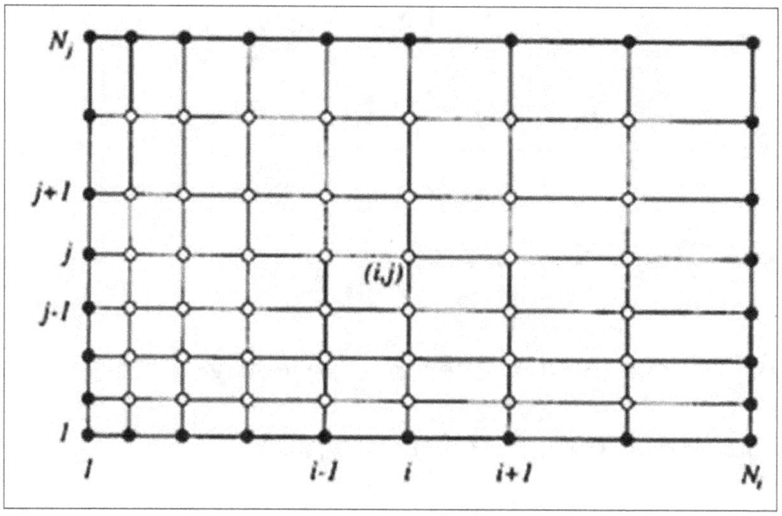

Figure-2. Grid with cartesian coordinates of nodes

If you recall the definition of derivative: $\left(\frac{\partial u}{\partial x}\right)_{x_i} = \lim_{\Delta x \to 0} \frac{u(x_i + \Delta x) - u(x_i)}{\Delta x}$

The equation represents slope of tangent to a curve u(x) which can be geometrically represented as shown in Figure-3.

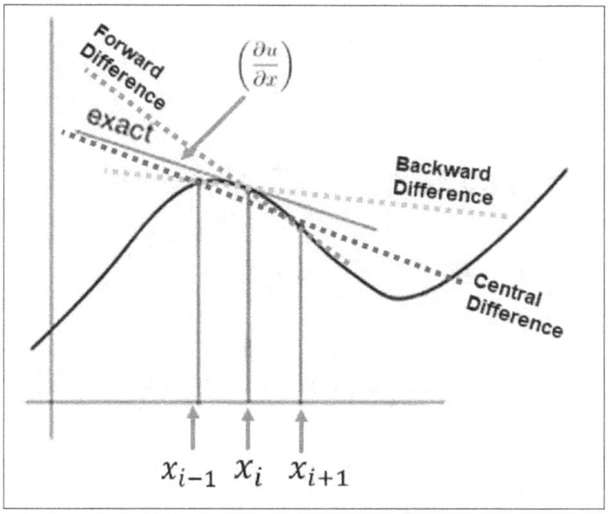

Figure-3. Geometrical interpretation of derivative

Now, assume that we have value of x_i,x_{i+1}, and x_{i-1} then there are three ways in which we can find the slope of curve.

Backward Difference which uses x_i and x_{i-1}.
Forward Difference which uses x_i and x_{i+1}.
Central Difference which uses x_{i+1} and x_{i-1}.

If we assume that Δx is difference between two consecutive nodes then lower the value of Δx more accurate we will get the value of slope.

For a uniform grid where Δx is same for each node then based on

Backward Difference : $\frac{du}{dx} \cong \frac{u_i - u_{i-1}}{\Delta x}$

Forward Difference : $\frac{du}{dx} \cong \frac{u_{i+1} - u_i}{\Delta x}$

Central Difference : $\frac{du}{dx} \cong \frac{u_{i+1} - u_{i-1}}{2\Delta x}$

Now, if you expand the backward difference derivative using Taylor's series then

Consider a function u(x) and its derivative at point x,

$$\left(\frac{\partial u}{\partial x}\right)_{x_i} = \lim_{\Delta x \to 0} \frac{u(x_i + \Delta x) - u(x_i)}{\Delta x}$$

If u(x + Δx) is expanded in Taylor series about u(x), we obtain

$$u(x + \Delta x) = u(x) + \Delta x \frac{\partial u(x)}{\partial x} + \frac{(\Delta x)^2}{2} \frac{\partial^2 u(x)}{\partial x^2} + \frac{(\Delta x)^3}{3!} \frac{\partial^3 u(x)}{\partial x^3} + \cdots$$

If we substitute this value in derivative equation then

$$\frac{\partial u(x)}{\partial x} = \lim_{\Delta x \to 0} \left(\frac{\partial u(x)}{\partial x} + \frac{\Delta x}{2} \frac{\partial^2 u(x)}{\partial x^2} + \cdots \right)$$

Based on this equation, we can write u in Taylor Series at i+1 and i-1 as:

$$u_{i+1} = u_i + \Delta x \left(\frac{\partial u}{\partial x}\right)_i + \frac{\Delta x^2}{2}\left(\frac{\partial^2 u}{\partial x^2}\right)_i + \frac{\Delta x^3}{3!}\left(\frac{\partial^3 u}{\partial x^3}\right)_i + \frac{\Delta x^4}{4!}\left(\frac{\partial^4 u}{\partial x^4}\right)_i + \cdots$$

$$u_{i-1} = u_i - \Delta x \left(\frac{\partial u}{\partial x}\right)_i + \frac{\Delta x^2}{2}\left(\frac{\partial^2 u}{\partial x^2}\right)_i - \frac{\Delta x^3}{3!}\left(\frac{\partial^3 u}{\partial x^3}\right)_i + \frac{\Delta x^4}{4!}\left(\frac{\partial^4 u}{\partial x^4}\right)_i + \cdots$$

Re-writing the above two equations, we get:

Forward difference : $\left(\frac{\partial u}{\partial x}\right)_i = \frac{u_{i+1} - u_i}{\Delta x} + O(\Delta x)$

Backward Difference : $\left(\frac{\partial u}{\partial x}\right)_i = \frac{u_i - u_{i-1}}{\Delta x} + O(\Delta x)$

Central Difference : $\left(\frac{\partial u}{\partial x}\right)_i = \frac{u_{i+1} - u_{i-1}}{2\Delta x} + O(\Delta x^2)$

Note that central difference takes second derivative of delta x so the value of error is lesser than compared to forward or backward difference. For example if forward or backward difference gives an error of 0.001 then second derivative will be 0.001 x 0.001 which gives 0.000001. This error value is a lot lesser.

You can learn more about these methods in books dedicated to Finite Difference Method and solution techniques.

INTRODUCTION TO AUTODESK CFD

Autodesk CFD is a powerful tool used to understand the behavior of fluid on a component design (Inside or Outside). The fluid can either be liquid or gas depends on the Designer's choice and real environment factors. To understand and calculate the effect of various natural and man-made process or operation had been a challenge for the humanity since history. This inspired the greatest scientist to develop the science of fluid dynamics and its equations to harness the power of operations. These equations are very difficult to solve and also consume lots of time. Equations like, Continuity Equation, X- Momentum Equation, Y- Momentum Equation, Z-Momentum Equation, and some equations are stated above. These equations are so complex that even sometimes scientist are unable to solve these equations by hand. Due to the complexity of solving these types of equation by hand, it led to a software revolution that uses computers to solve these types of equations and to predict the behavior of fluid in a real-time situation. With the use of these software, one can easily understand and predict the behavior of fluid on the design of product.

Use of Autodesk CFD

CFD is used in various aspects of a dynamics study. Fluids affect the properties of component, device, or structure through various ways. To predict these affect, we use the CFD based software. CFD is a important part of design process which benefits the areas like risk reduction, energy efficiency, and innovation. Following are some of the uses of CFD.

- **Increase Efficiency**

Fluids are all around us and they take energy to move from one place to another. By understanding the effects and forces of fluid dynamics, you can make a design of a particular product that uses less energy of fluid and also improve efficiency.

- **Risk Reduction**

You have heard these problems before, like product failure, vehicle failure, structure failure, computer overheats, structure collapse due to high winds. In these cases, there may be a reason of unfair prediction of structure or parts with respects to the fluids. By running CFD analysis throughout the design process, one can reduce the chances of failure of product by solving many issues before they turn into a problem.

- **Innovation throughout Insight**

The testing of prototype of a model in real situation could be costly and give discrete data. Also this process is time consuming. The CFD analysis in a software gives us a complete view of the flow and effects of fluid on the model structure. This can reduce the risk of failure of a component.

Applications of Autodesk CFD

- Optimization of HVAC designs.
- Validation of diverse design parameters.
- Aerodynamics

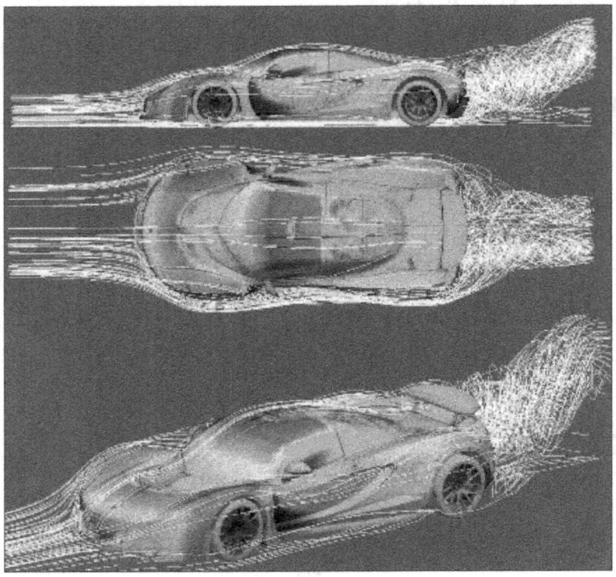

- Industrial Fluid Dynamics

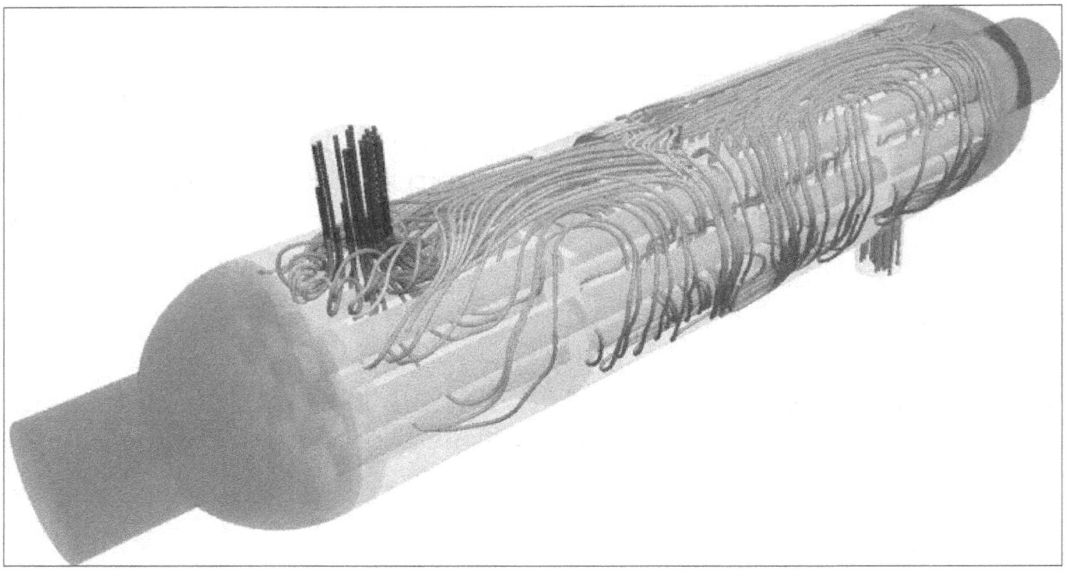

- Fluid Structure Interaction
- Heat Transfer
- Hydrodynamics
- Multi-phase Flows

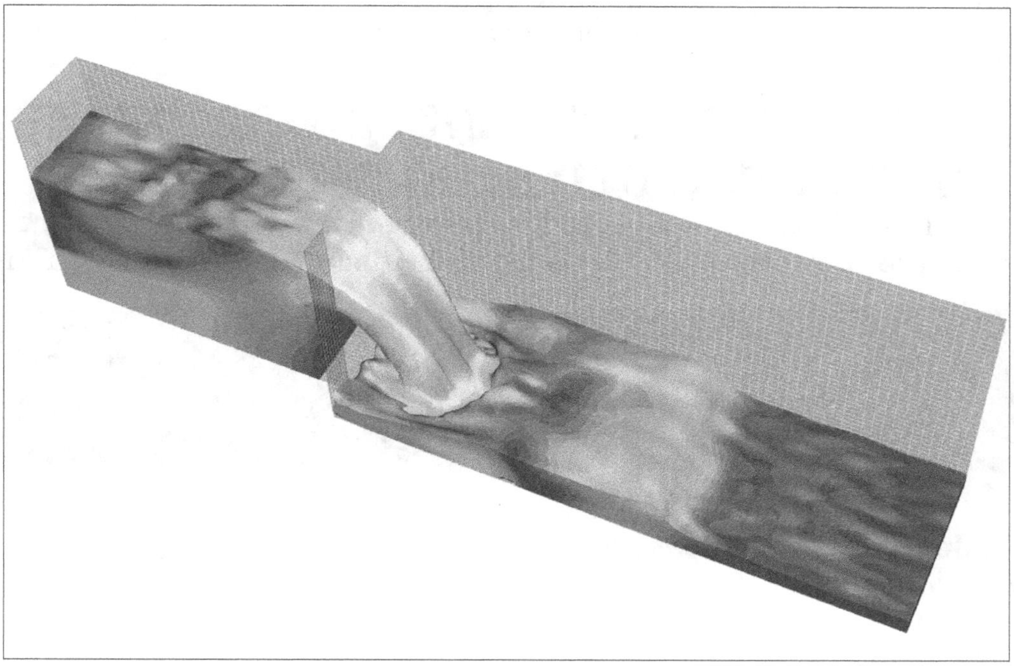

- CFD helps in design verification of systems like, displacement ventilation system, vestibule smoke system, natural ventilation system.

How does CFD works

CFD software uses computer to solve mathematical equations for the problem. The main component of CFD design cycle are listed below:

- The Designer or Analyst who states the problem to be solved.
- Scientific knowledge of model and methods, expressed mathematically.
- The software which embodies this knowledge and provides detailed instructions in the form of algorithm.
- The computer hardware which perform the actual calculations.
- The analyst who inspects and interprets the simulation results.

Advantages of Autodesk CFD

You can do CFD analysis throughout the design process to enhance the properties of structure to make a good design.

- Good insight into systems that might be difficult to prototype or test through experimentation.
- Ability to foresee design changes and optimize accordingly.
- Predict mass flow rates, pressure drops, mixing rates, heat transfer rates & fluid dynamic forces.

Sometimes, CFD is able to simulate real conditions like:

- Some flow and heat transfer processes cannot be tested, e.g. hypersonic flow.
- CFD provides the ability to theoretically simulate any physical condition
- CFD permits great control over the physical processes and offers the ability to isolate specific phenomena for study.

- CFD permits the analyst to examine a large number of locations in the area of interest and yields a comprehensive set of flow parameters for examination.

DOWNLOADING AND INSTALLING AUTODESK CFD STUDENT VERSION

- Reach the link : **https://www.autodesk.com/education/edu-software/overview** from your web browser. The web page will be displayed as shown in Figure-4.

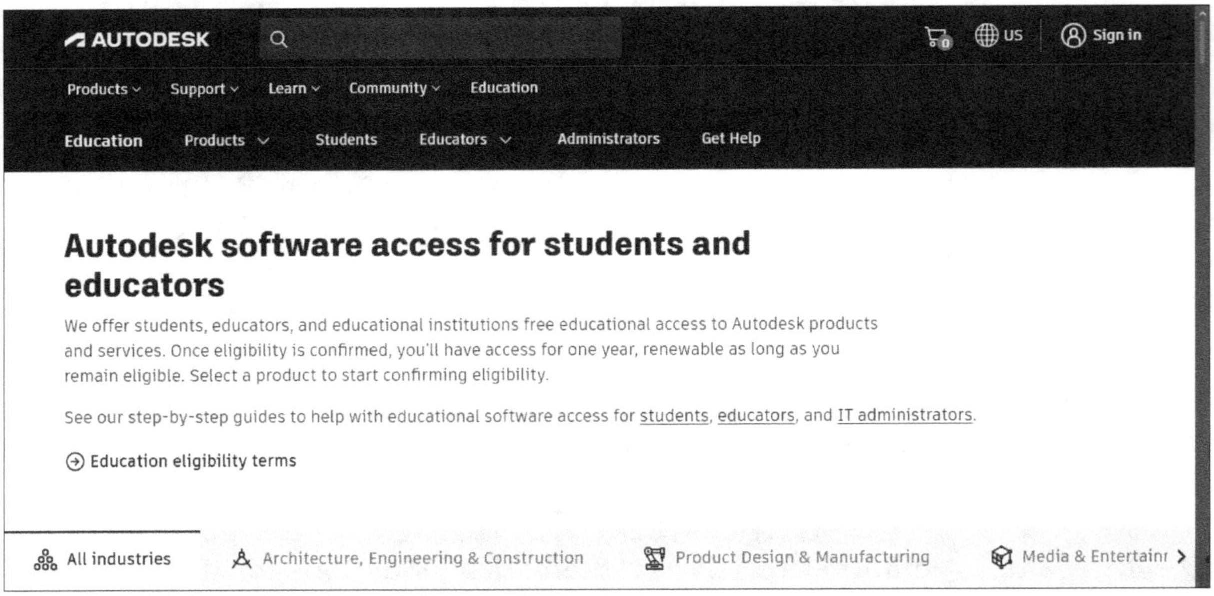

Figure-4. Autodesk website

- Click on the **Select** button for **Autodesk CFD Ultimate** from the webpage. The web page to define your current role will be displayed.
- Click on the **Select** button for Student from the page. Click on the **Continue** button from the notification shown on web page. The **Sign up** page will be displayed; refer to Figure-5.

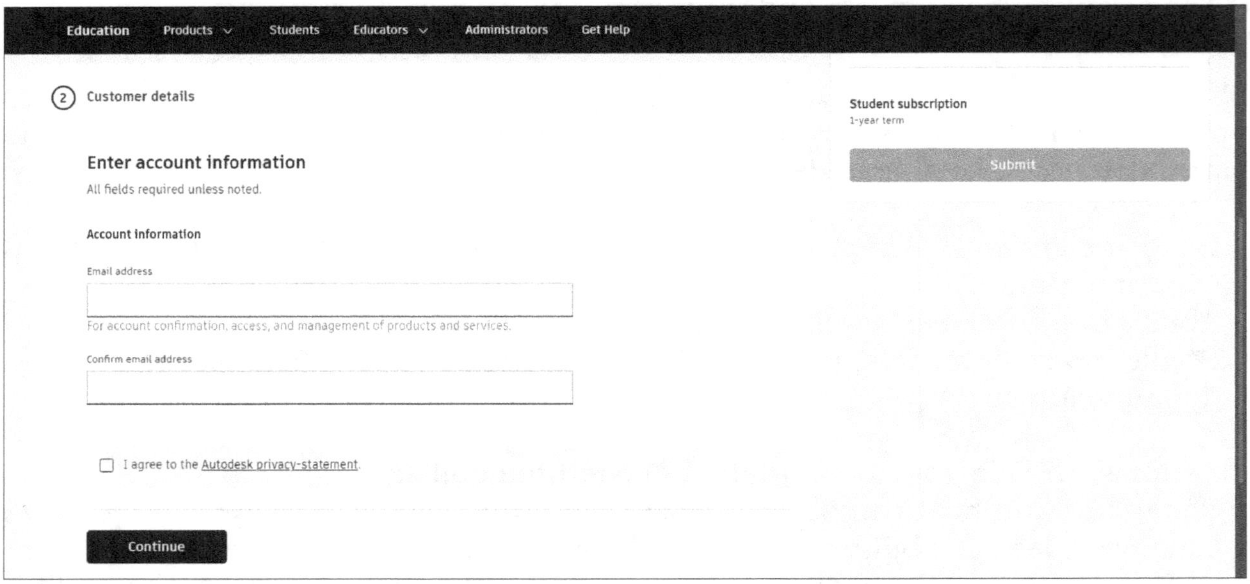

Figure-5. Sign up page

- Enter your student E-mail ID in the fields, select the check box, and click on the **Continue** button.
- Fill the other details as asked on webpage. After completion of these processes, you may be asked to upload your documentation like ID card scan or receipt to confirm your student status. Once your account is approved which can take up to 2 days, you need to sign-in to your Autodesk Account and search for the **Autodesk CFD software**.
- Click on the **Get product** button below the software name. The **Access** button will become active; refer to Figure-6. Click on this button to download the **Autodesk CFD software**.

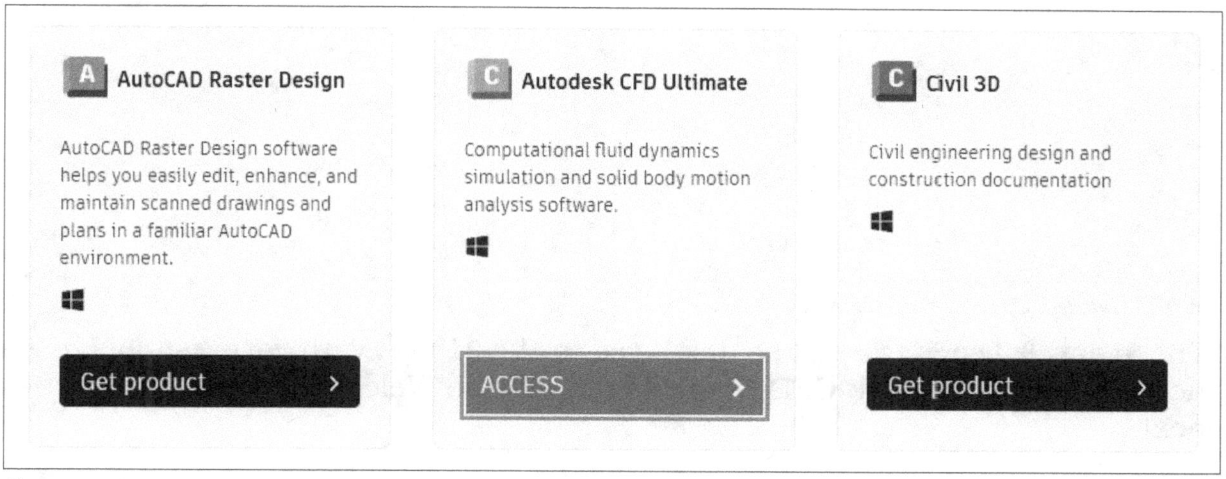

Figure-6. Access button

- Open the download setup file and follow the instructions as per the setup instruction. The software will be installed in a couple of minutes.

STARTING AUTODESK CFD

- To start **Autodesk CFD** from **Start** menu, click on the **Start** button in the **Taskbar** at the bottom left corner, click on **Autodesk** folder, and select the **CFD 2027** icon; refer to Figure-7. The Autodesk CFD software welcome window will be displayed; refer to Figure-8.

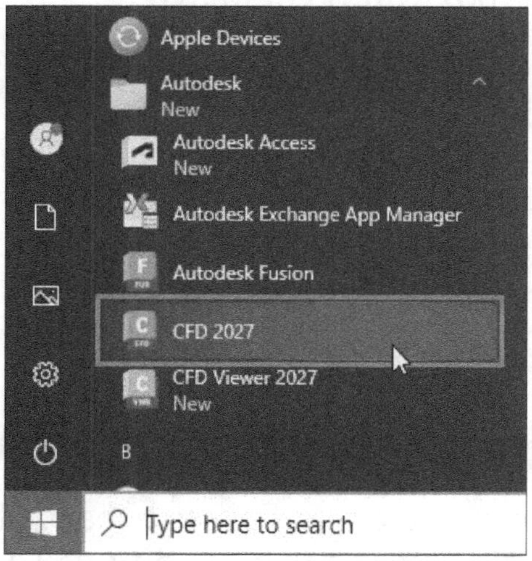

Figure-7. CFD 2027 icon from Start Menu

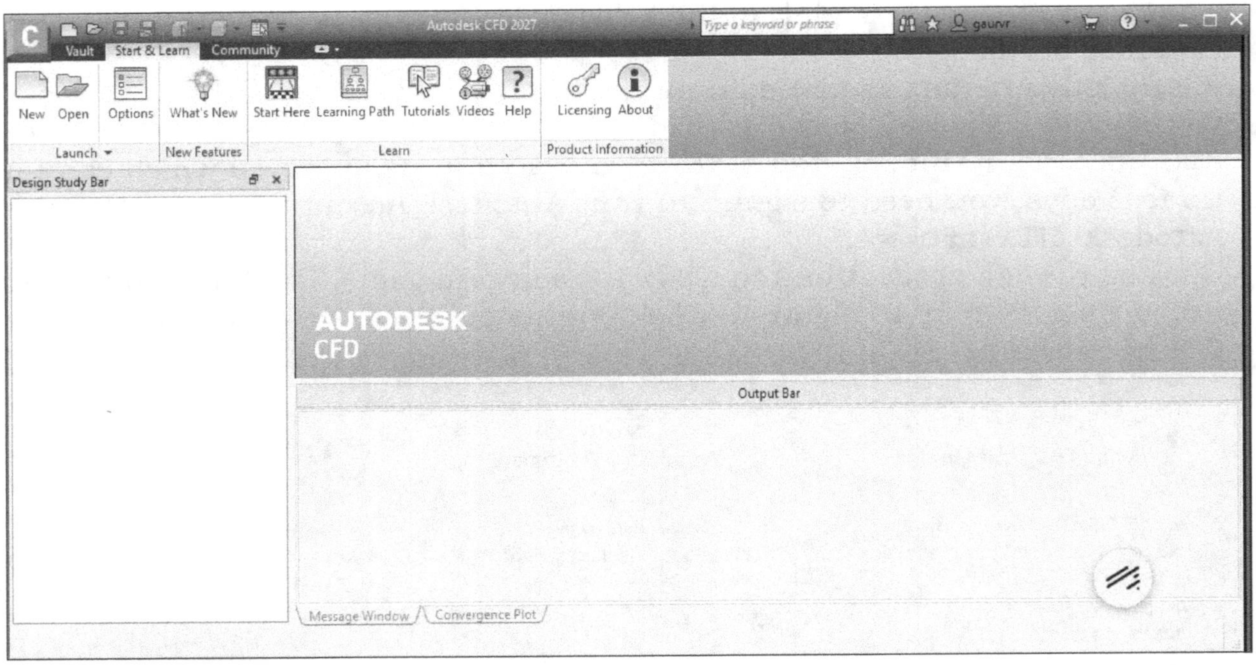

Figure-8. Autodesk CFD welcome window

- The **Start & Learn** tab will be displayed in the **Ribbon** with various tools to learn new topics of Autodesk CFD. Various tabs in the Welcome screen are discussed next.

Start & Learn tab

The tools of **Start & Learn** tab are used to explore and learn Autodesk CFD. There are also tools to create or open an analysis of CFD. These tools are discussed next.

New

The **New** tool is used to create a new study file in Autodesk CFD. The procedure to use this tool is discussed next.

- Click on the **New** button from **Launch** section to create a new design study. The **New Design Study** dialog box will be displayed; refer to Figure-9.

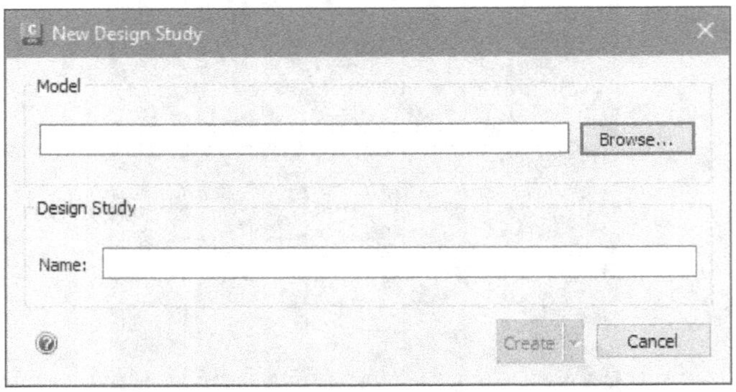

Figure-9. New Design Study dialog box

In Autodesk CFD, you cannot create or design a part file. This software is only for analysis of model or structure as per given condition. To create a part, you will need a CAD software like Autodesk Fusion, Autodesk Inventor, SolidWorks, AutoCad, etc. You can check our other books like, Autodesk Fusion Black Book, SolidWorks 2026 Black Book, and Autodesk Inventor 2027 Black Book to learn about these software.

- Click on the **Browse** button from **New Design Study** dialog box. The **Create New Design Study** dialog box will be displayed; refer to Figure-10.

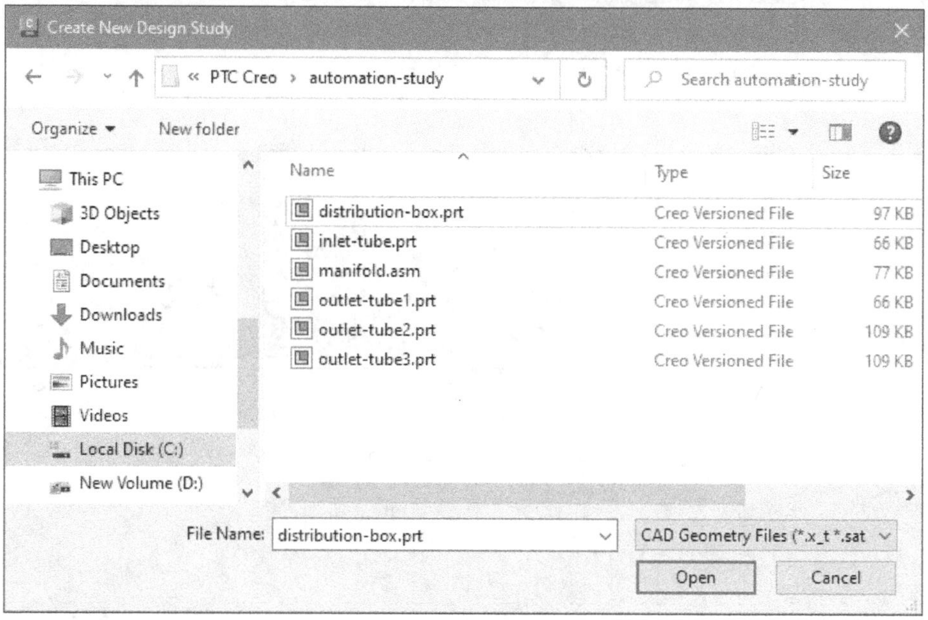

Figure-10. Create New Design Study dialog box

- Click on the **File Format selection** drop-down and select desired format for file to be opened; refer to Figure-11.

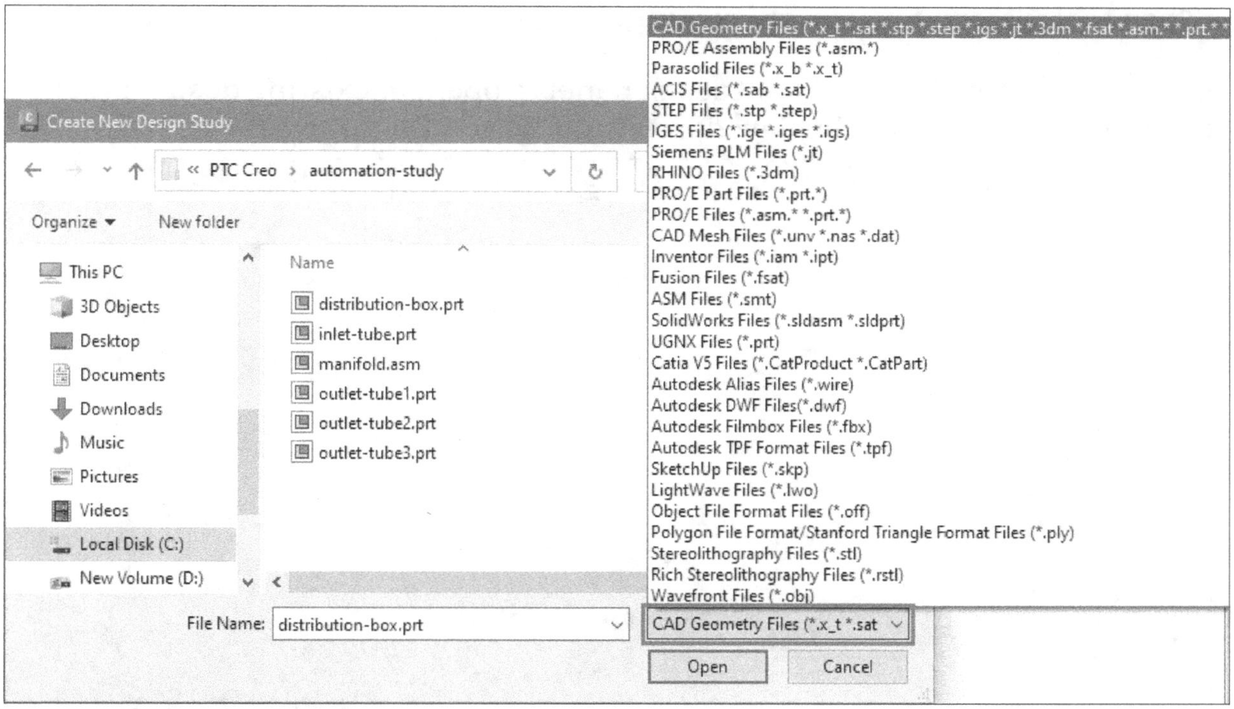

Figure-11. File Format Selection drop-down

- Select desired file from **Create New Design Study** dialog box and click on the **Open** button. You will return to **New Design Study** box where you can check the name of your selected file.
- Specify desired name for new design study and click on the **Create** button. The model will be displayed in graphics window along with all options activated; refer to Figure-12.

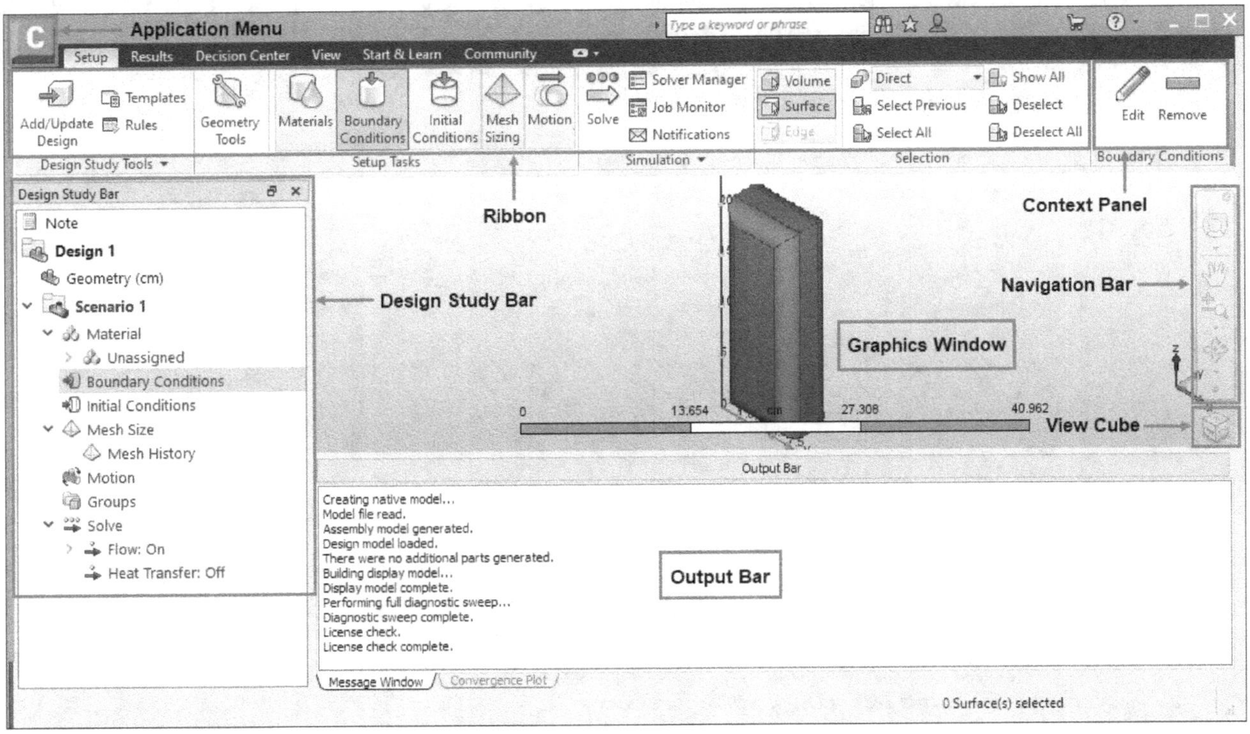

Figure-12. Model interface

Open

The **Open** tool is used to open an existing design study.

- Click on the **Open** button from **Launch** panel to open an existing design study. The **Open** dialog box will be displayed; refer to Figure-13.

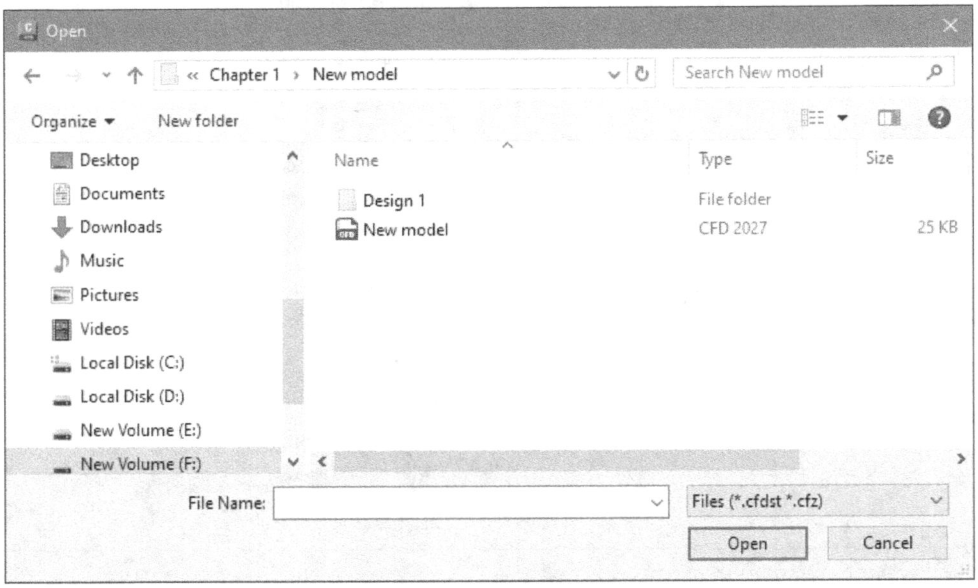

Figure-13. Open dialog box

- Select the design study file which you want to open and click on the **Open** button from **Open** dialog box. The file will open in Autodesk CFD along with the access of all tools. If you want to open previous version of current open project then click on the down arrow next to **Open** button in the **Open** dialog box and select the **Show previous versions** option; refer to Figure-14. Previous versions of project will be displayed in the dialog box.

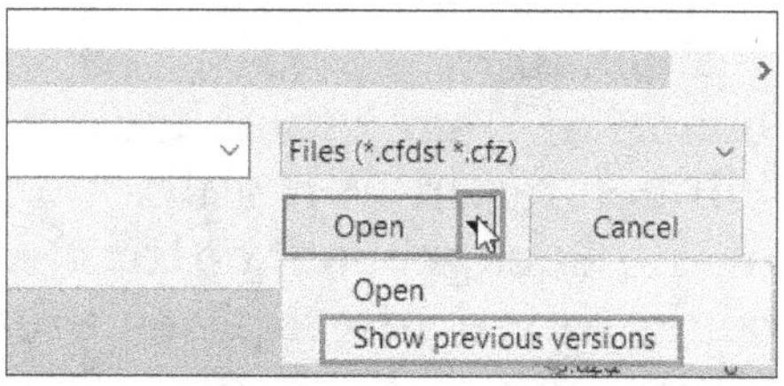

Figure-14. Show previous versions option

- Select desired version of project and click on the **Open** button.

Options

The **Options** tool is used to customize user interface to suit the work habits of designer and working environment.

- Click on the **Options** tool from **Launch** panel to customize the user interface, the **User Interface Preferences** dialog box will be displayed; refer to Figure-15.

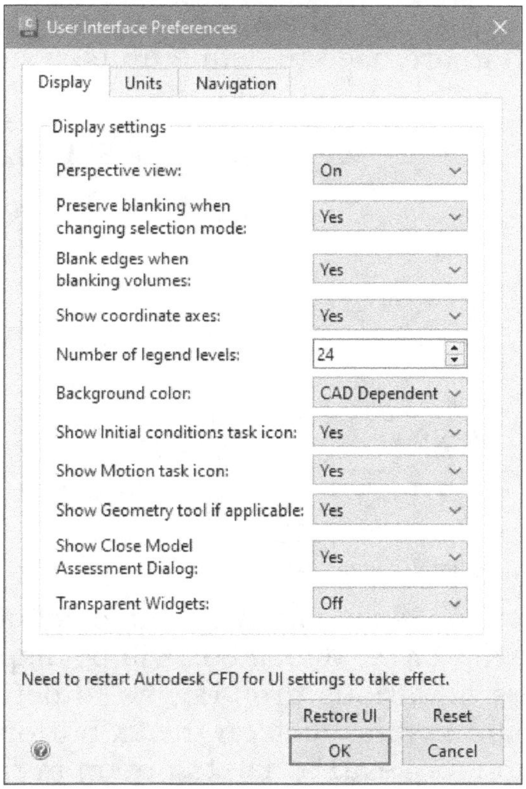

Figure-15. User Interface Preferences dialog box

Display Tab

- Select the **On** option from the **Perspective view** drop-down to display model in perspective display style. If the **Off** option is selected in the **Perspective view** drop-down then model will be displayed orthographic view style.
- Select the **Yes** option from the **Preserve blanking when changing selection mode** drop-down to keep blanking of model elements active even after changing the selection mode. Here, blanking means hiding. Use this option when you have a complex model and you need to select inner elements of the model.
- Select the **Yes** option from the **Blank edges when blanking volumes** drop-down to hide edges of model as well when you blanking is applied to volume.

- Select the **Yes** option from the **Show coordinate axes** drop-down to display coordinate axes in the graphics area.
- Set desired value in the **Number of legend values** drop-down to specify maximum number of legends that will be shown in result.
- Select desired option from the **Background color** drop-down to define how color will be displayed at the background in graphics area. Select the **CAD Dependent** option to display background color based on origin software of model used in project. Select the **User Defined** option to manually define color of background.
- Select **Yes** option from the **Show Initial conditions task icon** drop-down to display initial conditions icon in the **Design Study Bar**.
- Select **Yes** option from the **Show Motion task icon** drop-down to display motion icon in **Design Study Bar**.
- Similarly, set the options to display geometry tool and close model assessment dialog.
- Select **On** or **Off** option from **Transparent Widgets** drop-down to keep the dialogs transparent or opaque, respectively while moving the mouse away.

Units Tab

The options in the **Units** tab are used to define units system for setup and results; refer to Figure-16.

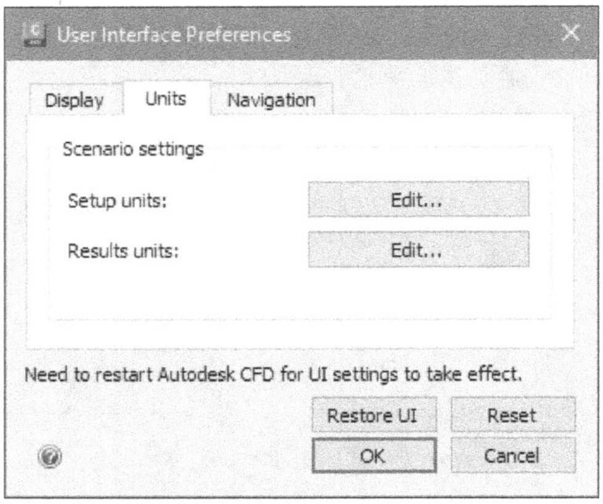

Figure-16. Units tab

- Click on the **Edit** button for **Setup units** option to define unit system for analysis setup. The **Default Setup Units** dialog box will be displayed; refer to Figure-17. Set desired parameters in various drop-downs to define respective unit types. After setting desired parameters, click on the **OK** button.
- Click on the **Edit** button for **Results units** option in the dialog box. The **Scalar Results Default Units** dialog box will be displayed; refer to Figure-18. Specify desired units for various results in the dialog box and click on the **OK** button.

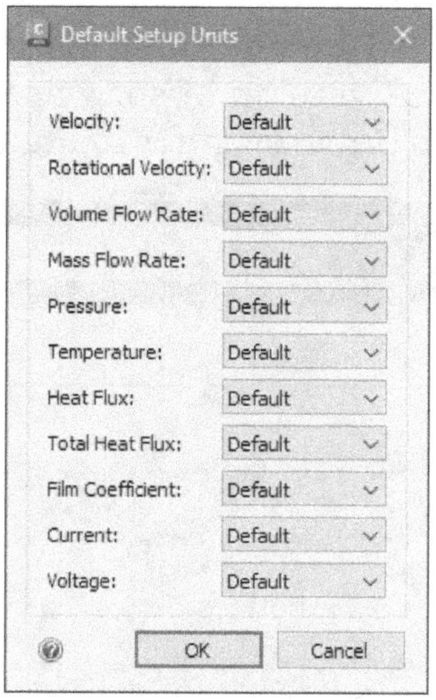

Figure-17. Default Setup Units dialog box

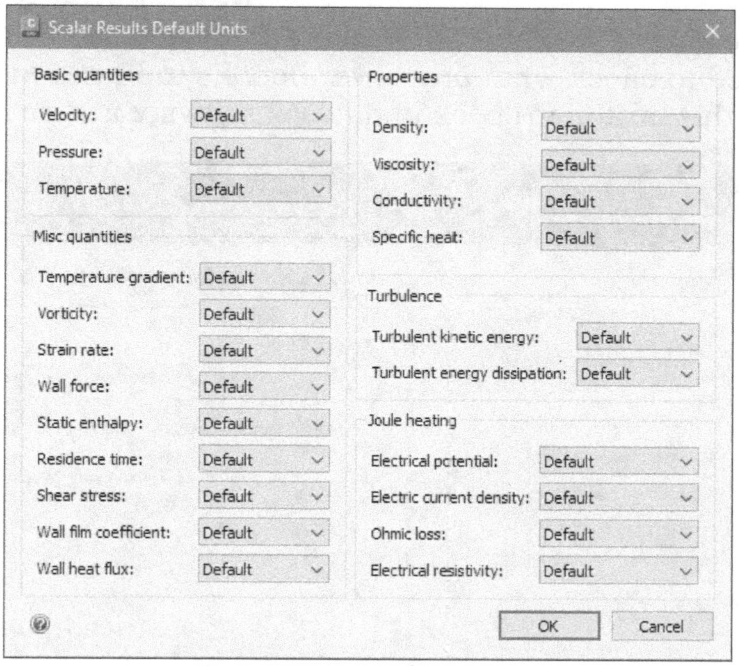

Figure-18. Scalar Results Default Units dialog box

Navigation Tab

The options in the **Navigation** tab are used to define how standard navigation operations will work in the software like zoom in/out, pan, and so on; refer to Figure-19.

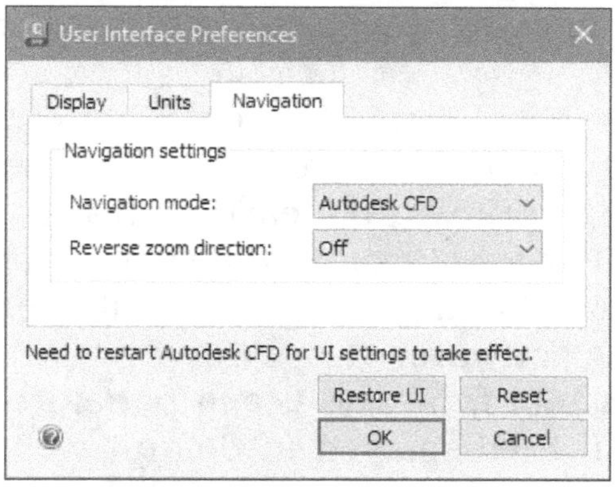

Figure-19. Navigation tab

- Select desired option from the **Navigation mode** drop-down to use navigation style of respective software. For example, if you want to use navigation style of SolidWorks then select the **SolidWorks** option from the drop-down.
- If you want to reverse the direction zoom then select the **On** option from the **Reverse zoom direction** drop-down in the dialog box.
- Click on the **Restore UI** button to restore the user interface of Autodesk CFD to default.
- Click on the **Reset** button to reset default values of **User Interface Preferences** dialog box.
- After specifying the parameters, click on the **OK** button. The changes to customize the user interface will be saved. Note that you need to restart the software before changes take effect in software.

New Features

The **What's New** tool in the **New Features** panel of **Start & Learn** tab in the **Ribbon** is used to check what are new functions/updates in current version of software. Click on this button to check updates of software in default web browser; refer to Figure-20.

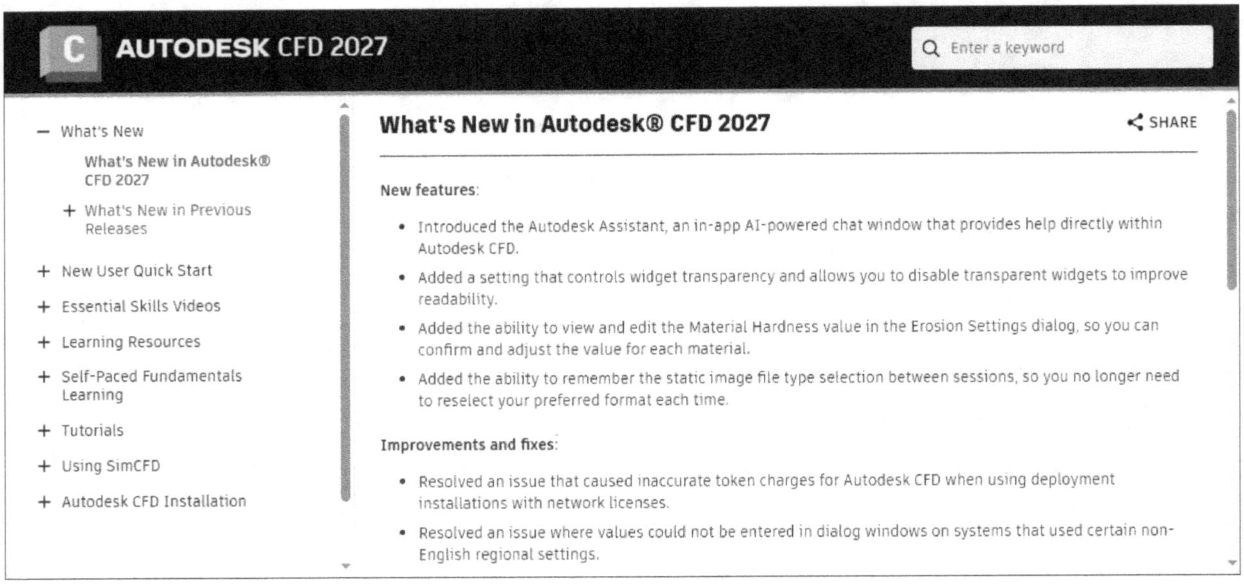

Figure-20. Whats New in Autodesk CFD

Learn

The tools and buttons of **Learn** panel in **Start & Learn** tab of **Ribbon** are used to help you to learn basics of the software. Various tools in this panel are discussed next.

- Click on the **Start Here** tool from the **Learn** panel in the **Start & Learn** tab of **Ribbon**. A web page will be displayed in default web browser showing basic information of software to put you on learning track.
- Click on the **Learning Path** tool from the **Learn** panel in the **Start & Learn** tab of **Ribbon**. A web page will be displayed in default web browser showing the self learning paths for using software.
- Click on the **Tutorials** tool from the **Learn** panel in the **Start & Learn** tab of **Ribbon**. A web page will be displayed in default web browser showing links to tutorials provided by Autodesk for beginner's learning; refer to Figure-21.

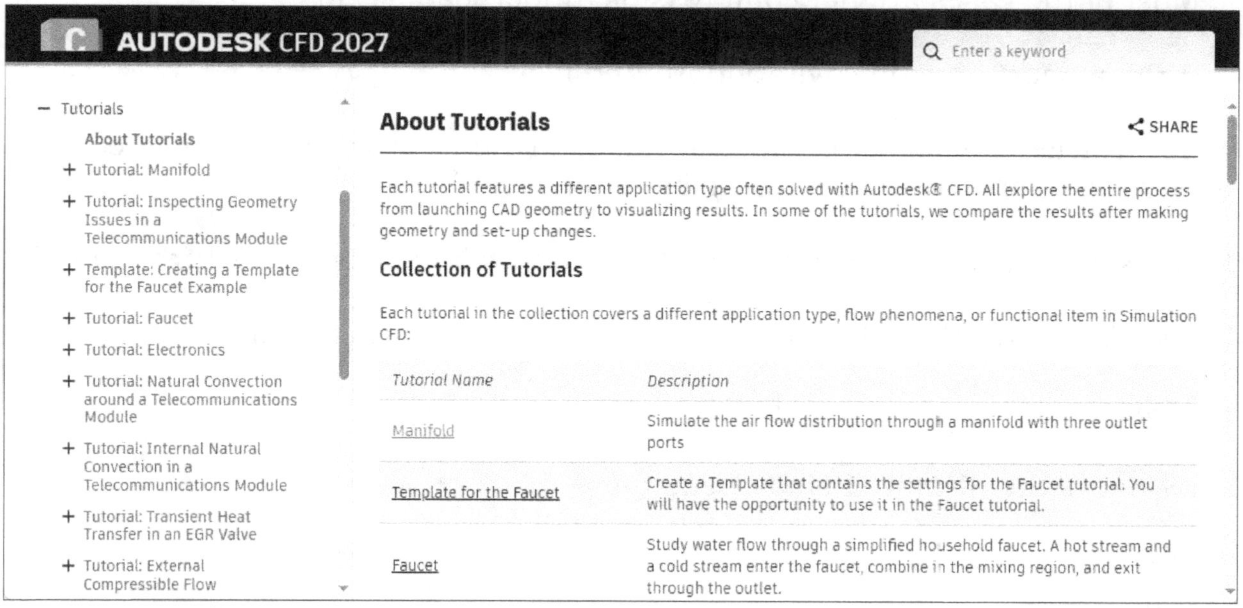

Figure-21. Tutorials page

- Click on the **Videos** tool from the **Learn** panel to check videos of basic operations like applying material, boundary conditions, running simulation, and so on.
- Click on the **Help** tool from the **Learn** panel to check documentation of software.

Product Information

The tools of **Product Information** panel provide the information about software version and available license for the installed software.

SELF-ASSESSMENT

Q1. Discuss the difference between weight density and mass density.

Q2. As the temperature of liquid rises, its density is reduced and vice-versa is also true. (T/F)

Q3. As the temperature of gas rises, its density is reduced and vice-versa is also true. (T/F)

Q4. Resistance to the free flow of fluid can be expressed in terms of viscosity. (T/F)

Q5. Which of the following fluid types is compressible under load?

a. Ideal Fluid
b. Real Fluid
c. Newtonian Fluid
d. Non-Newtonian Fluid

Q6. For which of the following fluid types, shear stress is directly proportional to shear strain under load?

a. Ideal Fluid
b. Real Fluid
c. Newtonian Fluid
d. Non-Newtonian Fluid

Q7. Most of the gases are not compressible under load. (T/F)

Q8. Write a short note on cavitation in fluid flow.

Q9. The Navier-Stokes equations are the elemental partial differentials equations that describe the flow of incompressible fluids. (T/F)

Q10. At Reynolds number larger than 30, fluid flow in pipe becomes turbulent. (T/F)

Q11. Explain Navier-Stokes equations of Newtonian viscous fluid.

Q12. Discuss the basic steps of CFD.

Q13. What is the SI unit of Mass Density?

A. N/m^3
B. kg/m^3
C. $N \cdot s/m^2$
D. $Pa \cdot s$

Q14. What is the Specific Gravity of a fluid defined as?

A. Ratio of volume to temperature
B. Ratio of viscosity to density
C. Ratio of weight density of fluid to weight density of reference fluid
D. Ratio of pressure to density
Q15. How does the density of a gas change with an increase in temperature?

A. It remains constant
B. It decreases
C. It increases
D. It first increases then decreases

Q16. What is the unit of viscosity in SI units?

A. N/m^3
B. kg/m^2
C. $N \cdot s/m^2$ or $Pa \cdot s$
D. m^2/s

Q17. Which of the following statements is true about Ideal Fluids?

A. They are compressible and have high viscosity
B. They are real and used in experiments
C. They are incompressible and have no viscosity
D. They are always Newtonian

Q18. What type of fluid has shear stress directly proportional to shear strain?

A. Non-Newtonian Fluid
B. Real Fluid
C. Newtonian Fluid
D. Ideal Plastic Fluid

Q19. Which equation represents the relationship between pressure, volume, and temperature for a gas?

A. F = ma
B. P.V = RT
C. V = IR
D. P = ρgh

Q20. What is the value of gas constant R for air?

A. 1000 J/kg-K
B. 8314 J/kg-mole K
C. 287 J/kg-K
D. 1.225 kg/m^3

Q21. What does an isothermal process imply in gas dynamics?

A. Temperature remains constant
B. Heat transfer is zero
C. Density remains constant
D. Pressure remains constant

Q22. What does Pascal's Law state?

A. Pressure is only vertical in a static fluid
B. Pressure is same in all directions in a static fluid
C. Pressure increases with depth
D. Pressure is dependent on temperature only

Q23. Which of the following is not a method of fluid flow analysis?

A. Control Volume
B. Differential
C. Spectroscopic
D. Experimental

Q24. What is the Eulerian method focused on in fluid mechanics?

A. Tracking individual particles
B. Measuring density change of one particle
C. Analyzing field variables at fixed points
D. Observing compressibility directly

Q25. What is cavitation in fluid flow?

A. Formation of gas due to low pressure
B. Formation and collapse of bubbles causing surface erosion
C. Movement of particles at high velocity
D. Sudden change in viscosity

Q26. In the differential approach, what is the purpose of meshing?

A. To reduce volume of fluid
B. To divide the fluid into small elements for numerical solution
C. To compress the fluid data
D. To extract heat energy from flow

Q27. What does CFD stand for?

A. Constant Flow Dynamics
B. Computational Flow Distribution
C. Computational Fluid Dynamics
D. Continuous Fluid Description

Q28. Which of the following is considered the "third approach" in the study of fluid dynamics?

A. Experimental Dynamics
B. Computational Fluid Dynamics
C. Theoretical Dynamics
D. Laminar Flow Analysis

Q29. What are the Navier-Stokes equations used to describe?

A. Electric and magnetic fields in fluids
B. Static energy transfer
C. The relation between velocity, pressure, temperature, and density in a moving fluid
D. The reaction of solids under stress

Q30. What does dynamic viscosity measure?

A. The temperature change in a fluid
B. The pressure of a fluid in a pipe
C. The force needed to overcome internal molecular friction in a fluid
D. The weight of a fluid in vacuum

Q31. Which property is defined as the ratio of dynamic viscosity to density?

A. Static pressure
B. Kinematic viscosity
C. Reynolds number
D. Second viscosity coefficient

Q32. What is the Kronecker delta primarily used for?

A. Describing heat transfer
B. Defining mass balance in control volume
C. Representing discrete delta functions
D. Calculating laminar flow

Q33. What is the Reynolds number used to predict?

A. Heat transfer behavior
B. Flow behavior—laminar or turbulent
C. Velocity of sound in a medium
D. Pressure change in pipe flow

Q34. What does the Conservation of Mass imply in fluid dynamics?

A. Fluids increase in volume under heat
B. Mass cannot be created or destroyed
C. Pressure is inversely related to volume
D. Density is always constant

Q35. What form does the momentum equation in CFD take?

A. F = m/v
B. E = mc^2
C. F = m.a
D. W = F.d

Q36. Which force is represented by ρ.g in the momentum equations?

A. Viscous force
B. Shear force
C. Surface force
D. Body force

Q37. What is assumed constant for incompressible flow in Navier-Stokes equations?

A. Pressure
B. Density
C. Volume
D. Temperature

Q38. What does a Mach number less than 0.3 indicate about the fluid?

A. It is compressible
B. It is laminar
C. It is turbulent
D. It is incompressible

Q39. What is the Favre averaging technique mainly used for?

A. Averaging pressure fields
B. Solving incompressible flows
C. Simplifying compressible flow equations using density-weighted averaging
D. Ignoring turbulent effects in compressible flows

Q40. What is the first step in the process of solving a Computational Fluid Dynamics problem?

A. Discretization of Model
B. Getting Solution
C. Creating Mathematical Model
D. Post Processing

Q41. What is the process of converting a mathematical model into finite elements called?

A. Finite Analysis
B. Discretization
C. Mathematical Simplification
D. Meshing

Q42. In CFD, what are the elements called after discretization?

A. Grids
B. Meshes
C. Cells
D. Nodes

Q43. Which of the following is not a mesh-based method of discretization?

A. Finite Volume Method
B. Finite Pointset Method
C. Finite Element Method
D. Finite Difference Method

Q44. What is the key requirement not included in numerical scheme characteristics?

A. Accuracy
B. Stability
C. Convergence
D. Elasticity

Q45. In the Finite Difference Method, which approach uses xi and xi-1?

A. Central Difference
B. Forward Difference
C. Backward Difference
D. Finite Volume

Q46. What setting in the Display Tab hides the model edges when a volume is blanked?

A. Show coordinate axes
B. Preserve blanking
C. Blank edges when blanking volumes
D. Background color

Q47. What does the Navigation Tab mainly control in Autodesk CFD?

A. File import format
B. Simulation accuracy
C. Zoom, pan, and view styles
D. Meshing quality

Q48. Which panel includes tools for video tutorials and learning paths in Autodesk CFD?

A. Learn Panel
B. New Panel
C. Open Panel
D. Features Panel

FOR STUDENT NOTES

Chapter 2

Model Setup in Autodesk CFD

Topics Covered

The major topics covered in this chapter are:

- ***Edge Merge***
- ***Void Fill***
- ***ViewCube***
- ***Navigation bar***
- ***Diagnostics***
- ***Mesh Refinement Regions***

INTRODUCTION

In the last chapter, we have learned many things about CFD, fluid mechanics, and Autodesk CFD like first time user interface which will be useful for upcoming chapters. In this chapter, we will learn about various tools to create a design study, applying material, creating mesh, and running the simulation.

MODEL SETUP IN AUTODESK CFD

To create a design study in Autodesk CFD, you will need a pre-created design model created with the help of Autodesk CFD supported software which were discussed in last chapter.

- Open Autodesk CFD software by double-clicking on icon from desktop. You can also open the same from Start menu. The welcome window of Autodesk CFD will be displayed.
- Click on the **New** button of **Launch** panel from **Start & Learn** tab. The **New Design Study** dialog box will be displayed. Select the file which you want to open and click on the **Create** button. The software will start to read file design and status will be displayed in **Output bar**.
- Sometimes, when there is some error with the design or there is a need to improve the quality of model for CFD, the **Geometry Tools** dialog box will be displayed; refer to Figure-1.

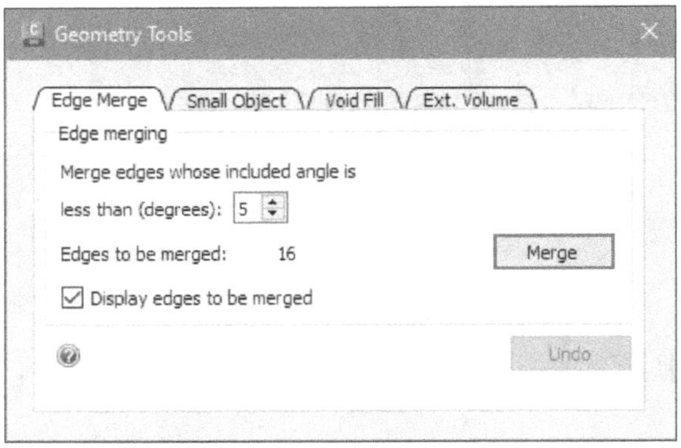

Figure-1. Geometry Tools dialog box

You can also open the **Geometry Tools** dialog box by clicking on the **Geometry Tools** button from **Setup Tasks** panel of **Setup** tab.

Edge Merge

Options in the **Edge Merge** tab are used to unite edges that share a common vertex at an inflection angle less than a specified tolerance. This tool is helpful in generating mesh and reducing computer time because it reduces the number of small edges in the design to make analysis faster; refer to Figure-2.

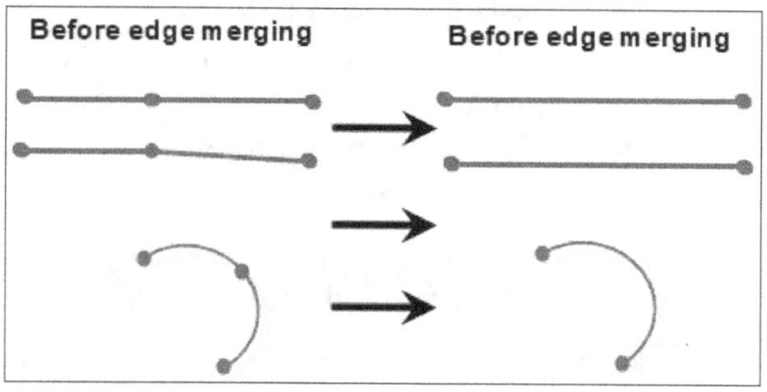

Figure-2. Edge merging

- The **Inclination** angle is determined by value of included tangency angle which has a maximum limit of 15 degrees. All the small edges that have inclination angle less than this value will be merged. The edge merging will have no effect on vertex where two or more edges are joining. Also, it will have no effect on edges whose angle is greater than the specified angle. Click in the edit box from **Edge Merge** tab and specify desired value in degree to merge the edges whose included angle is less than the specified value. On specifying the value, software will automatically calculate the number of edges which are going to merge and the value is displayed in **Edge Merge** tab.
- Select the **Display edges to be merged** check box from the **Edge Merge** tab to view the edges to be merged. The edges will be displayed along with the arrows; refer to Figure-3.

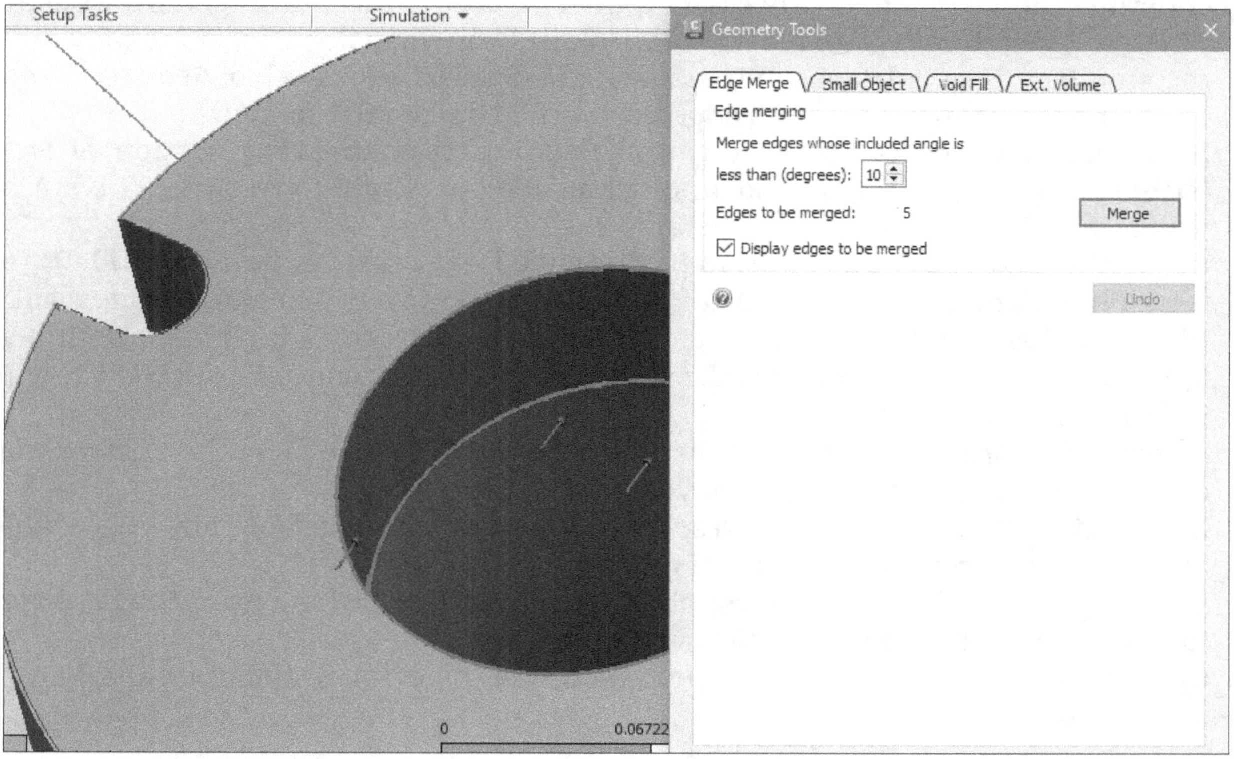

Figure-3. Displaying edges to be merged

- After specifying the parameters, click on the **Merge** button from the **Edge Merge** tab. The selected edges will be merged.
- Click on the **Undo** button from **Edge Merge** tab to undo the action of edge merging.

Small Object

The **Small Object** tab is used to remove geometry from model, like surfaces and edges, which are too small to see/create in the mesh; refer to Figure-4. The process of removing small edges and surfaces from model will decrease the time taken by computer for analysis processing and mesh generation.

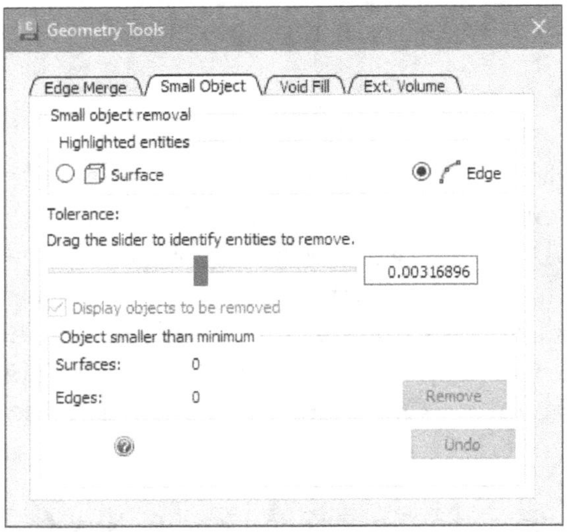

Figure-4. Small Object tab

- Sometimes, there are some small surfaces and edges in the design of model which consume more time and processing power to create mesh and generate results. When we open this type of file in Autodesk CFD, the software automatically detect the smaller edges/surfaces and displays the **Small Object** tab of **Geometry Tools** dialog box to minimize excess edges or surfaces from the model.
- Select the **Surface** radio button from **Highlighted entities** section of **Small Object** tab to highlight the extra small surface of model to remove. The surface will be highlighted along with the arrows.
- Select the **Edge** radio button from **Highlighted entities** section of **Small Object** tab to highlight the small edges of model to be removed. The small edges will be highlighted along with the arrows generated by software to highlight small surfaces.
- Move the slider to set the tolerance value. You can also manually specify the value in **Tolerance** edit box.
- Select the **Display objects to be removed** check box to view the surfaces and edges which are going to be removed.
- In **Object smaller than minimum** section, the number of surfaces and edges which are going to be removed will be displayed.
- After specifying the parameters, click on the **Remove** button from **Small Object** tab. The small surface and edges will be removed.
- Click on the **Undo** button from the dialog box to revert to default values in the dialog box.

Void Fill

Mostly CAD models consist of solid body and fluid flow inside them or around them, but sometimes there are some openings in the solid body as a part of geometry model where the working fluid enters or leaves. In such case, the geometric model is not suitable for a flow analysis. The **Void Fill** options are used to create capping surfaces that bound a water-tight internal void on the openings of solid body. The surfaces and volumes that are created, are actual geometries that can have boundary conditions, material, and other CFD parameters. When creating a cap on the opening, always remember to not overlap void fill volume with other volume.

- Select desired radio button from **Model entity selection** section of **Void Fill** tab.
- The **Edge** radio button is selected by default. You need to select the edge from model to close the opening; refer to Figure-5.

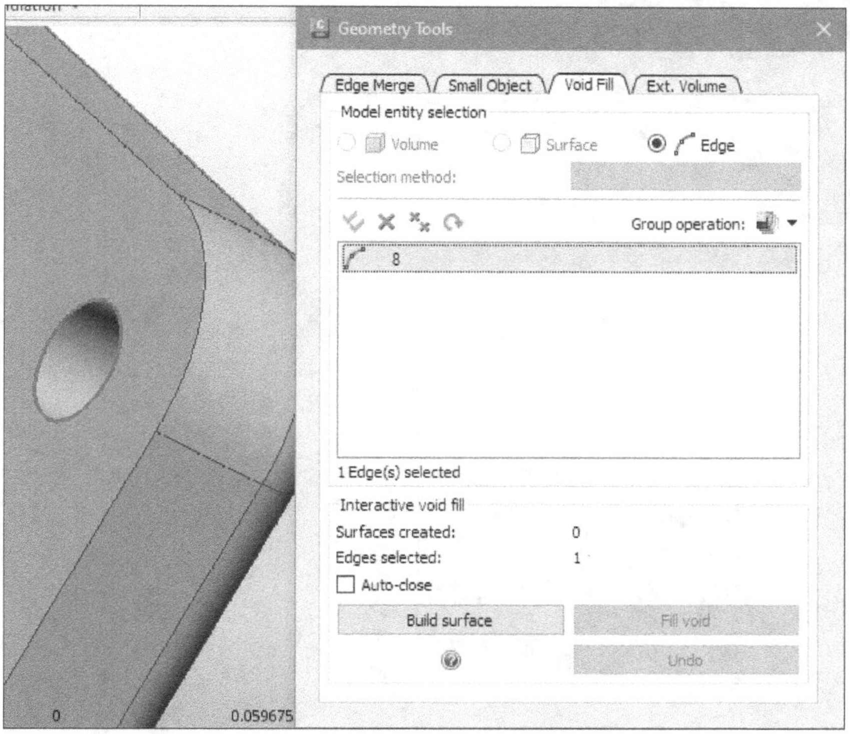

Figure-5. Void Fill tab

- On selection of edge from model, the number of edges will be displayed in Edges selection box.
- After selecting the required edges, click on the **Build surface** button from **Void Fill** tab. The surface will be created based on the selected edge; refer to Figure-6.
- The dialog box will be updated after creating surface. You can see the number of created surfaces next to **Surface created**. The **Fill Void** button will be activated on creation of surfaces.
- Click on the **Fill Void** button from the **Fill Void** dialog box. If the void fill region is created, a message "There was 1 additional part generated", will be displayed in the **Message** box; refer to Figure-7.

To fill a void: The created surfaces should form a closed volume.

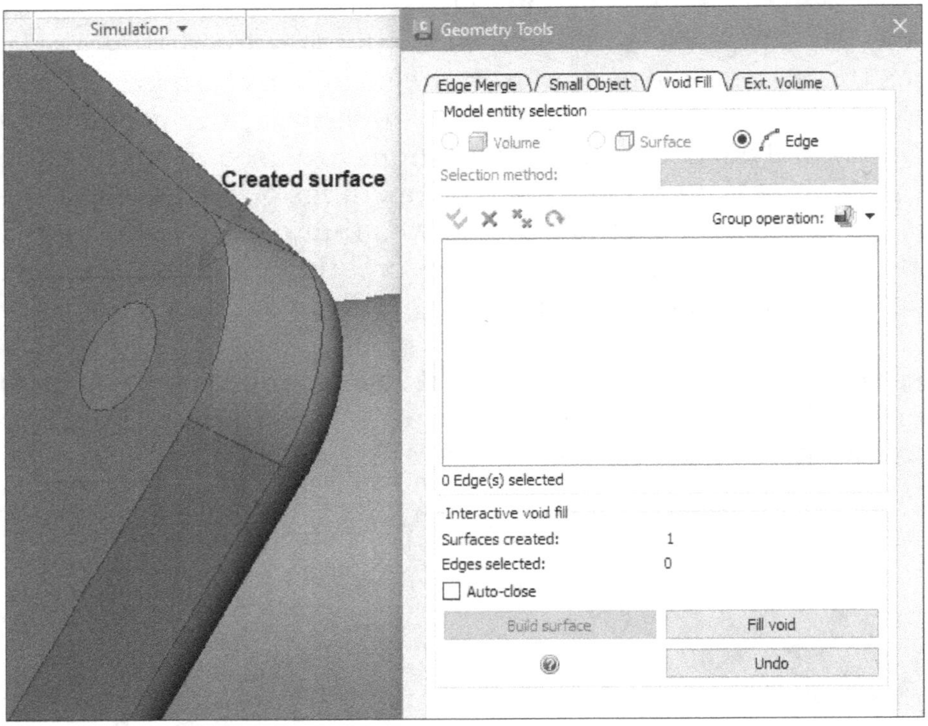

Figure-6. Created surface

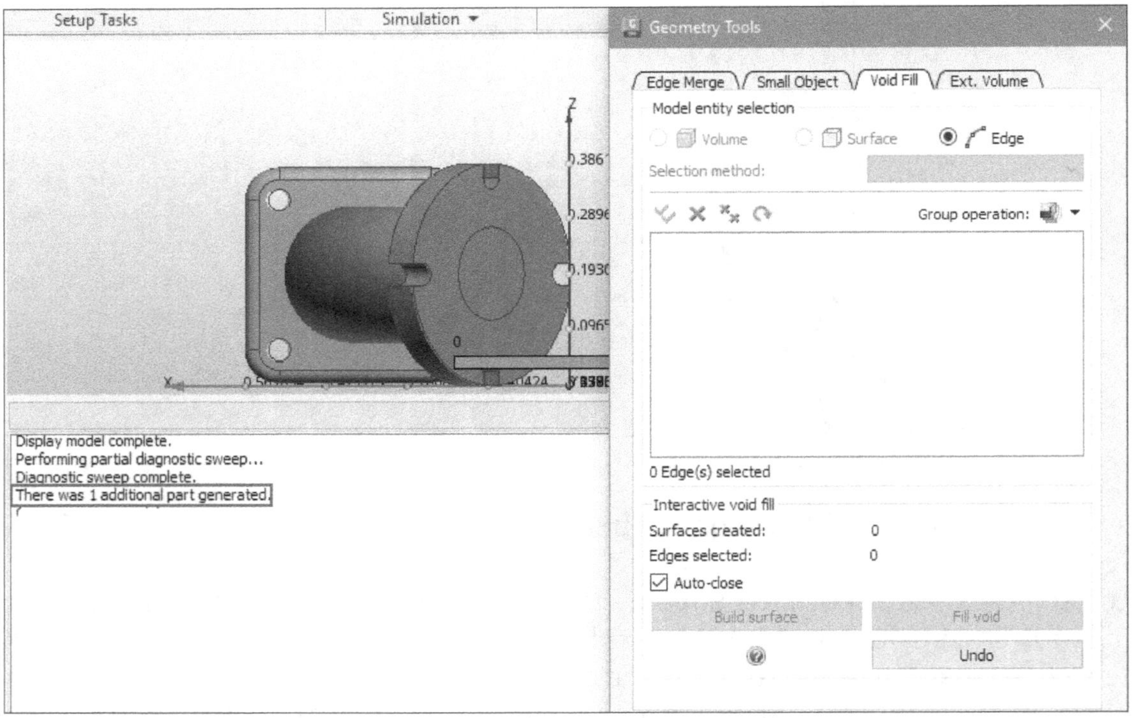

Figure-7. Created Fill Void

Ext. Volume

The options in the **Ext. Volume** tab are used to define external fluid volume for different analyses like wind analysis on motorcycle, aircraft, and other objects. In most cases, the volume that surround the model is not included as part of model design. For analysis, one needs to add the surrounding in the form of external volume of fluid to the model with the help of **Ext. Volume** tab. It adds the surrounding fluid to the model without adding it to the CAD geometry.

- Click on the **Ext. Volume** tab from the **Geometry Tools** dialog box. The preview of external volume will be displayed; refer to Figure-8.

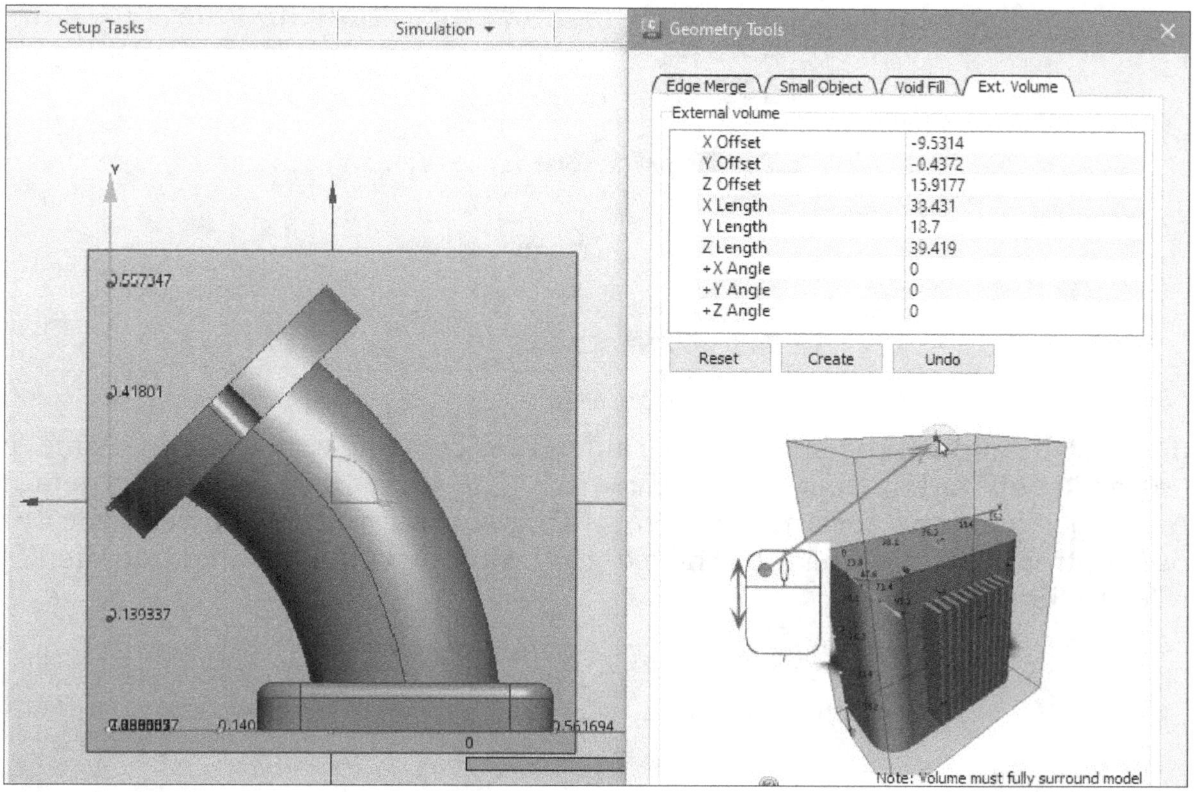

Figure-8. Automatically created external volume

- Always remember while creating surrounding that whole model should be immersed in the fluid or we can say, the external volume should totally cover the model. To resize the external volume as per requirement, click and hold the left mouse button on a grab handle and drag mouse to resize the length; refer to Figure-9.

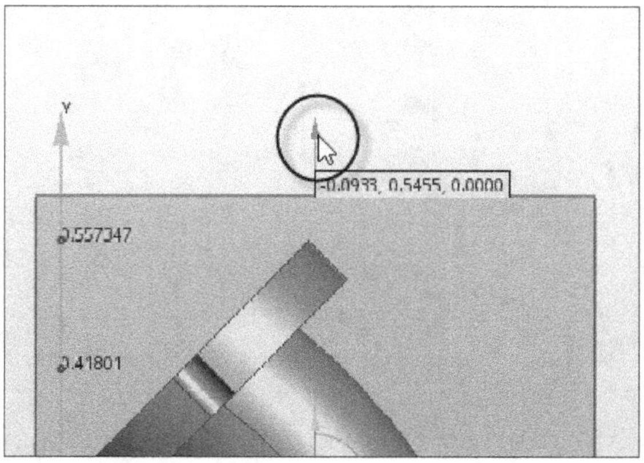

Figure-9. Resize the external volume

- On grabbing the drag handle, the color of arrow will be changed from blue to red. Adjust the length of external volume as required. If you want to specify the length of external volume manually, click on the value of parameter from **Ext. Volume** tab and specify desired value; refer to Figure-10.

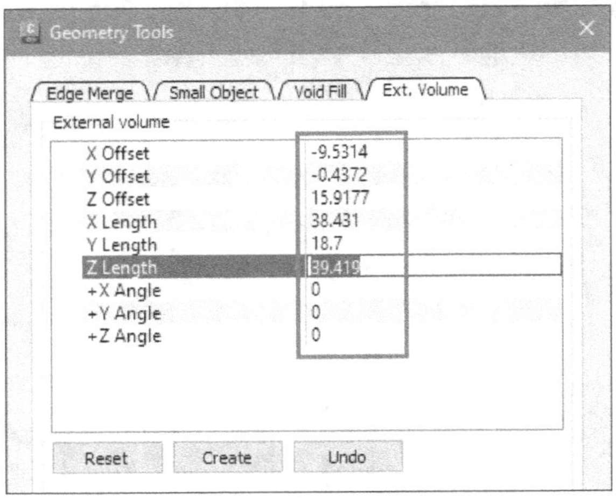

Figure-10. Specifying manually

- If you want to reset the specified parameter for creating an external volume, click on the **Reset** button from **Ext. Volume** tab. The values will be reset to default.
- After specifying the parameters to set up an external volume, click on the **Create** button from **Ext. Volume** tab. The external volume will be created and displayed; refer to Figure-11.

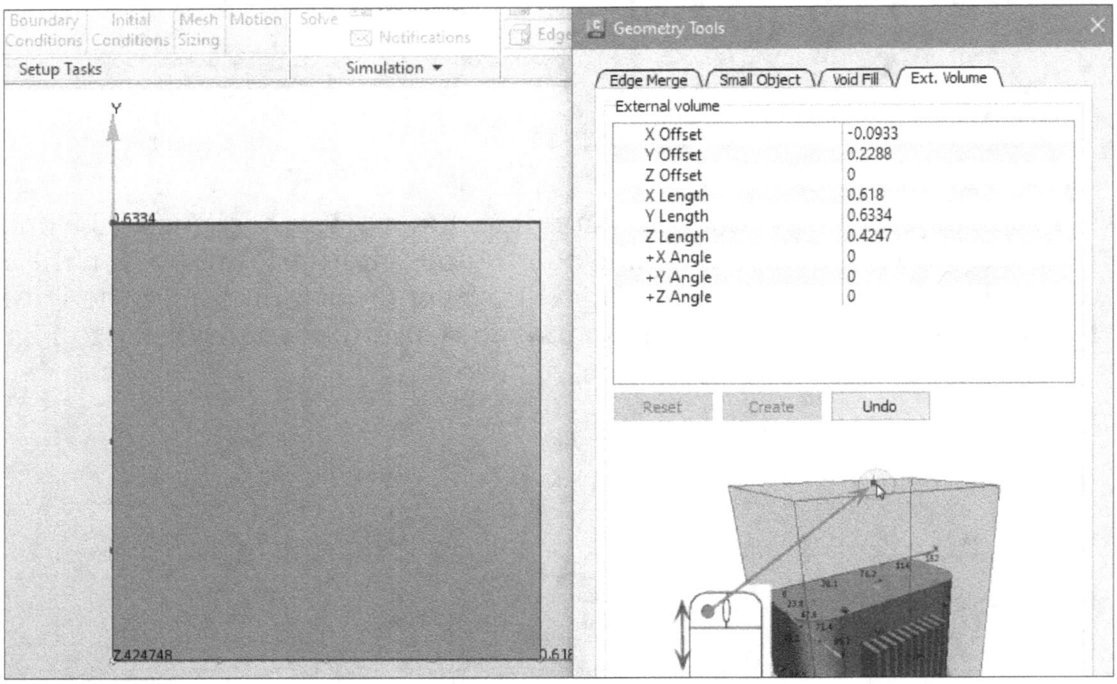

Figure-11. Created external volume

- To undo the process of creating the external volume around the model, click on the **Undo** button from **Ext. Volume** tab. The **Warning** box will be displayed asking you whether to undo the process or not; refer to Figure-12.

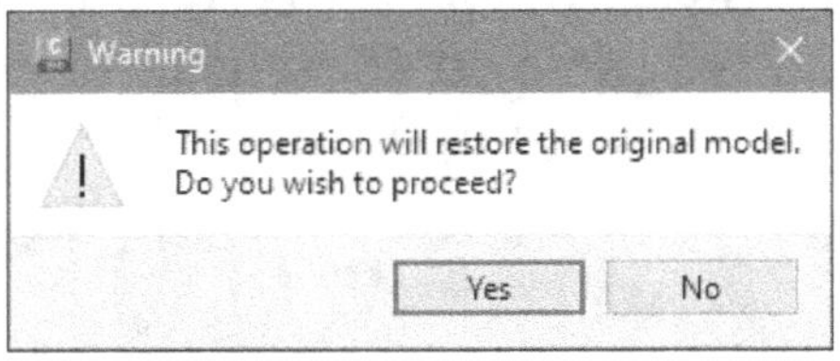

Figure-12. Warning box

- Click on the **Yes** button from **Warning** box. The created external volume will be deleted and model will be returned to its initial position.

NAVIGATION

The **Navigation bar** is a user interface element where you can access the model through different aspects; refer to Figure-13. There are two types of navigation tools, i.e. Unified navigation tools and product-specific tools. The Unified navigation tools are those tools that can be found in almost all Autodesk software. The Product-specific tools are those tools which are software specific. The tools of **Navigation bar** are discussed next.

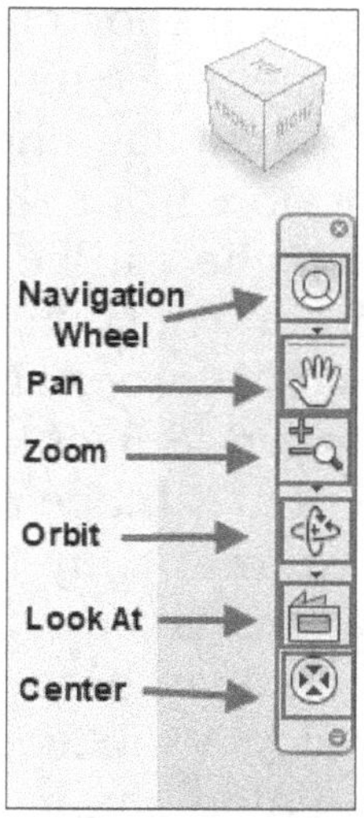

Figure-13. Navigation bar

ViewCube

ViewCube is used to display orientation of model and reorient the model; refer to Figure-14.

Figure-14. View Cube

- Names of the views are displayed on the faces of **ViewCube**. To orient the model in a particular view, click on the respective view name. The model will be displayed as per clicked view.
- Click on the **Home** button from **ViewCube** to quickly move to the Isometric view.
- Right-click on the **ViewCube** to modify advanced view options; refer to Figure-15. Select the **Perspective** option from the shortcut menu to display model in perspective view. By default, the model is displayed in orthographic view. Select the **Set Current View as Home** option from the shortcut menu to set current displaying view of model as home view. Select the **Reset Home** option from the shortcut menu to reset home view to default. Select the **Set Current View as Front** option from the shortcut menu to make current view of model as front view. Select the **Reset Front** option from the shortcut menu to reset front view to default.

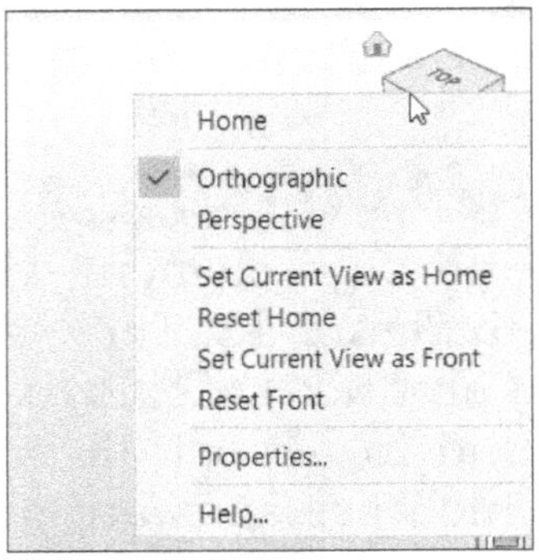

Figure-15. Shortcut menu for ViewCube

- Select the **Properties** option from the shortcut menu to define general properties of ViewCube. The **ViewCube Properties** dialog box will be displayed; refer to Figure-16. Select the **Show the ViewCube** check box to display **ViewCube** in the graphics area. Select desired option from the **On-screen position** drop-down to define the position where **ViewCube** will be placed in graphics area. Using the options in the **ViewCube Size** drop-down, you can define size of **ViewCube**. Similarly, select desired option from the **Inactive opacity** drop-down to define up to which level the transparency will be applied. Select the **Snap to closest view** check box to snap cursor automatically to nearest face of **ViewCube**. Select the **Fit-to-view on view change** check box to automatically fit view to screen based on selected face of **ViewCube**. Select the **Use animated transitions when switching views** check box to play animation when switching views. Select the **Show the compass** check box to display compass below **ViewCube**. After setting desired parameters, click on the **OK** button from the dialog box.

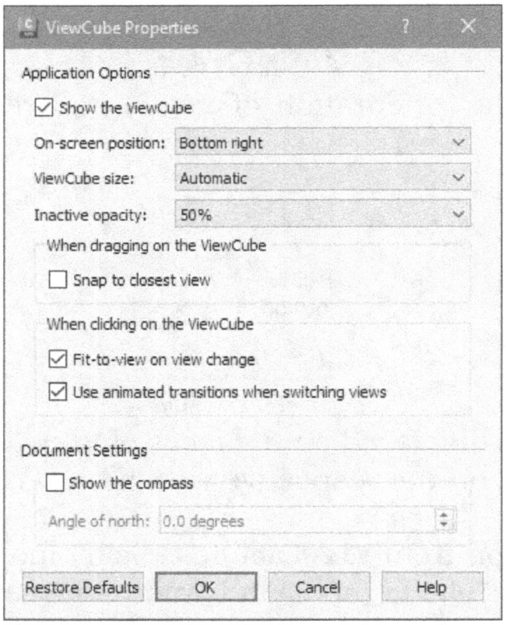

Figure-16. ViewCube Properties dialog box

Full Navigation Wheel

Full Navigation Wheel, also known as wheels, are menus that provide 2D and 3D navigation commands from a single source. These menus are known as tracking menus, which means they follow your cursor. **Full Navigation wheel** consists of many navigation commands into a single interface. The procedure to use this is discussed next.

- Click on the **Full Navigation Wheel** button from **Navigation bar**. The **Navigation Wheel** will be attached to the cursor; refer to Figure-17.

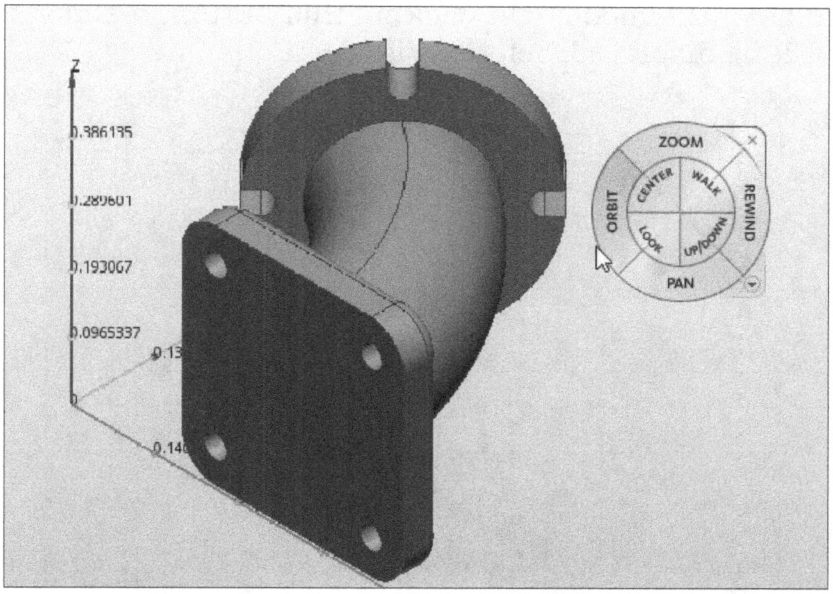

Figure-17. Navigation wheel

- Click and hold the left mouse button on **ZOOM** button from **Navigation Wheel** and move the cursor upward and downward to Zoom-in and Zoom-out respectively.
- Click and hold the left mouse button on **ORBIT** button from **Navigation Wheel** and move the cursor as per requirement to move the model.
- Click and hold the left mouse button on **PAN** button from **Navigation Wheel** and move the cursor as required to move the model.
- Click and hold the left mouse button on **REWIND** button from **Navigation Wheel** and move the mouse towards left or right to rewind the last action. On selecting **Rewind** button, an array of pictures will be displayed from which you can select desired previous state of model; refer to Figure-18.

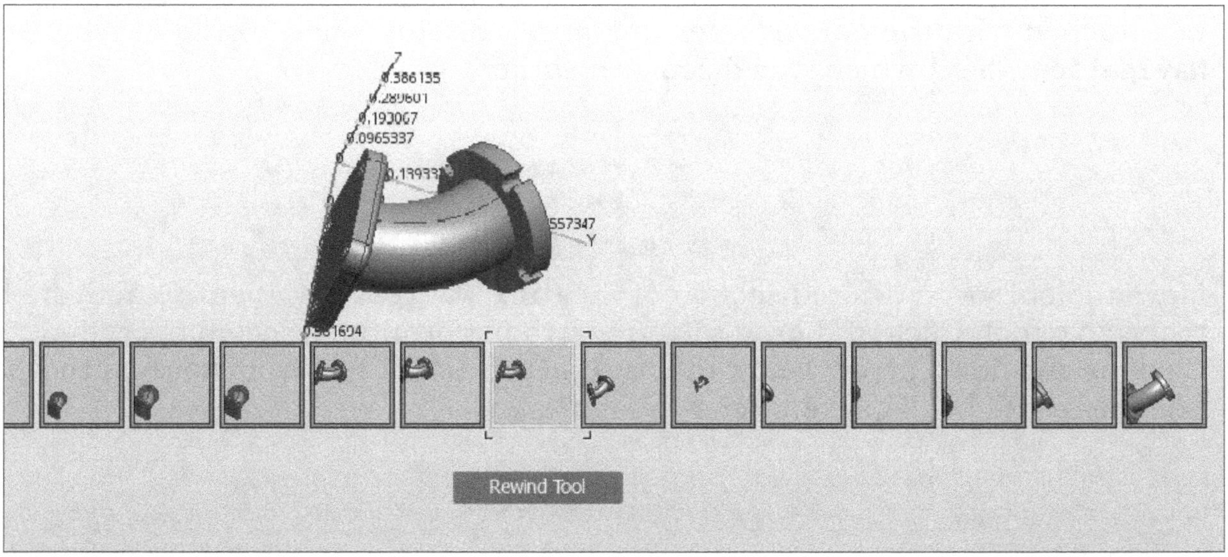

Figure-18. Rewind tool

- Click and hold the left mouse button on **CENTER** button from **Navigation Wheel** and select a point on the graphics window and release the left mouse button. The model moves so that the selected point is at the centre of screen.

- Click and hold the left mouse button on **UP/DOWN** button from **Navigation Wheel** and move the cursor towards up or down to adjust the height of current viewpoint along the Z-axis of the model. On clicking this button, a slider to navigate from up to down will be displayed; refer to Figure-19.

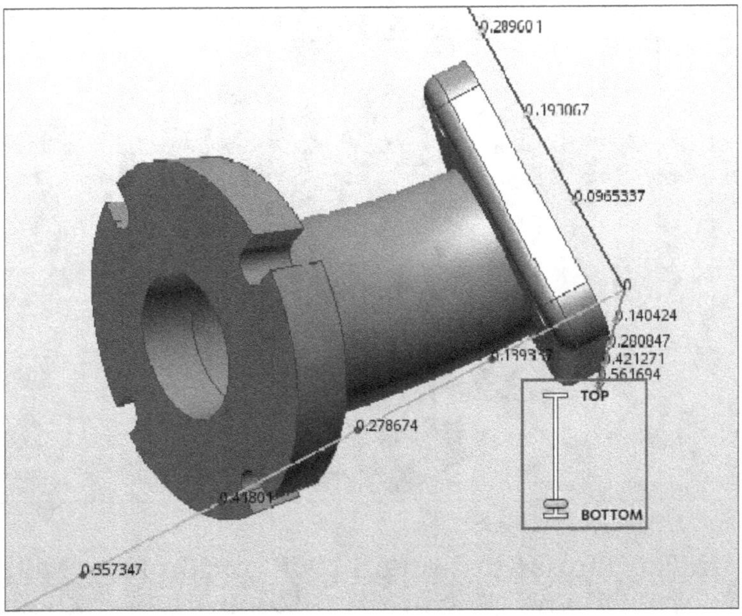

Figure-19. UP DOWN slider

- Click and hold the left mouse button on **Look** button from **Navigation Wheel** and move the cursor to rotate the current view vertically and horizontally. While rotating, your line of sight rotates about the current eye position like turning your head.
- Click again on the **Navigation Wheel** button from **Navigation bar** to deactivate the **Navigation Wheel**.
- Click on the **Mini Full Navigation Wheel** button from **Navigation Wheel** drop-down of **Navigation bar** to activate the mini navigation wheel. The wheel will be attached with the cursor; refer to Figure-20. This wheel works like the **Full Navigation Wheel** which was discussed earlier.

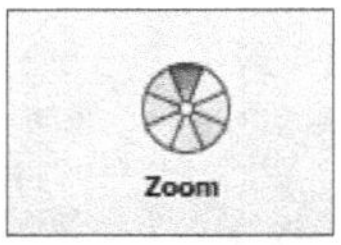

Figure-20. Mini Navigation Wheel

- Move the cursor in desired section of the **Mini Navigation Wheel** to activate the respective tool. Click and drag the cursor to perform the selected operation.
- Click on the down arrow below the **Navigation wheel** tool from **Navigation bar**. The menu will be displayed; refer to Figure-21.

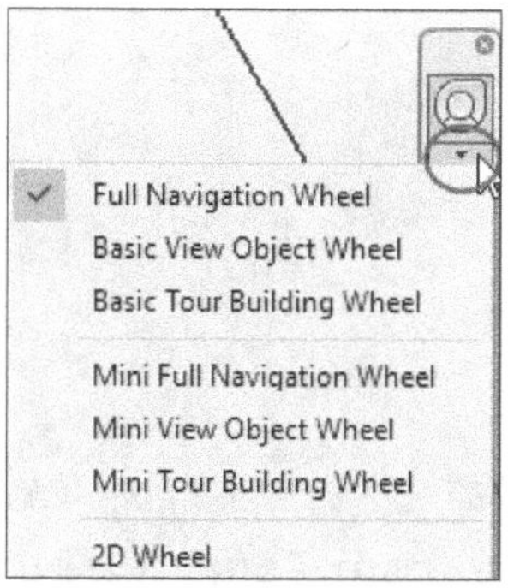

Figure-21. Navigation Wheel drop-down

View Object Wheel

- Click on the **Basic View Object Wheel** button from the drop-down to activate the **View Object Wheel**. The **View Object Wheel** is used to view individual objects or features in model; refer to Figure-22.

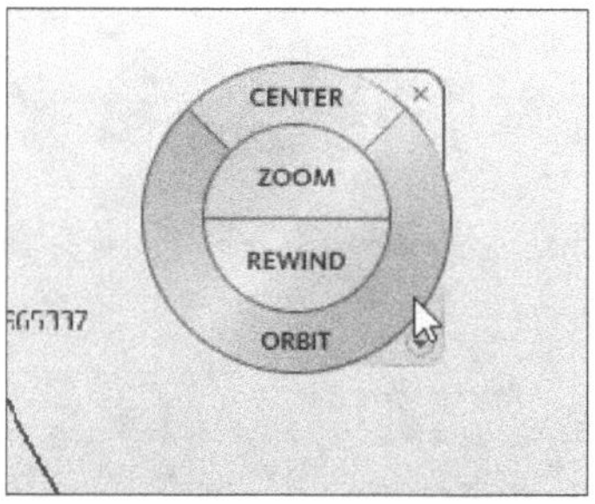

Figure-22. View Object Wheel

- The buttons of **View Object Wheel** are same as discussed in **Full Navigation Wheel** section.
- Click on the **Mini View Object Wheel** button from **Navigation Wheel** drop-down of **Navigation bar** to activate the mini object wheel. The wheel will be attached with the cursor; refer to Figure-23.

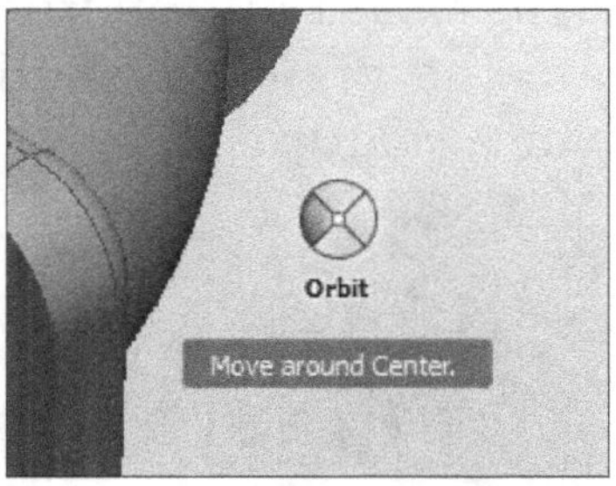

Figure-23. Mini Object Wheel

- The working of this wheel is same as discussed earlier.

Tour Building Wheel

- Click on the **Basic Tour Building Wheel** tool from the **Navigation Wheel** drop-down of **Navigation bar** to activate the **Tour Building Wheel.** The wheel will be attached to the cursor; refer to Figure-24. The **Tour Building Wheel** is used to move through model like building, assembly line, ship, or oil rig.

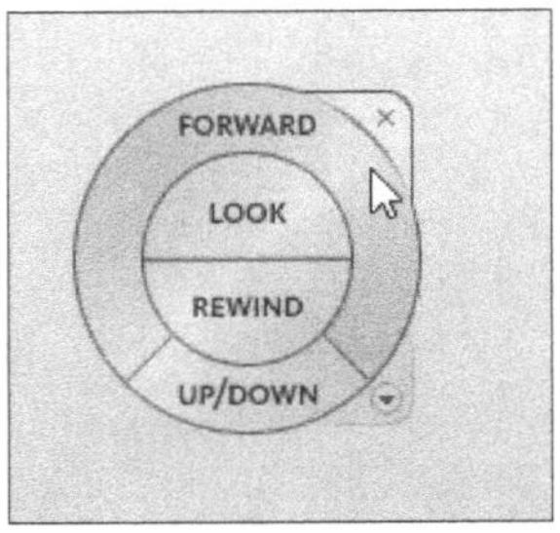

Figure-24. Tour Building Wheel

- Click and hold **Forward** button from **Tour Building Wheel** to adjust the distance between the current point of view and defined pivot point of the model. Move the cursor forward and backward to zoom in and out through the model respectively.
- You can also activate the **View Object Wheel** and **Tour Building Wheel** from **Navigation Wheel** drop-down of **Navigation Wheel**; refer to Figure-25.

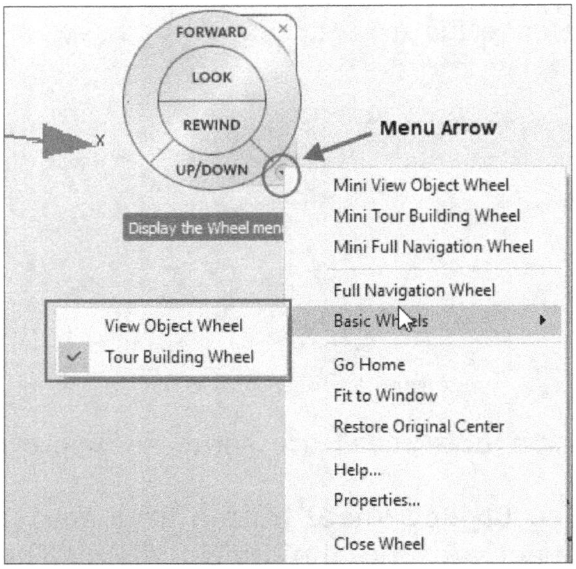

Figure-25. Menu arrow of navigation wheel

- Click on the **Mini Tour Building Wheel** button from **Navigation Wheel** drop-down of **Navigation bar** to activate the mini tour building wheel. The wheel will be attached with the cursor; refer to Figure-26.

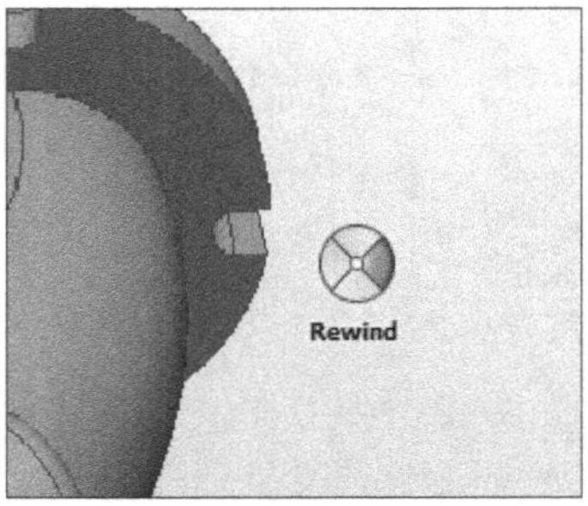

Figure-26. Mini Tour building wheel

- The working of this wheel was discussed earlier.

2D Wheel

The **2D Wheel** provides the basic navigation command for 2D navigation. This wheel is useful when you don't have a mouse with scroll wheel. The procedure to activate this wheel is discussed next.

- Click on the **2D Wheel** button from **Navigation Wheel** drop-down of **Navigation bar** to activate the 2D Wheel. The wheel will be attached to the cursor; refer to Figure-27.

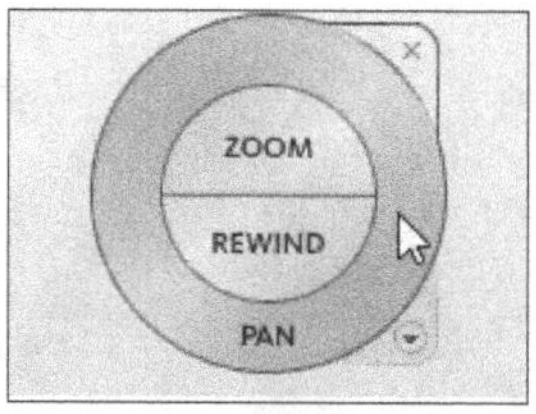

Figure-27. 2D Wheel

- The tools of 2D navigation wheel were discussed earlier.

Zoom

The **Zoom** tool is used to increase or decrease the magnification of current view of model.

- Click on the **Zoom** button from **Navigation bar**. The tool will be activated and a magnifier will be displayed in place of your mouse cursor.
- To zoom in and zoom out, roll up and roll down the middle mouse button.
- To deactivate the **Zoom** tool, click again on the **Zoom** button from **Navigation bar**. You can also press left click of mouse anywhere on the graphics window to do the same work.
- Click on the **Zoom (Fit All)** button from **Navigation Wheel** drop-down of **Zoom** button, so that entire model is visible; refer to Figure-28.

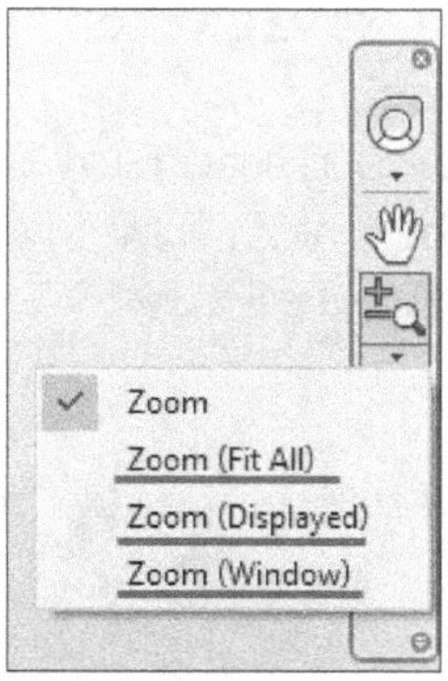

Figure-28. Zoom menu arrow

- Click on the **Zoom (Displayed)** button from **Navigation Wheel** drop-down of **Zoom** button to zoom the displayed view or visible parts of model to the screen.
- Click on the **Zoom (Window)** button from **Navigation Wheel** drop-down of **Zoom** button to zoom selected region. You need to select a region of model to zoom with the help of box selection; refer to Figure-29.

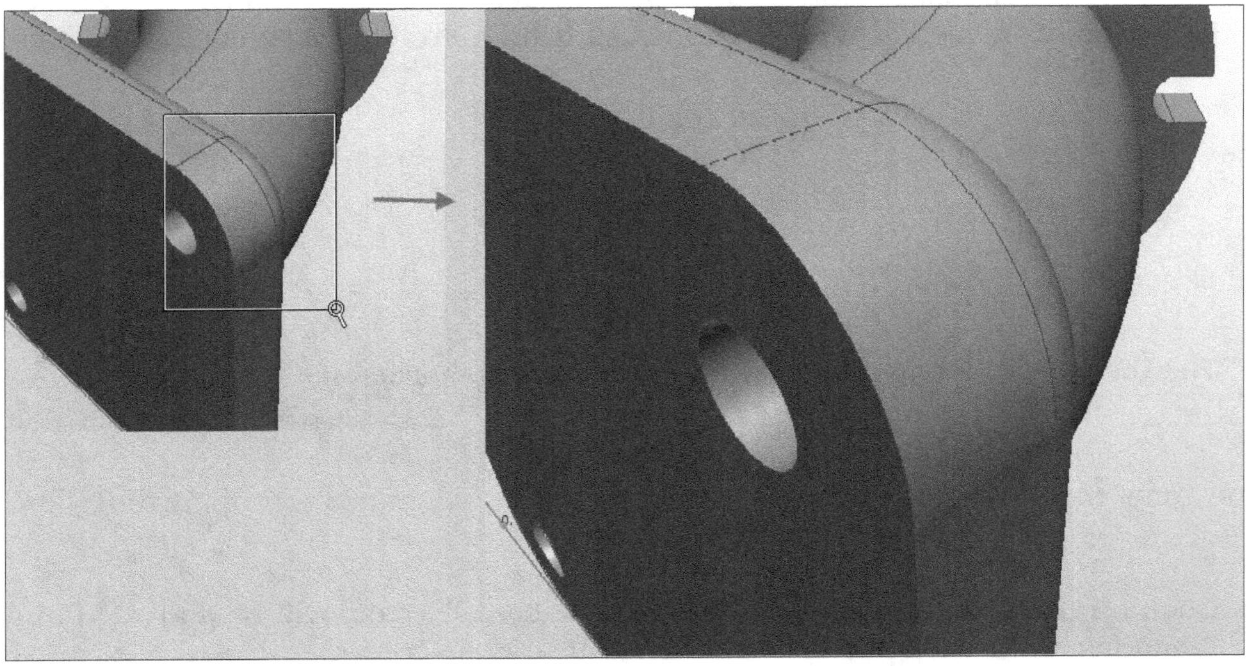

Figure-29. Zoom window selection

Orbit

The **Orbit** tool is used to change the orientation of a model. The procedure to use this tool is discussed next.

- Click on the **Orbit** button from **Navigation bar**. The tool will be activated and cursor will change to orbit shape.
- Press and hold the left mouse button, and move the cursor to change the orientation of model; refer to Figure-30. When you have reached at desired orientation, leave the left mouse button.

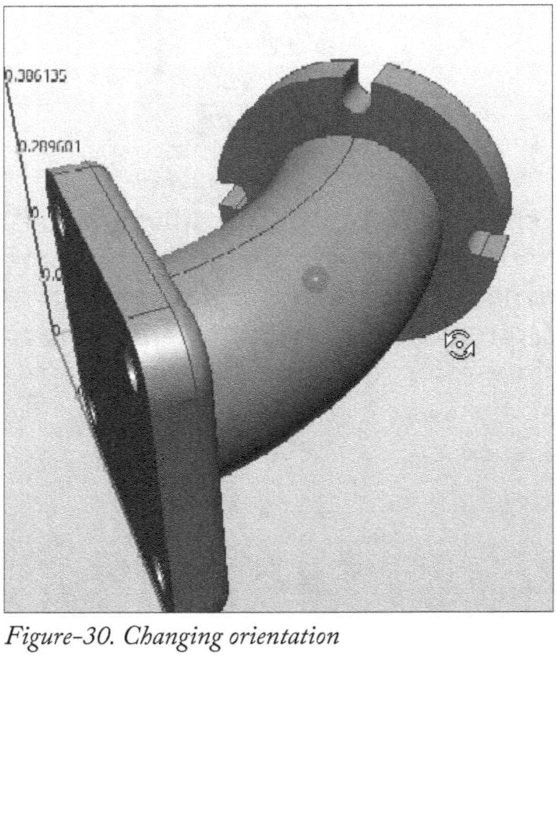

Figure-30. Changing orientation

- Click on the **Orbit (Constrained)** tool from arrow menu of **Orbit** button to rotate about a single axis. This tool is equivalent to moving the eye position about the model in latitude and longitude.

Look At

The **Look At** tool is used to focus on a specific face. The procedure to use this tool is discussed next.

- Click on the **Look At** tool from **Navigation bar**. The tool will be activated and the cursor will be modified accordingly.
- Click on the particular face from the model; the face will be displayed parallel to the screen; refer to Figure-31.

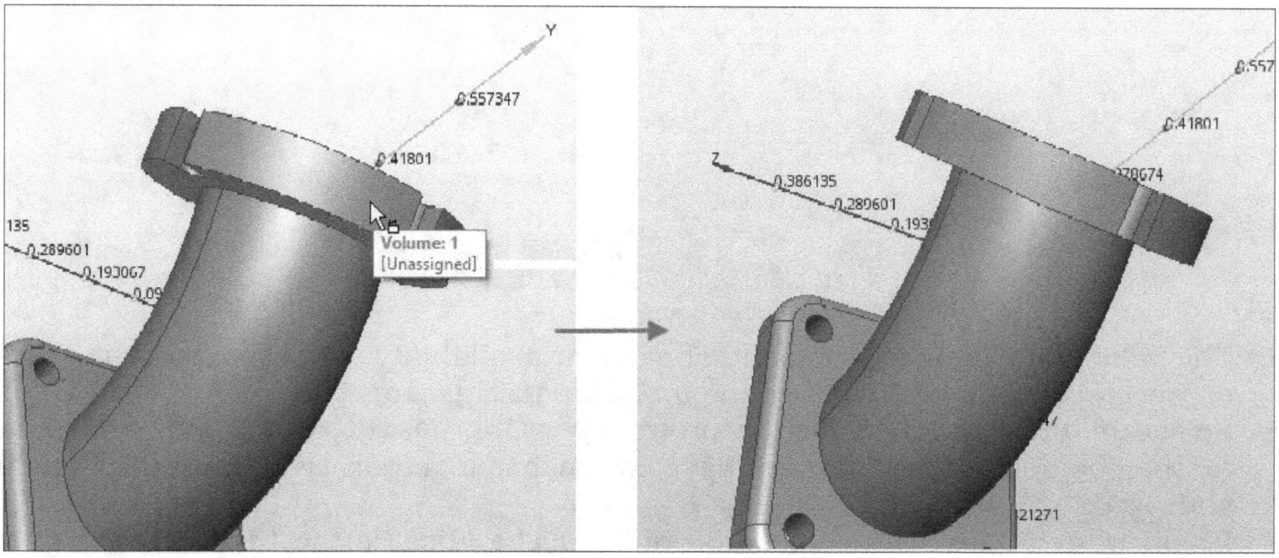

Figure-31. Using Look At tool

Customize Menu

The default position of **Navigation bar** is at the top right side of the Graphics window. The **Customize menu** of **Navigation bar** is used to change the position of **Navigation bar**. The procedure to use **Customize menu** is discussed next.

- Click on the small arrow on the lower right corner of the **Navigation bar**. The menu will be displayed; refer to Figure-32.

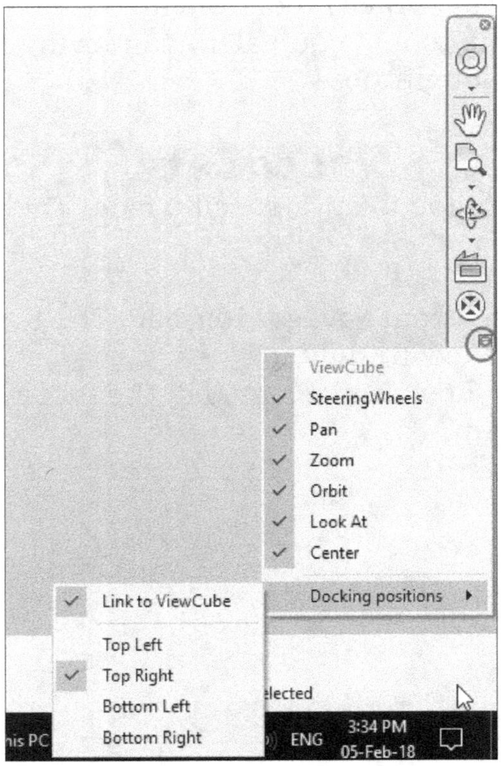

Figure-32. Customize menu

- The ticks in front of tools in menu show their availability in **Navigation bar**. Click on specific tool to add/remove the tool from **Navigation bar**.
- Select the **Link to ViewCube** button from **Docking positions** cascading menu to tie the position of **ViewCube** and **Navigation bar** together. By default, this tool is activated.
- If you want to change the position of **ViewCube**, disable the **Link to ViewCube** button and move the **Navigation bar** manually by using drag and drop at the top edge **Navigation** bar.
- Click on the **Top Left**, **Top Right**, **Bottom Left**, **Bottom Right** button from **Docking positions** cascading menu to move the **ViewCube** and **Navigation bar** together towards top left, top right, bottom left, and bottom right, respectively.

Context Toolbar

The **Context Toolbar** provide convenient access to frequently-used functions specific to the current task. The procedure is discussed next.

- Left-click in the Graphics Window. The **Context Toolbar** will be displayed; refer to Figure-33.

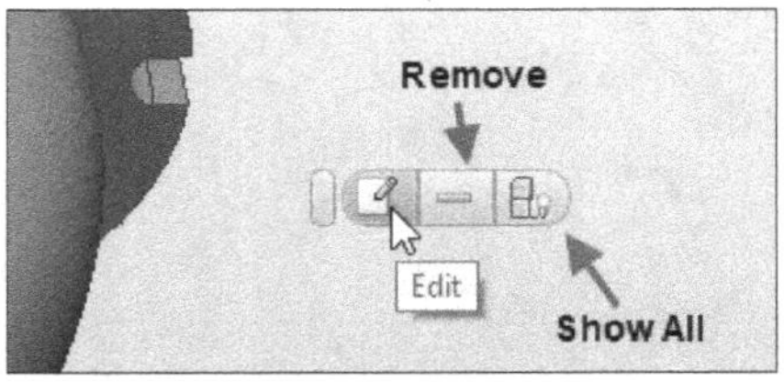

Figure-33. Context Toolbar

- Left-click on the **Edit** button of **Context Toolbar** is used to assign or modify the last material setting.

- Left-click on the **Remove** button of **Context Toolbar** is used to deselect the last command.
- Left-click on the **Show All** button of **Context Toolbar** is used to show all hidden entities.
- Left-click on the **Hide** button of **Context Toolbar** is used to hide the selected entity.

Meshing Context Toolbar

The **Meshing Context Toolbar** is used to control and define mesh. The procedure to use tools of this is toolbar are discussed next.

- To use the **Meshing Context Toolbar**, select the **Mesh Sizing** toggle button from the **Setup Tasks** panel of **Setup** tab in the **Ribbon** and select the model from Graphics window with the help of left-click of mouse. The **Meshing Context Toolbar** will be displayed along with the changed color; refer to Figure-34.

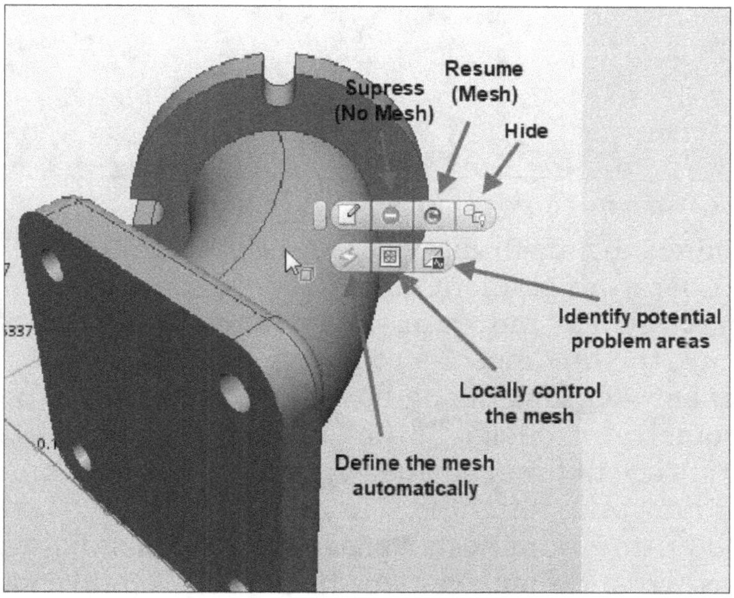

Figure-34. Meshing Context Toolbar

- The **Define the mesh automatically** button is used to apply sizing of mesh automatically. Click on this button, the mesh will be generated automatically on the model.
- You can also use this tool from **Automatic Sizing** section of **Setup** tab after selecting the **Mesh Sizing** tool from the **Setup Tasks** panel in the **Ribbon**; refer to Figure-35.

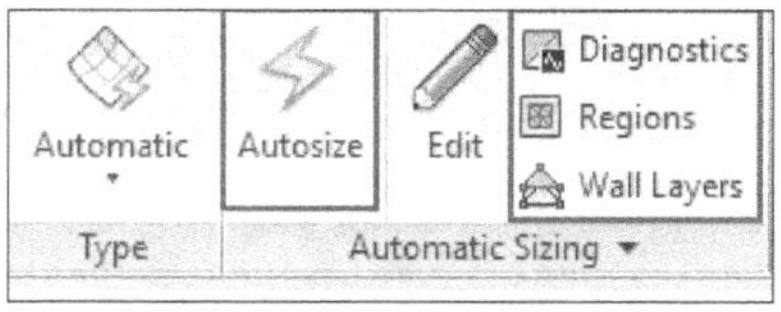

Figure-35. Automatic Sizing section

Mesh Refinement Region

- The **Locally control the mesh** button in toolbar is used to construct refinement regions of mesh. Click on this button, the **Mesh Refinement Regions** dialog box will be displayed; refer to Figure-36. You can also use this tool by clicking on **Regions** button from **Automatic Sizing** section of **Setup** tab.

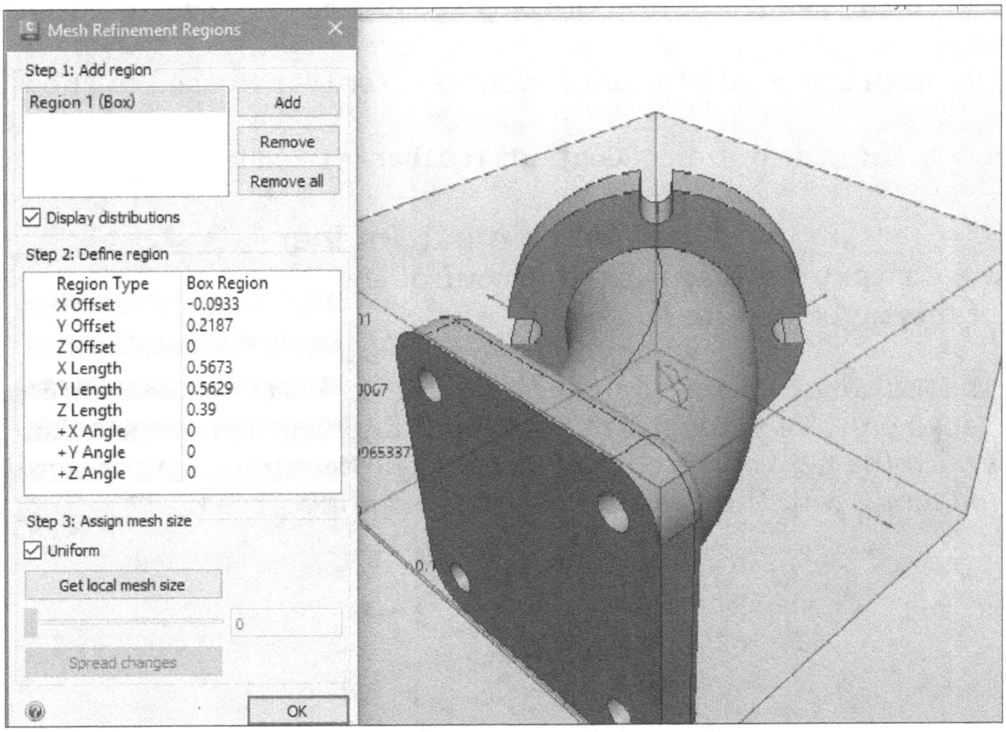

Figure-36. Mesh Refinement Regions dialog box

- The basic guidelines for mesh distribution is that it must be efficient to resolve the flow and temperature gradient effectively. In some regions, the coarser mesh is sufficient where the flow moves in single direction. But in case of flow through various directions, the fine mesh is required.
- The **Mesh Refinement Regions** dialog box is used to create a mesh in a particular area, where geometry of design is not available. It is important to note that refinement regions are not real geometry, and cannot hold any other settings like boundary conditions and material.
- Click on the **Add** button from **Mesh Refinement Regions** dialog box, the **Region 1 (Box)** will be created and displayed on the model. To add more region box, click again on the **Add** button.
- Click in the **Region Type** drop-down from **Step 2: Define region** area of the **Mesh Refinement Regions** dialog box and select the shape of region from the list; refer to Figure-37.

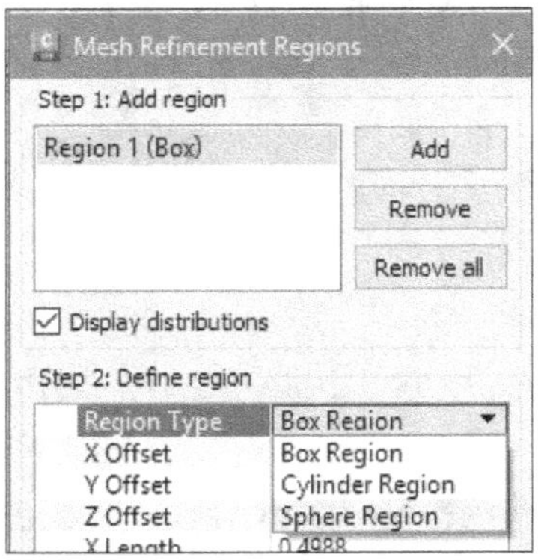

Figure-37. Selecting region type

- Click in the edit boxes from **Step 2: Define region** area section of **Mesh Refinement Regions** dialog box and specify desired values to set the shape & size of refinement region.

- You can also adjust the shape and size of refinement region by moving the drag handle from Graphics window.
- If you want to change the shape of region then select desired shape option from the **Region Type** drop-down; refer to Figure-38.

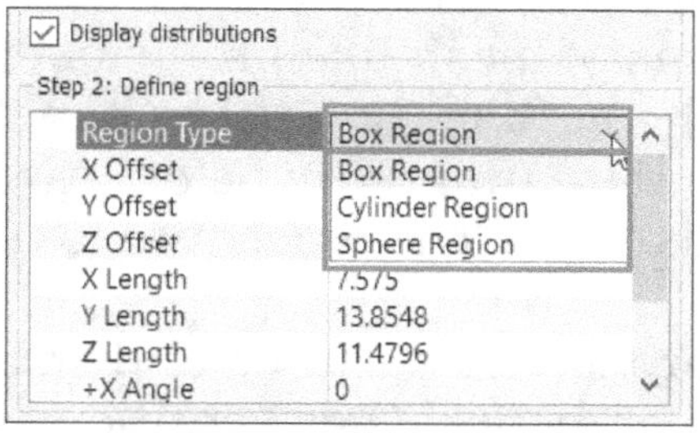

Figure-38. Region Type drop-down

- Select the **Uniform** check box from **Step 3: Assign mesh size** area section to create a mesh with single size element because the mesh in the selected region is based on geometry enclosed within the region.
- Clear the **Uniform** check box to allow non uniform mesh size for producing more efficient mesh at complex regions.
- Click on the **Get local mesh size** button from **Mesh Refinement Regions** dialog box to define a varying mesh. The mesh size edit box will be activated.
- Specify desired value in the edit box or set the value by moving the mesh size slider. The lower the size, more fine the size of **Mesh Size Refinement** region.
- Click on the **Spread Changes** button from **Mesh Refinement Region** dialog box to propagate the effect of mesh in selected region.
- To remove desired region, select the region box from **Mesh Refinement Regions** dialog box and click on the **Remove** button. The selected region will be removed.
- If you want to remove all the region, click on the **Remove All** button from **Mesh Refinement Region dialog** box.
- After specifying the parameters, click on the **OK** button from **Mesh Refinement Region** dialog box. The refinement region will be created on the model; refer to Figure-39.

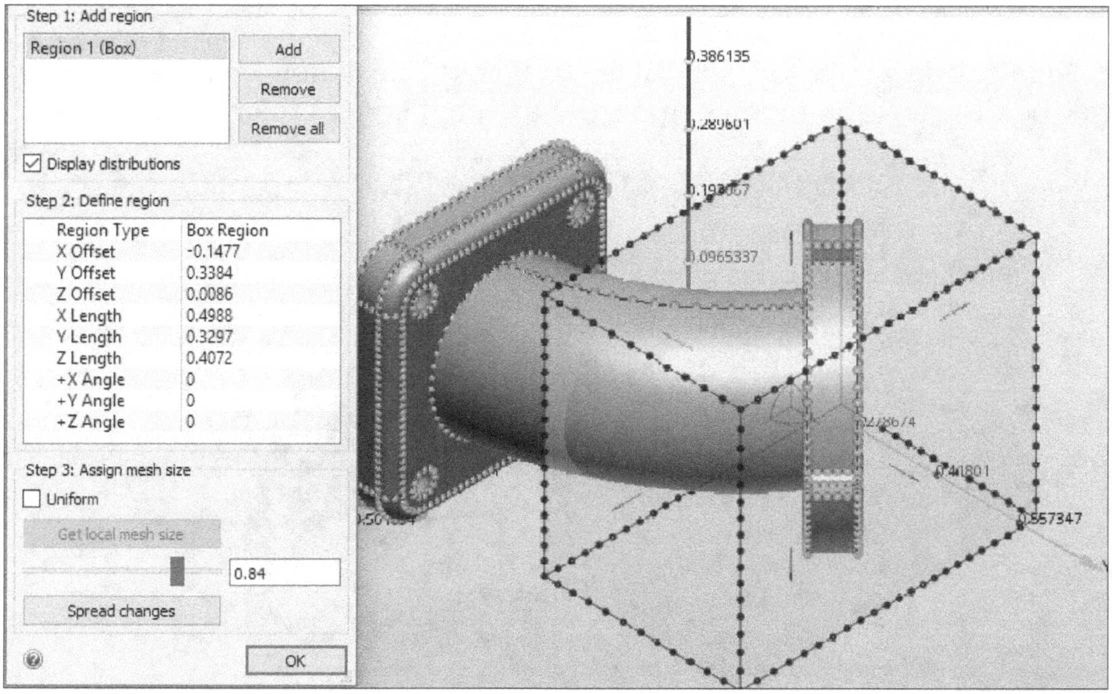

Figure-39. Selected mesh refienement region

- The created refinement regions will be added in **Design Study Bar** with their names as Automatic size and Region (Box) in **Mesh History** node.

Identify potential problem areas

The **Identify potential problem areas** tool is used to run a diagnostic on the model to identify the problems of mesh like problematic surfaces. You can also use the **Diagnostics** tool from the **Automatic Sizing** panel of **Setup** tab in the **Ribbon**. Identifying these problems and locating them before running an analysis is necessary to reduce the effort and wasted time. The procedure to use this tool is discussed next.

This diagnostic function searches for surfaces and edges that are extremely thin & small relative to other parts of model. These entities are caused by poor geometric design or the result of multiple design format conversion throughout the life of model designing.

- Click on the **Identify potential problem areas** button from **Meshing Context Toolbar**. The **Diagnostics** dialog box will be displayed; refer to Figure-40.

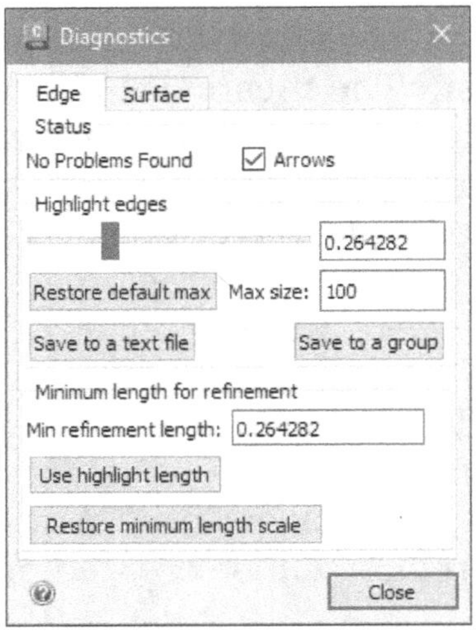

Figure-40. Diagnostics dialog box

- The **Edge** tab is active by default in **Diagnostics** dialog box. Select the **Arrows** check box to view the arrows upon the affected edges; refer to Figure-41.

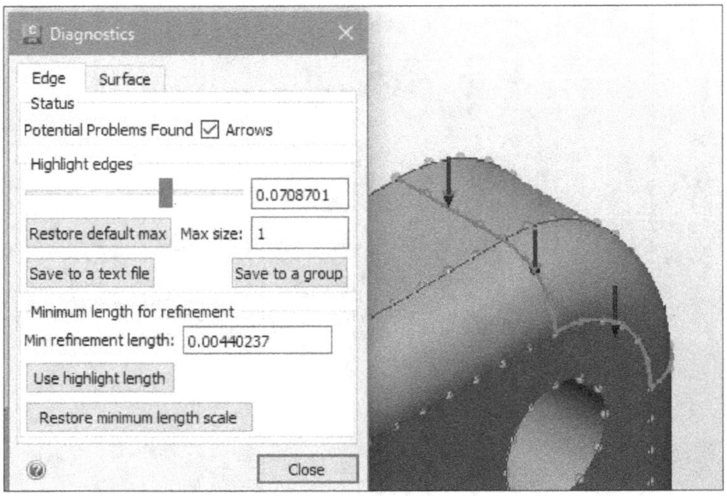

Figure-41. Arrows on highlighted areas

- Click in the **Highlight edges** edit box and specify the size value to define safe lower limit of edges. The edges which have size below specified value will be highlighted. You can also specify the value by moving the **Highlight Edges** slider.
- Click in the **Max size** edit box and specify the maximum value to locate the edges of size less than specified value. Edges will be highlighted accordingly.
- Click on the **Restore default max** button to reset maximum value for edge highlight.
- Click on the **Save to a text file** button to save the data of displayed edge in the format of text file. The **Save File** dialog box will be displayed. Specify desired location and click on the **Save** button.
- Click on the **Save to a group** button from **Diagnostics** dialog box to save the displayed edge to a group. The **Add to Group** dialog box will be displayed.
- Click in the **Min refinement length** edit box and specify desired value of edge length.
- Click on the **Use highlight length** button to select the length of highlighted edges of the model in the **Min refinement length** edit box.
- Click on the **Restore minimum length scale** button from **Diagnostics** dialog box to reset the specified data.
- Click on the **Surfaces** tab from **Diagnostics** dialog box, the tools to detect thin surfaces will be displayed; refer to Figure-42. Options in the **Surface** tab are used to identify potentially problematic surface that may cause problem when generating mesh, like silvers surface, thin annular surface, and surface with cusps.

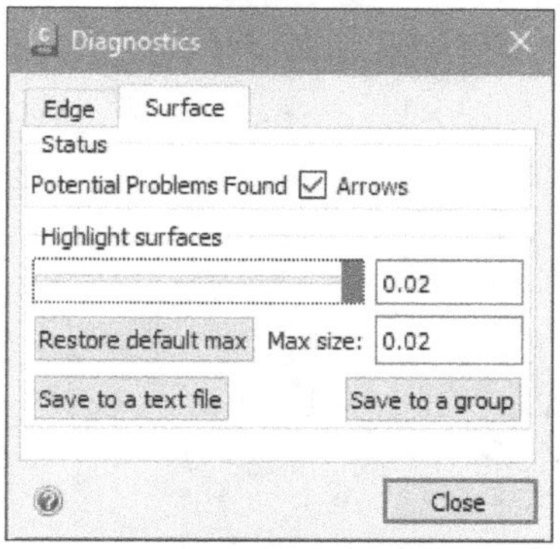

Figure-42. Surfaces tab of Diagnostics dialog box

- Move the **Highlight surfaces** slider or specify the value manually in the **Highlight Surfaces** edit box to specify upper limit for detecting the surfaces with edge length less than the specified value.
- Check the **Status** after specifying the value. When status shows "**No Problems Found**" then there is no problem in the design of model. But, if status shows "**Potential Problems Found**" then some surfaces of model have thickness less than the specified value in **Highlight Surfaces**.
- Other tools of **Surfaces** tab are same as discussed in **Edge** tab.
- After checking the parameters, click on the **Close** button to exit dialog box.

Suppress (no mesh)

The **Suppress** tool is used to suppress the selected body. The suppressed body is removed temporarily from the model so that it cannot interfere in analysis. The procedure is discussed next.

- Click on desired part of model to be suppressed. The **Meshing Context Toolbar** will be displayed.

- Click on the **Suppress** button from the displayed menu. If you had not created any mesh on the selected part then the part will be suppressed. But if, you have created any mesh on the selected part, then **Suppress Confirmation** dialog box will be displayed; refer to Figure-43.

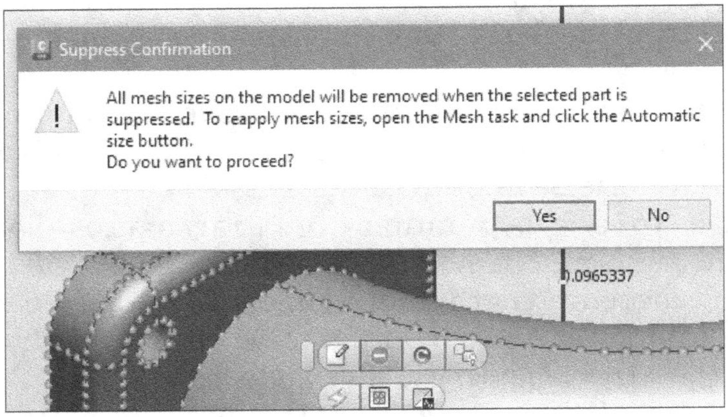

Figure-43. Suppress Confirmation box

- Click on the **Yes** button to confirm, the part will be suppressed.

SELF-ASSESSMENT

Q1. You can create 3D model of product in Autodesk CFD to perform analysis. (T/F)

Q2. Using the options of Small Object tab in Geometry Tools dialog box, you can delete small surfaces which cannot be meshed in Autodesk CFD. (T/F)

Q3. The working model which has openings for fluid entry and exit are not suitable for analysis in Autodesk CFD. (T/F)

Q4. Which of the following navigation wheels is used to navigate through buildings like assembly line, rig, and ship?

a. Mini Object Wheel
b. Basic Tour Building Wheel
c. Full Navigation Wheel
d. Mini View Object Wheel

Q5. Which of the following options cannot be used to rotate the model?

a. Orbit
b. Pan
c. ViewCube
d. Look At

Q6. The .... tool is used to increase or decrease the magnification of current view of model.

Q7. The .... toolbar provide convenient access to frequently-used functions specific to the current task.

Q8. Which of the following options is used to seal openings of the model which can later be used to define boundary conditions?

a. Edge Merge
b. Small object
c. Void Fill
d. Ext. Volume.

Q9. When there is some error with the design or there is a need to improve the quality of model imported in CFD project then the .... dialog box will be displayed after opening model.

Q10. You can open the Geometry Tools dialog box by clicking on the .... button from Setup Tasks panel of Setup tab.

Q11. On using Edge merge function to improve model quality, all the small edges that have inclination angle more than 15 degree get merged. (T/F)

Q12. The options in .... tab of Geometry Tools dialog box are used to remove geometry from model, like surfaces and edges, which are too small to see/create in the mesh.

Q13. The options in .... tab are used to create capping surfaces that bound a water-tight internal void on the openings of solid body.

Q14. Write down the steps to change view style from orthographic to perspective.

Q15. What must you have before creating a design study in Autodesk CFD?

A. A saved simulation study
B. A design model created in unsupported software
C. A pre-created design model created using Autodesk CFD-supported software
D. A completed mesh structure

Q16. What does the Geometry Tools dialog box assist with?

A. Adding lighting effects
B. Opening new projects
C. Improving model quality for CFD
D. Saving the design study

Q17. What is the maximum limit for the tangency angle used in edge merging?

A. 5 degrees
B. 10 degrees
C. 15 degrees
D. 20 degrees

Q18. What happens when you click the "Display edges to be merged" checkbox?

A. The mesh is finalized
B. Only the merged edges disappear
C. Edges to be merged are shown with arrows
D. The simulation runs automatically

Q19. What is the purpose of Void Fill in Autodesk CFD?

A. To add external volumes
B. To delete unneeded geometry
C. To create capping surfaces for internal voids
D. To enhance rendering

Q20. What message appears after a successful void fill?

A. "1 edge removed successfully"
B. "Geometry error detected"
C. "There was 1 additional part generated"
D. "Simulation complete"

Q21. Which type of analysis is the Ext. Volume tab used for?

A. Mesh smoothing
B. External fluid flow analysis
C. Electrical simulations
D. Material optimization

Q22. What is important when creating an external volume?

A. It should match the color of the model
B. It should only touch the base of the model
C. The model should be completely immersed in the external volume
D. The external volume should be smaller than the model

Q23. How can you resize the external volume manually?

A. Move the model inwards
B. Click Reset repeatedly
C. Click and drag grab handles or specify values
D. Click Export tab

Q24. What is the primary function of the Navigation bar in Autodesk software?

A. To create new models
B. To edit materials
C. To access the model through different aspects
D. To export files

Q25. Which of the following tools is considered a Unified navigation tool?

A. ViewCube
B. Tour Building Wheel
C. Meshing Context Toolbar
D. Customize Menu

Q26. What view is shown when you click the Home button on the ViewCube?

A. Front View
B. Top View
C. Isometric View
D. Perspective View

Q27. What is the effect of selecting the “Snap to closest view” checkbox in ViewCube Properties?

A. Automatically animates the view
B. Snaps cursor to nearest face of ViewCube
C. Resets the home view
D. Enables 2D navigation

Q28. What happens when you click the Full Navigation Wheel button?

A. A box selection appears
B. Cursor disappears
C. A navigation wheel attaches to the cursor
D. ViewCube gets hidden

Q29. Which button on the Navigation Wheel allows you to move the model horizontally or vertically?

A. PAN
B. ZOOM
C. ORBIT
D. CENTER

Q30. What is the function of the REWIND button in Navigation Wheel?

A. Zooms out the model
B. Resets all views
C. Moves the model forward
D. Lets you select and go back to a previous view state

Q31. Which tool is used to reorient the model view by rotating vertically and horizontally from eye position?

A. Look
B. Orbit
C. Pan
D. Center

Q32. Which Navigation Wheel allows you to move through environments like buildings or ships?

A. 2D Wheel
B. View Object Wheel
C. Full Navigation Wheel
D. Tour Building Wheel

Q33. What is the primary function of the 2D Wheel?

A. Rotate the model
B. Provide navigation when scroll mouse is unavailable
C. Display animation
D. Reset the model orientation

Q34. Which tool allows zooming selected region using box selection?

A. Zoom (Fit All)
B. Zoom (Window)
C. Zoom (Displayed)
D. Zoom (Home)

Q35. What does the Orbit (Constrained) tool help you do?

A. Rotate in any direction freely
B. Zoom with constraints
C. Rotate about a single axis
D. Reset the view to home

Q36. What is the purpose of the Look At tool?

A. Hide selected face
B. View selected face parallel to the screen
C. Show all entities
D. Zoom selected region

Q37. What is the Customize Menu used for in the Navigation bar?

A. Change units
B. Change Navigation bar position and visibility
C. Modify mesh parameters
D. Create new materials

Q38. What does enabling the "Link to ViewCube" option do?

A. Locks the ViewCube
B. Synchronizes position of ViewCube and Navigation bar
C. Disables docking
D. Adds custom tools

Q39. Which tool in the Context Toolbar is used to show all hidden entities?

A. Hide
B. Show All
C. Edit
D. Remove

Q40. Which panel contains the Mesh Sizing toggle for activating Meshing Context Toolbar?

A. Zoom Panel
B. Setup Tasks panel
C. View Panel
D. Edit Panel

Q41. What does selecting the Uniform checkbox in Mesh Refinement dialog do?

A. Prevents mesh generation
B. Hides mesh
C. Creates a mesh with single size elements
D. Allows varying mesh sizes

Q42. What happens when you click the Get local mesh size button?

A. Refines mesh manually
B. Opens the Orbit view
C. Enables mesh size editing
D. Removes all regions

Q43. What is the purpose of the Identify potential problem areas tool?

A. Add new geometry
B. View all commands
C. Detect thin or small surfaces and edges
D. Customize interface

Q44. What does the Surface tab in Diagnostics dialog help identify?

A. Incorrect lighting
B. Missing views
C. Potentially problematic surfaces like thin or silver surfaces
D. Animation errors

Q45. What is the function of the Suppress button in Meshing Context Toolbar?

A. Highlights geometry
B. Hides mesh settings
C. Temporarily removes part from model
D. Changes color of toolbar

FOR STUDENT NOTES

Chapter 3

Creating Analysis Model

Topics Covered

The major topics covered in this chapter are:

- ***Applying Materials***
- ***Boundary Conditions***
- ***Initials Conditions***
- ***Generating Mesh***
- ***Motion tool***

INTRODUCTION

In the last chapter, we have learned the interface of software and tools for navigation through the model. In this chapter, we will learn the procedure of applying material, boundary condition, initial Conditions, and other parameters on the model.

APPLYING MATERIALS

Material is a key input for any analysis. The result of analysis is directly related to material of the object. There are few properties of material like, ultimate strength, hardness, and young's modulus which play important role in success/failure of the object under specified load. Also, material determines the application of object in real world. For example, we do not use glass to make pistons in engine. That's why, the selection of material should be good enough to perform the analysis. The procedure to apply material is discussed next.

- Open the Autodesk CFD from **Start** menu or from Desktop icon. The Autodesk CFD will open and welcome screen will be displayed.
- Click on the **New** button from **Ribbon** and open desired part file which is compatible with Autdodek CFD to work with. The part file will be displayed along with all activated tools for creating an analysis; refer to Figure-1. The procedure to create a new analysis has been discussed in previous chapter.

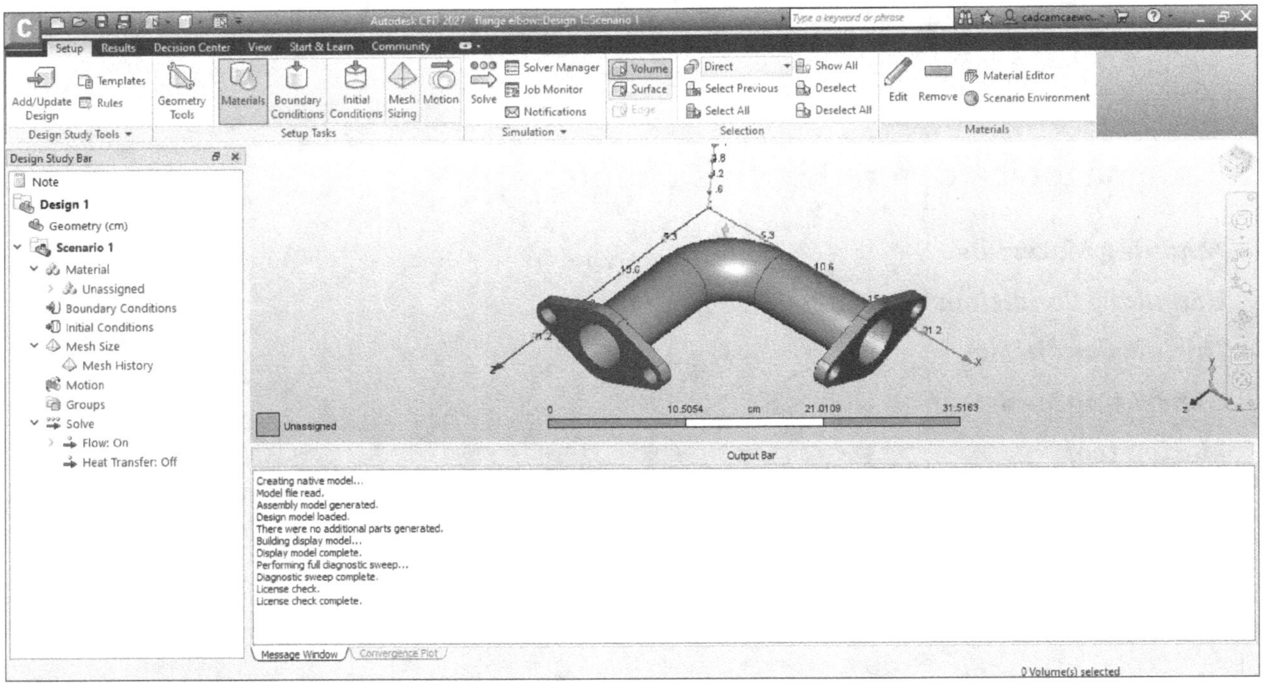

Figure-1. Welcome screen for elbow design

- On starting the analysis, the **Design Study Bar** will be displayed at the left in the application window. Various options are available in the **Design Study Bar** to assign material, apply boundary condition, create mesh, and so on.
- After adding model in Autodesk CFD, the first step for running an analysis is to assign material to the model. Whether it is blank space in the form of air or a metal part, you need to assign proper material to the model. The analysis of model depends on the type of material assigned to various components of model.

First Method

- Click on the **Materials** button from **Setup Tasks** panel of **Setup** tab and then click on the **Edit** button from **Materials** panel; refers to Figure-2. The **Materials** dialog box will be displayed; refer to Figure-3.

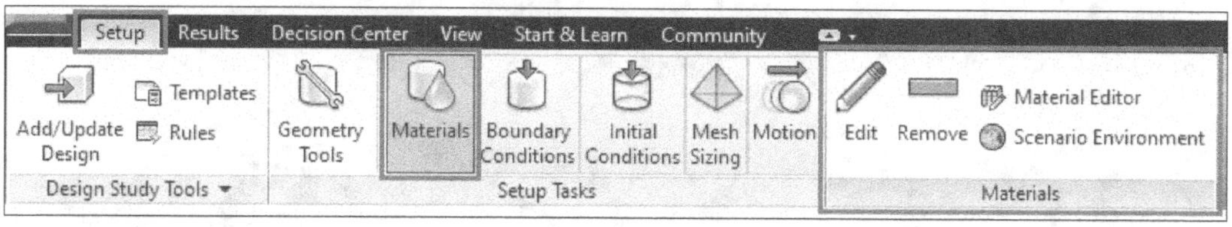

Figure-2. Setup tab

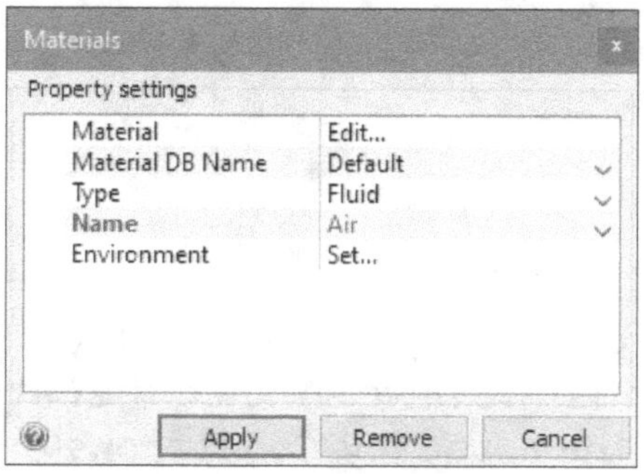

Figure-3. Materials dialog box

- The parameters and details of **Materials** dialog box will be discussed later in this chapter.

Second Method

- Right-click on the unassigned part of model from **Design Study Bar**. The right-click shortcut menu will be displayed; refer to Figure-4.

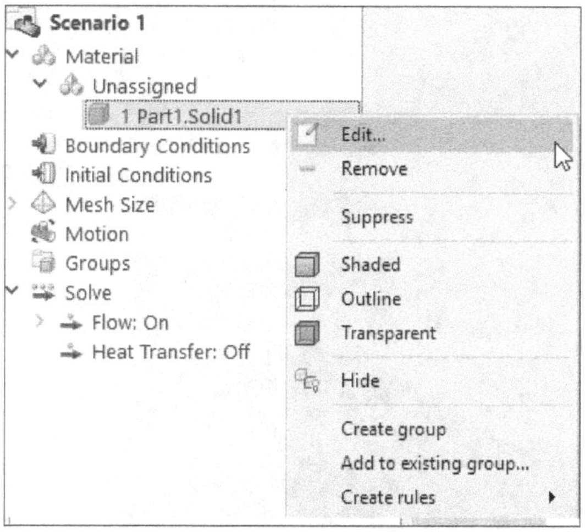

Figure-4. Material right-click menu

- Click on the **Edit** button from the displayed menu. The **Materials** dialog box will be displayed.

Third Method

- Click on the **Materials** button from **Setup Tasks** panel of **Setup** tab. The material options will be activated.

- Left-click on the model, the context toolbar will be displayed. Click on the **Edit** button from the displayed toolbar; refer to Figure-5. The **Materials** dialog box will be displayed.

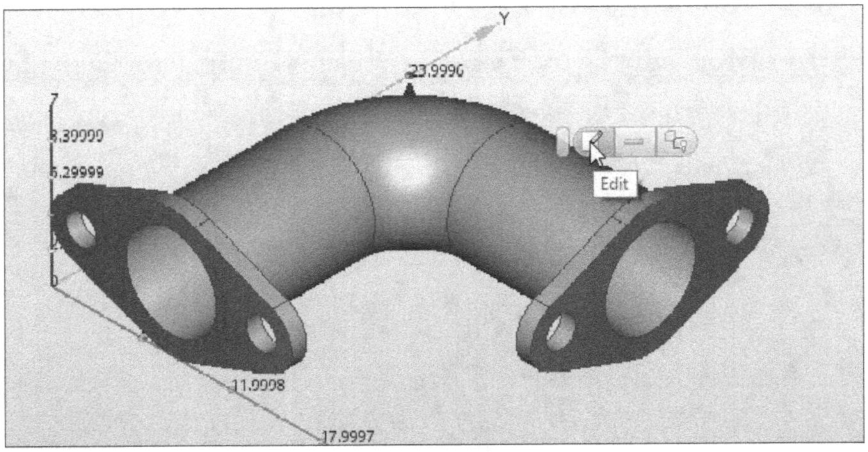

Figure-5. Context toolbar of model

- When we click anywhere in the graphic window then the context toolbar for material is displayed because we have selected the **Materials** tool from **Setup Tasks** panel. If we had selected the **Boundary Conditions** button or **Initial Conditions** button or any other tool, the context toolbar related to that selected parameter would have displayed instead of **Materials** dialog box.

Fourth Method

- After selecting **Materials** tool from **Setup Tasks** panel in the **Ribbon**. Right-click anywhere on the Graphics window. The right-click shortcut menu will be displayed; refer to Figure-6.

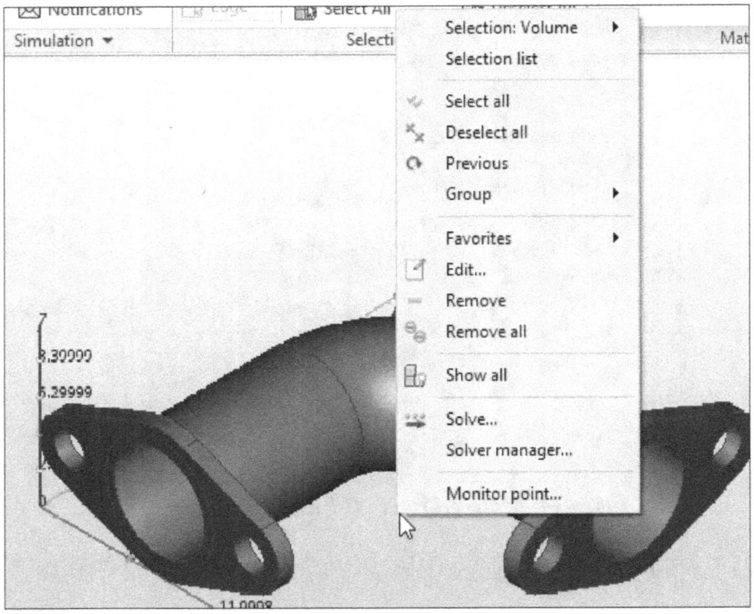

Figure-6. Right-click menus for Material

- Click on the **Edit** button from right-click menu. The **Materials** dialog box will be displayed.

- Make sure, the **Default** option is selected in **Material DB Name** drop-down, because the default list contains all the materials which are going to be used while performing analysis. If you want to use any other material library then select it from **Material DB Name** drop-down.
- Click in the **Type** drop-down from **Materials** dialog box and select desired material category; refer to Figure-7. If you want to use a gas or liquid type material then select the Fluid option.
- Each material type list contains various materials of same kind. Click in the **Name** drop-down from the **Materials** dialog box and select desired material; refer to Figure-8.

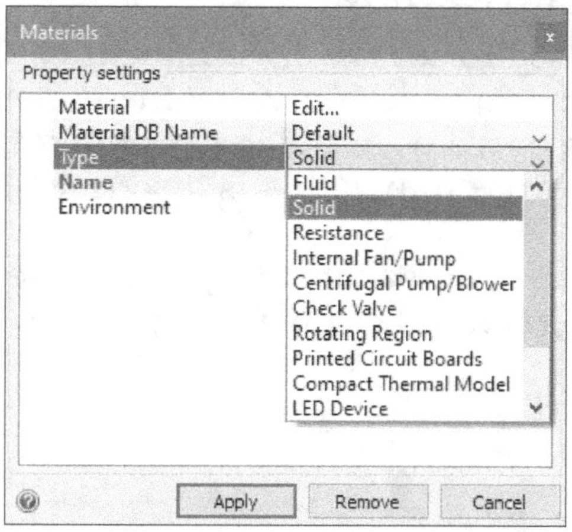

Figure-7. Material type drop-down

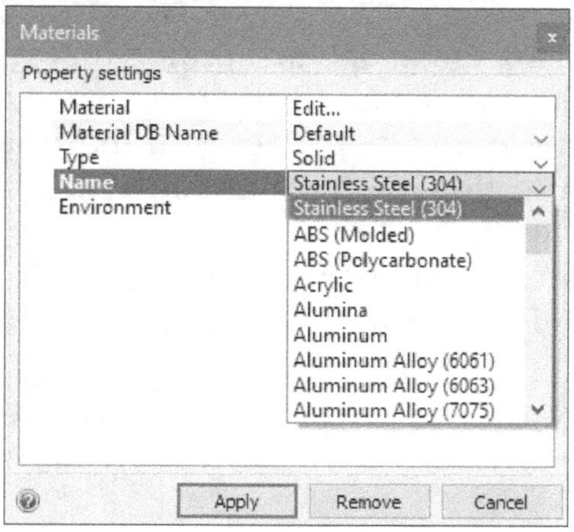

Figure-8. Selecting material for model

- Click on the **Set** button for **Environment** option, the **Material Environment** dialog box will be displayed; refer to Figure-9. The environment settings are applicable only to solid and fluid materials.

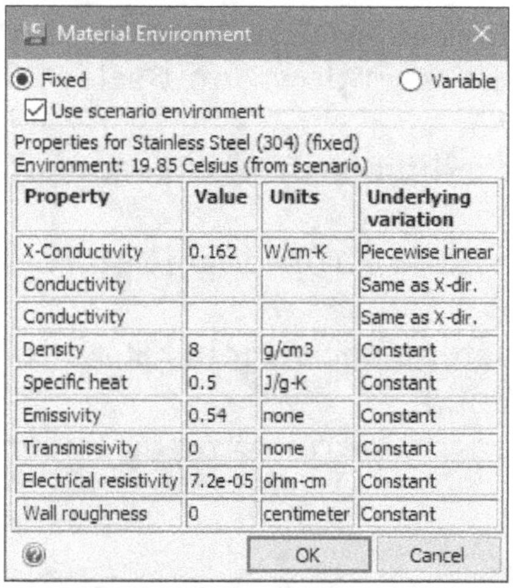

Property	Value	Units	Underlying variation
X-Conductivity	0.162	W/cm-K	Piecewise Linear
Conductivity			Same as X-dir.
Conductivity			Same as X-dir.
Density	8	g/cm3	Constant
Specific heat	0.5	J/g-K	Constant
Emissivity	0.54	none	Constant
Transmissivity	0	none	Constant
Electrical resistivity	7.2e-05	ohm-cm	Constant
Wall roughness	0	centimeter	Constant

Figure-9. Material Environment dialog box

- For some analysis, material property are constant with respect to time and for other simulations, the material properties needs to vary with time. For example, in case of natural convection and high-speed compressible simulations, the material properties vary.
- Select the **Fixed** radio button from **Material Environment** dialog box to keep environment properties constant.
- Select the **Variable** radio button from **Material Environment** dialog box to vary properties as defined in the material. Note that, only properties defined with a variable method will vary.

- By default, the **Use scenario environment** check box from **Material Environment** dialog box will be selected which means it uses the data specified in **Scenario Environment** dialog box. Clear the **Use scenario environment** check box to set the temperature and pressure different from **Scenario Environment** dialog box.
- Click in the **Temperature** edit box and specify desired value.
- Click in the **Temperature unit** drop-down and select desired unit.
- Similarly, specify pressure and pressure unit as desired.
- Click on the **OK** button from dialog box to apply parameters. The **Materials** dialog box will be displayed again. Click on the **Apply** button to apply material.

Scenario Environment

The **Scenario Environment** dialog box is used to set the environment conditions for an individual material. Sometime, the scenario environment value is not sufficient to define the material property, if materials operates at different conditions, like two types of fluid flowing in a model. The procedure to use this is discussed next.

- Click on the **Scenario Environment** tool from **Materials** panel of **Setup** tab in **Ribbon**. The **Scenario Environment** dialog box will be displayed; refer to Figure-10.

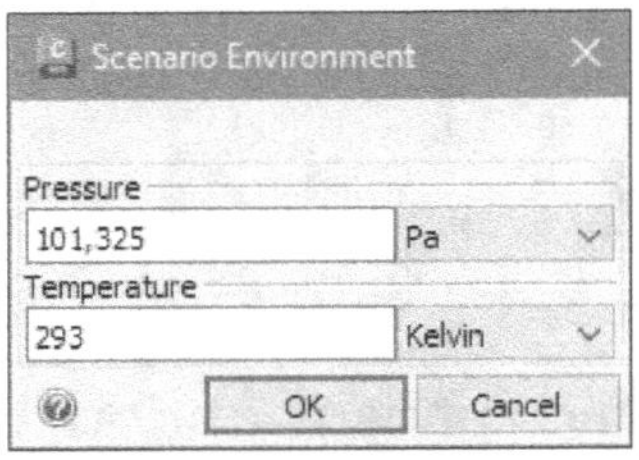

Figure-10. Scenario Environment dialog box

- Click in the **Pressure** edit box from the **Scenario Environment** dialog box and specify desired value.
- Click in the **Pressure unit** drop-down and select desired unit for pressure from the displayed list.
- Click in the **Temperature** edit box from **Scenario Environment** dialog box and specify desired value.
- Click in the **Temperature unit** drop-down and select desired unit for pressure from the displayed list.
- After specifying the parameters, click on the **OK** button. The parameters for scenario environment will be specified.
- After specifying desired parameters from the **Material Environment** dialog box, click on the **OK** button.

Material Editor

- Click on the **Edit** button from **Materials** dialog box; refer to Figure-11. The **Material Editor** will be displayed; refer to Figure-12.

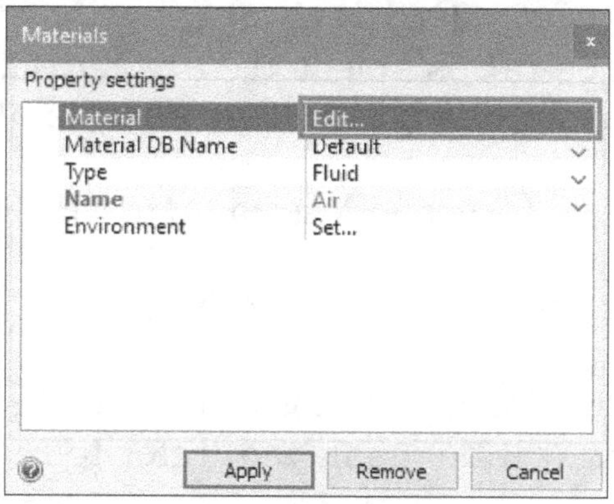

Figure-11. Edit button in Material dialog Box

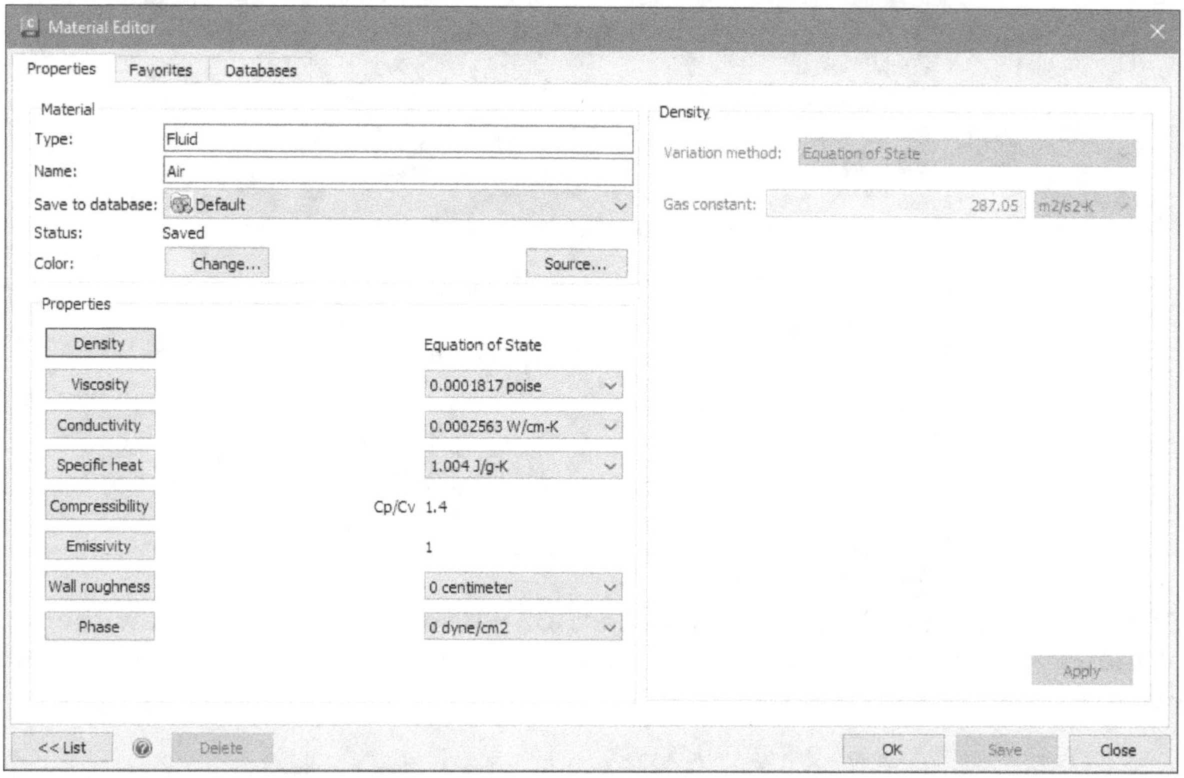

Figure-12. Material Editor dialog box

- You can also open the **Material Editor** dialog box from **Materials** panel of **Setup** tab by clicking on **Material Editor** button; refer to Figure-13.

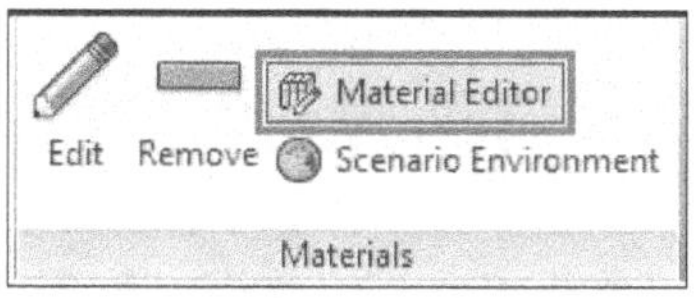

Figure-13. Material Editor button

- The **Material Editor** dialog box is used to view the parameters of default fluid. You can also create a new material as per your desired parameters in **Material Editor** dialog box.
- There are three tabs in the **Material Editor** dialog box, i.e. **Properties** tab, **Favorites** tab, and **Database** tab. The options in these tabs are discussed next.

Properties tab

- By default, the properties tab is selected in **Material Editor** dialog box. In the **Properties** tab, you cannot change the parameters of a material, you can check the parameters.
- Select desired button from the **Properties** area of the dialog box to check respective properties.
- The **Save to database** option shows the database in which the selected material is saved.
- Click on the **Change** button next to **Color** option to change the color of model. The **Select Color** dialog box will be displayed; refer to Figure-14.

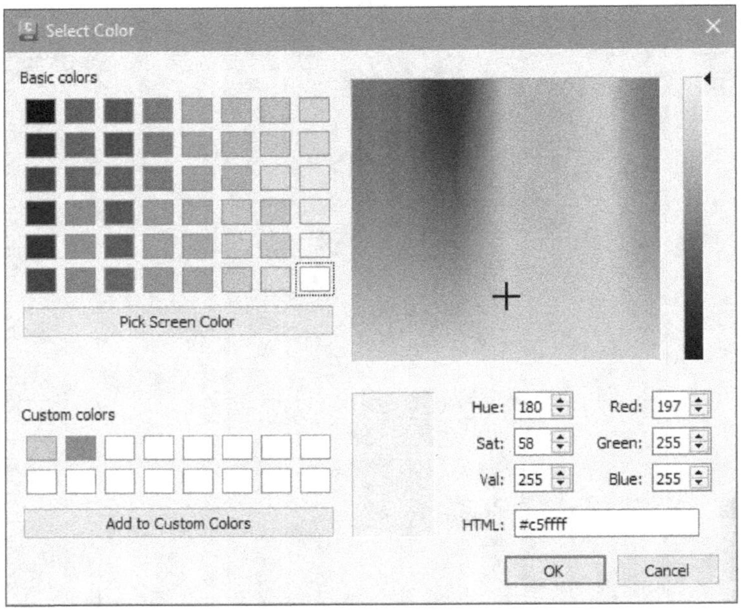

Figure-14. Select Color dialog box

- Click on the **Source** button from **Material Editor** dialog box to view the source of material. The **Material Values Source** dialog box will be displayed; refer to Figure-15.

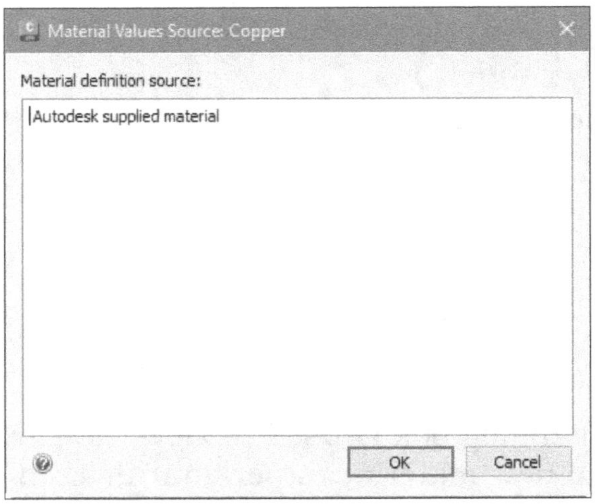

Figure-15. Material Values Copper box

- Check the source of material and click on the **OK** button. You will be returned to **Material Editor** dialog box.
- The parameters of selected material are shown under **Properties** section.
- Click on the **<<List** button from **Material Editor** dialog box to view the list of all fluid present in Autodesk CFD; refer to Figure-16.

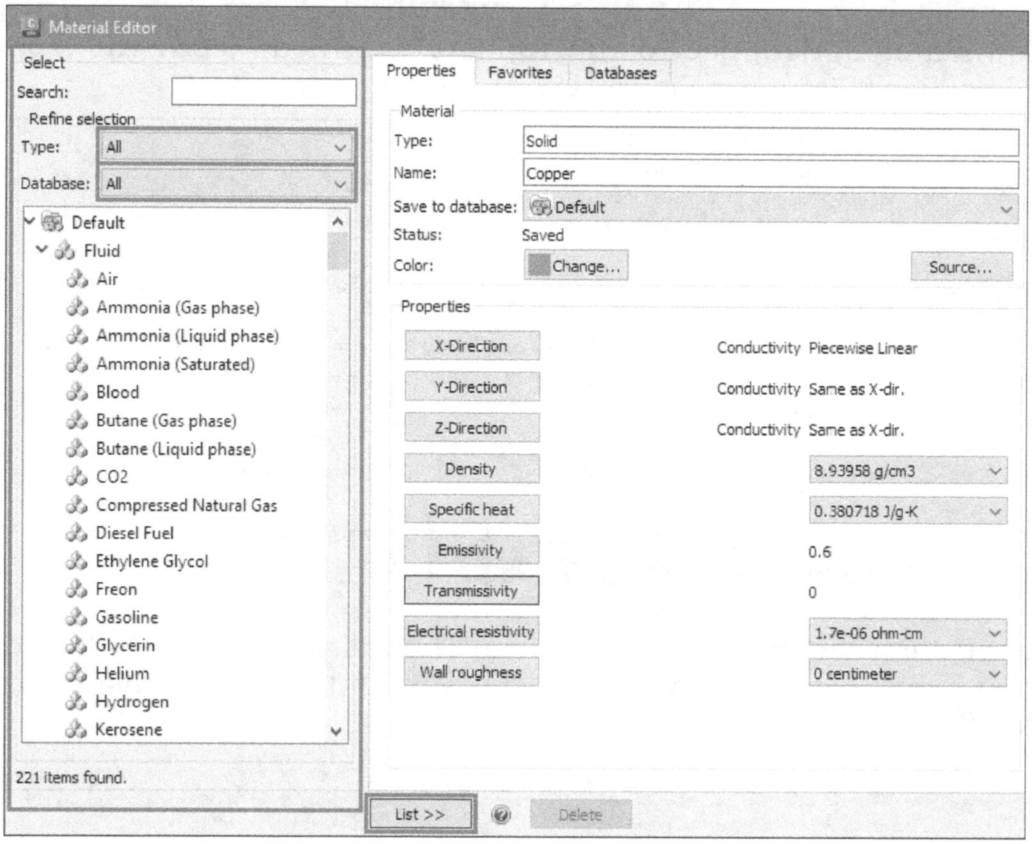

Figure-16. List button

- If you want to search a material from list of material to save time, click in the **Search** edit box and specify the name of desired material.
- Click on the **Type** drop-down from **Select** section and select desired type of material type. After selection of material type, the materials of selected type will be displayed.
- Click on the **Database** drop-down from the **Refine selection** section and select desired database to only view the material of selected database.
- Click on desired material from the list. The properties will be displayed at right.
- If you use some of the materials frequently for analyses then you can add these material to your favorite material list. To do so, right-click on the material, a right-click menus will be displayed; refer to Figure-17.

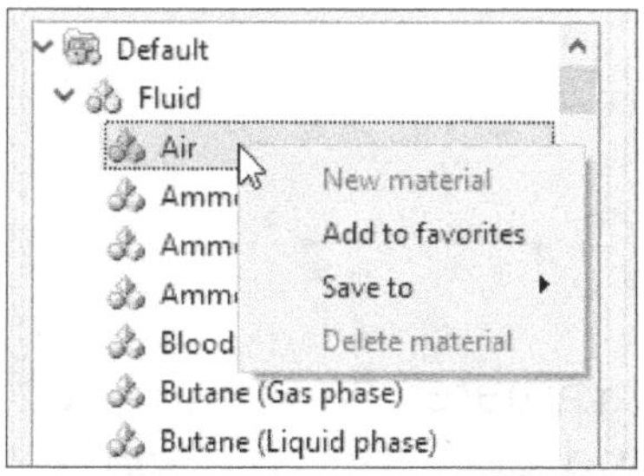

Figure-17. Add to favorites button

- Click on the **Add to favorites** button from the displayed list, the selected material will be added to favorite material list and a red star will be displayed on the material icon.
- You can also save the selected material to **My Material** database by clicking on the **My Materials** button from **Save to** cascading menu of right-click shortcut menu.

Adding New Material

To add new material, right-click on the **My Materials** node. The right-click shortcut menu will be displayed; refer Figure-18.

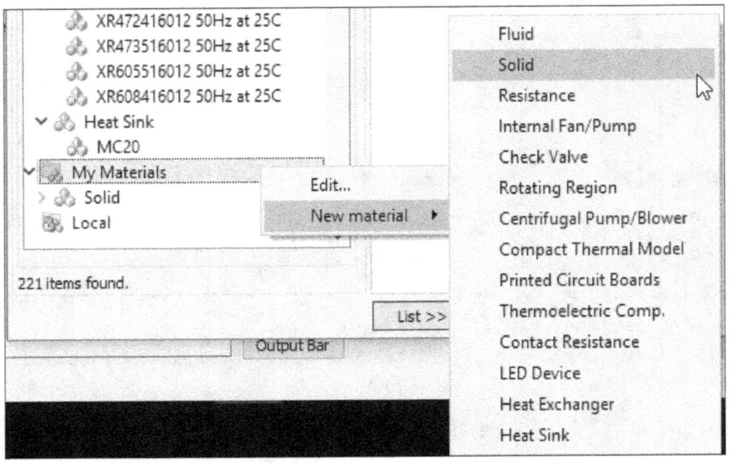

Figure-18. Adding new Material

- Hover the cursor to **New Material** option. The cascading menu will be displayed.
- Click on desired material type. The **Properties** tab will be displayed; refer to Figure-19.

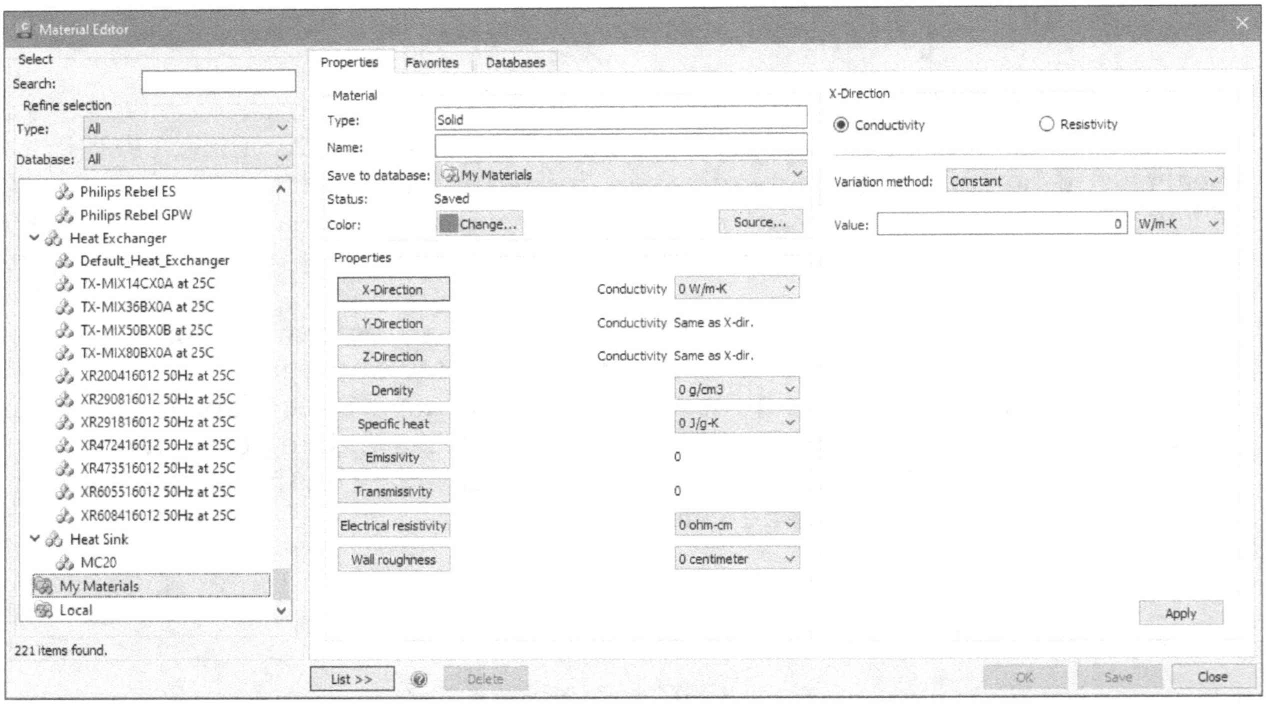

Figure-19. Specifying properties of new material

- Specify the properties & parameters as required in **Material Editor** dialog box to create a new material and click on the **Apply** button to apply parameters to new material.
- Click on the **Save** button from **Material Editor** dialog box. The material will be created and could be used in current analysis. The newly created material will be added under **My Material** database.
- If you want to remove selected material then click on the **Remove** button from **Material** dialog box. The material will be removed from model and model material will be **Unassigned**.

- After specifying the parameters, click on the **Apply** button from **Materials** dialog box. The selected material will be applied on the model.

APPLYING BOUNDARY CONDITIONS

The **Boundary Conditions** option is used to create flow inlet and outlet boundary conditions as well as wall conditions of selected fluid-contacting faces for both internal and external flow analyses. Also, thermal wall conditions can be created on selected external walls for internal flow analyses with enabled heat conductions in solid. For 3D models, you can apply these conditions to model surfaces and for 2D models, you can apply boundary conditions to edges.

Boundary conditions connect the model with surroundings. Without boundary conditions, the analysis cannot be defined. Generally, boundary conditions can be defined in two state i.e. steady state and transient state. Steady state boundary condition persist throughout the analysis process and transient boundary condition vary with time throughout the process. The procedure to use this tool is discussed next.

- Open desired model in Autodesk CFD and apply the material as required.
- Before applying the boundary conditions on the surface of model, you need to enable the **Boundary Conditions** task by clicking on it from the **Setup Tasks** panel of **Setup** tab in the **Ribbon**; refer to Figure-20. The **Boundary Conditions** tool will be enabled.

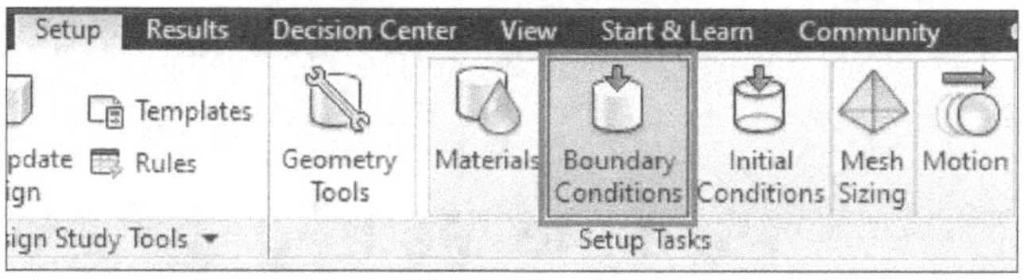

Figure-20. Boundary Conditions tool

- When you are applying **Boundary Conditions** in a fluid flow model then you need to make sure you have applied proper lids on the openings of model.
- There are various methods to apply the boundary conditions to the model which are discussed next.

First Method

- After activating the **Boundary Conditions** tool from the **Setup Tasks** panel, click on the **Edit** button from **Boundary Conditions** panel of **Setup** tab; refer to Figure-21. The **Boundary Conditions** dialog box will be displayed; refer to Figure-22.

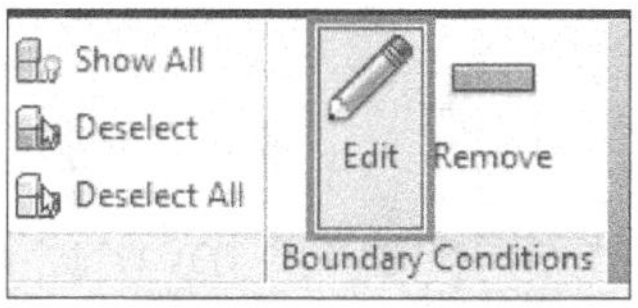

Figure-21. Edit button of Boundary conditions tool

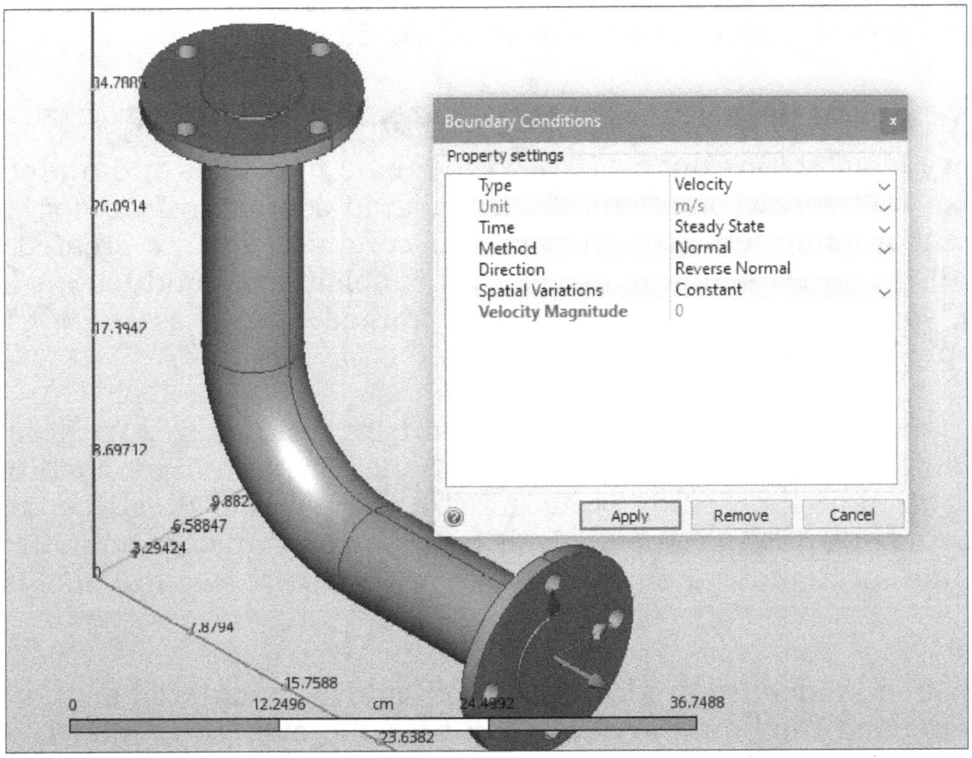

Figure-22. Boundary Conditions dialog box

- Set desired parameters for boundary conditions in the dialog box.
- To apply the boundary condition on a particular surface, you need to click on the surface from model before clicking on **Apply** button from **Boundary Conditions** dialog box.

Second Method

- Right-click on the **Boundary Conditions** option from **Design Study Bar**, the right-click shortcut menu will be displayed; refer to Figure-23.

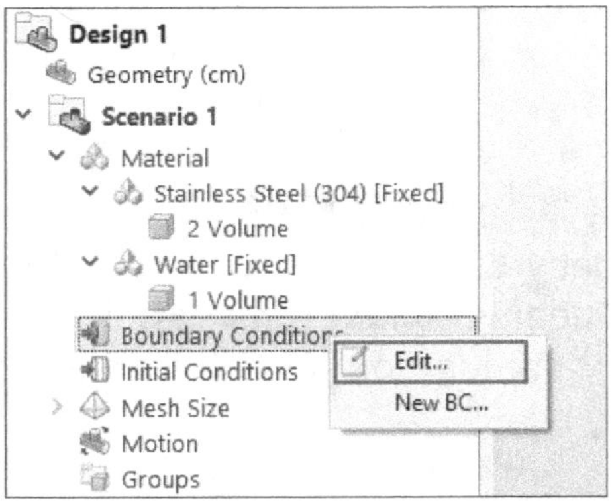

Figure-23. Edit button from Boundary Conditions option

- Click on the **Edit** button from displayed menu. The **Boundary Conditions** dialog box will be displayed as discussed earlier with parameters of earlier specified boundary conditions.
- Click on the **New BC** tool from displayed shortcut menu to create a new boundary condition. The **Boundary Conditions** dialog box will be displayed.
- To apply the boundary condition on a particular surface, you need to click on the surface from model before clicking on **Apply** button from **Boundary Conditions** dialog box.

Third Method

- After activating **Boundary Conditions** tool from **Setup Tasks** panel, left-click on the surface to which you want to apply boundary conditions. The **Context Toolbar** will be displayed; refer to Figure-24.

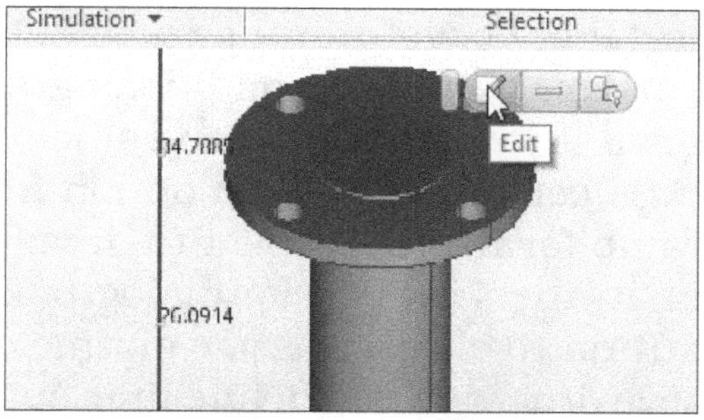

Figure-24. Context Toolbar for Boundary Condition

- Click on the **Edit** button from displayed menu. The **Boundary Conditions** dialog box will be displayed; refer to Figure-25.

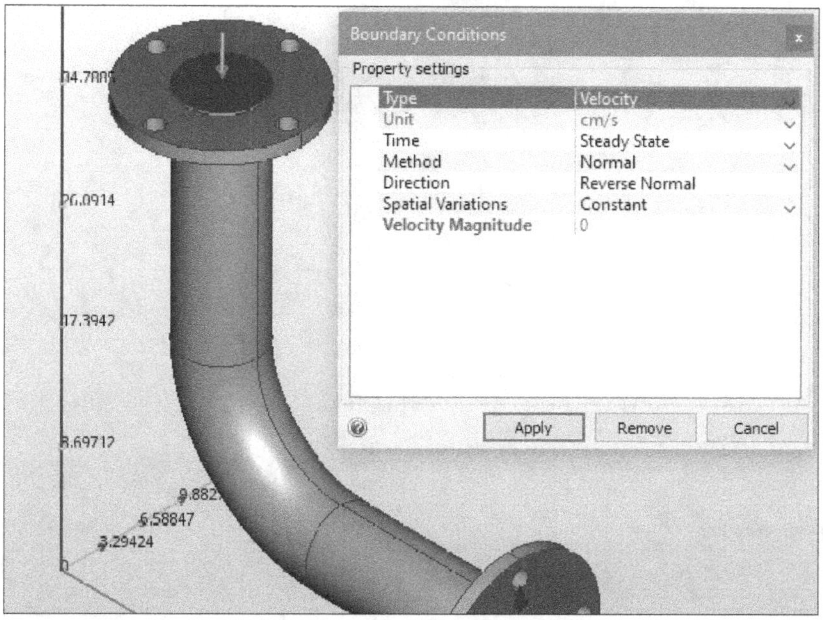

Figure-25. Boundary Conditions dialog box after selecting face

- There are various types of boundary conditions available in Autodesk CFD, which you can apply on the model as required. Some important boundary conditions are given next.

Velocity

Velocity boundary condition is commonly used as inlet boundary condition in a model. It is the speed at which fluid or solid is moving in given direction. Velocity boundary condition can be specified normal to the selected surface. You can apply the velocity to outlet of a model but the direction should be outward of the model. The method to apply velocity boundary condition is given next.

- Click in the **Type** drop-down from **Boundary Conditions** dialog box and select desired boundary condition. In our case, we are selecting **Velocity** boundary condition.
- Click in the **Unit** drop-down from **Boundary Conditions** dialog box and select desired unit. In our case, we are selecting **m/s** unit.

- Click in the **Time** drop-down from **Boundary Conditions** dialog box and select the desired option. Select **Steady State** option if you want to set fixed values of boundary conditions with respect to time. Select the **Transient** option if you want to specify time curve for variation of boundary condition values. On selecting **Transient** option, the dialog box will be displayed as shown in Figure-26. Select desired option from the **Time Curve** drop-down to define time curve form to be followed for generative variable boundary condition parameter. Select the **Constant** option from the drop-down if you want to keep value of parameter constant with respect to time change. Select the **Ramp Step** option from the drop-down to vary value of parameter in ramp form with respect to time; refer to Figure-27. Specify desired constant values in the **Time Curve** dialog box for different time ranges and click on the **Plot** button to check preview of time curve. Select the **Periodic** option from the **Time Curve** drop-down to define time curve as exponential function Similarly, you can use other options in the drop-down to create respective type of time curve for defining parameter value over time.

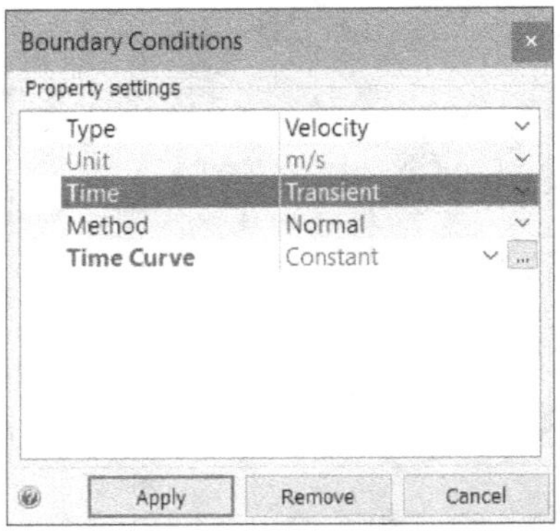

Figure-26. Velocity Boundary Conditions dialog box

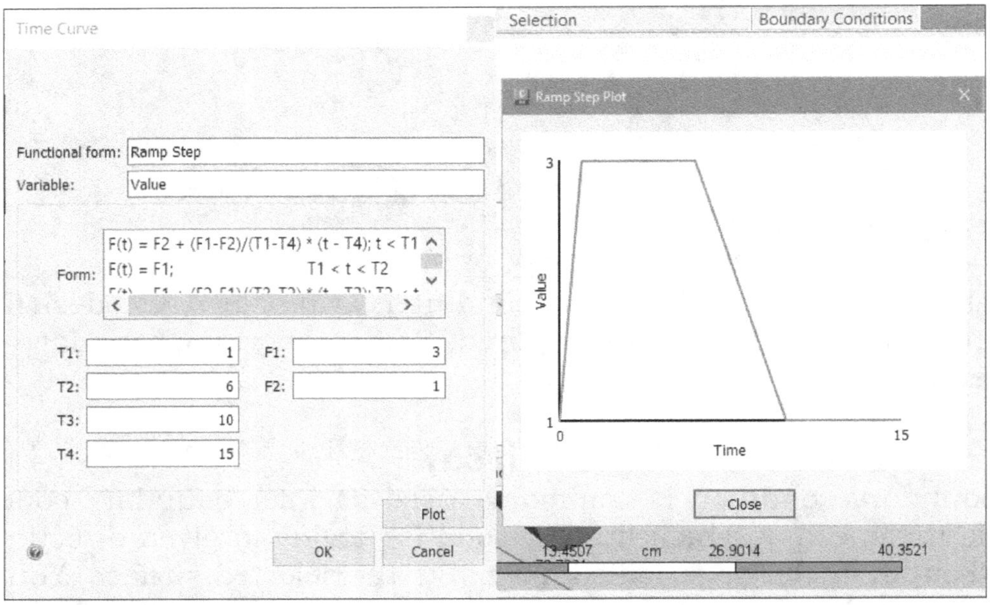

Figure-27. Ramp time curve

- Click in the **Method** drop-down from **Boundary Conditions** dialog box and select desired option from the drop-down. Select the **Normal** option to apply velocity normal to the selected surface and select the **Component** option to specify velocity along three major axes. Note that you can define time curve for each component of boundary condition parameter if **Transient** option is selected in the **Time** drop-down.

- Click on the **Reverse Normal** button from **Boundary Conditions** dialog box to reverse the direction of fluid velocity. On clicking this button, you could notice the change in direction of Normal arrow pointing toward or away from the selected surface.
- Click in the **Spatial Variations** drop-down from **Boundary Conditions** dialog box and select **Constant** option to define variations as constant. Select **Fully Developed** option to specify the entrance of the model as fully developed. Pipe and ducts flow are assumed to be fully developed. The fully developed flow profile is more realistic than a uniform (slug) profile as it completely fills the cross-section of boundary. Select **Linear Variations** option to vary velocity or temperature boundary condition in one dimension across a boundary surface. After selecting the **Linear Variations** option, click on **...** the button in **Direction** field and define direction of velocity to be varied linearly. Click on the **...** button in **Velocity Curve** field to modify velocity curve parameters in the **Velocity Curve** dialog box. Note that you can apply variation only to velocity or temperature parameter.
- If the **Constant** option is selected in the **Spatial Variations** drop-down then click in the **Velocity Magnitude** edit box from **Boundary Conditions** dialog box and specify the value of boundary condition as desired.
- After specifying the parameters, click on the **Apply** button to create boundary condition on selected surface; refer to Figure-28. A colored line will be created on the selected surface and the created boundary condition will be mentioned at lower left of the screen; refer to Figure-29.

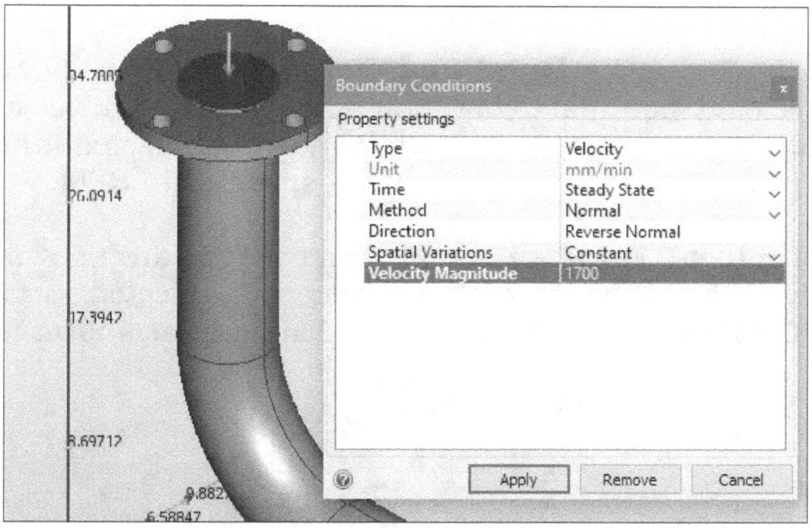

Figure-28. Applied boundary condition

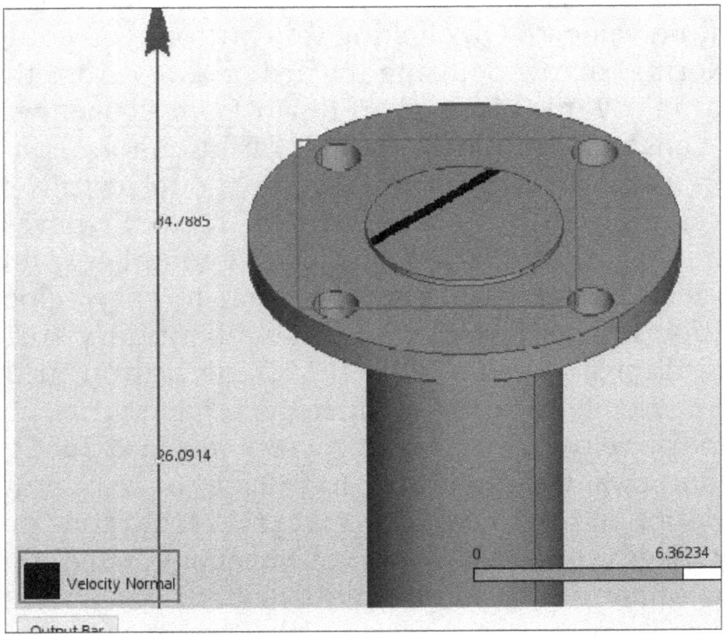

Figure-29. Colored strip

- If you want to delete the boundary current condition, click on the **Remove** button from the **Boundary Conditions** dialog box. The current boundary condition will be deleted from the selected surface.

Rotational Velocity

The Rotational Velocity boundary condition applies rotational velocity to a wall and is used for simulating a rotating object surrounded by selected fluid, like a rotating plate in a fluid. Rotational velocity is generally specified in RPM.

- Select the **Rotational Velocity** option from the **Type** drop-down in the **Boundary Conditions** dialog box to apply rotational velocity to selected surfaces. The options in **Boundary Conditions** dialog box will be displayed as shown in Figure-30.

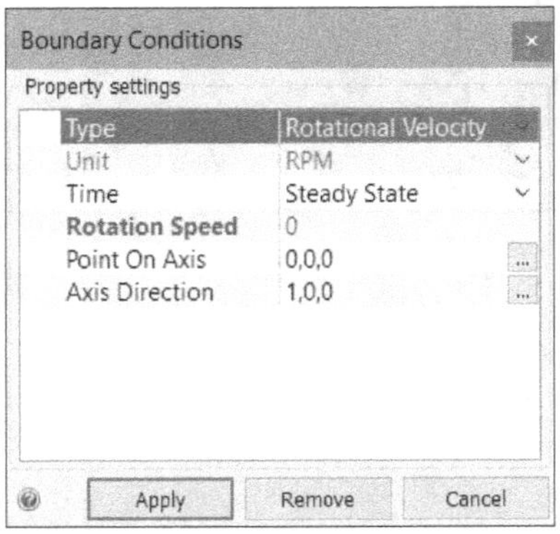

Figure-30. Rotational velocity boundary conditions

- Select desired unit for rotational speed from **Unit** drop-down and specify the rotational speed value in the **Rotation Speed** edit box of the dialog box.
- Click in the **Point On Axis** field and then click on the **Select surface** button from the displayed dialog box; refer to Figure-31. You will be asked to specify location centroid for rotational speed axis. Select desired circular surface to be used as reference for defining rotational axis location.

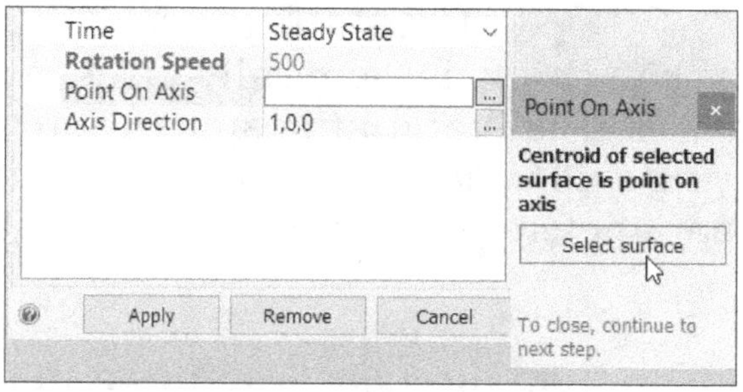

Figure-31. Point On Axis dialog

- Click in the **Axis Direction** field and set desired direction for rotational axis about which selected surface will rotate.
- After setting desired parameters, click on the **Apply** button to apply boundary condition.

Volume Flow Rate

The Volume Flow Rate Boundary Condition is applied to planar openings of model. Generally, it is used in inlet conditions and also when the density of fluid is constant throughout the analysis. This boundary condition can also be applied to flow outlet, if the direction of flow is outward of model. When applying this boundary condition to multiple surfaces of the model at same time, the flow direction must be the same.

- Select the **Volume Flow Rate** option from the **Type** drop-down in the **Boundary Conditions** dialog box to apply specified amount of fluid flow rate through selected surface. The options in **Boundary Conditions** dialog box will be displayed as shown in Figure-32.

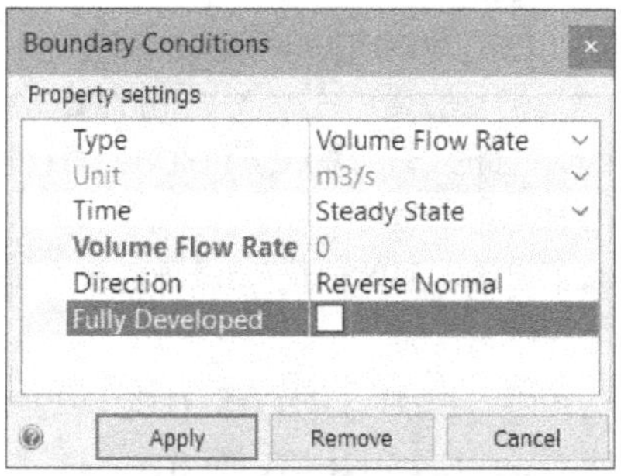

Figure-32. Volume flow rate boundary condition

- Specify desired value of rate of fluid flow in the **Volume Flow Rate** edit box.
- Select the **Fully Developed** check box if the flow of fluid is saturated and fills the full boundary.
- Specify other parameters as discussed earlier and click on the **Apply** button to apply the boundary conditions.

Mass Flow Rate

The Mass Flow Rate boundary condition is applied to planar inlets and outlets. It is the amount of material flowing through the boundary. It is generally used as inlet boundary condition. This boundary condition can also be applied to flow outlet, if the direction of flow is out of model. If you are applying this boundary condition to multiple surfaces of the model at same time then the flow direction must be the same. The procedure to apply mass flow rate boundary condition is similar to volume flow rate.

Pressure

The Pressure boundary condition is generally used as outlet condition. The recommended outlet condition is static atmospheric pressure of 1 atm for open environment. After applying this condition, no other condition are needed to apply at outlet for flow related parameters. The procedure to apply this boundary condition is given next.

- Select the **Pressure** option from the **Type** drop-down in the **Boundary Conditions** dialog box. The options will be displayed as shown in Figure-33.

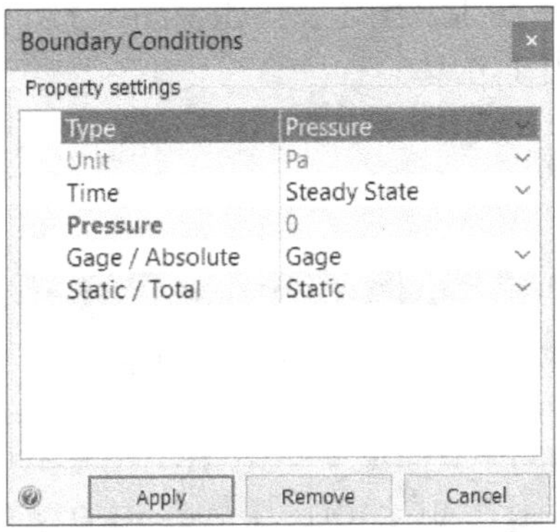

Figure-33. Pressure Boundary condition

- Select the **Gage** option from the **Gage/Absolute** drop-down to use relative pressure on selected face/surface. Generally gage pressure is measured with respect to atmospheric pressure. For example, if you inflate car type with air and measure it using Tire pressure gauge then pressure shown by gauge will be in reference to standard environmental pressure. Select the **Absolute** option from the **Gage/Absolute** drop-down to measure pressure using absolute **0** value as reference.
- Select the **Static** option from the **Static/Total** drop-down to specify fixed pressure of fluid. The **Static** option is generally preferred for incompressible fluid flow. Select the **Total** option from the **Static/Total** drop-down to include both static as well as dynamic pressure of fluid.
- Specify other parameters as discussed earlier and click on the **Apply** button.

Temperature

The Temperature boundary condition is used to apply temperature condition at desired location on the model. Note that temperature condition can be fixed or changing with respect to time. The procedure to apply temperature boundary condition is similar to applying pressure condition.

Slip/Symmetry

The Slip/Symmetry boundary condition causes the fluid to flow along a wall instead of stopping at wall due to friction. Slip walls are useful for defining symmetric planes. The Slip condition can be used with a very low fluid viscosity to simulate Euler flow. In case of axisymmetric analysis, you do not need to apply symmetric condition manually because it is set automatically along the axis.

Unknown

The Unknown boundary condition is used when you have to apply open boundary condition where no other constraints are applied. Mostly, this boundary condition is used at the outlet of compressible flow analysis like for supersonic flow, where neither the outlet pressure nor the velocity are known. There is no value associated with unknown condition.

Scalar

The Scalar boundary condition is a unit less quantity ranging from 0 to 1 that represent the concentration of the scalar quantity for tracking concentrations of fluids when two or more similar fluids are involved in study.

Humidity

The Humidity is a unit less quantity ranging between 0 to 1 that represent relative humidity (water content). Here, 1 represent a humidity level of 100%.

Quality

The Quality boundary condition is unit less parameter used to represent vapour content in steam or other saturated mixtures. Here, 1 represents 100% of vapour content and 0 represents 0% of vapour content in mixture.

Heat Flux

The Heat Flux boundary condition is applied to define amount of heat applied to per unit area of the model surface. Heat flux should be applied to outer wall surfaces only. The procedure is same as discussed earlier.

Total Heat Flux

The Total Heat Flux boundary condition is applied to define total heat applied on full extent of the selected surface. Total heat flux should be applied to outer wall surfaces only.

Film Coefficient

The Film Coefficient boundary condition works similar to heat convection coefficient boundary condition. Film coefficient defines rate at which heat energy is released from selected surface to the environment/other connected bodies. Film Coefficient boundary condition simulates natural convection from exterior surfaces to regions that are outside of the physical model (but not included). Several engineering resources recommend a film coefficient value between 5 and 25 W/m^2K as a good approximation for natural convection. The choice of value is influenced by the physical size of the physical (not-modeled) air volume as well as by the strength of any exterior air circulation. Note that external walls that do not have any applied heat transfer conditions (temperature, film coefficient, radiation, heat flux, etc.) are considered perfectly insulated.

Radiation

The Radiation boundary condition is applied to define heat radiation emissivity rate for selected surface. You need to specify emissivity rate and reference temperature for defining radiation boundary condition.

External Fan

The External Fan boundary condition is used to apply forced flow of fluid (gases) through selected boundary. Note that slip factor plays important role in flow generated by external fan. The slip factor is the ratio of the true rotational speed of the flow to the rotational speed of the fan blades. Autodesk® CFD determines the flow tangential velocity component by multiplying the slip factor by the user-supplied fan rotational speed. The default slip factor is 1.0. This means that the rotational speed of the flow is the same as the rotational speed of the fan.

Current

The Current boundary condition is used to apply electric current to selected surface for performing Joule heating analysis. Heat is generated by flow of current through the metal. Note that current value specified for this boundary condition is total current not the current density.

Voltage

The Voltage boundary condition is used to apply electric voltage to selected surface for performing Joule heating analysis. The use of this boundary condition is similar to current boundary condition. A voltage difference can be applied to the solid to represent a potential difference. In this mode, do not specify a Current condition.

Periodic

The Periodic boundary condition is used to apply cyclic symmetry to model for faster calculations of analysis. To simulate transparent media that is completely immersed in the working fluid, only the material transmissivity needs to be specified. To simulate transparency through surfaces on an exterior solid, the Transparent boundary condition is also required. Periodic boundary conditions are a convenient way to include the effect of multiple repeating features in a simplified model. Because of the repeating geometry, the flow upstream and downstream of a device will be the same for each passage.

Note that mesh enhancement is automatically disabled when periodic boundary conditions are applied. This is done to improve solution stability. To enable mesh enhancement: open the **Mesh** quick edit dialog, click the **Enhancement** button, and select the **Enable mesh enhancement** check box.

Transparent

The Transparent boundary condition is applied to define computation of radiation heat transfer through transparent media. The level of transmissivity is defined as a material property in the **Materials** dialog box. To simulate transparent media that is completely immersed in the working fluid, only the material transmissivity needs to be specified. To simulate transparency through surfaces on an exterior solid, the Transparent boundary condition is also required.

- Similarly, you can create the boundary condition at outlet of the model; refer to Figure-34.

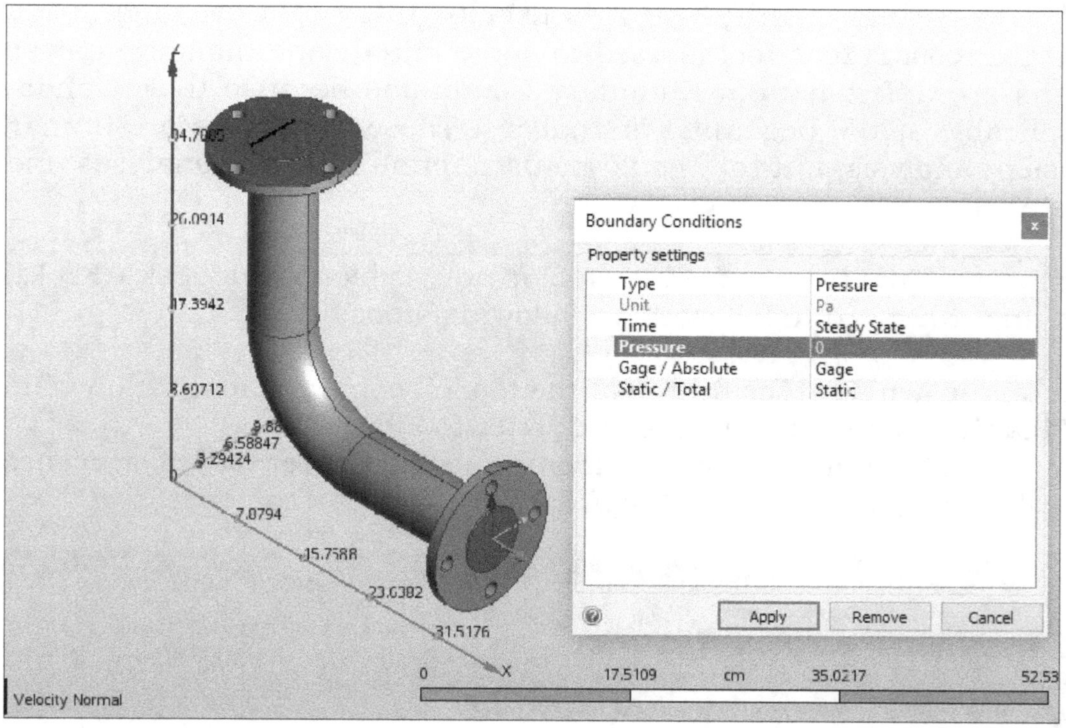

Figure-34. Outlet condition

- In most fluid flow cases, we use **Pressure** boundary condition at outlet for a natural outlet.
- The colored strip will be created after clicking on **Apply** button from the **Boundary Conditions** dialog box; refer to Figure-35.

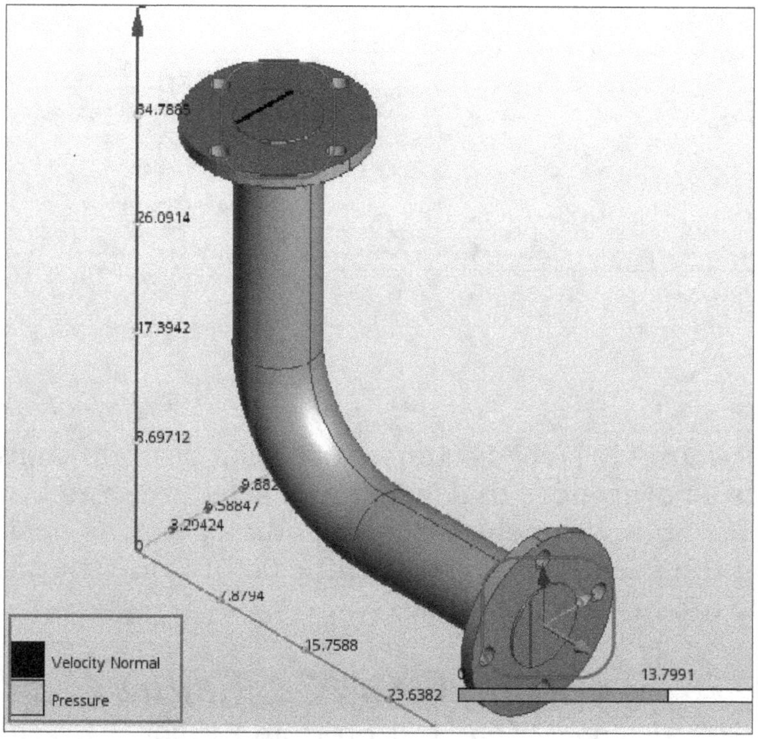

Figure-35. Colored strips of boundary conditions

INITIAL CONDITIONS

The **Initial Conditions** tool is used to apply initial conditions in analysis. These conditions are different from Boundary Conditions because these conditions are only applicable at the beginning of analysis. These conditions are primarily used for transient analysis, but they could be used for steady state analyses under some circumstances.

Sometimes, the **Initial Conditions** tool is not visible to Autodesk CFD **Ribbon**. To activate this, you need to follow these following steps:

- Click on the **Application** button at the top left corner of application window. The **Application** menu will be displayed; refer to Figure-36.
- Click on the **Options** button from menu, the **User Interface Preferences** dialog box will be displayed; refer to Figure-37.

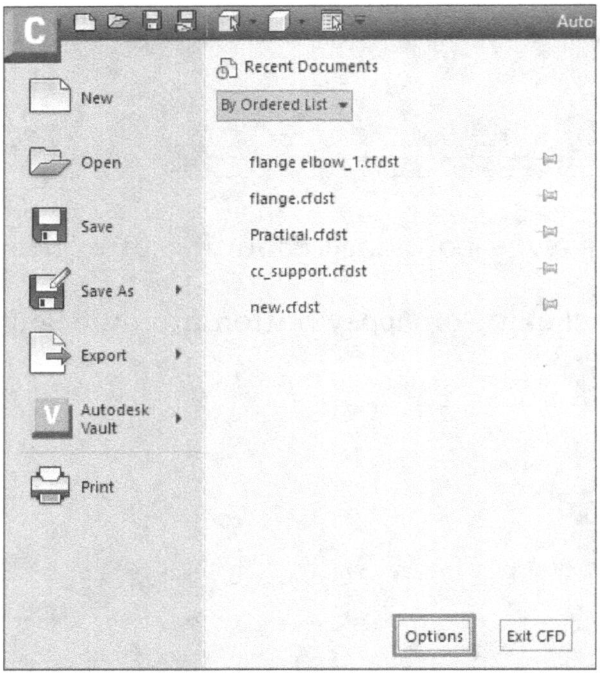

Figure-36. Application menu

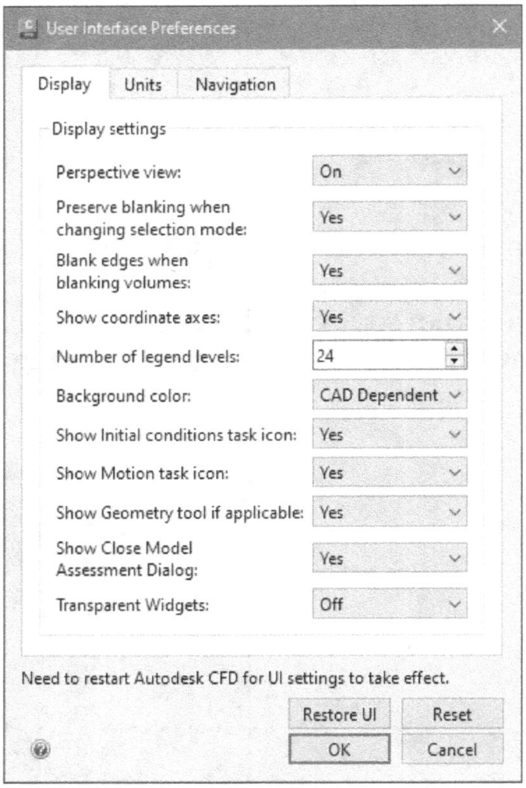

Figure-37. User Interface Preferences dialog box

- Click on the **Show Initial conditions task icon** drop-down from **Display** tab of **User Interface Preferences** dialog box and select the **Yes** button. You can also set other settings and parameters from this dialog box as desired.
- After specifying the parameters, click on the **OK** button. The **Initial Conditions** tool will be activated in the **Ribbon**.

Applying Initial Conditions

- Click on the **Initial Conditions** button from **Ribbon**. The **Initial Conditions** tools will be activated.
- The method of opening the **Initial Conditions** dialog box is similar to the methods which were discussed in last section, i.e. by clicking **Edit** button.

- Click on the **Edit** tool from **Initial Conditions** panel of **Setup** tab; refer to Figure-38. The **Initial Conditions** dialog box will be displayed; refer to Figure-39.

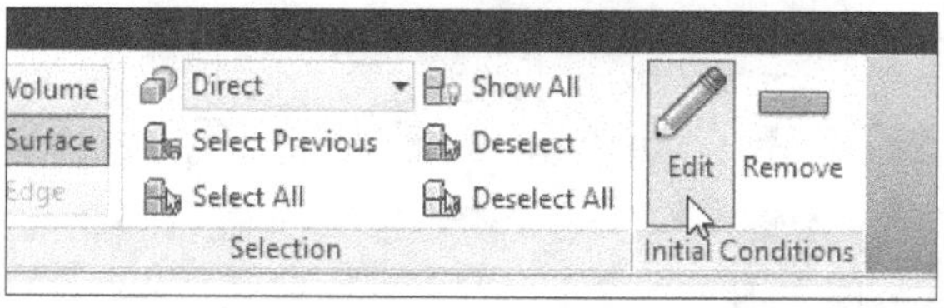

Figure-38. Edit button of Initial Conditions tool

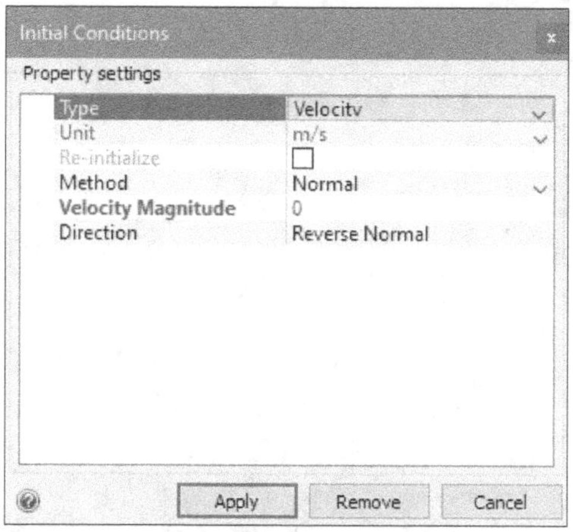

Figure-39. Initial Conditions dialog box

- Click on the surface of the model where you want to apply initial boundary condition.

Note: You can apply the initial boundary condition to a specific volume of model. What you need to do is select the **Volume** button from **Selection** panel in place of **Surface** button; refer to Figure-40. In our case, we are selecting the **Surface** button to apply initial condition.

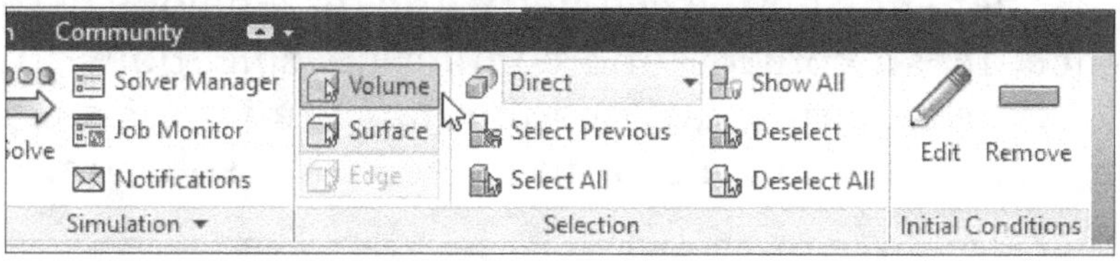

Figure-40. Selection panel

- Click in the **Type** drop-down from **Initial Conditions** dialog box and select desired initial boundary condition. These conditions have already been discussed earlier.
- Click in the **Unit** drop-down from **Initial Conditions** dialog box and select desired unit of selected condition type.
- The **Re-initialize** check box of **Initial Conditions** is activated when you had done a simulation before. This tool is used to reset the condition on the selected parts, like to re-initialize the temperature after flow simulation to see how the temperature varies with time.
- Click in the **Method** drop-down from **Initial Conditions** dialog box and select the required option as discussed earlier.
- Click in the **Velocity Magnitude** edit box from **Initial Conditions** dialog box and specify desired value of the selected conditions. The name of this edit box will be changed as per selected condition.
- Click in the **Direction** drop-down and select the required option.

- After specifying the parameters, click on the **Apply** button from **Initial Conditions** dialog box; refer to Figure-41. The initial condition will be created and added in **Design Study Bar**.

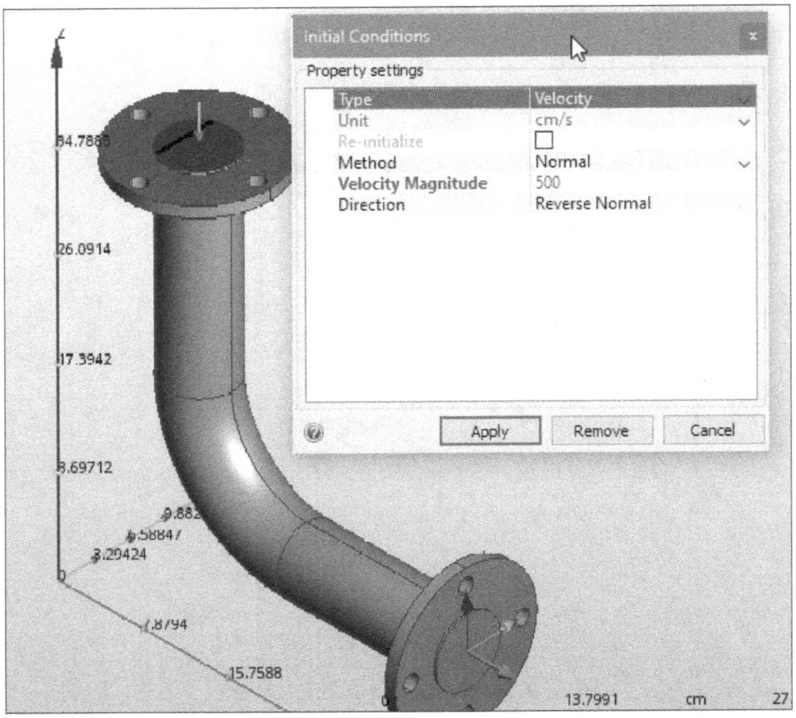

Figure-41. Applying Initial conditions

GENERATING MESH

The **Mesh** tool is used to display the computational mesh cells and mesh related parameters at the calculation moment selected for getting the results. The software estimates a global element size for the model taking into consideration its volume, surface area, and other geometric details. The size of the generated mesh (number of nodes and elements) depends on the geometry and dimensions of the model, element size, mesh tolerance, mesh control, and contact specifications. In the early stages of design analysis where approximate results may suffice, you can specify a larger element size for a faster solution. For a more accurate solution, a smaller element size may be required.

Meshing generates 3D tetrahedral solid elements, 2D triangular shell elements, and 1D beam elements. A mesh consists of one type of elements unless the mixed mesh type is specified. Solid elements are naturally suitable for bulky models. Shell elements are naturally suitable for modeling thin parts (sheet metals), and beams and trusses are suitable for modeling structural members.

The procedure to create the mesh of the solid is given next.

- Click on the **Mesh Sizing** tool from **Setup Tasks** panel to activate mesh tool; refer to Figure-42. The **Mesh Sizing** tool will be activated and other tools related to mesh will be displayed.

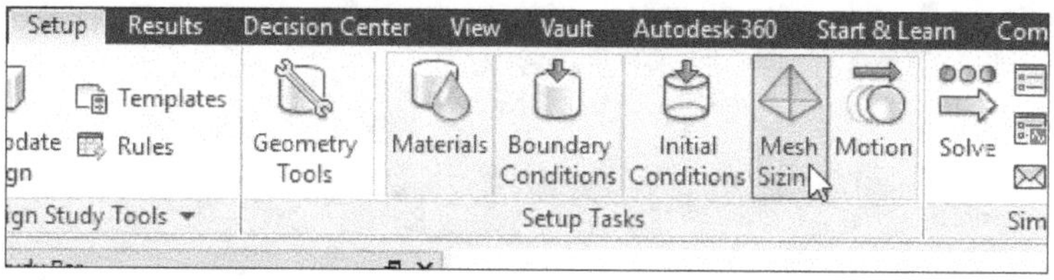

Figure-42. Mesh Sizing tool

Automatic Mesh Generation

- Click on the **Automatic** button from **Type** panel of **Setup** tab to enable automatic mesh sizing of the model; refer to Figure-43.

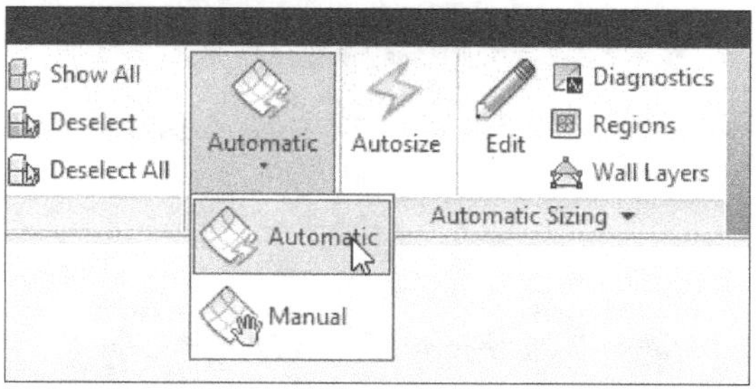

Figure-43. Type panel

- Click on the **Autosize** button from **Automatic Sizing** panel to generate mesh automatically. The mesh will be generated in the form of blue dots on the edges of model; refer to Figure-44.

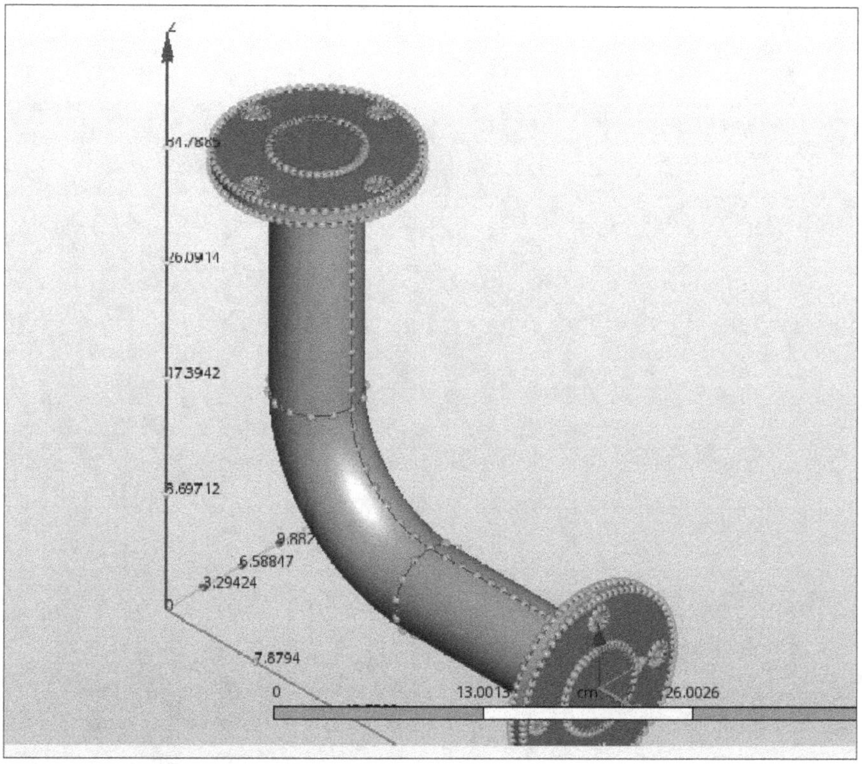

Figure-44. Automatically generated mesh

- The generated mesh will also be displayed in **Design Study Bar**; refer to Figure-45.

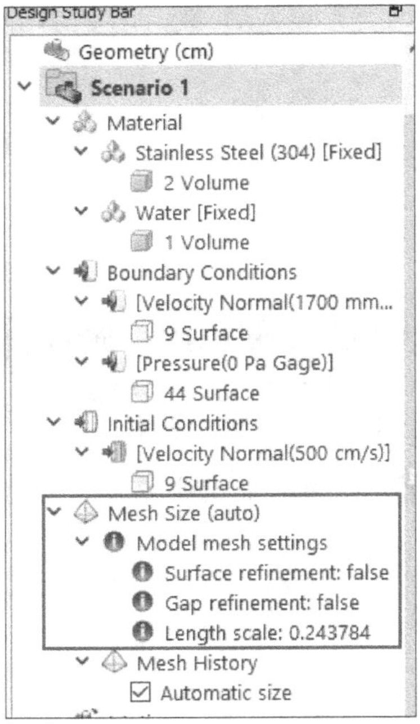

Figure-45. Automatic mesh in Design Study Bar

- If you want to refine the mesh of the model, right-click on the **Surface Refinement** option from **Design Study Bar** and click on the **Edit** button; refer to Figure-46. The **Mesh Sizes** dialog box will be displayed; refer to Figure-47.

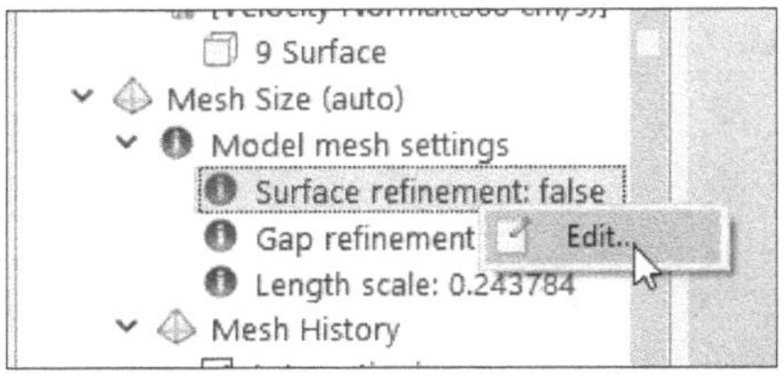

Figure-46. Edit button of Surface refinement

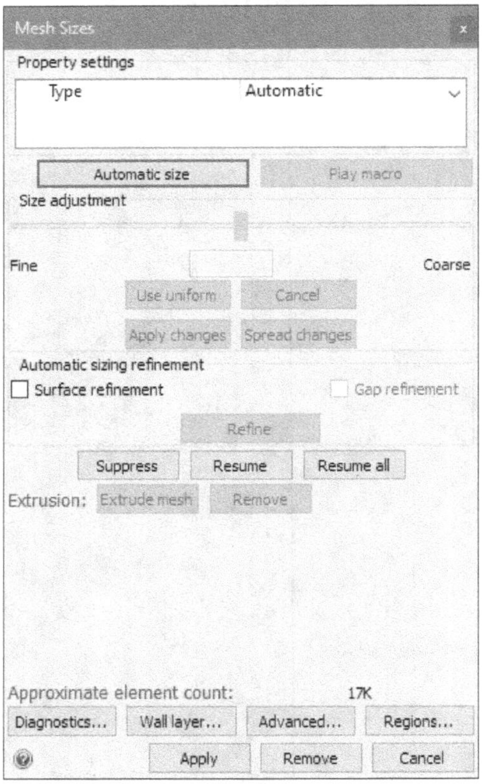

Figure-47. Mesh Sizes dialog box

- Select the **Surface Refinement** check box from **Automatic sizing refinement** section, the **Refine** button to refine the surface will be activated.
- Click on the **Refine** button, the mesh will be refined using Autosize parameters.

- Select the **Gap Refinement** button from **Automatic sizing refinement** section to refine the gap present in the model. You can also open the **Mesh Sizes** dialog box by clicking on the **Edit** button from right-click menus of **Gap Refinement** option of **Design Study Bar**.
- Click on the **Refine** button, the mesh will be refined.
- After specifying the parameters, click on the **Apply** button from **Mesh Sizes** dialog box. The changes will be updated.

Manual Mesh Generation

- Click on the **Manual** button from **Type** panel of **Setup** tab; refer to Figure-48. The tools will be updated in the **Ribbon** as per **Manual** tool.

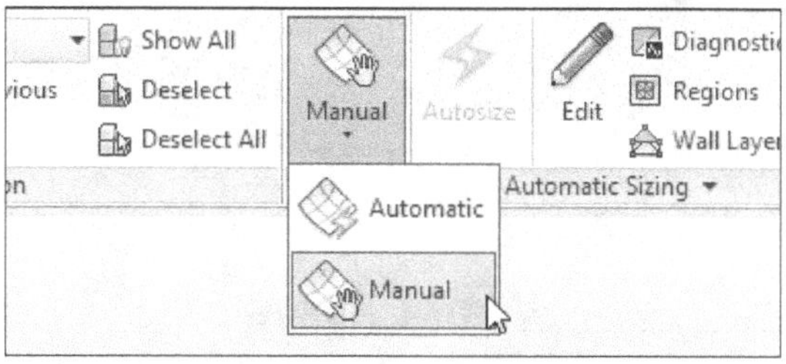

Figure-48. Manual button Type panel

- Click on the **Edit** button from **Automatic Sizing** panel of **Setup** tab, the manual **Mesh Sizes** dialog box will be displayed; refer to Figure-49.

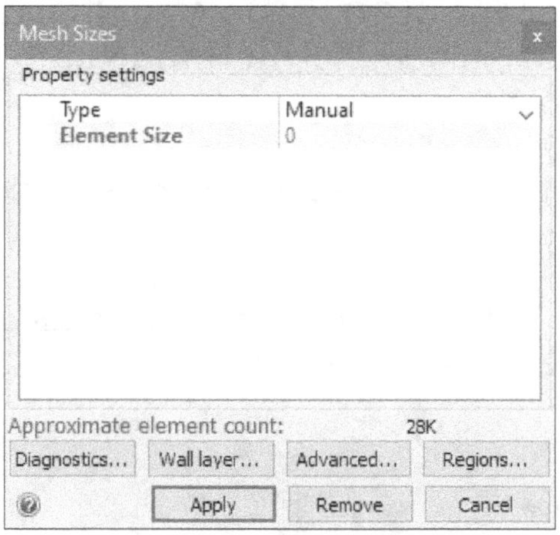

Figure-49. Manual Mesh Sizes dialog box

- To create mesh manually, you need to select the Surface, Volume, or Edge separately from the model to create the mesh of that selected part.
- To select the **Volume**, **Surface**, or **Edge**, you will need to activate the respective button from **Selection** panel; refer to Figure-50.

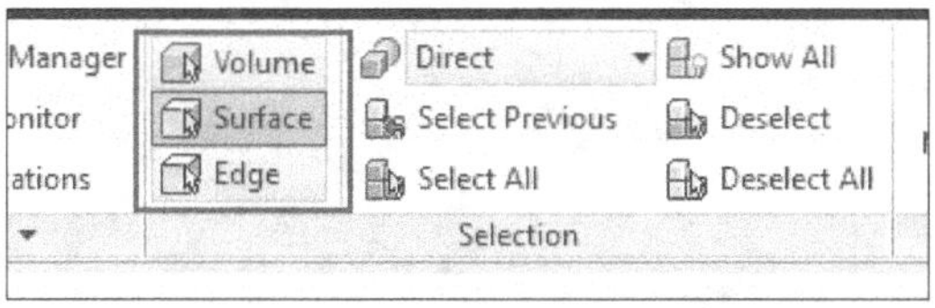

Figure-50. Selection panel

- Click on the **Element Size** edit box from **Mesh Sizes** dialog box and specify the value; refer to Figure-51. Less the value of **Element Size**, more coarse the mesh will be.

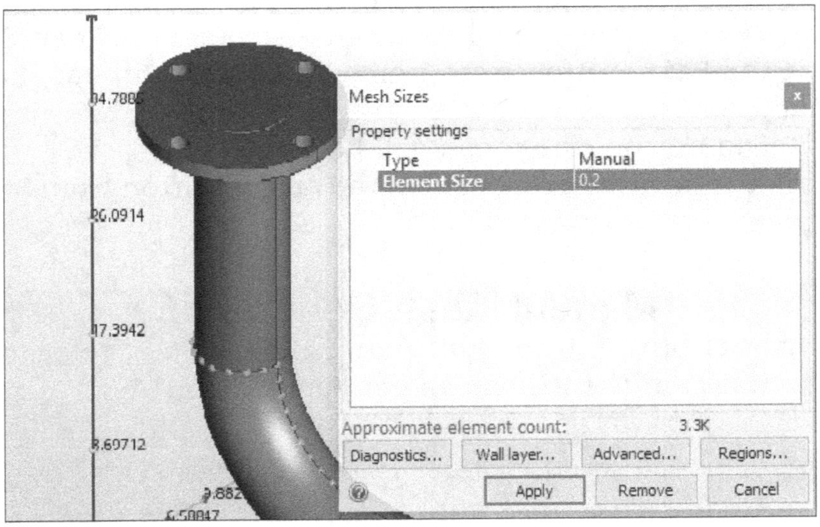

Figure-51. Entering value for manual mesh

Wall Layers

The **Wall layers** tool is used to add element layer along all fluid walls and solid-fluid interface. It increases the original size of mesh to a great extent to produce a smooth distribution along corners, where original mesh is unable to reach. The **Wall layer** tool ensures proper spreading of mesh across small gaps and corners. This tool create layers before construction of 3D mesh. A gradual transition between surfaces ensure gradual variations in element height throughout the mode. The procedure to use this tool is discussed next.

Note: It is not possible to add layers to imported mesh, because wall layers are added before the generation of mesh.

- Click on the **Wall layer** button from **Mesh Sizes** dialog box, the **Wall Layer** dialog box will be displayed; refer to Figure-52.

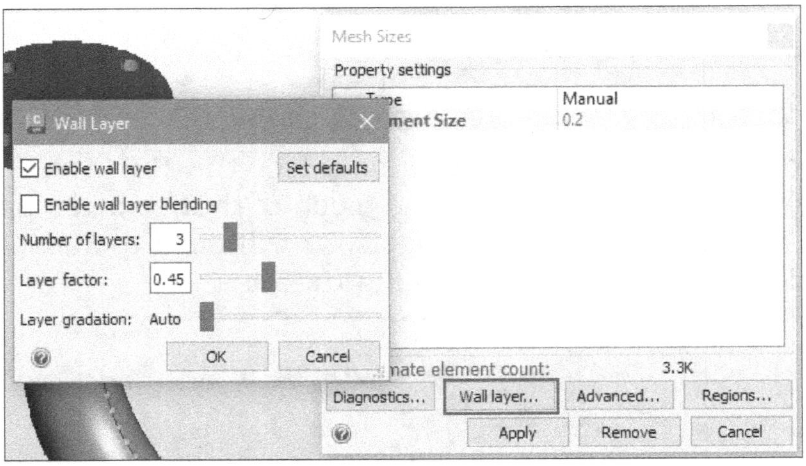

Figure-52. Wall Layer dialog box

- Select the **Enable Wall Layer** check box from **Wall Layer** dialog box to activate the tools related to wall layer. This check box is activated by default.

- Select the **Enable Wall Layer** blending check box from **Wall Layer** dialog box to create a more gradual transition in the selected region. By default, the transition between wall layer region and original mesh is instantaneous from highly anisotropic to isotropic.
- Click in the **Number of layers** edit box and specify the value to control the number of layers of prismatic element. In some rotating-region analyses, you can improve the stability of layers by specifying the value to 1. You can also set the **Number of Layers** by moving the respective slider.
- Click in the **Layer factor** edit box from **Wall Layer** dialog box and specify the value to control the thickness of layer. The method of determining the layer height of a particular surface is by multiplying the Layer factor to the local isotropic length scale. You can also specify the value of **Layer Factor** by moving respective slider.
- Move the **Layer gradation** slider from **Wall Layer** dialog box to control the rate of growth of wall layers near wall. More the wall layer, more will be computational time. As the number of wall layers increases, the layer thickness often has a tendency to become uniform.
- Click on the **Set Defaults** button from **Wall Layer** dialog box to reset the specified parameters of **Wall Layer** dialog box.
- After specifying the parameters, click on the **OK** button from **Wall Layer** dialog box. You will be returned to **Mesh Sizes** dialog box.

Advanced

The **Advanced** button is used to specify several additional parameters for controlling mesh distribution over a selected part, surface, edge, and model. The procedure to use this button is discussed next.

- Click on the **Advanced** button from **Mesh Sizes** dialog box, the **Advanced Meshing Controls** dialog box will be displayed; refer to Figure-53.

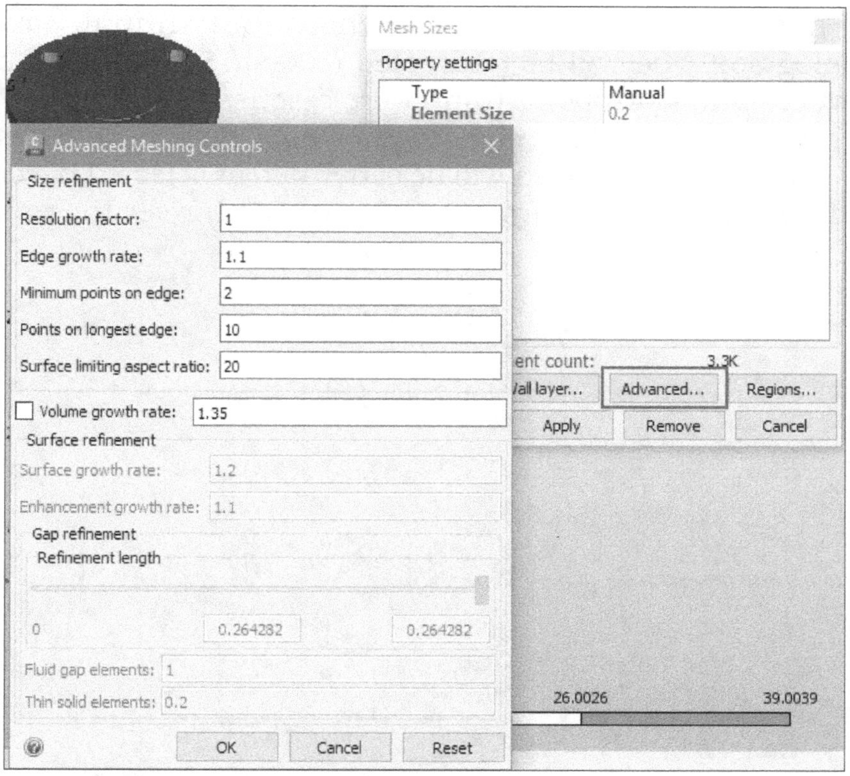

Figure-53. Advanced Meshing Controls dialog box

- Click in the **Resolution factor** edit box from **Advanced Meshing Controls** dialog box to specify desired value to control relative fineness of the mesh in response to the curvature of model entities. The effects of Resolution factor are localized to region of high curvature. Smaller the value of Resolution factor, more fine will be the mesh on model with curvature. The model regions without curvature are not affected by this parameter. The acceptable range of this parameter is from 1 to 3. Beyond this range, values are rejected.
- Click in the **Edge growth rate** edit box and specify the value to control the quality of mesh distribution computed by automatic sizing. The smaller value of **Edge growth rate** cause slower variation in distribution from regions of high to low curvature. The 1.1 and 1.5 value of Edge growth rate represent 10% and 50% growth rate.
- Click in the **Minimum points on edge** edit box and specify the value to define minimum number of points on edge. For entities lacking curvature, a minimum level of resolution is guaranteed by this parameter.
- Click in the **Points on longest edge** edit box and specify the value to define the points on longest edge of selected part. This tool is more relevant for geometry with no curvature, like surrounding box from external flow. This tool may create more points on longest edge as compared to the value specified in Longest Edge parameter.
- Click in the **Surface limiting aspect ratio** edit box and specify the value to introduce a constraint on length scale to ensure they are not larger than a specified factor of the dimensions of the surface. This tool is generally used in Automatic sizing of a mesh. This affects the distributions on edges bounding high aspect-ratio surfaces.
- Click in the **Volume growth rate** edit box and specify the value to control the volume elements grow. The range of specifying the value is between 1.01 to 2.0. In this, the value of 1.1 and 1.4 cause the growth rate of 10% and 40% respectively.
- Other parameters of this dialog box were discussed earlier.
- After specifying the parameters, click on the **OK** button from **Advanced Meshing Controls** dialog box. You will be redirected to **Mesh Sizes** dialog box.
- The **Diagnostics** and **Regions** buttons were discussed earlier.
- After specifying the parameters, click on the **Apply** button from **Mesh Sizes** dialog box; refer to Figure-54. The mesh will be generated at selected part as per specified parameter. In our case, the coarser mesh is created; refer to Figure-55.

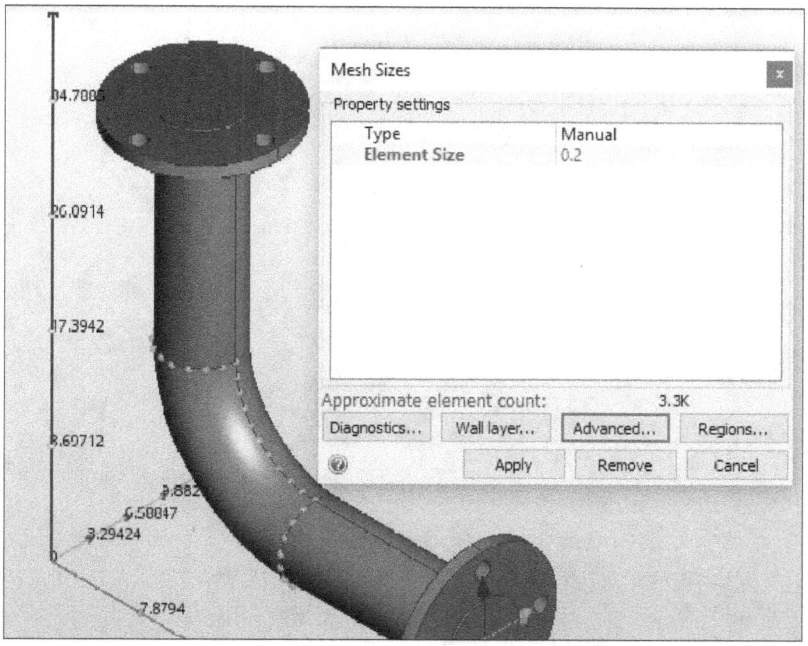

Figure-54. Mesh Sizes dialog box along with selected surface

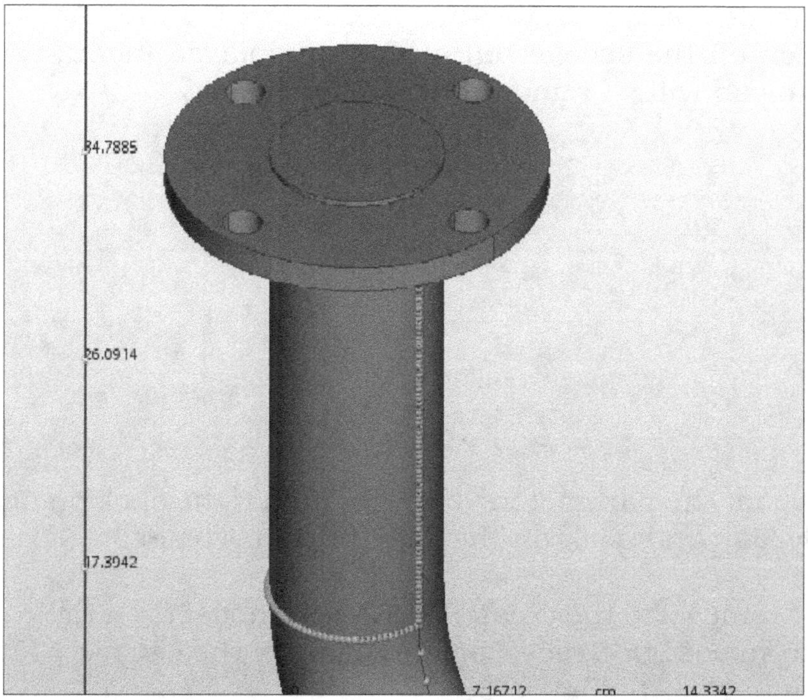

Figure-55. Generated mesh

- The notification of created mesh will also be added in **Design Study Bar**; refer to Figure-56.

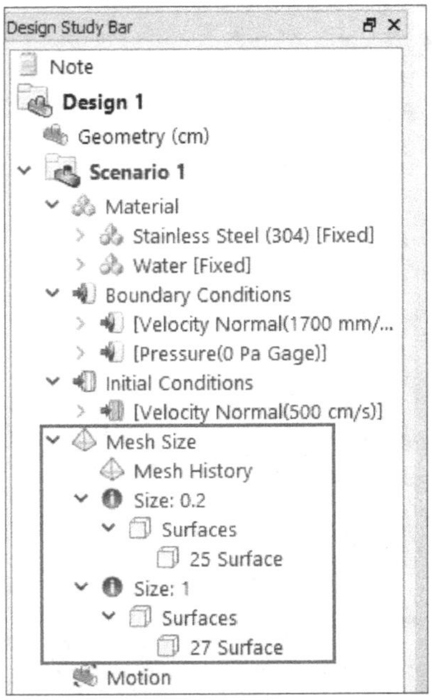

Figure-56. Mesh displayed in Design Study Bar

- If you want to delete any mesh then right-click on the **Surfaces** node of that mesh and click on the **Remove** button from displayed menu; refer to Figure-57. The selected mesh will be removed from model.

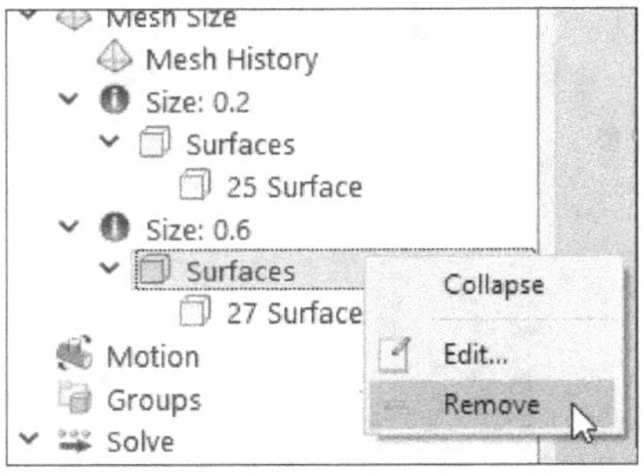

Figure-57. Right-click menu of mesh

- If you want to edit the parameters of mesh, then right-click on desired mesh from **Design Study Bar** and click on the **Edit** button. The **Mesh Sizes** dialog box will be displayed.
- If you want to remove all the created mesh of a model then right-click on the **Mesh Size** option from **Design Study Bar** and click on the **Remove All** button from the displayed menu; refer to Figure-58.

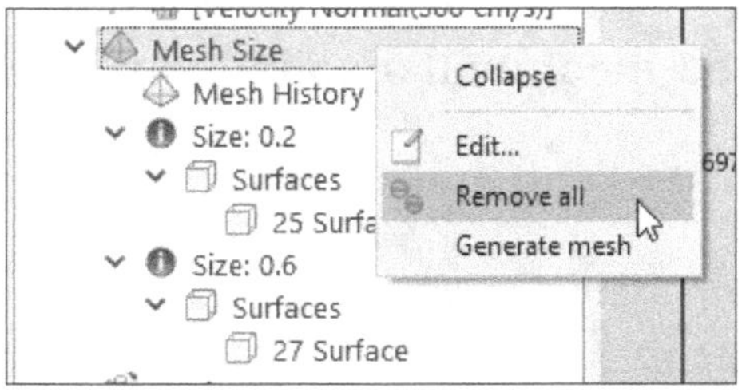

Figure-58. Right-click menu of Mesh Size

- If you click on the **Generate mesh** button from right-click menus, the software start analysis of the model. The tools used to solve the analysis will be discussed in next chapter.

MOTION

The **Motion** tool is used to analyze the interaction between moving part of model to the surrounding fluid. The movement of the part can be angular and linear. With this tool, we can analyze the motion on fluid medium as well as flow induced forces on the model. The procedure to use this tool is discussed next.

- Click on the **Motion** button from the **Setup Tasks** panel in the **Ribbon** to activate the tool. The tools related to **Motion** will be displayed in **Motion** panel; refer to Figure-59.

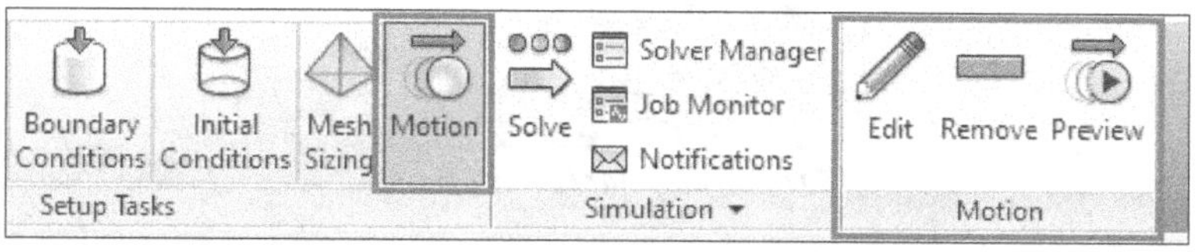

Figure-59. Motion panel

- Click on the **Edit** button from **Motion** panel in **Setup** tab. The **Motion** dialog box will be displayed; refer to Figure-60.

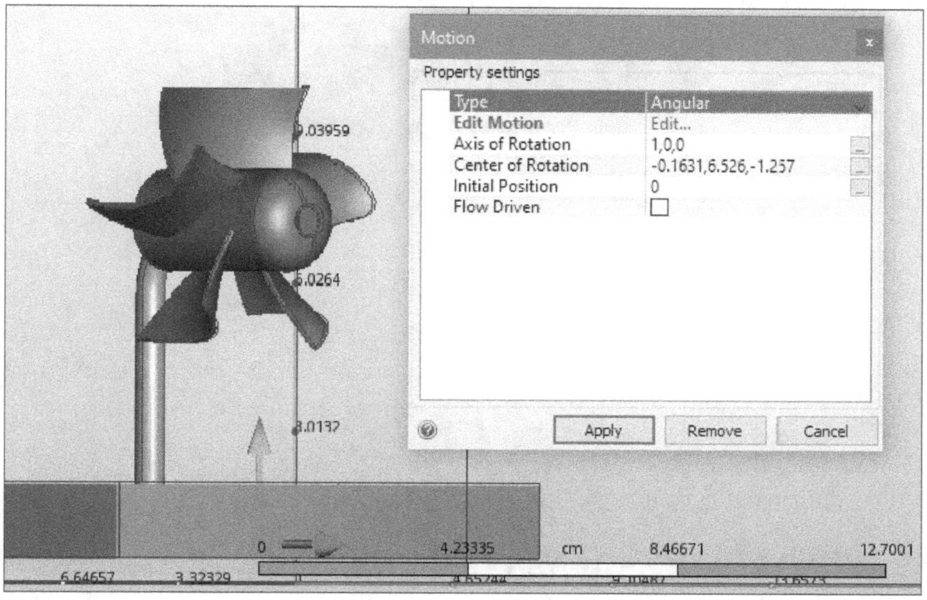

Figure-60. Motion dialog box

Types of Motion

Click on the **Type** drop-down from **Motion** dialog box, the motion type list will be displayed. There are seven types of motion available in Autodesk CFD, which are discussed below.

Angular Motion

The **Angular** motion is the rotation of a part about an axis. Some examples are, displacement pumps, Gear pumps, check walls, Fan, Centrifugal pumps, etc. The component in angular motion can have paths that interfere like gear teeth, fan blades, etc. The **Motion** dialog box for angular option is displayed as shown in Figure-61.

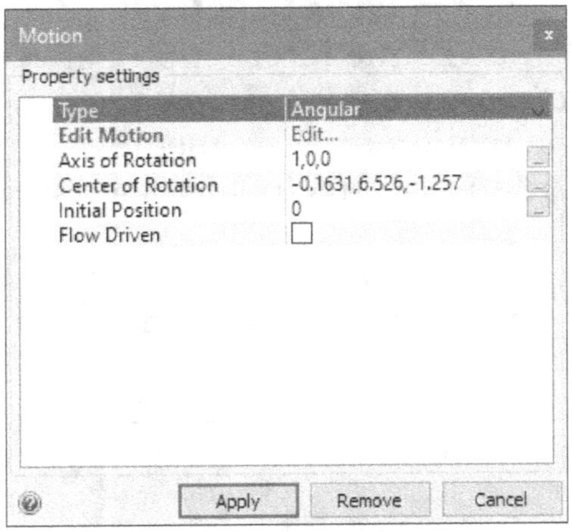

Figure-61. Angular Motion dialog box

Linear Motion

The **Linear** motion is the motion of an object in a straight line. Some examples are, piston cylinder mechanism, values opening and closing, reciprocating motion, etc. The **Motion** dialog box for linear option is displayed as shown in Figure-62

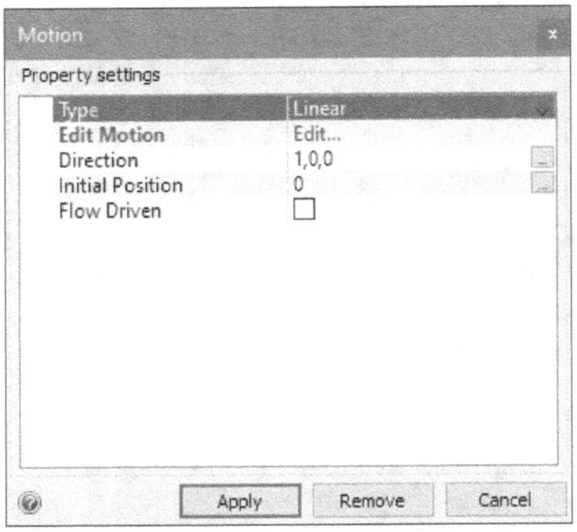

Figure-62. Linear Motion dialog box

Combined Linear/Angular

The **Combined Linear/Angular** motion is used where we need to apply both the motions, i.e. angular motion and well as linear motion. The selected part will follow combined linear and angular motion. The directions of both the motions need to be specified in **Motion** dialog box. For flow induced rotation, torque is used to compute angular accelerations. The linear position of object is determined by user specifications or a result of flow induced forces.

If linear and angular motions are flow induced, it could be assumed that the two motions are uncoupled and work independently to each other. The axis of rotation is determined by translation of object. Some examples of Combined Linear/Angular motion are, rack and pinion gear, tightening screw, and so on. The **Motion** dialog box for combined linear/angular motion is shown in (Change all the others in the same way) Figure-63.

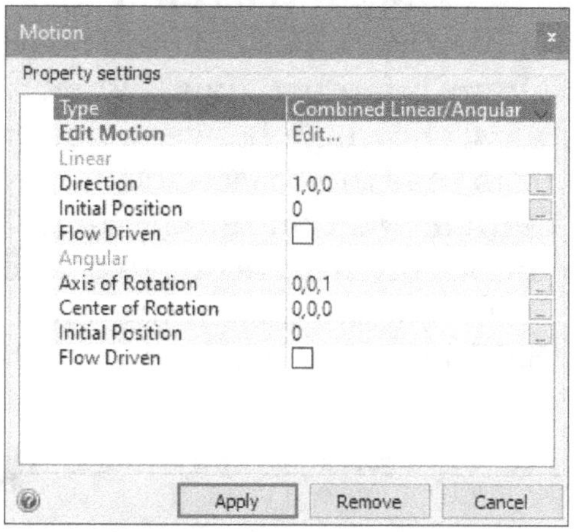

Figure-63. Combined Linear Angular dialog box

Combined Orbital/Rotational Motion

The **Combined Orbital/Rotational Motion** is used where the orbital motion and rotation motion works together. In this, the object rotates about its axis of rotation and also orbits about an axis parallel to its axis of rotation. Example are epicyclic gear, solar system, and so on. The orbital speed of object is usually slower than the primary rotational speed. The **Combined Orbital/Rotational** motion dialog box for combined linear/angular motion is shown in Figure-64.

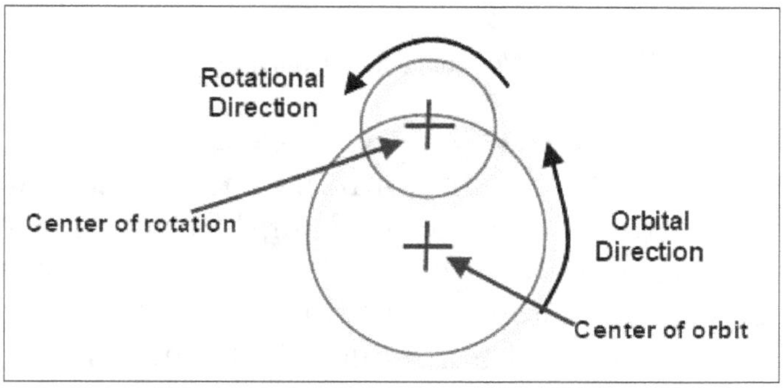

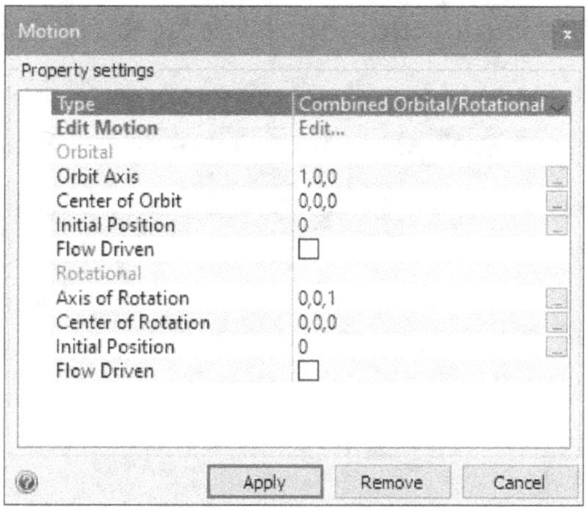

Figure-64. Combined Orbital Rotational motion dialog box

- The rotational and orbital motion of a component can either be user-prescribed or flow driven.

Nutating Motion

The **Nutating Motion** is used in several types of liquid flow meters. In Nutating motion, object is inclined at an angle to reference axis. When the normal vector of object rotates about the reference axis, the angle between normal vector and reference axis remains constant. The result is that the object actually wobbles about the reference axis, but does not change angular position relative to it. For example, coin wobbling along its edge. In Nutating motion, the user needs to define three parameters to set-up nutating motion which are, tilt axis, the axis of nutation (Nutating axis), and centre of nutation. The **Nutating Motion** dialog box of combined linear/angular motion is shown in Figure-65.

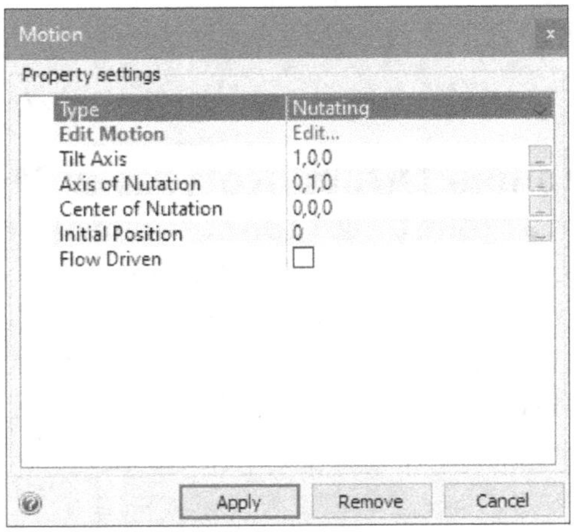

Figure-65. Nutating Motion dialog box

Sliding Vane Motion

Sliding Vane motion is a combination of angular motion and linear motion. In this, the path of linear translation is user defined, and is not changed by the rotational motion. The location of the axis of rotation is specified by the user. Example of this motion is sliding-vane positive displacement pumps. In this type of pump, the pistons rotate about the specified line of the impeller, but translate radially. The direction of linear motion changes at every angular motion and the axis of rotation remains constant. The **Sliding Vane** dialog box of combined linear/angular motion is shown in Figure-66.

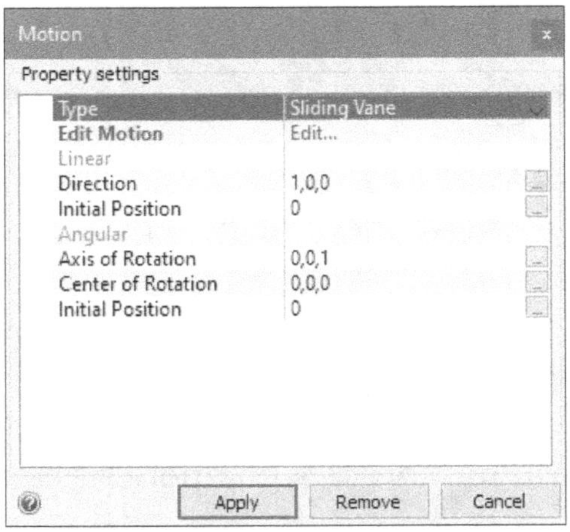

Figure-66. Sliding Vane motion dialog box

Free Motion

The **Free Motion** allows motion of component in any direction. This is most easy type of motion for all and it can be used to stimulate partially constrained movement of objects within an active flow field. This motion type is flow driven and is defined by enabling or disabling any of the six degrees of freedom. The **Free Motion** dialog box of combined linear/angular motion is shown in Figure-67.

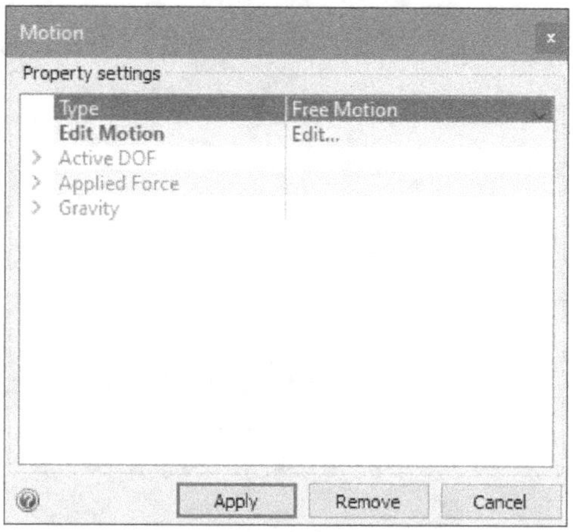

Figure-67. Free Motion dialog box

Let's get back to specifying parameters for **Motion** dialog box.

- Click in the **Type** drop-down from **Motion** dialog box and select the required motion type. In our case, we are selecting **Angular** motion type.
- Click on the component from model at which you want to apply angular motion; refer to Figure-68.

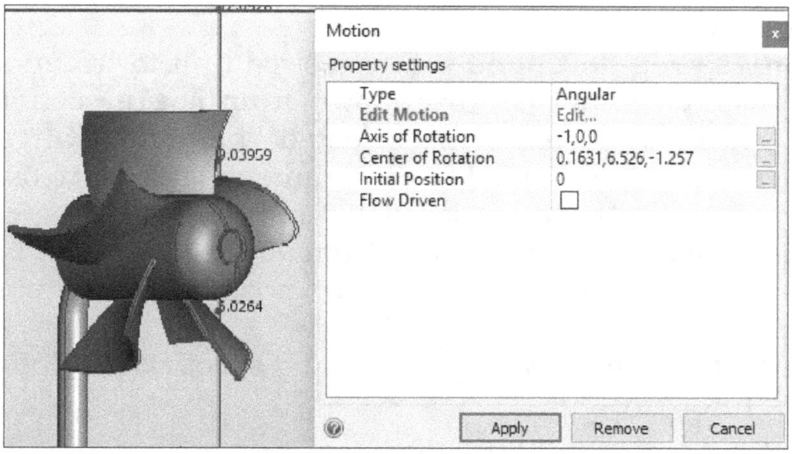

Figure-68. Selected component for angular motion

- Click on the **Edit** button from **Edit Motion** field of the **Motion** dialog box. The **Motion Editor** dialog box will be displayed; refer to Figure-69.

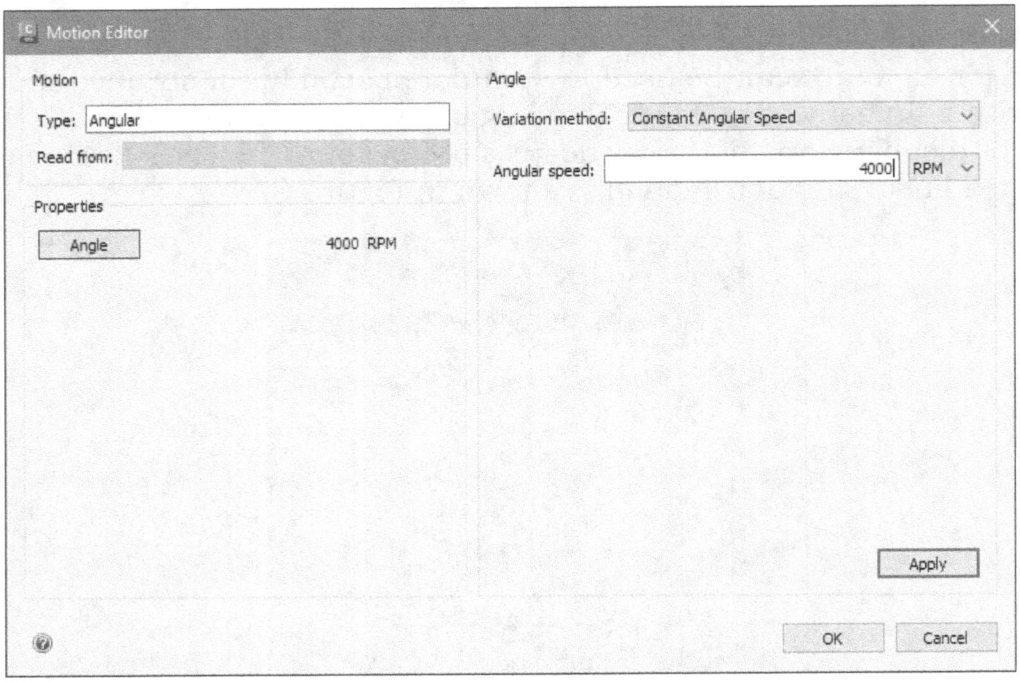

Figure-69. Motion Editor dialog box

- The selected **Angular** motion type is displayed in **Motion Editor** dialog box. If we had selected any other motion type then the selected motion type will be displayed here along with related parameters.
- Click in the **Variation method** drop-down from **Angle** section and select the **Constant Angular Speed** option to specify a constant angular speed for the selected part throughout the process.
- Click in the **Angular speed** edit box from **Angle** section and specify the rotation speed of selected part.
- Click in the **Units** drop-down and select desired unit for rotation.
- Click in the **Variation method** drop-down from **Angle** section and select the **Oscillating** option to oscillate the selected component angularly through a prescribed angle range in specified time. Parameters related to **Oscillating** option will be displayed in the **Angle** section of **Motion Editor** dialog box.
- Click in the **Half period time** edit box from **Angle** section and specify the value of time taken by object to rotate from start position to end position of angular displacement.
- Click in the **Angular Displacement** edit box and specify the value of included angle of stroke; refer to Figure-70.

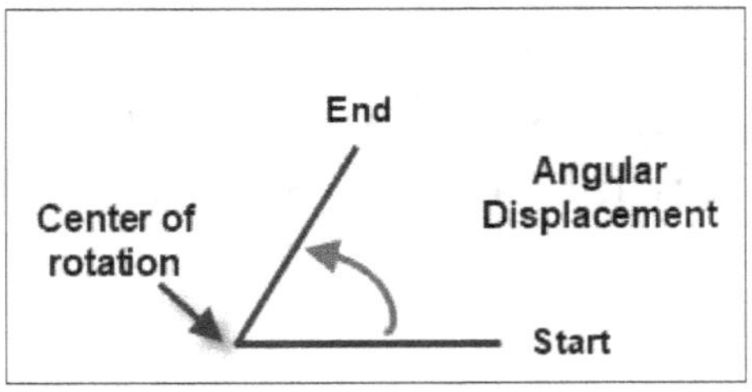

Figure-70. Angular Displacement

- Click in the **Variation method** drop-down from **Angle** section and select the **Table** option to specify angular position at specific times.

- Enter the data of Angle and Time in the table as desired.
- Select the **Cyclical** check box from **Angle** section of **Motion Editor** dialog box to repeat only forward sweeps through the angle table.
- Select the **Reciprocating** check box from **Angle** section of **Motion Editor** dialog box to repeat forward and reverse sweeps through the angle table.
- After specifying the parameters from **Motion Editor** dialog box, click on the **Apply** button and then **OK** button, You will be redirected to **Motion** dialog box.

Axis of Rotation

- The **Axis of Rotation** button of **Motion** dialog box is used to set the axis of rotation of selected component. The rotational direction of component is selected as per right hand thumb rule. You need to choose the X,Y, or Z axes to choose Cartesian direction as the axis of rotation.
- On clicking the **Axis of Rotation** button from **Motion** dialog box, the **Axis of Rotation** box will be displayed; refer to Figure-71.

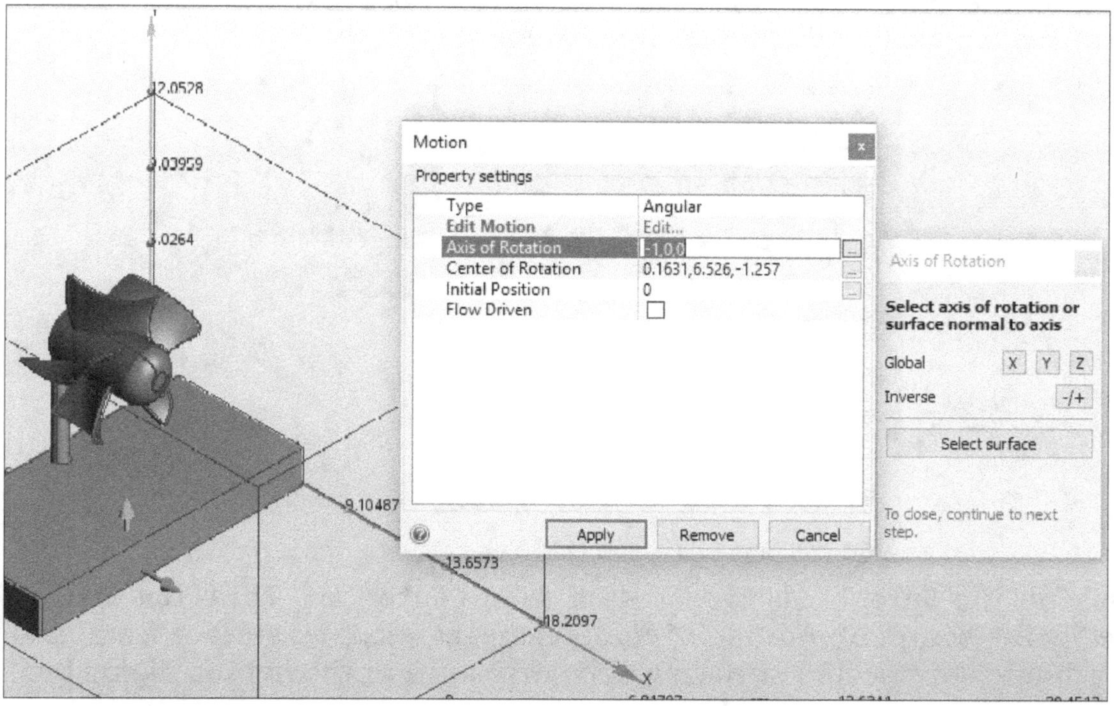

Figure-71. Axis of rotation box

- Click on the X,Y, or Z from **Axis of Rotation** box to set the direction of rotation of selected component as per right hand thumb rule; refer to Figure-72. In our case, we have selected the X axis.

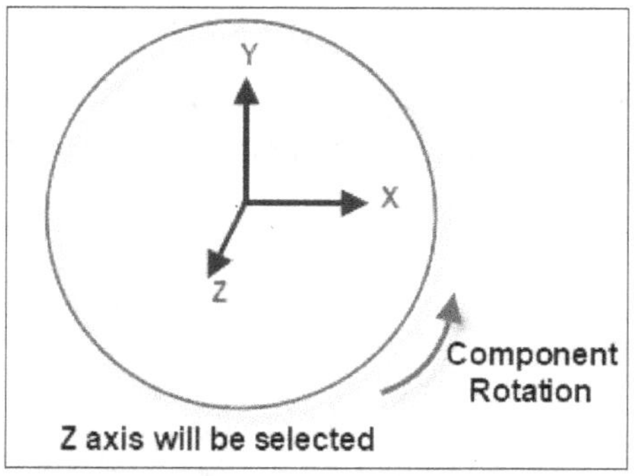

Figure-72. Selection of direction

- Click on the **Inverse** button to reverse the rotation direction of selected component.
- The **(0,0,0)** from **Axis of Rotation** button of **Motion** dialog box is equals to **(X,Y,Z)** of **Axis of Rotation** box. Which means, when you select the X axis from **Axis of Rotation** box, **1** will be displayed in **Motion** dialog box in place of X, and if you also have selected the **Inverse** button from **Axis of Rotation** dialog box, **(-1,0,0)** will be displayed in **Axis of Rotation** button of **Motion** dialog box.
- Click on the **Select surface** button from **Axis of Rotation** dialog box to specify the rotation direction of component by selecting a surface from mode. The surface selection will be activated. The **Surface** will be selected and coordinates of surface will be displayed.

Center of Rotation

The **Center of Rotation** is used to specify the point through which axis of rotation passes. The procedure to use this is discussed next.

- Click on the **Center of Rotation** button from **Motion** dialog box. The **Center of Rotation** box will be displayed; refer to Figure-73.

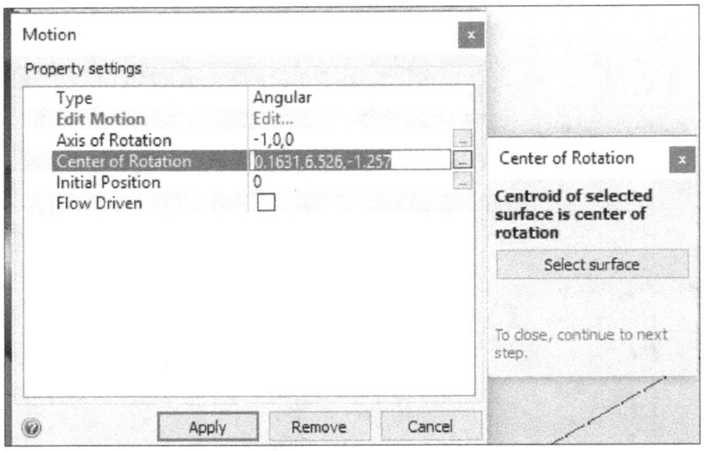

Figure-73. Center of Rotation box

- Click on the **Select Surface** button from **Center of Rotation** dialog box to specify the centre of rotation of component by selecting surface from model. The coordinates of selected surface will be displayed in the **Motion** dialog box.

Initial Position

The **Initial Position** button is used to specify the initial angular position of the part from the as-built position of model. This tool is very helpful for fine tuning the model when the original position of the model is not appropriate. The procedure to use this is discussed next.

- Click on the **Initial Position** button from **Motion** dialog box. The **Initial Position** edit box will be activated and **Initial Position** box will be displayed; refer to Figure-74.

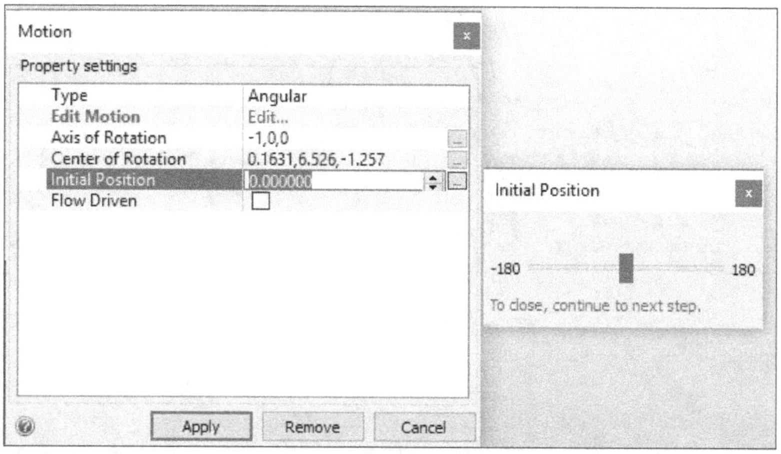

Figure-74. Initial Position box

- Enter desired value in **Initial Position** edit box or move the **Initial Position** box slider to specify the initial position value. When you move the **Initial Position** slider, selected component will also move, respectively.

Flow Driven

The **Flow Driven** check box of **Motion** dialog box is used to apply minimum and maximum limit of rotation to selected components. In some cases, we do not want a full 360° rotation of component, what we want is a restricted rotation of component. In this type of condition, the **Flow Driven** tool is used. The procedure to use this option is discussed next.

- Select the **Flow Driven** check box from **Motion** dialog box. The **Minimum Bound** and **Maximum Bound** options will be activated and displayed in **Motion** dialog box; refer to Figure-75.

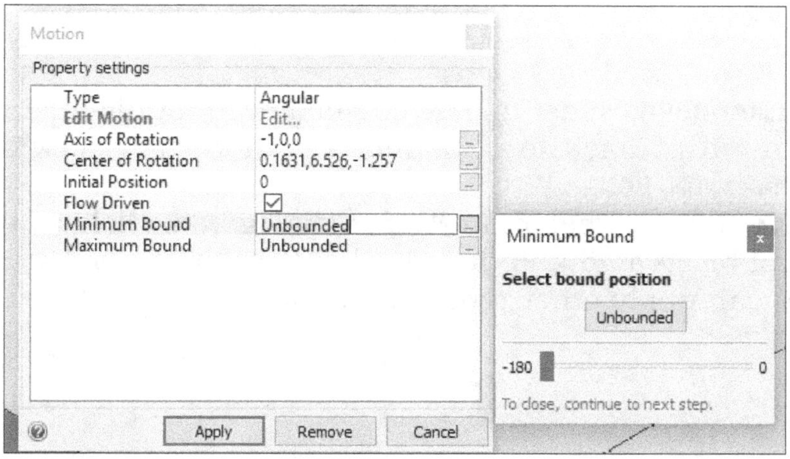

Figure-75. Flow Driven check box

- The default value of **Maximum Bound** and **Minimum Bound** is set to **Unbounded** in **Motion** dialog box.
- Click in the **Minimum Bound** field, the **Minimum Bound** box will be displayed; refer to Figure-76.

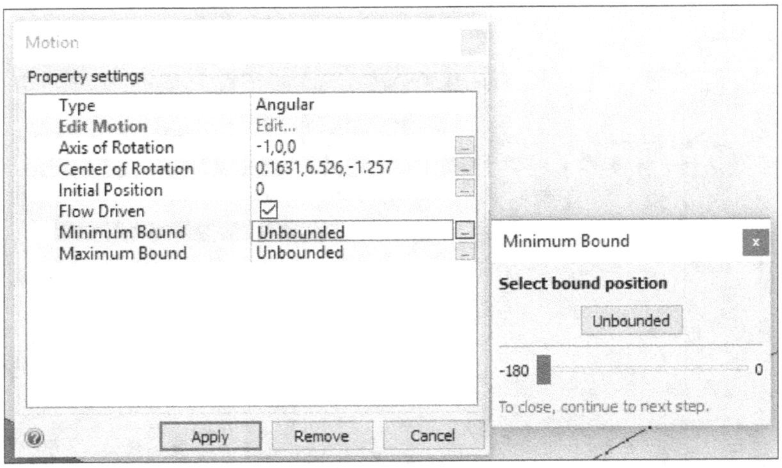

Figure-76. Minimum Bound box

- Move the **Minimum Bound** slider to desired minimum rotation limit of the component.
- Click in the **Maximum Bound** field from **Motion** dialog box. The **Maximum Bound** box will be displayed; refer to Figure-77.

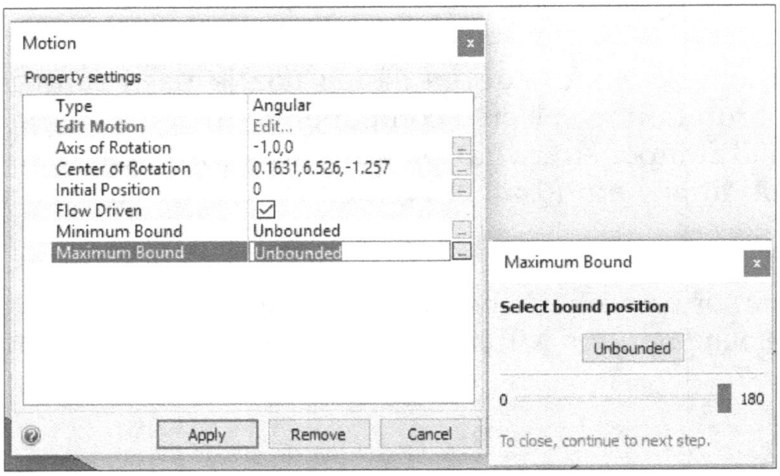

Figure-77. Maximum Bound box

- Move the **Maximum Bound** slider to desired maximum rotational limit of component. If you want to return back to unbound condition than click on the **Unbounded** button from **Maximum Bound** box.
- After specifying the parameters in **Motion** dialog box, click on the **Apply** button. The motion will be created and displayed in **Design Study bar**.
- Similarly, you can apply other types of motions to selected components.

SELF-ASSESSMENT

Q1. Material is a key input for any analysis in Autodesk CFD. (T/F)

Q2. Which of the following tools is used to set temperature and pressure conditions for fluid naturally flowing in the computational domain?

a. Scenario Environment tool
b. Materials tool
c. Geometry tools
d. Initial Conditions tool

Q3. In Autodesk CFD, there is no need to assign material to surroundings when performing external volume analysis as air is by default selected as the material (T/F)

Q4. The Scenario Environment dialog box is used to set the environment conditions for an individual material. (T/F)

Q5. For 2D models, the boundary conditions are applied to model surfaces. (T/F)

Q6. For 2D models, the boundary conditions are applied to edges. (T/F)

Q7. Velocity boundary condition can only be used as inlet boundary condition in a model. (T/F)

Q8. The .... option in Time Curve drop-down of Boundary Conditions dialog box is used to define Boundary Conditions as exponential function of time.

Q9. The Volume Flow Rate Boundary Condition is applicable when the density of fluid is constant throughout the analysis. (T/F)

Q10. The Mass Flow Rate boundary condition can be applied as both inlet and outlet boundary conditions. (T/F)

Q11. What is the difference between gage pressure and absolute pressure?

Q12. The .... option of Static/Total drop-down is used when both static as well as dynamic pressure of fluid are included in analysis.

Q13. In the early stages of design analysis where approximate results may suffice, you can specify a larger element size for a faster solution. (T/F)

Q14. Which of the following element types is suitable for meshing thin sheet metal parts?

a. 3D tetrahedral solid elements
b. 2D triangular shell elements
c. 1D beam elements
d. 1D truss elements

Q15. In .... motion, object is inclined at an angle to reference axis. When the normal vector of object rotates about the reference axis, the angle between normal vector and reference axis remains constant.

Q16. What is the first step after adding a model in Autodesk CFD for analysis?

A. Apply boundary condition
B. Create mesh
C. Assign material
D. Open Material Editor

Q17. What does the "Use scenario environment" checkbox do in the Material Environment dialog box?

A. Locks the properties to system defaults
B. Uses data specified in Scenario Environment dialog box
C. Prevents editing pressure and temperature
D. Automatically selects the hardest material

Q18. What should be selected in the Material DB Name drop-down to get all standard materials?

A. My Materials
B. External Library
C. Default
D. General

Q19. Which material type should be selected for gas or liquid materials?

A. Solid
B. Alloy
C. Fluid
D. Composite

Q20. How can you vary the properties of a material with time in simulations?

A. Select Fixed radio button
B. Set high pressure values
C. Select Variable radio button
D. Change color of the material

Q21. What tool is used to define environment conditions for individual materials?

A. Scenario Environment
B. Simulation Settings
C. Environment Manager
D. Pressure Tab

Q22. In which tab of the Material Editor can you check parameters of a material?

A. Database
B. Properties
C. Favorites
D. Environment

Q23. How can you add frequently used materials to your favorite material list?

A. Drag and drop into Favorites tab
B. Select and press Ctrl + F
C. Right-click and select "Add to favorites"
D. Copy material name to Favorites box

Q24. Where are new materials saved after creation?

A. Main Library
B. Autodesk Cloud
C. My Material database
D. Setup Tasks tab

Q25. Which section in the Material Editor helps filter materials based on type and database?

A. Search bar
B. Refine selection section
C. Properties section
D. Database toolbar

Q26. What happens when you remove a selected material from the model?

A. It is deleted permanently
B. It changes to Default material
C. Model material becomes Unassigned
D. A warning message appears

Q27. What is the primary purpose of boundary conditions in Autodesk CFD?

A. To define material properties
B. To connect the model with surroundings
C. To create the mesh
D. To apply forces

Q28. Which boundary condition represents fluid speed at the model boundary?

A. Pressure
B. Volume Flow Rate
C. Velocity
D. Mass Flow Rate

Q29. Which state of boundary condition varies with time?

A. Static
B. Periodic
C. Steady
D. Transient

Q30. Before applying boundary conditions, what must be ensured in a fluid flow model?

A. Material is not applied
B. Velocity is zero
C. Proper lids are applied on openings
D. Only 3D model is used

Q31. Which method allows editing boundary conditions directly by right-clicking from the Design Study Bar?

A. First Method
B. Second Method
C. Third Method
D. Initial Conditions Method

Q32. What is selected to specify velocity normal to the surface?

A. Gage option
B. Component option
C. Normal option
D. Transient option

Q33. What type of variation simulates a realistic entrance flow profile in pipes or ducts?

A. Constant
B. Linear
C. Fully Developed
D. Periodic

Q34. Which boundary condition is typically used for simulating rotating walls?

A. Pressure
B. Rotational Velocity
C. Heat Flux
D. Slip/Symmetry

Q35. What unit is typically used for rotational velocity?

A. m/s
B. °C
C. RPM
D. W/m^2K

Q36. Which boundary condition is used when fluid density remains constant throughout the analysis?

A. Velocity
B. Volume Flow Rate
C. Mass Flow Rate
D. Temperature

Q37. Which boundary condition is recommended as an outlet condition in open environment?

A. Velocity
B. Mass Flow Rate
C. Pressure
D. Unknown

Q38. What does the Scalar boundary condition represent?

A. Humidity level
B. Vapour content
C. Fluid temperature
D. Concentration of scalar quantity

Q39. Which boundary condition is used to represent vapour content in steam?

A. Heat Flux
B. Scalar
C. Quality
D. Humidity

Q40. Which boundary condition defines the rate of heat energy released from a surface to the environment?

A. Temperature
B. Radiation
C. Film Coefficient
D. Total Heat Flux

Q41. The External Fan boundary condition uses which factor to determine tangential velocity component?

A. Velocity Magnitude
B. Emissivity
C. Slip Factor
D. RPM

Q42. Which electrical condition applies total current to a surface for Joule heating analysis?

A. Voltage
B. Current
C. Scalar
D. Heat Flux

Q43. Which boundary condition simulates multiple repeating geometry features for faster calculations?

A. Transparent
B. Periodic
C. Pressure
D. Quality

Q44. What is the role of Transparent boundary condition in analysis?

A. Simulate radiation through transparent media
B. Define electric voltage
C. Apply natural convection
D. Apply unknown boundary

Q45. What is the main difference between initial and boundary conditions?

A. Boundary conditions are used only in 2D models
B. Initial conditions apply at the start of analysis
C. Initial conditions override all boundary settings
D. Boundary conditions are for electrical analysis only

Q46. What must be selected from the Selection panel to apply the initial boundary condition to a specific volume of the model?

A. Surface button
B. Volume button
C. Edge button
D. Region button

Q47. What does the Re-initialize checkbox in the Initial Conditions dialog box do?

A. It saves simulation data
B. It re-applies boundary conditions to the entire model
C. It resets the initial condition on selected parts after a previous simulation
D. It refines the mesh

Q48. What type of elements are generated by meshing in a bulky model?

A. Shell elements
B. Beam elements
C. Solid elements
D. Mixed elements

Q49. What does the Surface Refinement checkbox do when selected?

A. Displays mesh statistics
B. Activates the Refine button for surface mesh refinement
C. Applies temperature constraints
D. Applies boundary conditions

Q50. In manual meshing, which parameter controls the fineness of the mesh?

A. Gap refinement
B. Wall layers
C. Element size
D. Resolution factor

Q51. Why can't wall layers be added to an imported mesh?

A. Because imported mesh is incompatible
B. Because layers are added before mesh generation
C. Because imported models are 2D
D. Because imported mesh is already refined

Q52. What is the purpose of the Layer factor in the Wall Layer dialog box?

A. To control the number of layers
B. To define the axis of rotation
C. To control the thickness of the layer
D. To refine mesh gaps

Q53. What is the acceptable range of the Resolution factor in Advanced Meshing Controls?

A. 0.5 to 2
B. 2 to 5
C. 1 to 3
D. 1.5 to 4

Q54. What value of Edge growth rate represents a 50% growth rate?

A. 1.2
B. 1.5
C. 2.0
D. 1.1

Q55. Which tool analyzes the interaction between moving parts and surrounding fluid?

A. Mesh
B. Motion
C. Volume
D. Initial Conditions

Q56. Which motion type involves both rotation and orbital motion?

A. Combined Linear/Angular
B. Nutating Motion
C. Sliding Vane Motion
D. Combined Orbital/Rotational Motion

Q57. Which motion type is used in displacement pumps and fan blades?

A. Nutating Motion
B. Free Motion
C. Angular Motion
D. Linear Motion

Q58. Which Motion option allows oscillating a component angularly through a prescribed angle?

A. Constant Angular Speed
B. Oscillating
C. Table
D. Free Motion

Q59. Which method specifies angular position at specific times?

A. Oscillating
B. Constant Angular Speed
C. Table
D. Nutating

Q60. Which axis can be selected to define rotation direction in Axis of Rotation dialog box?

A. Any face
B. Custom axis
C. X, Y, or Z
D. Mesh axis

Q61. What is the default setting for Maximum Bound in Flow Driven conditions?

A. 360°
B. Unbounded
C. 180°
D. 90°

Chapter 4

Solving Analysis

Topics Covered

The major topics covered in this chapter are:

- ***Control Tab***
- ***Adaptation Tab***
- ***Physics Tab***
- ***Convergence Plot***

INTRODUCTION

In last chapters, we have learned about tools used for preparation of the analysis. The understanding of those tools is vital to perform the analysis and generate valid result of an analysis. In this chapter, we will learn about the tools used to perform analysis and check different results.

SOLVING ANALYSIS

To solve an analysis, you need to apply the materials and boundary condition to the model. These tools were discussed in last chapters. After applying the boundary condition, you need to create a mesh of required shape and size. This can be done automatically as well as manually as discussed in previous chapter. After creating mesh, the next step is to solve the analysis which is discussed next.

There are various methods to solve the analysis, which are discussed next.

Method 1

In this method, we will discuss the procedure of activating the **Solve** tool from **Design Study Bar**.

- Right-click on the **Solve** button from **Design Study Bar**. The right-click menu will be displayed; refer to Figure-1.
- Click on the **Solve** button from displayed right-click menu. The **Solve** dialog box will be displayed; refer to Figure-2.

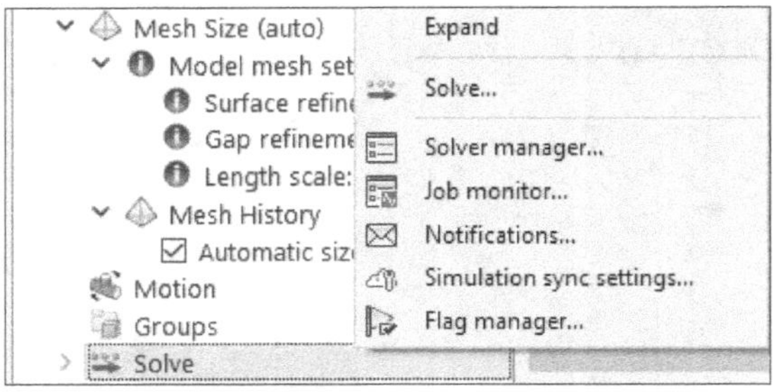

Figure-1. Right-click menu of Solve button

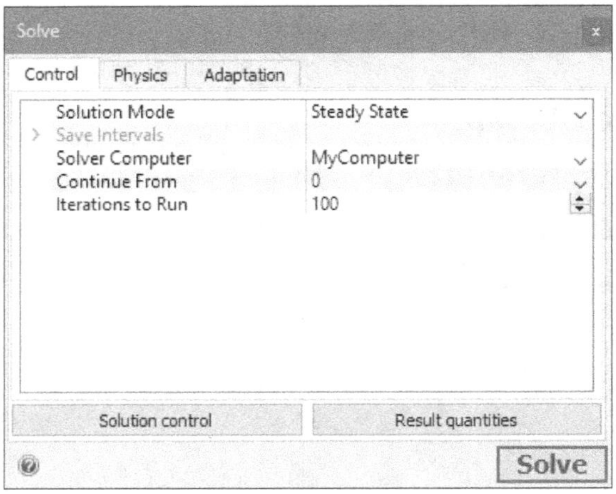

Figure-2. Solve dialog box

Method 2

- Right-click on the canvas window outside the model, the right-click menu will be displayed; refer to Figure-3.

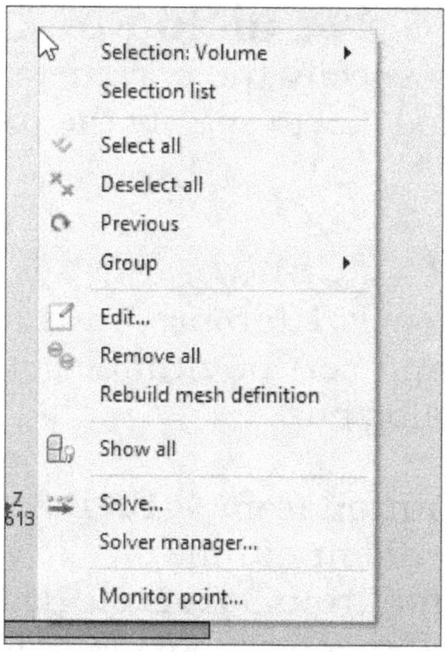

Figure-3. Right-click menu of graphics window

- Click on the **Solve** button from the displayed menu, the **Solve** dialog box will be displayed.

Method 3

- Click on the **Solve** button from **Simulation** panel of **Setup** tab; refer to Figure-4, the **Solve** dialog box will be displayed; refer to Figure-5.

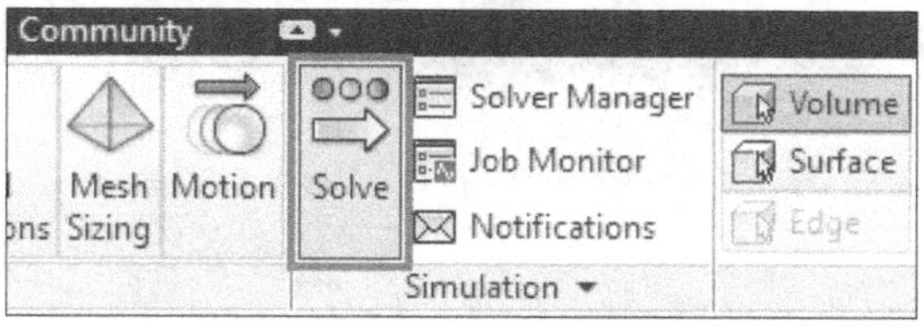

Figure-4. Solve button from Simulation Panel

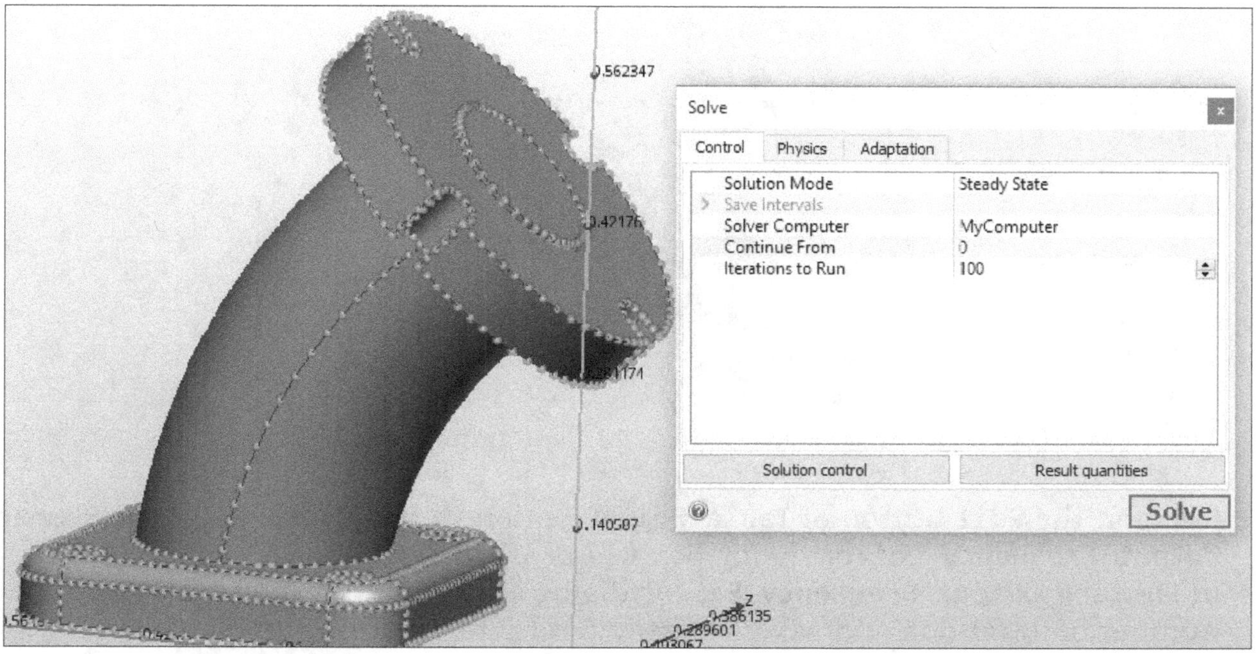

Figure-5. Solve dialog box along with model

Solve dialog box

The **Solve** dialog box is used to specify the parameters for performing a simulation. There are three tabs in this dialog box to specify the parameters, which are discussed next.

Control tab

The tools and parameters of **Control** tab are used to specify analysis parameters, like transient or steady state and set the number of iterations. The **Control** tab is by default selected in **Solve** dialog box.

- Click on the **Steady State** button from **Solution Mode** drop-down of **Control** tab to make the analysis independent of time.
- Click on the **Transient** button from **Solution Mode** drop-down of **Control** tab to make the analysis to be time-dependent. All motion analyses will run as a Transient analyses. You can switch between the two modes anytime during an analysis.

Save Interval

- Double-click on the **Save Intervals** node button from **Control** tab of **Solve** dialog box to specify the time intervals for saving results and information in Autodesk CFD. The default value is specified at 0, which means result are saved only when the analysis completes the specified iterations or stops manually.
- Select the **Table** check box from **Save Intervals** section to save iterations or time steps at varying interval. The **Table Editor** button will be displayed; refer to Figure-6.

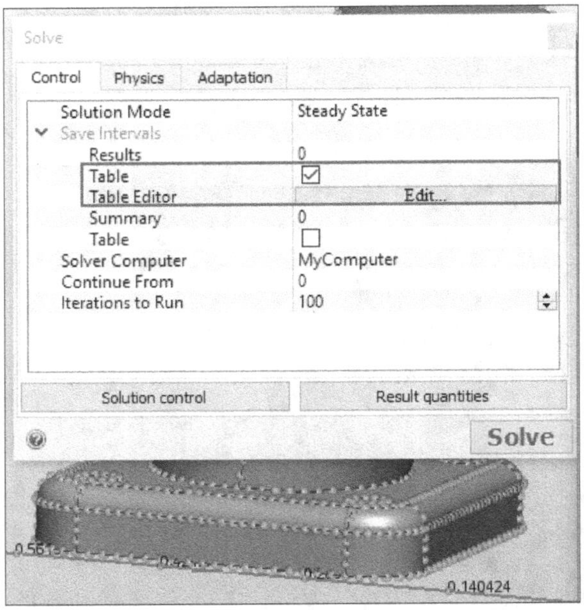

Figure-6. Table Editor button

- Click on the **Edit** button of **Table Editor** option to specify the data, the **Summary Output Frequency Editor** dialog box will be displayed.
- In **Summary Output Frequency Editor** dialog box, you need to specify the data of number of iterations and save frequency; refer to Figure-7.

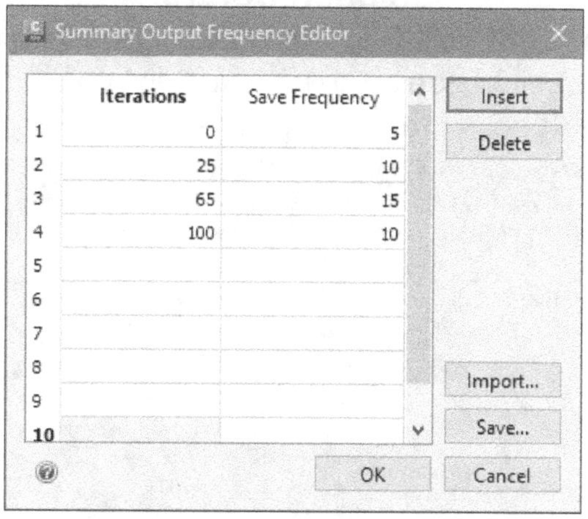

Figure-7. Adding data in Summary Output Frequency Editor dialog box

- For example in above dialog box, starting from step 0, output will be saved at every 5 iterations. At step 25, output will be saved at every 10 iterations. At step 65, the output will be saved at every 15 iterations. Finally, from step 100, output will be saved at every 10 iterations. If more than 100 steps are needed for analysis like 300 steps, then results will be saved at every 10 iterations.
- Click on the **Insert** button from **Summary Output Frequency Editor** dialog box to insert a row above the selected row.
- Click on the **Delete** button to remove the selected row from the table.
- Click on the **Import** button to import the data for current analysis.
- Click on the **Save** button to save the table data. The **Save** dialog box will be displayed. Select desired location from **Save** dialog box and click on **Save** button. The data will be saved at desired location.
- After specifying the parameters, click on the **OK** button. You will be redirected to **Solve** dialog box.
- Click in the **Solver Computer** drop-down and select desired solver to solve the current analysis. You can also solve the current analysis using cloud solver if you have cloud credits. For cloud solver, you will need a internet connection.
- Click in the **Continue From** edit box and specify desired iteration number from where solver will start solving analysis. Suppose, you have performed an analysis earlier on the current model, and after updating the model you want to continue the model from a specific value in between 1 to 100. Then, you can simply enter desired value in **Continue From** edit box. The analysis will start from specified value.

If the last iteration or time step is selected, then all selected saved iterations will be deleted from the current analysis. If you have changed mesh definitions, boundary conditions, or material of model then these are automatically incorporated into the analysis. After changing these parameters, you have to reset the **Continue From** value to 0, if not, following cases may arrive:

1. The current results are interpolated into new mesh
2. A new mesh will be generated.
3. The analysis iteration count reset to 0.

- Click in the **Iterations to Run** edit box from **Solve** dialog box and specify the value of iterations for current analysis.

Solution Control

- Click on the **Solution control** button of **Control** tab from **Solve** dialog box to enable or disable the **Intelligent Solution Control** tool. The **Solution Controls** dialog box will be displayed; refer to Figure-8.

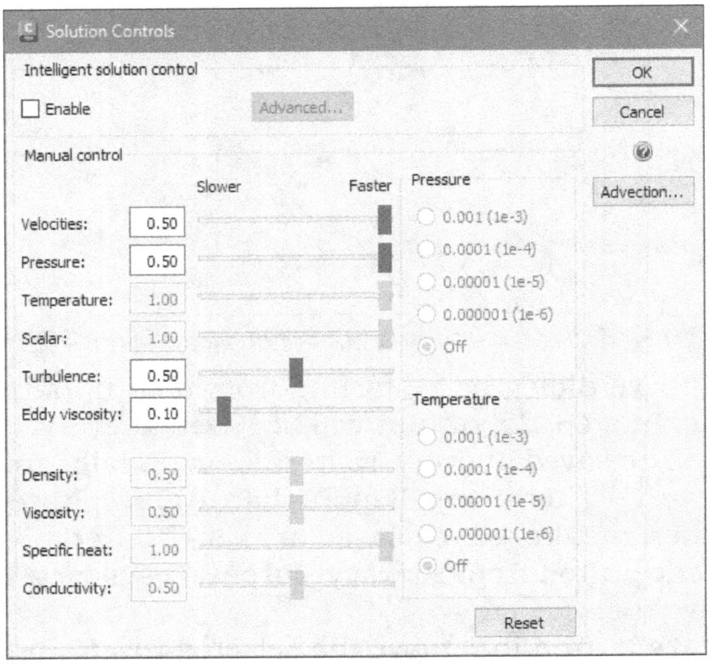

Figure-8. Solution Controls dialog box

- Select the **Enable** check box to control the convergence progression of the steady state stage of the analysis. Clear the **Enable** check box to disable **Intelligent Solution Control** tool.
- After clearing the check box, you need to specify various parameters manually to use **Solution control** tool.
- Click on the **Advection** button from **Solution Controls** dialog box to control the solution progression rate so that chances of divergence are minimized.
- After specifying the parameters, click on the **OK** button from **Solution Controls** dialog box. You will be returned to **Solve** dialog box.

Result quantities

The **Result Quantities** button is used to display or hide the result parameters that are available after the analysis is complete. The procedure to use this button is discussed next.

- Click on the **Result quantities** button from **Solve** dialog box. The **Result Quantities** dialog box will be displayed; refer to Figure-9.

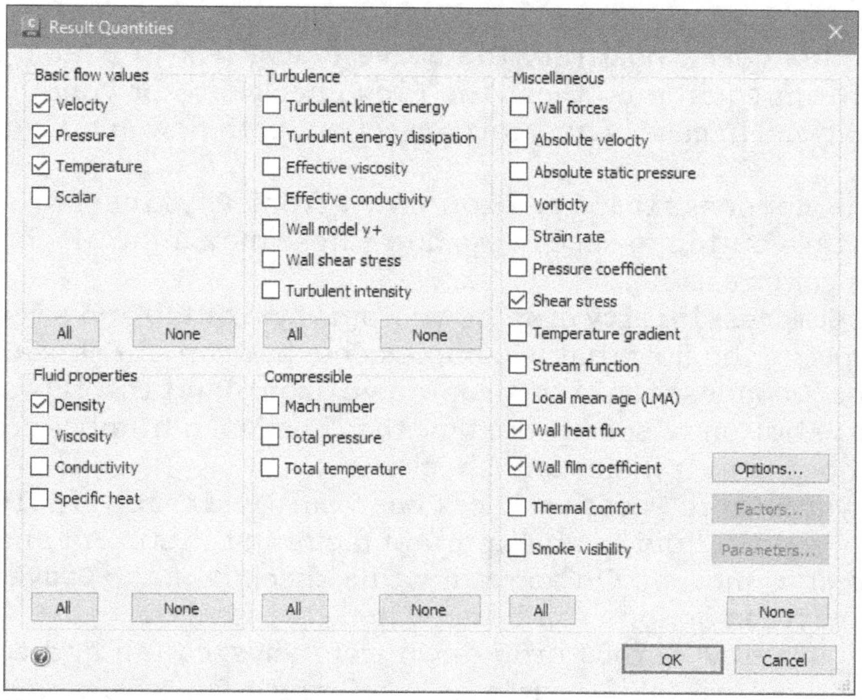

Figure-9. Result Quantities dialog box

- Select the check boxes of those quantities which you want to display in results after analysis. If you want to view all parameters, click on the **All** button from **Result Quantities** dialog box.
- If you want to deselect all the quantities then click on the **None** button.
- After selecting desired quantities, click on the **OK** button from **Result quantities** dialog box. You will be returned to **Solve** dialog box.

Physics tab

The **Physics** tab is used to define simulation conditions and solution parameters. The options in this tab are discuss next.

- Click on the **Physics** tab from **Solve** dialog box. The options in the dialog box will be displayed as shown in Figure-10.

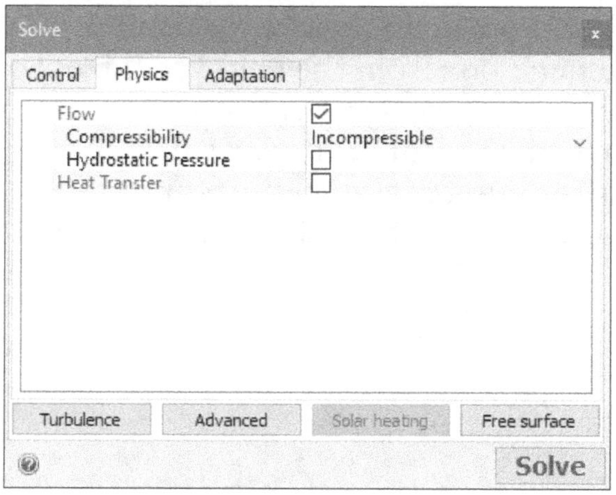

Figure-10. Physics tab

Flow

- Select the **Flow** check box from the **Solve** dialog box to enable fluid pressure and momentum equations. Clear the **Flow** check box for conduction-only heat transfer analysis. In case of natural convection, both flow and heat transfer must be enabled.
- Click in the **Compressibility** drop-down from **Physics** tab and select the **Incompressible** button to specify the flow whose maximum Mach number is less than 0.3 as compressible.
- Click in the **Compressibility** drop-down from **Physics** tab and select the **Subsonic** button to specify the flow that is compressible but contain shock.
- Click in the **Compressibility** drop-down from **Physics** tab and select the **Compressible** button to specify the flow that has Mach number greater than 0.8 with or without heat transfer and shock.
- Select the **Hydrostatic Pressure** check box from **Physics** tab of **Solve** dialog box to specify the weight of fluid as an important factor in the current analysis, whether fluid is at rest or moving. On activating this check box, the **Gravity Method** and **Gravity Direction** options will be activated.
- Click in the **Gravity Method** drop-down from **Physics** tab and select the **Earth** option when you are taking earth as a reference for creating analysis. In this case, you need to specify the direction of gravity by entering the value in **Gravity Direction** button. Suppose your model is constructed such that "down" is negative Z direction, the unit vector for gravity should be (0,0,-1). If you are selecting **Component** option in place of **Earth** option then you need to specify the magnitude and direction vector in the **Gravity Components** field. The **Components** option is generally used in flows with hydrostatic pressure and buoyancy driven flows.

Heat Transfer

- Select the **Heat Transfer** check box from **Physics** tab of **Solve** dialog box to specify the transfer of heat in the flow. Clear this check box to specify the simulation to be adiabatic. On selecting **Heat Transfer** check box, more options related to this will be activated.
- Select the **Auto Forced Convection** check box from **Physics** tab to automatically stage a forced convection analysis into separate flow and heat transfer stages. Using this option, the flow and heat transfer can be solved separately because the flow does not depend on temperature distribution.
- Select the **Radiation** check box from the **Physics** tab of **Solve** dialog box to include surface-to-surface radiation effects in heat transfer analysis. The **Radiation** option is generally used when field temperature near model is very high. On selecting this check box, the **Solar heating** button becomes active. Click on this button to set solar radiation parameters. The **Solar Heating Dialog** box will be displayed; refer to Figure-11.

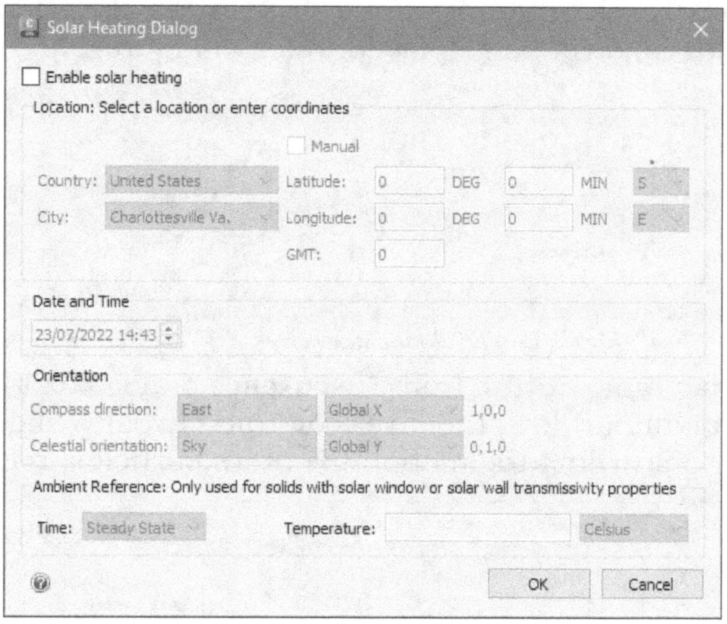

Figure-11. Solar Heating Dialog box

Solar heating plays an important role in designing homes and building. Engineers need to understand and account for the effects of solar heating on performance and efficiency of structures. Solar heating works with Radiation solver and supports radioactive heat transfer through transparent media. The procedure to use this is discussed next.

- Select the **Enable solar heating** check box from the **Solar Heating Dialog** box. Tools of solar heating will be activated.
- Select the geographical location as selecting country from **Country** drop-down and city from **City** drop-down. The **Latitude**, **Longitude**, **GMT**, **DEG**, and **MIN** will be specified by default. If you want to set these parameters manually then select the **Manual** check box.

Note - **Latitude** must be between -90 to 90 degrees, **Longitude** must be between -180 and 180 degrees, and the **GMT** must be between -12 to 12.

- Set the date and time from **Date and Time** section of **Solar Heating Dialog** box by using up and down arrows.
- Select the required orientation of solar heating from **Orientation** section of **Solar Heating Dialog** box.
- Select the **Steady State** button from **Time** drop-down to assign temperature to the outer surfaces of the model. Click in the **Temperature** edit box and enter desired value to specify ambient reference temperature.
- Select the **Transient** button from **Time** drop-down to specify how the **Ambient Temperature** varies with time using the **Time Curve** table. Click on the **Time Curve** drop-down and select the required option to specify time curve.
- After specifying the parameters, click on the **OK** button from **Solar Heating Dialog** box. You would be returned to **Solve** dialog box.

Turbulence

The **Turbulence** button is used to specify flow turbulence for the fluid. The procedure to use this option is discussed next.

- Click on the **Turbulence** button from the **Physics** tab of the **Solve** dialog box. The **Turbulence** dialog box will be displayed; refer to Figure-12.

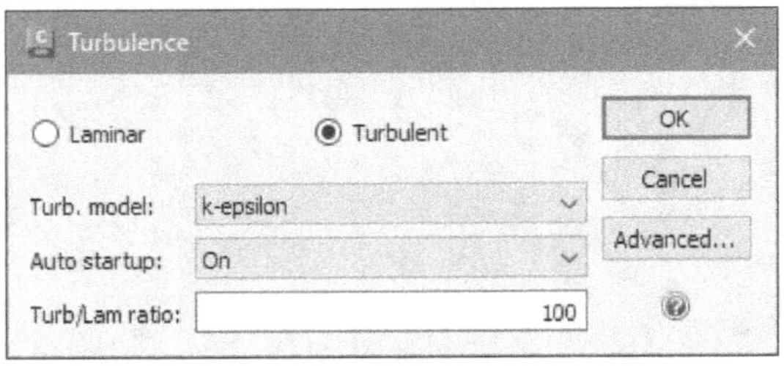

Figure-12. Turbulence dialog box

- Select the **Laminar** radio button from **Turbulence** dialog box to specify the flow as laminar flow. In laminar flow, the layers of fluid particles slide over the adjacent particle without disturbing the motion of others particles; refer to Figure-13.

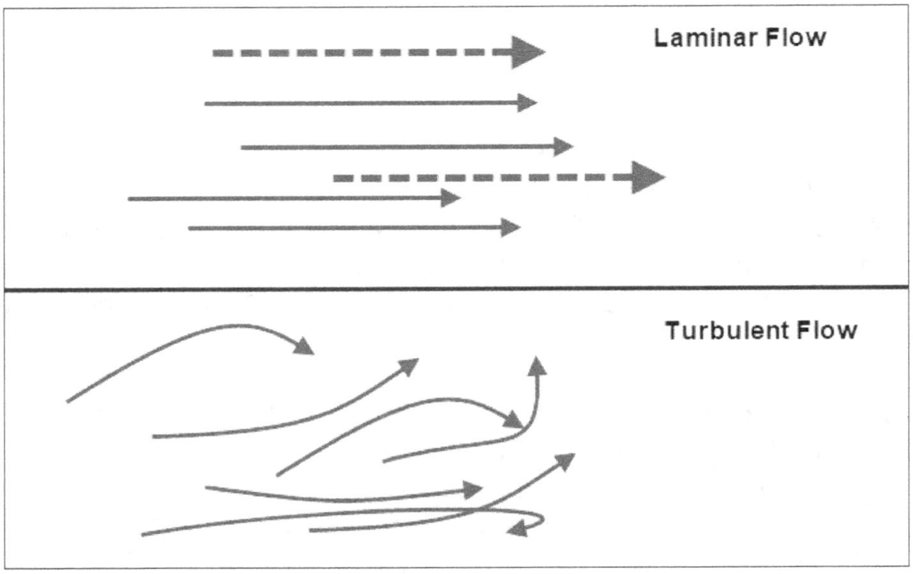

Figure-13. Laminar and Turbulent Flow

- Select the **Turbulent** radio button from **Turbulence** dialog box to specify the flow as turbulent. In turbulent flow, the fluid properties of flow vary rapidly with time. The velocity, pressure, density, and other flow properties show random changes.
- Click in the **Turb. model** drop-down and select desired turbulence model. You can learn about these options from Help page of the software.
- Click in the **Auto startup** drop-down from **Turbulence** dialog box and select required option to run **Automatic Turbulent Start-up** algorithm as per command. Select the **Lock On** button from **Auto startup** drop-down to keep ATSU on during the entire analysis until you shut it down. If you are having convergence difficulties after 50 iterations, then you must enable **Lock On** button. If ATSU is already turned on then you should run at least 200 iterations to ensure convergence of the turbulent flow simulation. Select the **Extended** option from **Auto startup** drop-down to activate an extended version of ATSU. This method is generally used for compressible analyses. At least 400 iterations should run in this algorithm.
- Click in the **Turb/Lam ratio** edit box from **Turbulence** dialog box and specify the ratio of value to estimate the effective viscosity at the beginning of turbulent flow analysis. The default value of this option is generally suitable for most flows.
- Click on the **Advanced** button from **Turbulence** dialog box to specify advanced parameters of turbulence flow in the **Advanced Turbulence Parameters** dialog box; refer to Figure-14.

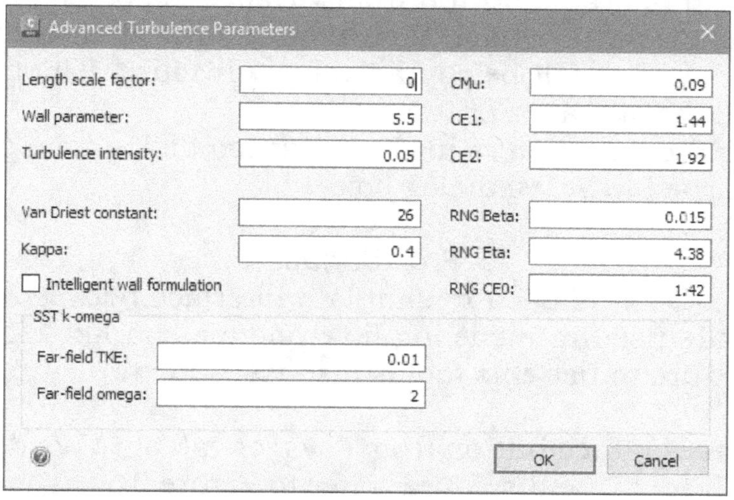

Figure-14. Advanced Turbulence Parameters dialog box

- After specifying the parameters, click on the **OK** button from **Turbulence** dialog box. You will be returned to **Solve** dialog box.

Advanced

The **Advanced** button in the **Solve** dialog box is used to set humidity, quality, and cavitation properties. The procedure to use this button is discussed next.

- Click on the **Advanced** button from **Solve** dialog box. The **Advanced** dialog box will be displayed; refer to Figure-15.

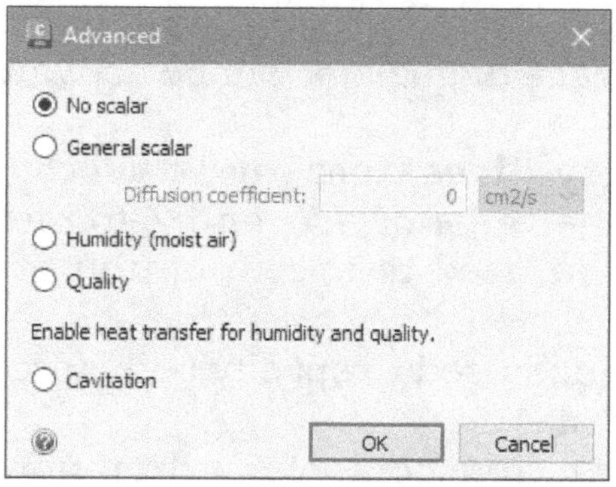

Figure-15. Advanced dialog box

- Select the **No scaler** radio button from the **Advanced** dialog box to not involve scalar calculation as a part of analysis.
- Select the **General scalar** radio button from the **Advanced** dialog box to specify the value of scalar as a part of analysis. The **Diffusion Coefficient** edit box will be activated.
- Click in the **Diffusion Coefficient** edit box and specify the value to control mass diffusion of the scalar quantity into the surrounding field. The zero value of **Diffusion Coefficient** will prevent any diffusion of scalar quantity.
- Select the **Humidity (moist air)** radio button from **Advanced** dialog box to simulate moist gas. In that case, both the relative humidity and condensed water can be visualized. Note that, in this software condensation of moist gas can be modeled but it cannot be possible to model the evaporation of water into gas stream.
- Select the **Quality** radio button of **Advance** dialog box to simulate a homogeneous mixture of vapor and liquid. If scalar is 0 then there will be no vapour. If scalar is 1, there will be all vapour and no liquid.

- Select the **Cavitation** radio button from **Advance** dialog box to predict the small collection of bubbles in a model due to fluid flow. When cavitation is selected, fluid pressure does not fall below the vapor pressure. If not selected, the fluid pressure will fall below vapor pressure.
- After specifying the parameters in the **Advanced** dialog box, click on **OK** button. You will be returned to **Solve** dialog box.

Free Surface

The **Free surface** button is used to simulate interface between liquids and gases. This tool is generally used in modeling flow phenomena like sloshing, waves, and spilling. The procedure to use this tool is discussed next.

- Click on the **Free surface** button from **Physics** tab of **Solve** dialog box. The **Free Surface** dialog box will be displayed; refer to Figure-16.

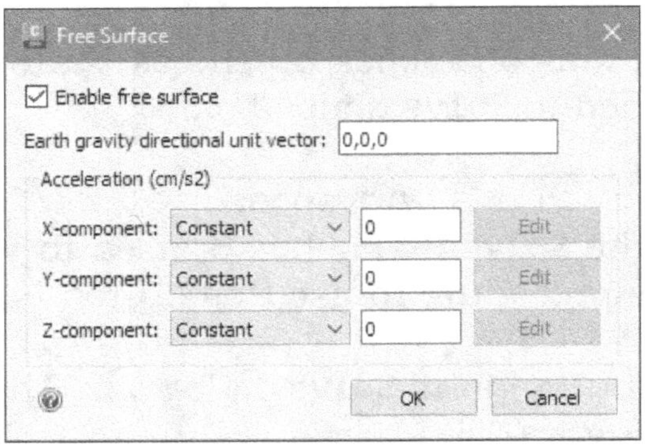

Figure-16. Free Surface dialog box

- The options of **Free Surface** dialog box will be activated on selecting **Enable free surface** check box.
- Click in the **Earth gravity directional unit vector** edit box from **Free Surface** dialog box and specify the value of X,Y, and Z to include the effects of elevation change on the liquid. You need to specify a unit gravity vector to indicate the direction of pull.
- The **Acceleration** section is used to specify body forces experienced by fluid, like a fluid transportation tank.
- Select the **Constant** option from component drop-downs to simulate acceleration that does not vary with time and click in the adjacent edit boxes to specify acceleration values.
- Select the **Piecewise Linear** option from component drop-down to define a time variation of acceleration component. The **Edit** button will be activated.
- Click on the **Edit** button to specify acceleration time data. The **Acceleration Curve Editor** dialog box will be displayed; refer to Figure-17.

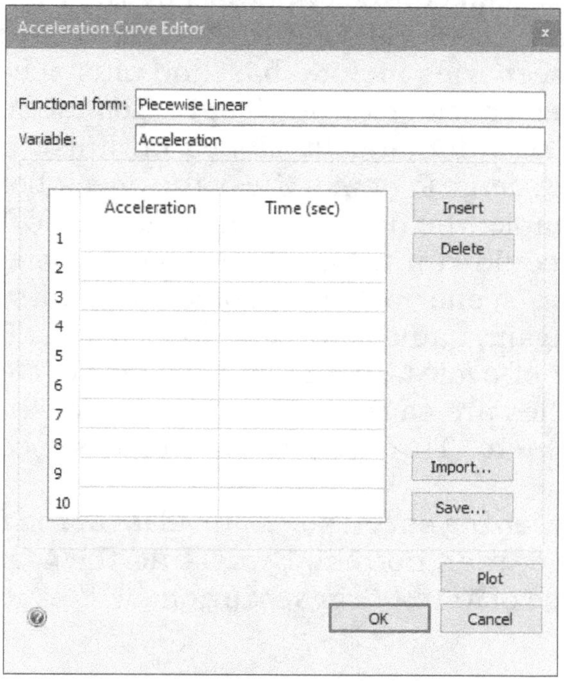

Figure-17. Acceleration Curve Editor dialog box

- Specify the values of accelerations with respect to time in **Acceleration Curve Editor** dialog box and click on the **OK** button. You will be returned to **Free Surface** dialog box.
- After specifying the parameters in **Free Surface** dialog box, click on the **OK** button. You will be returned to the **Solve** dialog box.

Adaptation tab

The options of **Adaptation** tab are generally used to improve the mesh by running the analysis multiple times. At the end of each run, this tool modifies the mesh as per result and uses this mesh for next cycle. The procedure to use this is discussed next.

- Click on the **Adaptation** tab from **Solve** dialog box. The **Adaptation** tab will be displayed; refer to Figure-18.

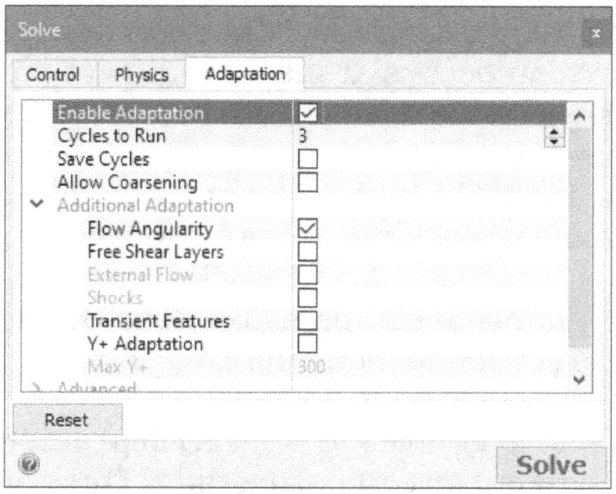

Figure-18. Adaptation tab of Solve dialog box

- Select the **Enable Adaptation** check box from the **Adaptation** tab of **Solve** dialog box to activate mesh adaptation for the current study. When it is enabled, a baseline scenario will run to completion.

- Click in the **Cycles to Run** edit box and specify the number of cycles which you want to run for refining mesh. By default, 3 cycles are specified for this. Note that the total number of scenarios include baseline plus specified number of cycles.
- Select the **Save Cycles** check box from **Adaptation** tab to save each intermediate mesh. Scenario will be automatically cloned on finish and the cycle number is appended to the base scenario name. Clear the check box to save only final mesh and results. For example: the default name is scenario 1 at the beginning of the process. Scenario 1 could run to completion and cloned, named as Scenario 1-Mesh 1. The mesh on scenario 1 is adapted to results and run to completion. Scenario 1 is cloned again, named as Scenario 1 Mesh 2. This process will continue till specified number of cycles. At the end, Scenario 1 contains the final mesh, and intermediate cycles are saved in Scenario 1 - Mesh 1, Scenario 2 - Mesh 2, Scenario 3 - Mesh 3, etc. Throughout the process, scenario 1 will always the active scenario.
- Select the **Allow Coarsening** check box from **Adaptation** tab of **Solve** dialog box to make the mesh coarser than normal. By default, the **Adaptation** tool only refines mesh and with the use of **Allow Coarsening** check box, it prevents the mesh from growing too fine.

Additional Adaptation

The **Additional Adaptation** option complements the primary options for defining mesh adaptation. The procedure to use these options is discussed next.

- Click on the **Additional Adaptation** node from the **Adaptation** tab of the **Solve** dialog box. The controls and parameters of **Additional Adaptation** will be displayed.
- Select the **Flow Angularity** check box from the **Adaptation** tab to improve the resolution in areas that contain large amounts of flow separation and circulatory flow.
- Select the **Free Shear Layers** check box from **Adaptation** tab to sharply define velocity gradient within a flow stream in case of pipe bend. The Free Shear Layers occur at the intersection between slow velocity flow and free velocity flow, like separate region. For accurate flow prediction, it is important that the distribution of mesh is fine enough to capture severe velocity gradient within the shear flow layers. In general, the free stream flow is pushed towards outside radius of pipe and flow separation region occurs at inside radius of pipe.
- The **External Flow** check box is available only if the **Free Shear Layers** check box is selected in the dialog box. The external flow option tunes mesh adaptation to refine the mesh of the model in high velocity gradient regions occurring between viscous and free-stream flows of large unbounded flow domains, like aerodynamics flows.
- The **Shock** option is available in compressible flow. Select the check box to enable this option. This option is used to focus the mesh on location and gradients across a sudden barrier, like a shock wave.
- Select the **Transient Features** check box from **Adaptation** tab, if flow has dynamic region like flow reattachment or vortex shedding. This performs three adaptations per error criteria before proceeding to next criteria. The result is that dynamic features are better resolved, but static regions are not.

- Select the **Y+ Adaptation** check box to specify the sensitivity of boundary element thickness. It is a non-dimensional distance between a wall node and its corresponding neighbor node.
- The **Max Y+** option is activated after selecting the **Y+ Adaptation** check box. Select the **Max Y+** check box to achieve desired accuracy by reducing or increasing the value. As per numerous study, the ideal range of **Max Y+** is between 35 and 350. The default value for **Max Y+** is 300.

Advanced

The tools of **Advanced** node are used to provide detailed control over the process of mesh generation. In the parameters of **Advanced** node, the parameters are provided with default values which were based of testing and most rigorous situation. The procedure to use this tool is discussed next.

- Click on the **Advanced** node from **Adaptation** dialog box of **Solve** dialog box. The advanced parameters will be displayed; refer to Figure-19.

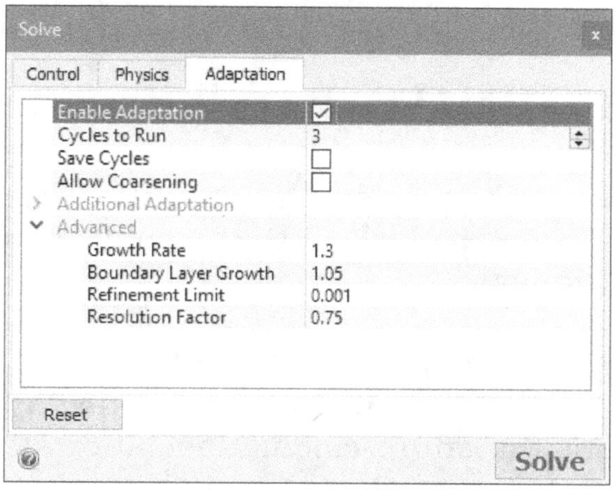

Figure-19. Advanced node of Solve dialog box

- Click in the **Growth Rate** edit box from **Advanced** node and specify the value to modify smoothness of volumetric mesh. The **Growth Rate** option works similar to **Mesh Autosize** tool.
- Click in the **Boundary Layer Growth** edit box and specify the value to modify the smoothness of boundary layer mesh.
- Click in the **Refinement Layer** edit box and specify the parameters to prevent over refinement of mesh when wall layer is disabled. When wall layers is enabled, the boundary layer specifies the minimum allowable length scale during adaptation, and **Refinement Layer** plays no role.
- Click in the **Resolution Factor** edit box and specify the value to make mesh finer. For greater refinement, specify the value less than 1.0. This reduces the error threshold by specified factor resulting in finer mesh.
- If you want to reset the values of **Adaptation** tab to default, click on the **Reset** button. The specified values will reset to default.
- After specifying the parameters, click on the **Solve** button from **Solve** dialog box. The analysis will start.
- On clicking the **Solve** button, the **Message Window** of **Output Bar** will be displayed and running calculation will be displayed in the **Message Window**; refer to Figure-20.

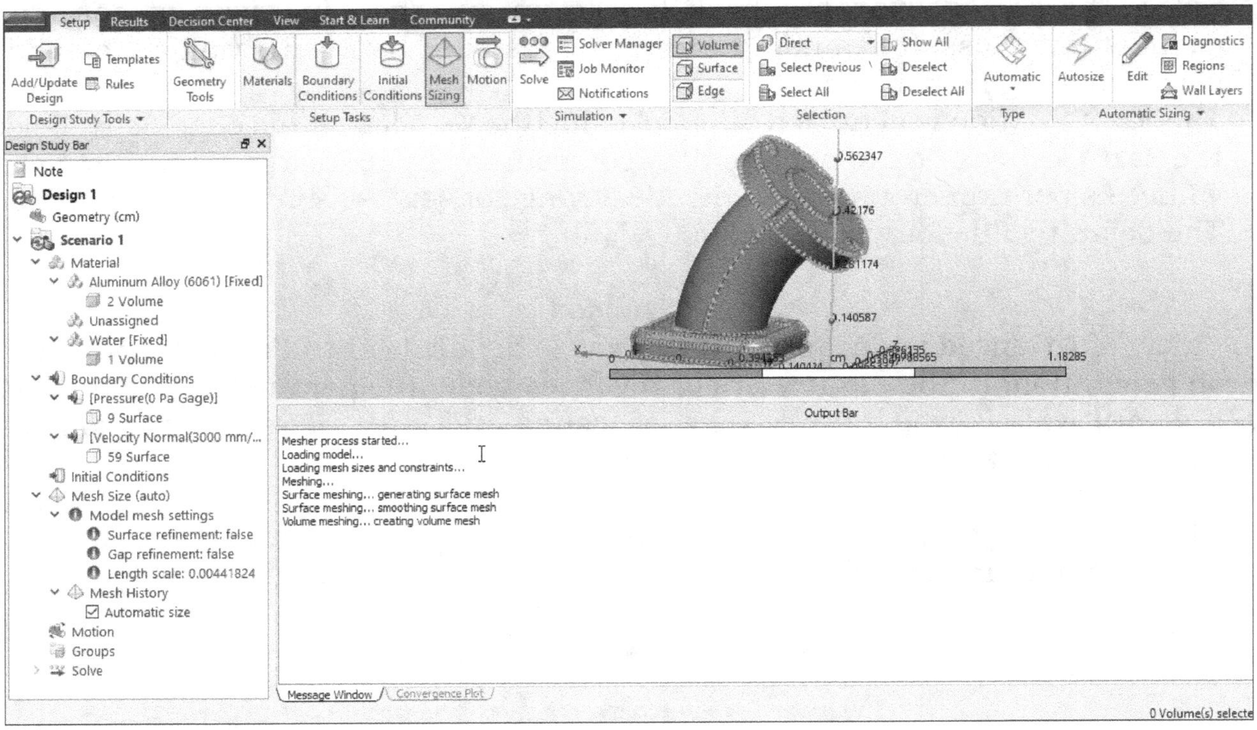

Figure-20. Running calculations

- The **Message Window** is used to view the ongoing processes of current project. Whatever action you do in Autodesk CFD, the notification, action, and result will be displayed in this window.

Convergence Plot

The **Convergence Plot** is used to view the convergence information and curves of each iteration throughout the entire calculation. After starting the calculation of analysis, you can view ongoing iterations throughout the process with the help of curves; refer to Figure-21.

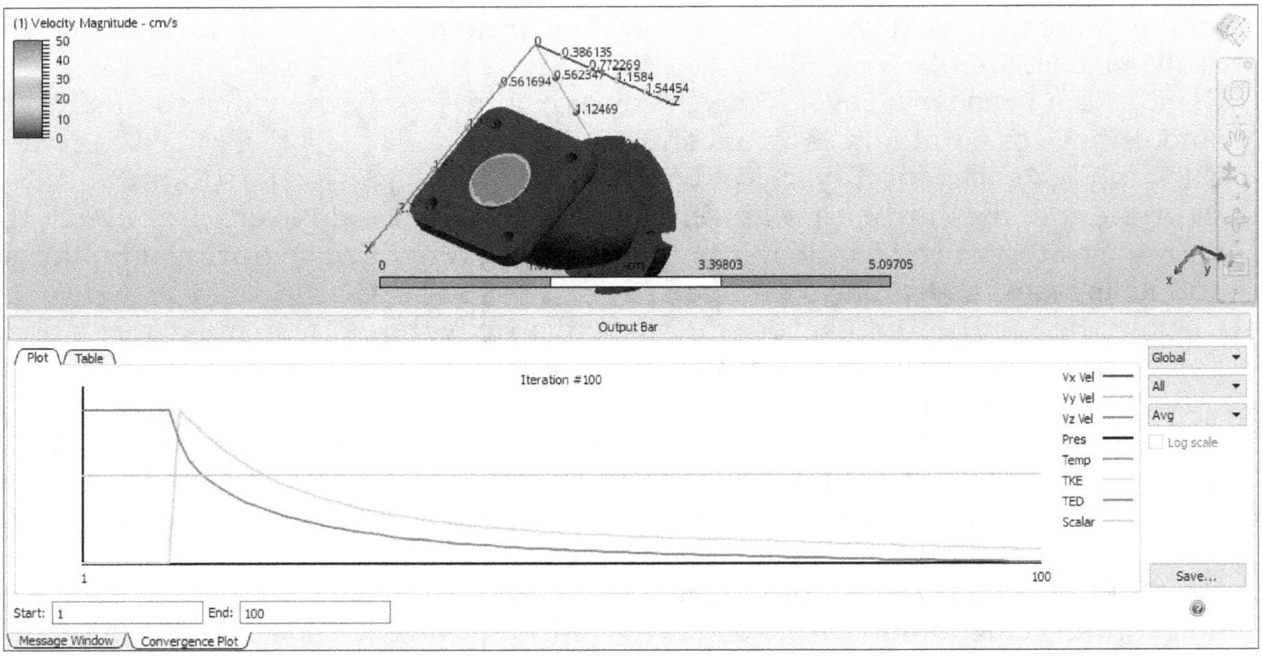

Figure-21. Curves plot

- The **Start** and **End** edit boxes in the **Plot** tab of **Convergence Plot** tab indicate the starting and ending number of iteration. If you want to see the iterations of the current plot from 10 to 70 then specify respective values in **Start** and **End** edit boxes. The graph will be displayed based on specified values; refer to Figure-22.

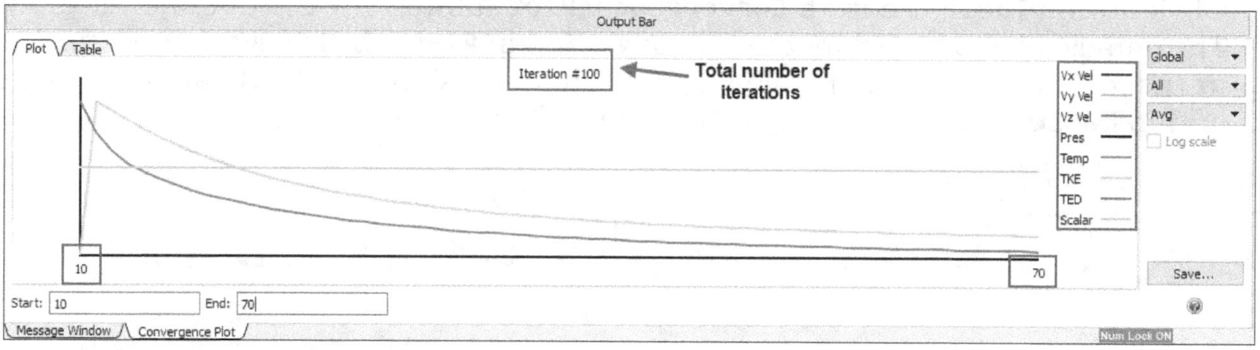

Figure-22. View particular number of Iteration

- The starting and ending number of iterations are displayed in the highlighted box.
- The highlighted box at the upper right corner of the above figure contains various parameters as given below,

Vx Velocity refers to velocity in X direction.
Vy Velocity refers to velocity in Y direction.
Vz Velocity refers to velocity in Z direction.
Pres. refers to pressure
Temp refers to temperature
TKE refers to two equation Turbulence.
TED refers to turbulent kinetic energy.
Scalar refers to scaler quantity.

- The **Global** button on the right of **Convergence Plot** tab is used to view the graph of global parameters in convergence plot.
- If you want to view the graph of particular parameter then click on the **All** drop-down and select desired parameter. The graph related to that parameter will be displayed; refer to Figure-23.

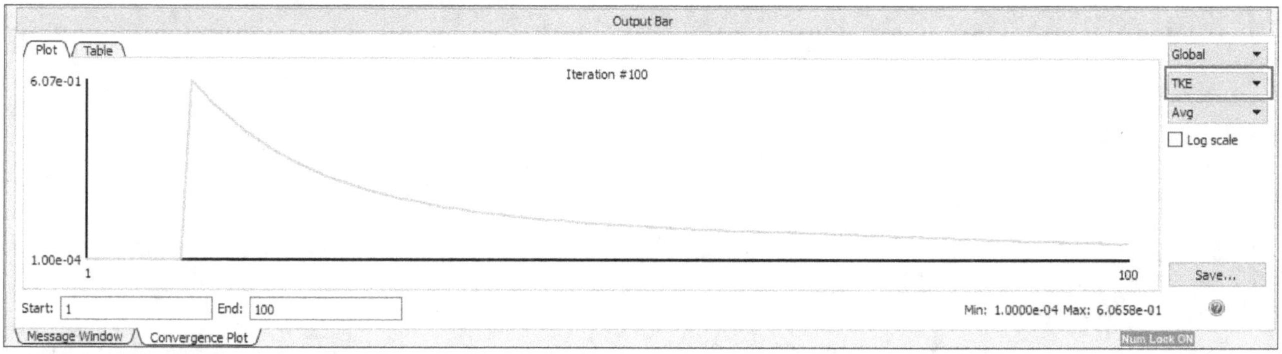

Figure-23. TKE graph

- You can also view the graph from a specific start and end value by specifying the same in **Start** and **End** edit box.
- Click in the **Avg** drop-down from **Convergence Plot** tab to view different values of plotted quantities.

- Click on the **Save** button to save the current data of iterations. The **Save Iteration History** dialog box will be displayed. Select the folder, where you want to save the data in **.CSV** format and click on the **Save** button. The file will be saved in specified folder.
- Click on the **Table** tab from **Convergence Plot** tab to view the data of iterations. The data is all about parameters which we saw in **Plot** tab of **Convergence Plot** tab in the form of graph; refer to Figure-24. The data shown in **Plot** tab is graphical and in **Table** tab, the data is in the form of numerical values.

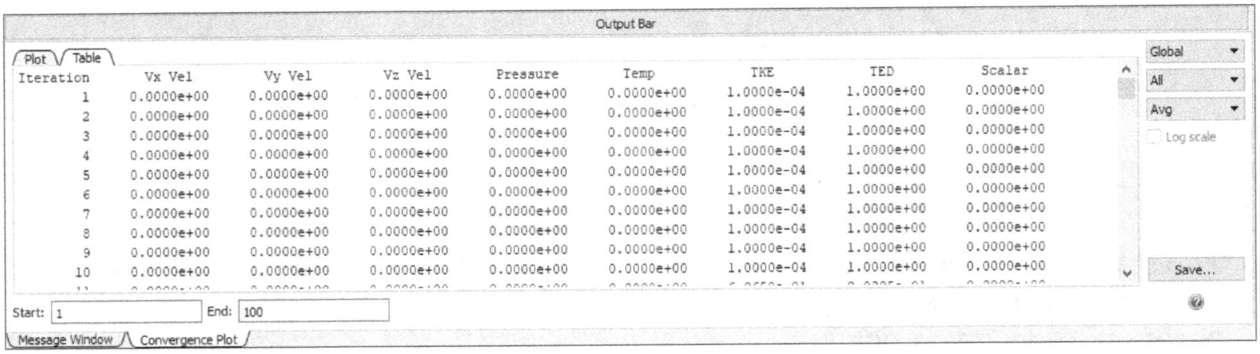

Figure-24. Table tab of Convergence tab

Solve Manager

The **Solver Manager** is used to manage multiple scenarios in a queue. This tool is used, when we have to assign the processes to start in numerical order. The procedure to use this is discussed next.

- Click on the **Solver Manager** button from **Simulation** panel of **Setup** tab, the **Solver Manager** dialog box will be displayed; refer to Figure-25.

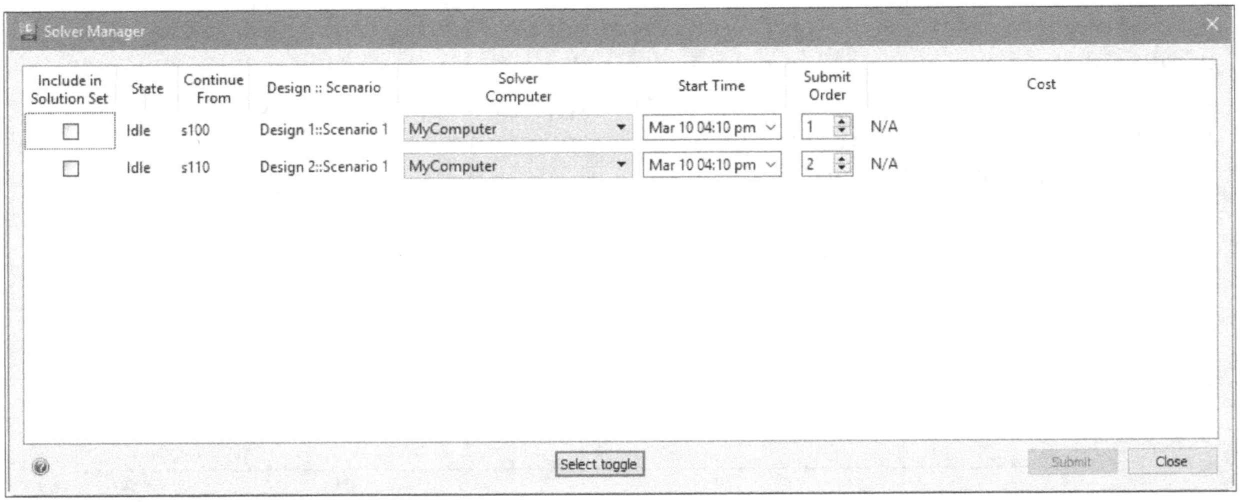

Figure-25. Solver Manager dialog box

- Select desired check box from the **Include in Solution Set** column to include the analysis to be solved. If you do not want to solve any of the analysis from **Solver Manager** then clear the check box next to it.
- Click in the **Solver Computer** drop-down and select desired machine for solving analysis. You can select computer or Autodesk Cloud computer for solving analysis.
- Click in the **Start Time** drop-down and select desired start time for the analysis.
- Select the order number from **Submit Order** drop-down to specify the order in which analyses should be solved.

- Click on the **Select toggle** button from **Solver Manager** to toggle solver on or off for the studies.
- After specifying the parameters, click on the **Submit** button. The state will be changed from **Idle** to **Submitted** in **Solver Manager** and the process to solve analyses will start as per specified data.

Job Monitor

The **Job Monitor** is used to check real time information of analyses. It can be used to monitor the status of simulations running in the cloud, stops running simulations, and run simulation jobs in background . The procedure to use this is discussed next,

- Click on the **Job Monitor** button from **Simulation** panel of **Setup** tab. The **CFD Job Monitor** dialog box will be displayed; refer to Figure-26.

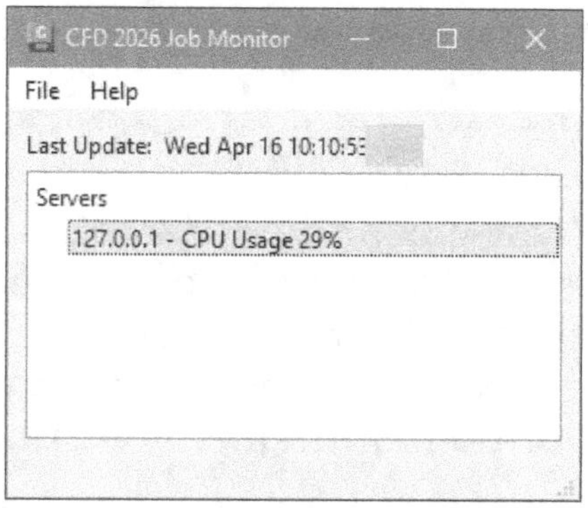

Figure-26. CFD Job Monitor dialog box

- You can check the status of analyses and processing power of system used by them in this dialog box. If you want to remove any of the analysis, right-click on it and click on the **Remove Job** button. The result of the selected analysis will be lost.
- After checking the status of analysis, close the dialog box.

Notifications

The notifications are the e-mail sent by Autodesk CFD when your analysis has completed a specific milestone. The procedure to enable notification is discussed below.

- Click on the **Notifications** button from **Simulation** panel of **Setup** tab. The **Solver Notifications** dialog box will be displayed; refer to Figure-27.

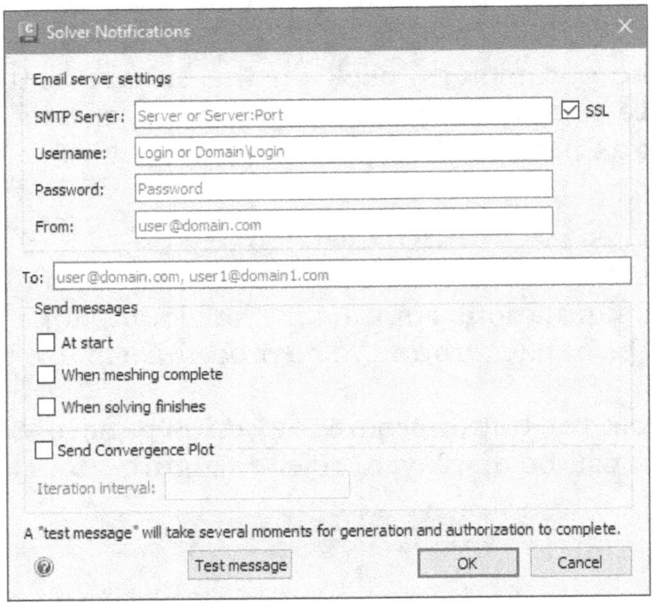

Figure-27. Solver Notifications dialog box

- Click in the **SMTP Server** edit box and enter the name of your SMTP server. You can enter either the server or the server:port. Some common 3rd party servers are smtp.gmail.com:587 and smtp.mail.yahoo.com:465.
- Click in the **Username** edit box from **Solver Notifications** dialog box and specify the username as login id or domain name. For public email server, this is often your email address.
- Click in the **Password** edit box and specify the password of the username which you have entered earlier.
- Click in the **From** edit box and enter your email address. This email address must match the above entered username. This email address will appear in **From** field on emails sent through this service.
- Click in the **To** edit box and enter the target email address for notifications. You can enter multiple addresses in the edit box separated by comma.
- To receive notifications as a text message, enter the mobile number as per vendor specifications.
- Select the appropriate option check box from **Send messages** area of **Solver Notifications**, as per requirement.
- Select the **Send Convergence Plot** check box to select the events that trigger a notification. The **Iteration Interval** edit box will be activated. In this edit box, enter the number of iterations that should elapse between plot images.
- After specifying the parameters, click on the **Text message** button from **Solver Notifications** dialog box to confirm.
- After clicking **OK** button, notifications are sent for all subsequent analyses launched from your computer, under your window login. The analysis conclusion notification contains the status file. If an error occurs, this file includes the error message.

Note: If Notification e-mails are not delivered to Inbox, check your "Spam" or similar folder.

SMS Address for receiving text messages, by phone vendor.

- T-Mobile: phonenumber@tmomail.net
- Virgin Mobile: phonenumber@vmobl.com

- Cingular: phonenumber@cingularme.com
- Sprint: phonenumber@messaging.sprintpcs.com
- Verizon: phonenumber@vtext.com
- Nextel: phonenumber@messaging.nextel.com
- US Cellular: phonenumber@email.uscc.net
- SunCom: phonenumber@tms.suncom.com
- Powertel: phonenumber@ptel.net
- AT&T: phonenumber@txt.att.net
- Alltel: phonenumber@message.alltel.com
- Metro PCS: phonenumber@MyMetroPcs.com

These numbers are subject to change. Please consult your mobile number phone vendor for more information.

Monitor Point

The **Monitor Point** tool is used to place some point in the model so that basic degree of freedom are plotted in convergence plot throughout the analysis. These points provide a way to track convergence at some specific location of the model. The procedure to use this tool is discussed next.

- Click on the **Monitor Point** tool from the **Simulation** panel drop-down of **Setup** tab. The **Runtime Monitor Points** dialog box will be displayed; refer to Figure-28.

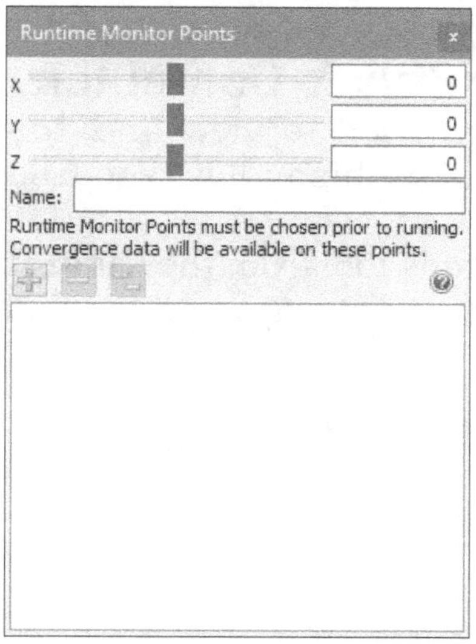

Figure-28. Runtime Monitor Points dialog box

- To add points, move the triad axis and click on the **Add a point** button from **Runtime Monitor Points** dialog box; refer to Figure-29.

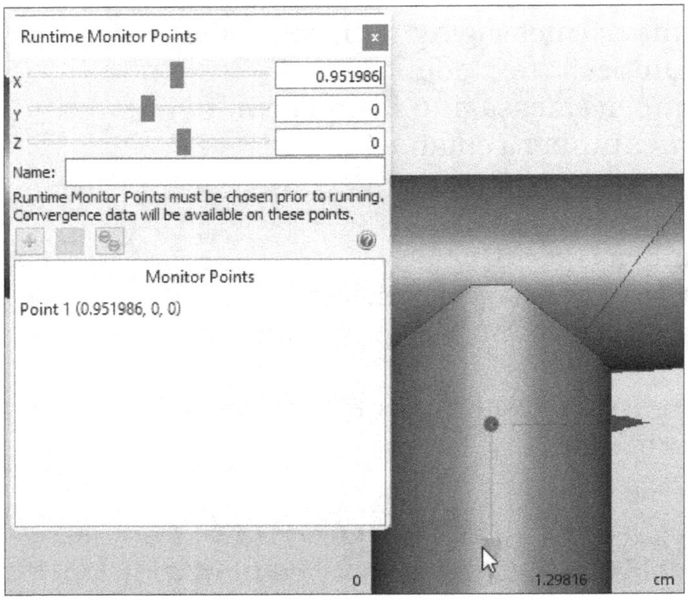

Figure-29. Adding Monitor points

- You can add as many points as you want for convergence plot using the same procedure.
- You can create monitor points after the completion of iterations and then run additional iterations. The plotted monitor point data will start at intermediate iteration instead of at the beginning of the calculation.

Solver Computers

The **Solver Computers** tool is used to view and edit the configurations of solver computers. The procedure to use this tool is discussed next.

- Click on the **Solver Computers** tool from the **Simulation** panel drop-down in **Setup** tab. The **Solver Computers and Configurations** dialog box will be displayed; refer to Figure-30.

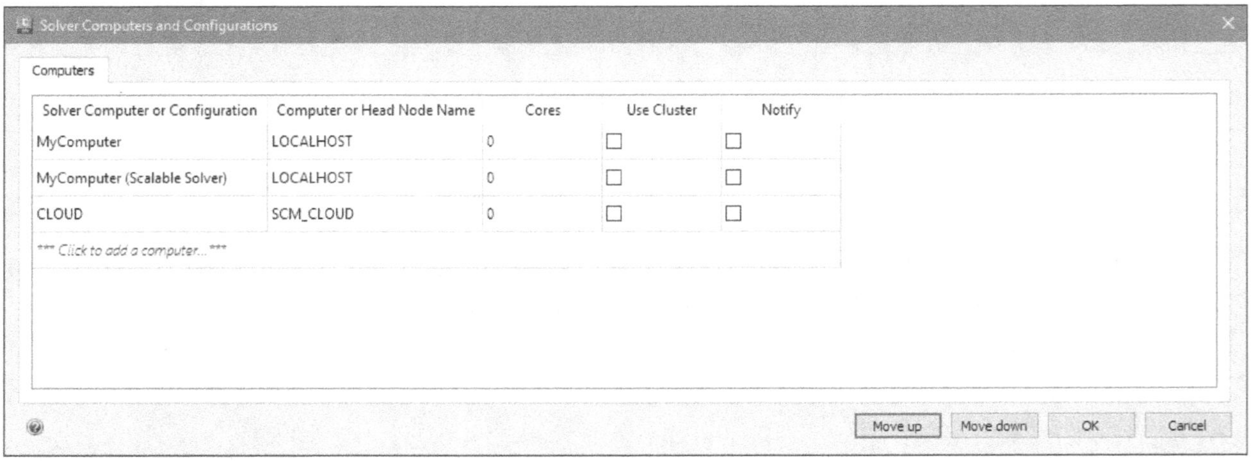

Figure-30. Solver computer and configurations dialog box

- Double-click in the **Cores** edit box and specify the number of cores which you want to use for solving analysis.
- Select the **Use Cluster** check box for desired solver to use the respective cluster for solving the analysis. Computer Clusters are set of computers that works together so that they can be viewed and worked as single system.

- Select the **Notify** check box to get notifications while using respective solver.
- Click on the **Click to add a computer** button to add a custom solver as per requirement. The **Solver Computer** dialog box will be displayed; refer to Figure-31.

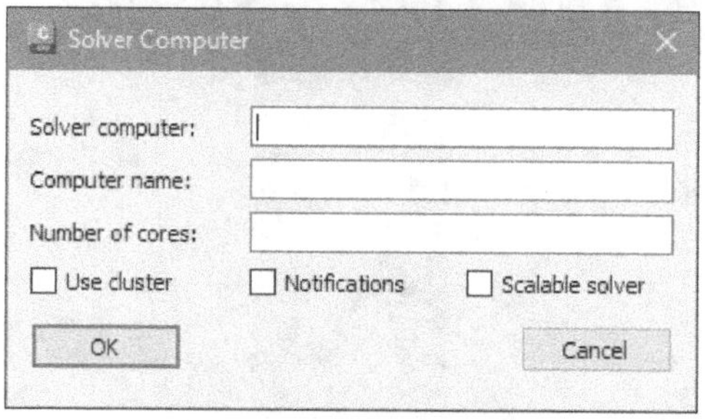

Figure-31. Solver Computer dialog Box

- Specify desired parameters from the **Solver Computer** dialog box and click on the **OK** button. The solver will be added in **Computers** tab.
- After specifying desired parameters in **Solver Computers and Configurations** dialog box and click on **OK** button.

Selection panel

The **Selection** panel contains various tools to select or deselect the model and its entities. The tools of this panel are discussed next.

- Click on the **Volume** button from the **Selection** panel to enable volume selection. This tool is used when you want to select volume from model to perform an operation; refer to Figure-32.

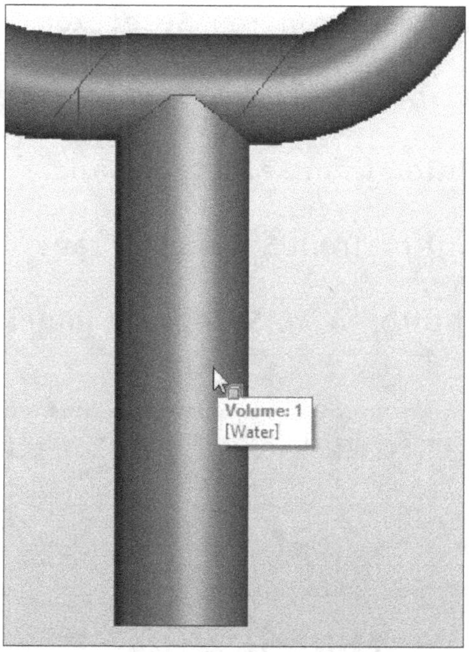

Figure-32. Selecting volume

- Click on the **Surface** button from the **Selection** panel to enable surface selection. This tool is used when you want to select surface of a model for performing further operations; refer to Figure-33.

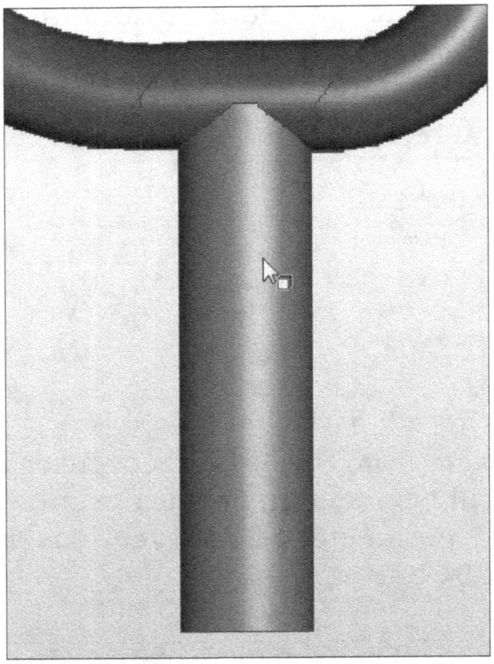

Figure-33. Surface Selection

- Click on the **Edge** button from **Selection** panel to enable edge selection. This button is not available when working with 3D geometry.
- Click on the **Select by** drop-down and select the **Direct** option to select volume and surface. If you have selected **Volume** button then the volume of model will be highlighted. If you have selected **Surface** button then surface of components will be highlighted on hovering the cursor on model.
- Click on the **Select Previous** button from **Selection** panel to select last previously selected item.
- Click on the **Select All** button from **Selection** panel to select every entity of current selection mode.
- Click on the **Show All** button from **Selection** panel to select resume the visibility of all hidden items.
- Click on the **Deselect** button from **Selection** panel to deselect current selected entity.
- Click on **Deselect All** button from **Selection** panel to deselect all the selected entities; refer to Figure-34.

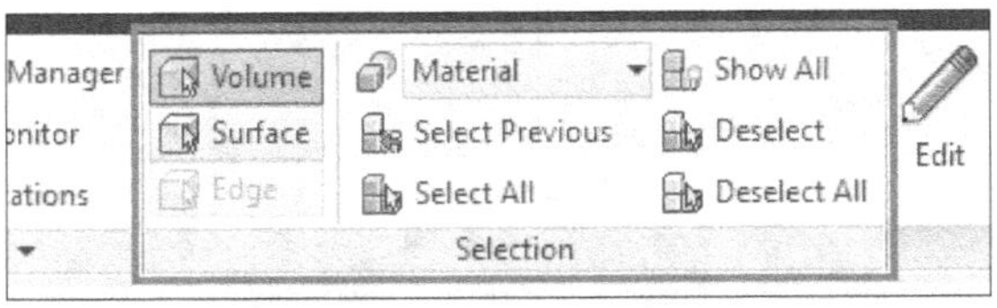

Figure-34. Selection panel

Materials panel

The **Materials** panel provides the tools to edit and remove the material from component. The tools of this panel is discussed below.

- Click on the **Edit** button from **Materials** panel to edit the material properties of selected component. Before clicking on **Edit** button, you will need to select the component. The **Materials** dialog box will be displayed. The options of this dialog box have already been discussed.

- Click on the **Remove** button to remove existing material from the component.
- Click on the **Material Editor** button from **Materials** panel to view the properties of material. The **Material Editor** dialog box will be displayed. The options of this dialog box have already been discussed.
- Click on the **Scenario Environment** button from **Materials** panel to edit the scenario environment. The **Scenario Environment** dialog box will be displayed which has been discussed earlier.

DESIGN STUDY TOOL PANEL

The **Design Study Tool** panel is used to define the structure of the design study. In this, you can add or update the design, and assign the structure of a fully defined scenario. The procedure to use this tool is discussed next.

Add/Update Design

The **Add/Update Design** tool is used to add or update existing model. This tool is generally used when you clone the design to perform some more analyses after changing or modifying the components. The procedure to use this tool is discussed next.

- Click on the **Add/Update Design** button from the **Design Study Tools** panel of **Setup** tab in the **Ribbon**. The **Add Geometry File** dialog box will be displayed; refer to Figure-35.

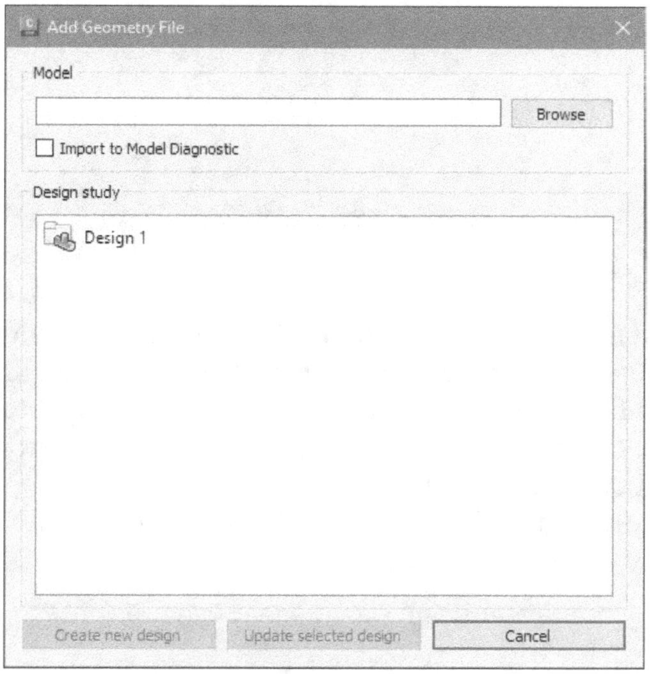

Figure-35. Add Geometry File dialog box

- Before proceeding to the next step, you should have a CAD model modified as required.
- Click on the **Browse** button from **Add Geometry File** dialog box. The **Add Geometry** dialog box will be displayed. Select the file, which you want to update and click on the **Open** button. The file will be displayed in **Model** edit box of **Add Geometry File** dialog box.
- Select the required design from **Design Study** section, which you want to update or modify the existing decision.

- Click on the **Create new design** button to create a new design using the geometry.
- Click on the **Update selected design** button to replace the geometry of selected design with new geometry. The geometry will be updated and displayed.

Templates

A **Template** is a file that contains the model settings for one or more scenarios that define the design. Templates provide consistency for design studies that contain similar settings.

- Click on the **Templates** tool from the **Design Study Tools** panel of **Setup** tab in the **Ribbon**. The **Template Manager** will be displayed; refer to Figure-36.

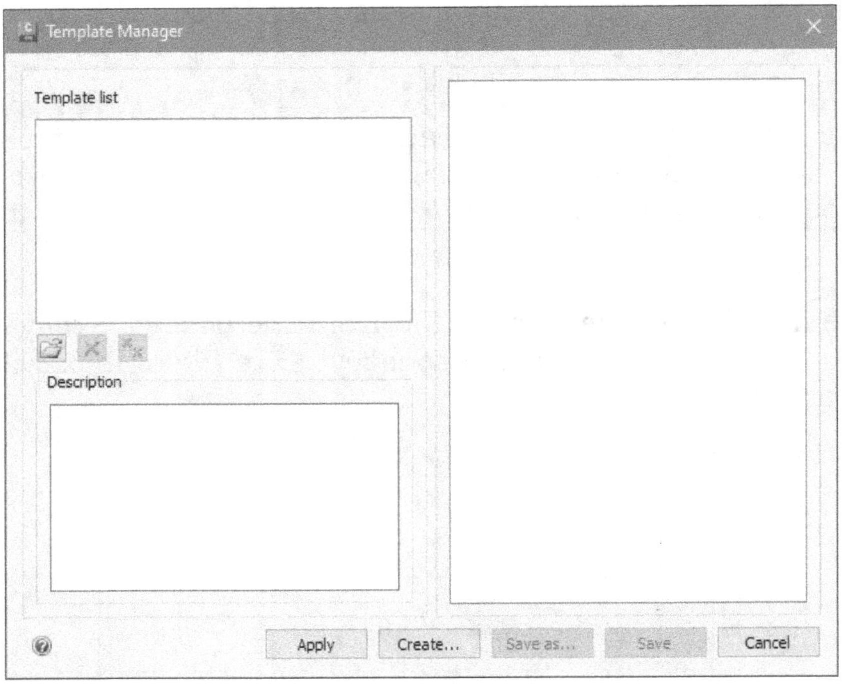

Figure-36. Template Manager dialog box

- Click on the **Create** button from **Template Manager** dialog box to create a new template file. The **Create a new template file** dialog box will be displayed. Specify the location of the file where you want to save the template file.
- Specify the name of template and click on **Save** button. The template will be displayed in **Template list** section.
- Click on desired template, the details will be displayed at the right of **Template Manager** dialog box; refer to Figure-37.

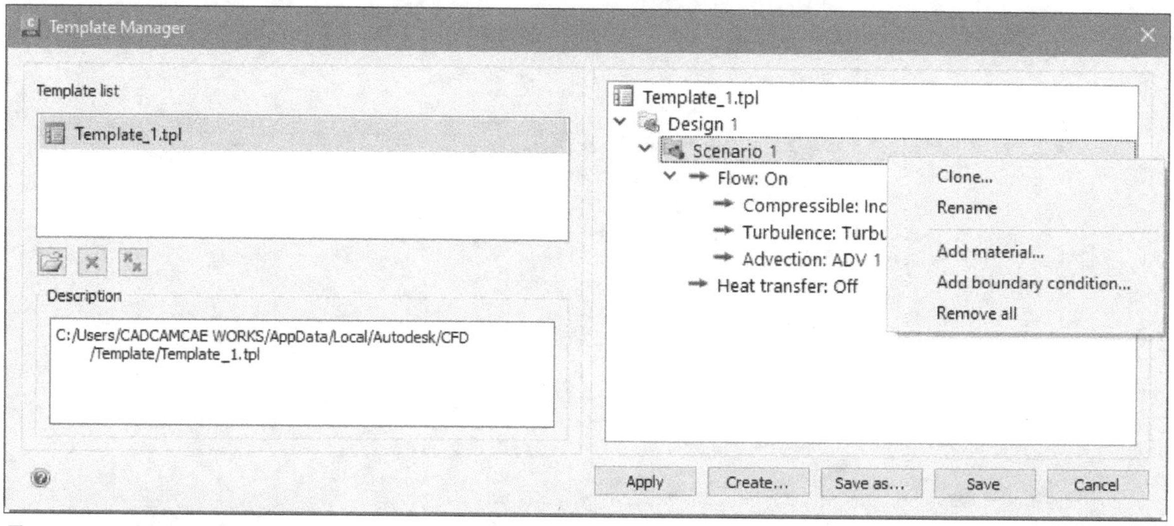

Figure-37. Added template

- To add material, boundary condition, or clone the template, click on the respective button from right-click menu.
- After selecting the template, click on the **Apply** button to apply selected template.

Rules

The **Rules** button is used to create associations between CAD and CFD settings. You can use these rules to automatically assign settings to frequently recurring CAD components. Rules are usually applied automatically when the design study is launched. The procedure to use this is discussed next.

- Click on the **Rules** button from the **Design Study Tools** panel in the **Setup** tab of **Ribbon**. The **Rule Manager** will be displayed; refer to Figure-38.

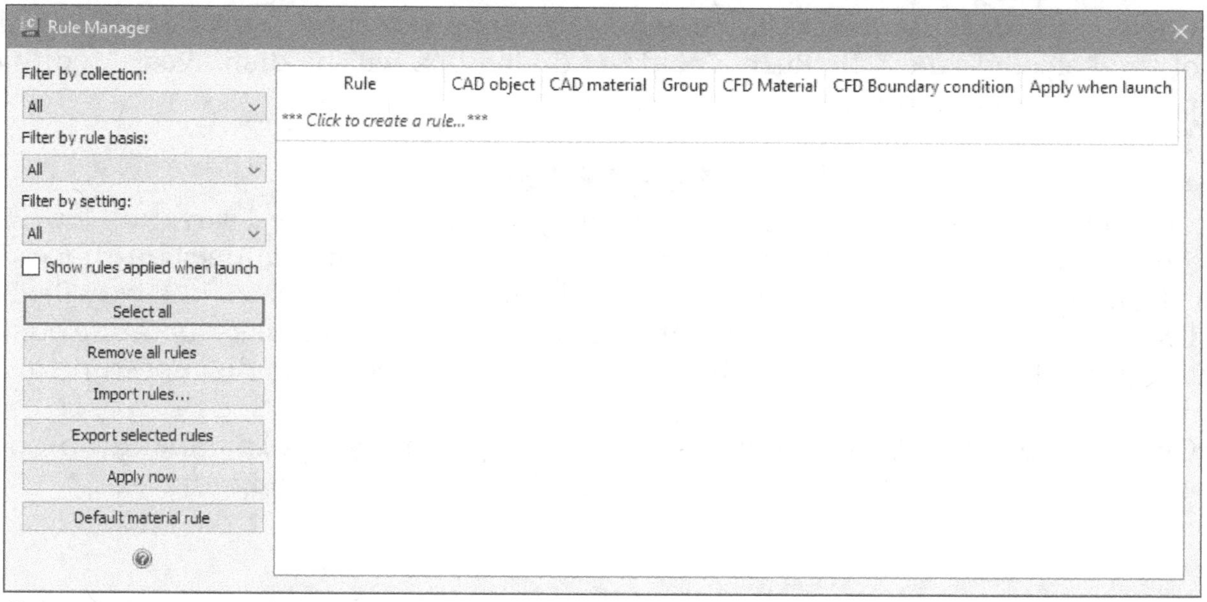

Figure-38. Rule Manager dialog box

- Click on the **Click to create a rule** button. The **Rule Creation** dialog box will be displayed; refer to Figure-39.

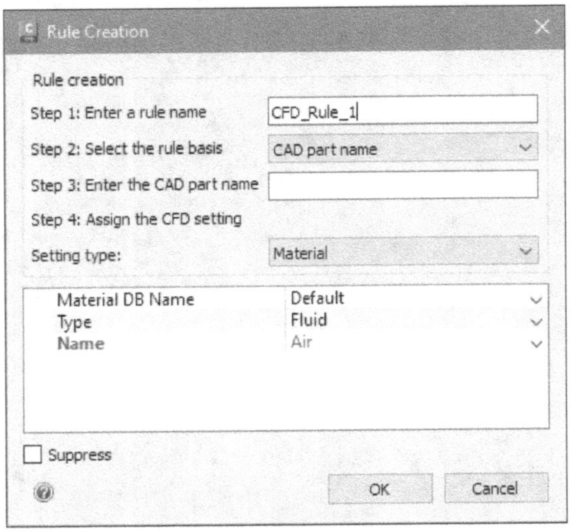

Figure-39. Rule Creation dialog box

- Specify the parameters to create rule and click on **OK** button from the **Rule Creation** dialog box. The rule will be created and displayed in **Rule Manager** dialog box.
- Click on the **Select all** button from **Rule Manager** to select all the listed rules.
- Click on the **Remove all rules** button from **Rule Manager** to remove all created rules.
- Click on the **Import rules** button to import the pre-created rules. The **Open a setup file or a rule file** dialog box will be displayed. Select the file and click on the **Open** button. The rule will be listed in **Rule Manager** dialog box.
- Click on the **Export Selected rules** button from **Rule Manager** to export the selected rule for future reference. The **Export a rule file** dialog box will be displayed. Select desired folder where you want to save the rule file and click on **Save** button. The rule will be added in the list.
- Click on **Apply Now** button to apply the selected rule to current model.
- Click on the **Default material rule** button to apply or change the default material of the selected rule. The **Rule Creation** dialog box will be displayed. Modify the parameters as required.

Script Editor

The Autodesk CFD Application Programming Interface provides ways to work with Autodesk CFD functionality that are not readily available in the user interface. The API is a platform for customization, and can benefit design process. It is very flexible, and can be used for a wide variety of tasks, like, crating custom tasks, creating custom result quantities, etc. The procedure to use the script editor is discussed next.

- Click on the **Script Editor** button from **Design Study Tools** panel drop-down, the **CFD Script Editor** dialog box will be displayed; refer to Figure-40.

Figure-40. Script Editor

- Create the script as required using the Python language programming.

Flags

The **Flags** button is used to modify many different aspects of Autodesk CFD by creating different configurations. The procedure to use this button is discussed next.

- Click on the **Flags** button from **Design Study Tools** panel drop-down, the **Flag Manager** dialog box will be displayed; refer to Figure-41. The **Flag Manager** organizes and provides visibility to the collection of flags.

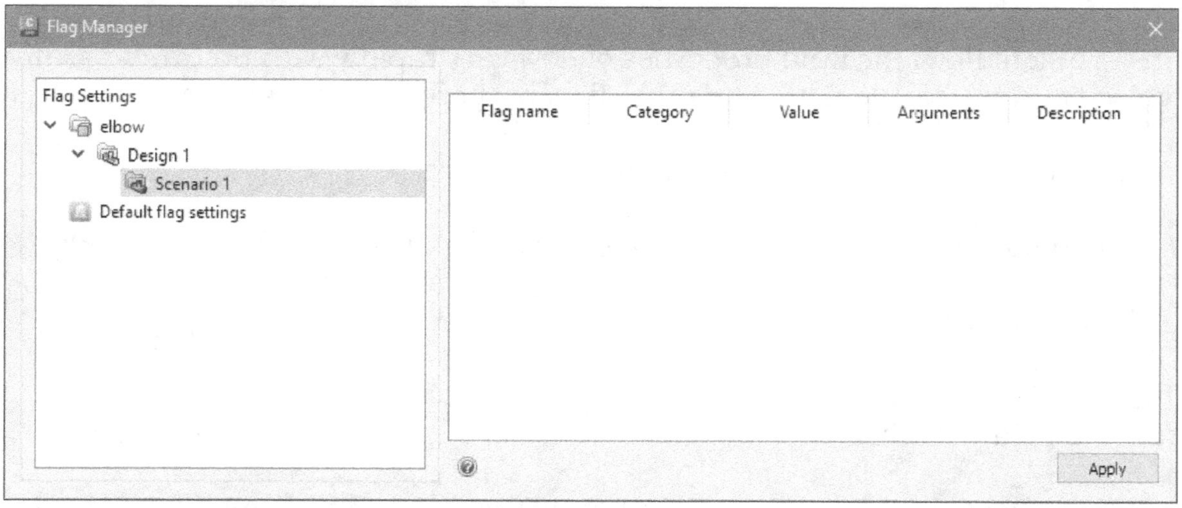

Figure-41. Flag Manager dialog Box

- You can add flag to the scenario by clicking on **Add** button from right-click menu. The **Add New Flag** dialog box will be displayed. Specify the flag name and click on **OK** button. The flag will be displayed.
- Select the flag and click on **Apply** button to apply the flag.

SELF ASSESSMENT

Q1. Select the Transient button from Solution Mode drop-down of Solve dialog box if you want to solve time-dependent analysis. (T/F)

Q2. If the save interval in Solve dialog box is set to 0 then results and information of analysis is saved instantly after modification in Autodesk CFD. (T/F)

Q3. Click on the .... button from Solution Controls dialog box to control the solution progression rate so that chances of divergence are minimized.

Q4. Which of the following is not a basic flow value displayed in results of CFD in Autodesk CFD?

a. Velocity
b. Pressure
c. Temperature
d. Viscosity

Q5. Define the term Subsonic flow.

Q6. For defining Solar radiation location, Latitude must be between ...... to ...... degrees, Longitude must be between .... and .... degrees.

Q7. In laminar flow, the layers of fluid particles slide over the adjacent particle without disturbing the motion of others particles. (T/F)

Q8. In turbulent flow, the fluid properties of flow vary rapidly with time and parameters like velocity, pressure, density, and other flow properties show random changes. (T/F)

Q9. What is the use of Free surface tool?

Q10. Which step must be performed before solving an analysis in Autodesk CFD?

A. Assign heat transfer options
B. Create a mesh
C. Open the Physics tab
D. Activate solar heating

Q11. What does the "Steady State" button in the Control tab do?

A. Enables time-dependent simulation
B. Makes analysis independent of time
C. Enables radiation heat transfer
D. Displays result quantities

Q12. What will happen if mesh definitions are changed but Continue From value is not reset to 0?

A. Solve dialog will not open
B. The current results are deleted permanently
C. Analysis restarts with fresh values
D. Results are interpolated into new mesh

Q13. What is the purpose of the Intelligent Solution Control tool?

A. Control mesh parameters
B. Specify boundary conditions
C. Control convergence progression
D. Set gravity direction

Q14. Which check box must be selected to enable fluid pressure and momentum equations?

A. Compressibility
B. Flow
C. Hydrostatic Pressure
D. Advection

Q15. What type of convection does the "Auto Forced Convection" check box handle?

A. Natural
B. Mixed
C. Forced
D. Radiative

Q16. What does selecting the "Compressible" option in Compressibility dropdown imply?

A. Mach number < 0.3
B. Flow with or without heat transfer and shock
C. Conduction-only heat transfer
D. Buoyancy-driven flow

Q17. What should you select in Turbulence settings to simulate compressible analyses?

A. Laminar flow
B. Lock On
C. Extended
D. Turb/Lam ratio

Q18. What does enabling "Cavitation" do in Advanced settings?

A. Simulates turbulent flows
B. Prevents pressure below vapor pressure
C. Simulates free surface effects
D. Prevents mass diffusion

Q19. Which condition activates Gravity Method options like Earth and Component?

A. Selecting Transient
B. Selecting Flow
C. Selecting Hydrostatic Pressure
D. Selecting Compressibility

Q20. What does the "Free Surface" tool simulate?

A. Heat transfer in gases
B. Evaporation of liquids
C. Interface between liquids and gases
D. Moist air properties

Q21. What is the use of the "General scalar" option in Advanced settings?

A. Model evaporation
B. Visualize condensed water
C. Control scalar diffusion
D. Control solar heating

Q22. Which option allows the mesh to be coarser than normal?

A. Save Cycles
B. Y+ Adaptation
C. Allow Coarsening
D. Flow Angularity

Q23. What is the purpose of selecting the 'Flow Angularity' checkbox in Additional Adaptation?

A. To improve mesh near external boundaries
B. To improve resolution in areas with flow separation
C. To increase time step
D. To smoothen mesh transitions

Q24. What is the ideal range for Max Y+ value based on studies?

A. 5–50
B. 10–100
C. 35–350
D. 100–1000

Q25. What does the 'Growth Rate' option in Advanced node control?

A. Pressure limits
B. Thermal conductivity
C. Smoothness of volumetric mesh
D. Simulation speed

Q26. What does the 'Resolution Factor' do when set below 1.0?

A. Increases error tolerance
B. Makes the mesh finer
C. Increases boundary layer size
D. Stops adaptation

Q27. What does the Solver Manager allow you to do?

A. Track fluid velocity in the model
B. Manage multiple scenarios in a queue
C. Change fluid properties
D. Display pressure contours

Q28. What can you do in the Job Monitor dialog box?

A. Change material types
B. Save mesh as PDF
C. Monitor status of running analyses
D. Export mesh to CAD

Q29. What do you enter in the SMTP Server field under Notifications?

A. CFD project name
B. Job ID
C. Email server address
D. Mesh cycle count

Q30. What does the 'Send Convergence Plot' checkbox activate?

A. Submit Order dialog
B. Iteration Interval input
C. Graph view mode
D. Advanced Simulation

Q31. Which vendor uses phonenumber@tmomail.net for SMS notifications?

A. Verizon
B. T-Mobile
C. Metro PCS
D. AT&T

Q32. What is the purpose of Monitor Point tool?

A. Save iterations
B. Run simulations in batch
C. Plot degrees of freedom during analysis
D. Set up solver configurations

Q33. What is a 'Cluster' in the context of Solver Computers?

A. A saved mesh
B. A hardware group for parallel processing
C. A default node
D. A plot of pressure vs time

Q34. What does the "Scenario Environment" button allow you to do?

A. Add a new rule
B. Edit the scenario environment
C. Open the Script Editor
D. Export templates

Q35. What is the purpose of the "Add/Update Design" button?

A. Add a new rule
B. Modify flags
C. Add or update a model
D. Create a new script

Q36. Which button lets you replace the geometry of a selected design with a new one?

A. Edit
B. Create new design
C. Apply
D. Update selected design

Q37. What does the Templates tool manage?

A. Script settings
B. Rules for geometry
C. Model settings for design scenarios
D. Edge selections

Q38. What happens when you click the "Default material rule" button?

A. Opens Script Editor
B. Opens the Flag Manager
C. Modifies default material parameters
D. Applies a new surface

Q39. Which programming language is used in Script Editor?

A. Java
B. Python
C. C++
D. JavaScript

Q40. What is the main purpose of Script Editor in Autodesk CFD?

A. Hide components
B. Create or customize tasks
C. Clone templates
D. Edit scenario environments

Q41. What does the Flags button allow you to manage?

A. Material properties
B. Script tasks
C. Various configurations in Autodesk CFD
D. Volume Selections

FOR STUDENT NOTES

Chapter 5

Analyzing Results

Topics Covered

The major topics covered in this chapter are:

- ***Results tab***
- ***Result Tasks panel***
- ***Review panel***
- ***Image panel***

INTRODUCTION

In the last chapter, you have learned the process to solve the analysis with the use of software. In this chapter, you will learn to analyze results with the help of various tools.

RESULTS TAB

The **Results** tab is generally used to analyze the results of a simulation study with the help of various panels, like **Image** panel, **Results Tasks** panel, **Reporting** panel, **Review** panel, and **Iteration/Step** panel; refer to Figure-1. Note that you can check the process of analysis in **Output** tab. Every action of an analysis is displayed in **Output Bar**; refer to Figure-2. The results options are discussed next.

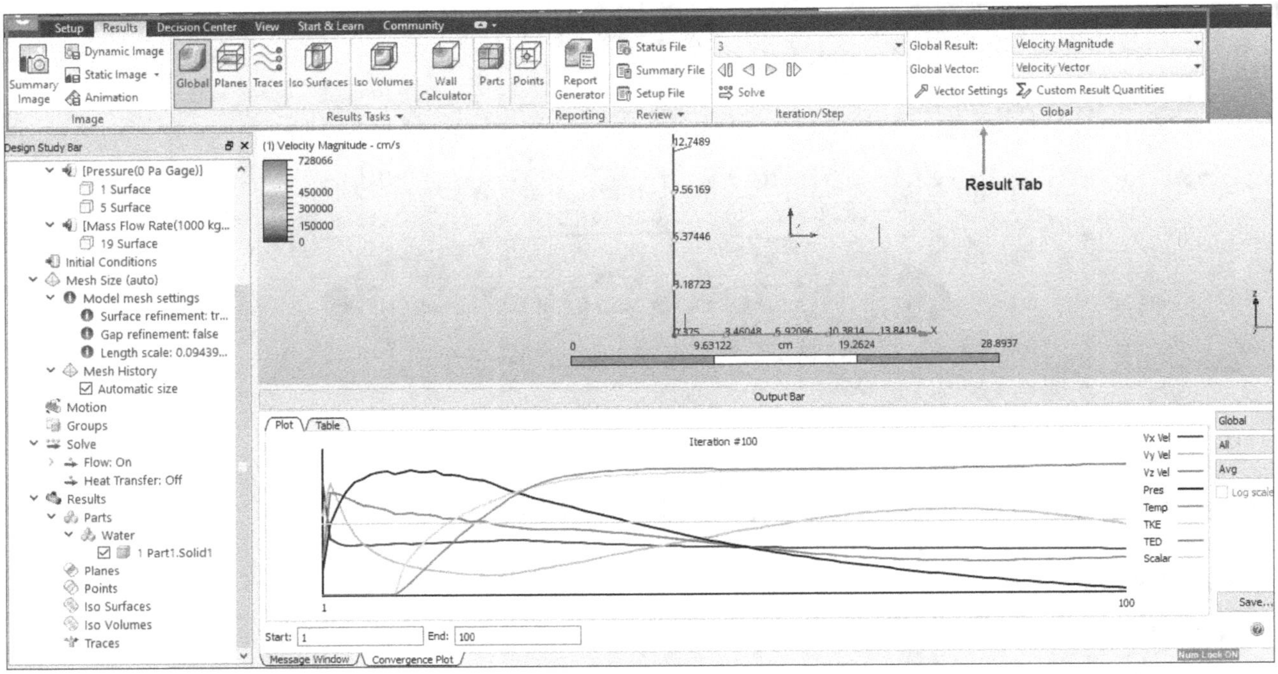

Figure-1. Results tab

Figure-2. Output Bar

Results Tasks panel

The tools in **Result Tasks** panel are used to visualize the simulation results. These tools are discussed next.

Global

The **Global** tool is used to control the display of results and vectors on model surfaces. The procedure is discussed next.

- After the completion of analysis, click on the **Global** button from **Results Tasks** panel. The **Global** tool will be activated and **Global** context panel will be displayed at the right in **Ribbon**; refer to Figure-3.

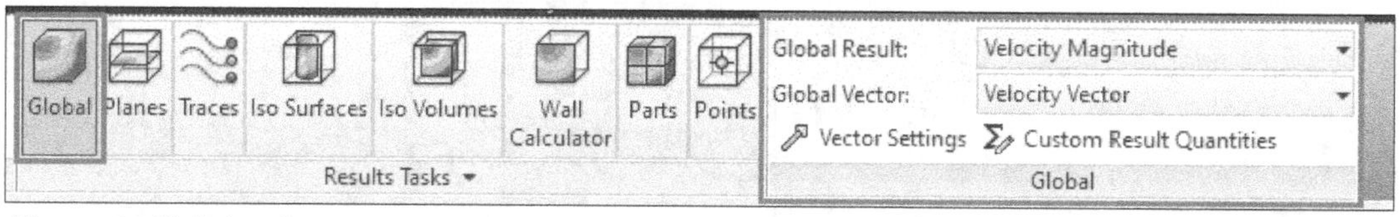

Figure-3. Global tool

- Click in the **Global Result** drop-down from **Global** context panel and select desired parameter which you want to display on the model surfaces; refer to Figure-4.

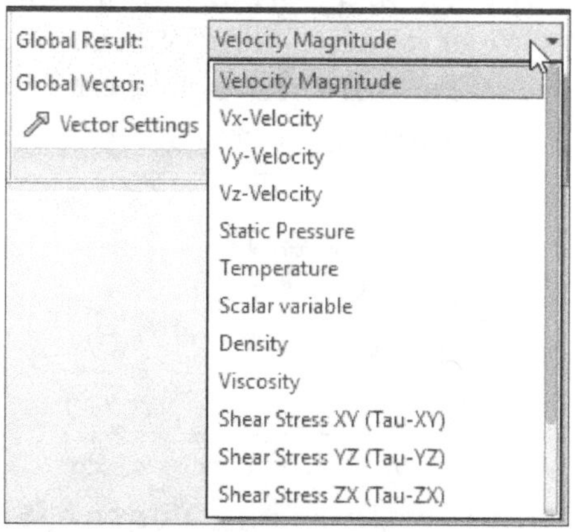

Figure-4. Global Result drop-down

- On selecting any scalar quantity from **Global Result** drop-down, the plot will be displayed at the right of canvas screen as per analysis results and results on model will be displayed accordingly; refer to Figure-5.

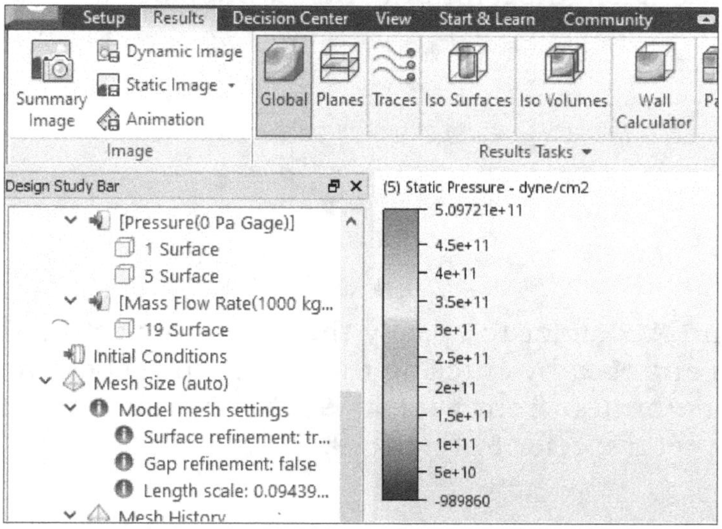

Figure-5. Plot Static Pressure

- Click on the **Global Vector** drop-down from **Global** context panel and select the vector quantity to be displayed on surface of model; refer to Figure-6. Vector quantity is used to show the direction of related result.

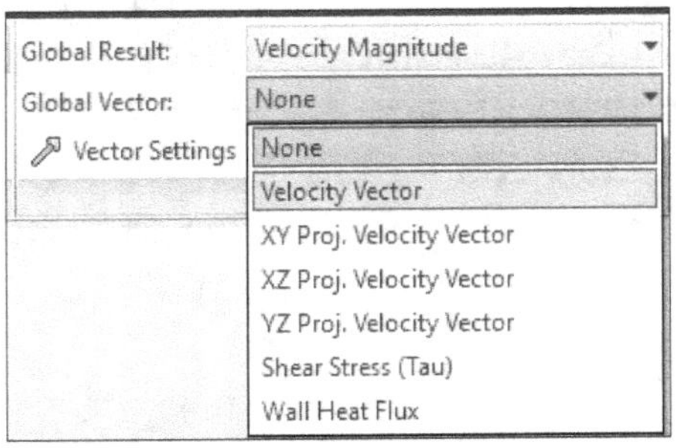

Figure-6. Global Vector drop-down

Vector Settings

- Click on the **Vector Settings** button from **Global** context panel to specify parameters for selected vector result. The **Vector Settings** dialog box will be displayed; refer to Figure-7. The options in **Vector Settings** dialog box are used to specify the length and intensity of vectors.

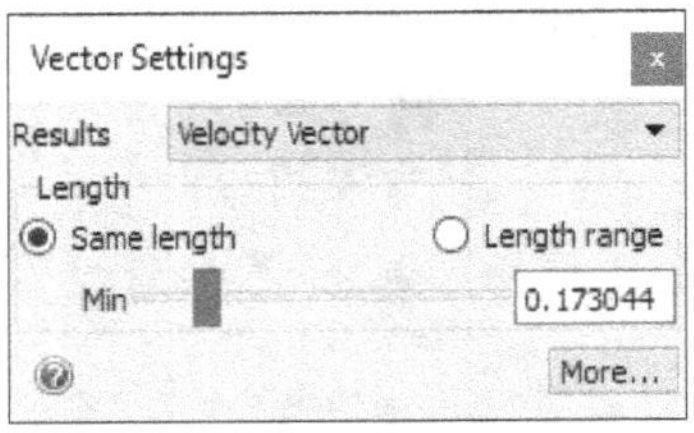

Figure-7. Velocity Vector diaog box

- Select the **Same Length** radio button from **Vector Settings** dialog box to apply same length to all the vectors on both sides of flow.
- Move the length slider or specify the length value numerically in **Length** edit box to specify the length of vector. The maximum value of **Length** edit box is 0.999.
- Select the **Length Range** radio button from **Vector Settings** dialog box to display vectors with different lengths for input and output sides of model; refer to Figure-8.

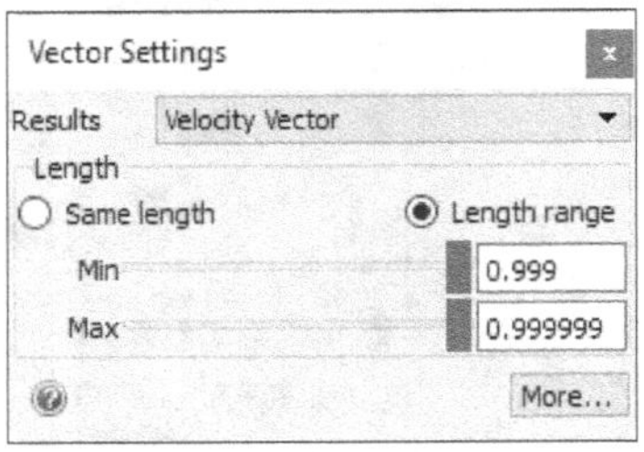

Figure-8. Length Range radio button

- Move the **Min** and **Max** slider to specify the length of vector. You can also specify the value of **Min** and **Max**, by entering the values in respective edit boxes.
- Click on the **More** button from **Vector Settings** dialog box to define advanced parameters for vectors; refer to Figure-9.

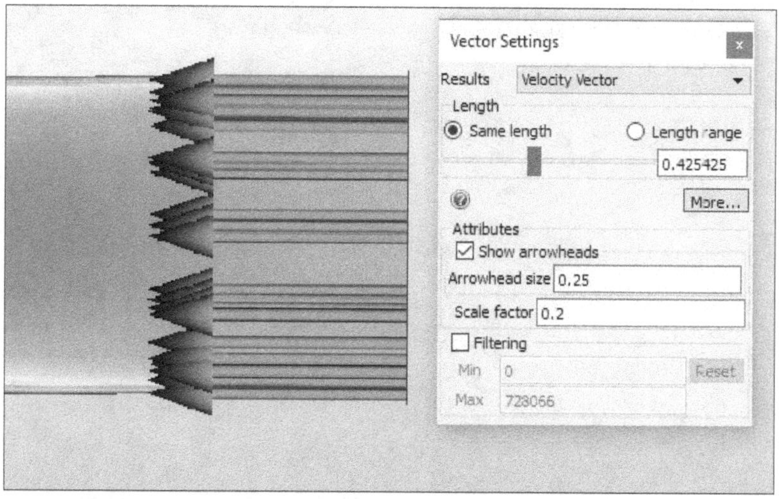

Figure-9. Parameters of More button

- Select the **Show arrowheads** check box from the **Attributes** section to display the arrow head in vector arrows of result. Clear the check box to hide arrow heads.
- Click in the **Arrowhead size** edit box from **Attributes** section and enter the value to increase or decrease the size of arrowhead.
- Click in the **Scale factor** edit box from **Attributes** section and specify desired value to increase or decrease the size of vector with respect to model length.
- Select the **Filtering** check box from **Vector Settings** dialog box to show regions where the active vector value is within specified range. After selecting this check box, specify desired values in **Min** and **Max** edit boxes of **Filtering** section to define range.
- Click on the **Reset** button to reset the **Filtering** values.
- After specifying the parameters in **Vector Settings** dialog box, close the dialog box by clicking on the **Close** button.

Custom Result Quantities

The **Custom Result Quantities** button is used to create custom result quantities to analyze and visualize results as per your requirement. Sometimes, we have to work on custom and different mechanism to find out the outcomes. In such a case, this tool is used to build a quantity which support mechanism and working of machine. The procedure to use this is discussed next.

- Click on the **Custom Result Quantities** button from the **Global** contextual panel. The **Custom Result Quantities** dialog box will be displayed; refer to Figure-10.

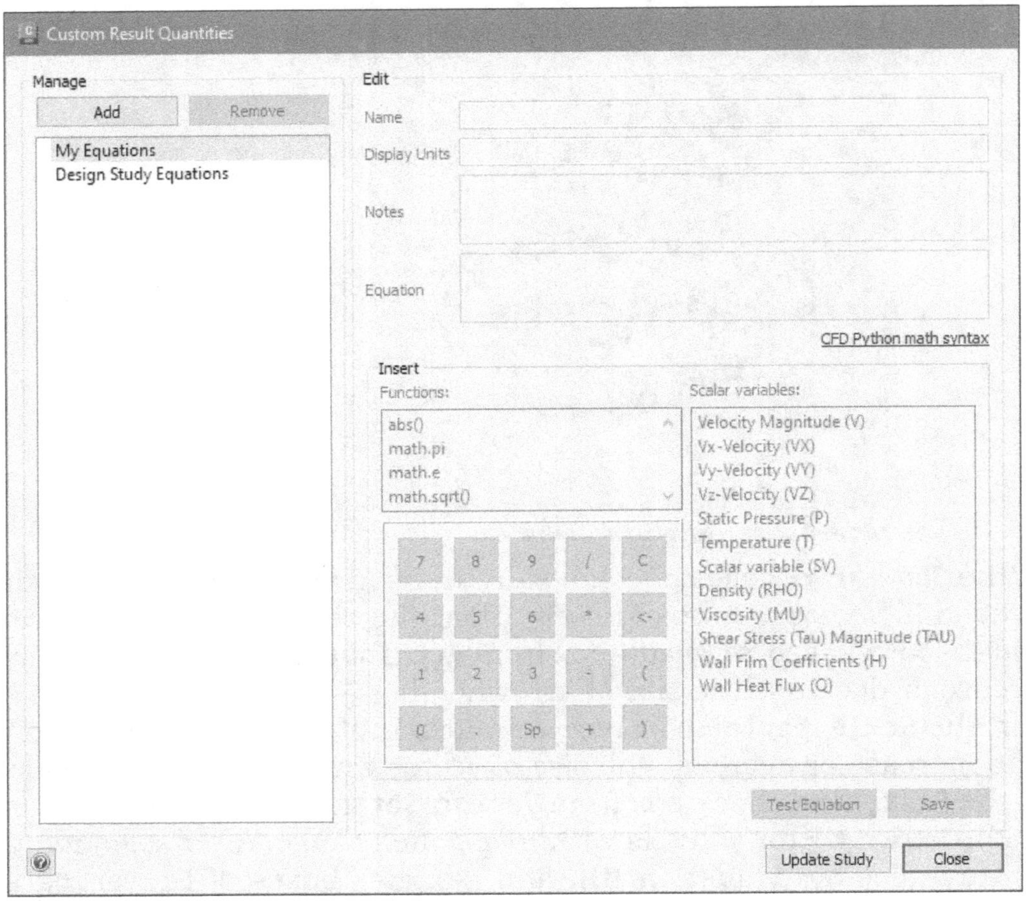

Figure-10. Custom Result Quantites dialog box

- Click on the **Add** button from the **Custom Result Quantities** dialog box to add a new quantities. All the edit box of **Custom Result Quantities** dialog box will be enabled.
- Specify desired values in edit boxes like **Name**, **Display Units**, and **Notes**.
- Double-click on desired parameter from the **Scalar variables** area and apply desired formula using options in the **Functions** area of the dialog box. Click on **Test Equation** button to test the equation.
- After testing, click on the **Save** button. The quantity will be created and displayed in **Global** context panel. Click on the **Update Study** button if you want to update a parameter already being used in the study.
- After specifying the parameters, click on the **Close** button from **Custom Result Quantity** dialog box. You will be returned to **Result** tab. The procedure to create custom quantity will be discussed later in this chapter.

Planes

The **Planes** tool is used to visualize 3D result data on specified planes. The procedure to use this tool is discussed next.

- Click on the **Planes** tool from the **Results Tasks** panel of **Results** tab in the **Ribbon**. The **Plane** tool will be activated and **Planes** context panel will be displayed at the right in the **Ribbon**; refer to Figure-11.

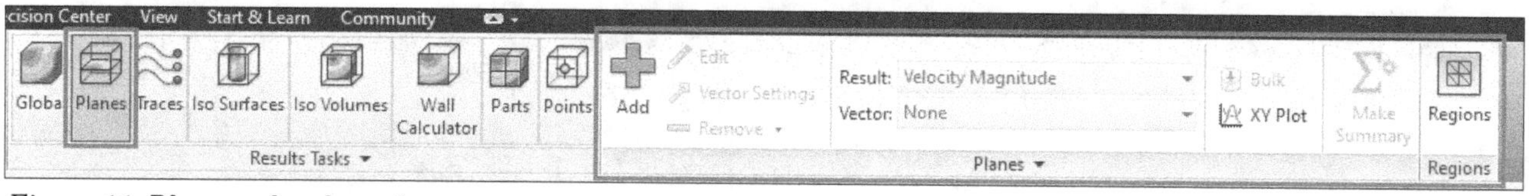

Figure-11. Planes tool and panel

- Click on the **Add** button from **Planes** context panel to add a plane on the model to view the result. A plane will be displayed in the model and all tools of **Plane** context panel will be activated; refer to Figure-12.

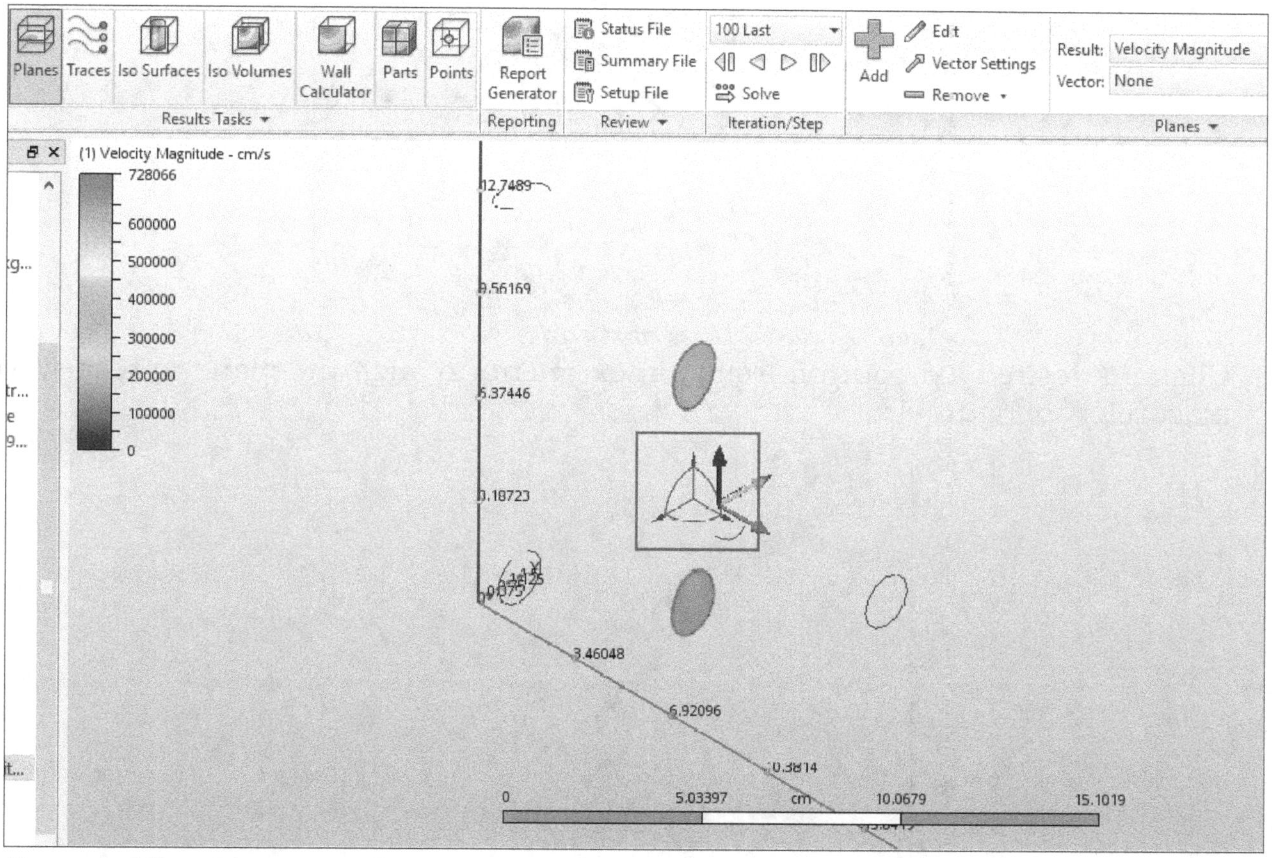

Figure-12. Adding plane

- You can move the added plane with the help of **Plane Controls** displayed on the model. What you need to do is, just grab the desired arrow with left-click of mouse and drag to the position where you want to place your plane. The plane will start moving in direction of selected arrow.
- You can change the plane angle or rotate the plane by dragging the arc of **Plane Control**.
- If you want to align the plane to desired axis then left-click on the plane. A context menu will be displayed; refer to Figure-13

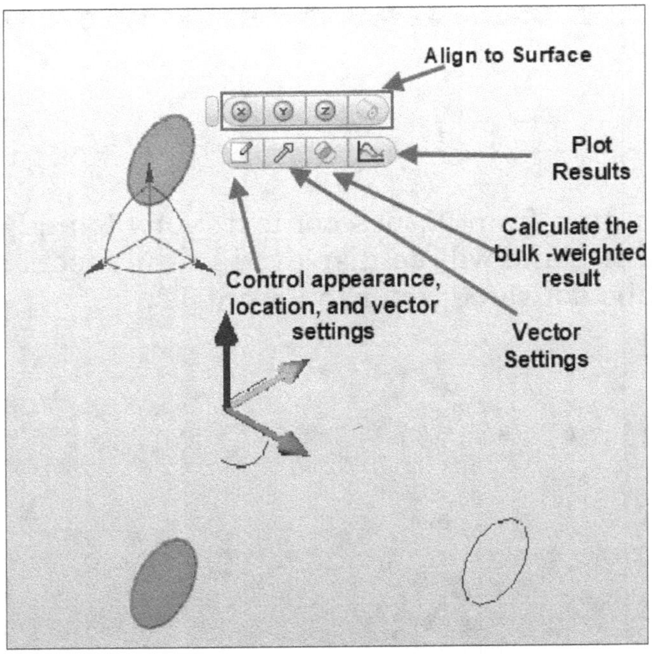

Figure-13. Left-click plane context menu

- Click on desired axis button from context menu to align the plane to respective axis; refer to Figure-14.

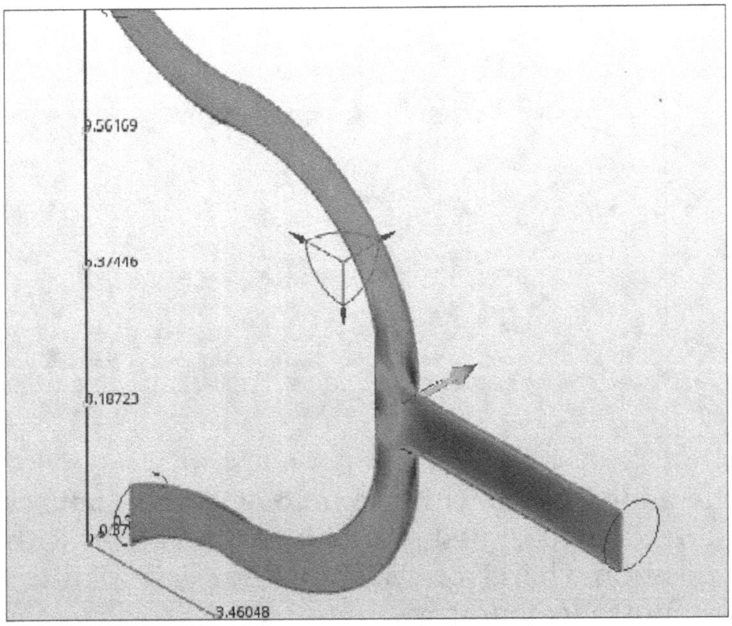

Figure-14. Plane aligned to Y axis

- Click on the **Align to Surface** button from context menu and click on the surface to align the added plane.
- Click on the **Control appearance, location, and vector settings** button from context panel to change appearance and location of plane. The **Plane Control** dialog box will be displayed; refer to Figure-15.

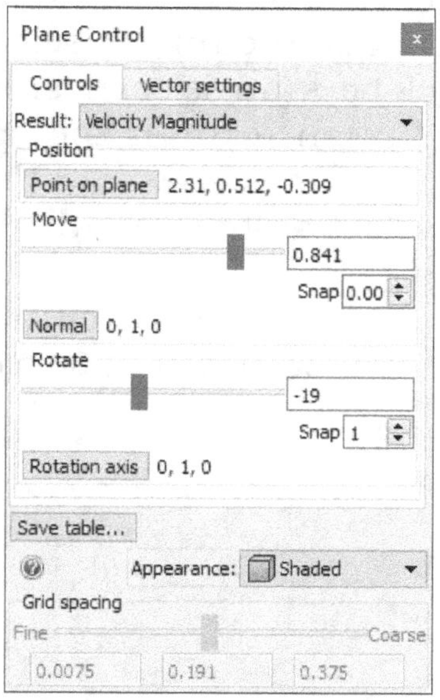

Figure-15. Plane Control dialog box

- The options of **Plane Control** dialog box will be discussed later in this chapter.
- Click on the **Vector Settings** button from context menu to change the plane vector setting with this tool. The **Vector Settings** tab of **Plane Control** dialog box will be displayed. The options of **Vector Settings** tab will be discussed later in this chapter.

Bulk Results

- Click on the **Calculate bulk-weighted results** button from context menu to calculate the bulk-weight results. The **Bulk Results** dialog box will be displayed; refer to Figure-16.

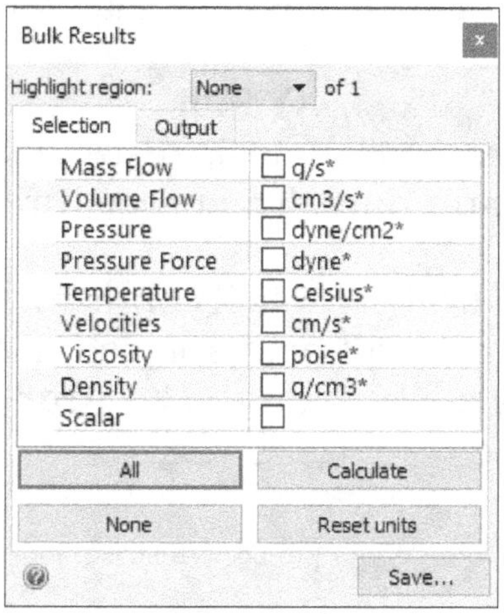

Figure-16. Bulk Results dialog box

- You can also open the **Bulk Results** dialog box by clicking on **Bulk** button from **Planes** panel; refer to Figure-17.

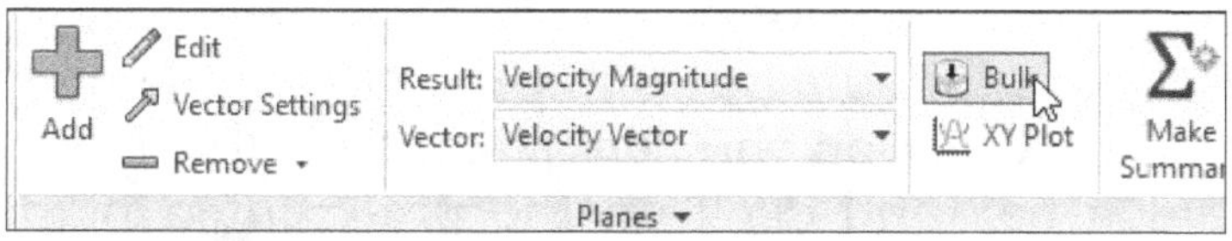

Figure-17. Bulk Button

- The **Bulk Results** dialog box calculates and shows bulk-weighted results on a result pane.

- Select the required check boxes of quantities from **Selection** tab of **Bulk Result** dialog box. If you want to change the unit of selected quantity then click in the **Unit** drop-down next to check box and select desired unit from displayed unit list.
- Click on the **Reset units** button to reset the specified units of quantities in **Selection** tab.
- Click on the **All** button to select all the quantities and click on the **None** button to deselect all the quantities.
- After selecting the quantities, click on the **Calculate** button from the **Bulk Result** dialog box. The bulk results will be added in **Output** tab; refer to Figure-18.

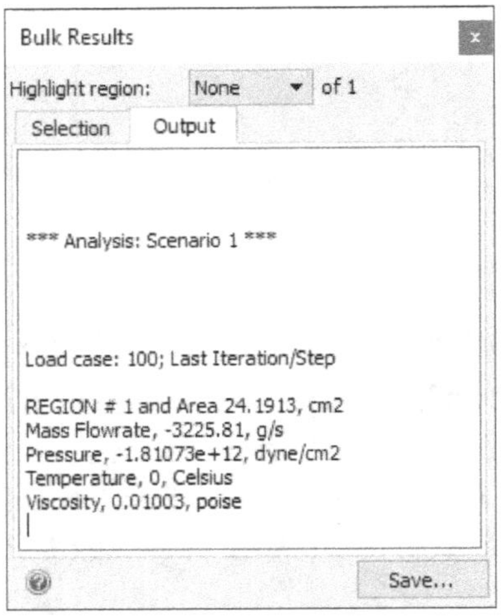

Figure-18. Output tab of Bulk Results dialog box

- Click on the **Save** button from **Output** tab to save the current data of bulk result. The **Save Bulk Data** dialog box will be displayed.
- Select desired location in your computer to save the file, and click on **Save** button. The data will be saved in selected location.
- Click on the **Close** button of **Bulk Results** dialog box to exit the dialog box.

XY Plot

The **XY Plot** is used to create graph of analysis result quantity. This tool is a convenient way to extract and present result data. The procedure to use this is discussed next.

- Click on the **XY Plot** button from left-click context menu after clicking on the added plane. The **XY Plot** dialog box will be displayed; refer to Figure-19. You can also open **XY Plot** dialog box by clicking on the **XY Plot** button from the **Planes** panel.

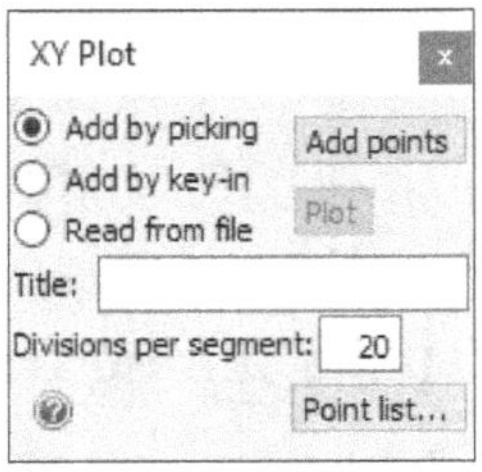

Figure-19. XY Plot

- Select the **Add by picking** radio button from **XY Plot** dialog box to add points by clicking on the plane. Click on the **Add points** button next to the radio button from **XY Plot** dialog box and click on the pre-created plane to specify points; refer to Figure-20. You can add as many points as you want but you need to add minimum 2 points. The plot will pass through selected points showing how the parameter varies from one selected point to another.

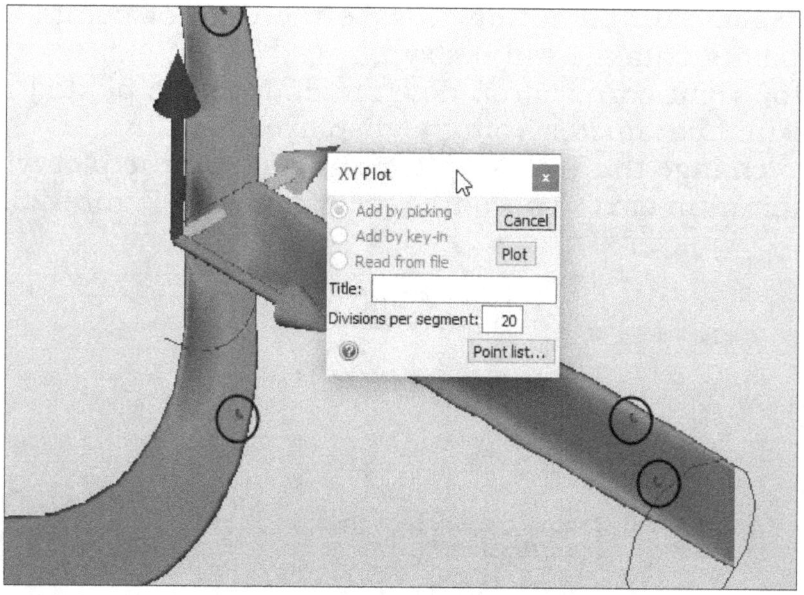

Figure-20. Adding points

- Click on the **Point list** button from **XY Plot** dialog box to view the list of added points; refer to Figure-21. Click again on the **Point List** button to hide the shown list.
- Click on the **Plot** button from **XY Plot** dialog box to show the plot. The **XY Plot: Plot 1** will be displayed; refer to Figure-22.

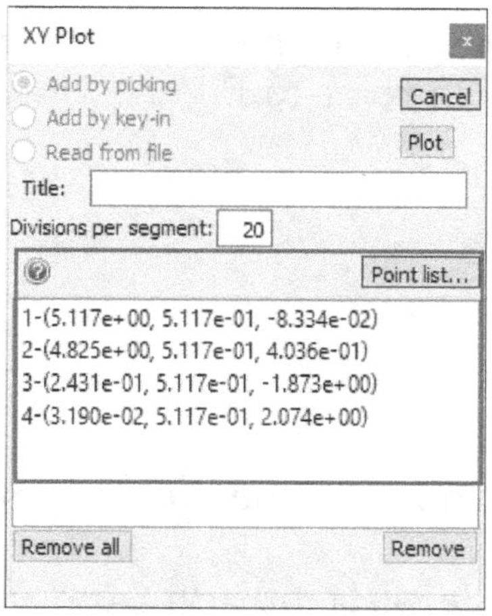

Figure-21. Points list

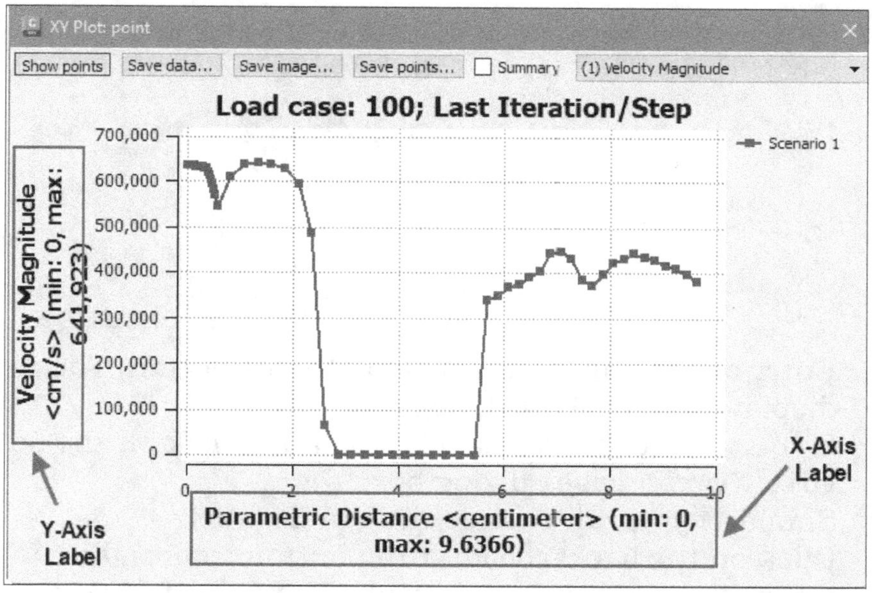

Figure-22. XY Plot : Plot 1

- You can customize the result of the plot by using the various button from dialog box.
- Click on the **Show points** toggle button to display/hide points in graph.
- Click on the **Save data** button to save the current data for future reference in CSV format. The **Save** dialog box will be displayed. Set desired location to save the file and click on the **Save** button from **Save** dialog box.
- Click on the **Save image** button to save current screen of graph. The **Save Image** dialog box will be displayed. Save the image at desired location. You can also set desired file extension for image from **Save as type** drop-down of **Save Image** dialog box. The default file extension for saving image files is **.bmp**.

- Click on the **Save points** button to save the data of points in a file. The file extension of points data file will be .xyp.
- Click in the top right corner drop-down to change the plotted result parameter and select desired parameter from the displayed list.
- If you want to change the Y-axis unit, right-click on the plot window and select the desired unit from **Units** cascading menu; refer to Figure-23.

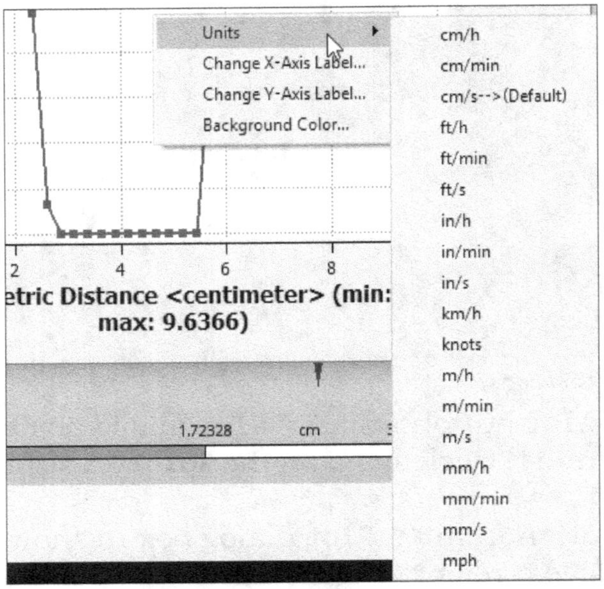

Figure-23. Selecting Units for Y-axis

- Click on the **Change X-Axis Label** button from right-click menu to change or create label. The **Edit X-Axis Label** dialog box will be displayed; refer to Figure-24.

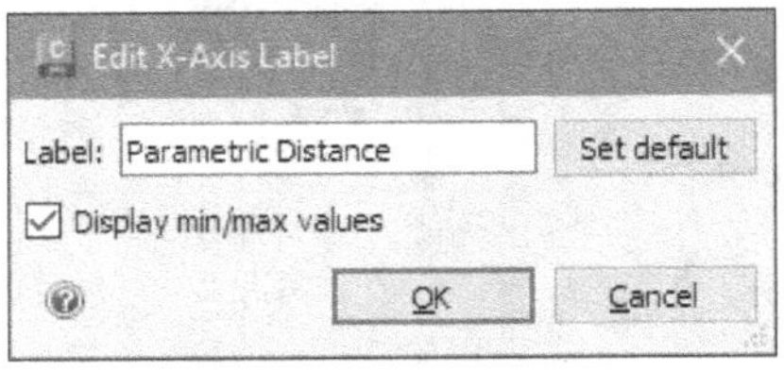

Figure-24. The Edit X-Axis Label dialog box

- Enter desired label and click on the **OK** button. The new label will be created and displayed in **XY Plot** dialog box.
- If you want to set the label to default, click on the **Set default** button from the **Edit X-Axis Label** dialog box.
- Similarly you can change the Y-Axis label.
- Click on the **Background color** button from right-click shortcut menu to change the background color of graph. The **Select Color** dialog box will be displayed; refer to Figure-25.

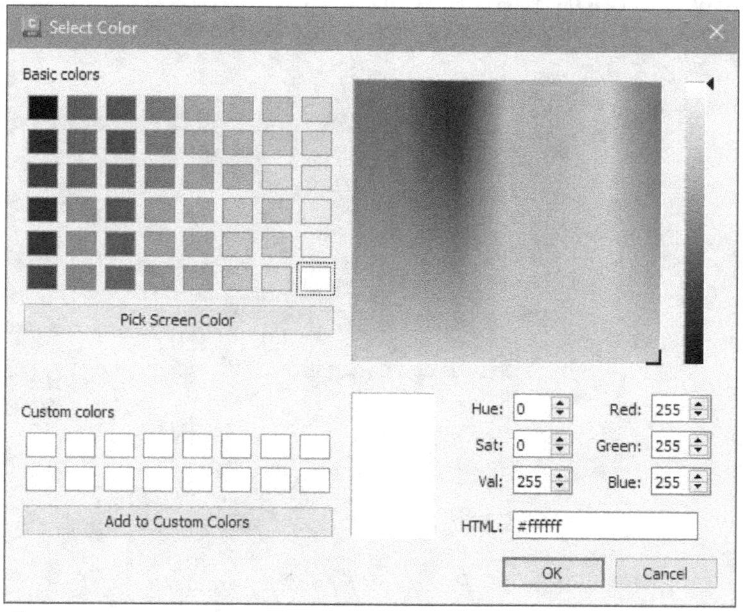

Figure-25. Select Color dialog box

- Select desired color and click on the **OK** button. The background color will be changed with the selected one.
- After checking the plot, click on the **Close** button from **XY Plot: Plot 1** dialog box. You will be returned to **XY Plot** dialog box.

Add by key-in

- Select the **Add by key-in** radio button from the **XY Plot** dialog box to add the points by specifying their particular X,Y, and Z coordinate values.
- Click in the **Add** edit box and enter the coordinates separated by comma. You can view the coordinates value of a particular point from **Status bar**; refer to Figure-26.

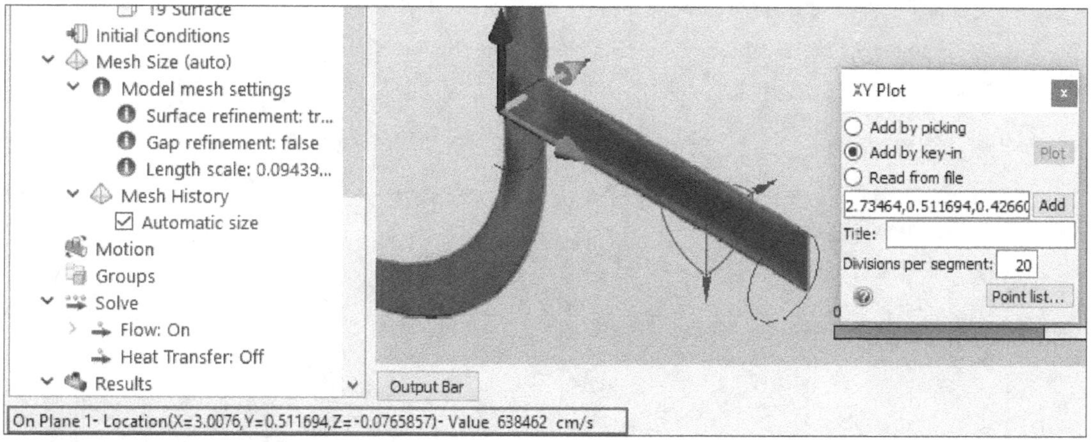

Figure-26. Entering coordinates value

- When you move the cursor on the added plane, the coordinates value of that particular point will be displayed in **Status Bar**. After specifying the values, click on the **Add** button of **XY Plot** dialog box. The point will be added. Repeat this step to add more points.
- Click in the **Title** edit box and specify the name of title which you want to give to current plot.
- Click in the **Divisions per segment** edit box from **XY Plot** dialog box and specify the value to change the plot resolution. The default number of divisions between every point is 20.

- If you want to view the coordinates of specified points then click on the **Points list** button from the **XY Plot** dialog box. The list will be displayed; refer to Figure-27.

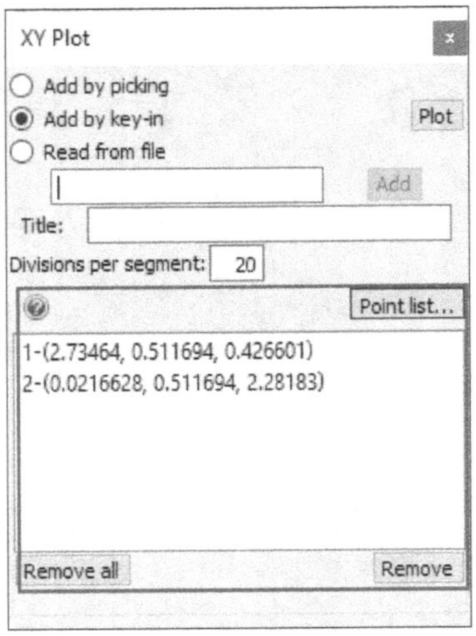

Figure-27. Points List for added coordinates

After specifying the parameters, click on the **Plot** button from the **XY Plot** dialog box. The **XY Plot: Pot 2** will be displayed. The options of the plot have been discussed earlier.

Read from file

- Select the **Read from file** radio button from **XY Plot** dialog box to input the data from a earlier saved file. The procedure to save a file has been discussed earlier.
- Click on the **Browse** button from **XY Plot** dialog box. The **Open XYPlot Points File** dialog box will be displayed; refer to Figure-28.

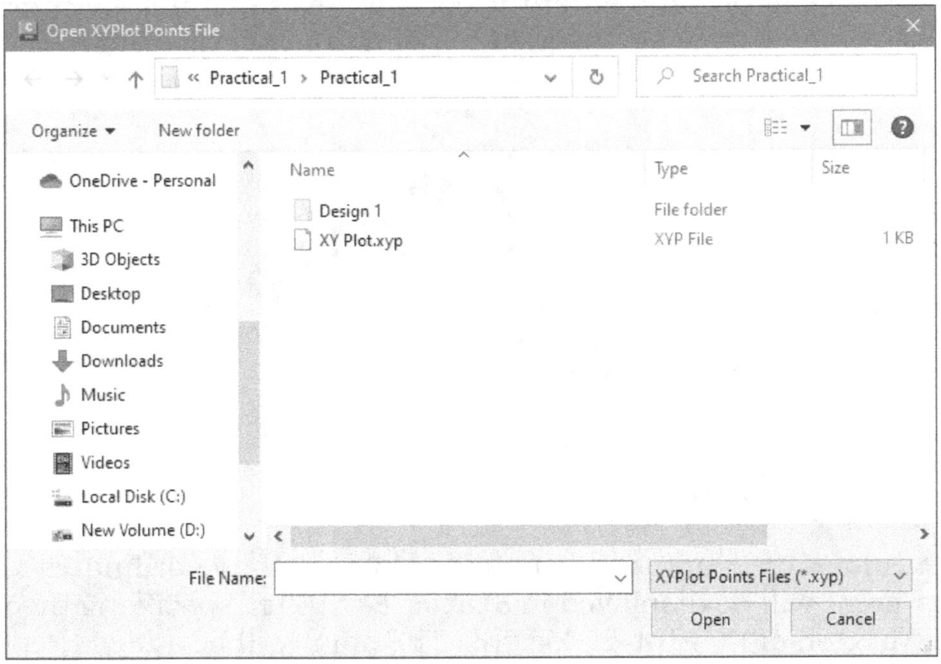

Figure-28. Open XYPlot Points File dialog box

- Select desired file and click on the **Open** button. The file will open in **XY Plot** dialog box and the data related to this file will be automatically updated in **XY Plot** dialog box; refer to Figure-29.

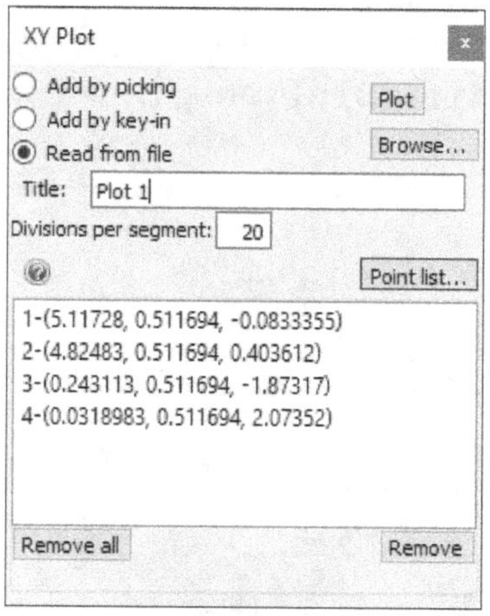

Figure-29. Updated XY Plot dialog Box

- Click on the **Plot** button from **XY Plot** dialog box to view the plot of specified points.
- After checking the plot and performing desired operation. Close the **XY Plot** dialog box to exit.

Editing Plane for XY Plot

The **Edit** tool is used to align, move, and rotate the added plane. The procedure to use this is discussed next.

- Click on the **Edit** button from **Planes** panel of **Result** tab in the **Ribbon**. The **Plane Control** dialog box will be displayed; refer to Figure-30.

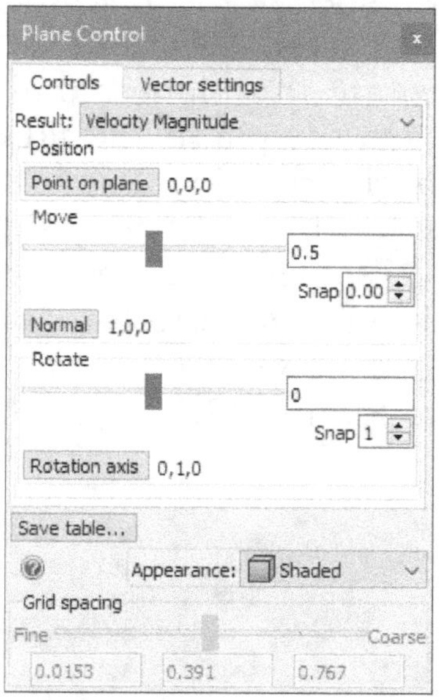

Figure-30. Plane Control dialog box

- There are two tabs available in the **Plane Control** dialog box which are **Controls** and **Vector settings** tabs. First, we will discuss the **Controls** tab and then **Vector settings** tab.

Controls tab

- Click in the **Result** drop-down from the **Plane Control** dialog box and select desired quantity which you want to view on the added plane. On selecting the quantities, the visualization and appearance of plane also change.

- The coordinates in **Position** section show the location of plane. To change the location, click on the **Point on plane** button from the **Position** section of **Plane Controls** dialog box. The **Edit point on plane** dialog box will be displayed; refer to Figure-31.

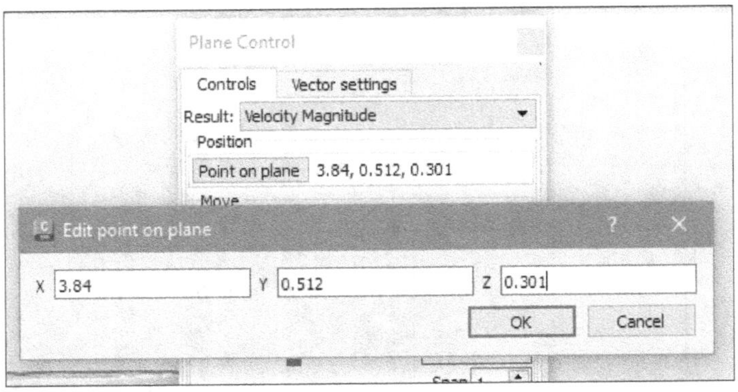

Figure-31. Edit point on plane dialog box

- Specify desired coordinates in **X**, **Y**, and **Z** edit boxes, and then click on **OK** button. The plane will move to specified coordinates.
- Drag and move the **Move** slider in **Plane Control** dialog box to move the plane at desired location. You can also do the same by entering the value manually in **Move** edit box.
- If you want to rotate the plane in desired direction then click on the **Normal** button from **Move** section. The **Edit plane normal** dialog box will be displayed.
- Specify desired values in **X**, **Y**, and **Z** edit boxes to define component of direction vector for plane. If you have entered 1 in **X** edit box then the plane will be perpendicular to X axis, if you specify 1 in **Y** edit box while others are 0 then plane will become perpendicular to Y axis.
- Move the **Rotate** slider to rotate the plane along selected axis. First, you need to specify the axis about which the plane should move using the **Rotation axis** button. The procedure to specify rotation axis is same as discussed above.
- Click on the **Save table** button from the **Plane Control** dialog box to save the plane table data. The **Save Plane Data** dialog box will be displayed. Specify the location as desired and click on **Save** button to save the file.
- Click in the **Appearance** drop-down and select desired option to change the appearance of plane; refer to Figure-32.

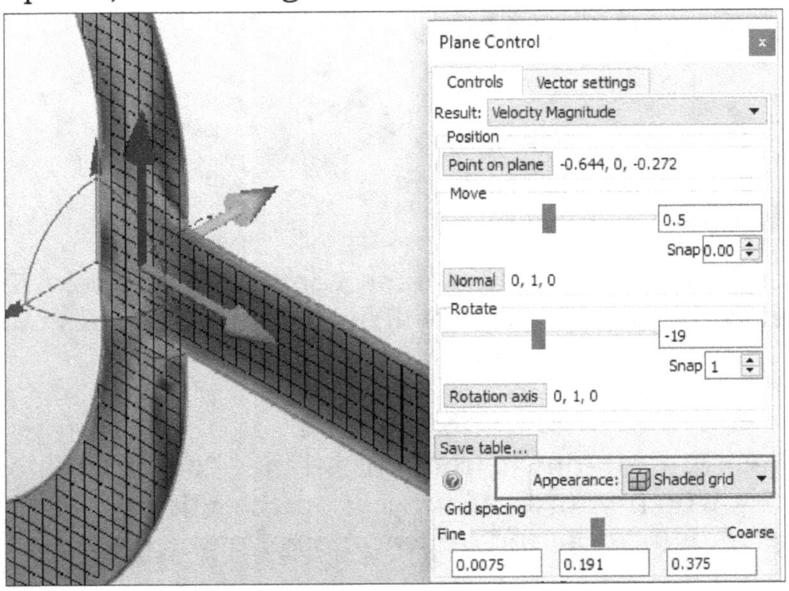

Figure-32. Selecting Appearance of plane

- The **Grid spacing** section is only available on selecting **Shaded grid** and **Outline grid** option.
- Move the **Grid spacing** slider to specify spacing between grids. Move the slider towards **Fine** option to decrease the spacing between grids and move the slider towards **Coarse** option to increase the spacing of grids. You can also specify these values manually.

Vector Settings tab

The **Vector settings** tab is used to apply and modify the display of vector on the plane. It is generally used to observe the flow of particles inside the model. The procedure to use this tool is discussed next.

- Click on the **Vector settings** tab of **Plane Control** dialog box. The parameters related to **Vector Settings** tab will be displayed; refer to Figure-33.

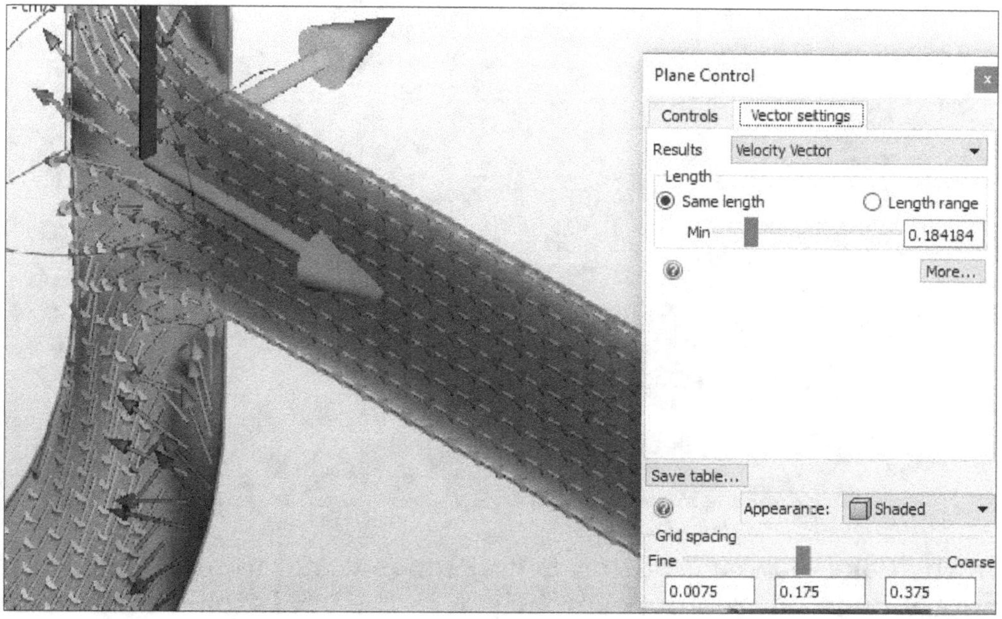

Figure-33. Vector settings tab

- The **Vector Settings** tab was discussed earlier in **Global** section of this chapter. You can also open the **Vector Settings** tab by clicking on **Vector Settings** tool from **Planes** panel; refer to Figure-34.

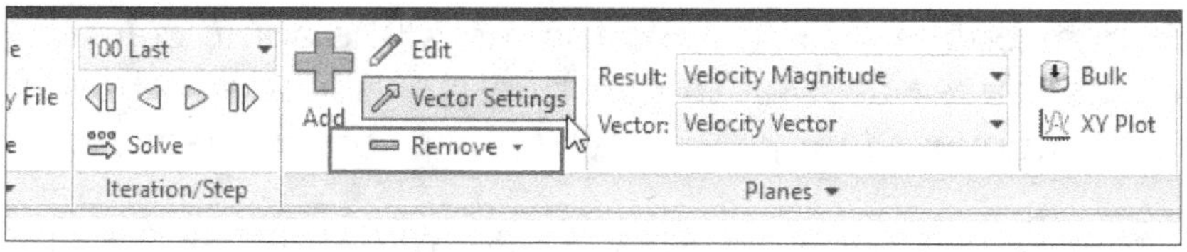

Figure-34. Vector Settings button

- After specifying the parameters in the **Plane Control** dialog box, close the dialog box. You will be returned to **Results** tab.
- Click on the **Remove** button from the **Plane** panel to remove the planes from the model. If you have added multiple planes to the model, click on the **Remove All** button from the **Remove** drop-down. All planes will be deleted.
- Select the **Show Outline** check box from **Planes** panel drop-down to view outline of model in the plane; refer to Figure-35.

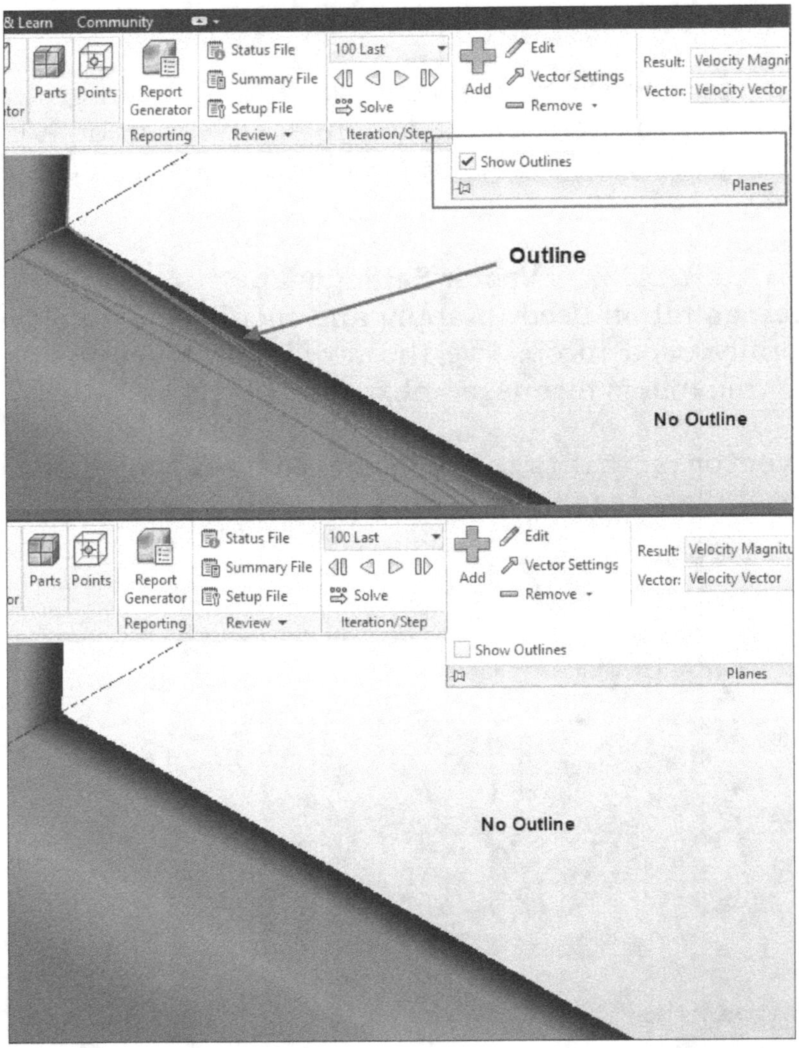

Figure-35. Outline of plane

- Click on the **Make Summary** button from **Planes** panel to make the selected plane as summary plane for results comparison in the **Decision center**. The **Decision center** will be discussed later.

Traces

The **Traces** tool is used to understand the behavior of flow inside the model, around the corners, and near edges. The **Traces** tool acts like some colored droplet injected into flow. We can use these droplet to identifies the location where fluid changes its direction and how it moves. The procedure to use this is discussed next.

- Click on the **Traces** tool from **Results Tasks** panel of **Results** tab. The tools for applying **Traces** will be activated; refer to Figure-36.

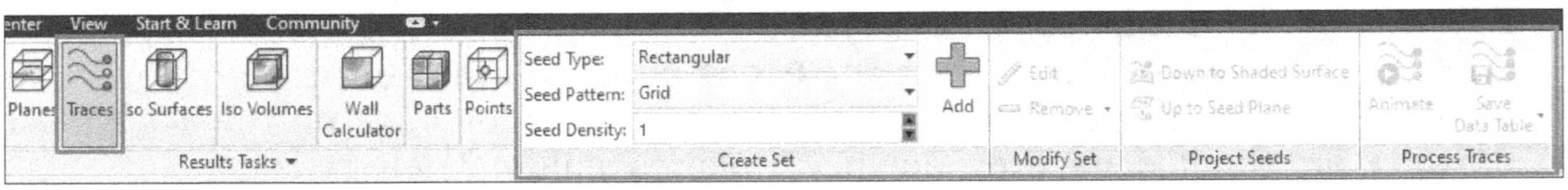

Figure-36. Traces tool

- To apply **Traces** tool, you will need to add a plane near the inlet flow of the model. The reason behind this is to place some colored particles on that plane so that the placed particles will move as per the given flow in and around the model.

Create Set panel

The **Create Set** panel is used to specify the basic parameters of adding traces to a plane. These parameters are discussed next.

Point Type Traces

- Click in the **Seed Type** drop-down and select the **Point** option to display flow of single point as per analysis. Click on the **Add** button from the **Create Set** panel and click on the plane at desired locations. The flow will be traced automatically; refer to Figure-37. You can add as many points as required on the plane.

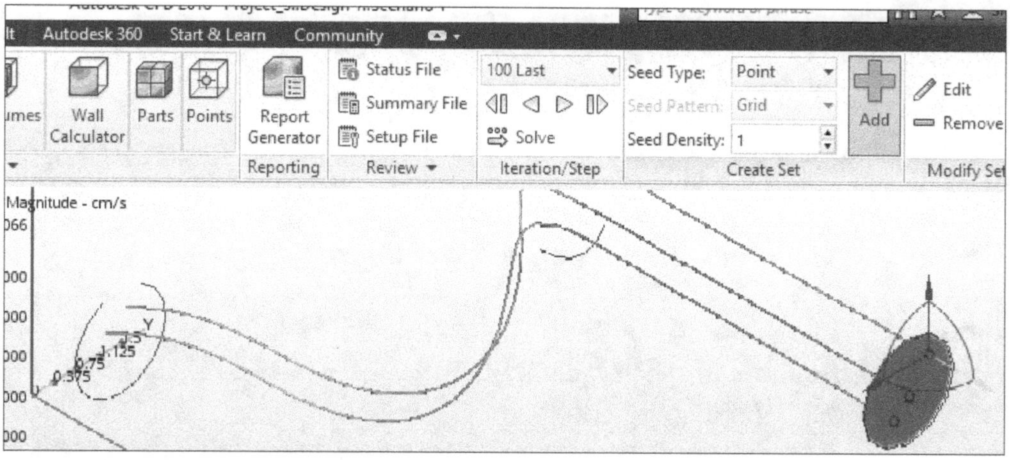

Figure-37. Traces with Point option

Line Type Traces

- Click in the **Seed Type** drop-down and select **Line** option to add a line of points on the plane. Click on the **Add** button from **Create Set** panel and click to specify end points of line. The particles will be traced; refer to Figure-38.

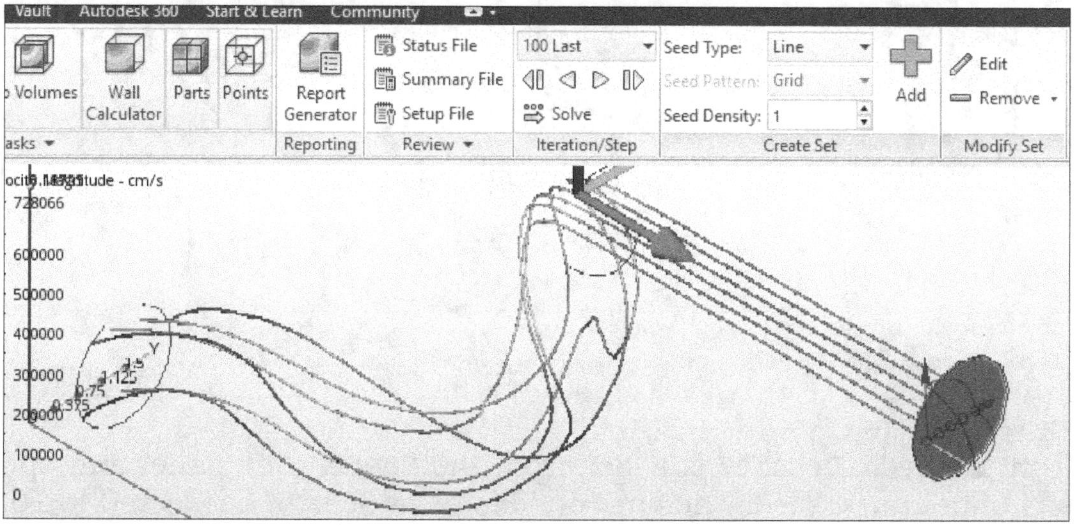

Figure-38. Line option of traces

Ring Type Traces

- Click in the **Seed Type** drop-down and select **Ring** option to add points in ring like structure on the plane. Now, click on **Add** button and click at the plane to specify center point of ring. Click again at desired location to define the diameter of ring. The particles will be traced in or around model as per flow; refer to Figure-39.

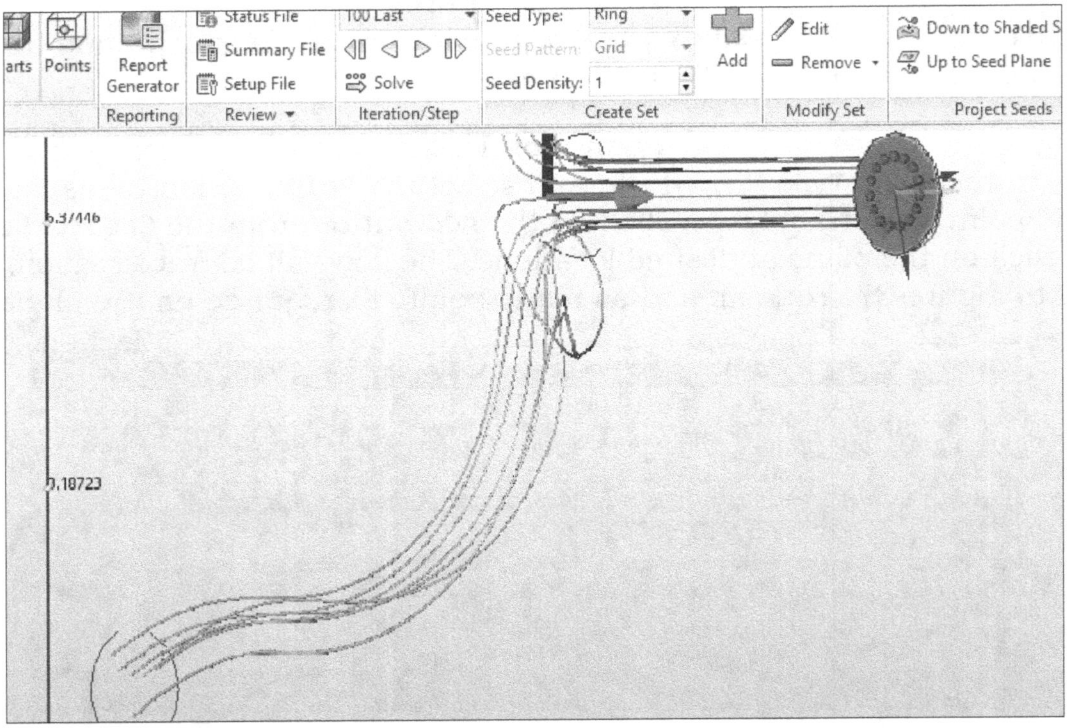

Figure-39. Ring option of traces

Circular Type Traces

- Click in the **Seed Type** drop-down and select **Circular** option to add points in circular structure. The points will combine to form a circular shape of points.
- Click in the **Seed Pattern** drop-down and select the desired pattern in which points will be placed inside the circle; refer to Figure-40.

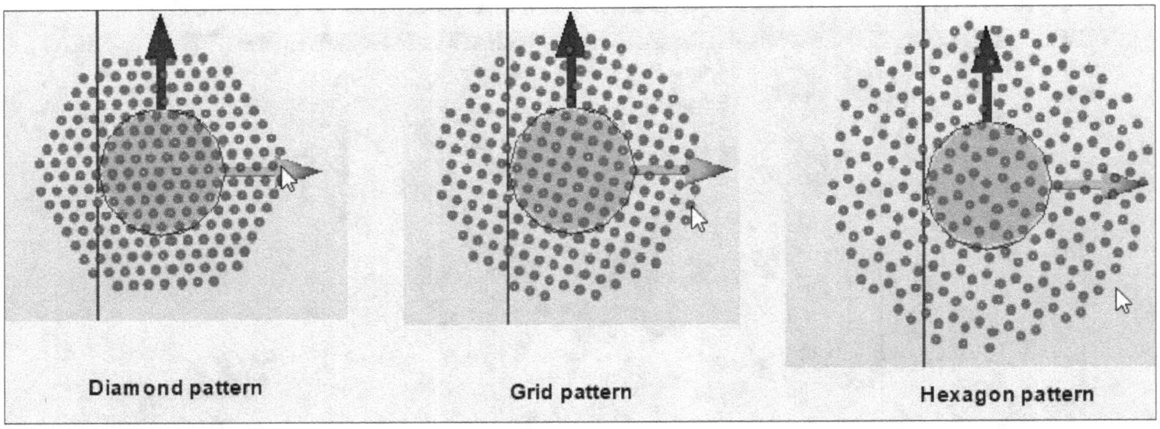

Figure-40. Seed pattern

- Click in the **Seed Density** edit box from the **Create Set** panel and specify the density of points or seed. The limit of density value is in between 0 to 10. Higher the density value, more the gap between seeds or points.
- After specifying desired parameters, click on the **Add** button from the **Create Set** panel and then click on the plane to specify center of the circle. Click again at desired location on plane to specify diameter of circle. The seeds will be traced as per flow inside the model; refer to Figure-41.
- Similarly, you can create rectangular shape of seeds using **Rectangular** option of **Seed Type** drop-down from **Create Set** panel.

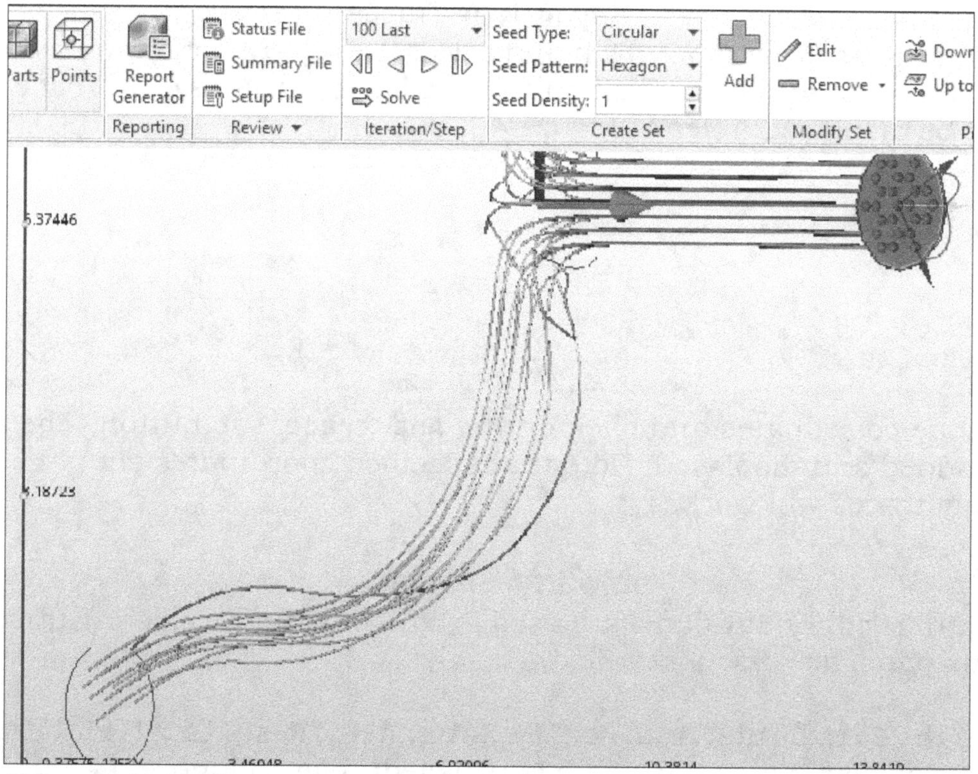

Figure-41. Circular Shape

Region Type Traces

- Click on the **Seed Type** drop-down and select **Region** option to generate trace for whole selected faces/surfaces. Now, click on the plane at which seeds will be placed, the particles will displayed as per the parameters set in **Create Set** panel of **Ribbon** while tracing the path; refer to Figure-42.

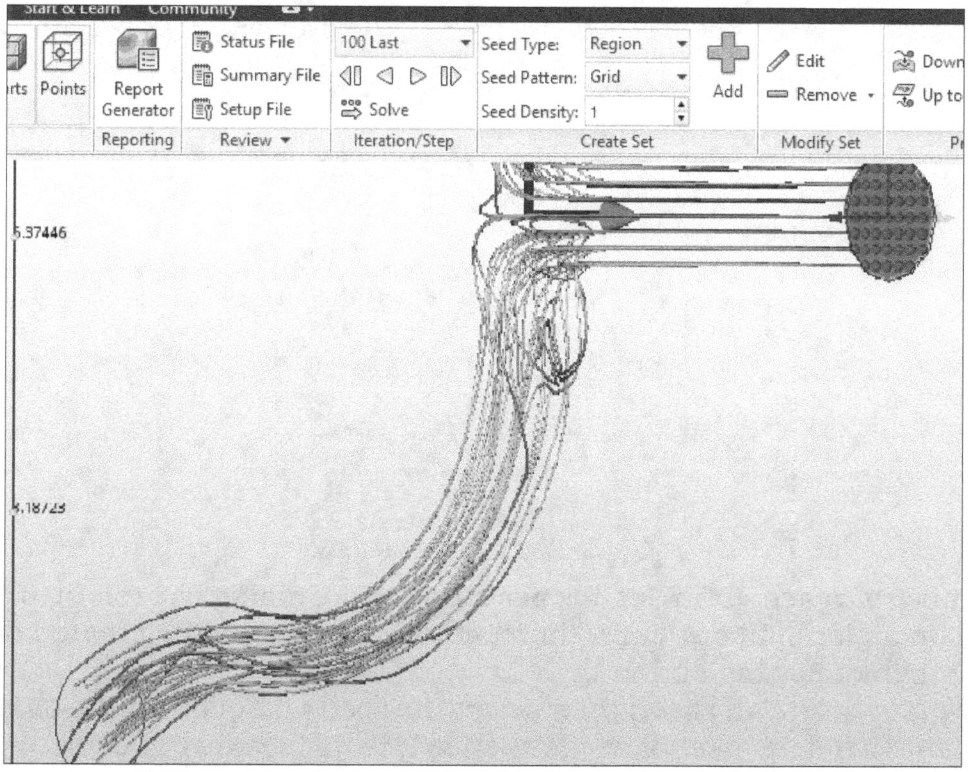

Figure-42. Region option of traces

Key in Type Traces

- Click in the **Seed Type** drop-down and select the **Key in** option to create the seeds by specifying coordinates. Click on the **Add** button, the **Key In Trace Set** dialog box will be displayed; refer to Figure-43.

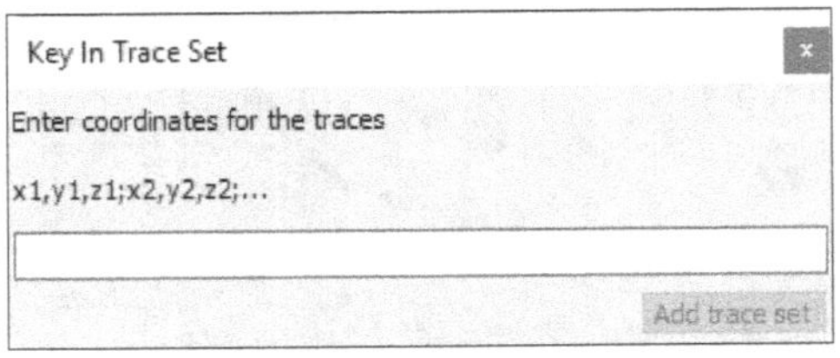

Figure-43. Key In Trace Set dialog Box

- Specify the coordinates and click on the **Add trace set** button. The trace point will be added and displayed. Note that specified coordinates should lie on plane, then only traces will work.

Modify Set panel

The tools in the **Modify Set** panel are used to edit and remove existing traces. Various tools in this panel are discussed next.

- Click on the **Edit** button from **Modify Set** panel of **Results** tab in the **Ribbon**. The **Edit Traces Set** dialog box will be displayed; refer to Figure-44.

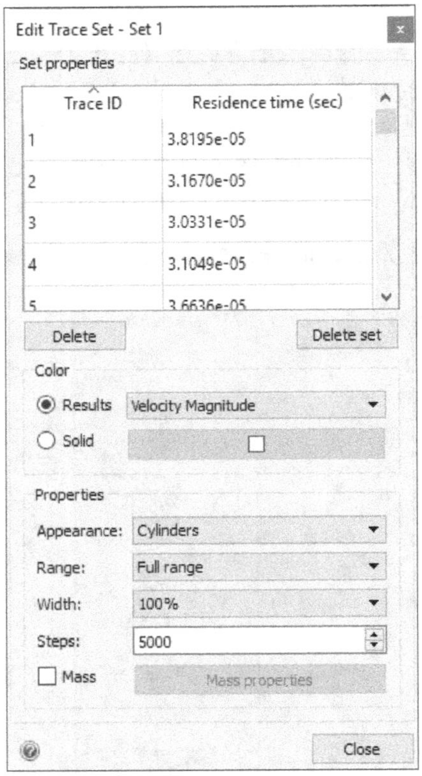

Figure-44. Edit Trace Set dialog box

- The number of **Trace ID** in **Set Properties** area of dialog box refers to the number of seeds on a plane. In our case, there are 45 seeds or points created on the plane with the help of **Region** option.
- If you want to delete any seed then select the seed and click on the **Delete** button. If you want to delete a set of seeds then select the seeds and click on the **Delete set** button.

- Click in the **Results** drop-down and select desired result quantity which you want to see. Select the **Result** radio button to activate this drop-down.
- Select the **Solid** radio button from the **Color** section to specify desired color to the traces. The default color of traces is white.
- To change the color, click on the **Solid** check box which is in front of **Solid** radio button. The **Select Color** dialog box will be displayed; refer to Figure-45.

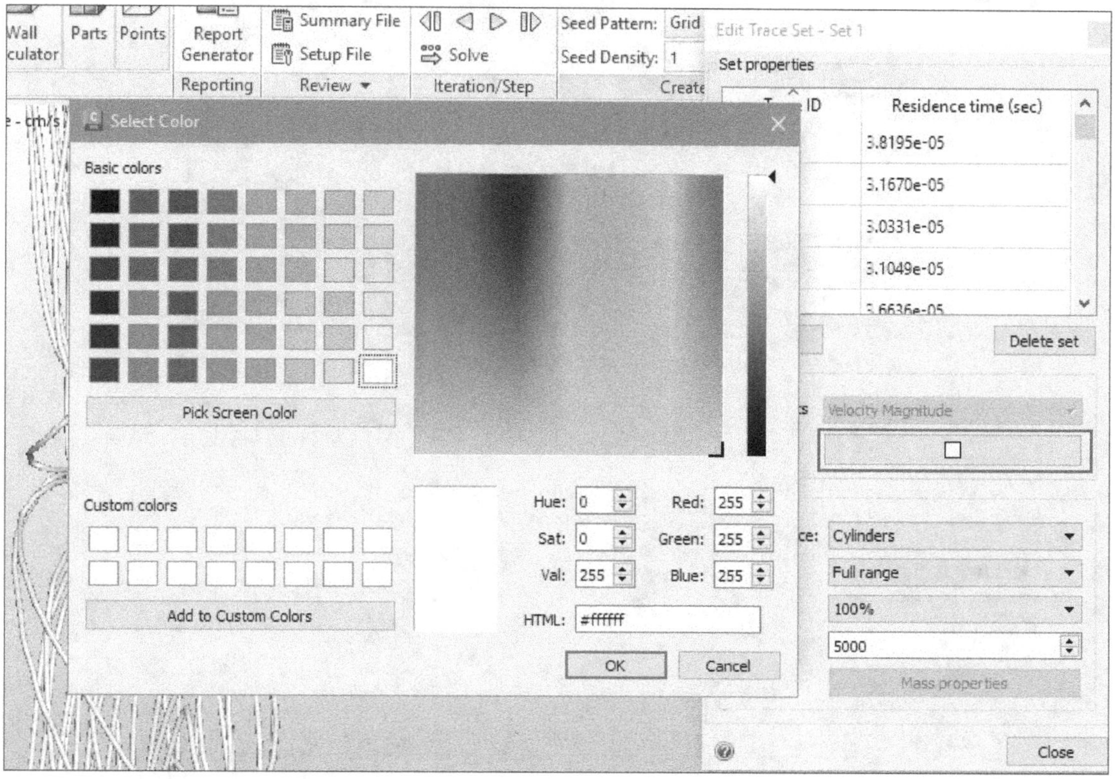

Figure-45. Select Color dialog box

- Select desired color and click on the **OK** button from **Select Color** dialog box. The color of traces will be changed to selected color.
- Click in the **Appearance** drop-down from **Properties** section of **Edit Trace Set** dialog box and select desired appearance of traces. There are 5 types of appearances available in **Appearance** drop-down.
- Click in the **Range** drop-down from **Properties** section to set desired range of traces. Select the **Forward** button to view traces towards the fluid flow. Select the **Backward** button to view traces against the fluid flow; refer to Figure-46. Select the **Full Range** button to display traces in both directions i.e. forward and backward direction.
- Click in the **Width** drop-down from the **Properties** section and select the width of traces appearance.
- Click in the **Steps** edit box and specify the value of traces. Here, step implies the length of traces inside the model; refer to Figure-47.

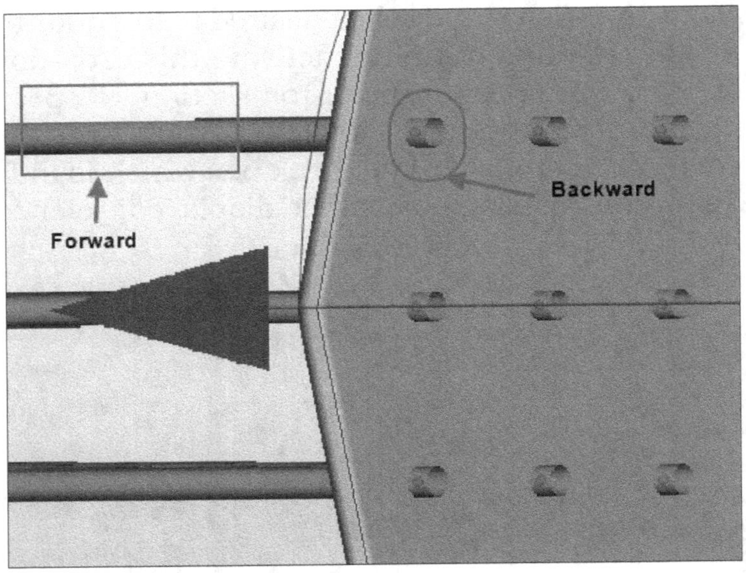

Figure-46. Forward and backward range

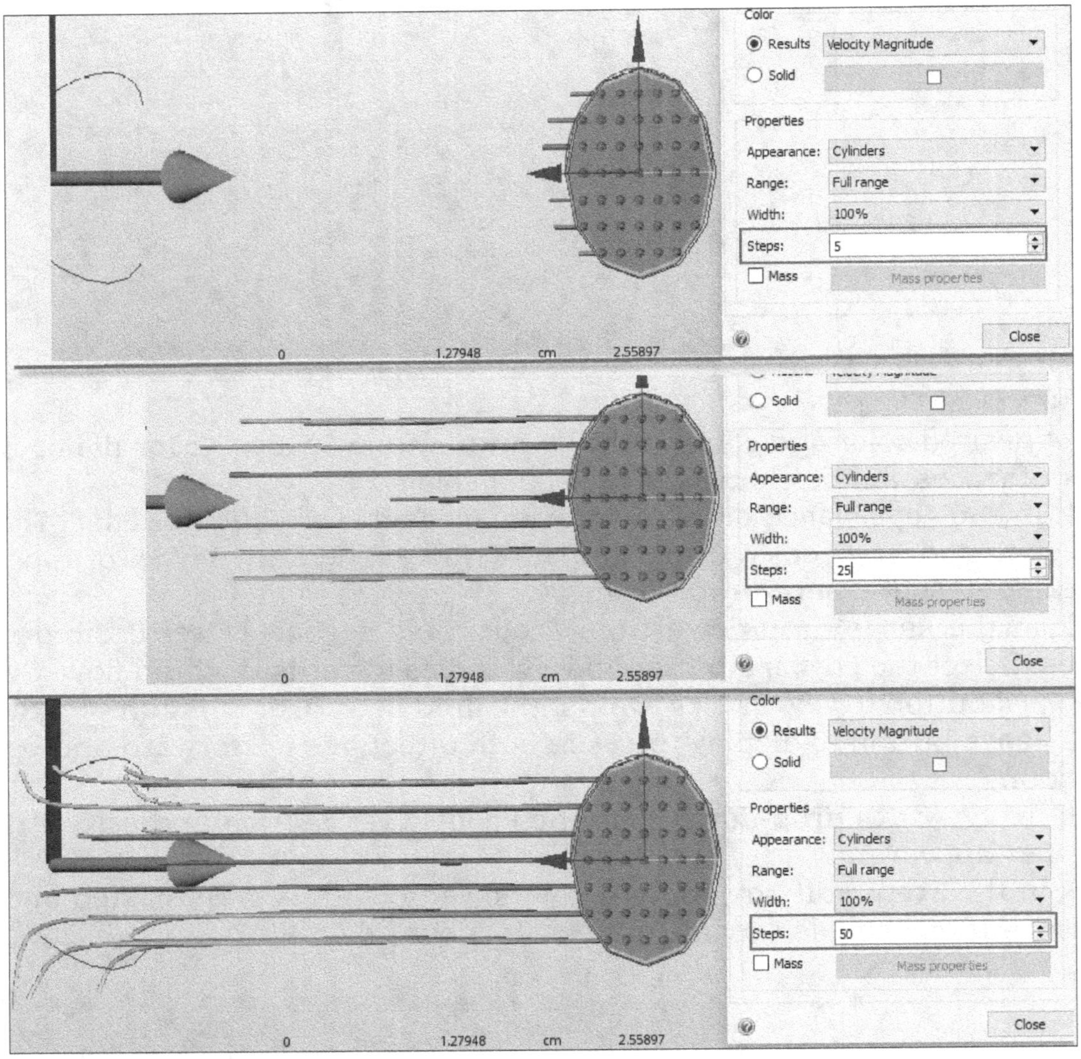

Figure-47. Steps

- Select the **Mass** check box from **Properties** section to apply some mass to the particles or seeds. This tool help us to observe the real time condition by applying mass to the seeds which are flowing along the flow inside the model. The resulting trace behaves like a physical substance within the flow system; refer to Figure-48.

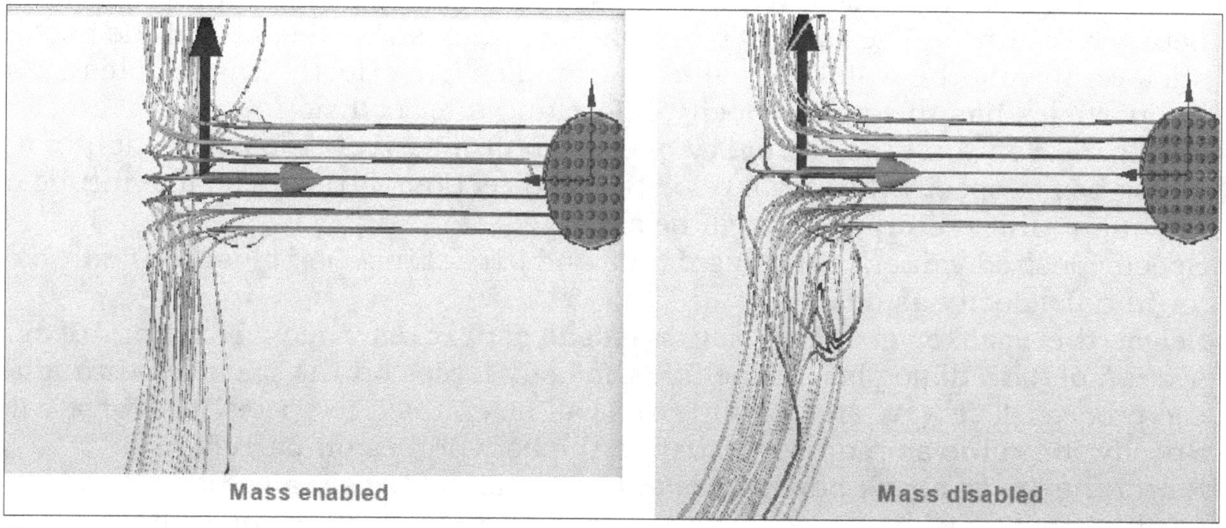

Figure-48. Mass enabled and disabled

- You can see the difference in above figure. In left figure, the particles are acting like they are containing some mass and are flowing in a restricted manner inside the boundary of model. In right figure, you can see the particles are moving freely.
- On selecting the **Mass** check box, the **Mass properties** button will be activated. Click on the **Mass properties** button to view and edit the mass properties of the particles. The **Mass** dialog box will be displayed; refer to Figure-49.

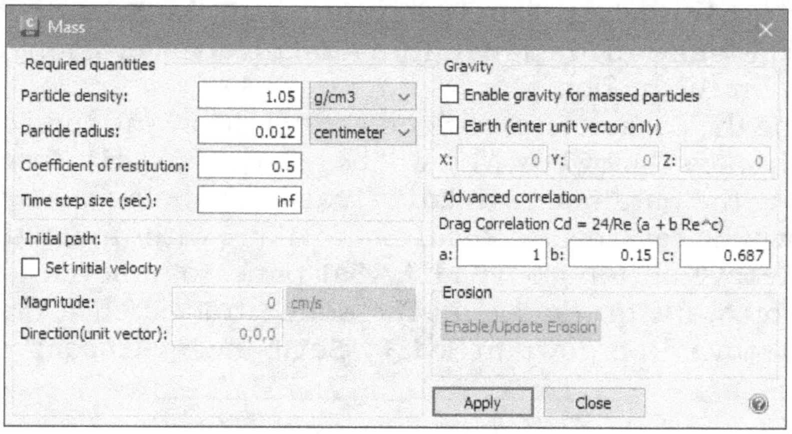

Figure-49. Mass dialog box

- Click in the **Coefficient of restitution** edit box from **Mass** dialog box to specify the coefficient value. It is the measure of bounce amount between two objects, or we can say the ratio of velocities of objects before and after collision. Mathematically it can be described as:

$$C = \frac{V_{2f} - V_{1f}}{V_{2i} - V_{1i}}$$

V_{1f} - Velocity of first object
V_{2f} - Velocity of second object
i - initial velocity
f - final velocity

- The default value of **Coefficient of restitution** is 0.5 and can be specified in between 0.01 to 1. The value 0.01 implies the inelastic collision and the particles stick on hitting the wall. The value of 1 implies as perfectly elastic collision and the particles has the same velocity before and after collision.
- Select the **Set initial velocity** check box from **Initial path** section of **Mass** dialog box to specify the initial velocity and direction of trace. The magnitude and direction (unit vector) option will be activated.
- Specify desired values in the **Magnitude** and **Direction (unit vector)** edit boxes for initial velocity as desired.
- Select the **Enable gravity for massed particles** check box from **Gravity** section of **Mass** dialog box to include the body forces on the particles throughout the process. The **X**, **Y**, and **Z** edit boxes will be enabled to specify the force value. Specify the value as required to define the body forces on particle.
- Select the **Earth** check box from **Gravity** section of **Mass** dialog box to enable the earth's gravity on the trace particle. Now, you need to enter the unit vector in X, Y, and Z component to specify the direction of earth's gravity.
- The **Drag Correlation** characteristics of each particle only affect the motion not the flow of particle. Particle traces are purely a post processing tool and does not effect the flow field at all. The drag correlation is basically used for massed particles. The equation of **Drag Correlation** is available in the **Advanced Correlation** area of the dialog box. Specify the values of a, b, and c constants in their respective edit boxes to change the drag as required.
- Click on the **Enable/Update Erosion** button from the **Mass** dialog box to reduce erosion for the sake of design improvement. The erosion will be updated automatically on the model.
- After specifying the parameters, click on **Apply** button and then click on the **Close** button from the **Mass** dialog box. You will be returned to **Edit Trace Set** dialog box.
- After specifying the parameters in **Edit Trace Set** dialog box, click on the **Close** button. You will be returned to **Results** tab along with updated model.
- Click on the **Remove** button from **Modify Set** panel to remove the last added trace particles. If you want to remove all the added traces, click on the **Remove All** button from **Remove** drop-down in **Modify Set** panel of **Ribbon**; refer to Figure-50.

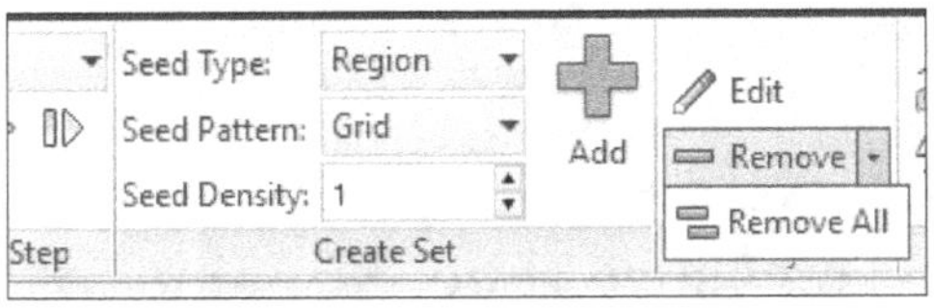

Figure-50. Remove and Remove All button

Project Seeds panel

The tools of **Project Seeds** panel are used to allow traces to be placed on desired surfaces or planes. These tools are generally used to position the traces on desired location to visualize flow very close to model boundaries and edges.

Down to Shaded Surface

The **Down to Shaded Surface** button of the **Project Seeds** panel is used for concentrating traces of the solid. This condition is used where flow is very close to the model and we need to study the effects of flow on the solid. The procedure to use this tool is discussed next.

- Create a seed distribution near the object that exceeds the size of object. You may have to create the seed grid of the solid and then move it near the object with the help of triad axis; refer to Figure-51.

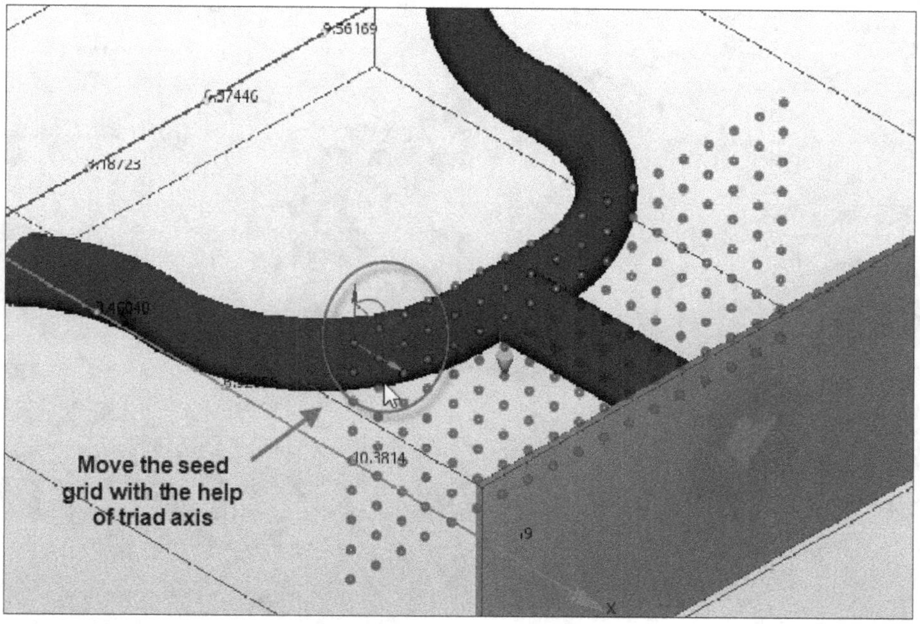

Figure-51. Creating seed distribution

- This tool works by projecting the seed traces in the negative direction of the yellow axis. You can rotate the triad axis to ensure the correct orientation.
- Now, select the model from **Results** of **Design Study Bar** and click on **Shaded** button from right-click menu; refer to Figure-52. The model will be displayed in shaded mode.

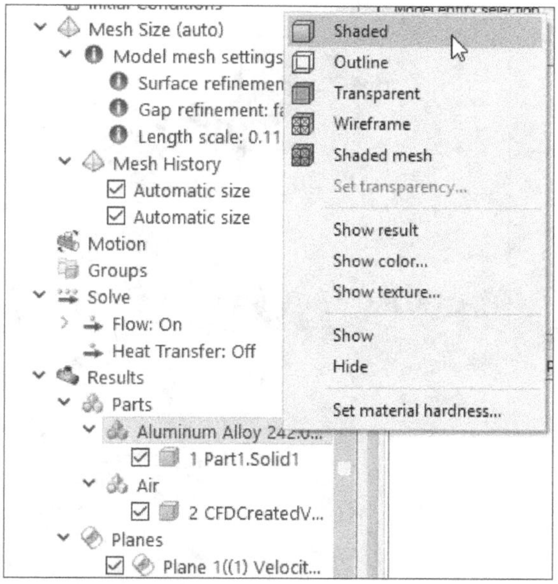

Figure-52. changing appearance

- Select the traces from **Results** and click on the **Down to Shaded Surface** button from **Projector Seeds** panel. The seeds will projected to the first shaded surface in line with negative yellow axis of triad; refer to Figure-53.

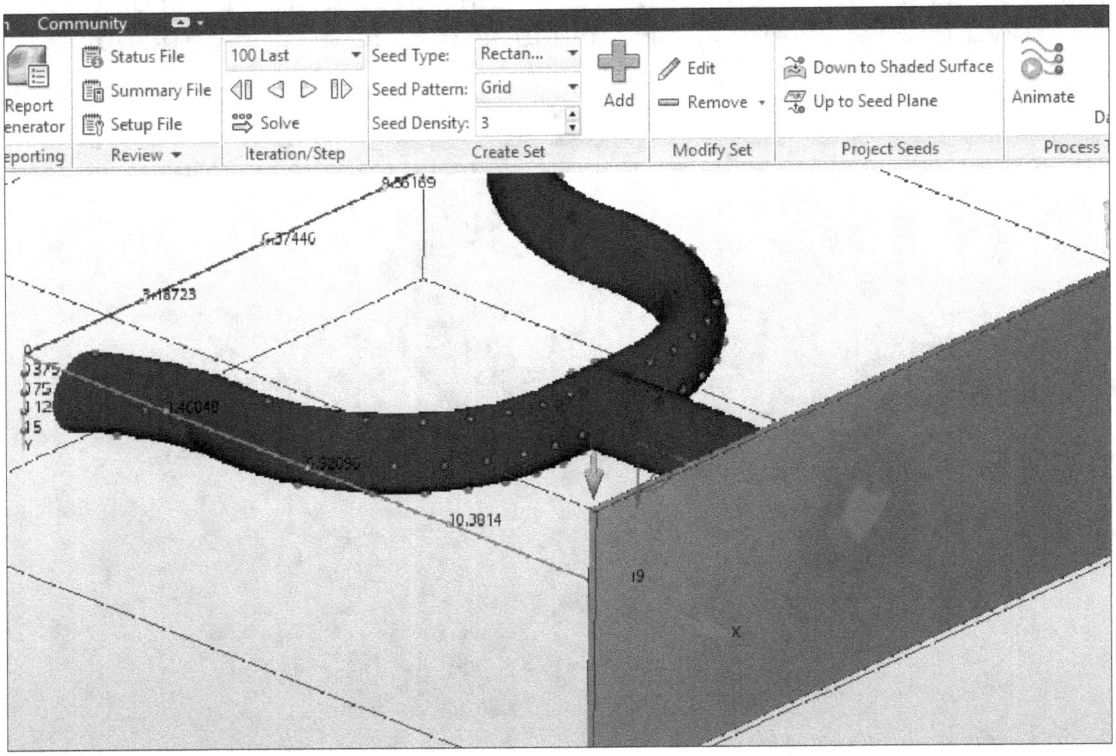

Figure-53. Seeds projected to surface

- To view the flow, drag the triad axis to a small distance away from model. The flow of traces will be displayed; refer to Figure-54. If no traces can be projected onto a surface, the trace distribution remains unchanged.

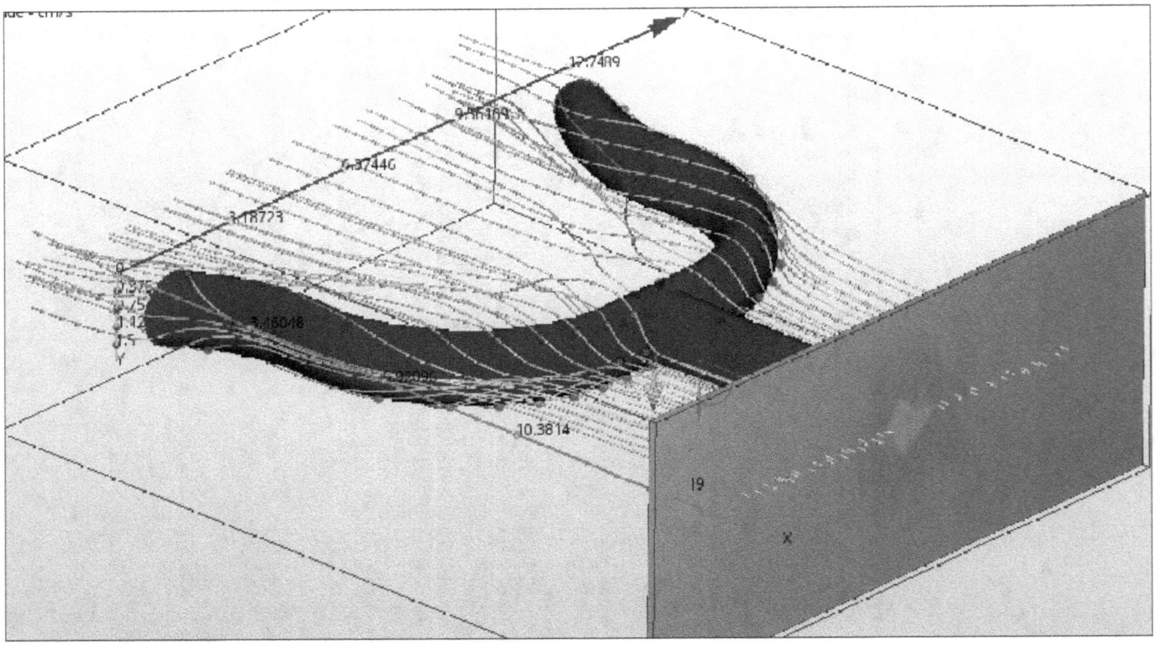

Figure-54. Flow as per traces

Up to Seed Plane

The **Up to Seed Plane** tool is used to project trace seeds that are distributed across a curved surface onto a plane. Click on **Up to Seed Plane** tool from **Project Seeds** panel, it moves the seed points to the plane defined by two blue axes in the triad; refer to Figure-55. This tool is used after applying the **Down to Shaded Surface** tool.

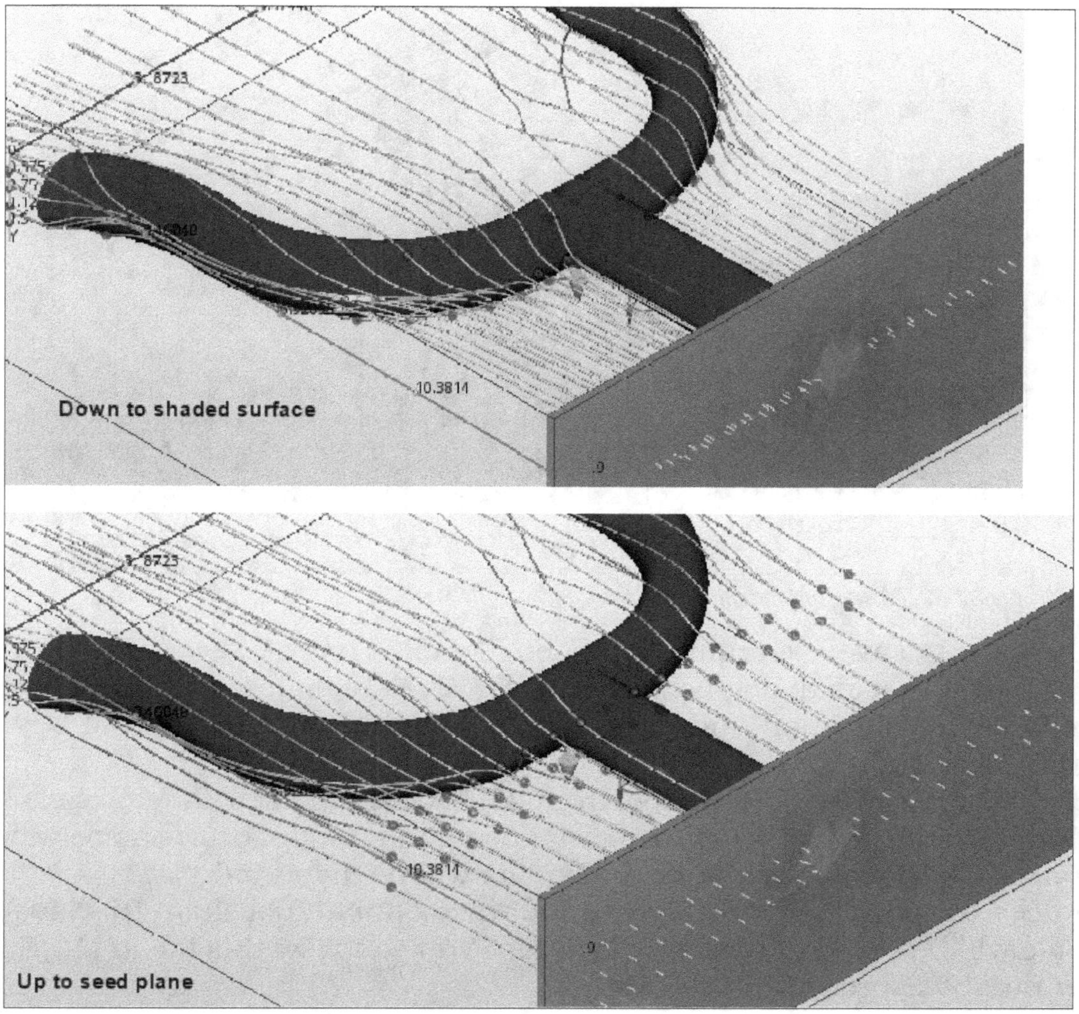

Figure-55. Before and after Up to seed plane tool

Process Traces panel

The tools in **Process Traces** panel are used to animate the traces and extract their data to external file. The **Process Traces** panel is generally used after applying traces to the model for analyzing the traces process by running their animation. The tools of this panel are discussed next.

- The **Animate** tool is used to view animation of existing traces. To do so, click on the **Animate** tool. The **Animate Traces** dialog box will be displayed; refer to Figure-56.

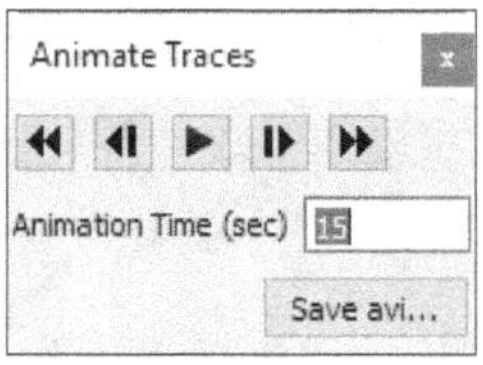

Figure-56. Animate Traces dialog box

- Click in the **Animation Time (sec)** edit box and specify desired value of duration up to which you want to play the animation of traces.
- The other tools in **Animate Traces** dialog box are common play & pause tools with which you are already familiar.
- After specifying duration of animation, click on the **Play** button. The animation will start playing; refer to Figure-57.

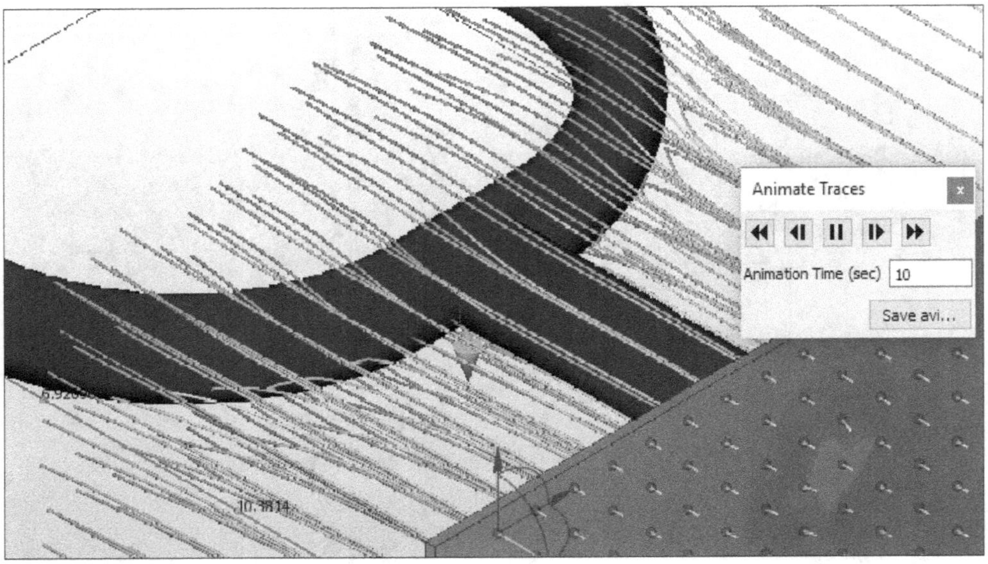

Figure-57. Playing animation

- If you want to save the animation video file, click on the **Save avi.** button from the **Animate Traces** dialog box. The **Save AVI File** dialog box will be displayed.
- Specify desired location and click on the **Save** button. The file will be saved in desired location.
- Click on the **Save Data Table** tool from the **Process Traces** panel to save the data of all traces from initial position to final position for all particles as per animation of traces. The **Save Trace Data** dialog box will be displayed.
- You need to specify location to save the trace data and click on the **Save** button. The file will be saved at specified location. You can view this file in MS Excel and other database processing software.

Iso Surfaces

The **Iso Surfaces** tool is a 3D visualization tool that shows values as well as physical shapes of flow characteristics. The physical shape of flow is useful for visualizing velocity distribution and thermal distribution in complicated flow paths of model. The **Iso Surfaces** tool is also used for determining the minimum and maximum values of quantities. An iso surface is a surface of constant value. The procedure to use this tool is discussed next.

- Click on the **Iso Surfaces** tool from the **Result Tasks** panel of the **Results** tab in the **Ribbon**. The **Iso Surfaces** panel will be displayed; refer to Figure-58.

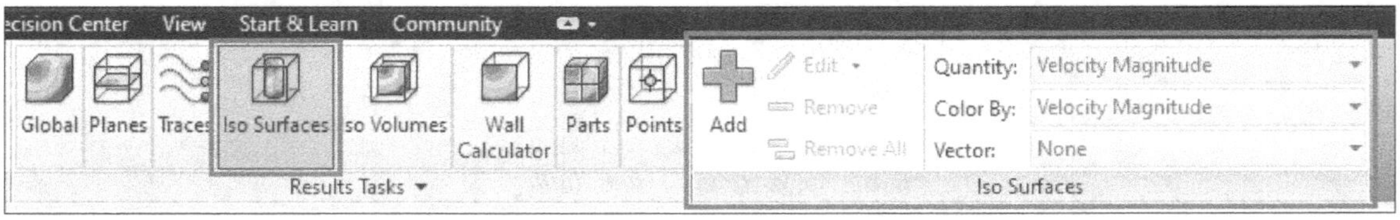

Figure-58. Iso surfaces tool and panel

- Click on the **Add** button from the **Iso Surfaces** panel. The iso surface will be added on model and in **Results** node of **Design Study Bar**; refer to Figure-59.

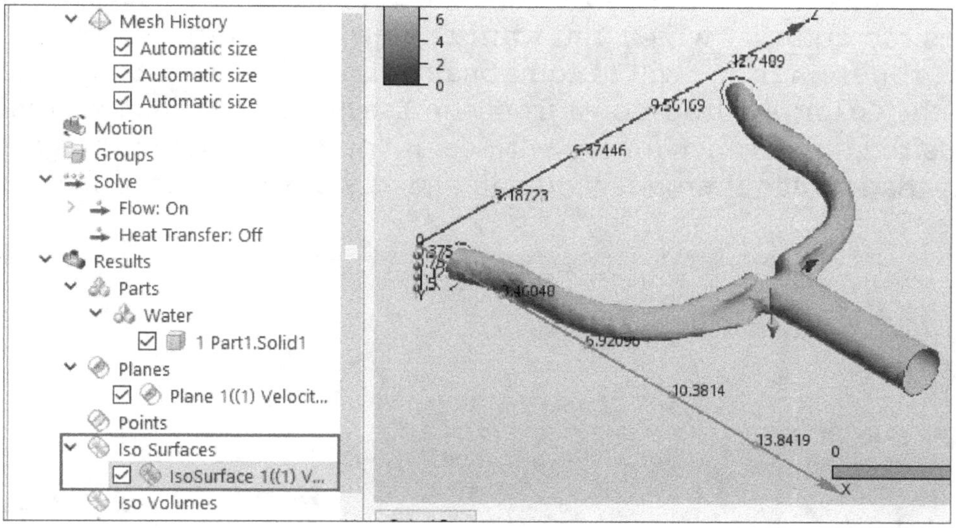

Figure-59. Iso surface

- Click on the **Edit** button from **Iso Surfaces** panel to edit quantity and appearance of the iso surface. The **Iso Surface Control** dialog box will be displayed; refer to Figure-60.

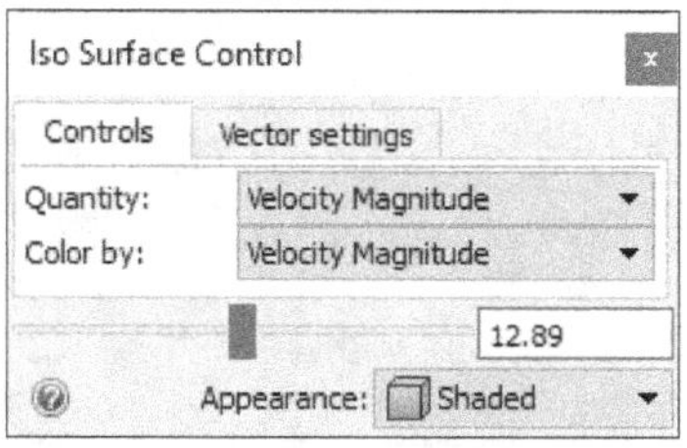

Figure-60. Iso Surface Control dialog box

- You can also open the **Iso Surface Control** dialog box by clicking on **Edit** button from the **Iso Surfaces** contextual toolbar; refer to Figure-61.

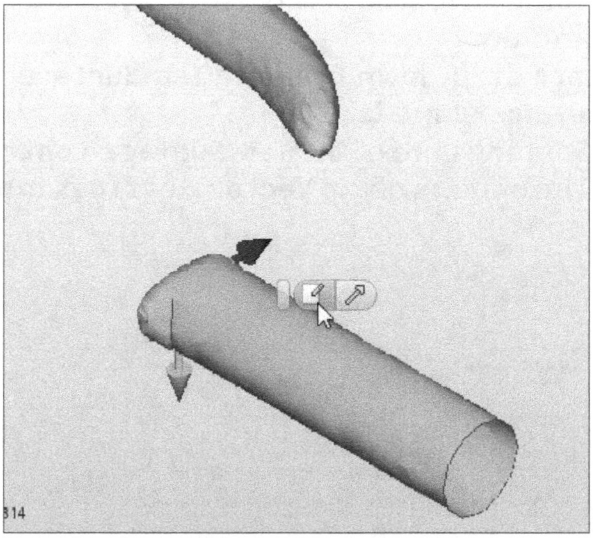
Figure-61. Right click menu of iso surface

- The **Quantity** option is the scalar result that determines the shape of iso surface, and **Color By** option determines the color. By default, these two options are same. If you want to see two different results together then you need to select different scalar results.

- Click in the **Quantity** drop-down from the **Iso Surface Control** dialog box and select desired quantity which you want to view in iso surface. As you change the quantity, the iso surface will automatically change as per selected quantity.
- Click in the **Color By** drop-down from the **Iso Surfaces Control** dialog box and select desired appearance for iso surface. If you select any parameter other than **Velocity Magnitude** then a legend will also displayed on graphics window; refer to Figure-62.

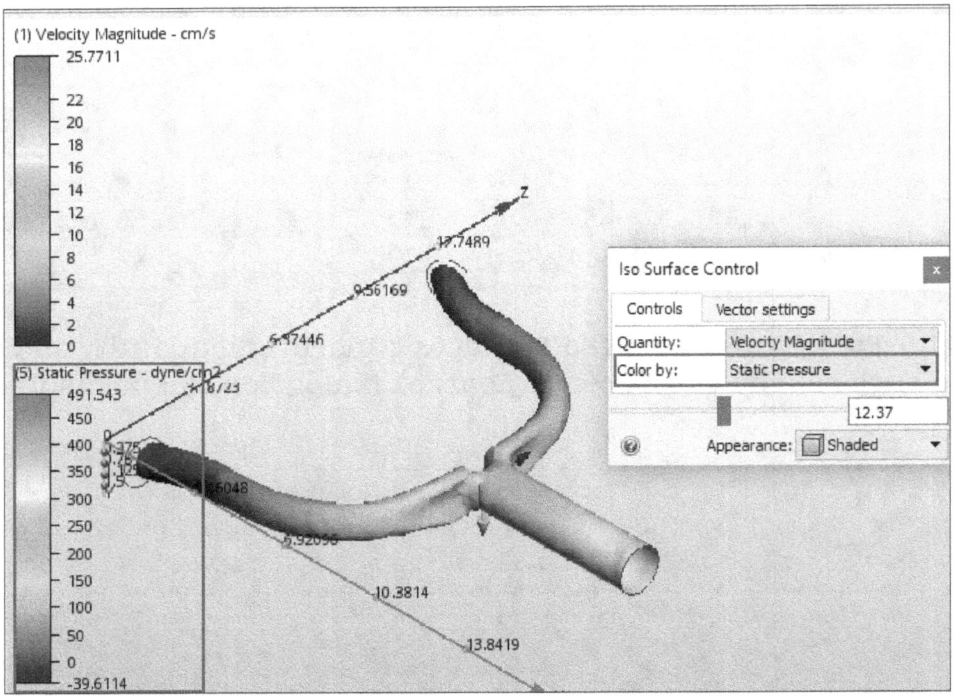

Figure-62. Changing color of iso surface

- The above figures shows the velocity magnitude at all location of model that have same static pressure.
- Move the slider to change the location of iso surface in the model. You can also specify the value manually.
- Click in the **Appearance** drop-down from the **Iso Surface Control** dialog box and select desired appearance of model.
- Click in the **Vector Settings** tab of the **Iso Surface Control** dialog box to change the vector settings. The options of the **Vector Settings** tab will be displayed; refer to Figure-63.

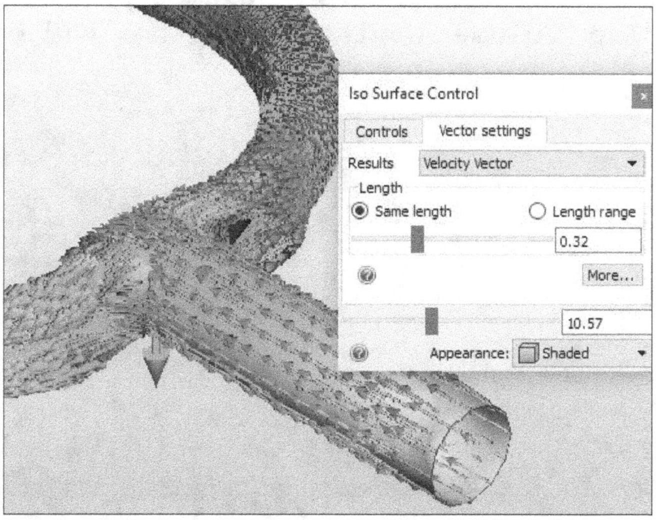

Figure-63. Vector Settings tab

- The options in this tab are same as discussed earlier.
- After specifying the parameters, close the **Iso Surface Control** dialog box. The applied changes will be reflected on the model.
- You can also do the same using **Quantity**, **Color By**, and **Vector** drop-downs in **Iso Surfaces** panel of **Result** tab; refer to Figure-64.

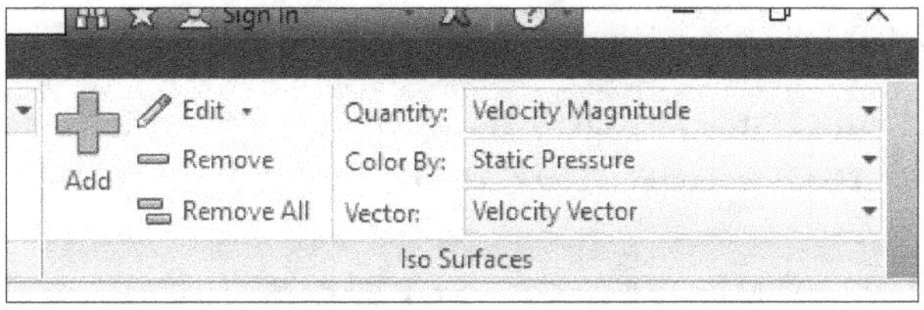

Figure-64. Tools of Iso Surfaces panel

- To remove a single iso surface or all iso surfaces, click on the **Remove** and **Remove All** button, respectively from the **Iso Surfaces** panel. The iso surfaces will be deleted.

Iso Volumes

The **Iso Volumes** tool is used to display result in the form of iso volume based on selected result parameters. Like, you can create an iso volume for velocity result so that you can check the change in velocity of fluid at different locations in the model. The procedure to use this tool is discussed next.

- Click on the **Iso Volumes** tool from **Results Tasks** panel of **Results** tab in the **Ribbon**. The tool will be activated and the **Iso Volumes** panel will be displayed; refer to Figure-65.

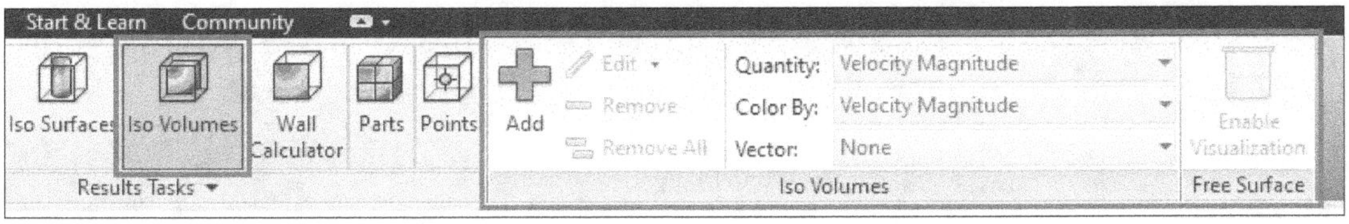

Figure-65. Iso Volumes tool and panel

- Most of the tools in **Iso Volumes** panel are disabled by default. To enable them, you need to add an iso volume by clicking on **Add** button. An iso volume will be displayed on model.

- Click on the **Edit** button from the **Iso Volumes** panel to edit the iso volume parameters. The **Iso Volume Control** dialog box will be displayed; refer to Figure-66.

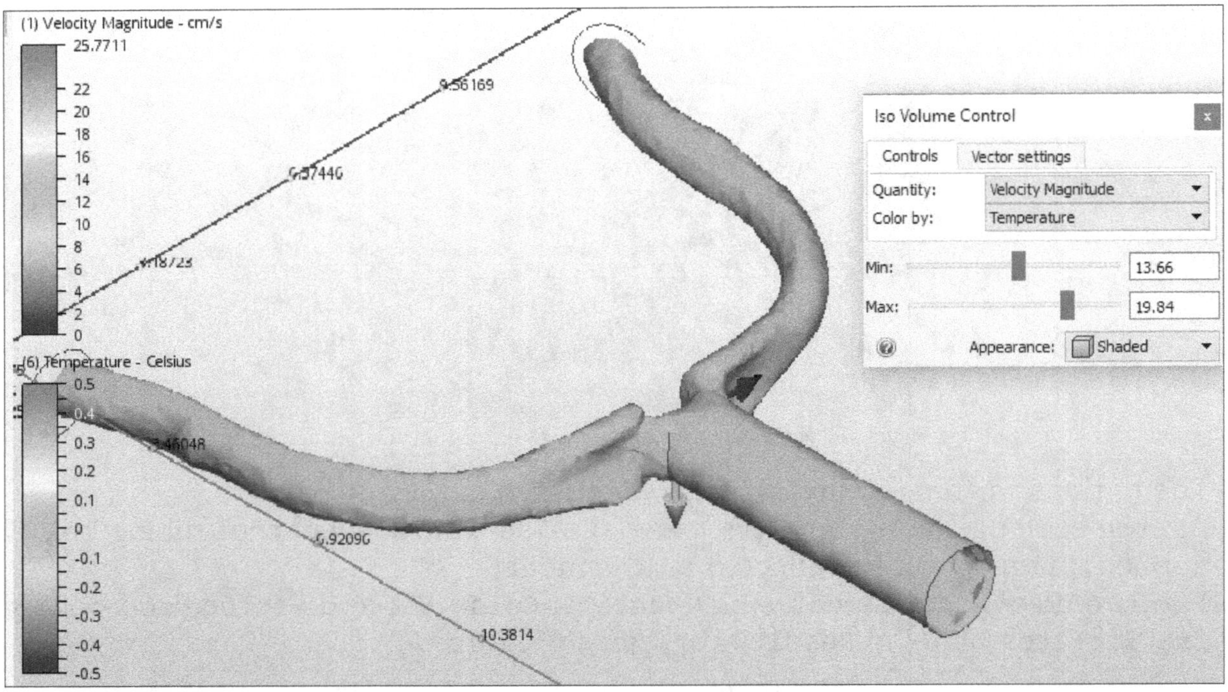

Figure-66. Iso Volume Control dialog box

- Set the **Minimum** and **Maximum** values by moving respective sliders. The iso volume as per specified minimum and maximum values of the result quantity will be displayed.
- Adjust the parameter of the **Vector Settings** tab in the **Iso Volume Control** dialog box as discussed earlier.
- After specifying the parameters, close the **Iso Volume Control** dialog box. The iso volume will be displayed as per specified parameters.
- The other tools is **Iso Volumes** panel are similar to **Iso Surfaces** panel, which was discussed earlier.

Wall Calculator

The **Wall Calculator** tool is used to calculate flow-induced forces on solid and wall surfaces. These forces are useful in many situations, like calculating the lift and drag on aerodynamics bodies. This tool can calculate pressure, wall temperature, heat flux, etc. The procedure to use this tool is discussed next.

- Click on the **Wall Calculator** button from the **Result Tasks** panel of the **Results** tab in the **Ribbon**. The **Wall Result** dialog box will be displayed; refer to Figure-67.

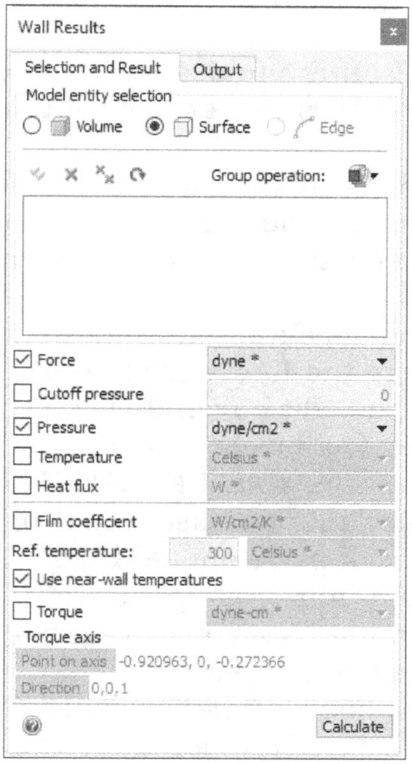

Figure-67. Wall Results dialog box

- Select the **Volume** or **Surface** radio button from the **Model entity selection** area to select entities of model for wall results.
- If you have selected **Volume** radio button then hover the mouse on model, the volume will be highlighted. Click to select highlighted model.
- If you have selected **Surface** radio button then hover the mouse on the model, the surfaces start to highlight. Click on the surface to assess wall results; refer to Figure-68.

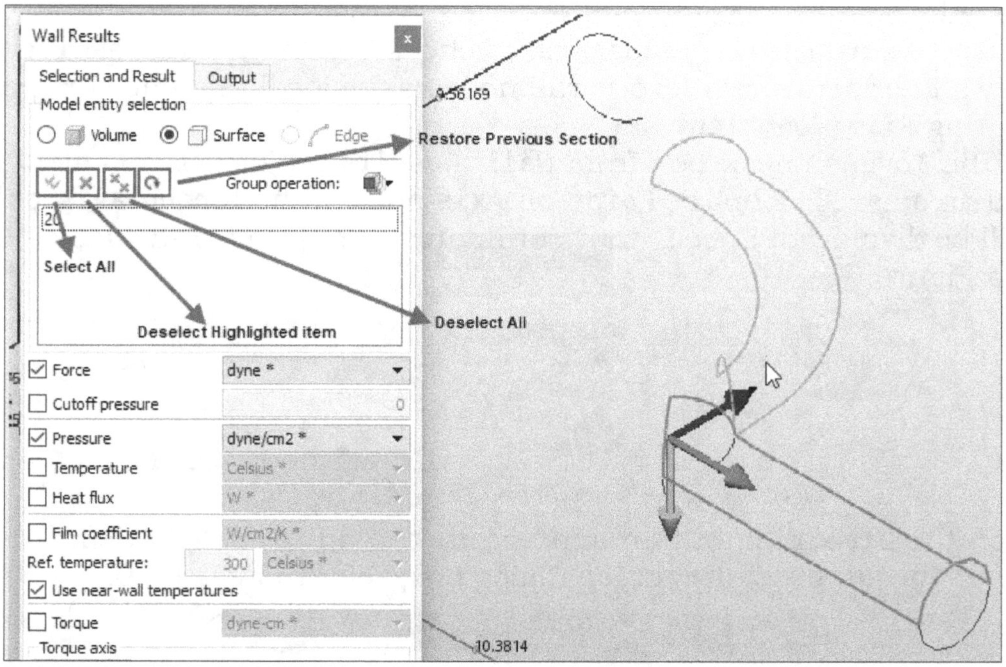

Figure-68. Selecting surfaces

- On selecting entities, the surfaces will be displayed in the **Wall Results** dialog box.
- Click on the **Select All** button to select all the surfaces/volumes present in model.

- Click on the **Deselect Highlighted Items** button to deselect the highlighted surface/volume.
- Click on the **Deselect All** button to deselect all the selected surface/volume.
- Click on the **Restore Previous Selection** button to restore the last deleted selection.
- Select the **Force** check box from **Wall Results** dialog box to calculate the force. Force components and magnitude are computed for each selected surface and the total force for all selected surfaces is also computed. Select the desired unit for force from the unit drop-down.
- Select the **Cutoff Pressure** check box from **Wall Results** dialog box to remove very low wall pressure from the force calculation. The **Cutoff pressure** edit box will be activated. Click in the edit box and specify the minimum pressure value. This value will be assigned to all locations with pressures.
- Select the **Pressure** check box from **Wall Results** dialog box to display the pressure for wall results. Specify the unit of pressure in drop-down next to the check box.
- Select the **Temperature** check box from **Wall Results** dialog box to display unit on wall surface. Specify the unit of temperature in drop-down next to the check box. Temperature values on walls are not available during the analysis. They are computed after the analysis is completed.
- Select the **Heat Flux** check box from **Wall Results** dialog box to display heat flux in wall results. **Heat Flux** is based on thermal residual from heat transfer solution. The value of heat flux is not accessible from intermediate saved iterations or time steps on the **Wall Result** dialog box.
- Select the **Film Coefficient** check box from **Wall Results** dialog box if you want to calculate film coefficient on wall.
- Click in the **Ref. temperature** edit box and specify desired reference temperature value to calculate film coefficient which is based on heat flux and temperature difference between the specified reference temperature and wall temperature. Note that this edit box is not available if **Use near-wall temperatures** check box is stopped.
- Select the **Use near-wall temperatures** check box from **Wall Results** dialog box to use wall temperature at every wall node as the local reference temperature for calculating **Film Coefficient**.
- Select the **Torque** check box from **Wall Results** dialog box to calculate torque around an axis. Click on the **Point on Axis** button, the **Torque axis point** dialog box will be displayed. Specify the coordinates as required and click on **OK** button; refer to Figure-69.

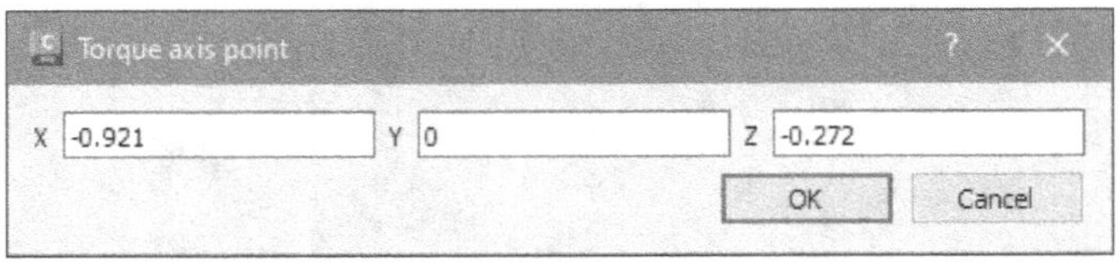

Figure-69. Torque axis point dialog Box

- Click on the **Direction** button and specify the unit vector to define direction of torque in **Torque axis direction** dialog box; refer to Figure-70.

Figure-70. Torque axis direction dialog box

- After specifying the parameters in **Wall Result** dialog box, click on the **Calculate** button to calculate the wall results. The result of all selected surfaces will be displayed in **Output** tab; refer to Figure-71.

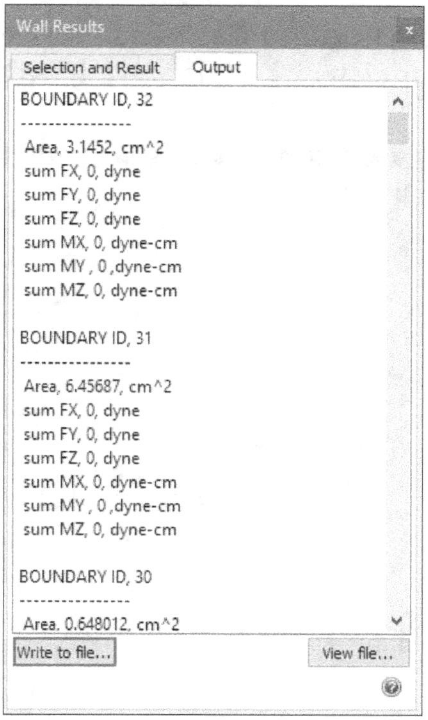

Figure-71. Output tab of Wall Results dialog box

- Click on the **Write to file** button from **Wall Results** dialog box to save this data to an excel .CSV file. The **Save Wall Data** dialog box will be displayed; refer to Figure-72. Specify the desired location and click on the **Save** button. The file will be saved at specified location.

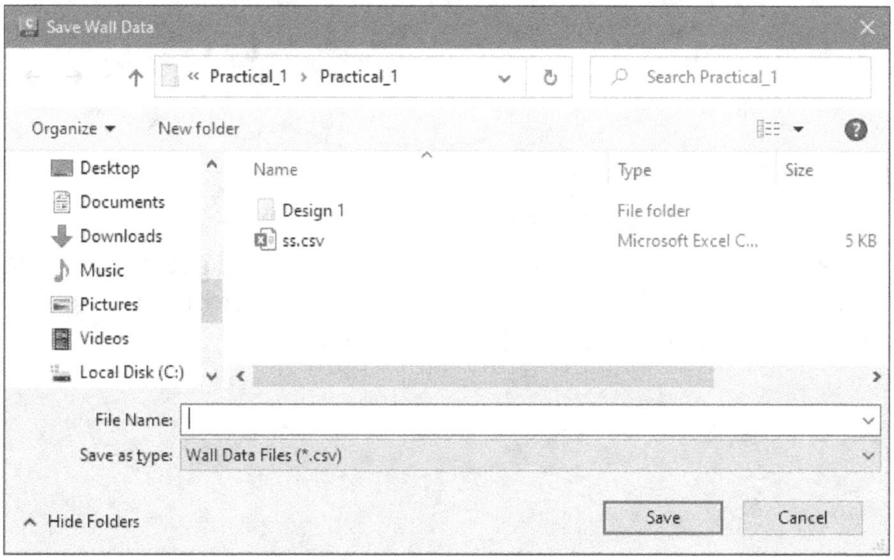

Figure-72. Save Wall Data dialog box

- Click on the **View File** button from **Wall Results** dialog box to open an existing .CSV file. The data of selected file will be displayed in **Output** tab.
- Click on **Close** button at the top right corner of dialog box to close the **Wall Results** dialog box.

Parts

The **Parts** tool is used to assess results on selected parts. The procedure to use this tool is discussed next.

- Click on the **Parts** tool from **Results Tasks** panel of **Result** tab; refer to Figure-73. The **Parts** contextual panel will be displayed with **Parts** dialog box; refer to Figure-74.

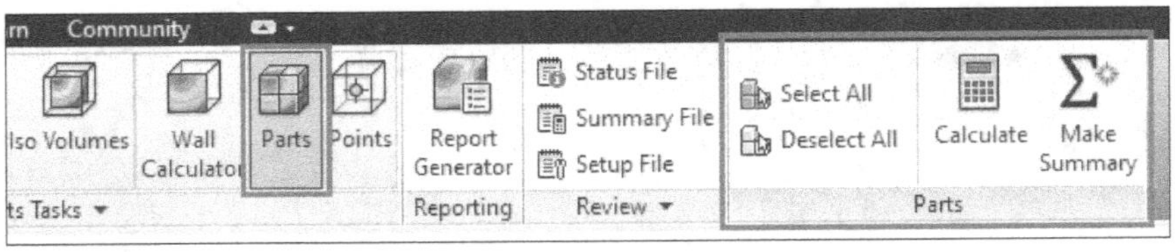

Figure-73. Parts panel

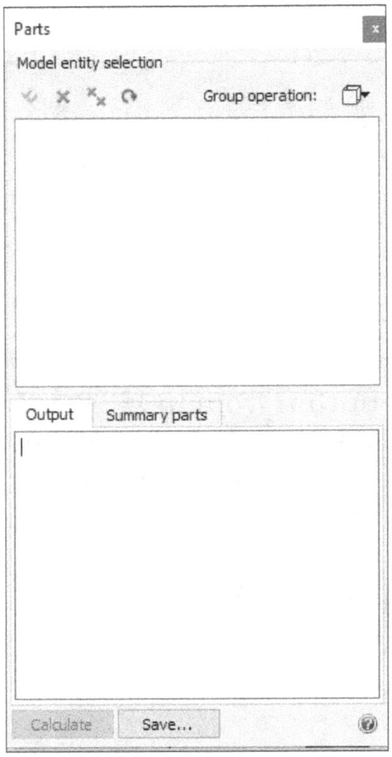

Figure-74. Parts dialog box

- To compare parts, you need to click on the parts from graphics area, the selected part will displayed in **Parts** dialog box and the boundaries of selected parts will be highlighted in pink color; refer to Figure-75.

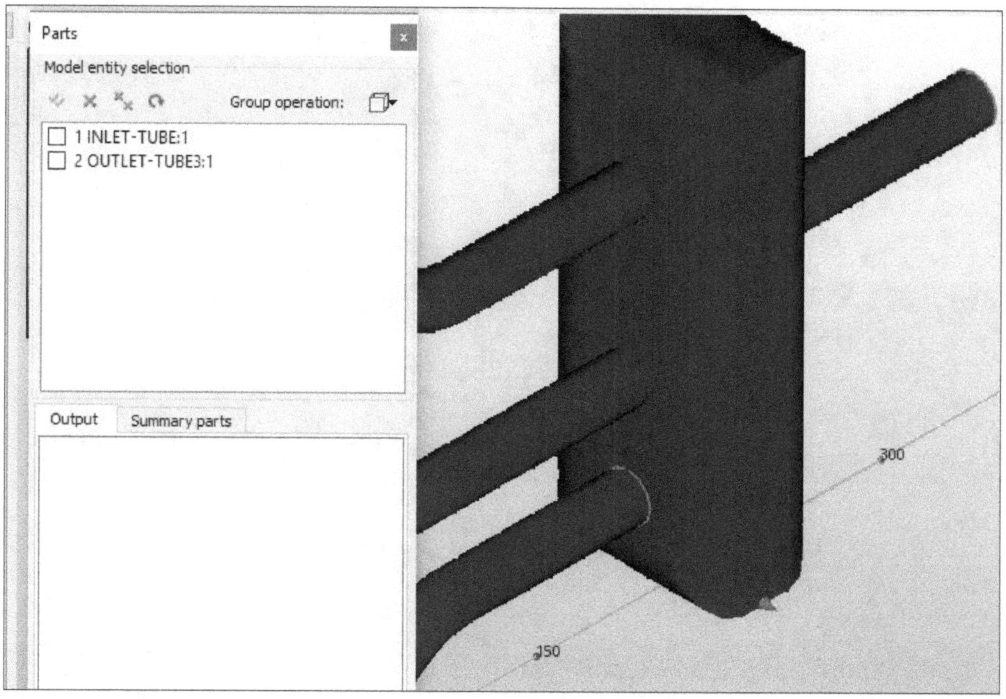

Figure-75. Selected parts

- Select the check box of components from **Parts** dialog box to select or deselect the parts for comparison.
- Click on the **Calculate** button from **Parts** dialog box. The results will be displayed in **Output** tab; refer to Figure-76.

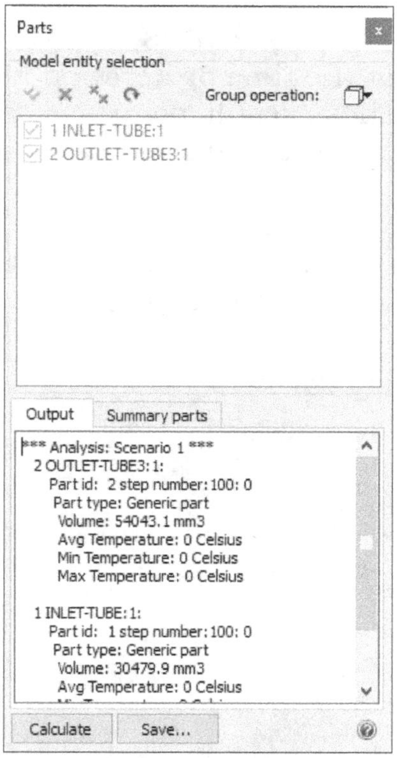

Figure-76. Calculated results of parts

- Click on the **Make Summary** button from **Parts** panel to designate a part as a summary part.
- Click on the **Summary Parts** tab of **Parts** dialog box to view the list of summary parts; refer to Figure-77.

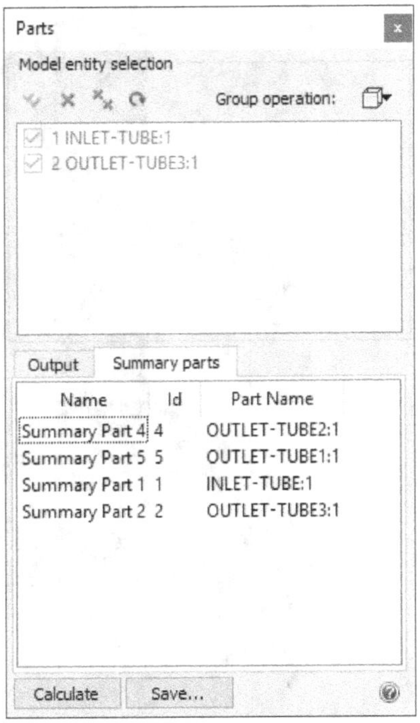

Figure-77. Summary Parts tab

- Click on the **Save** button from **Parts** dialog box to save the summary part data. The **Save Summary Part Data** dialog box will be displayed. Specify desired location to save the file and click on the **Save** button. The data will be saved in .TXT format file.

Points

The **Points** tool is used to plot the time or iteration history at a specific location in model using Result Points. These result points act as summary points to assess critical values and to compare result with other scenarios. The procedure to use this tool is discussed next.

Before starting this tool, you need to specify a result save interval in **Solve** dialog box; refer to Figure-78. This cause the software to save intermediate time steps throughout the calculation. You may need to run the analysis again.

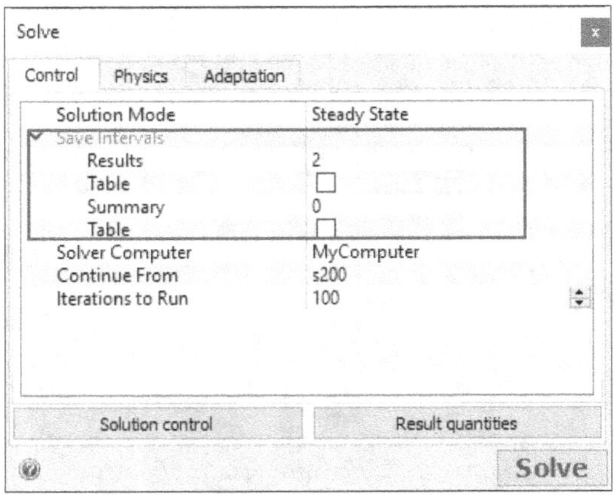

Figure-78. Save Intervals form

- Click on the **Points** tool from the **Results Tasks** panel of **Results** tab. The **Points** dialog box will be displayed; refer to Figure-79.

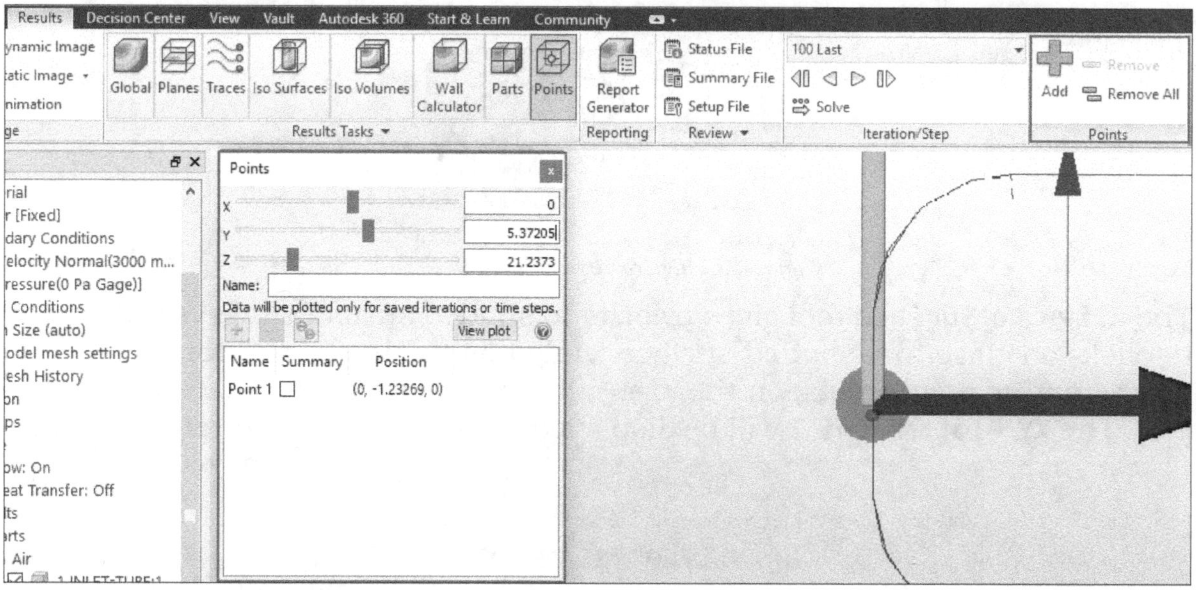

Figure-79. Points dialog box and Points panel

- Move the **X**, **Y**, and **Z** slider to specify location of point. You can also specify point by moving triad axis. If you want to manually specify the coordinates for result point then click in the **X**, **Y**, and **Z** axis edit boxes and specify respective value.
- After specifying the location of point, click on the **Add** button from **Points** dialog box, **Points** panel, or left-click contextual menu; refer to Figure-80. The coordinates of points will be displayed in **Points** dialog box; refer to Figure-81.

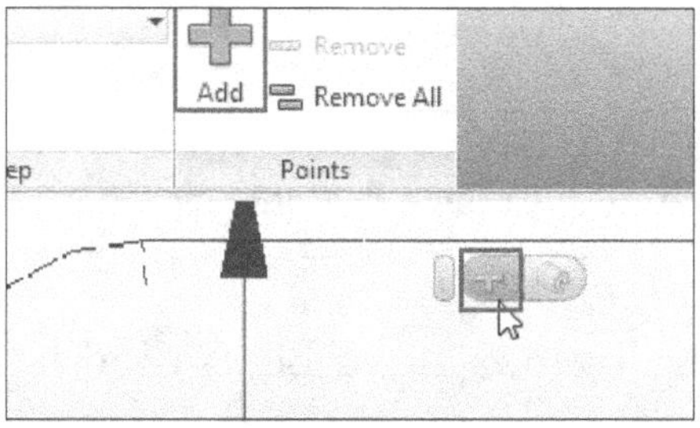

Figure-80. Add button

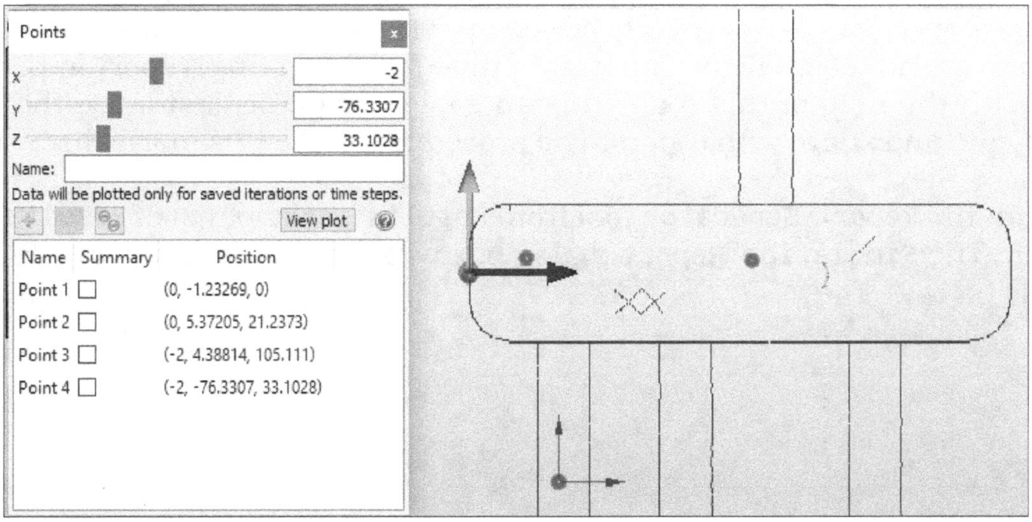

Figure-81. Added points

- If you want to create a point on geometry surface, then left-click on the model surface and select the **Align to Surface** button. This tool will be activated; refer to Figure-82. Click on the surface again to place the point.

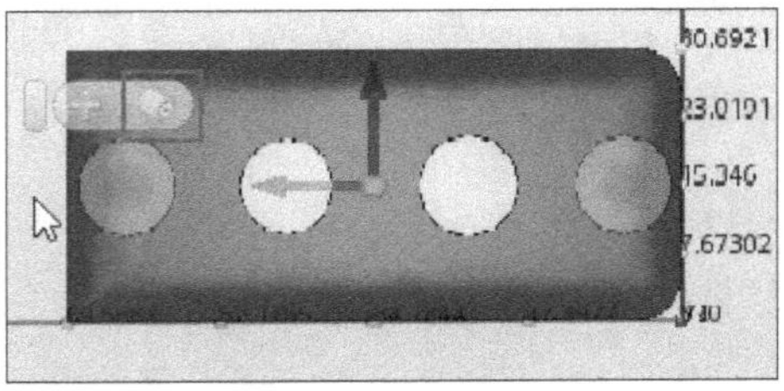

Figure-82. Align to surface button

- The **Align to Surface** tool gives priority to shaded surface. Always remember not to click too close to a shaded surface while positioning a monitor point.
- After creating points, click on the **View plot** button from **Points** dialog box to view plot. The **XY Plot: Point 2** will be displayed along with the plot; refer to Figure-83.

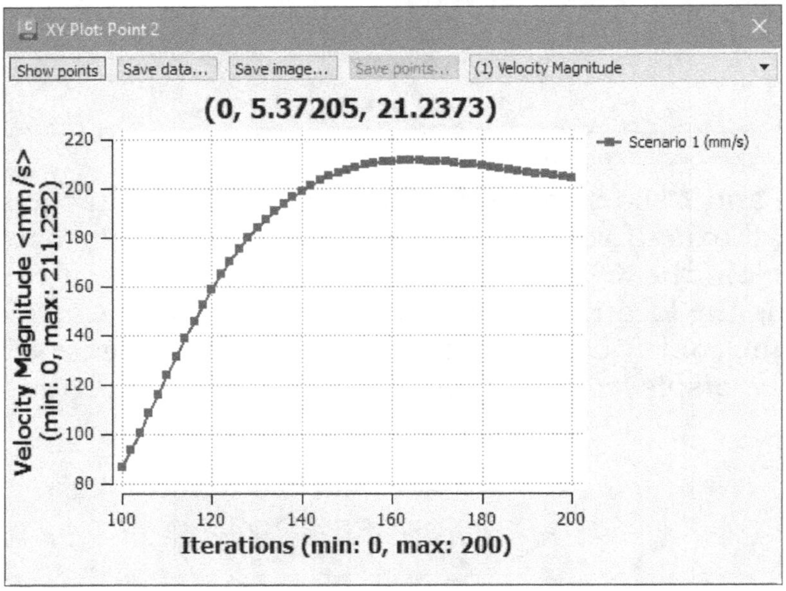

Figure-83. XY Plot : Point 2 dialog box

- The options of **XY Plot** dialog box have been discussed earlier.

Report Generator

The **Report Generator** tool is used to create final report of your simulation. Generally, you need to spend a significant amount of time for generating report in presentable format. With the help of this tool, you can easily create or customize the report to communicate and share with others. The procedure to use this tool is discussed next.

- Click on the **Report Generator** tool from **Results Tasks** panel of **Result** tab in the **Ribbon**. The **Simulation Report** dialog box will be displayed; refer to Figure-84.

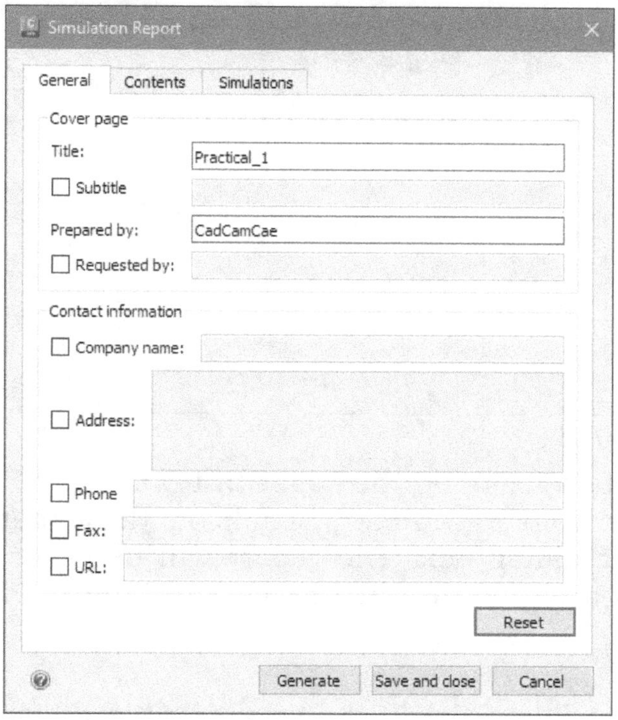

Figure-84. Simulation Report dialog box

- The options in **General** tab of the **Report Generator** dialog box are used to define information related to cover page of report and contact information of designing company. Select desired check boxes from this tab and specify related text information in respective fields.
- The options in the **Contents** tab are used to select the components of report to be generated; refer to Figure-85.

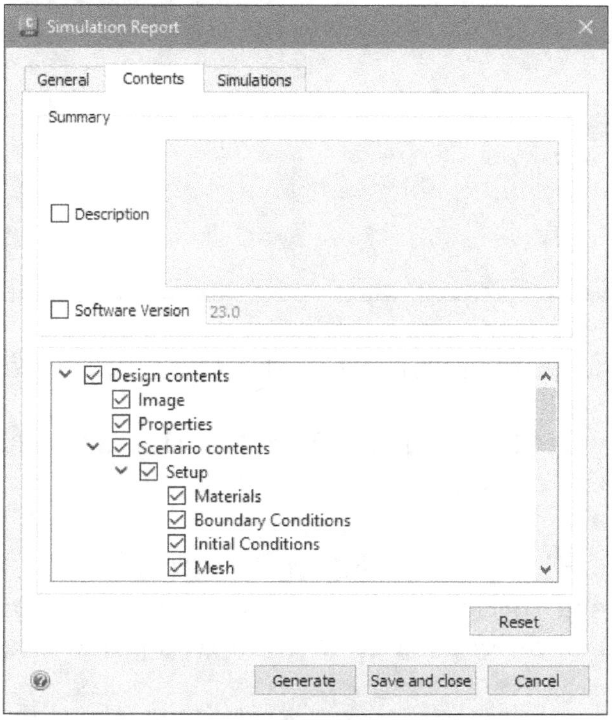

Figure-85. Contents tab of Simulation Report dialog box

- The options in the **Simulations** tab are used to define which designs and scenarios are to be included in your report; refer to Figure-86.

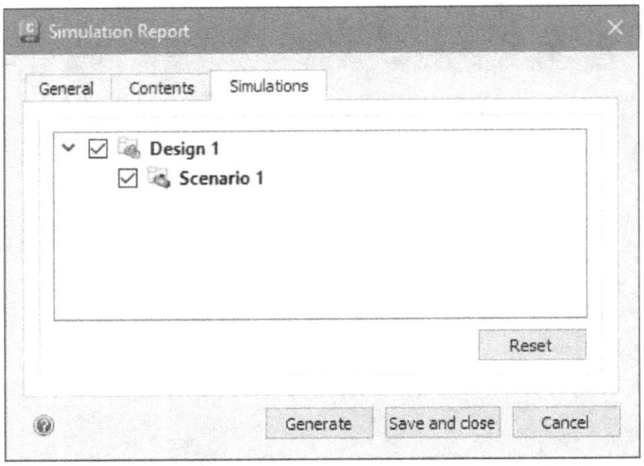

Figure-86. Simulations tab

- To reset specified data, click on the **Reset** button.
- After specifying desired parameters, click on the **Generate** button from the **Simulation Report** dialog box. The report will be generated and displayed in Microsoft word or other default word processor; refer to Figure-87.

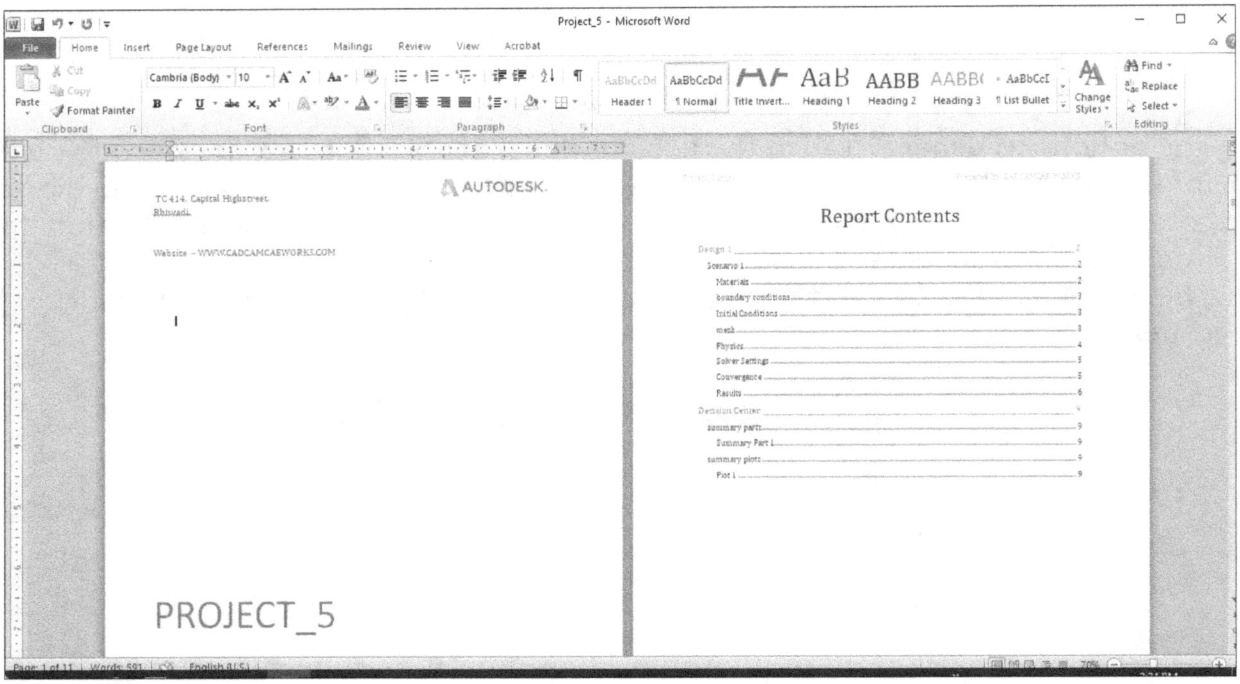

Figure-87. Generated report

- Save the file at desired location using the Save tool in default word processor application.
- Click on the **Save and Close** button from **Simulation Report** dialog box to save the data and close the dialog box.

Review Panel

The **Review** panel is used to view several information files produced during and at the end of the simulation process. The tools of this panel are discussed next.

Status File

- Click on the **Status File** button from **Review** panel to view information related to trouble shooting of an error occurred during analysis. The **Status** dialog box will be displayed; refer to Figure-88.

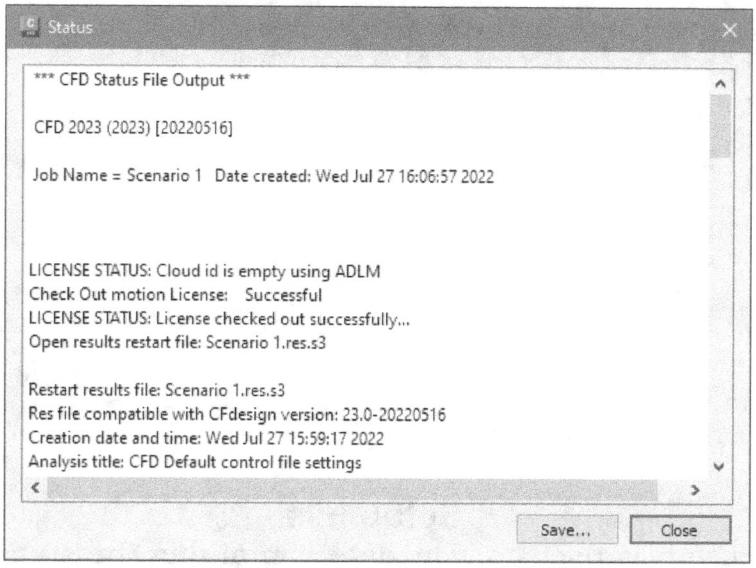

Figure-88. Status dialog box

- The convergence data in each degree of freedom is reported numerically for every iteration in status file. This data is useful for tracking convergence progress and complement the data displayed in the Convergence Plot.
- Click on the **Save** button if you want to save the data in a file. Click on the **Close** button to exit the dialog box.

Summary File

The **Summary File** button is used to view summary of various result and analysis parameters, like Tabulated minimum, maximum, and average nodal values for computed field variables like bulk pressure, temperature, wall heat transfer, and summary of fluid-induced forces.

- Click on the **Summary File** button from the **Review** panel in **Results** tab of **Ribbon**. The **Summary** dialog box will be displayed containing summary data; refer to Figure-89. Save the file as desired using the **Save** button in the dialog box.
- Click on the **Close** button to exit the dialog box.

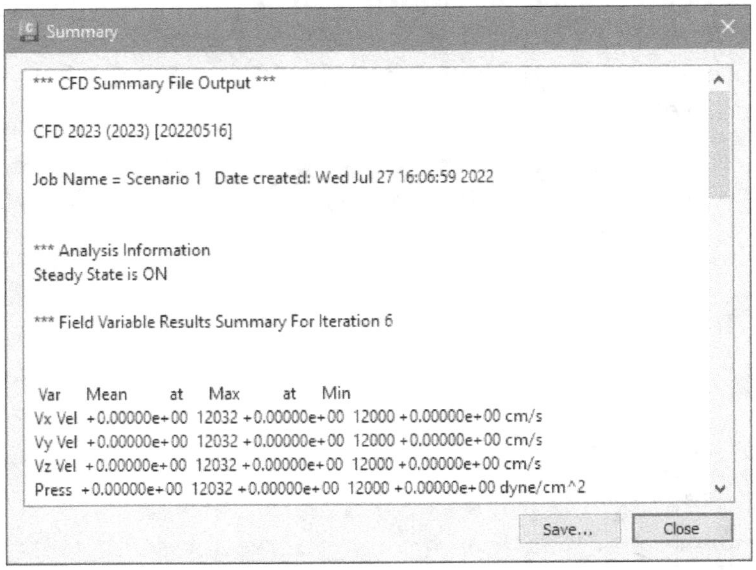

Figure-89. Summary dialog box

Setup File

The **Setup File** button is used to view data containing the summary of boundary conditions, materials, and solver options. The data of setup file is automatically saved at the conclusion of every simulation. The procedure to use this tool is discussed next.

- Click on the **Setup File** button from **Review** panel. The **Setup Parameters** dialog box will be displayed; refer to Figure-90. You can save the data in a file using the **Save** button.

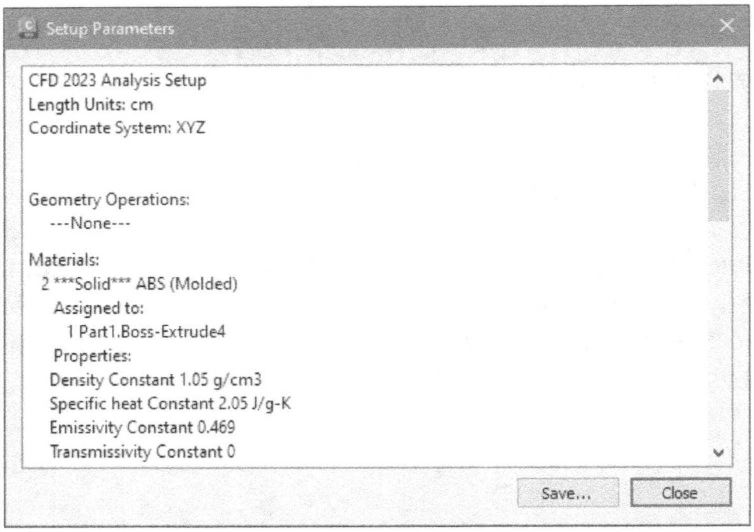

Figure-90. Setup Paramaters dialog box

Summary History File

The **Summary History File** is used to view the summary information. Every time when a simulation is stopped, the summary information of simulation is written to the summary file. This file can be used to view the history of summary information of each continuation of the simulation. Use Summary History File to understand the progression from one set of iterations to the next. The procedure to use this tool is discussed next.

- Click on the **Summary History File** button from **Review** panel drop-down; refer to Figure-91. The **Summary History** dialog box will be displayed; refer to Figure-92.

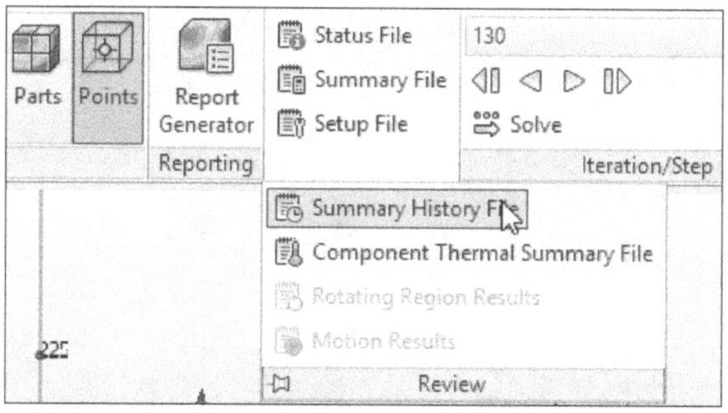

Figure-91. Summary History File button

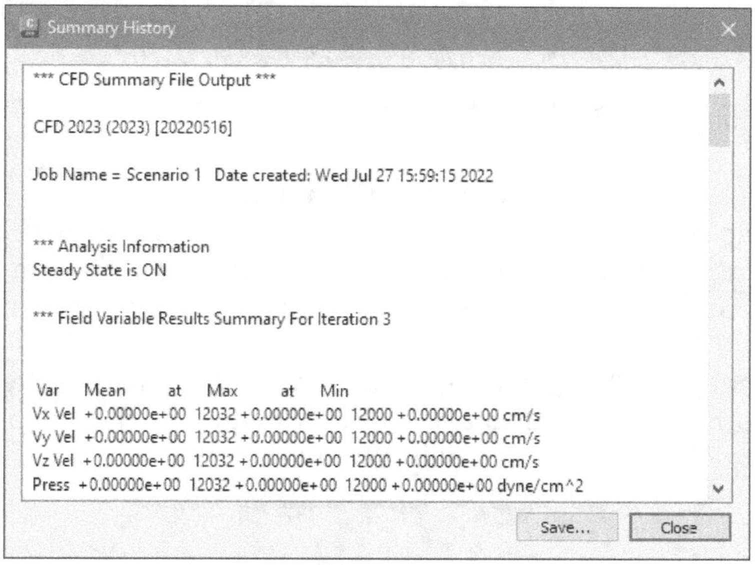

Figure-92. Summary History dialog box

- Save the file as discussed earlier, if needed.

Component Thermal Summary File

The **Component Thermal Summary File** button is used to view thermal summary file which contains the mean, maximum, and minimum temperatures for each solid part of model. This data is provided for each time step in a transient analysis. The component thermal summary file also contain temperature and heat flux data for compact thermal models and thermoelectric components. The procedure to use this is discussed next.

- Click on the **Component Thermal Summary File** tool from expanded **Review** panel in the **Results** tab of **Ribbon**. The **Component Thermal Summary** dialog box will be displayed; refer to Figure-93.

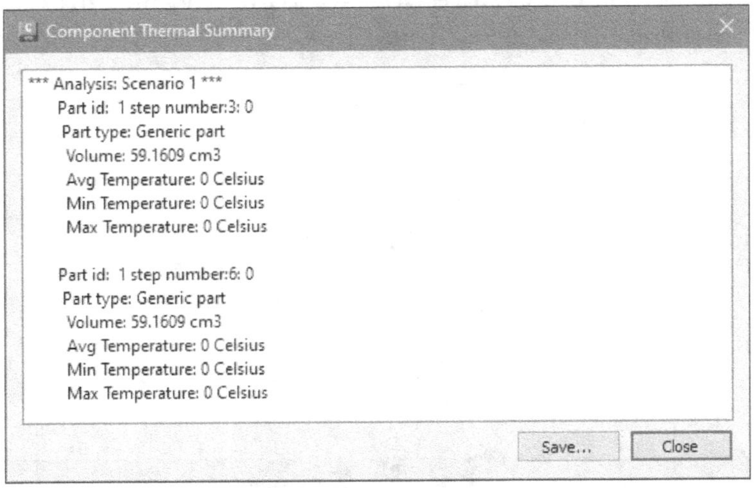

Figure-93. Component Thermal Summary dialog box

- Save the data in a file as discussed earlier.

Iteration/Step

The **Iteration/Step** panel is used to view or animate the saved results set for scenario. Each time an iteration is stopped, the results from last iteration are automatically saved. The procedure to use options of this panel are discussed next.

- Click in the **Iteration/Step** drop-down from the **Iteration/Step** panel and select desired iteration whose results are to be checked in the graphics area; refer to Figure-94. The selected iteration will be displayed.

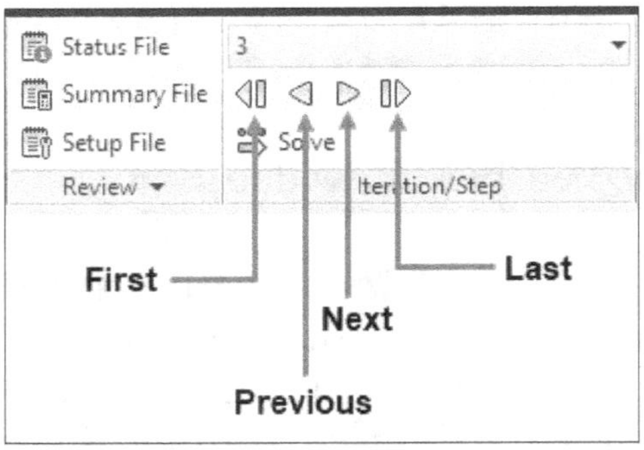

Figure-94. Iteration Step panel

- Note that by default, results from last saved iterations are displayed in graphics window. Using the **First**, **Previous**, **Next**, and **Last** buttons in the **Iteration/Step** panel, you can switch between various iterations.
- The procedure to use **Solve** tool has been discussed earlier.

Image Panel

The tools in the **Image** panel are used to create and share images of analyses for design collaboration and design comparison. The tools of this panel are discussed next.

Summary Image

The **Summary Image** tool is used to create snap of analysis in current orientation and visualization. With the help of this tool, you can compare results of different scenario using **Design Review Center** tool. This tool automatically compares the current configuration (orientation, result quantity, visualization features, etc.) with all selected scenario in the design study. The procedure to use this tool is discussed next.

- To compare summary images, you need to make separate analysis for the same model. Like, removing a outlet from the model or adding an inlet, etc. You can modify the model as per your requirement.
- After the first analysis, perform a result task like Global, planes, Iso surfaces, etc., and click on the **Summary Image** tool from the **Image** panel; refer to Figure-95. The snap will be captured and added in the **Summary images** of the **Decision Center** tab of **Ribbon**; refer to Figure-96.

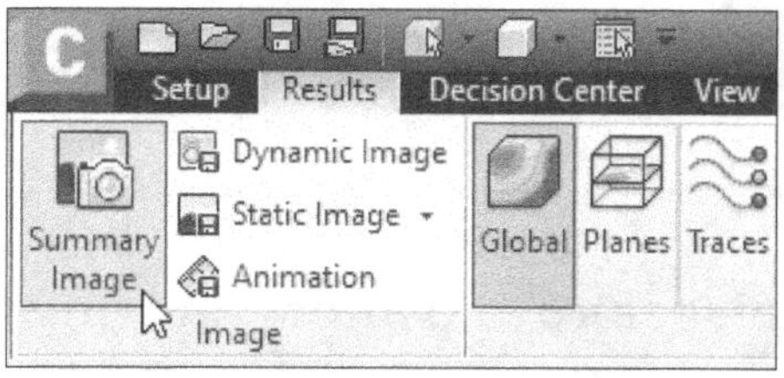

Figure-95. Summary Image button

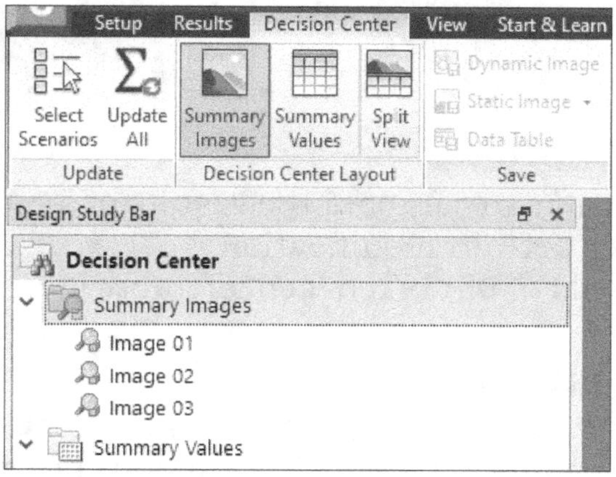

Figure-96. Decision Center tab

- The snap of current analysis will only be captured if you are at last iteration number. You can take as many snaps as you need for comparison. The snapped images will be stored in **Decision Center** tab. Added images will not be activated until you update the data.
- To update images, right-click on the **Summary Images** option from the **Design Study Bar** of when **Decision Center** tab is selected and select the **Update all images** option; refer to Figure-97. The images will be updated and displayed in the **Output Bar**; refer to Figure-98.

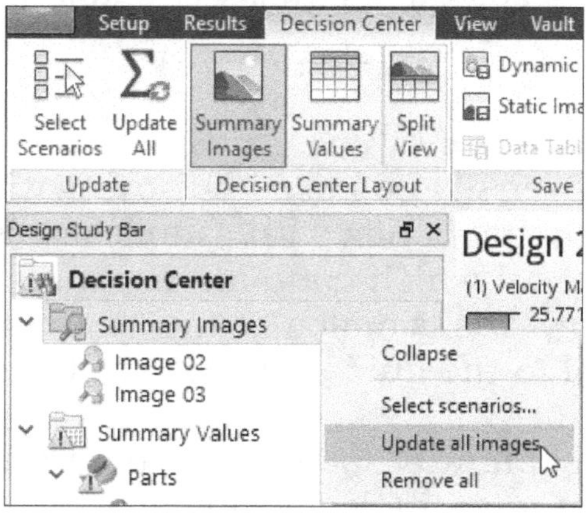

Figure-97. Updating images

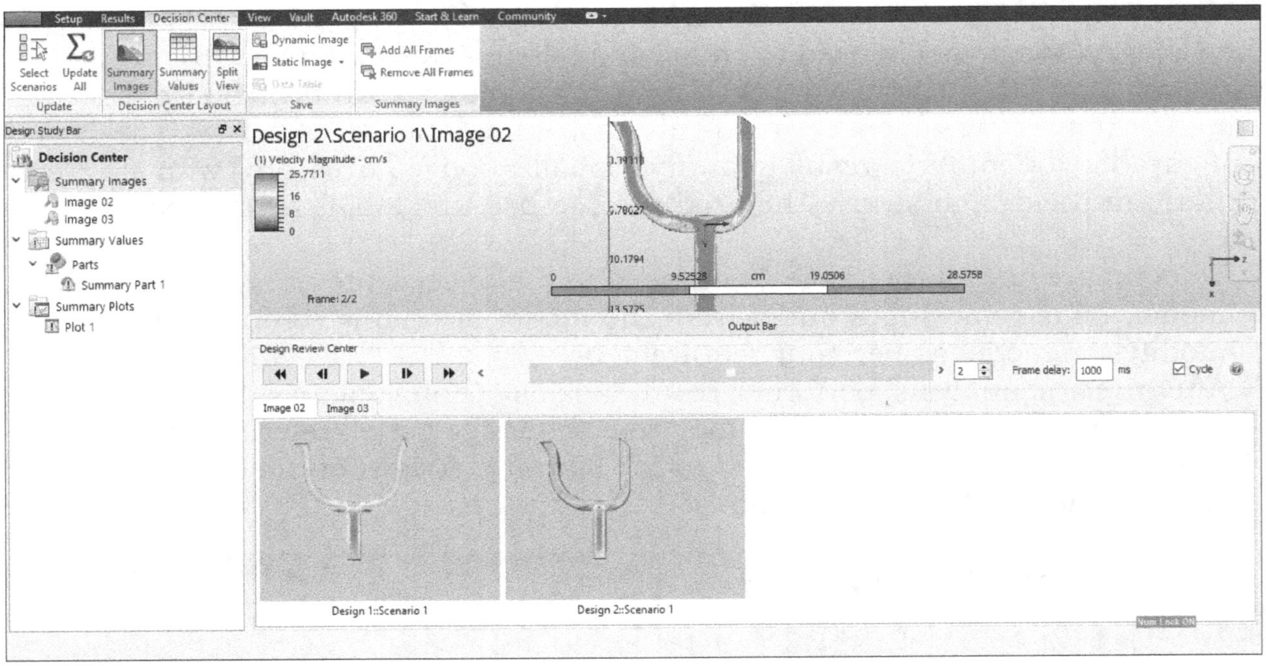

Figure-98. Comparing result

- Now, you can compare the results of a model, before and after changing the shape or after certain modification.
- The tools of **Decision Center** tab will be discussed in next chapter.

PRACTICAL

Let's create a custom quantity as **Kinetic Energy**. Kinetic energy is the energy of object when it is in motion. The kinetic energy can be easily determined by an equation using the mass and velocity of that object.

$$KE = 0.5 \times \rho v^2$$

$$m = mass\ of\ object$$

$$\rho = density\ of\ fluid$$

The standard unit of kinetic energy is joules (J), which is equivalent to

$$1\ kg * m^2/s^2$$

- Let us assume a fluid of density 20 kg/m^3 is moving with the velocity of 1.26 m/s. Determine the kinetic energy of box with Autodesk CFD.
- You need to create a model which contains moving fluid. Add **External Volume** with the help of **Geometry Tools** dialog box.
- Specify desired material to the fluid and surroundings.

Now, we will create result quantity for fluid to determine its kinetic energy. The procedure to create custom quantity is given next.

- Click on the **Custom Result Quantities** button from the **Global** panel of **Results** tab in the **Ribbon**. The **Custom Result Quantities** dialog box will be displayed; refer to Figure-99.

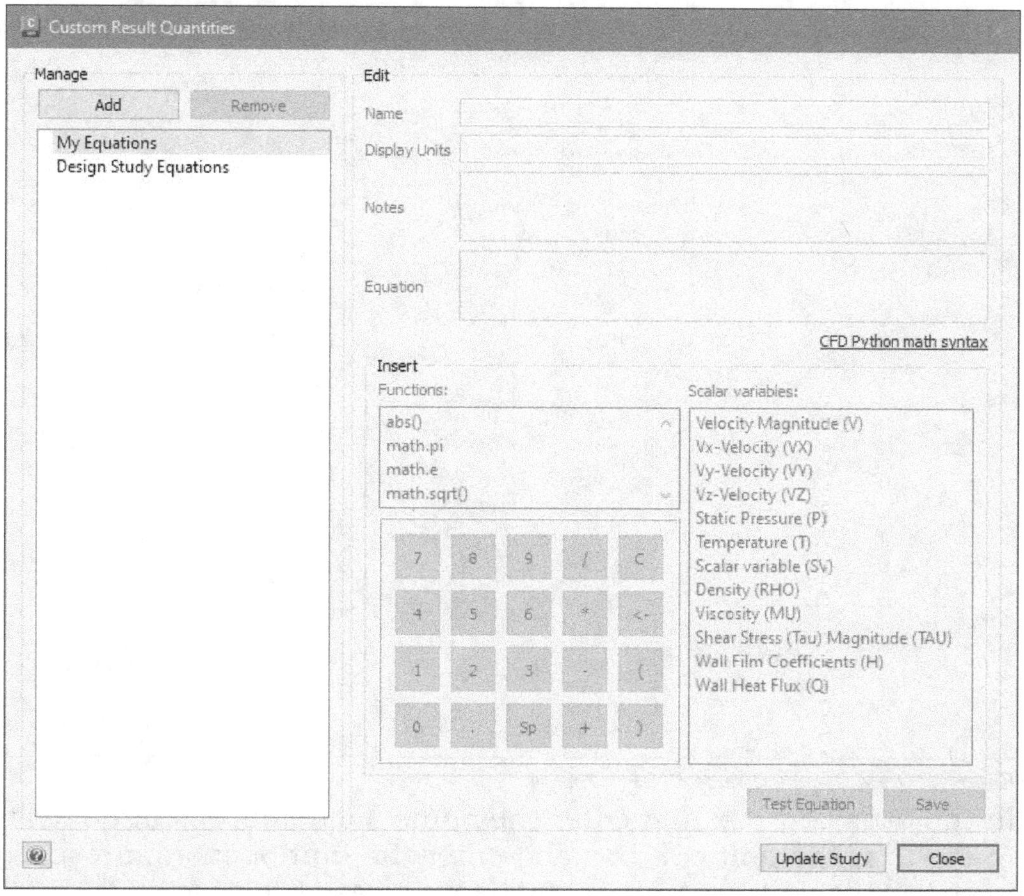

Figure-99. Custom Result Quantites dialog box

- Click on **Add** button to activate parameters for creating custom quantity and specify the data as displayed in Figure-100.

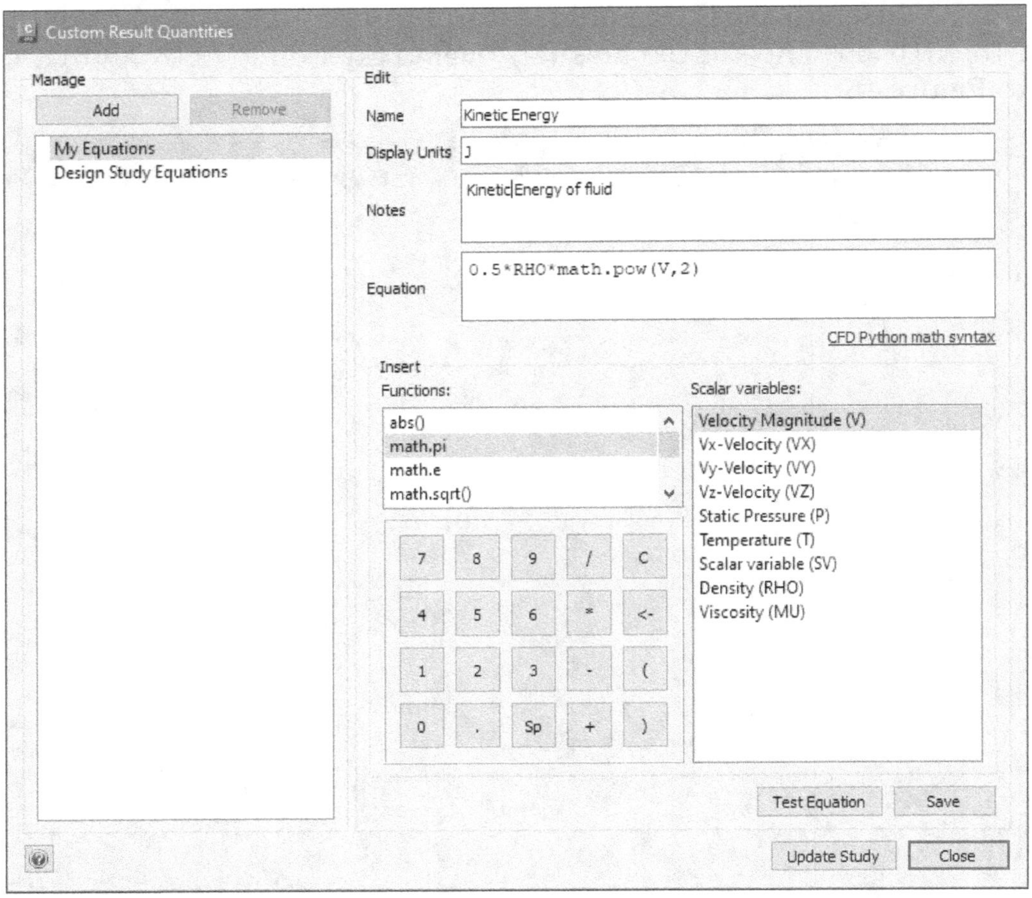

Figure-100. Added parameters for kinetic energy

- Click in the **Name** edit box and enter the name of custom result quantity.
- Click in the **Display** unit edit box and enter the unit of custom result quantity.
- Click in the **Notes** edit box and enter the notes as required.
- Click in the **Equation** edit box and enter the equation of quantity. For creating an quantity, you need to gather and understand the information of equation and its component. Like, what is velocity and its unit.
- To enter the variable in **Equation**, you need to double-click on the required variable from **Scalar** variables section.
- To apply math power, click on **Math.pow** button from **Functions** section and enter **(variable,variable unit)** inside brackets.
- After specifying the parameters, click on the **Test Equation** button from **Custom Result Quantities** dialog box. The **Custom Result Quantities - Test Equation** dialog box will be displayed; refer to Figure-101.

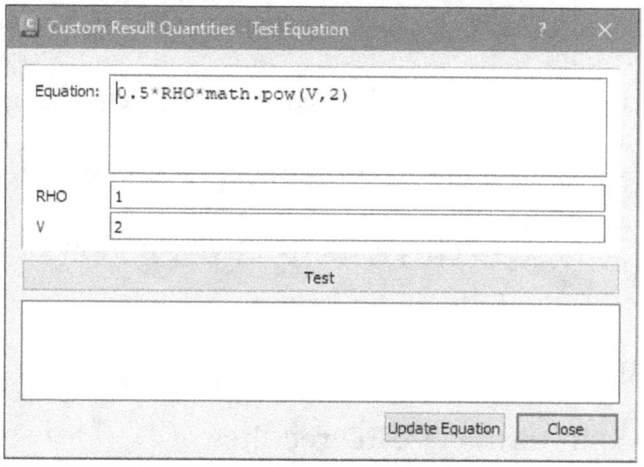

Figure-101. Custom Result Quantities Test Equation dialog box

- Click on the **Test** button, the feedback about equation will be displayed. Click on **Close** button to close the equation.
- Modify the data as per requirement and click on the **Save** button. The custom quantity will be added in the **Manage** section.
- Click on the **Update Study** button to update data and click on **Close** button. You will be returned to **Results** tab.
- Click in the **Global Results** drop-down to view recently created result quantity; refer to Figure-102.

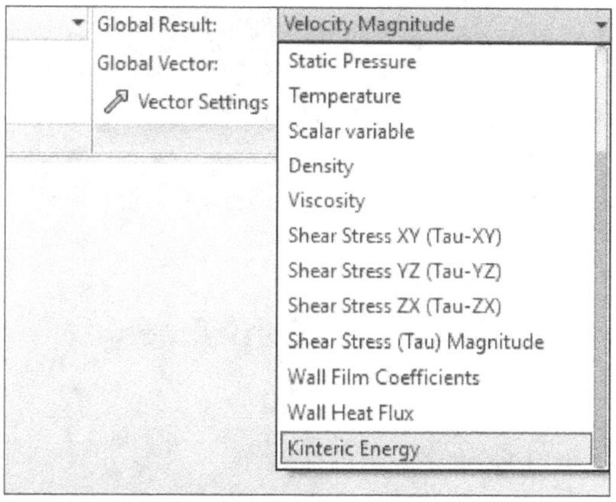

Figure-102. Kinetic Energy

- Now, you can use this result quantity in analysis of your model.

SELF ASSESSMENT

Q1. The .... tool is used to visualize 3D result data on specified planes.

Q2. The XY Plot is used to visualize 3D result data on specified planes. (T/F)

Q3. The .... tool is used to check the behavior of flow of fluid inside the model in CFD results.

Q4. What is Coefficient of restitution?

Q5. What is Iso surface in terms of CFD results?

Q6. What is the equation for Kinetic energy of a fluid?

Q7. The .... tool is used to control the display of results and vectors on model surfaces.

Q8. The **Custom Result Quantities** button is used to modify the results after performing analysis as per your requirement. (T/F)

Q9. The **Report Generator** tool is used to create graph of analysis result quantity. (T/F)

Q10. What is the use of **Summary File** button?

Q11. What does the Global tool allow users to control?

A. Size of canvas
B. Display of results and vectors on model surfaces
C. Simulation settings
D. Output tab parameters

Q12. Which option in the Vector Settings dialog box allows uniform vector lengths?

A. Filtering
B. Length Range
C. Same Length
D. Auto Scale

Q13. What is the maximum value you can set in the Length edit box?

A. 1.000
B. 0.999
C. 0.500
D. 1.500

Q14. What is the use of the Custom Result Quantities button?

A. To import data
B. To create and define custom result quantities
C. To view only default results
D. To edit vector lengths

Q15. Which action is used to test a custom equation in the Custom Result Quantities dialog box?

A. Click Save
B. Click Add
C. Click Test Equation
D. Click Apply

Q16. What does the Bulk Results dialog box calculate?

A. Pressure values
B. Surface velocity
C. Bulk-weighted results
D. Vector lengths

Q17. What file format is used when saving XY Plot points?

A. .bmp
B. .csv
C. .txt
D. .xyp

Q18. How can you change the background color of the XY Plot?

A. Using the Save dialog
B. By editing canvas
C. From right-click shortcut menu
D. Using the Global tool

Q19. Which feature allows you to specify a vector value range to be displayed?

A. Scale factor
B. Filtering
C. Arrowhead size
D. Background color

Q20. What is shown in the Output tab after clicking the Calculate button in the Bulk Results dialog box?

A. Raw image
B. Updated mesh
C. Bulk results
D. Custom parameters

Q21. What does the "Add by key-in" option in the XY Plot dialog box allow the user to do?

A. Add a title to the plot
B. Input data from a file
C. Add points by entering X, Y, and Z coordinates
D. Edit the plane direction

Q22. Where can you view the coordinates of a point while moving the cursor on the added plane?

A. Points list window
B. Edit tool
C. Status Bar
D. Plane Control dialog box

Q23. What is the default number of divisions between each point in the XY Plot?

A. 10
B. 15
C. 20
D. 25

Q24. What happens when you click the Points list button in the XY Plot dialog box?

A. Adds more points
B. Displays the coordinates of points
C. Removes all points
D. Saves the point data

Q25. Which button do you click to input data from a previously saved file in the XY Plot dialog box?

A. Add
B. Save
C. Browse
D. Plot

Q26. To make the plane perpendicular to the Y axis, what value should be entered in the Y edit box of the Edit plane normal dialog box?

A. 0
B. 1
C. -1
D. 10

Q27. What happens when the Grid spacing slider is moved toward the "Fine" option?

A. Grid lines become more widely spaced
B. The grid disappears
C. The spacing between grids decreases
D. Grid turns into a solid fill

Q28. What is the primary purpose of the Traces tool?

A. Create XY plots
B. Control lighting
C. Understand fluid flow behavior
D. Export result files

Q29. What is the function of the "Ring Type Traces"?

A. Create a square pattern of points
B. Add a flow boundary
C. Place points in a circular structure
D. Add points along a straight line

Q30. What is the limit range for Seed Density value in Circular Type Traces?

A. 1–5
B. 0–10
C. 5–20
D. 0–100

Q31. Which Seed Type option allows you to manually enter coordinates for traces?

A. Circular
B. Rectangular
C. Key in
D. Line

Q32. What does the Trace ID in the Edit Traces Set dialog box refer to?

A. A file path
B. Width of trace lines
C. Number of seed points
D. Color settings

Q33. What effect does checking the "Mass" checkbox have on the trace particles?

A. Changes their shape
B. Applies real-time physical behavior
C. Removes them
D. Makes them static

Q34. Which value of the Coefficient of restitution implies an inelastic collision?

A. 0.01
B. 0.5
C. 0.9
D. 1.0

Q35. What is the purpose of selecting the "Enable gravity for massed particles" option?

A. Display color
B. Control trace width
C. Apply body forces to particles
D. Activate seed density

Q36. What is the primary function of the tools in the Project Seeds panel?

A. To modify the physical shape of the model
B. To animate traces and extract data
C. To project traces onto desired surfaces or planes
D. To calculate forces on solid surfaces

Q37. When using Down to Shaded Surface, what mode must the model be in?

A. Wireframe
B. Transparent
C. Shaded
D. Hidden edges

Q38. What does the Up to Seed Plane tool require before being used?

A. Iso surface creation
B. Animation of traces
C. Application of Down to Shaded Surface
D. Wall result calculation

Q39. What dialog box is used to set animation duration for traces?

A. Save Trace Data dialog box
B. Animate Traces dialog box
C. Iso Surface Control dialog box
D. Wall Result dialog box

Q40. In which file format is the trace data saved for further analysis?

A. .TXT
B. .DOCX
C. .CSV
D. .AVI

Q41. What is the purpose of the Iso Surfaces tool?

A. To display model geometry
B. To calculate trace velocity
C. To visualize scalar flow quantities
D. To animate seed planes

Q42. What determines the shape of an iso surface?

A. Color By option
B. Model boundaries
C. Quantity option
D. Velocity vectors

Q43. What is shown when the Color By parameter is set to a non-default value in Iso Surfaces?

A. Flow direction
B. Model geometry
C. A legend in the graphics window
D. Seed plane

Q44. Which of the following actions allows you to move the location of an iso surface?

A. Change model color
B. Use triad axis
C. Move the slider or manually enter a value
D. Click the play button

Q45. What tool allows you to visualize variations of scalar quantities within a volume?

A. Iso Surfaces
B. Process Traces
C. Iso Volumes
D. Wall Calculator

Q46. What must you do to activate the controls in the Iso Volumes panel?

A. Click on Calculate
B. Click on Edit
C. Add an iso volume
D. Load a results file

Q47. What value does the Wall Calculator use to remove low-pressure zones from calculations?

A. Vector direction
B. Cutoff Pressure
C. Minimum temperature
D. Surface normal

Q48. What is required to calculate film coefficient in Wall Calculator?

A. Torque axis
B. Wall surface normal
C. Reference temperature
D. Surface gradient

Q49. What does the Use near-wall temperatures option do?

A. Stops all calculations
B. Ignores heat flux
C. Uses wall temperature as local reference
D. Uses average model temperature

Q50. How can torque be calculated in Wall Calculator?

A. Select axis and calculate automatically
B. Specify axis point and direction vector
C. Use default model orientation
D. Only from summary part

Q51. Which file format is used to save Wall Result data?

A. .AVI
B. .XLS
C. .TXT
D. .CSV

Q52. What is the function of the Parts tool?

A. Animate model parts
B. View wall forces
C. Assess results on selected parts
D. Display scalar result summary

Q53. What happens when you select a part in the Parts tool?

A. It is removed from the simulation
B. It is hidden
C. Boundaries are highlighted in pink
D. Animation starts

Q54. What does clicking on the Make Summary button do?

A. Saves the trace
B. Highlights part edges
C. Designates a part as summary part
D. Removes all data

Q55. How is summary part data saved using the Parts tool?

A. In .CSV format
B. In .DOCX format
C. In .TXT format
D. In .JPG format

Q56. What is the primary function of the Points tool in simulation results?

A. To adjust material properties
B. To specify simulation boundary conditions
C. To plot time or iteration history at a specific location
D. To view convergence data

Q57. Which dialog box must be configured before using the Points tool?

A. Report Generator
B. Simulation Report
C. Solve
D. Status

Q58. How can you manually specify the coordinates for a result point?

A. By clicking on surface only
B. By editing X, Y, Z axis values in edit boxes
C. By using automatic coordinate detection
D. By selecting default settings

Q59. What is the purpose of the Report Generator tool?

A. To display thermal data
B. To customize and generate simulation reports
C. To set up boundary conditions
D. To run real-time simulations

Q60. What is the function of the Status File tool in the Review panel?

A. View simulation results
B. Analyze heat transfer
C. Troubleshoot errors during analysis
D. Run new scenarios

Q61. What kind of data does the Summary File provide?

A. Only material types
B. Tabulated field variable values and forces
C. Animation of model
D. Graphic orientation

Q62. What does the Setup File include?

A. Simulation images
B. Cover page info
C. Summary of boundary conditions, materials, solver options
D. Comparison of model versions

Q63. What does the Component Thermal Summary File include?

A. Iteration time history
B. Mesh generation summary
C. Temperatures and heat flux for each part
D. Screenshot of model

Q64. What does the Iteration/Step panel allow you to do?

A. Save thermal data
B. Set up simulation
C. View or animate saved results
D. Generate report

Q65. What condition must be met to capture the snap using the Summary Image tool?

A. First iteration must be selected
B. Coordinates must be aligned
C. You must be at the last iteration number
D. You must enable Result Plane

Chapter 6

Comparing and Visualization

Topics Covered

The major topics covered in this chapter are:

- ***Decision Center***
- ***Update Panel***
- ***Decision Center Layout***
- ***Save panel***
- ***View tab***
- ***View Settings panel***

INTRODUCTION

In the last chapters, we have discussed various tools of result tab for analyzing the result and creating the summary file. In this chapter, we will learn the tools used to compare and visualize results.

DECISION CENTER

The **Decision Center** tab is used to compare results from multiple scenarios. There are various panels containing tools to compare results, which are discussed next.

Update Panel

The tools in **Update** panel are used to define scenarios which are reported in the Summary items for comparison. It is also used to ensure that all summary items are updated. The tools of **Update** panel are discussed next.

Select Scenarios

The **Select Scenarios** tool is used to select or deselect the scenarios. The procedure to use this tool is discussed below.

- Click on the **Select Scenarios** tool from the **Update** panel of **Decision Center** tab in the **Ribbon**. The **Select Scenarios** dialog box will be displayed; refer to Figure-1.

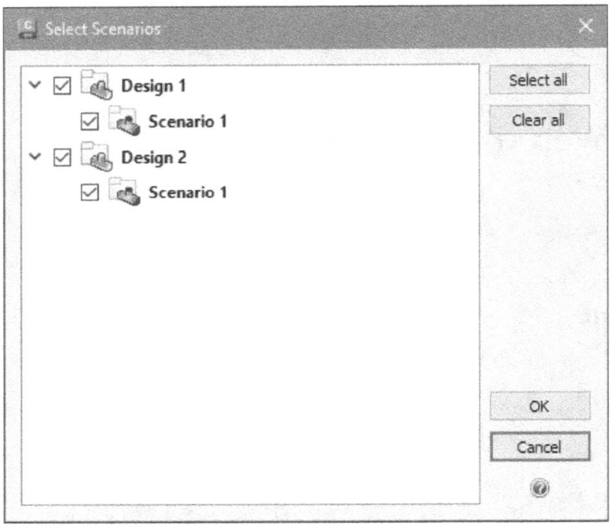

Figure-1. Select Scenarios dialog box

- Select check boxes for desired scenarios which you want to keep for comparison. Note that lesser the number of scenarios are selected, the quicker you will get the results of analysis.
- Click on the **Select All** button to select all scenario. If you want to clear all the selected scenarios then click on the **Clear All** button.
- After selecting desired scenarios, click on the **OK** button. The selected scenarios will be displayed.

Update All

The **Update All** tool is used to update all the summary data at once. The procedure to use this tool is discussed next.

- The exclamation symbol in **Design Study Bar** as displayed in Figure-2, means that a summary item has not been mapped to other scenarios, or results has changed and not mapped. In such cases, you need to update the items. To update these scenarios, click on the **Update All** button.

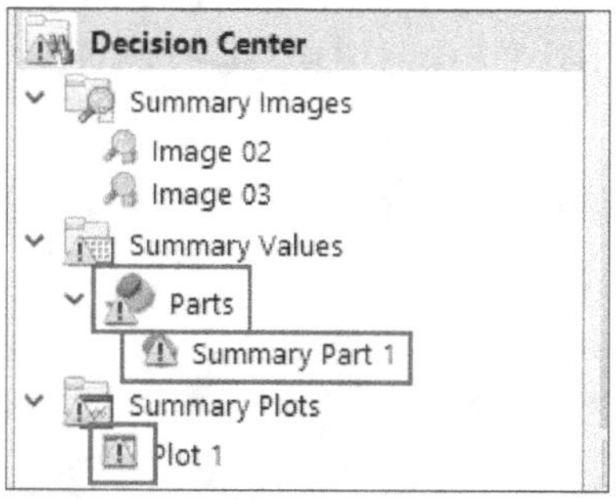

Figure-2. Scenarios to update

Decision Center Layout

The tools in the **Decision Center Layout** panel are used to configure the appearances of scenarios as per your requirement. The tools of this panel are discussed next.

Summary Images

- Click on the **Summary Images** button from the **Decision Center Layout** panel of the **Decision Center** tab in the **Ribbon** to display **Design Review Center**. The **Design Review Center** and **Summary Images** panel will be displayed; refer to Figure-3.

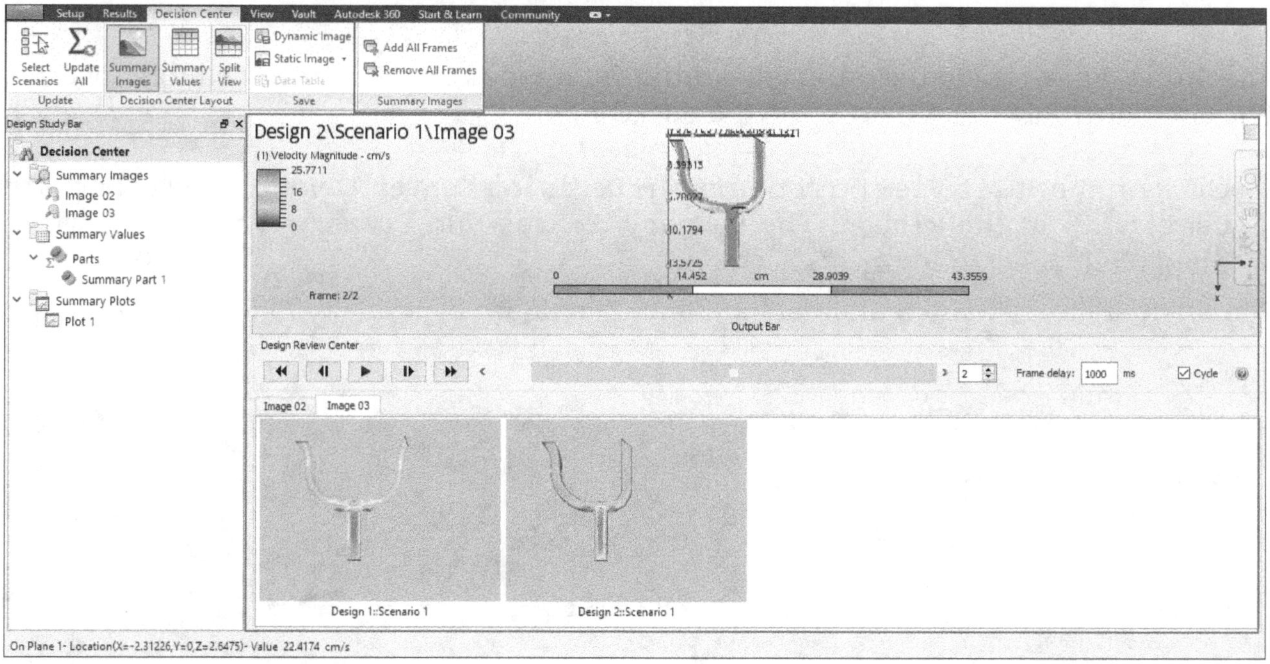

Figure-3. Summary Images button

- Click on the **Add All Frames** button from the **Summary Images** panel of **Decision Center** tab to add all the frames in **Design Review Center**. To remove all the frames, click on the **Remove All Frames** button.
- Use the **Design Review Center** tools to play video for comparison using summary images.

Summary Values

The **Summary Values** button is used to review only tabular data. The procedure to use this tool is discussed next.

- Click on the **Summary Values** button from **Decision Center Layout** panel of **Decision Center** tab. The tabular data will be displayed for comparison; refer to Figure-4.

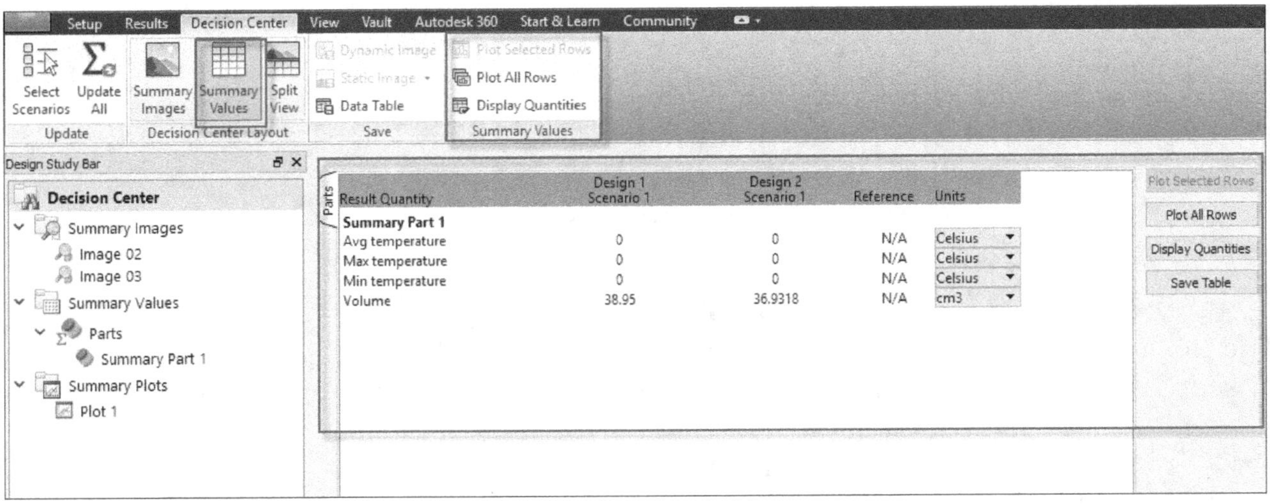

Figure-4. Summary Values button

- The tabular data hides the summary images from the view.

Split View

The **Split View** tool is used to view summary images and summary values together. The procedure to use this tool is discussed next.

- Click on the **Split View** button from the **Decision Center Layout** panel of **Decision Center** tab in the **Ribbon**. The **Summary Images** and **Summary Values** tab will be displayed; refer to Figure-5.

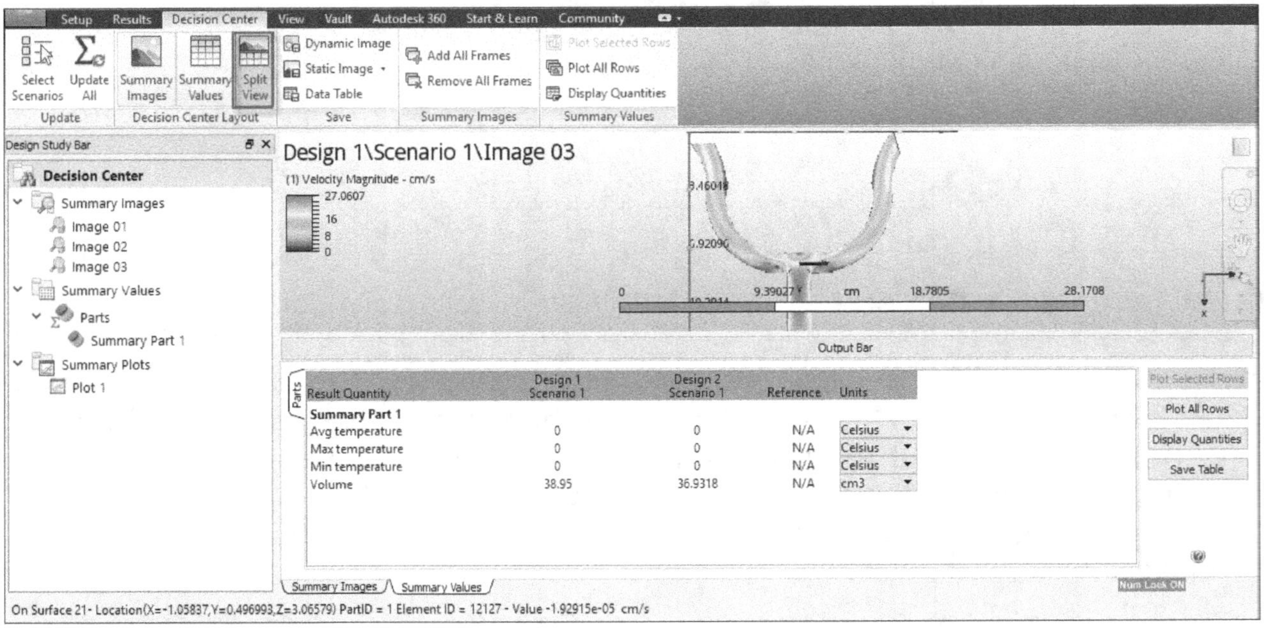

Figure-5. Split View button

Save panel

The tools in the **Save** panel are used to export visual and tabular data for sharing with others. The procedures to use these tools are discussed next.

Dynamic Image

The **Dynamic Image** tool is used to examine and share result data. The dynamic images can be navigated and animated to examine the simulation.

- Click on the **Dynamic Image** tool from the **Save** panel of the **Decision Center** tab in the **Ribbon**. The **Save Dynamic Image File** dialog box will be displayed; refer to Figure-6.

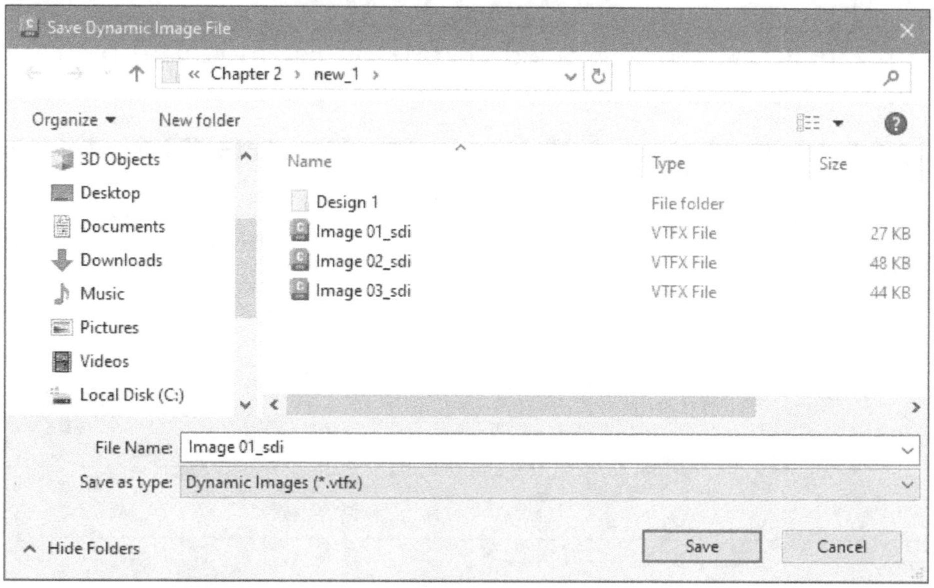

Figure-6. Save Dynamic Image File dialog box

- Specify the location where you want to save the file and click on **Save** button. The file will be saved at specified location.

Static Image

The **Static Image** tool is used to save an image of current view. The procedure to use this tool is discussed next.

- Click on the **Set Resolution** button from the **Static Image** drop-down of **Save** panel to set the resolution for saved static images and animation files; refer to Figure-7. The **Set Resolution** dialog box will be displayed; refer to Figure-8.

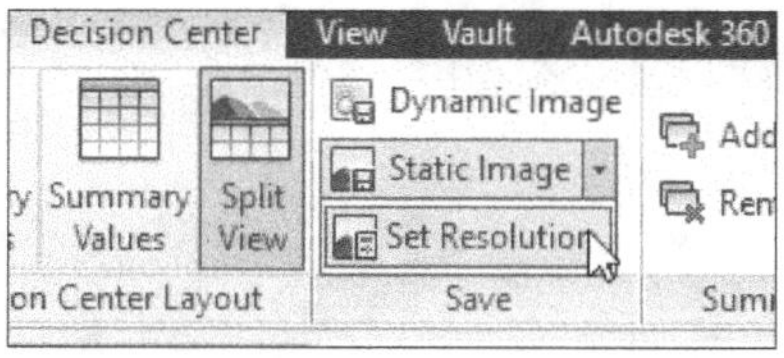

Figure-7. Set Resolution button

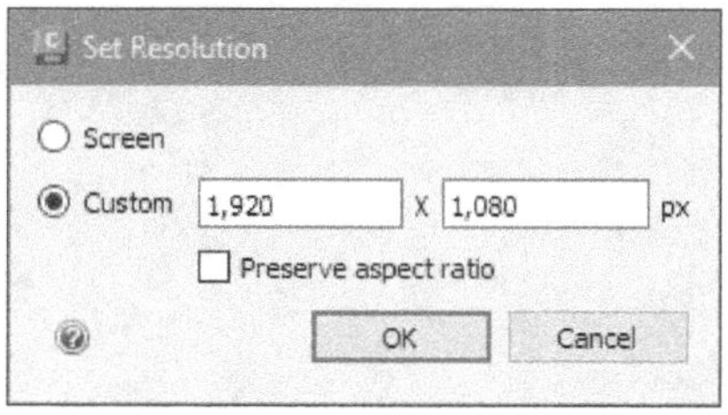

Figure-8. Set Resolution dialog box

- Select the **Screen** radio button from **Set Resolution** dialog box to use default screen resolution for image.

- Click on the **Custom** radio button from **Set Resolution** dialog box to manually set default resolution.
- Select the **Preserve aspect ratio** radio button to set the resolution of image in a balanced aspect ratio, which was defined by computer.
- After specifying the parameters, click on the **OK** button from **Set Resolution** dialog box. You will be returned to **Decision Center** tab.
- Click on the **Static Image** button from **Save** panel of **Decision Center** tab, the **Save Image** dialog box will be displayed.
- Specify the location and file format in which you want to save the image file, and click on the **Save** button. The file will be saved at specified location.

VIEW TAB

The options in the **View** tab are used to customize model appearance and user interface; refer to Figure-9. These tools are discussed next.

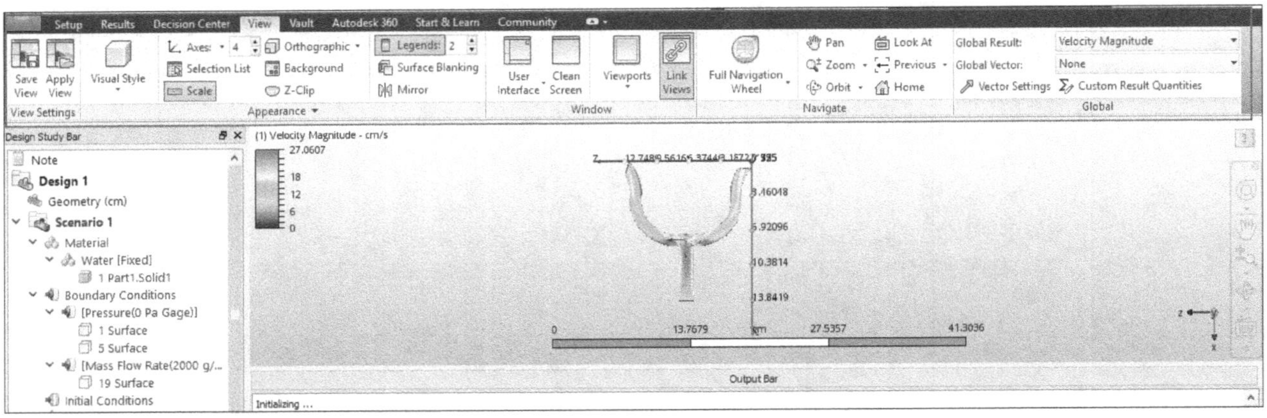

Figure-9. View tab

Appearance panel

The tools of **Appearance** panel are used to define model display and view styles. Most of the options of this panel are only available when results are displayed and the remaining are available for both setup and result views. The tools in this panel are discussed next.

Visual Style

- Click on the **Visual Style** drop-down from the **Appearance** panel and select desired visual style for the model; refer to Figure-10.

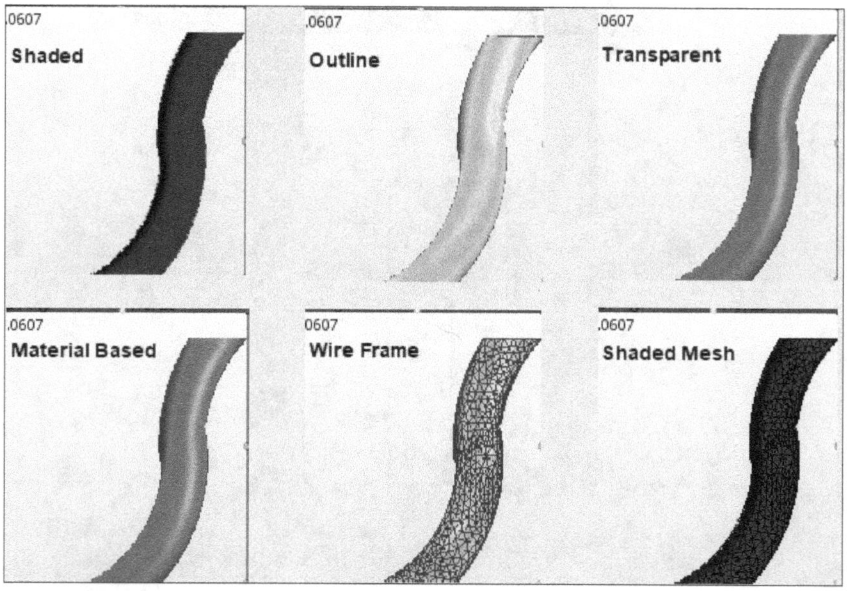

Figure-10. Visual Style

Axes

- Click in the **Axes** drop-down from the **Appearance** panel of the **View** tab in **Ribbon** and select required check boxes; refer to Figure-11. Clear the check boxes to hide respective interface elements; refer to Figure-12.

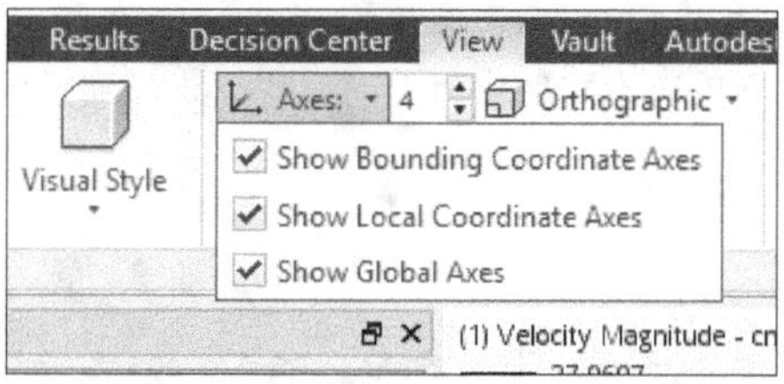

Figure-11. Axes drop-down

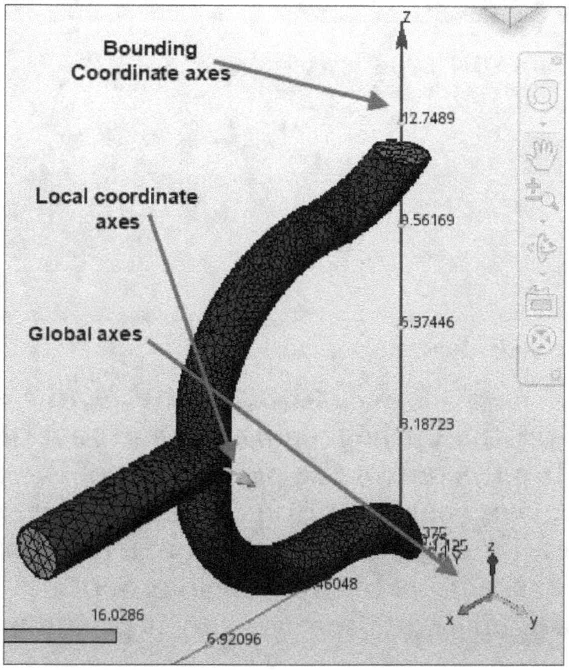

Figure-12. Axes option

- Click in the **Axis Gradient** edit box from **Appearance** panel and specify the value to define gradient lying on axis; refer to Figure-13.

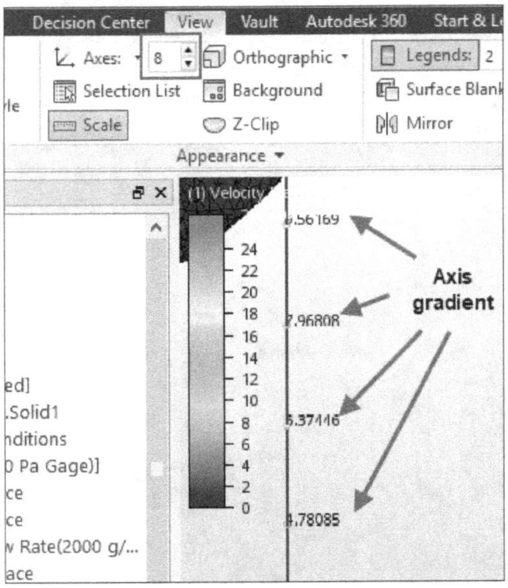

Figure-13. Axis Gradient

Scale

- Click on the **Scale** button from the **Appearance** panel of the **View** tab in the **Ribbon** to view model scale. Click again on this button to hide the scale from graphics area; refer to Figure-14.

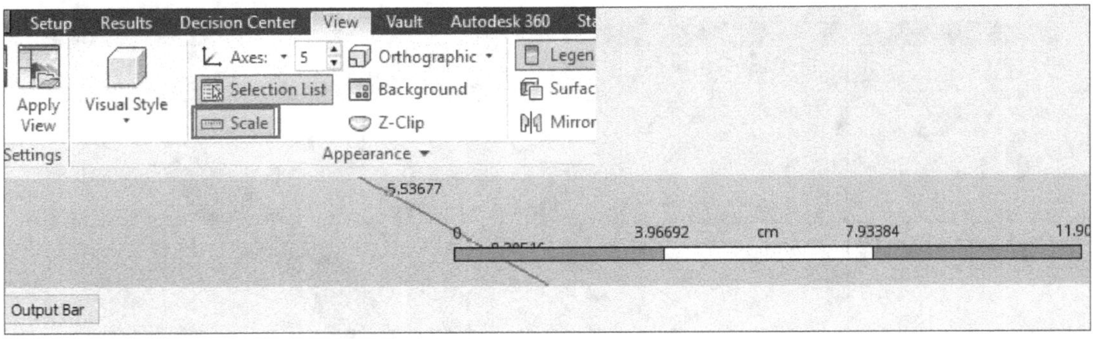

Figure-14. Scale

Orthographic and Perspective view

- Click on the **Orthographic** or **Perspective** button from the **Appearance** panel of **View** tab to control the depth view of the model; refer to Figure-15.
- The **Orthographic** button display model entities in their actual sizes. This button is useful for making selection when the model is aligned to Cartesian axis.
- The **Perspective** button provides depth to the model by reducing the size of objects that are far away from viewer. It provides more realistic view.

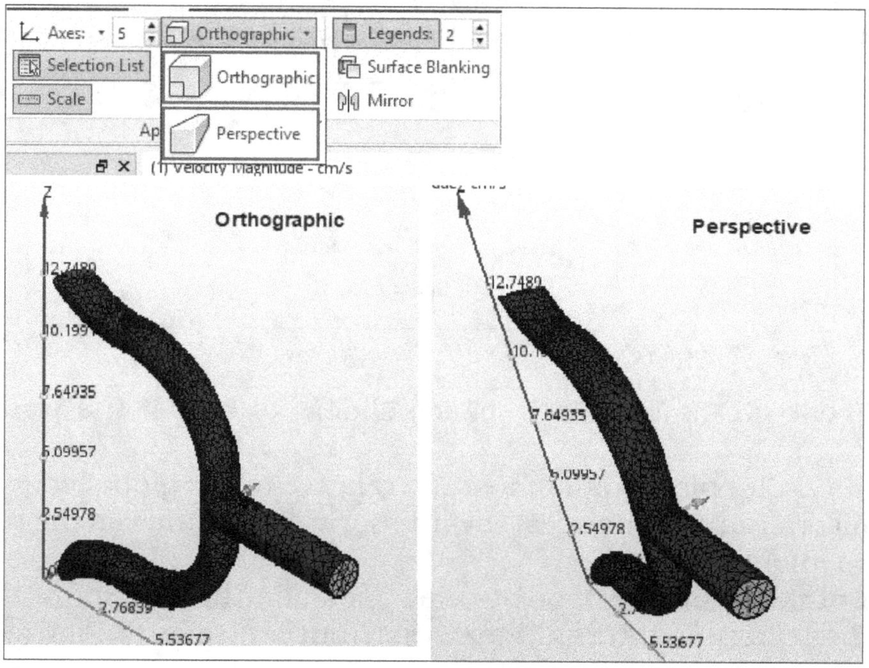

Figure-15. Orthographic and perspective

Background

The **Background** button is used to change the change the background color of graphics window where all the designing happens. The procedure is discussed next.

- Click on the **Background** button from the **Appearance** section of **View** tab in the **Ribbon**. The **Background Color** dialog box will be displayed; refer to Figure-16.

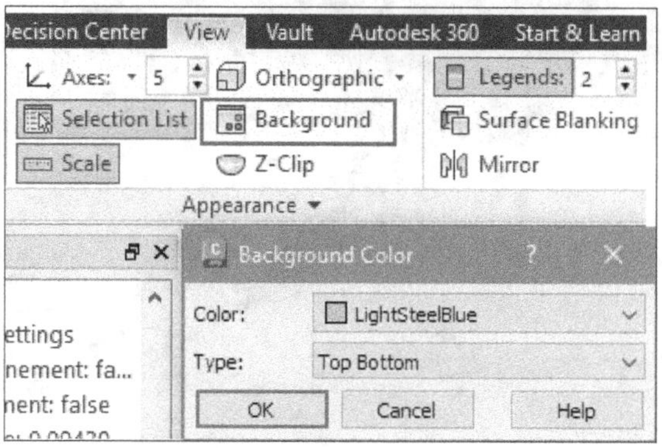

Figure-16. Background tool

- Click in the **Color** drop-down and select desired color which you want to apply on background.
- Click in the **Type** drop-down from the **Background Color** dialog box and select desired option to define pattern in which background will be created.
- After specifying desired color, click on the **OK** button from the **Background Color** dialog box. The background color of graphics window will be changed.

Z-Clip

The **Z-Clip** button is used to view interior of the model. The procedure to use this tool is discussed next.

- Click on the **Z-Clip** button from the **Appearance** panel of **View** tab in the **Ribbon**. The **Z-Clip Control and Crinkle Cut** dialog box will be displayed; refer to Figure-17.

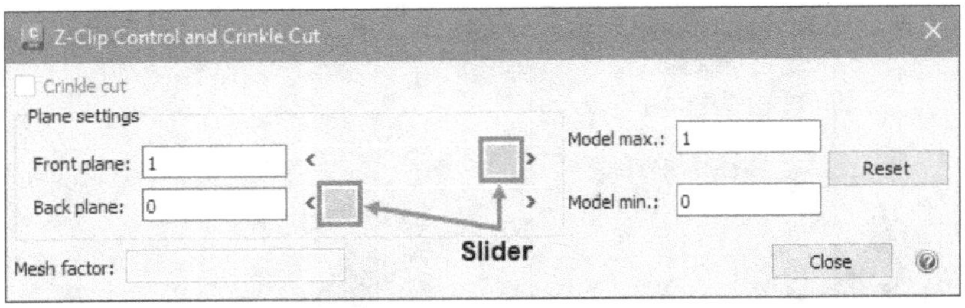

Figure-17. Z Clip Control and Crinkle Cut dialog box

- Move the **Front plane** and **Back plane** sliders to adjust the visibility of model interior.
- Note that the Z Clip plane remains static relative to the global coordinate system. As the model orientation changes, the interior view updates as the relative location of the Z Clip plane changes.
- Select the **Crinkle Cut** check box to view mesh on the interior of the model. This tool is used to examine internal mesh distribution; refer to Figure-18.

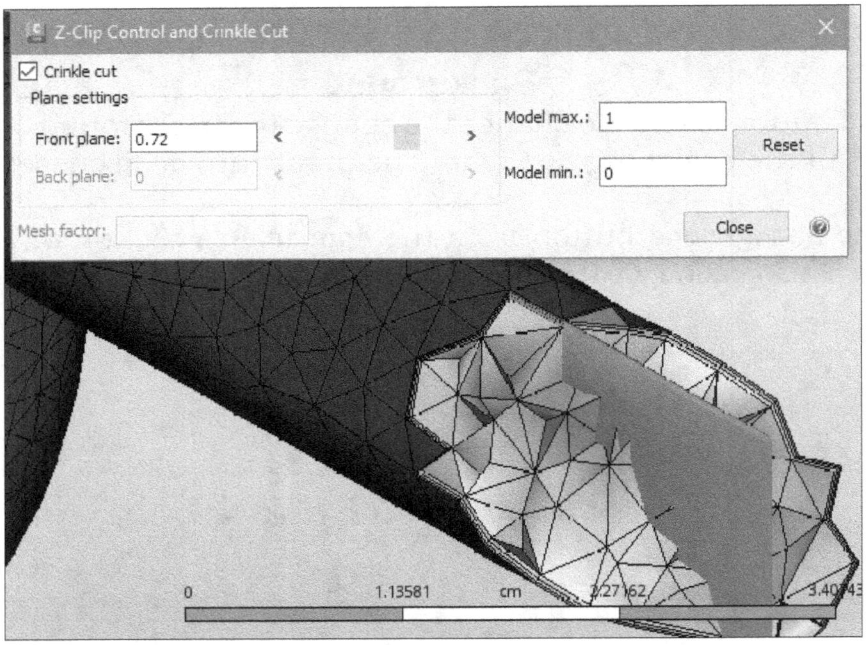

Figure-18. Crinkle cut

- Click on the **Reset** button to reset the previously specified parameters.
- After specifying the parameters, click on the **Close** button. You will be returned to **View** tab.

Legends

The **Legends** toggle is used to specify the number of legends on the screen. By default, the result legends will displayed when results are displayed.

- Click in the **Legends** edit box and specify the number of legends you want to display in the graphics window vertically. Software will automatically adjust the size of current legend based on the number specified. You can display a maximum of 5 legends in graphics window; refer to Figure-19. You can also use the spinner to specify number of legends.

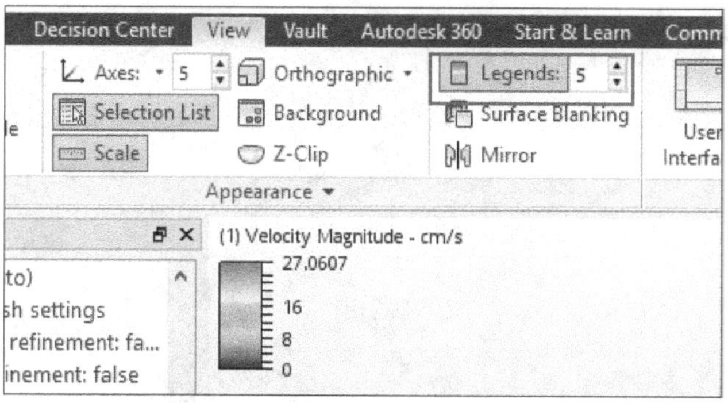

Figure-19. Legends

- Increase the legend value to reduce the legend size and decrease the value to increase legend size. The legends will be displayed vertically.

Surface Blanking

The **Surface Blanking** toggle button is used to display/hide surfaces when viewing results. Note that this tool is active only when you are viewing results.

- Click on the **Surface Blanking** toggle button from the **Appearance** panel of the **View** tab in the **Ribbon**. The tool will be activated; refer to Figure-20.

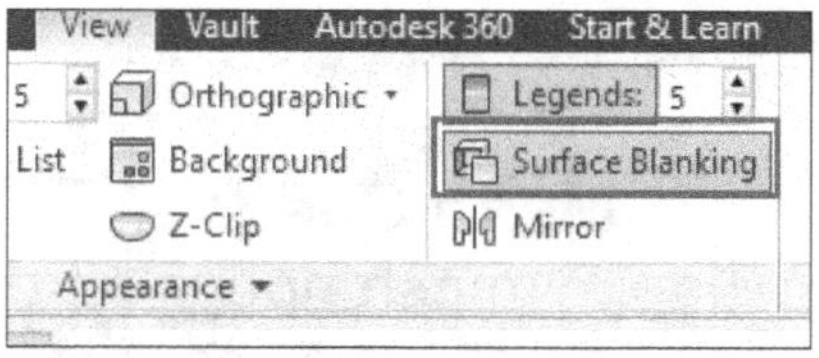

Figure-20. Surface Blanking button

Mirror

The **Mirror** tool is used to reflect the model and visualizations about selected plane. This tool is used when results are displayed. The procedure to use this tool is discussed next.

- Click on the **Mirror** tool from the **Appearance** panel of the **View** tab in the **Ribbon**. The **Mirror** dialog box will be displayed; refer to Figure-21.

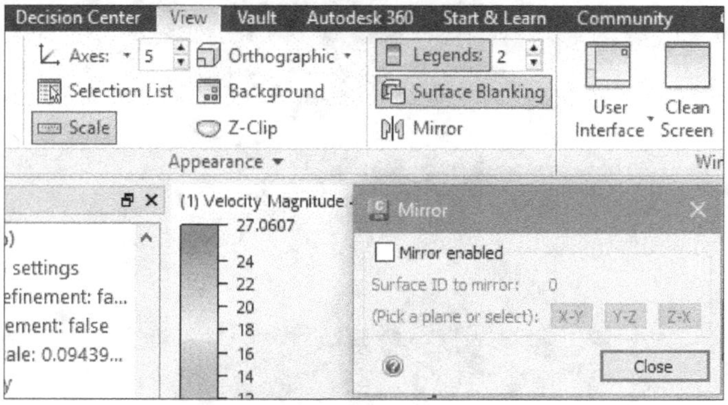

Figure-21. Mirror dialog box

- Select the **Mirror enabled** check box from **Mirror** dialog box to enable mirroring for current project. All tools of the **Mirror** dialog box will be activated.
- Select desired plane from the **Mirror** dialog box to define reflection; refer to Figure-22.

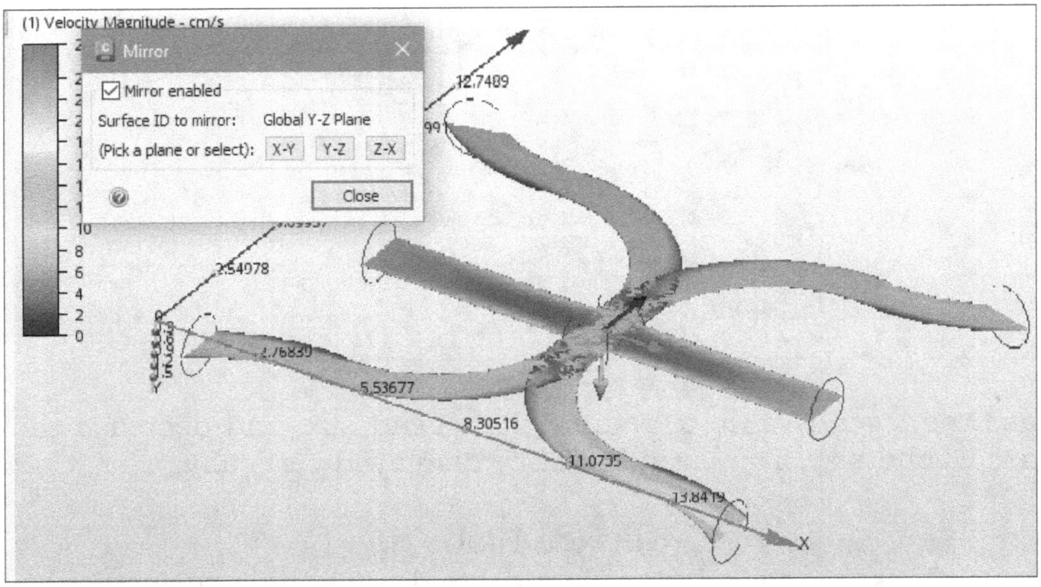

Figure-22. Selecting required plane

- After specifying the reflection plane, click on the **Close** button from the **Mirror** dialog box. The result of mirror will be displayed. Note that the mirror feature can be created about only one plane at a time.
- To disable mirroring, clear the **Mirror enabled** check box from the **Mirror** dialog box.

Mesh Seeds

The **Mesh Seeds** tool is used to display mesh nodes on the model after creating mesh; refer to Figure-23. Mesh seeds indicate the location of nodes when the mesh is generated. These seeds help us to identify the areas which need mesh adjustment. On complex models, mesh seeds can slow your computer performance. Note that this tool will be active only when if you have generated mesh and switched to **View** tab from **Setup** tab in the **Ribbon**.

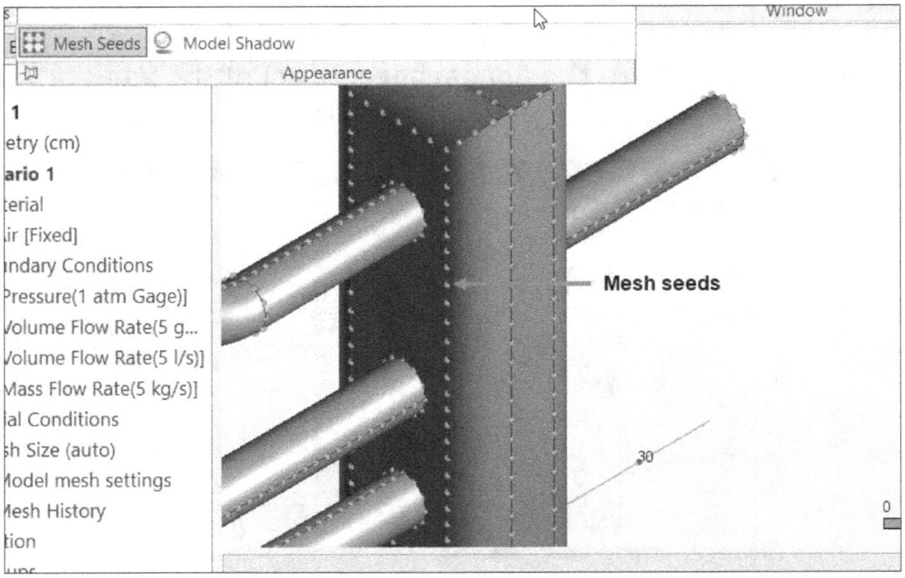

Figure-23. Mesh seeds

Model Shadow

The **Model Shadow** toggle button is used to display/hide the model shadow in graphics area. The procedure to use this button is discussed next.

- Click on the **Model Shadow** button from expanded **Appearance** panel of **View** tab in the **Ribbon**. The shadow will displayed just below the model geometry; refer to Figure-24.

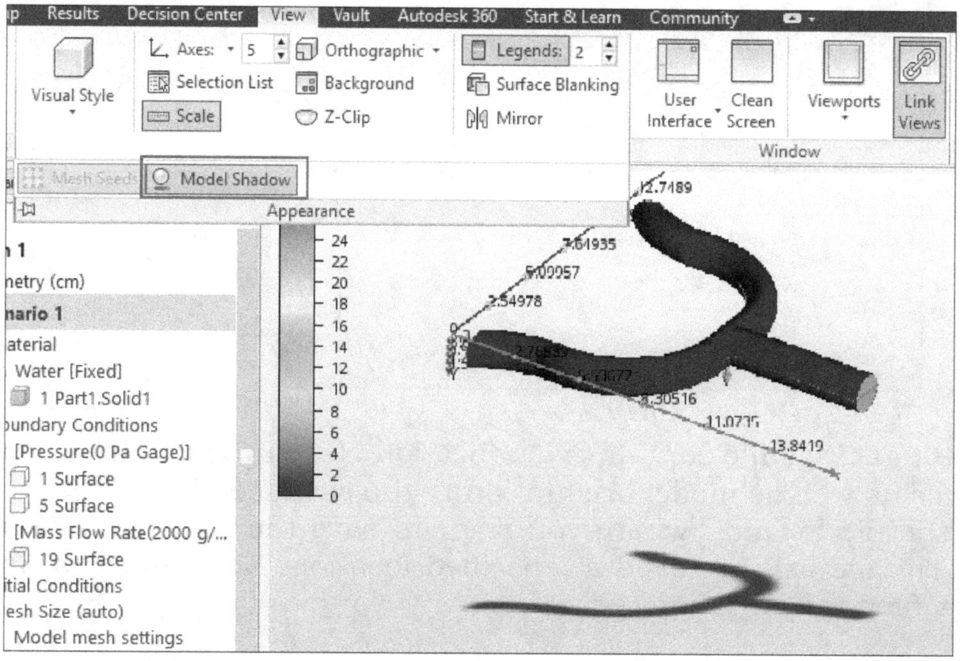

Figure-24. Model shadow

- Click again on the **Model Shadow** button to hide shadow of model.

View Settings panel

The tools of **View Settings** panel are used to save the current result view of model for future references and open earlier saved result views in graphics area. The tools of this panel are active when you have generated results and switched from **Results** tab to **View** tab in the **Ribbon**. Tools of this panel are discussed next.

Save View

- Click on the **Save View** button from **View Settings** panel of **View** tab to save view setting file. The **Save View Settings** dialog box will be displayed; refer to Figure-25.

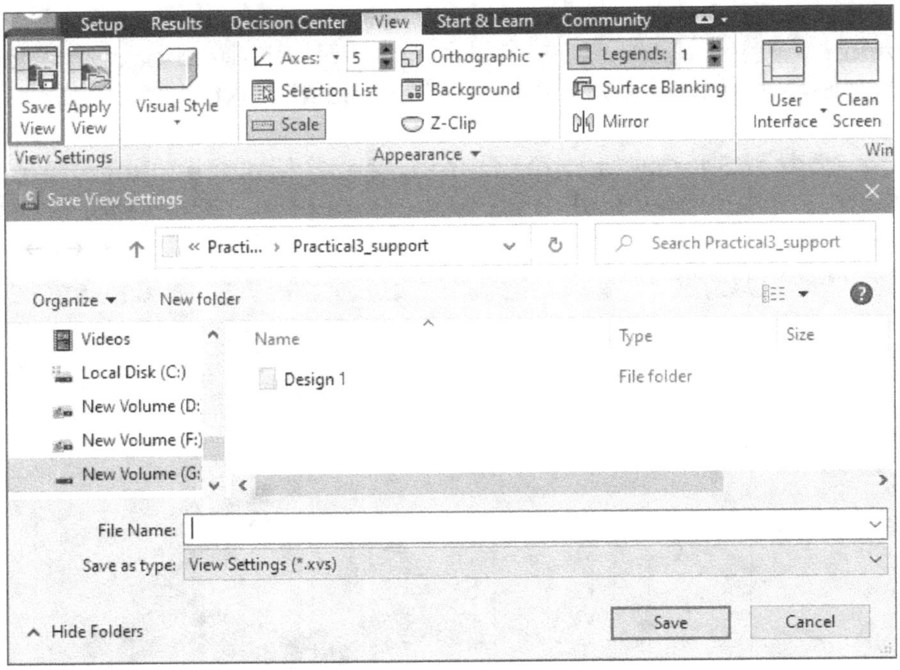

Figure-25. Save View Settings dialog box

- The **View Settings** file contains visualization elements like planes, iso-surfaces, and traces as well as model orientation to the save file.
- Specify the file location where you want to save the file and click on the **Save** button. The file will be saved at specified location. Now, you can use this **View Settings** file for future use.

Apply View

- Click on the **Apply View** button from the **View Settings** panel from **View** tab to apply view setting file of current scenario or another scenarios. The **Apply View Settings** dialog box will be displayed; refer to Figure-26.

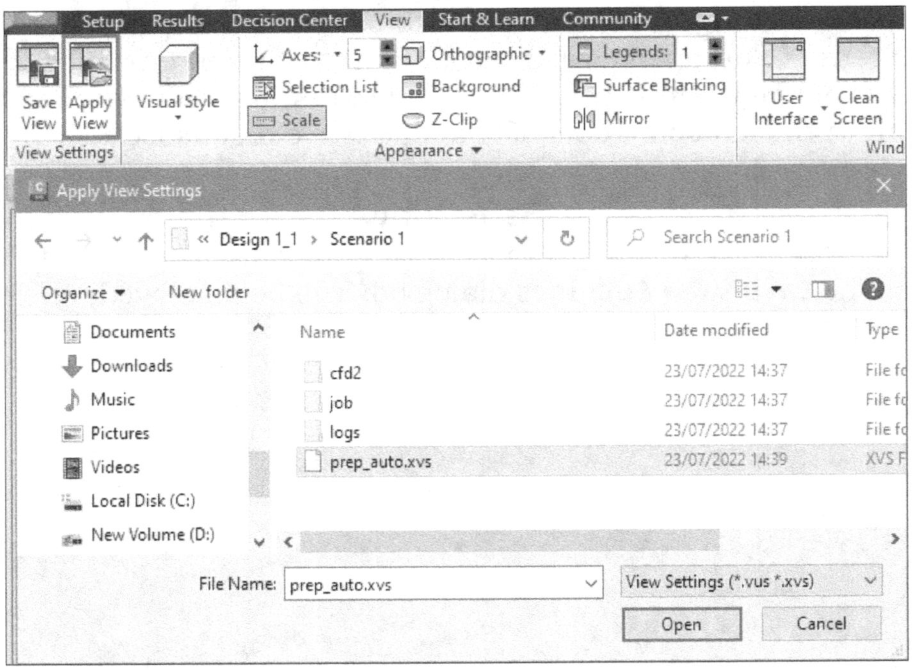

Figure-26. Applying View Settings dialog Box

- Select desired view settings file and click on the **Open** button. The view will be applied.

Window panel

The tools of **Window** panel are used to configure the graphics window. These tools are discussed next.

User Interface

The options in **User Interface** drop-down are used to hide or display various interface elements from the graphics window.

- Click on the **User Interface** drop-down from **Window** panel of **View** tab and select check boxes for the options that you want to display in graphics window; refer to Figure-27.

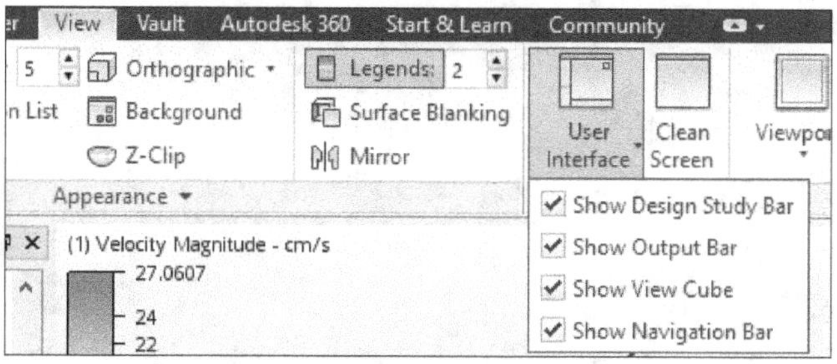

Figure-27. User Interface drop-down

- Clear desired check boxes from the **User Interface** drop-down to hide respective options from graphics window.

Clean Screen

The **Clean Screen** tool is used to maximize the graphics window.

- Click on the **Clean Screen** button from **Window** panel of **View** tab to hide **Design Study Bar**, **Status bar**, **Ribbon**, and **Output bar**. It will hide everything from graphic window other than model; refer to Figure-28.

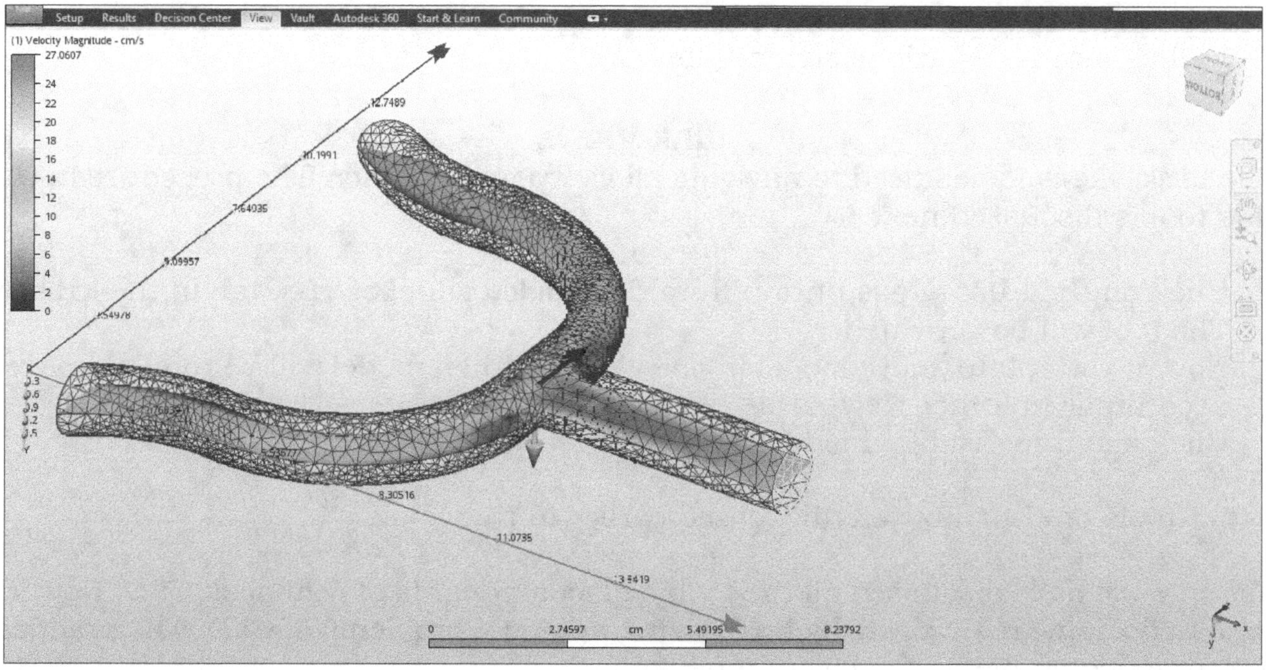

Figure-28. Clean Screen

- To display the interface components again, click on the **Clean Screen** button from the **Window** panel in **View** tab of the **Ribbon** after clicking on the **View** tab of **Ribbon**.

Viewports

The options in the **Viewports** drop-down are used to increase or decrease the number of viewports to be displayed in graphics area. The procedure is discussed next.

- Click on the **Viewports** drop-down from the **Window** panel of **View** tab and select desired option from the list; refer to Figure-29.

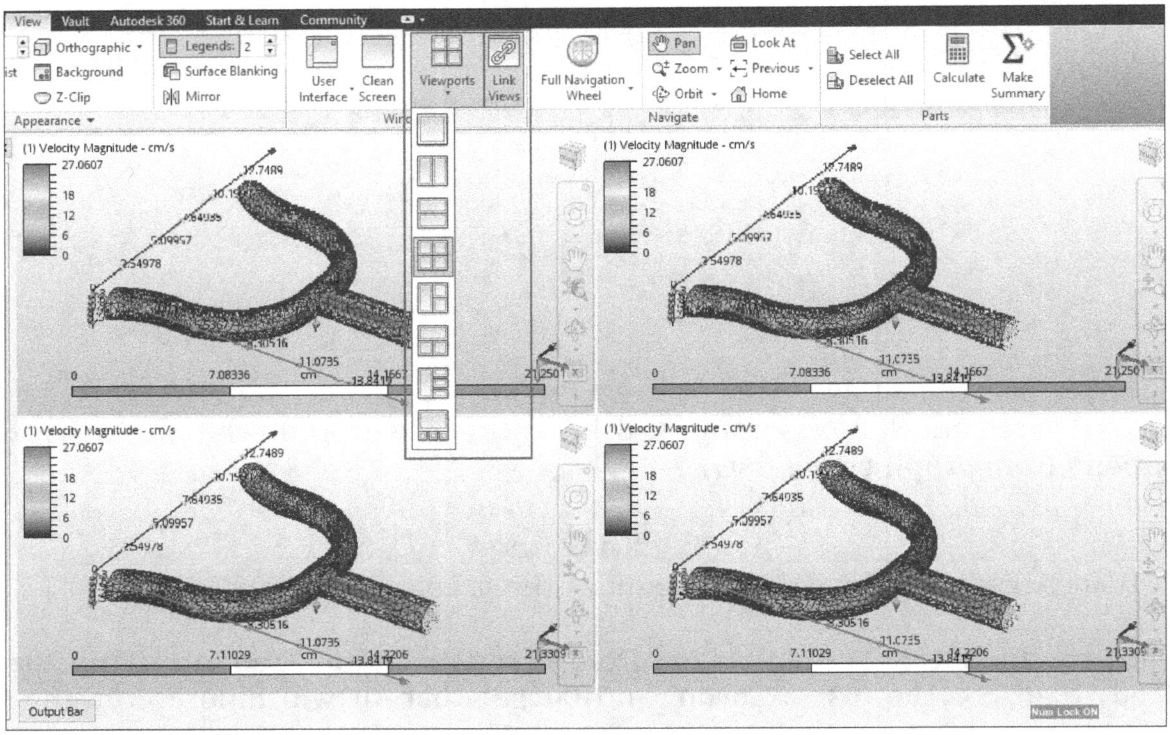

Figure-29. Viewports drop-down

- Multiple viewports are useful for assessing results from individual scenarios as well as multi-scenario design studies.

Link Views

The **Link Views** tool is used to navigate all viewports together. The procedure to use this tool is discussed next.

- Click on the **Link Views** button from the **Window** panel of **View** tab in the **Ribbon**. The tool will be activated.
- Now, if you rotate/move model in one viewport then model will be rotated/moved accordingly in other viewports.
- Click again to disable this tool.

Other tools of **View** tab were discussed earlier in this book.

Till now, we have discussed all the tools and components of Autodesk CFD. Now it's time to do some real work which is solving practical problems of CFD. The practical and practice problems are given in next chapter.

SELF ASSESSMENT

Q1. The options in .... tab of Ribbon are used to compare results generated from multiple scenarios.

Q2. The Split View tool is used to view summary images and summary values together when comparing results. (T/F)

Q3. The Dynamic Image tool is used to examine and share result data. (T/F)

Q4. The Static Image tool is used to save an image of current view. (T/F)

Q5. The Z-Clip button is used to view interior of the result model. (T/F)

Q6. The Clean Screen tool is used to close current design study and start a new design. (T/F)

Q7. The .... button is used to review only tabular data.

Q8. The tools of .... panel are used to define model display and view styles.

Q9. What is the primary purpose of the Decision Center tab?

A. To design new simulation models
B. To compare results from multiple scenarios
C. To set up mesh generation
D. To create 3D geometry

Q10. Which tool is used to select or deselect scenarios for comparison?

A. Update All
B. Summary Images
C. Select Scenarios
D. Split View

Q11. What does the exclamation symbol in the Design Study Bar indicate?

A. A tool is missing
B. Simulation has failed
C. A summary item is not mapped or results have changed
D. User interface elements are hidden

Q12. What does the Split View tool allow the user to do?

A. Export images
B. View summary images and values simultaneously
C. Hide interface elements
D. Save the simulation file

Q13. What kind of data is shown using the Summary Values button?

A. Graphical charts
B. Simulation logs
C. Tabular data
D. Animated images

Q14. Which tool is used to share result data with navigation and animation features?

A. Static Image
B. Update All
C. Summary Images
D. Dynamic Image

Q15. How can the background color of the graphics window be changed?

A. From Summary Images
B. Using the Background button in Appearance panel
C. From the Save View Settings
D. By enabling Clean Screen mode

Q16. What does the Z-Clip tool allow you to do?

A. Save mesh
B. View exterior surfaces
C. View model interior
D. Adjust viewport settings

Q17. What is the function of the Legends tool?

A. Play summary video
B. Adjust model scale
C. Specify number of result legends displayed
D. Enable mesh generation

Q18. When is the Surface Blanking tool active?

A. During simulation setup
B. Only when results are being viewed
C. When model is mirrored
D. While generating mesh

Q19. What is the use of the Mirror tool in the View tab?

A. Export static image
B. Mirror model and visualizations about a plane
C. Set visual style
D. Save background color

Q20. What are Mesh Seeds used to indicate?

A. Animation frames
B. Legend values
C. Mesh node locations
D. File formats

Q21. Which button is used to toggle the model shadow in the graphics area?

A. Surface Blanking
B. Split View
C. Model Shadow
D. Background

Q22. What does the Save View tool store?

A. Only model geometry
B. View settings including orientation and visualization elements
C. Animation timeline
D. Tabular comparison data

Q23. Which tool allows synchronization of navigation across multiple viewports?

A. Clean Screen
B. User Interface
C. Link Views
D. Summary Values

FOR STUDENTS NOTES

Chapter 7

Practical

Topics Covered

The major topics covered in this chapter are:

- ***Practical 1***
- ***Practical 2***
- ***Practical 3***

INTRODUCTION

In past chapters, we have learned the tools used to create a simulation study. We have also learned about tools which are used after performing simulation study to analyze results. In this chapter, we will create analyses on different scenario conditions.

PRACTICAL 1

In this practical, we will simulate the air flow distribution through a manifold which has two inlet and two outlet ports. The geometry consists of two inlet tubes, two outlet tubes and a distribution chamber; refer to Figure-1.

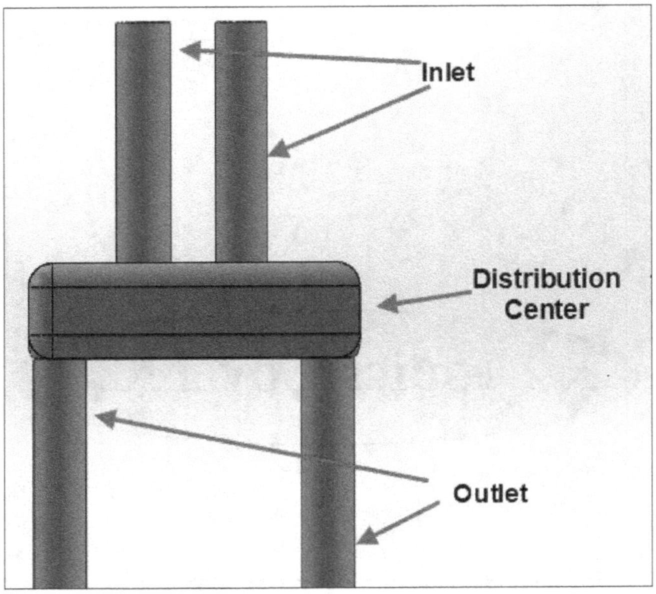

Figure-1. Practical 1

In this practical, our goal is to understand the effects of removing one of the inlet port. After running the initial scenario, we will clone the design, remove the 1st inlet tube from model, and compare the resultant flow distribution with the original design. We use the **Design Review Center** to visualize the effects of removing the inlet.

Opening the model

We are using SOLIDWORKS software for creating model here, but you can use any other CAD software supported by Autodesk CFD for importing CAD file. We have created the model and saved in respective folder of Autodesk CFD folder. We are using .IGS format to save part files because it is universally supported by all CAD software. You can use other formats to save your CAD model.

- Double-click on the **Autodesk CFD** icon from desktop. The welcome window of **Autodesk CFD** will be displayed. You can also open **Autodesk CFD** from **Start Menu**; refer to Figure-2.

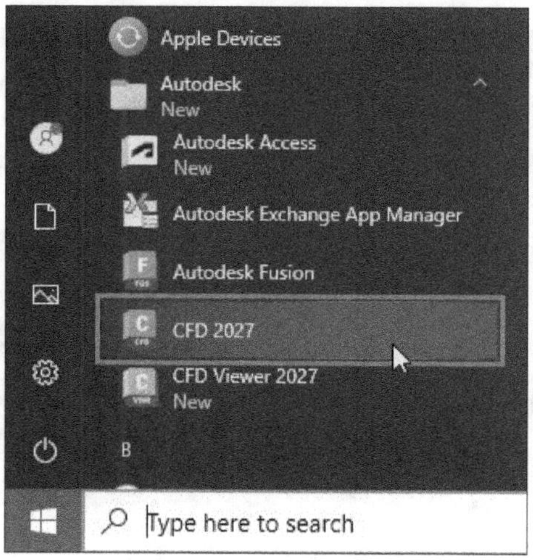

Figure-2. Opening Autodesk CFD from start menu

- Click on the **New** button from **Ribbon**; the **New Design Study** dialog box will be displayed; refer to Figure-3.

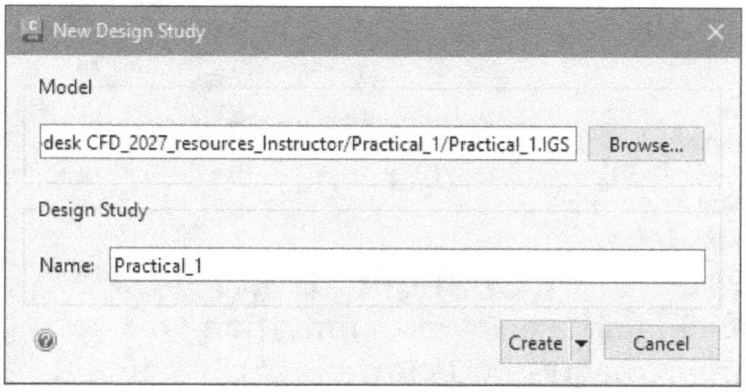

Figure-3. New Design Study dialog box for Practical 1

- Click on the **Browse** button from **New Design Study** dialog box and select **Practical 1.IGS** file from respective folder of resource kit for this book.
- Click in the **Name** edit box and specify the name as **Practical 1**. Click on the **Create** button. Software will start reading file.
- The **Geometry Tools** dialog box will be displayed asking you to merge the edges below specified angle. Click on the **Merge** button to merge edges. Close the **Geometry Tools** dialog box. The model will be displayed as shown in Figure-4.

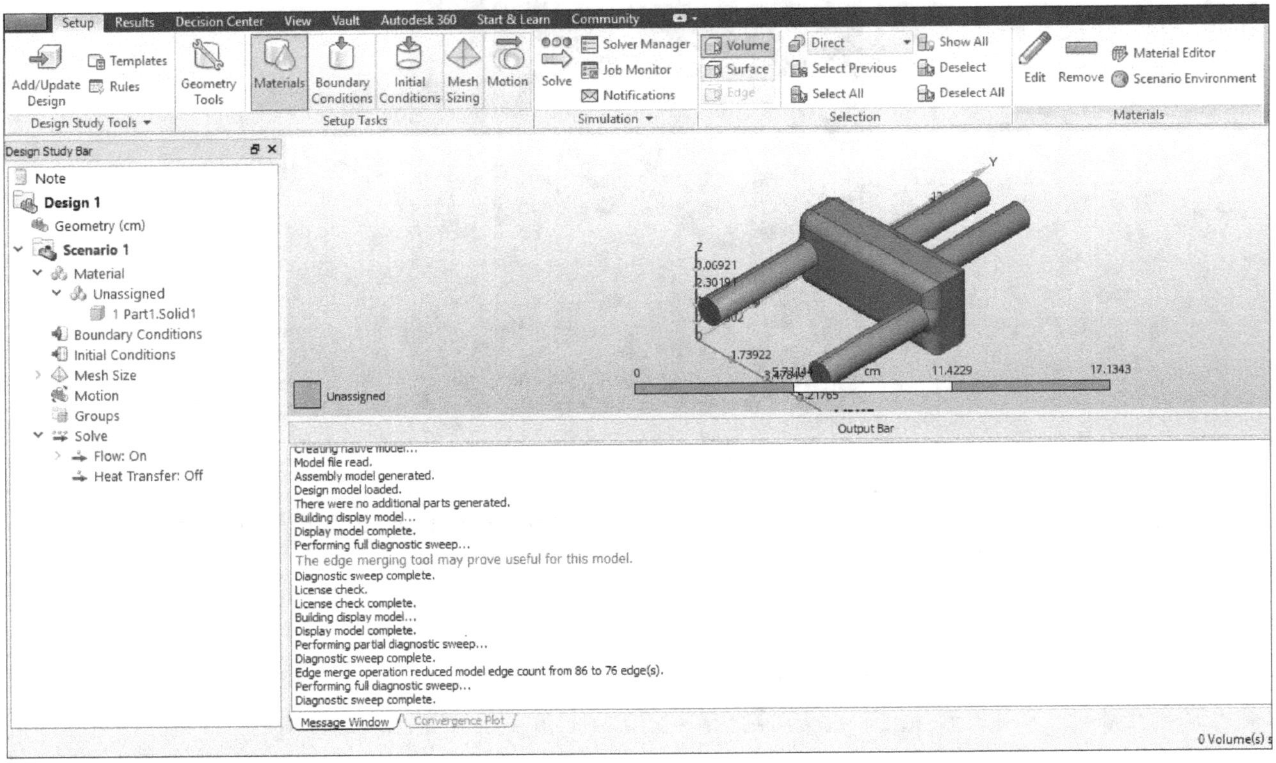

Figure-4. Practical 1 starting window

Changing Units

If the unit of your model is not selected to mm then you need to change the units to mm and the procedure is discussed below.

- Right-click on the **Geometry** from the **Design Study Bar** and select **mm** option from the **Change length units to** cascading menu; refer to Figure-5. The units will be changed to **mm**.

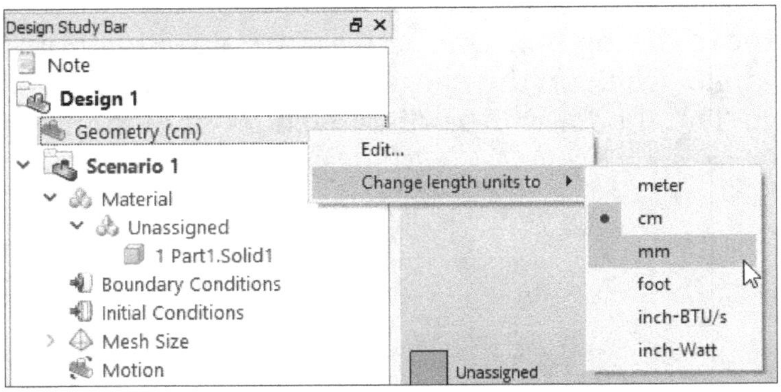

Figure-5. Changing units

Assigning Material

Now, its time to assign **Air** as fluid for the CFD model. The procedure to do so is discussed next.

- Right-click on the **Unassigned** branch from the **Design Study Bar** and select the **Edit** option. The **Materials** dialog box will be displayed; refer to Figure-6.

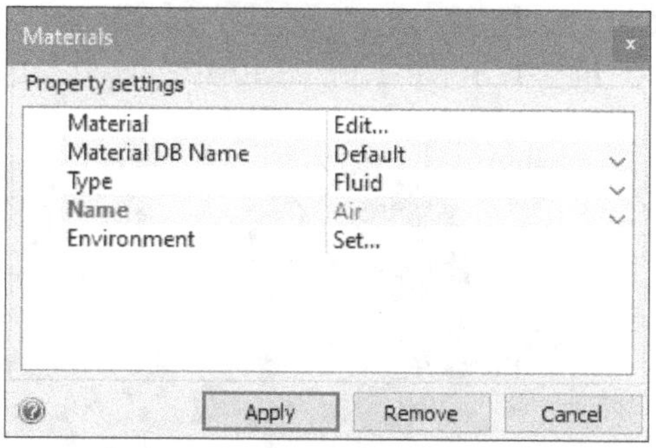

Figure-6. Specifying Air to model

- Select the **Type** as **Fluid** and **Name** as **Air** from list of **Materials** dialog box, and click on **Apply** button. The **Air** will be applied on model and mentioned in **Design Study Bar**. The color of model will be changed as per selected material.

Assigning Boundary Condition

Now, we will apply inlet boundary condition at two inlet and outlet boundary conditions at two outlet. The procedure is discussed next.

- Click on the **Boundary Conditions** tool from the **Setup** tab to enable this tool. Select the **Surface** button from the **Selection** panel to activate surface selection and click on **Edit** button from **Boundary Conditions** panel; the **Boundary Conditions** dialog box will be displayed; refer to Figure-7.

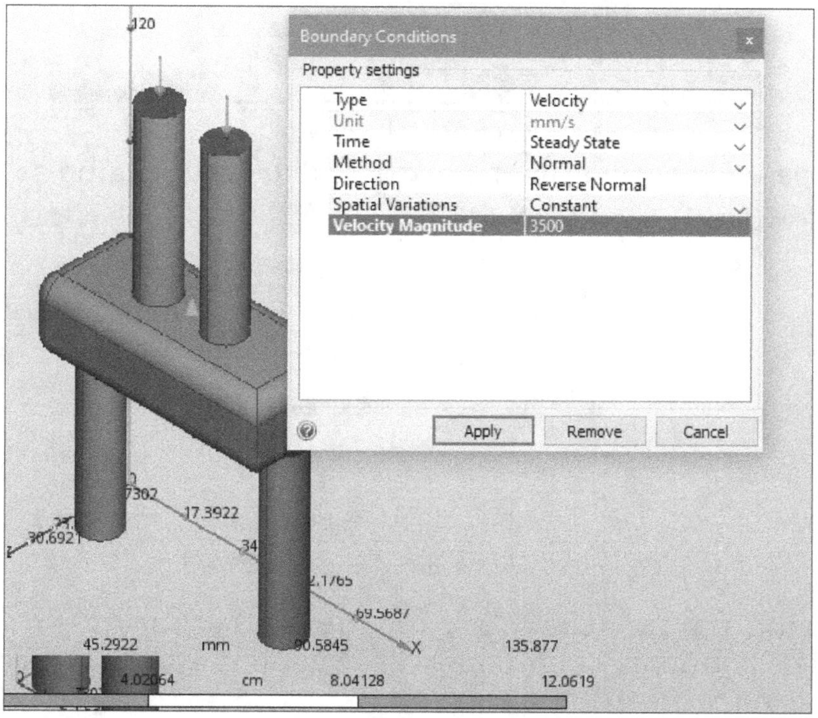

Figure-7. Applying boundary condition to Practical 1

- Select the inlet surfaces of model and specify the parameters of boundary condition as shown in above figure.
- Click on **Apply** button. The boundary conditions will applied.
- Now, rotate the model by pressing **SHIFT** and dragging model using MMB so that you can see surfaces of outlet pipes.

- Select the surfaces of two outlet pipes. Right-click on any of the surface and click on **Edit** button; refer to Figure-8. The **Boundary Conditions** dialog box will be displayed.

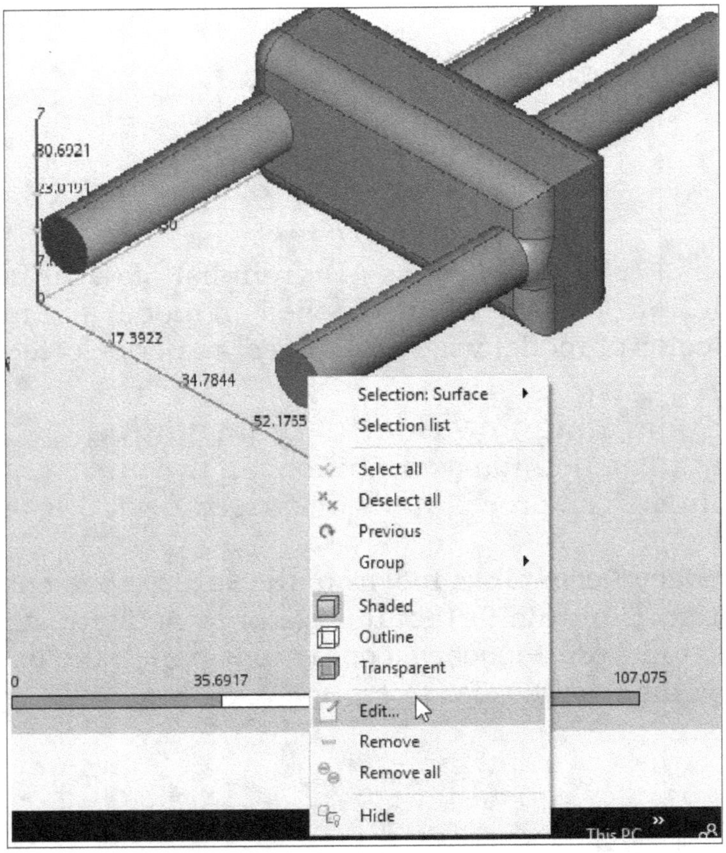

Figure-8. Selecting outlet surfaces of Practical 1

- Select the **Type** as **Pressure**, **Unit** as **atm**, and **Pressure** value as **1** from **Boundary Condition** dialog box; refer to Figure-9.

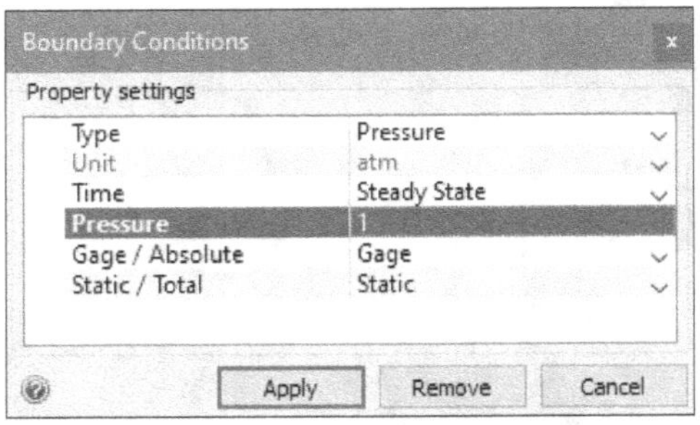

Figure-9. Outlet boundary condition Practical 1

- After specifying parameters, click on the **Apply** button to apply boundary conditions. The boundary conditions will be applied and displayed in the graphics window; refer to Figure-10.

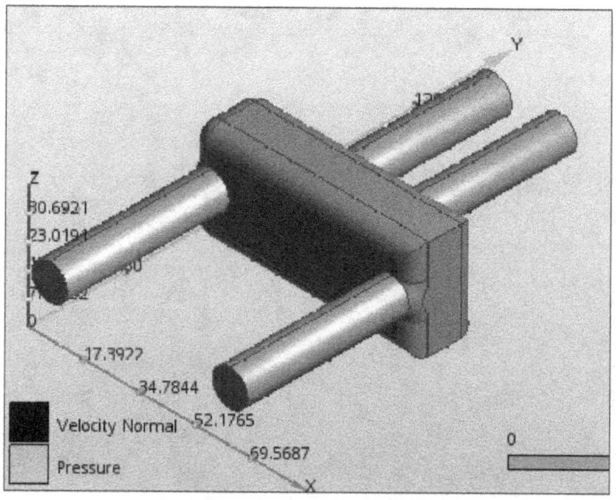

Figure-10. Displayed boundary conditions

Creating Mesh

For this model, you will create automatic mesh. The procedure is discussed next.

- Click on the **Mesh Sizing** tool from the **Setup Tasks** panel of the **Setup** tab in the **Ribbon** to activate this tool.
- Click on the **Autosize** tool from the **Automatic Sizing** panel of the **Setup** tab in the **Ribbon**. The mesh will be generated; refer to Figure-11.

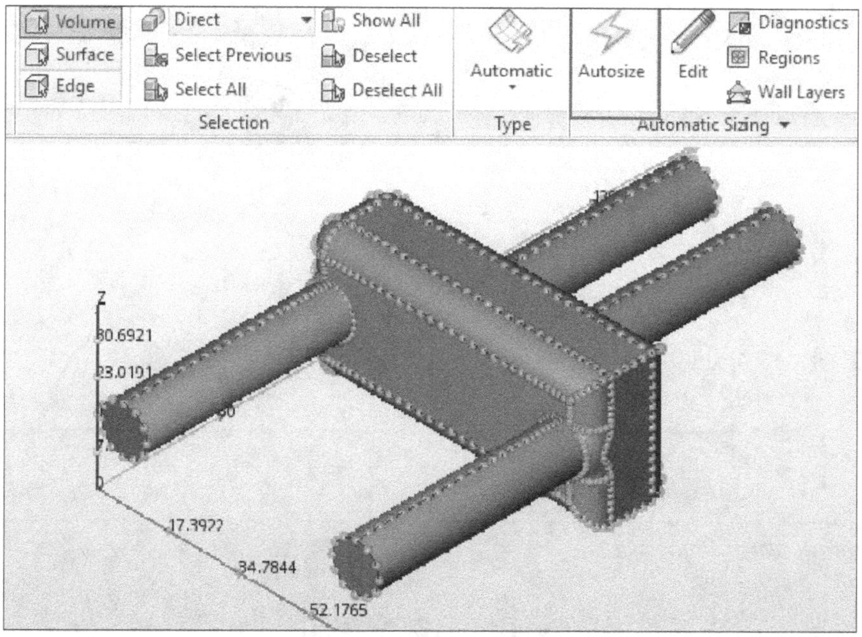

Figure-11. Generating mesh of practical 1

Solving Analysis

- Click on the **Solve** button from the **Simulation** panel in the **Setup** tab of the **Ribbon**. The **Solve** dialog box will be displayed; refer to Figure-12.

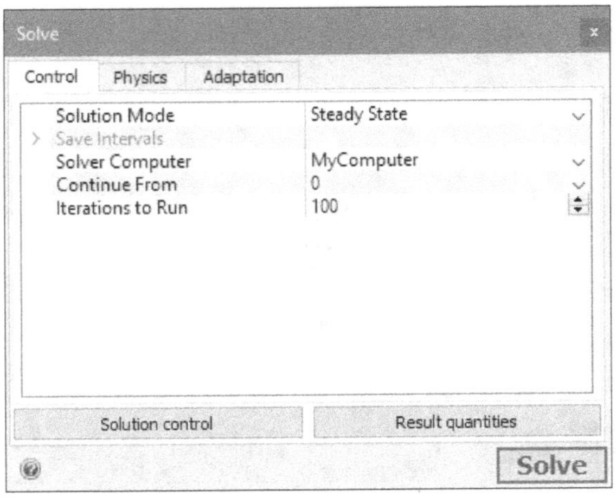

Figure-12. Solve dialog box

- Click in the **Iterations to Run** edit box and specify the value of iterations as **100**.
- Select the **Flow** check box from the **Physics** tab of the **Solve** dialog box and click on the **Solve** button. The data starts displaying in the **Output** tab and on completion of calculations; the **Convergence Plot** will be displayed; refer to Figure-13.

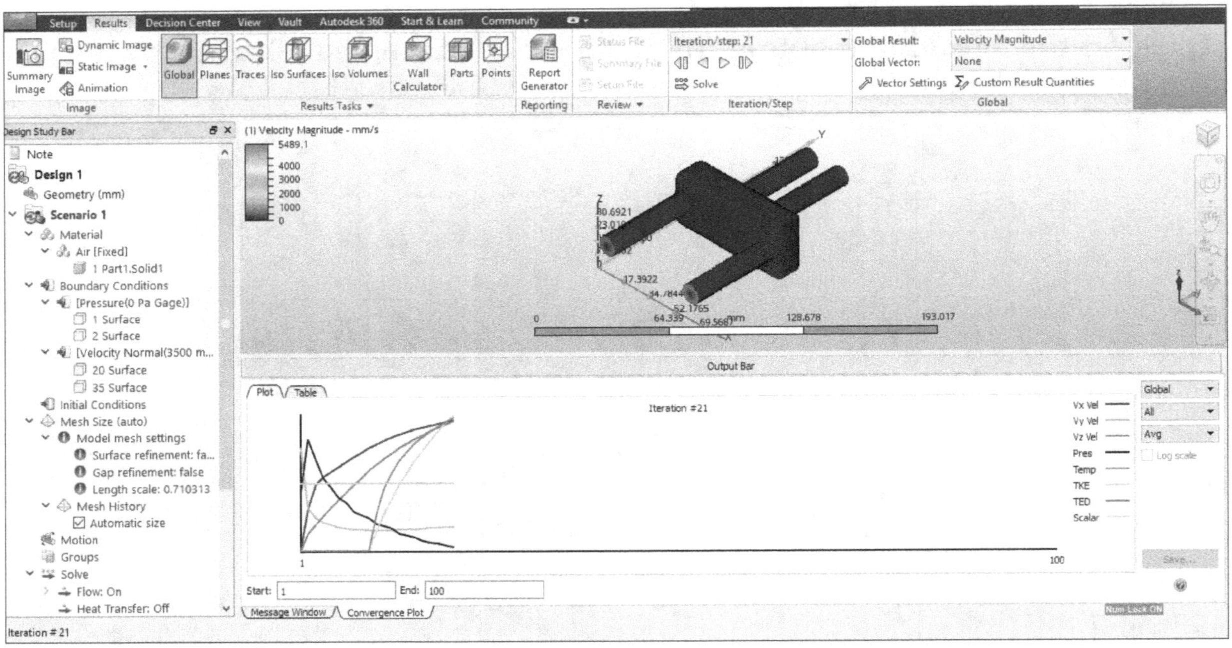

Figure-13. Convergence plot of Practical 1

Results of Design 1

Now, we will use a section plane to check results of analysis in the inner areas of model.

- Click on the **Planes** tool from **Results Tasks** panel of **Results** tab of the **Ribbon**. The related tools will be displayed.
- Click on the **Add** button from the **Planes** contextual panel; the plane will be added and displayed.
- Left-click on the plane and select the **Z axis** option from the displayed context menu; refer to Figure-14. The plane will be aligned to z axis.

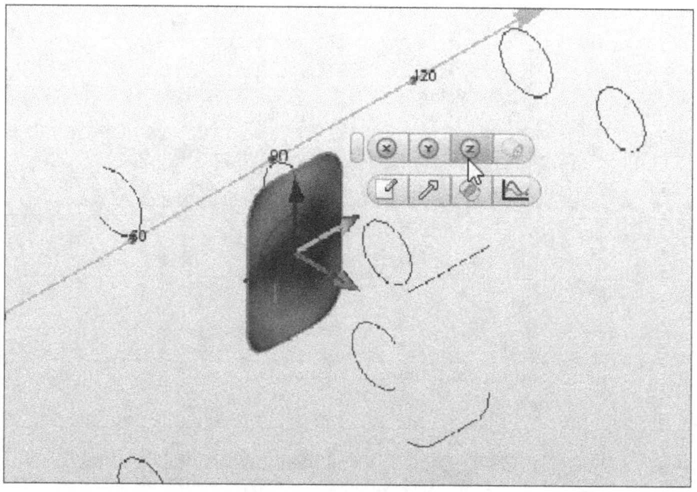

Figure-14. Aligning plane to z axis

- Click on the **Summary Image** button from **Image** panel of **Results** tab; the current image of plane will be saved and displayed in **Decision Center**; refer to Figure-15. If image is not displayed by default then click on the **Update All** tool from the **Update** panel of **Decision Center** tab in the **Ribbon**.

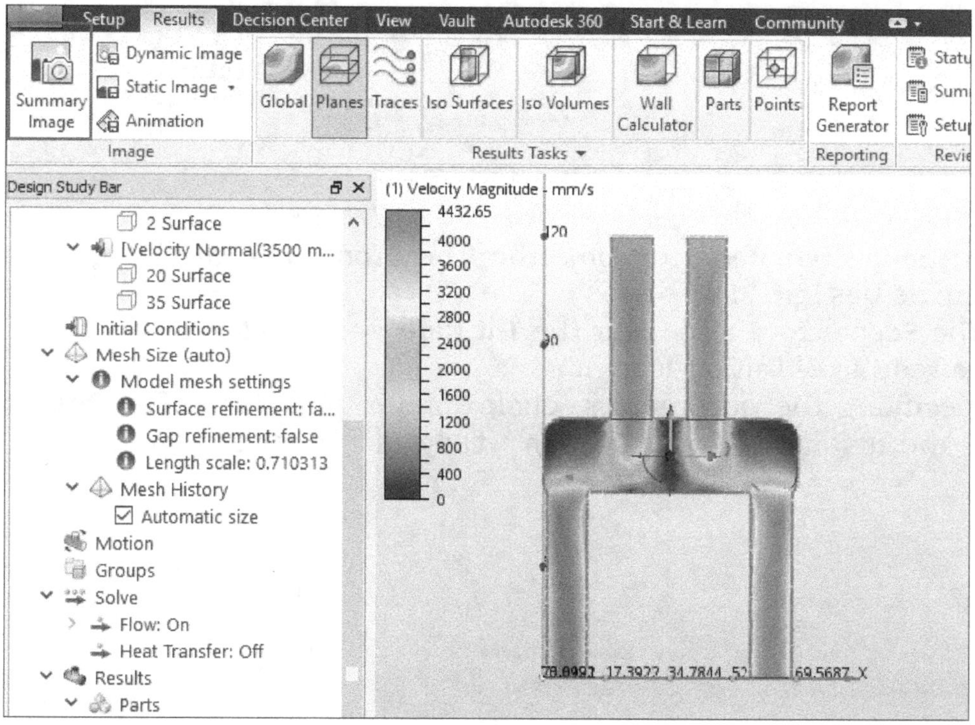

Figure-15. Creating summary image of Design 1

Cloning Model

Till now, we had solved the **Design 1** analysis. Before proceeding to view the results, we need to clone the current model to copy all the settings and current geometry to the other scenario. So that we can compare the results of initial model and last model. The procedure to do so is discussed next.

- Right-click on the **Design 1** option from the **Design Study Bar** when the **Setup** tab is active and select the **Clone** option; refer to Figure-16. The **Clone Design** dialog box will be displayed; refer to Figure-17.

Figure-16. Cloning design of practical 1

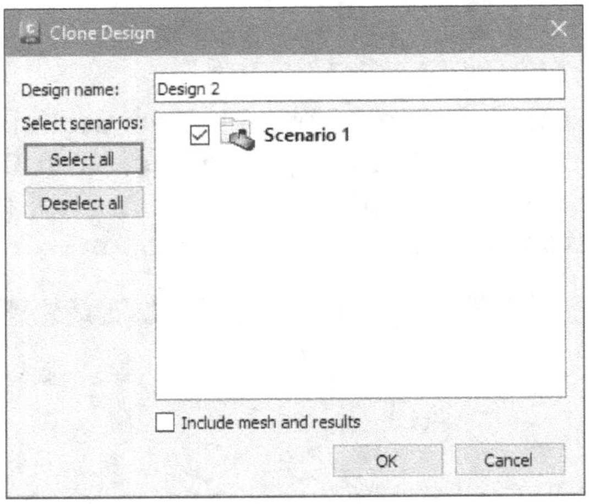

Figure-17. Clone Design dialog box of practical 1

- Click in the **Design name** edit box from the **Clone Design** dialog box and specify the name as **Design 2**.
- Select the **Scenario 1** and clear the **Include mesh and results** check box to not copy the results of initial design.
- After specifying the parameters, click on the **OK** button. The **Design 2** will be created and displayed in the **Design Study Bar**; refer to Figure-18.

Figure-18. Cloned Design 2

Suppressing one of the inlet tube

In this step, we will modify the CAD geometry by removing one inlet from the manifold. The following steps are created using SolidWorks. You can also use other software for performing model changes. You can learn about SolidWorks by using our SolidWorks 2026 Black Book.

- Open the **Practical 1** model in SolidWorks application. The file is available in respective folder of this book's resources.
- Suppress one of the inlets of model as shown in Figure-19 and save the file.

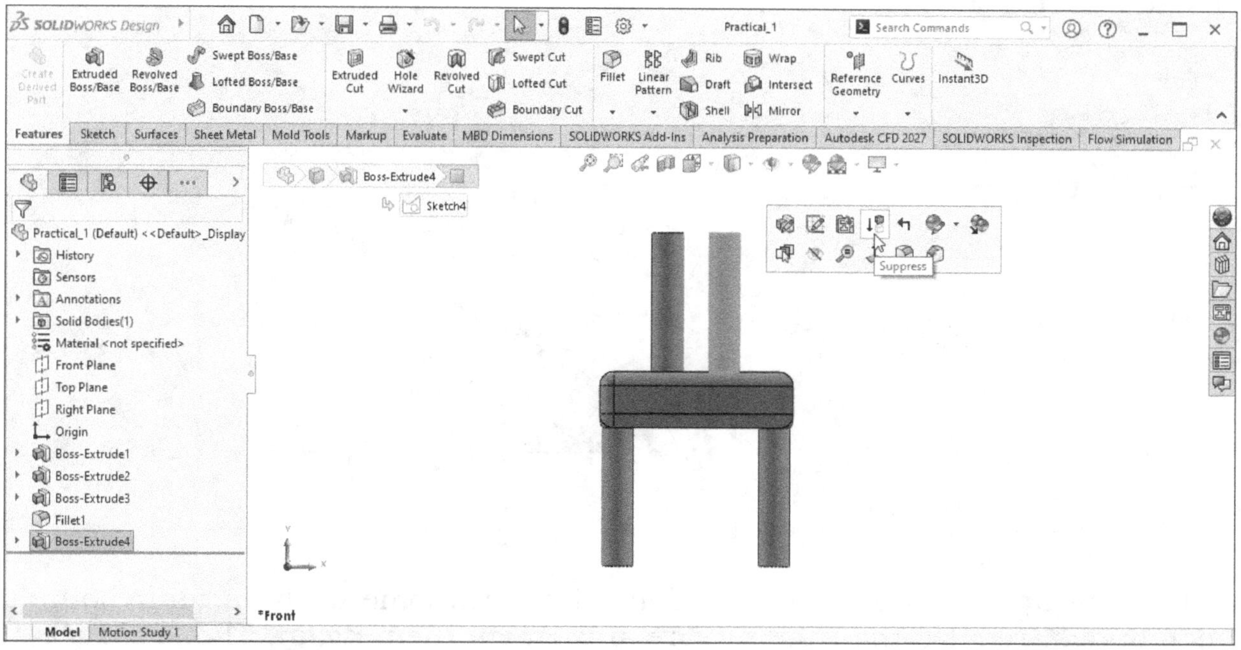

Figure-19. Suppressing inlet

- Now, click on the **Add/Update Design** button from **Design Study Tools** panel of **Setup** tab. The **Add Geometry File** dialog box will be displayed; refer to Figure-20.

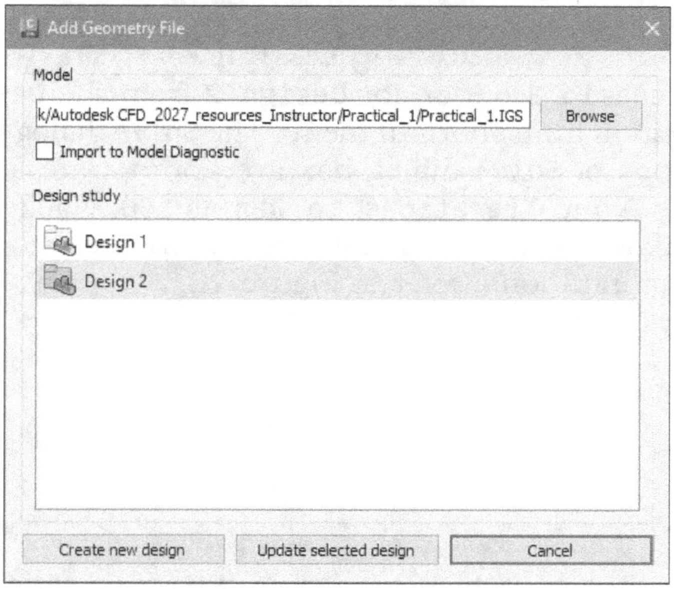

Figure-20. Updating Practical 1

- Click on the **Browse** button from **Add Geometry File** dialog box and select the updated part file (model file updated in SolidWorks).

- Select the **Design 2** option from the **Design study** area of dialog box to update the model in design 2 scenario and click on **Update selected design** button. The **Design 2** will be updated and displayed; refer to Figure-21.

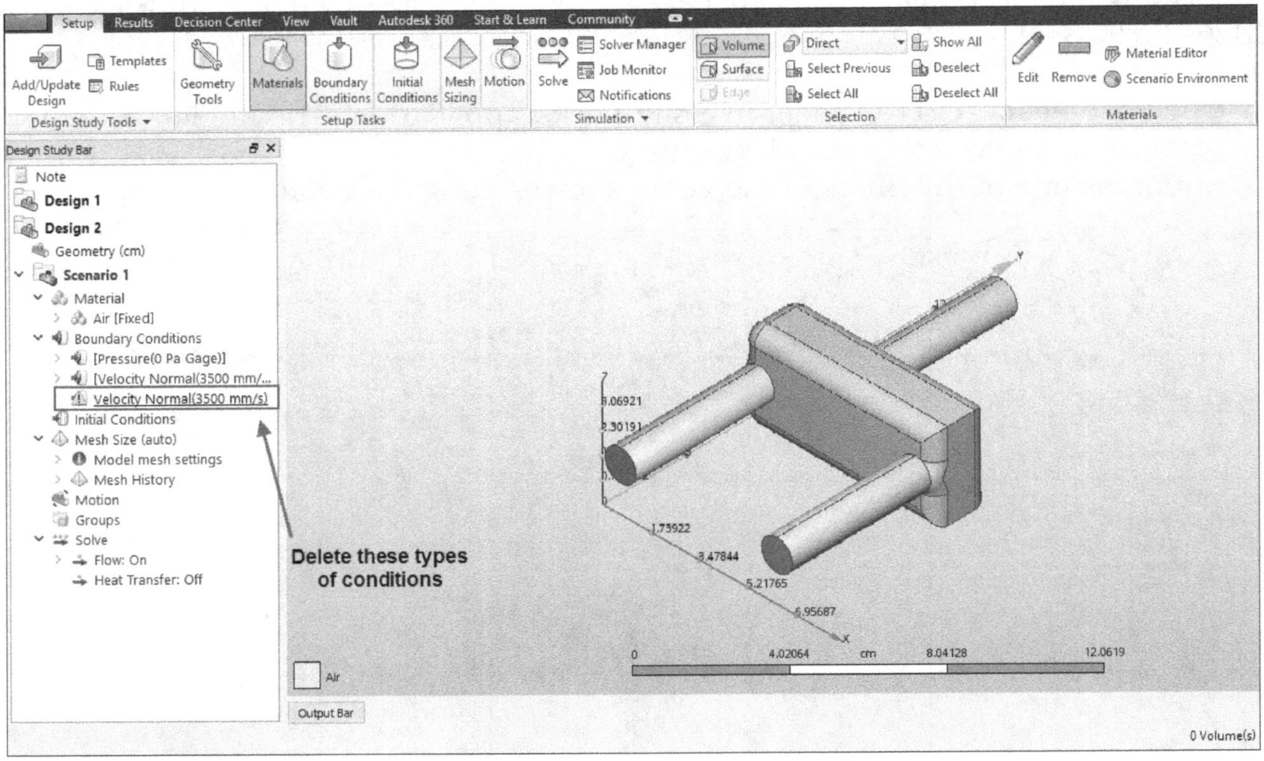

Figure-21. Updated Design 2

- Check the applied boundary conditions. If there is some kind of error in boundary conditions, remove the existing one and create them again. The **Pressure** and **Velocity** boundary conditions are same as we had applied in **Design 1** study. Remove the unnecessary boundary conditions.
- Till now, we had created both the design scenario and its time to solve the **Design 2**.

Solving Design 2

- Right-click on **Scenario 1** option for **Design 2** from the **Design Study Bar** and select the **Solve** option from shortcut menu. The **Solve** dialog box will be displayed.
- The default settings of **Solve** dialog box are appropriate for this scenario, like **Continue From** as **0** and **Iterations to Run** as **100**. Click on the **Solve** button from the **Solve** dialog box. The analysis will start and model will be displayed after completion of iterations; refer to Figure-22.

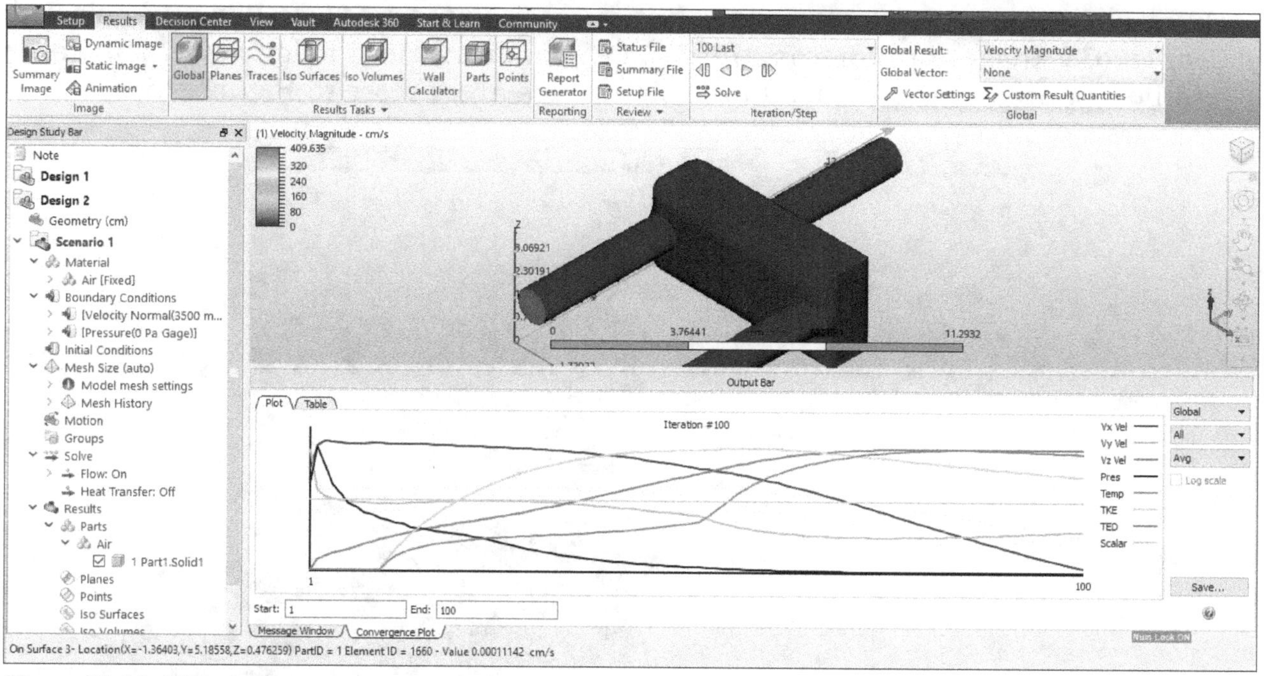

Figure-22. Model Design 2

- Click on the **Planes** tool from the **Results Tasks** panel of **Results** tab; the tools related to plane will be activated and displayed.
- Add a plane along **Z axis** as described in **Design 1**; refer to Figure-23.

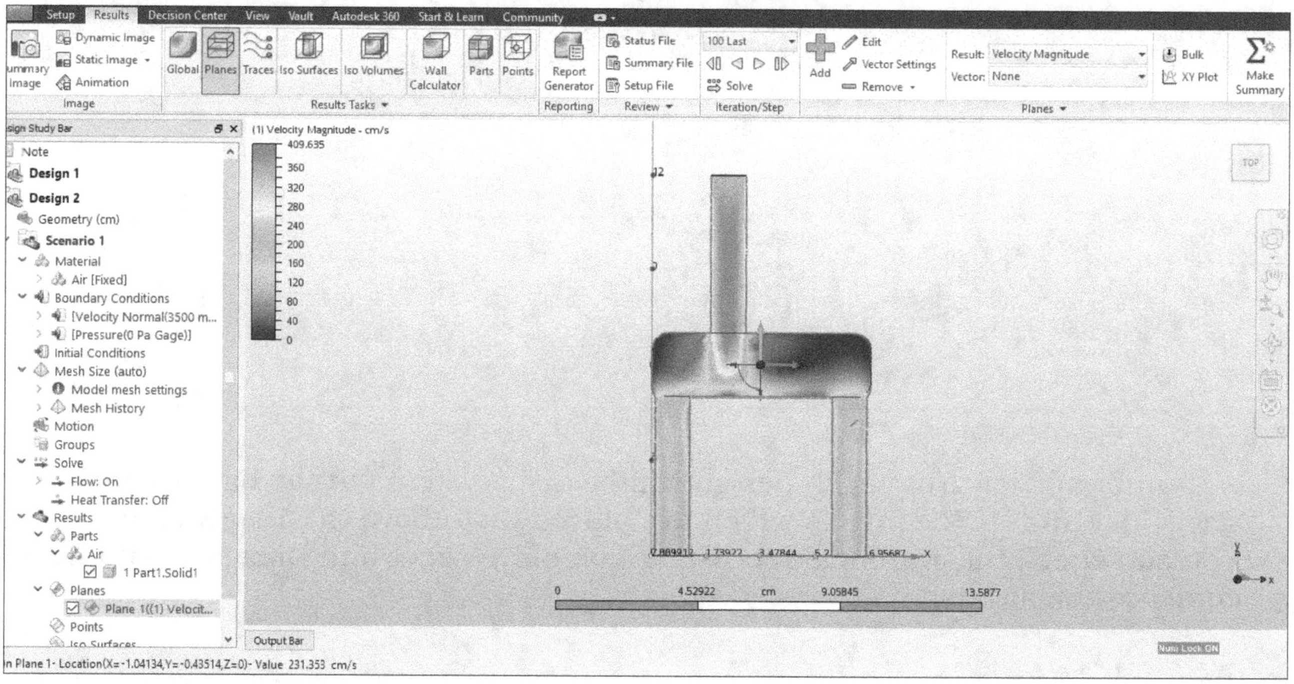

Figure-23. Added plane of Design 2

- Click on **Summary Image** tool from the **Image** panel of the **Results** tab in the **Ribbon** to take a snap of current result model.

Comparing Results

Now, we will compare graphical results of the **Design 1** and **Design 2** using the options of **Design Center** tab in the **Ribbon**. The procedure is discussed next.

- Click on the **Decision Center** tab from the **Ribbon**, the tools will be displayed.

- Right-click on the **Summary Images** option from **Design Study Bar** and select the **Update all images** option from the displayed menu; refer to Figure-24. The images will be updated and displayed in the graphics area; refer to Figure-25.

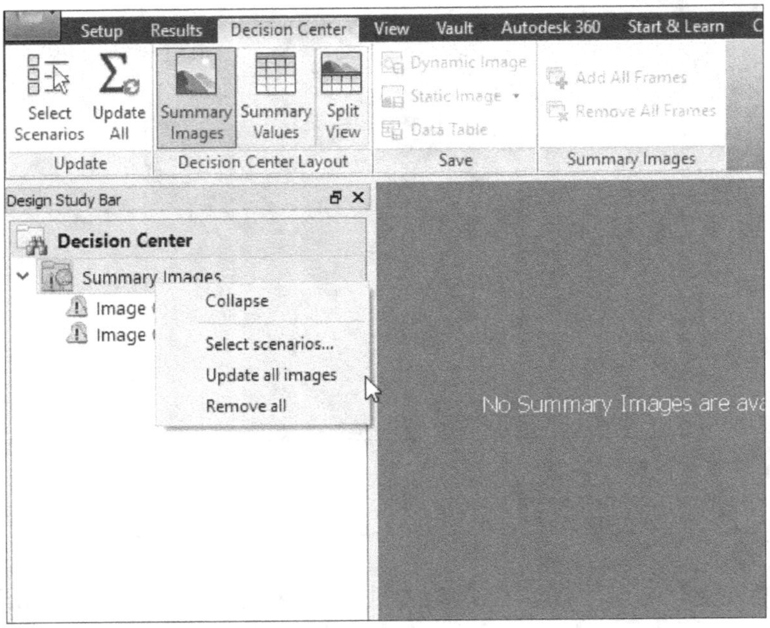

Figure-24. Updating images of Practical 1

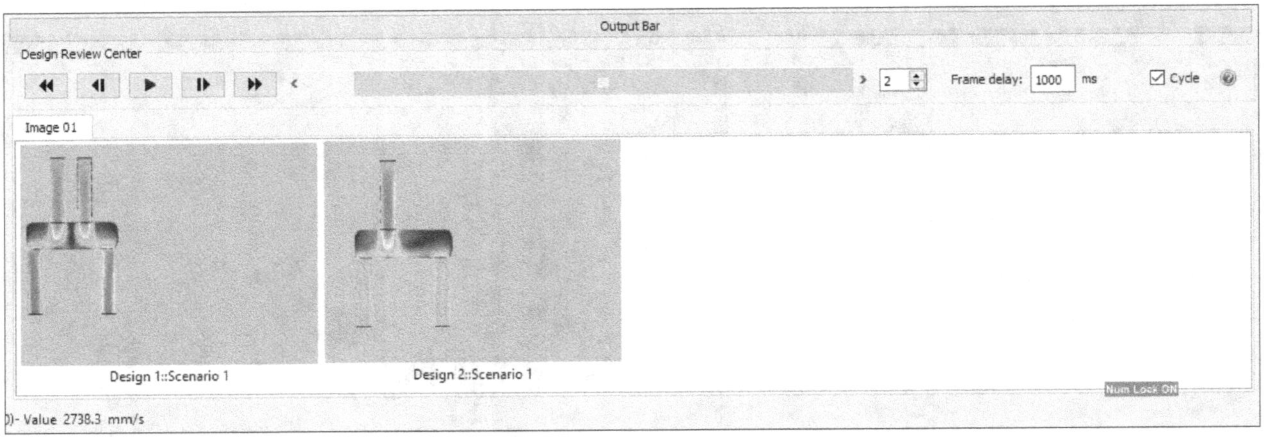

Figure-25. Design Review Center of Practical 1

- A thumbnail view from each design will be displayed in **Output** bar. To compare, use slider and VCR controls which are placed just above the **Image 01** tab.
- You can check the graphical representation of Design 1 and Design 2, and hence compare the air flow.

PRACTICAL 2

In this practical, we will simulate the flow and heat transfer within an electronics enclosure. The electronics model contain several components and we model them with Autodesk CFD as internal fan, capacitor, and so on; refer to Figure-26.

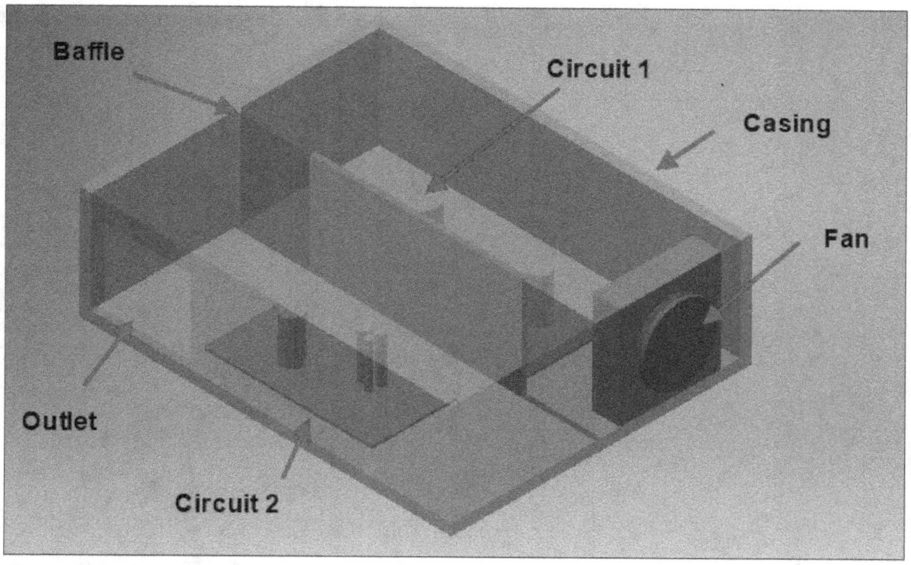

Figure-26. Practical 2

This CAD model is created in Autodesk Inventor. We have also published Autodesk Inventor 2027 Black Book if you need help in CAD modeling.

Opening Model

The procedure to open Practical 2 is discussed next.

- Double-click on the **Autodesk CFD** icon from **Desktop**. The welcome screen of **Autodesk CFD** will be displayed.
- Click on the **New** button from **Quick Access Toolbar**. The **New Design Study** dialog box will be displayed.
- Click on the **Browse** button and select the file **Practical 2 ASM.IAM** from Practical 2 folder (Download the files from our website i.e. www.cadcamcaeworks.com).
- Click in the **Name** edit box and specify the name as **Practical 2**; refer to Figure-27.

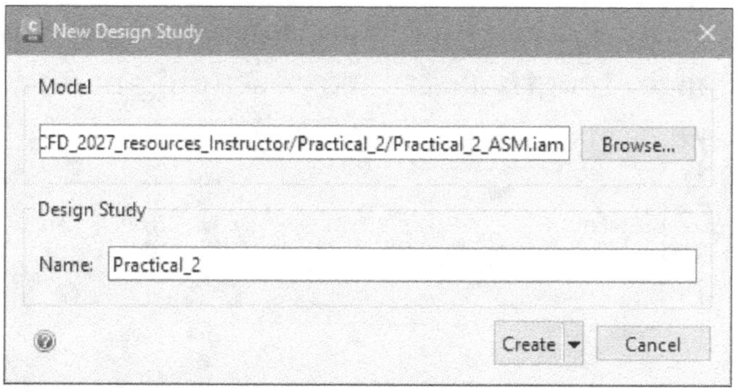

Figure-27. New Design Study dialog box for Practical 2

- After specifying the parameters, click on the **Create** button from **New Design Study** dialog box. The assembly file will be displayed in **Autodesk CFD**; refer to Figure-28. Click on the **Merge** button from the **Geometry Tools** dialog box and close the dialog box.

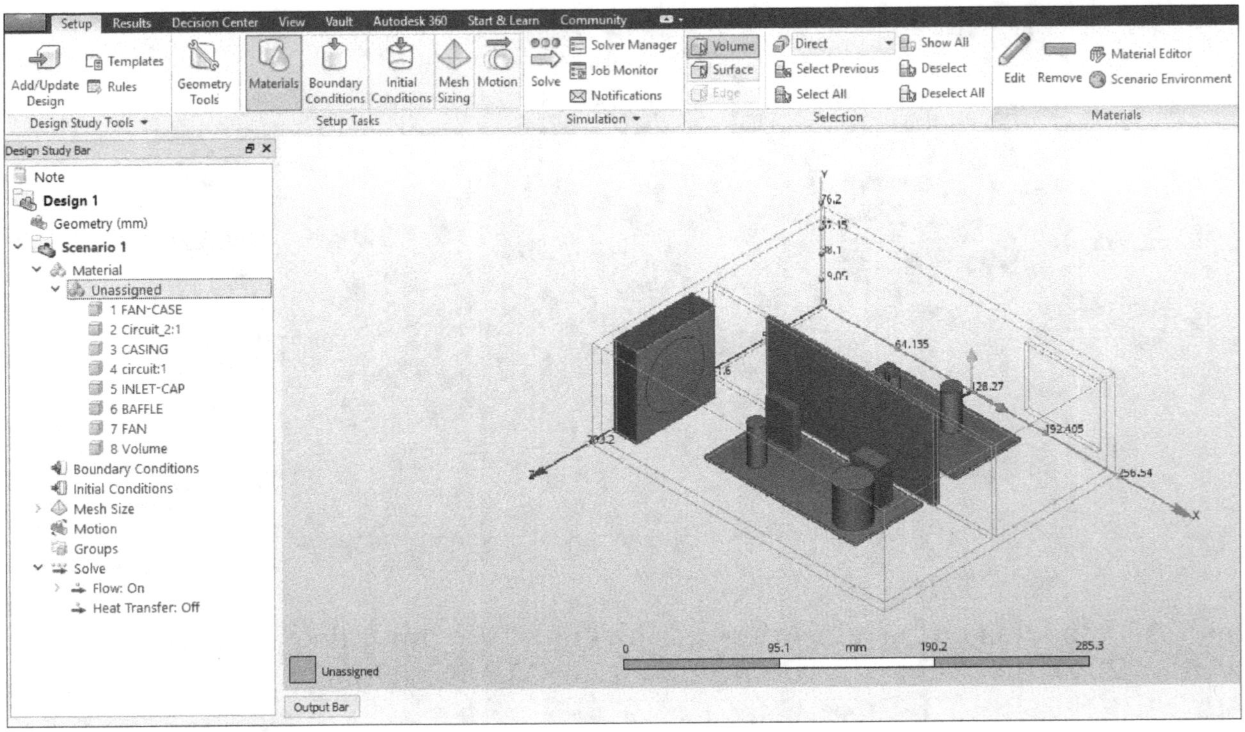

Figure-28. Displayed Practical 2

- The **Volume** and **Casing** option of **Design Study Bar** are set as outline for better visual appearance of other components.

Note: If **Geometry Tools** dialog box appears, merge the broken edges and proceed to the next step.

Changing Units

If the unit of current model is not in mm then change it. The procedure is discussed next.

- Right-click on the **Geometry** feature from **Design Study Bar** and select the **mm** option from the **Change length units to** cascading menu; refer to Figure-29.

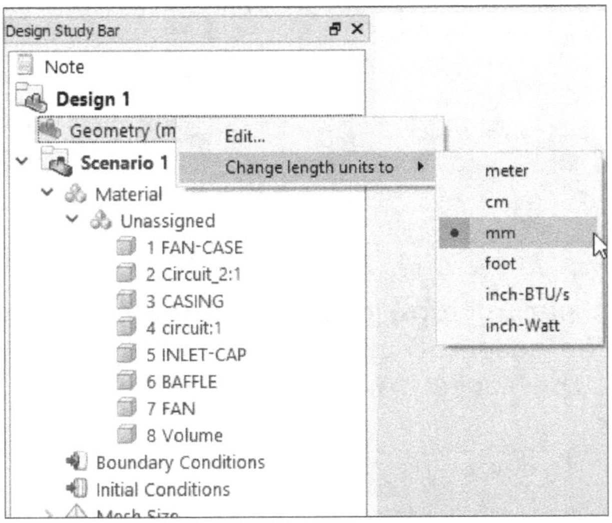

Figure-29. Changing units of Practical 2

- The unit of current model will change.

Creating Flow Volume

There are two fluid regions in the model. One is created automatically when the model is added in Autodesk CFD because it is fully enclosed in casing. The other is not fully bounded so we need to use **Void Fill Geometry** tool to create the other fluid volume. The procedure is discussed next.

- Right-click on the **Casing** and select the **Outline** option from the displayed menu to show model outlines only; refer to Figure-30.

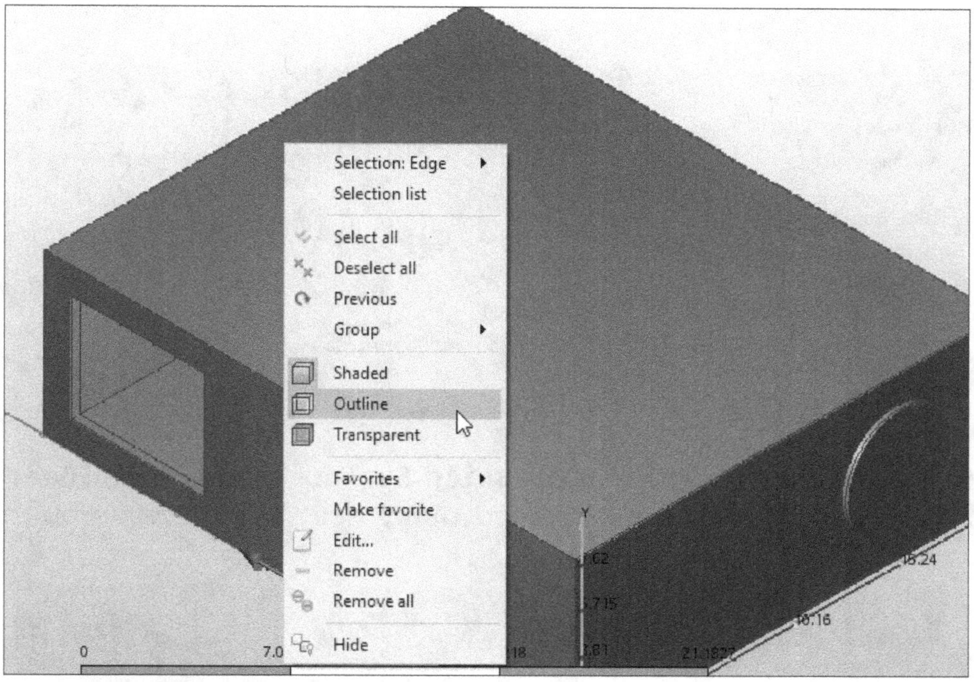

Figure-30. Selecting Outline visual style of Casing

- Click on the **Geometry Tools** button from the **Setup Tasks** panel of the **Setup** tab in **Ribbon**. The **Geometry Tools** dialog box will be displayed.
- Click on the **Void Fill** tab of **Geometry Tools** dialog box and select the two edges of outlet which are sharing the common vertex; refer to Figure-31. The other edges will be selected automatically and displayed in the **Model entity selection** section.

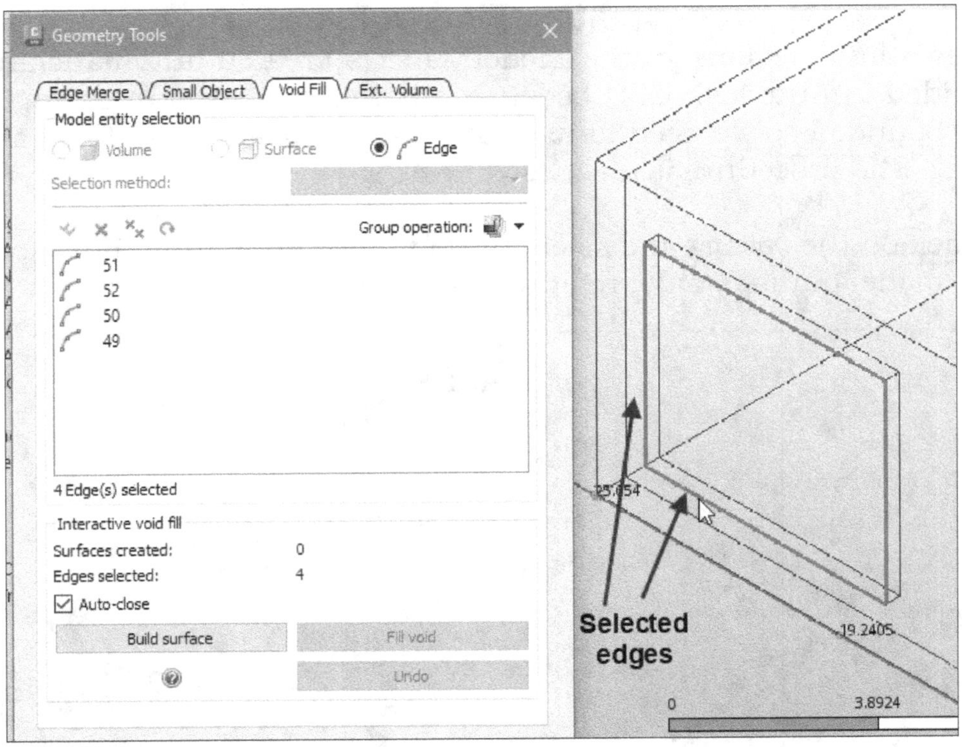

Figure-31. Selecting edges of outlet

- After selecting the edges, click on the **Build Surface** button of the **Geometry Tools** dialog box. The surface will be created using selected edges as boundary; refer to Figure-32.

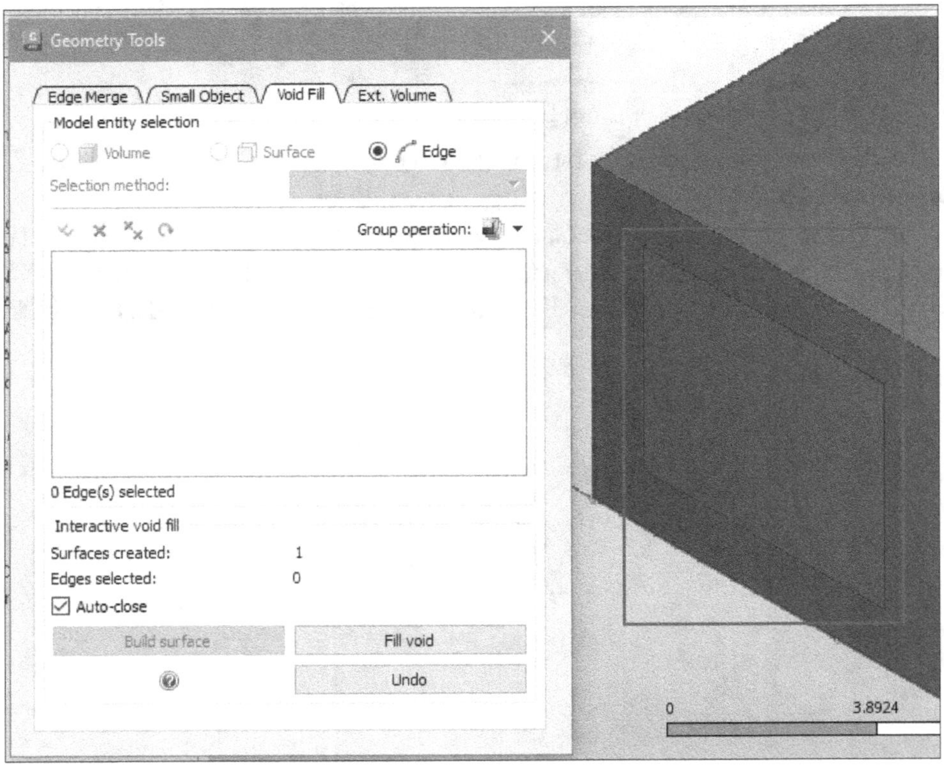

Figure-32. Created surface on outlet

- Click on the **Fill Void** button to complete the process of volume formation and close the **Geometry Tools** dialog box.

Creating groups of circuit boards

In this step, we will create a group of similar component to assigning materials, boundary conditions, and mesh sizes. The procedure to create a group is discussed next.

- Click on the **Materials** tool from **Setup Tasks** panel of **Setup** tab to activate the material task.
- Right-click on casing and click on **Hide** button from the displayed menu to hide casing; refer to Figure-33.

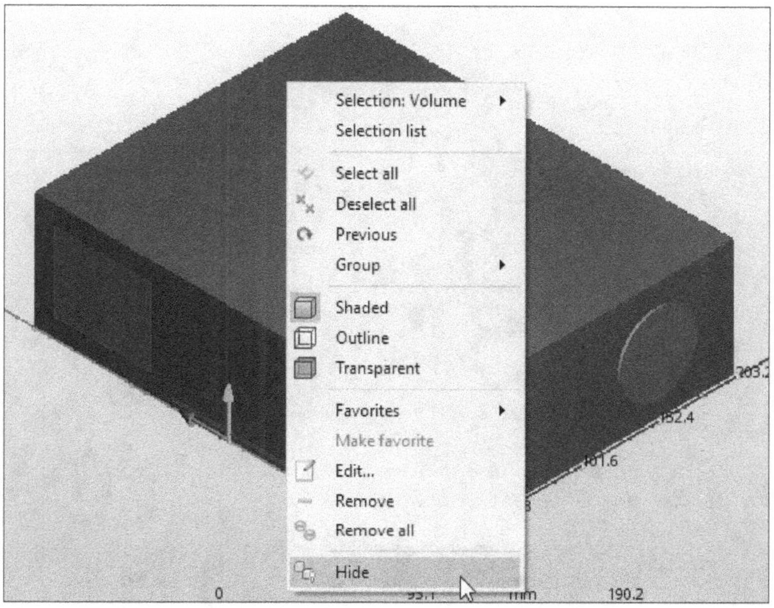

Figure-33. Hiding Casing

- Similarly, hide the **CFDCreatedvolume** and **Volume** by pressing **CTRL** key and middle mouse button. You can also hide the same with the help of previous method; refer to Figure-34.

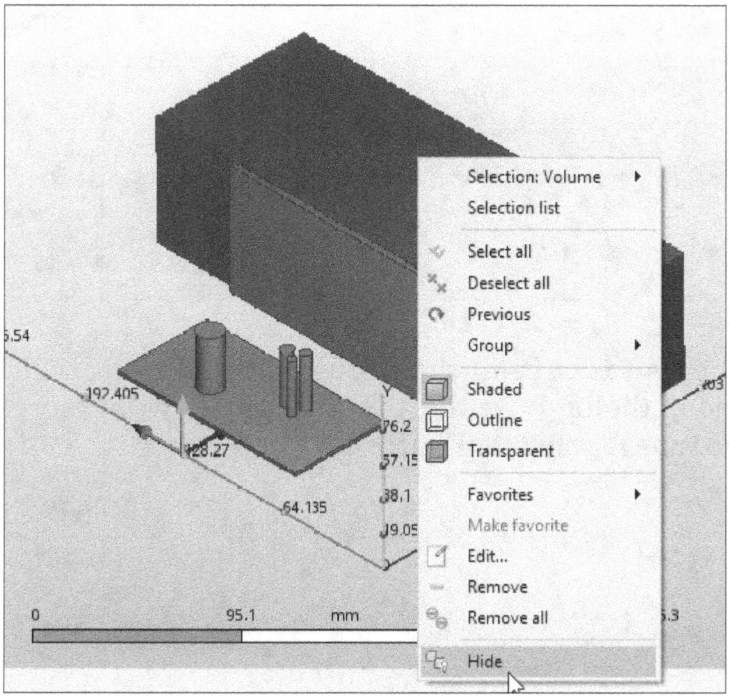

Figure-34. Hiding Volume

- Select the **Circuit 1** and **Circuit 2** objects from **Design Study Bar** and click on **Create Group** button from **Group** cascading menu of right-click menu; refer to Figure-35. The **Add to Group** dialog box will be displayed; refer to Figure-36.

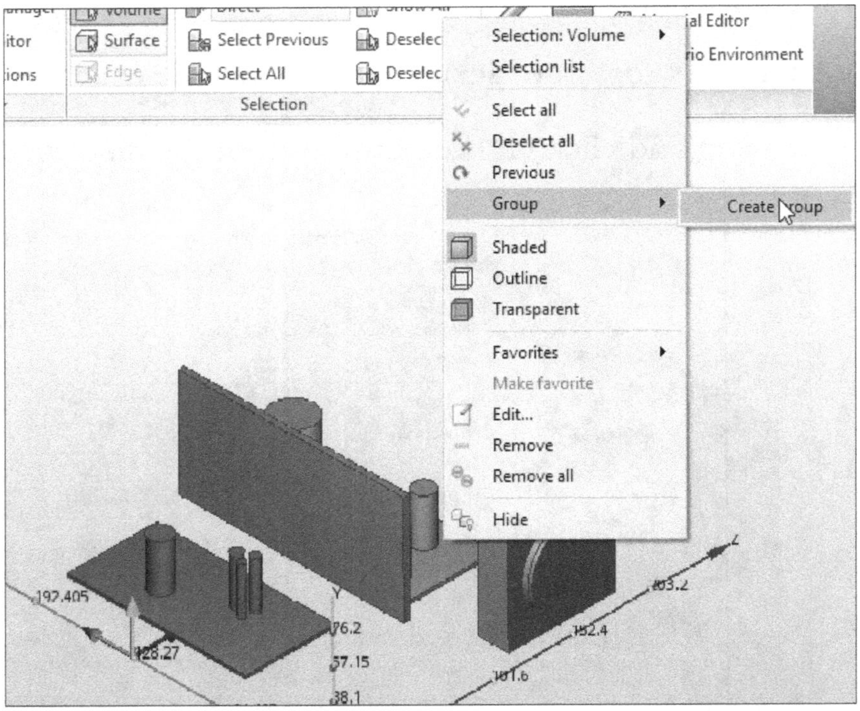

Figure-35. Creating Group of Circuit board

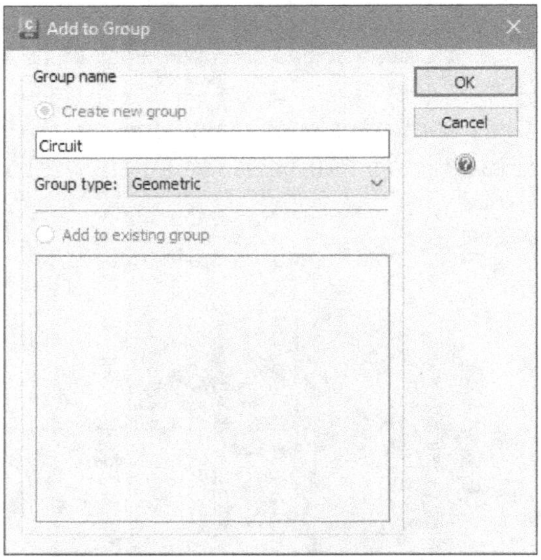

Figure-36. Creating group

- Specify the name as **Circuit** in the **Group Name** edit box. Click on the **OK** button from **Add to Group** dialog box; the **Circuit** group will be created and displayed as **Circuit -(Volume)**; refer to Figure-37.

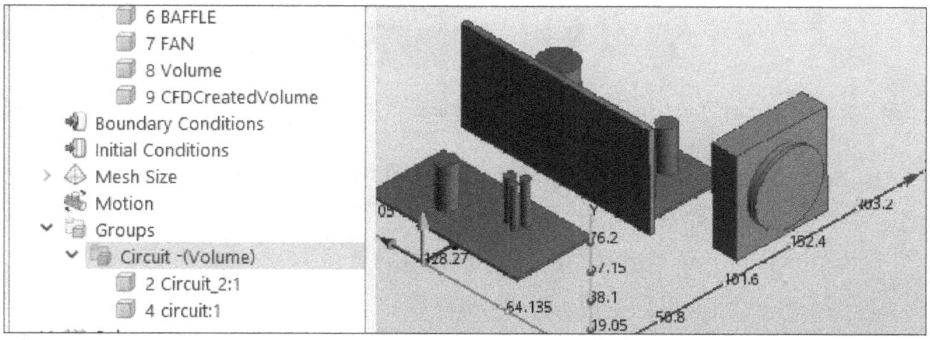

Figure-37. Circuit Volume

Assigning Material

Now, its time to assign material to all parts of model.

- Click on the **Materials** tool from **Setup Tasks** panel of **Setup** tab; the **Materials** task will be activated.
- Select the **Volume**, **Inlet-Cap**, and **CFDCreatedVolume** option from **Design Study Bar** and click on **Edit** button from **Materials** panel. The **Material** dialog box will be displayed.
- Select the **Material** as **Air** and click on **Apply** button; refer to Figure-38. The material will be applied and displayed on model.

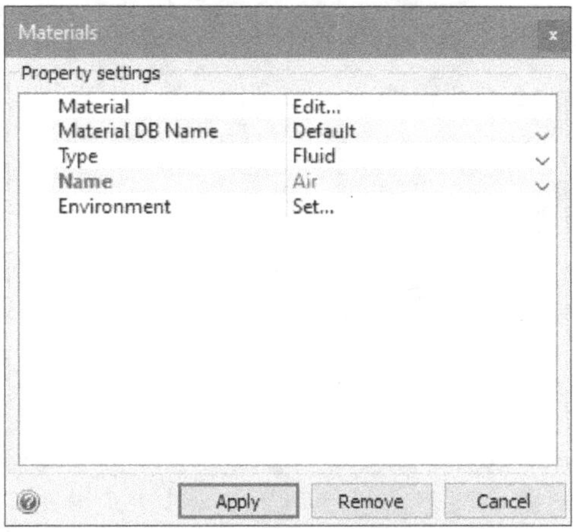

Figure-38. Applying Materials to Practical 2

- Now, select the **FAN-CASE**, **Casing**, **Circuit 1**, and **Circuit 2** from the **Design Study Bar** while holding **CTRL** key and right-click on any of the selected components. The right-click shortcut menu will be displayed.
- Select the **Edit** option from the shortcut menu. The **Material** dialog box will be displayed.
- Select the **Aluminum** as **Material** from **Solid** category and click on **Apply** button; refer to Figure-39. The selected material will be applied.

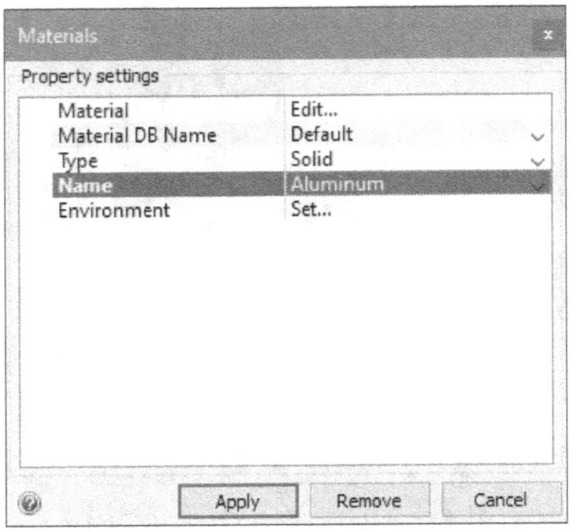

Figure-39. Applying Aluminum as material

Creating and applying Baffle material

- Select the **Baffle** component from **Design Study Bar** and click on **Edit** button from **Materials** panel of **Setup** tab; the **Materials** dialog box will be displayed. Select **Resistance** option from the **Type** drop-down in the dialog box.
- Click on **Edit** button from **Material** field in the dialog box. The **Material Editor** dialog box will be displayed; refer to Figure-40.

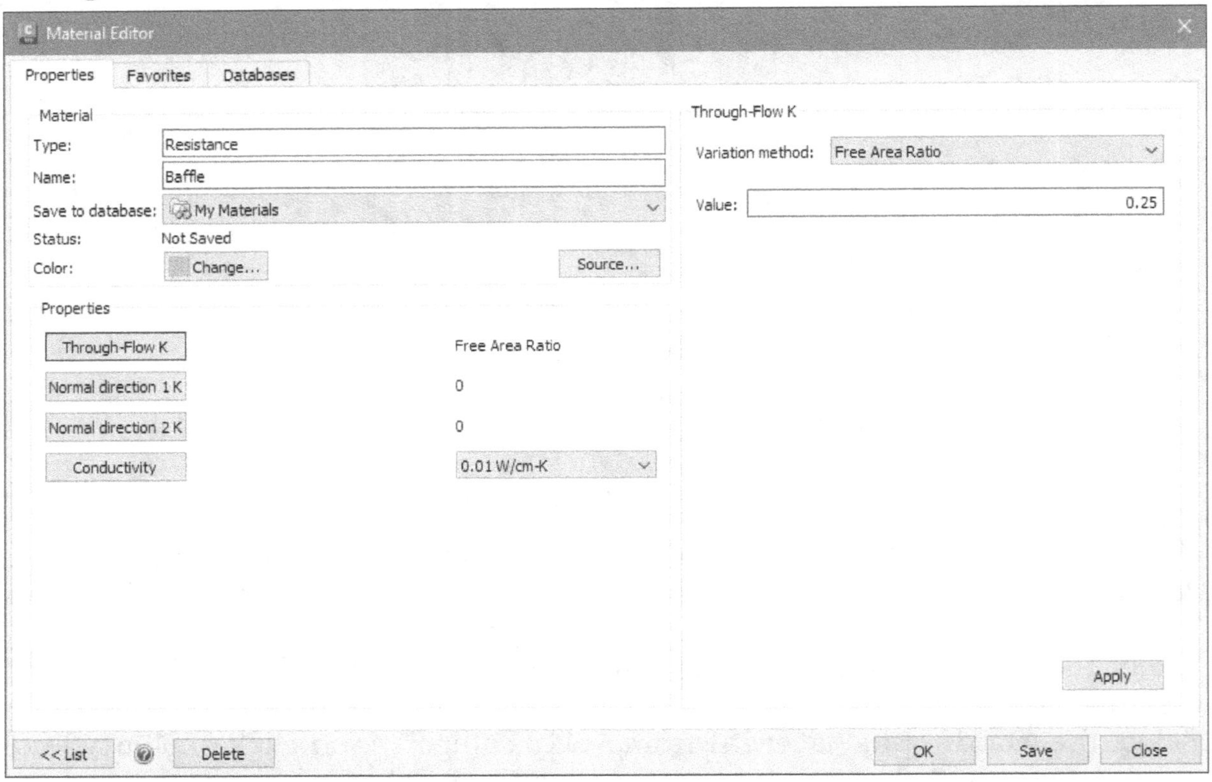

Figure-40. Creating material for baffle

- Click in the **Name** edit box from **Material Editor** dialog box and specify the name as **Baffle**.
- Select the **My Materials** option from **Save to database** drop-down to save the **Baffle** material in your selected list.
- Click on the **Through-Flow K** button. The parameters will be displayed at right of **Material Editor** dialog box.
- Click on the **Variation method** drop-down and select the **Free Area Ratio** option.
- Click in the **Value** edit box and specify the value as **0.25**.

- Click on the **Apply** button to apply changes to the resistance.
- Similarly, click on the **Normal direction 1K** button and specify the parameter of **Variation method** as **Free Area Ratio** with **Value** as **0**. After specifying parameters, click on **Apply** button to save the parameters.
- The parameters of **Normal direction 2K** are same as **Normal direction 1K** option.
- Click on the **Conductivity** button from **Material Editor** dialog box and specify the value of **Variation method** as **Constant** with **Value** as **0.2 W/mm-K**, and don't forget to click on **Apply** button.
- After specifying the parameters for **Baffle**, click on the **Save** button and then **OK** button from **Material Editor** dialog box. You will return to **Materials** dialog box and the **Baffle** material will be displayed in **Name** field.
- Click on the **Global X** button from the **Flow Direction** field in **Materials** dialog box; the **Flow Direction** dialog box will be displayed; refer to Figure-41.

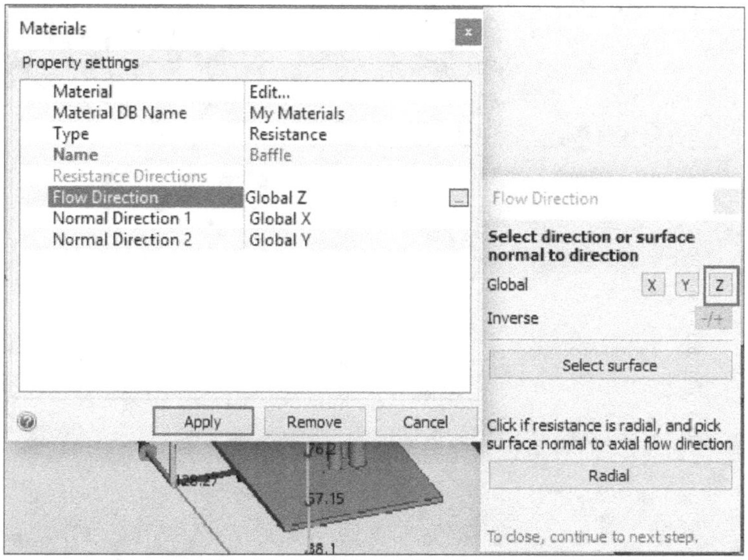

Figure-41. Flow Direction option

- Select the **Z** button from the **Flow Direction** dialog box and close it.
- Similarly, set **Global X** in **Normal Direction 1** and **Global Y** in **Normal Direction 2** fields.
- After specifying the parameters, click on the **Apply** button from **Materials** dialog box to apply **Baffle** resistance to model.

Creating Fan Material

- Select the **Fan** component from **Design Study Bar** and click on **Edit** button from **Materials** panel of **Setup** tab in **Ribbon**. The **Materials** dialog box will be displayed.
- Click on the **Type** drop-down from the **Materials** dialog box and select **Internal Fan/Pump** button to specify the material type.
- Click on the **Edit** button from **Material** option of **Materials** dialog box; the **Material Editor** dialog box will be displayed.
- Click in the **Name** edit box of **Material Editor** dialog box and specify the name as **Fan**.
- Click on the **Save to database** drop-down from **Material Editor** dialog box and select the **My Materials** option.
- Click on **Flow** button to specify the flow parameters. The parameters will be displayed at right.
- Click on the **Variation method** drop-down and select the **Constant** button.

- Click in the **Value** edit box and specify the value as **0.50**. Change the units to **m3/min** and click on **Apply** button to apply these parameters.
- Now, click on **Rotational Speed** button from **Material Editor** dialog box; the **Rotational Speed** section will be displayed at right.
- Click in the **Value** edit box of **Rotational Speed** section and specify the value as **1000**. Click on **Apply** button to apply these parameters.
- Click on the **Slip factor** button from **Material Editor** dialog box. The **Slip factor** area will be displayed at right.
- Click in the **Value** edit box of **Slip factor** area and specify the value as **1.** Rest of the parameters will be same as default. Click on the **Apply** button to apply the parameters.
- After specifying the parameters for **Fan**, click on the **Save** button and then on the **OK** button from **Material Editor** dialog box; refer to Figure-42. You will be returned to **Materials** dialog box.

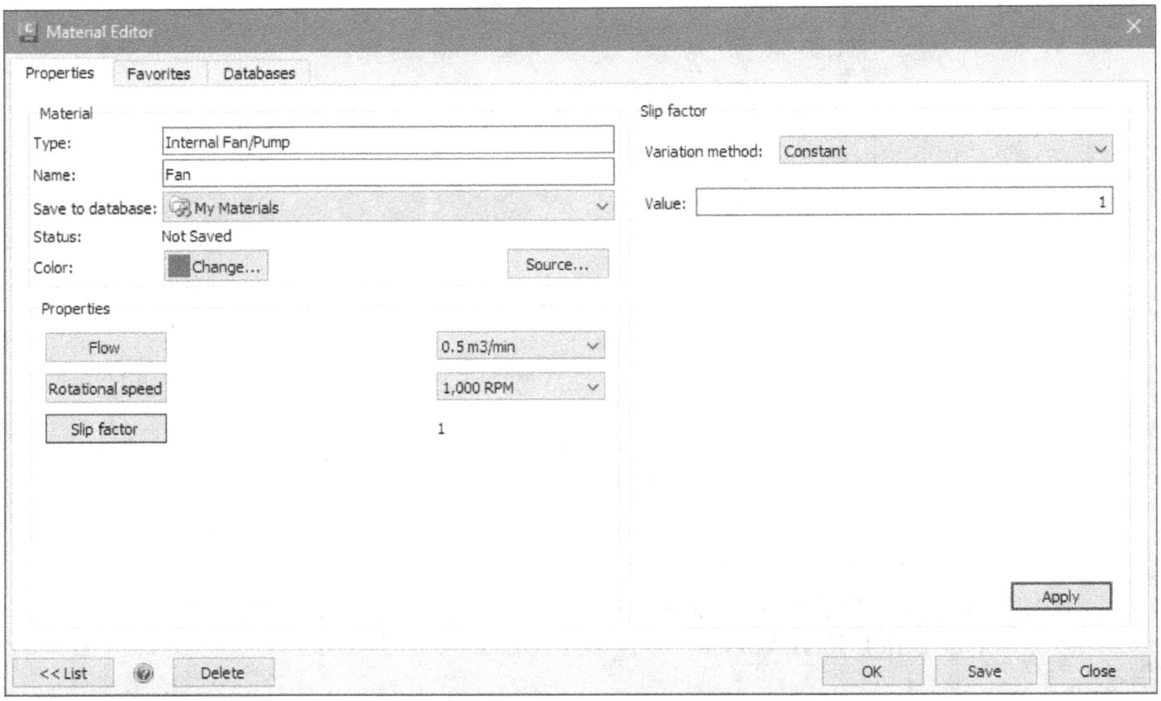

Figure-42. Fan material

- In **Materials** dialog box, select the **Name** as **Fan** and click on **Flow direction** button; the **Flow Direction** dialog box will be displayed; refer to Figure-43. Select the **X** button for direction from **Flow Direction** dialog box and click on **Apply** button from **Materials** dialog box.

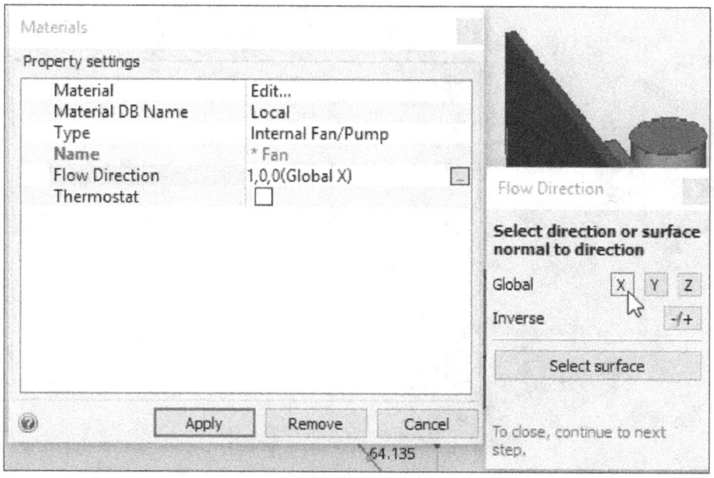

Figure-43. Specifying flow direction for Fan

Till now, we have applied materials to all component of model. Now, we will assign the boundary conditions.

Applying Boundary Conditions

In this section, we are going to apply boundary conditions to inlet and outlet of model.

- Click on the **Boundary Conditions** tool from **Setup** tab to activate boundary conditions task.
- Click on the **Surface** button from **Selection** panel to select surfaces from model.
- Select the inlet surface (outer surface of fan) and click on **Edit** button from **Ribbon**; the **Boundary Conditions** dialog box will be displayed.
- Specify the parameter of **Type** as **Pressure**, pressure value as **1 atm**, and click on the **Apply** button; refer to Figure-44. The pressure boundary condition will be applied.

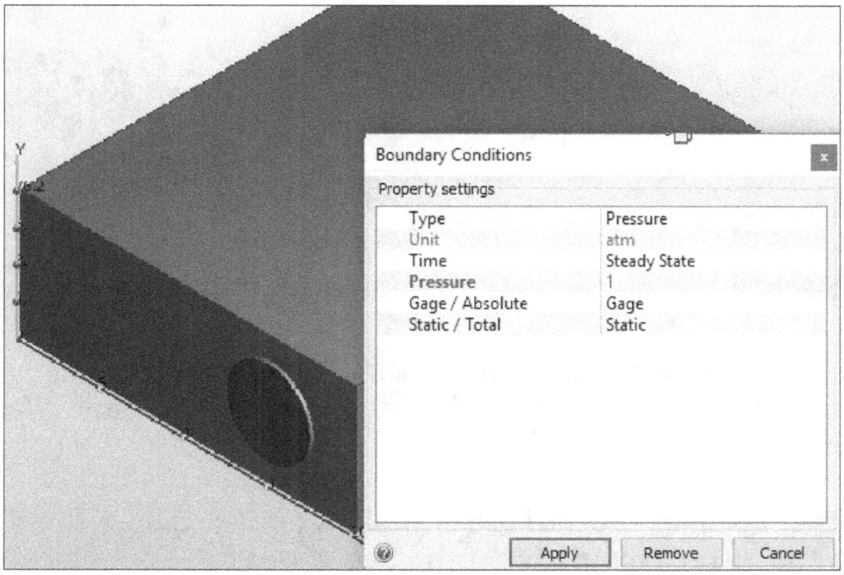

Figure-44. Applying inlet presure boundary condition

- Select the inlet surface again and click on **Edit** button. Specify the parameter **Type** as **Temperature**, **Unit** as **Celsius**, and **Temperature** as **25**, and click on **Apply** button; refer to Figure-45. The **Temperature** boundary condition will be applied at the inlet.

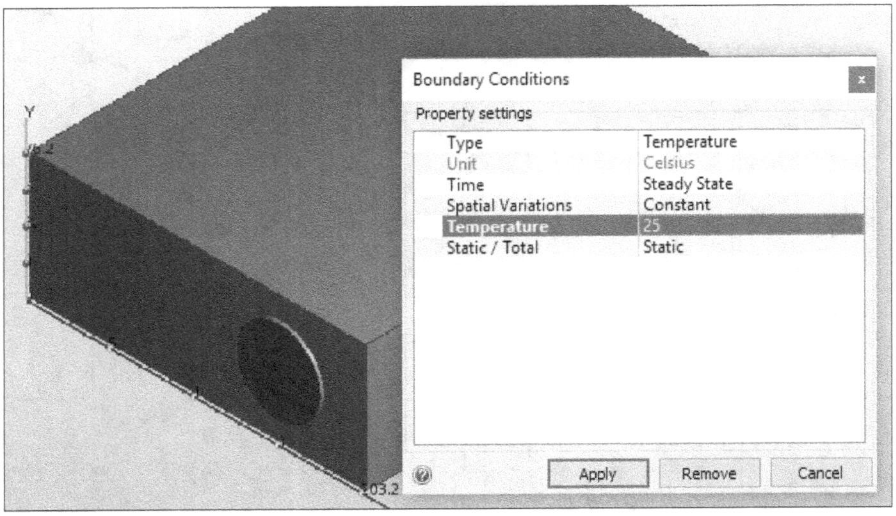

Figure-45. Applying inlet temperature boundary condition

Outlet Boundary condition

- Select the outlet surface of model and click on **Edit** button from **Boundary Conditions** panel; the **Boundary Conditions** dialog box will be displayed.
- Specify the parameter of **Type** as **Pressure**, **Unit** as **atm**, and **Pressure** as **1** in **Boundary Conditions** dialog box; refer to Figure-46.

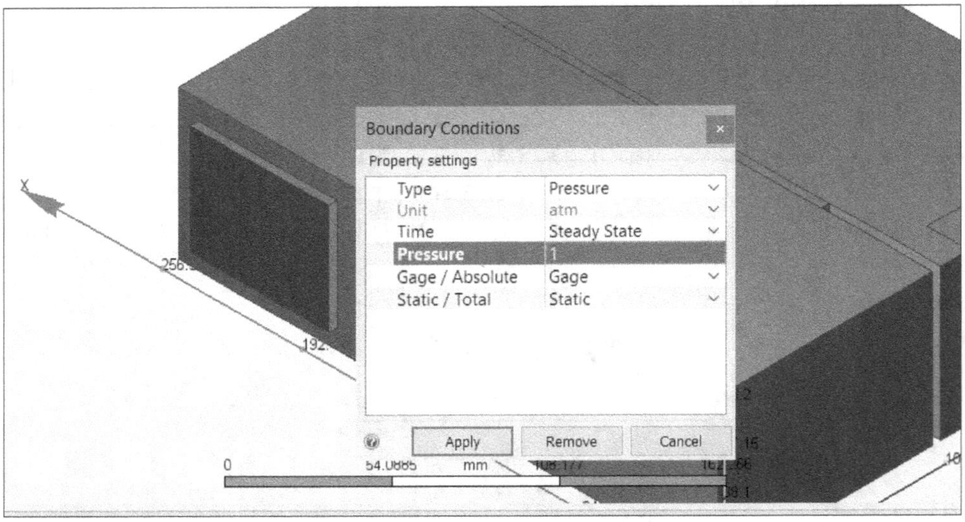

Figure-46. Outlet Boundary Conditions of Practical 2

- Click on the **Apply** button to apply the outlet boundary condition.

Heat Generation of Circuit Board

When electronic components work in circuit, they produce heat. We will now apply heat generation to the components.

- Make sure the **Boundary Conditions** task is active. Select the **Volume** selection button from the **Selection** panel of the **Setup** tab to select objects by volume.
- Hide the Casing, CFDCreatedVolume, and Volume by pressing **CTRL** key and middle mouse button.
- Now, select **Circuit 1** and **Circuit 2** from graphics area and click on **Edit** button from the **Ribbon**; the **Boundary Conditions** dialog box will be displayed.

- Specify the **Type** as **Total Heat Generation**, **Unit** as **W**, **Total Heat Generation** as **2** in **Boundary Conditions** dialog box; refer to Figure-47. Click on the **Apply** button from the dialog box. The **Total Heat Generation** boundary condition will be applied.

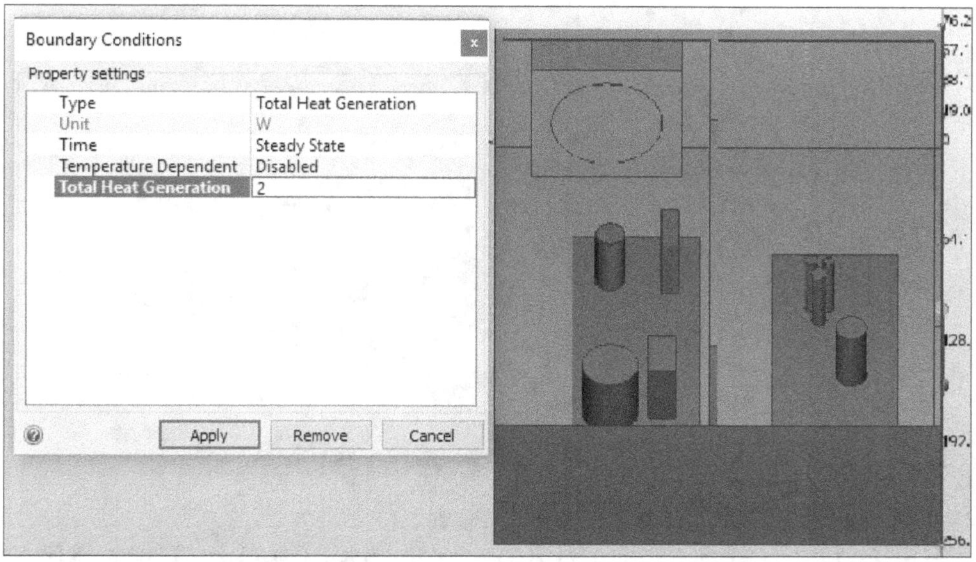

Figure-47. Applying Heat Generation Boundary Condition

- You can also do the same by selecting the previously created group i.e. **Circuit -(Volume)** and click on **Edit** button from **Boundary Conditions** panel. The **Boundary Conditions** dialog box will be displayed. Rest of the process to apply heat generation boundary condition is same as discussed earlier.

Mesh Generating

Till now, we have applied materials to all parts of model and boundary conditions to inlet and outlet surfaces. Now, we are ready to generate mesh and the procedure to do so is discussed next.

- Click on the **Mesh Sizing** tool from the **Setup Tasks** panel to activate the **Mesh Sizing** task.
- Click on the **Autosize** button from the **Automatic Sizing** panel of **Setup** tab in the **Ribbon**; the mesh will be generated and displayed on model; refer to Figure-48.

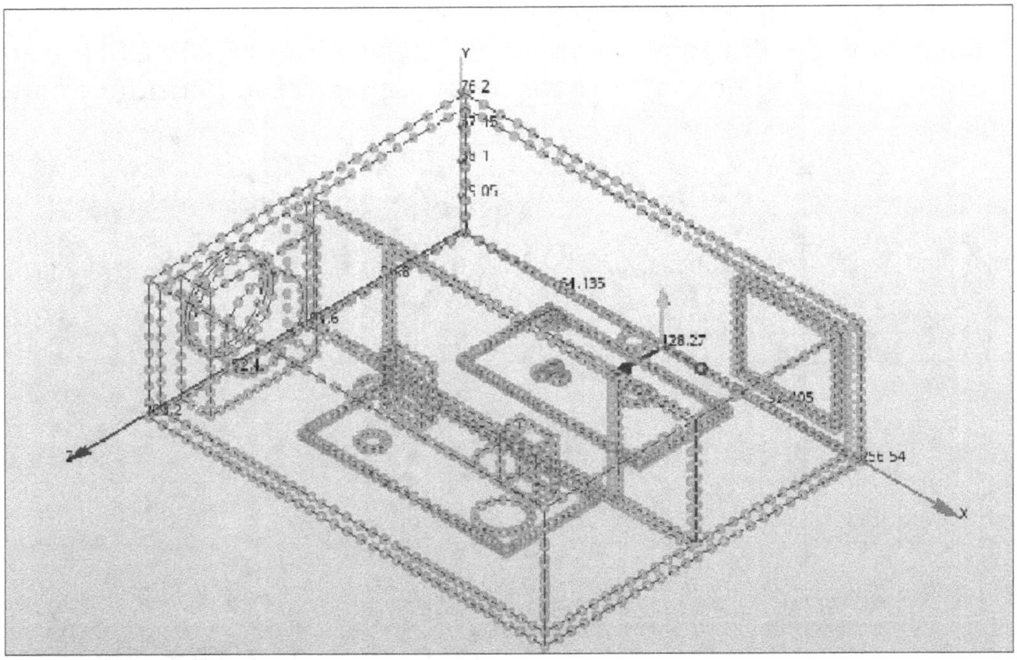

Figure-48. Mesh on Practical 2

- Click on the **`Edit`** button to edit the parameters of mesh. The **`Mesh Sizes`** dialog box will be displayed. The need of changing the parameters of mesh is because of some components on circuit board which are too small for analysis. If, we opt for automatic mesh then the automatically generated mesh will not be enough fine for our needs. So, we will now refine those parts to make them more convenient for analysis.
- Now, select all surfaces of available component on circuit board and move the slider of **`Size adjustment`** towards **`Fine`** and set **`0.50`** value; refer to Figure-49.

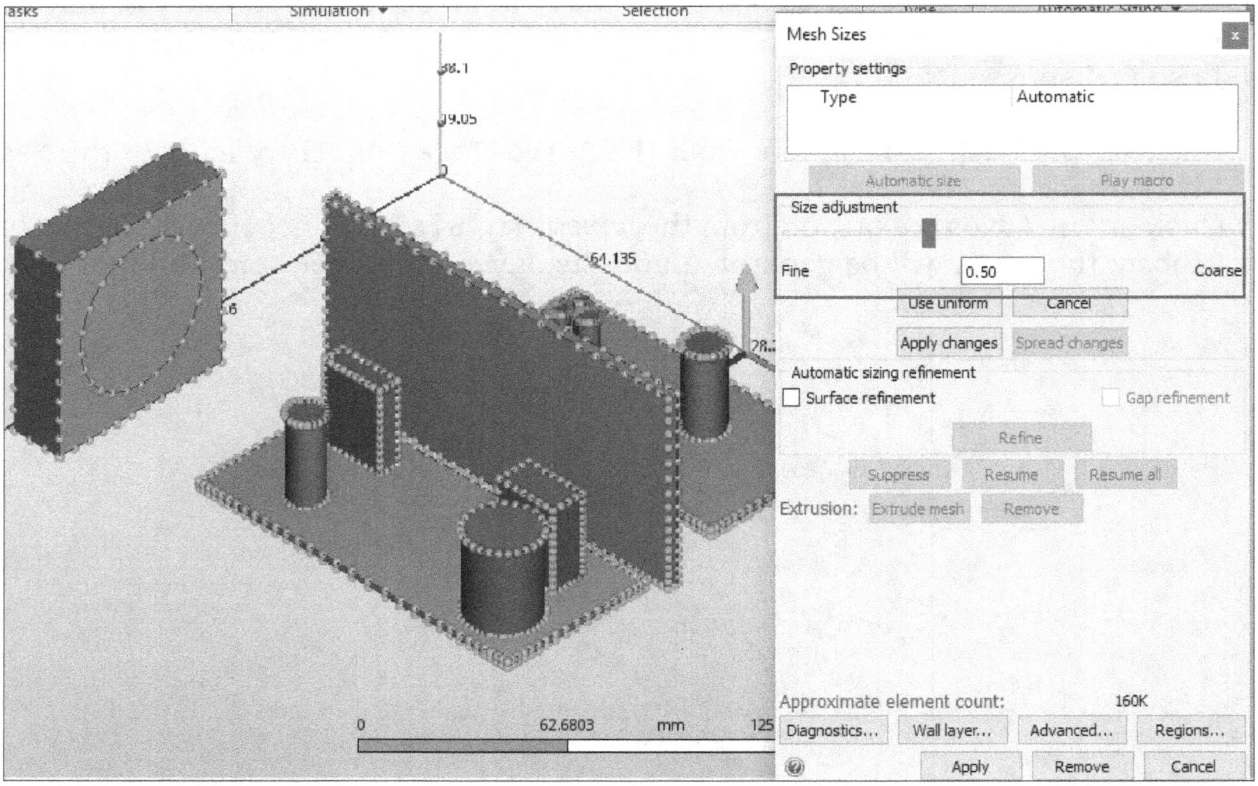

Figure-49. Adjusting mesh

- After adjusting the mesh, click on **Apply changes** and then **Spread changes** button from the Size adjustment area of dialog box.
- After setting mesh, click on **Apply** button from **Mesh Sizes** dialog box. You will return to **Setup** tab.

Solving Analysis

All the parameters needed to solve the analysis have been defined so we are ready to solve the analysis. The process is discussed next.

- Click on the **Solve** button from the **Simulation** panel of **Setup** tab in the **Ribbon**. The **Solve** dialog box will be displayed.
- Click on the **Physics** tab from the **Solve** dialog box and select the check boxes for **Flow**, **Heat Transfer**, and **Auto Forced Convection** options; refer to Figure-50.

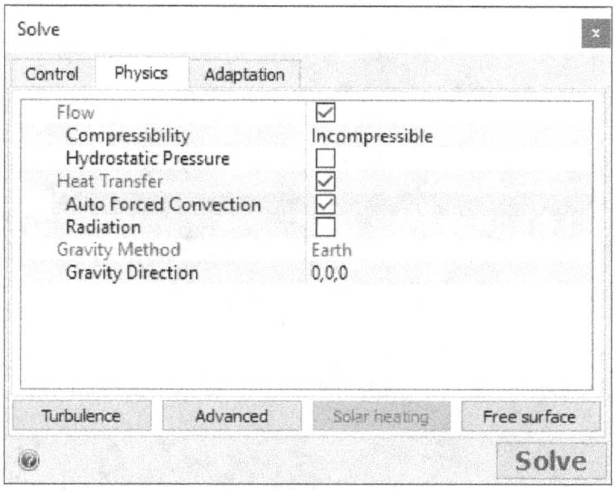

Figure-50. Physics tab of Practical 2

- Click on the **Control** tab and specify the value of **Iterations to Run** as **100**. Click on the **Solve** button to solve the analysis. The analysis will start to solve and progress will be displayed in **Convergence** tab; refer to Figure-51.

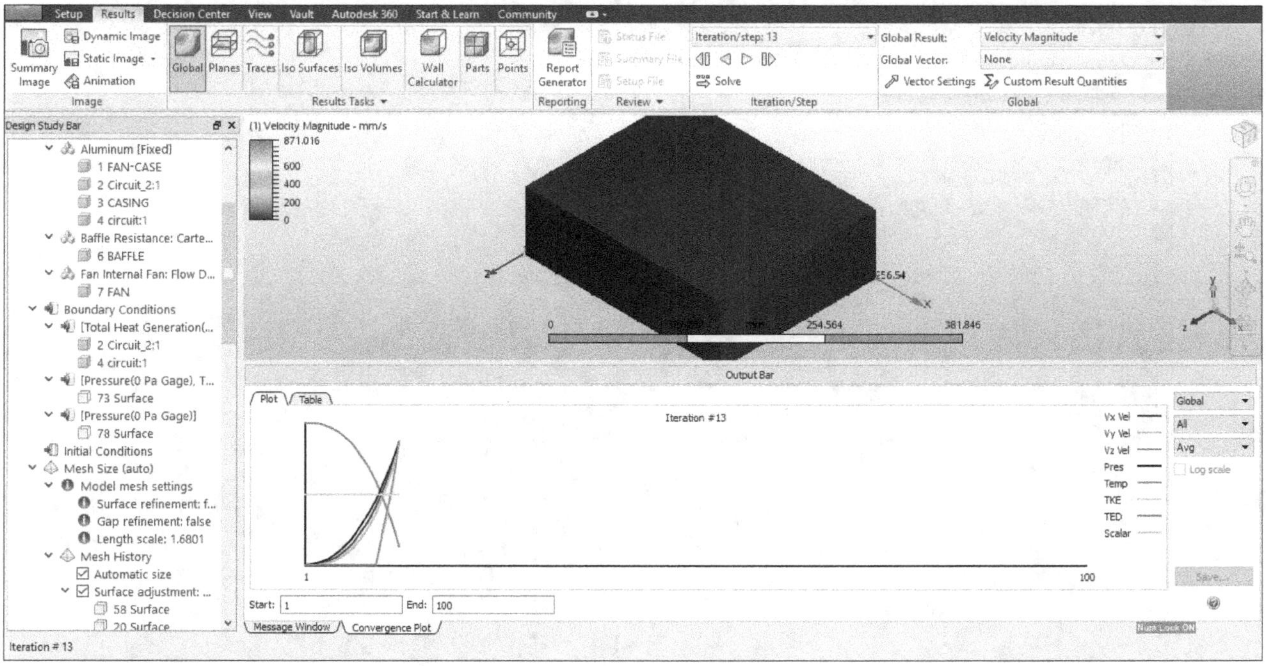

Figure-51. Convergence tab of Practical 2

- The **Auto Forced Convection** causes the analysis to automatically run in two stages. The first stage is flow-only and the other stage solves the heat transfer only, and runs to an additional 100 iterations. We had set the numbers of iterations to 100 in **Solve** dialog box to reduce the overall time of exercise. Increase the number of iterations to 300 to run the analysis for converging automatically.

Results

After the analysis is complete, the **Output Bar** and **Results** tab will be displayed. It's time to check the result of analysis.

Planes

- Click on the **Planes** button from the **Results** tab and click on the **Add** button from **Planes** panel. The plane will be created along X axis.
- Click on the added plane and select **Y** axis from context menu; refer to Figure-52.

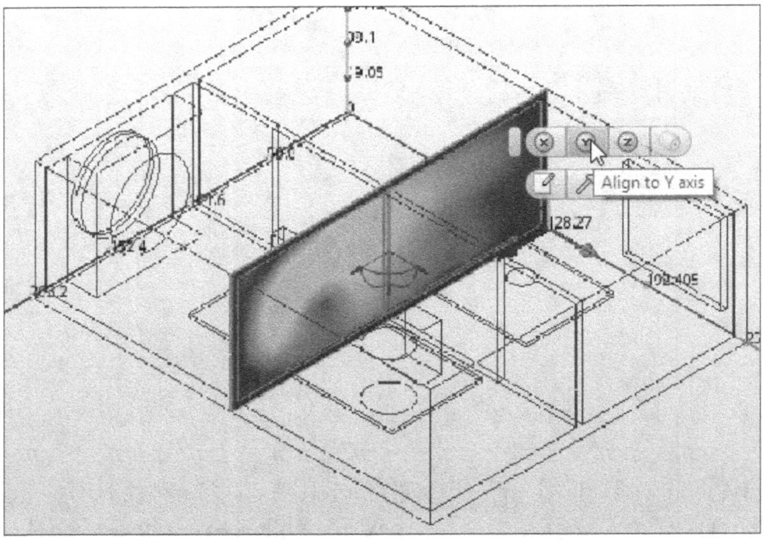

Figure-52. Plane along Y axis

- Move the plane downward by dragging the triad axis normal to plane; refer to Figure-53.

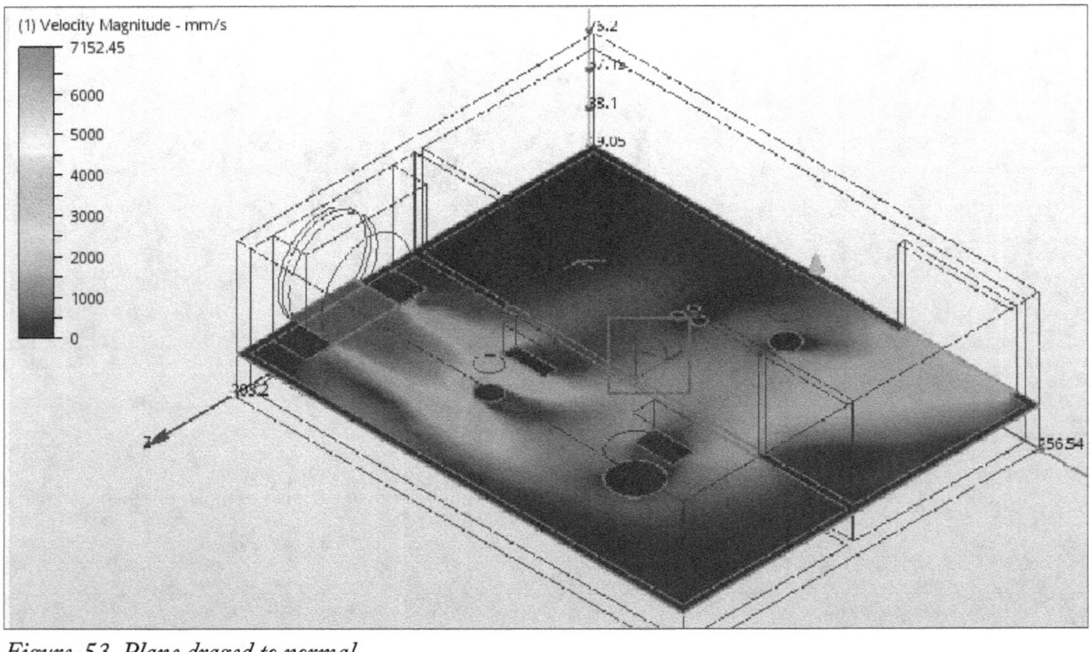

Figure-53. Plane draged to normal

Velocity Vector

- To display vectors, click on the **Vector** drop-down from the **Planes** panel and select the **Velocity Vector** option. The vectors will be displayed on added plane.
- Click on the **Edit** button from **Planes** panel to edit the vector spacings. The **Plane Control** dialog box will be displayed.
- Move the **Grid Spacing** slider towards **Fine** side from the **Plane Control** dialog box to increase the number of vectors on plane and to decrease the spacing between vectors; refer to Figure-54.

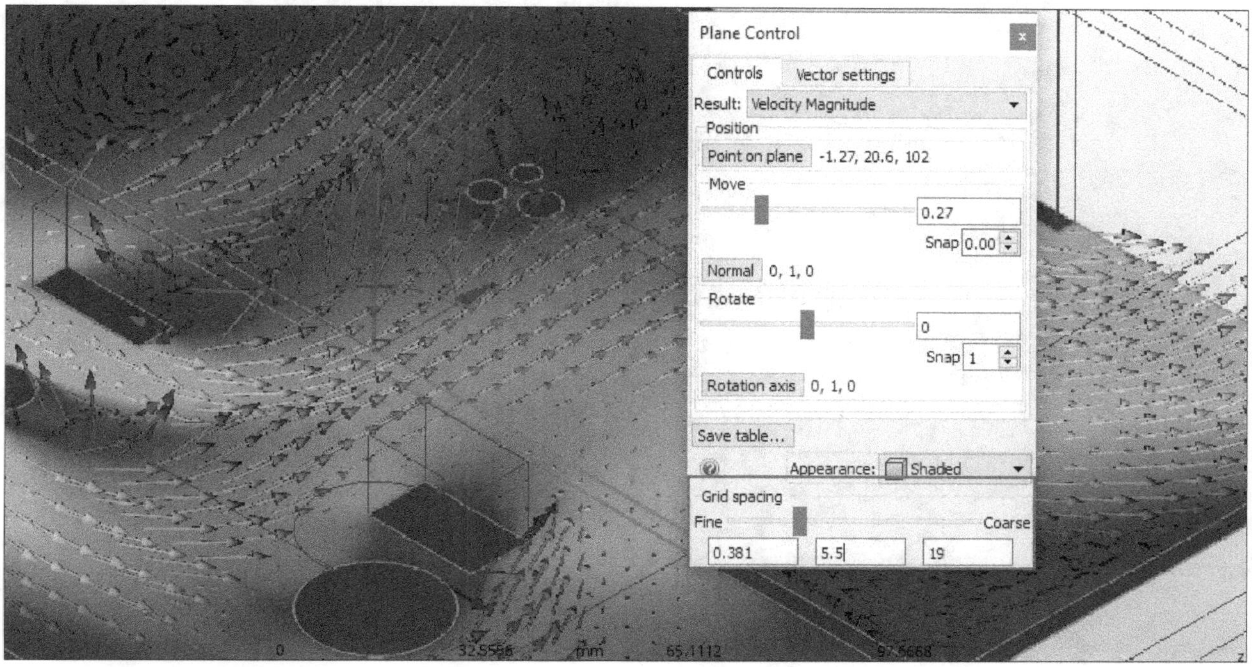

Figure-54. Grid Spacing

- Click on the **Vector settings** tab from the **Plane Control** dialog box and specify the parameters as displayed in Figure-55.

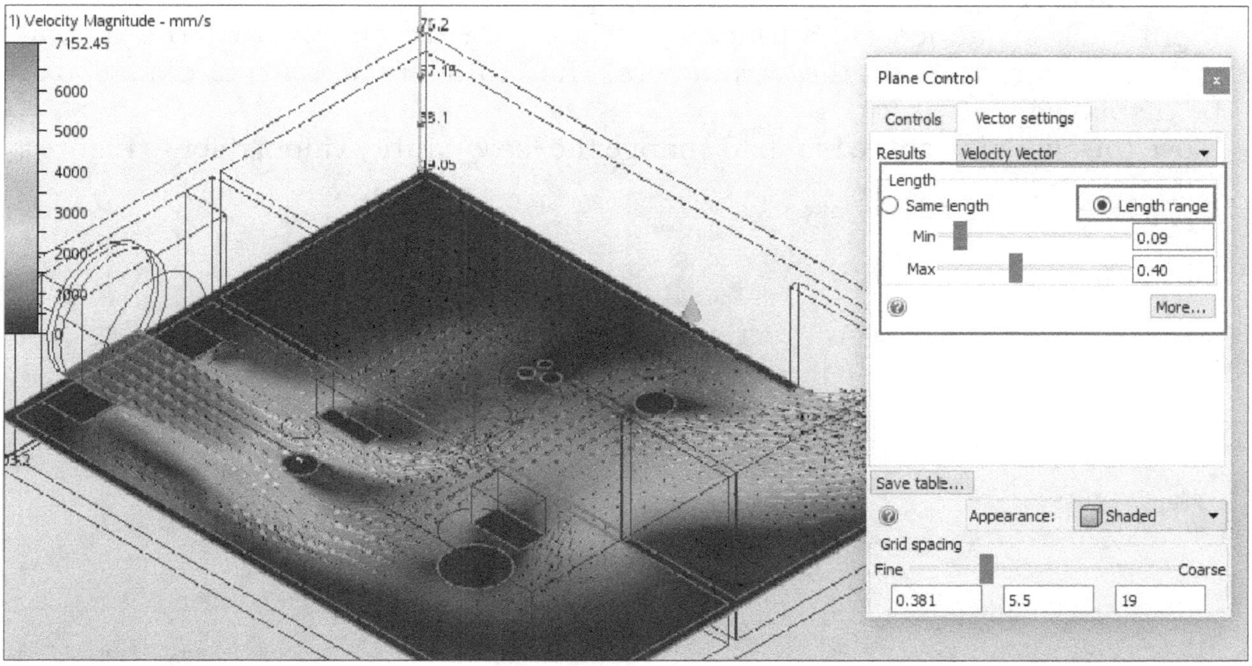

Figure-55. Vector Settings tab of Practical 2

- To clearly view the vectors, change the visual style of plane from **Shaded** to **Outline** by selecting the **Outline** option from the **Plane** right-click menu; refer to Figure-56.
- Close the **Plane Control** dialog box.

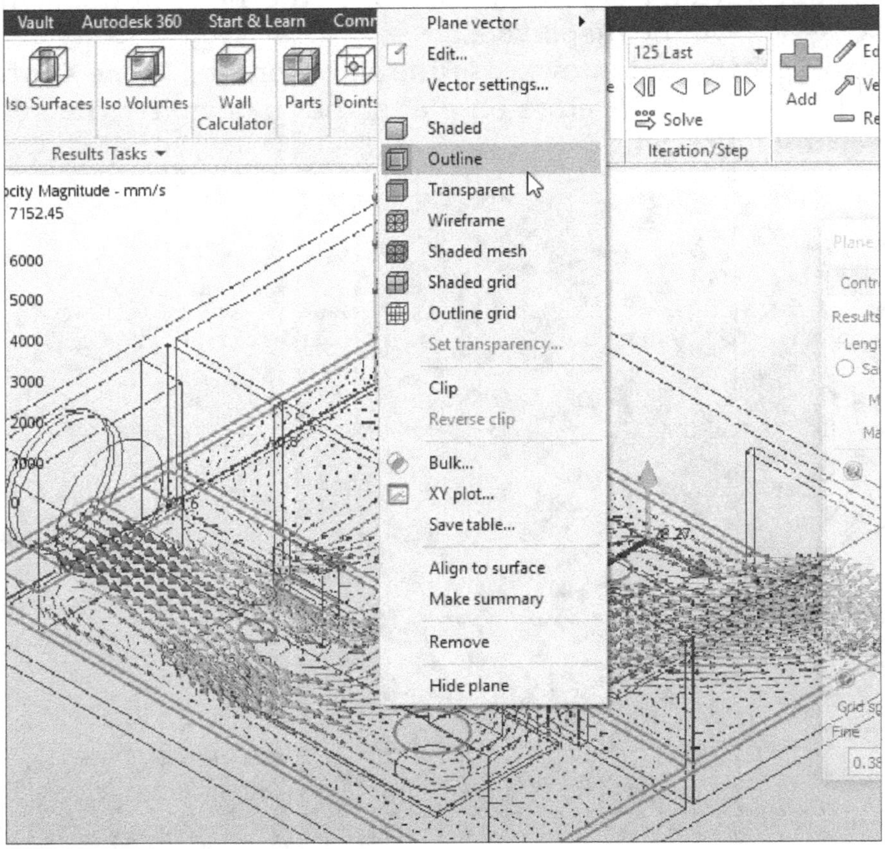

Figure-56. Changing Appearance of plane

Iso Surfaces

- Click on the **Iso Surfaces** tool from **Results Tasks** panel of **Results** tab and click on the **Add** button to add an iso surface plane.
- Right-click on added Iso-surface and click on **Edit** option from the displayed right-click menu to edit the parameters. The **Iso Surface Control** dialog box will be displayed.
- Move the slider in **Controls** tab to change the Iso Quantity value; refer to Figure-57.

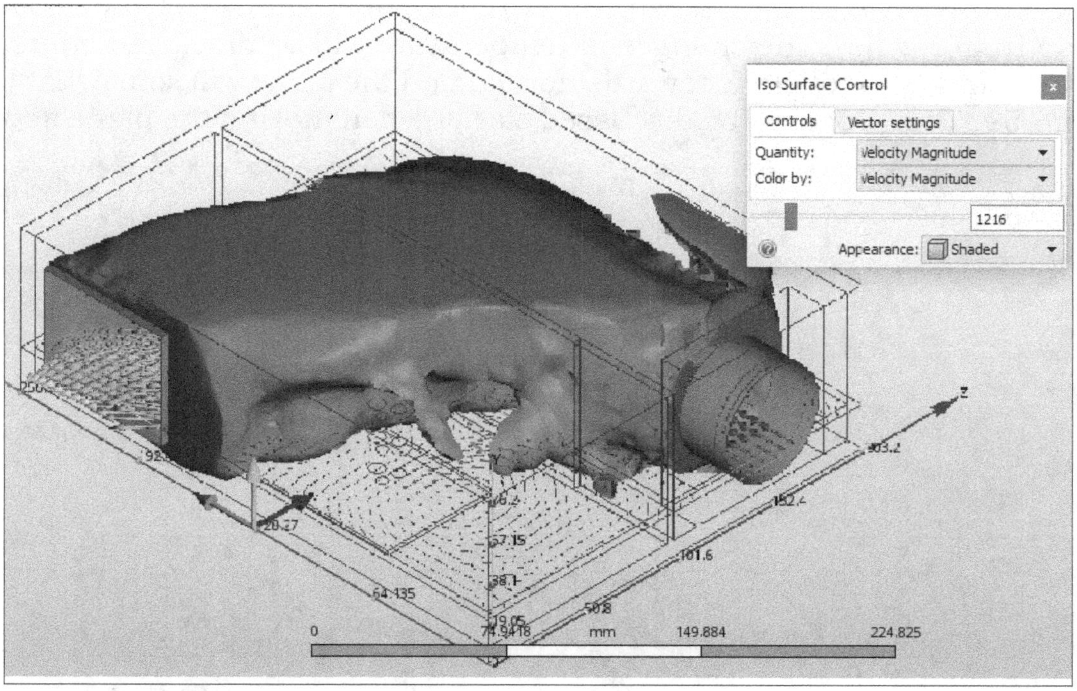

Figure-57. Specifying parameters of iso surfaces

- The **Iso Surface** is generally used to understand how the flow influence the heat transfer. Regions where movement of air is low leads to poor heat transfer and high component temperatures.
- After checking the results, remove the iso-surface by clicking **Remove** button from right-click shortcut menu of **IsoSurface** of **Design Study Bar**; refer to Figure-58.

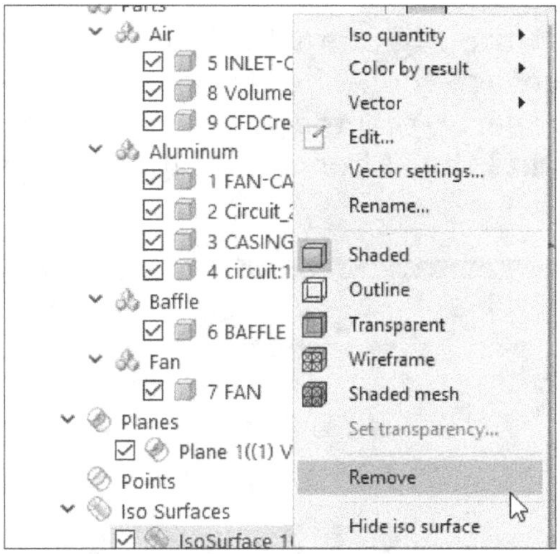

Figure-58. Removing iso surface

- Similarly, remove the previously created plane. We are removing these for better appearance in next step. Note that you can also clear the check boxes of results to remove them.

Temperature Results

- Click on the **Planes** tool from the **Results Tasks** panel of the **Results** tab and click on **Add** button to add a plane.
- Click on the recently created plane and click on Y axis to align the plane towards y-axis.

- Click on the **Results** drop-down from **Planes** panel and select the **Temperature** option from the list. The changes in temperature will be displayed on plane.
- Move the triad axis of plane towards normal and the plane will somewhat look like Figure-59. This process was discussed earlier when moving the plane downward.

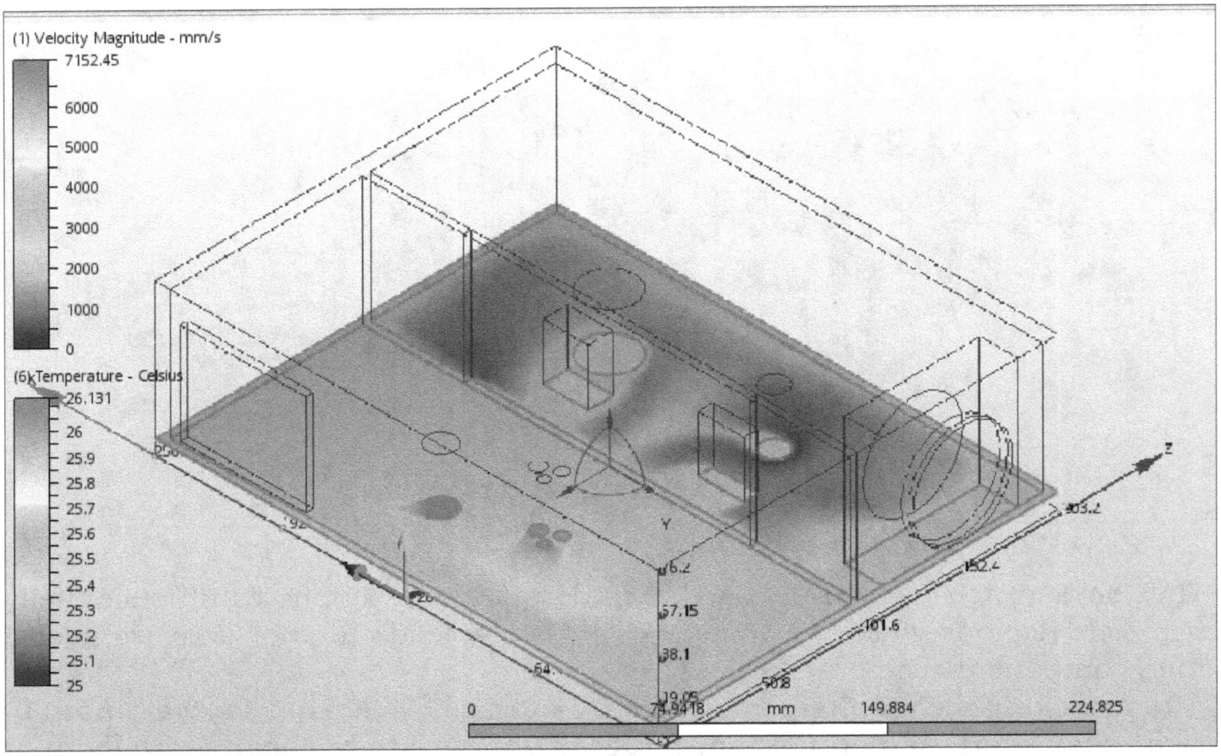

Figure-59. Temperature plane

- Similarly, you can view the regions where temperature are highest and lowest with the help of **Iso Surface** tool. The process is same as discussed earlier.
- To view **Iso Surface** properly, you may need to change the visual style of created plane from **Shaded** to **Outline**. After applying **Iso Surface**, the model will look like Figure-60.

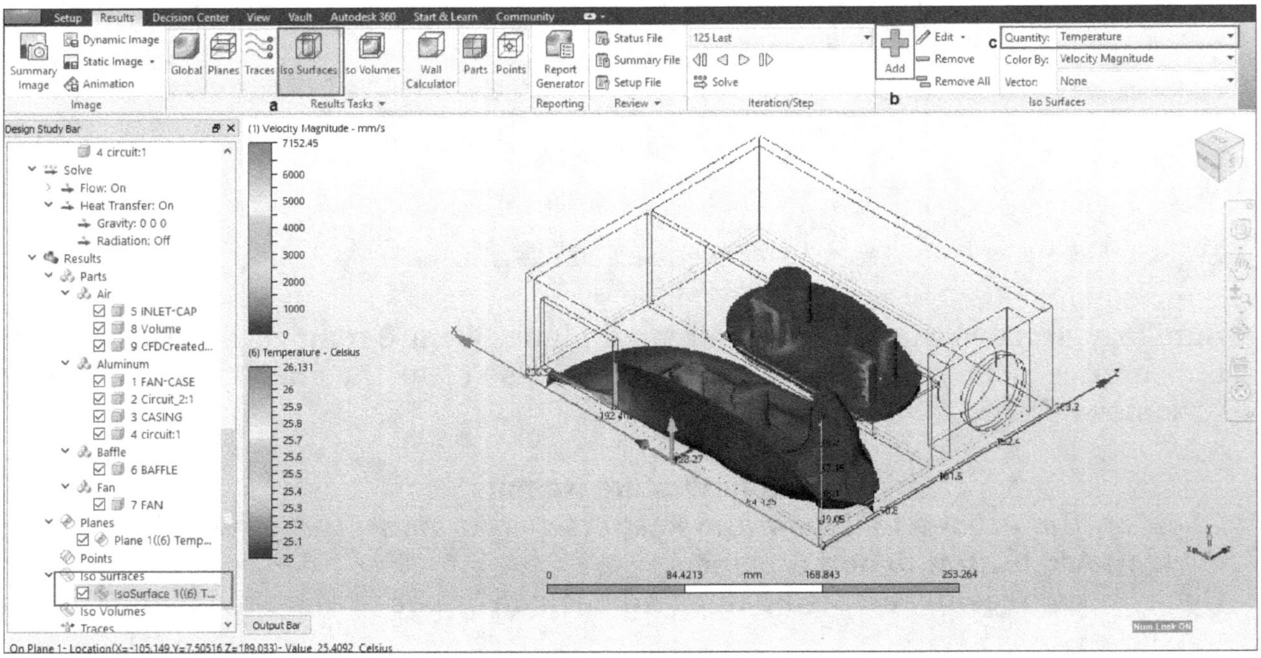

Figure-60. Added Iso Surface for temperature

Summary Parts

The **Summary Parts** tool is used for quick comparing of two parts, like temperature. To compare results of several parts, make them summary parts. In the below procedure, we compare the temperature of two circuit board.

- Click on the **Parts** tool from the **Results Tasks** panel of the **Results** tab in **Ribbon**. The **Parts** dialog box will be displayed in graphic window.
- Click on the **Group** operation button from **Parts** dialog box and select **Circuit** group. The **Circuit 1** and **Circuit 2** will be displayed in **Parts** dialog box; refer to Figure-61.

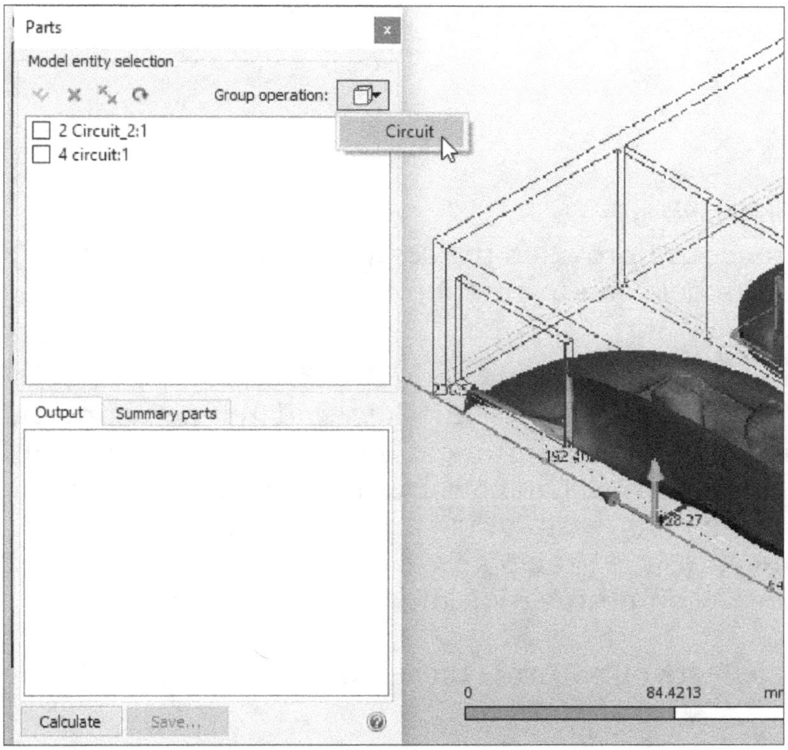

Figure-61. Selecting Circuit group

- Select the **Circuit 1** and **Circuit 2** check box to designate these parts as summary parts and click on the **Calculate** button.
- Click on the **Decision Center** tab to compare result. The added summary values will be displayed in **Design Study Bar**.
- To update all these values, click on the **Update All** button from **Update** panel. The values will be updated and displayed; refer to Figure-62.

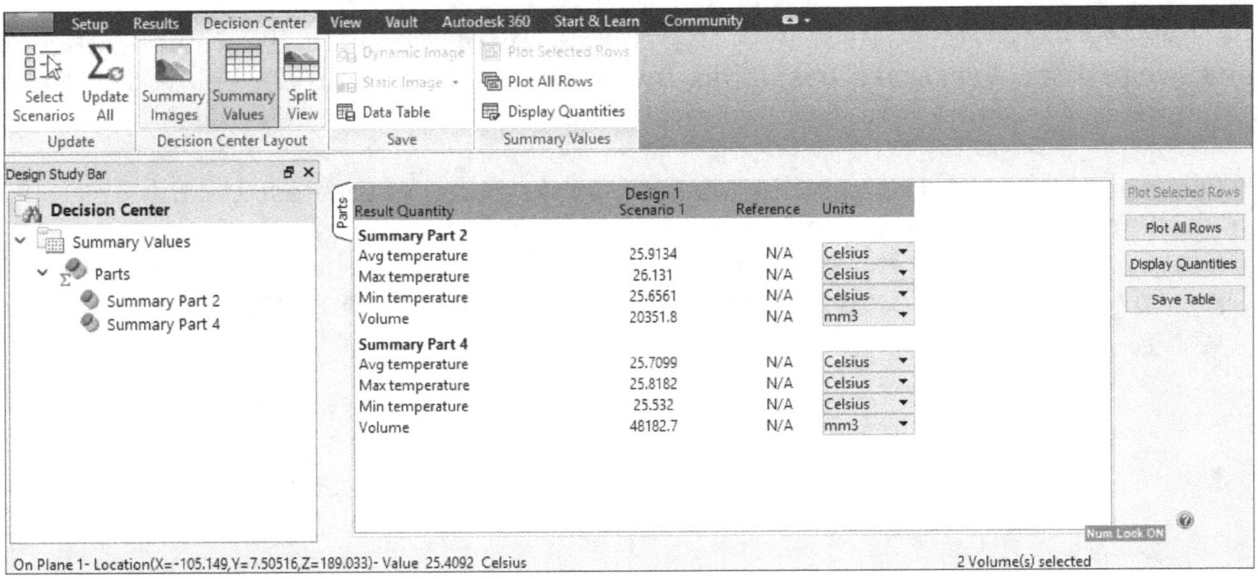

Figure-62. Comparing Values of Practical 2

The discussed procedure provides the result in simple data. It is now easier to plot and compare results between to components.

PRACTICAL 3

In this practical, we will simulate air flow and temperature distribution due to natural convection in a telecommunication model. The Practical 3 contains many heat generating components. The flow around the model is done naturally (with the use of gravity) and density variations caused by gradients in air temperature also known as buoyancy. In this practical, we are going to create the analysis of natural convection inside telecommunication module.

We will study the effects of natural convection inside the model; refer to Figure-63.

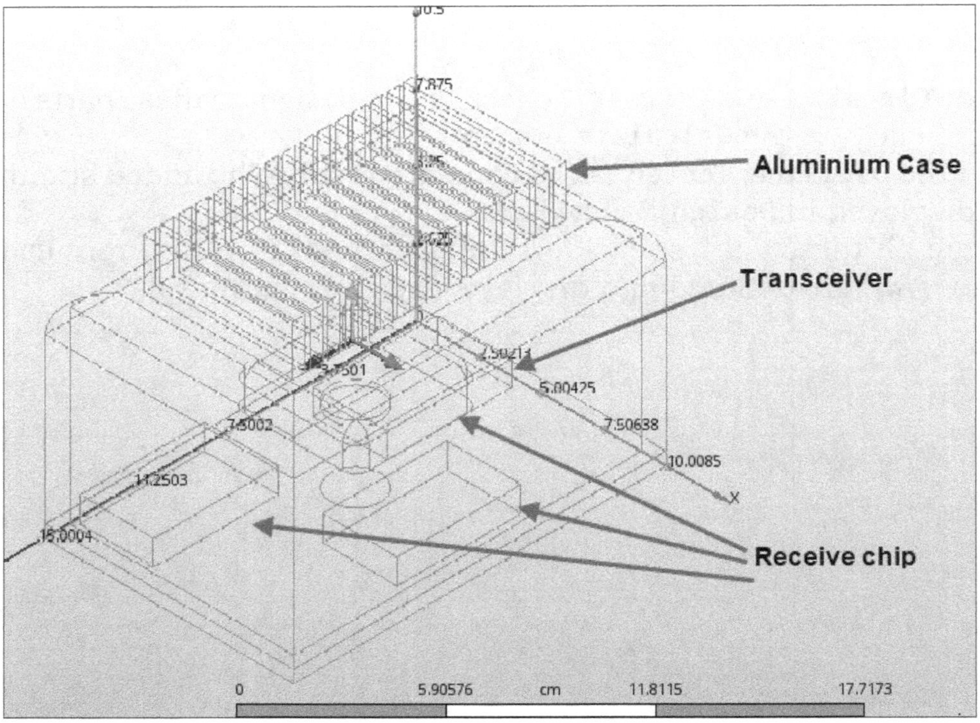

Figure-63. Practical 3

Opening the model

- Double-click on the Autodesk CFD icon from Desktop or click from the Start menu. The welcome screen of Autodesk CFD will be displayed.
- Click on the **New** button from **Ribbon** and open the file **Telecommunication Module Assembly.iam** with the name design study as **Practical 3**; refer to Figure-64.

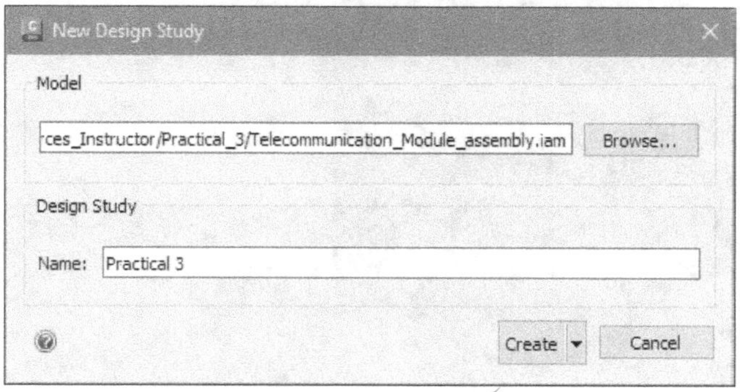

Figure-64. Opening Practical 3

- Click on **Create** button from **New Design Study** dialog box; The **Geometry Tools** dialog box will be displayed; refer to Figure-65.

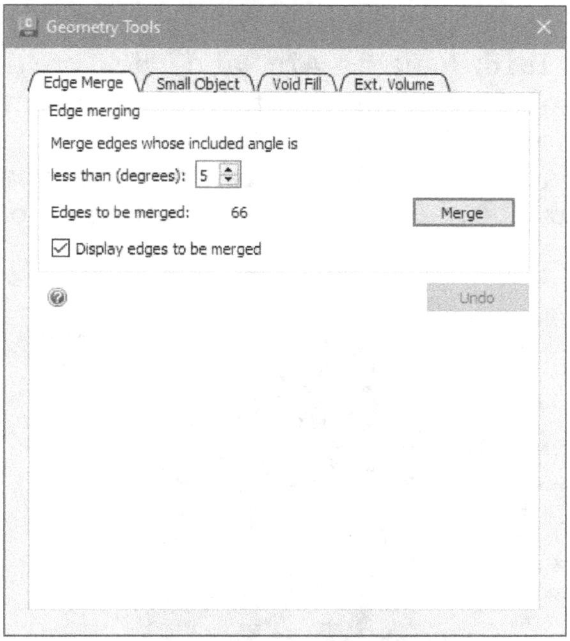

Figure-65. Geometry Tools dialog box of Practical 3

- Click on the **Merge** button to merge small edges and close the dialog box.
- Change the units of model from **CM** to **MM**, from **Design Study Bar**.

Applying Materials

- Click on the **Materials** tool from **Setup Tasks** panel of **Setup** tab to activate the **Materials** task.
- Select the **Outer case** and click on **Edit** button from **Materials** panel. The **Materials** dialog box will be displayed.
- Select the **Type** as **Solid**, **Name** as **Aluminium**, and click on **Apply** button; refer to Figure-66. The material will be applied to selected components.

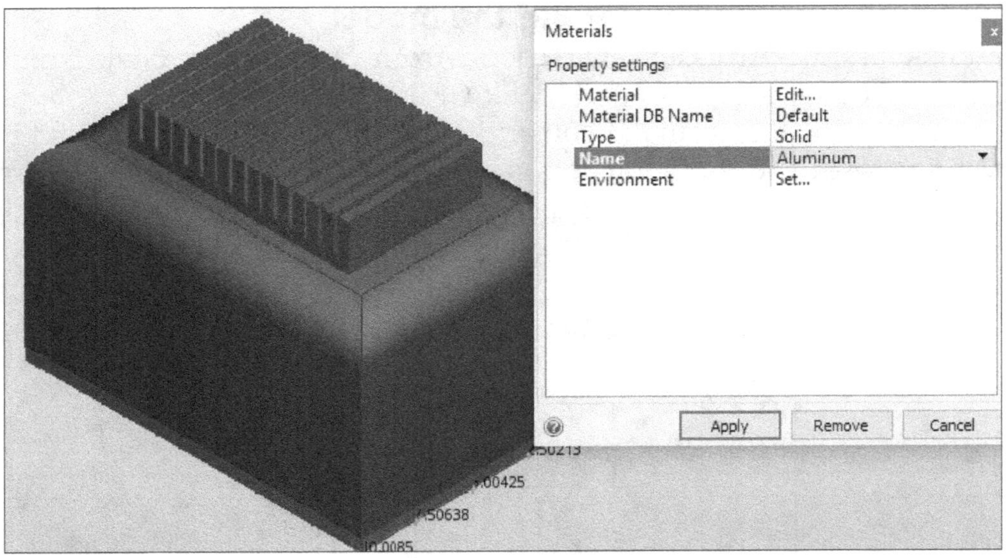

Figure-66. Applying Aluminium on outer case

- Hide the **Outer** case to assign material to inner area with the help of **CTRL** key and middle mouse button.
- Select the internal area and click on **Edit** button. The **Materials** dialog box will be displayed.
- Select the **Type** as **Fluid**, **Name** as **Air**, and click on the **Set** button from the **Materials** dialog box to set properties to vary with temperature. The **Material Environment** dialog box will be displayed.
- Select the **Variable** radio button from **Material Environment** dialog box and click on **OK** button; refer to Figure-67. You will be returned to **Materials** dialog box.

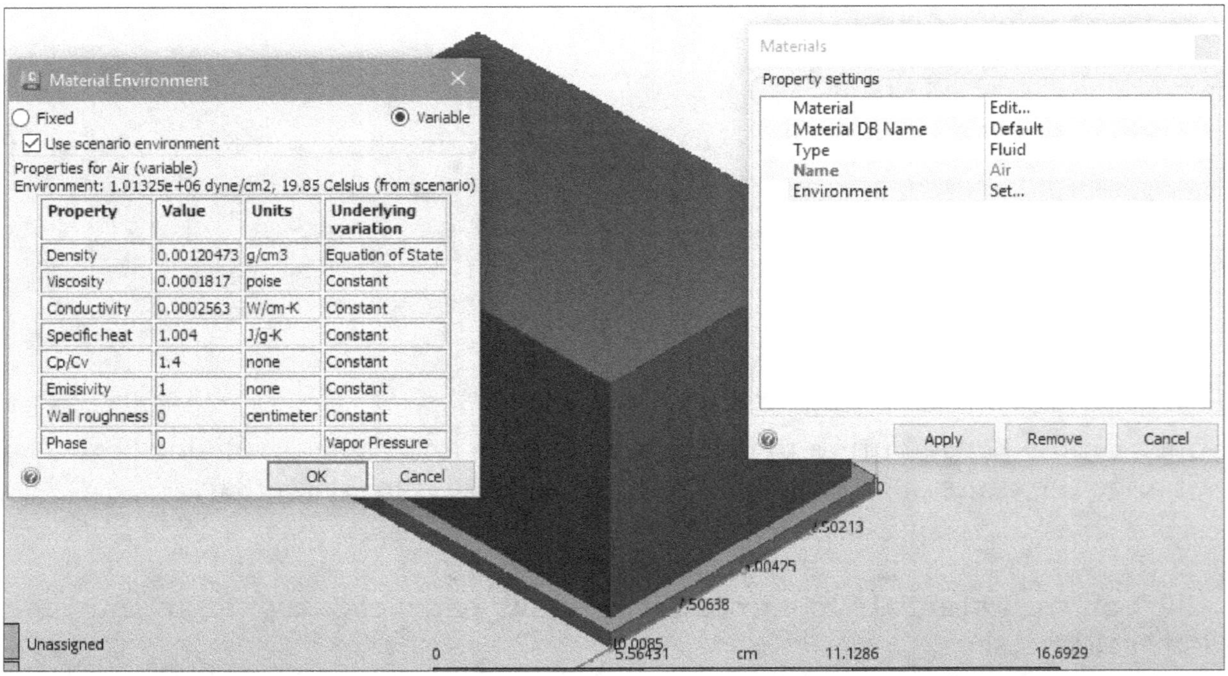

Figure-67. Specifying variable condition

- Click on **Apply** button from **Materials** dialog box to apply the boundary condition.
- Now, we will apply materials to other parts like **Receiver** and **Transceiver**.
- First of all, hide the case and air volume from the model and select all three receiver and transceiver from **Design Study Bar**; refer to Figure-68.

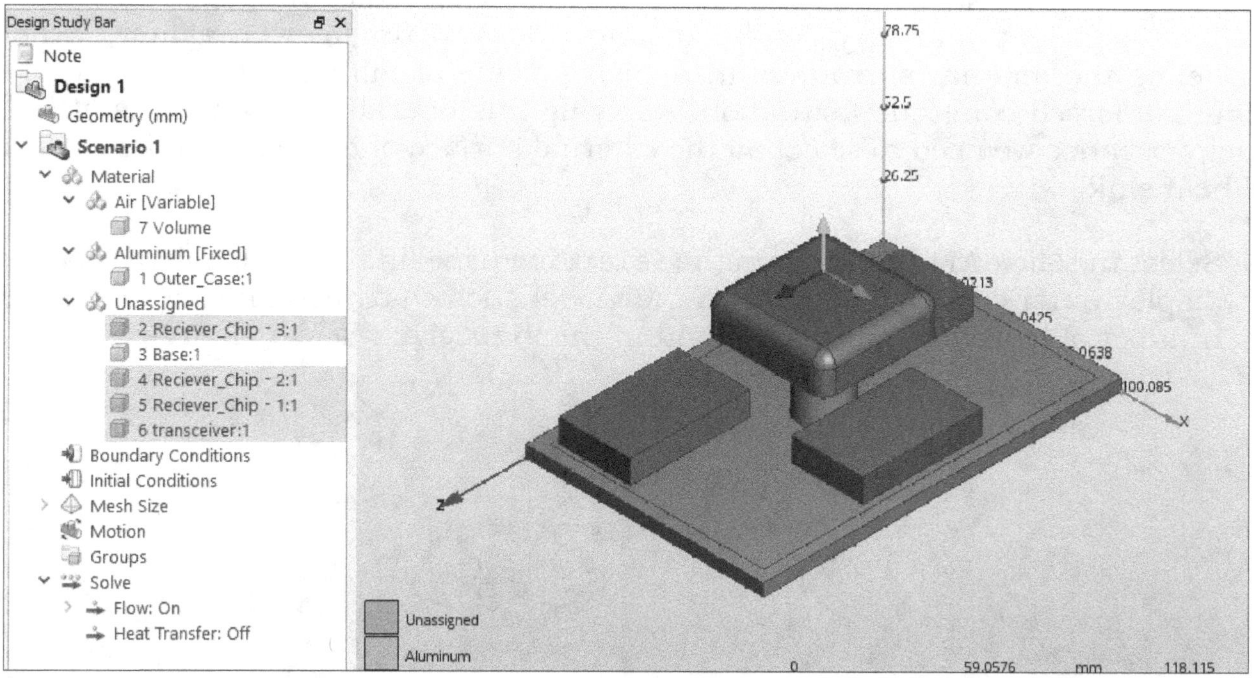

Figure-68. Selecting other components

- Right-click on any of the selected components and click on **Edit** button from menu. The **Materials** dialog box will be displayed.
- Select the **Type** as **Solid**, **Name** as **Silicon** from **Materials** dialog box, and click on **Apply** button to apply. The selected material will be applied.
- Select the **Base** component and click on **Edit** button. The **Materials** dialog box will be displayed.
- Select the **Type** as **Solid**, **Name** as **PCB 12-Layer(X)**, and click on **Apply** button. Selected material will be applied. The material we applied is a solid with conductivity equivalent to a 12-layer PCB.
- Till now, we had applied materials to all components of model and it is time to apply boundary conditions.

Boundary Conditions

- Click on **Boundary Conditions** tool from **Results Tasks** panel of **Setup** tab in Ribbon. The **Boundary Conditions** task will be activated.
- Select the **Volume** button from **Selection** panel of **Setup** tab in **Ribbon** to activate selection of volume from model.
- Hide the **Outer** case and air volume from model as discussed earlier. Select the **Receiver 1**, **Receiver 2**, and **Receiver 3** components.
- Click on the **Edit** button from **Boundary Conditions** panel in the **Setup** tab of **Ribbon**. The **Boundary Conditions** dialog box will be displayed.
- Click in the **Total Heat Generation** edit box from **Boundary Conditions** dialog box and specify the value as **6**. Click on the **Apply** button to set value. The boundary condition will be applied and displayed in graphics area as well as in **Design Study Bar**.
- Select the **Transceiver** from model and click on **Edit** button. The **Boundary Conditions** dialog box will be displayed.
- Click in the **Total Heat Generation** edit box and specify the value as **10**. Click on the **Apply** button to apply the boundary condition.

Assigning Film Coefficient boundary conditions

A Film Coefficient Boundary Condition simulates exposure to external flow, without modeling the air that surrounds it. A higher value of Film Coefficient is used to simulate forced convection situation. Applying this boundary condition is little bit tricky because we need to select all the external surface of model, even the surfaces of heat sink.

- Select the **Show All** button from the **Selection** panel in the **Setup** tab of **Ribbon** to display outer case of model. Align the model such that you can easily count the number of heat fins, i.e Left or Right in the **ViewCube**; refer to Figure-69.

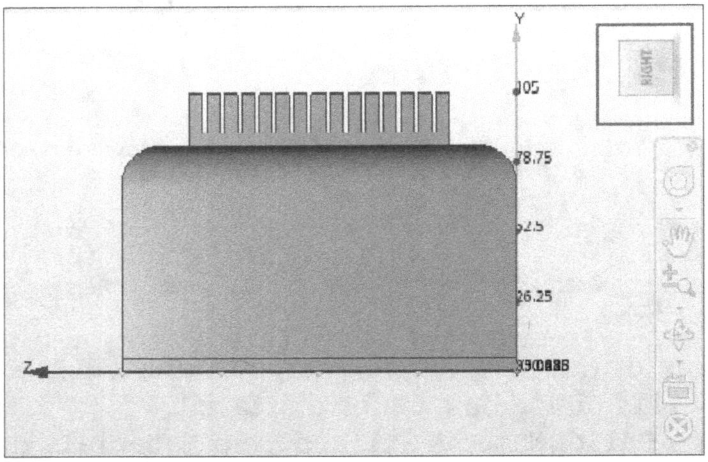

Figure-69. Align model to Right

- Make sure the **ViewCube** is set to **Orthographic** view so that you can easily select surfaces of the fins. If not enabled then select the **Orthographic** option from the **Orthographic** drop-down in the **Appearance** panel of **View** tab in the **Ribbon**.
- Select the **Surface** toggle button from **Selection** panel of **Setup** tab in the **Ribbon** to select surfaces of model.
- Using window selection, select the surfaces of fins by making a rectangle covering all fins; refer to Figure-70.

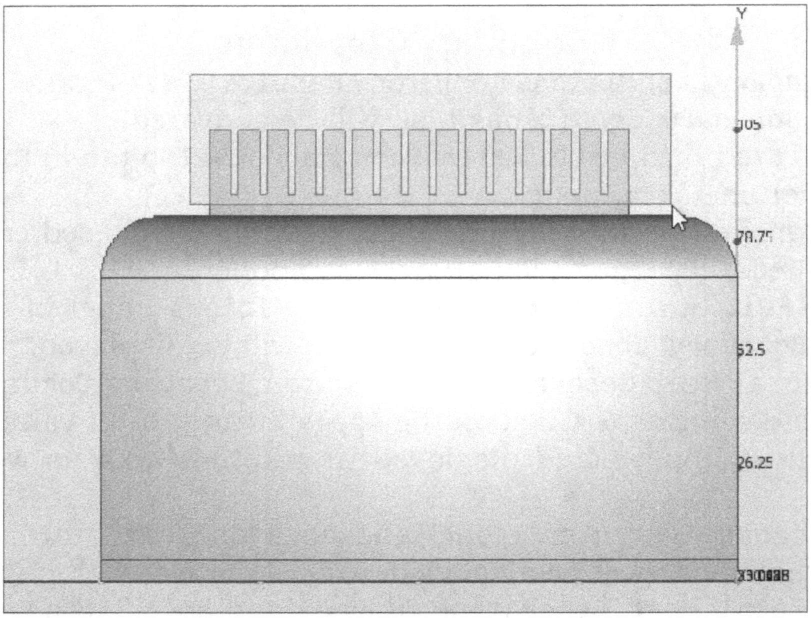

Figure-70. Selection of heat fins surfaces

- Select the remaining external surfaces of model; refer to Figure-71.

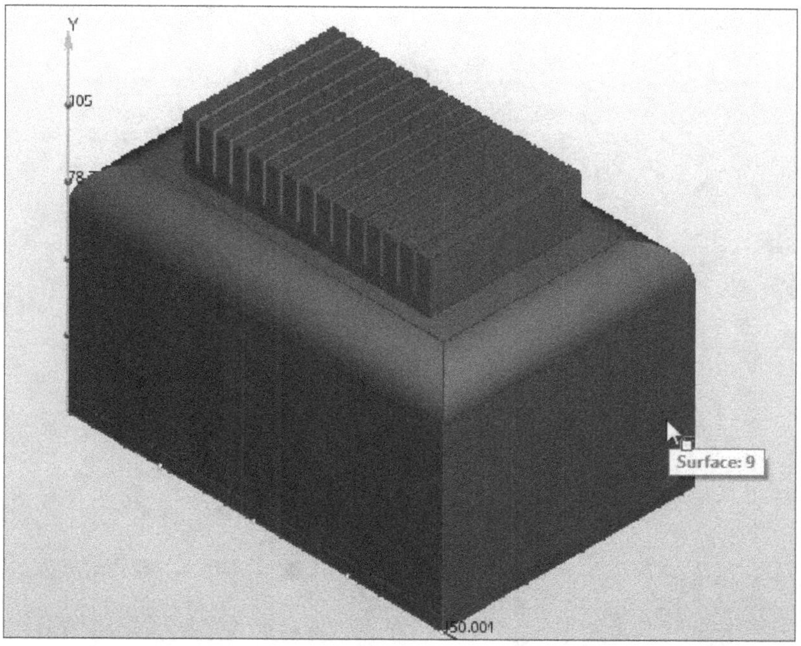

Figure-71. Selecting remaining surfaces

- After selecting all the external surfaces, click on the **Edit** button from the **Boundary Conditions** panel and specify the parameters as displayed in Figure-72.

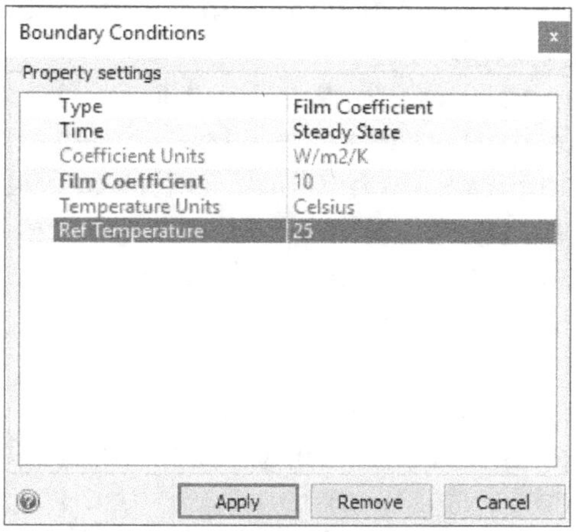

Figure-72. Parameters of Film Coefficient

- After specifying the parameters, click on the **Apply** button from the **Boundary Conditions** dialog box. The boundary condition will be applied.

Generating Mesh

Till now, we have applied material and boundary conditions to all components of model. Now, we will generate mesh for the model.

- Click on the **Mesh Sizing** tool from the **Setup Tasks** panel of the **Setup** tab in the **Ribbon**. The meshing tools will be activated.
- Click on the **Autosize** tool from the **Automatic Sizing** panel of the **Setup** tab in the **Ribbon**. The mesh will be displayed on model; refer to Figure-73.

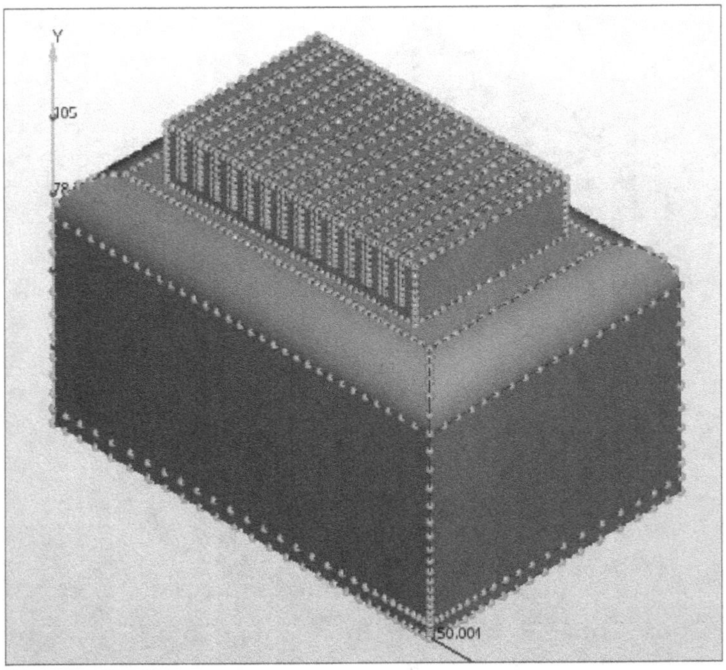

Figure-73. Mesh of Practical 2

Solving Analysis

- Click on the **Solve** tool from the **Simulation** panel of **Setup** tab in the **Ribbon**. The **Solve** dialog box will be displayed.
- Specify the value of **Iterations to Run** as **200** in the **Control** tab of dialog box.
- Click on the **Physics** tab and select the **Flow** & **Heat Transfer** check boxes.
- Select the **Gravity Method** as **Earth**. Click in the **Gravity Direction** edit box and specify the parameters as 0,-1,0. Here -1 refers to reverse direction of Y axis.
- After specifying the parameters, click on **Solve** button from the **Solve** dialog box. The software will start solving the analysis.

Note: If you want to generate mesh before using the **Solve** dialog box then right-click on the **Mesh Size** option from **Design Study Bar**. The right-click shortcut menu will displayed. Select the **Generate Mesh** option from the menu; refer to Figure-74. The mesh will be generated. Now, you can directly solve the analysis and the procedure is same i.e. by **Solve** dialog box.

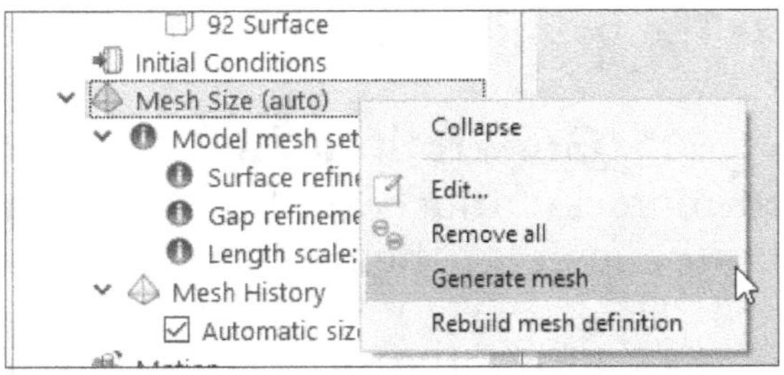

Figure-74. Generate Mesh button

- After generating mesh, system will start solving iterations; refer to Figure-75.

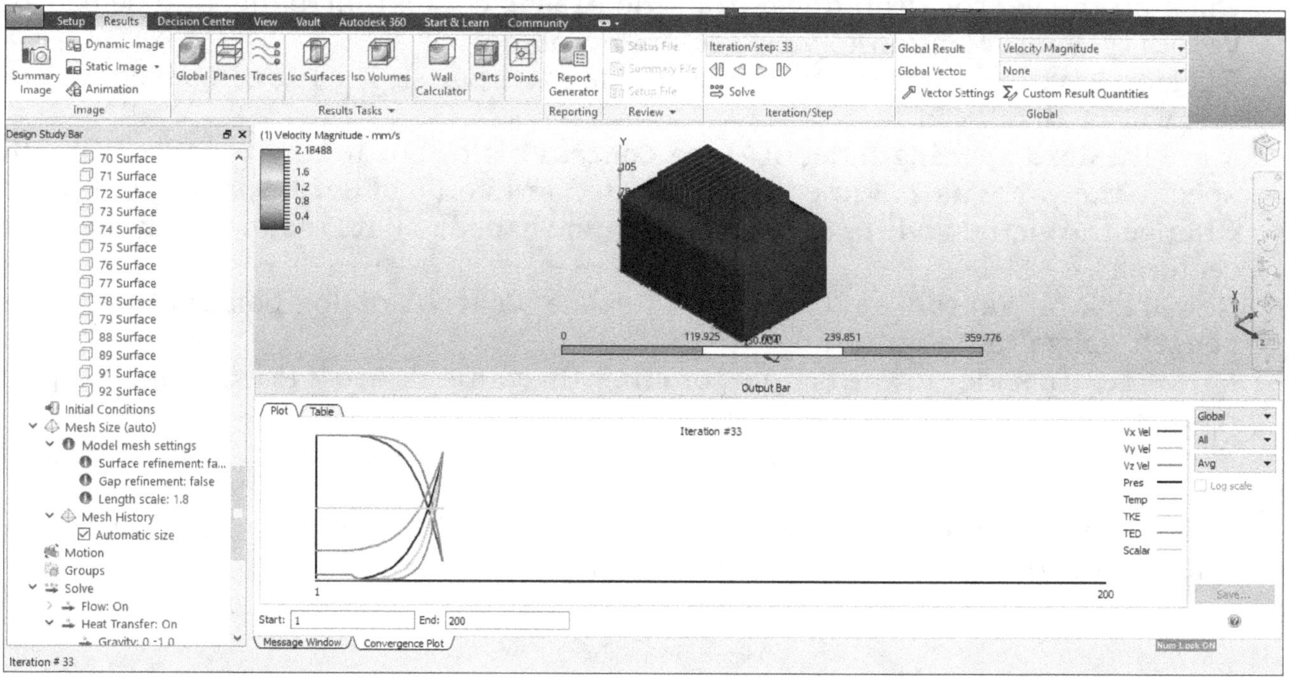

Figure-75. Analysis Processing for Practical 3

Results

After completion of iterations, the **Results** tab will be displayed. Now, we will examine the velocity results using a cutting plane and an iso surface.

- Click on the **Planes** tool from the **Results Tasks** panel of the **Results** tab in the **Ribbon** and click on the **Add** button from the **Planes** contextual panel. The plane along X axis will be created on model; refer to Figure-76.

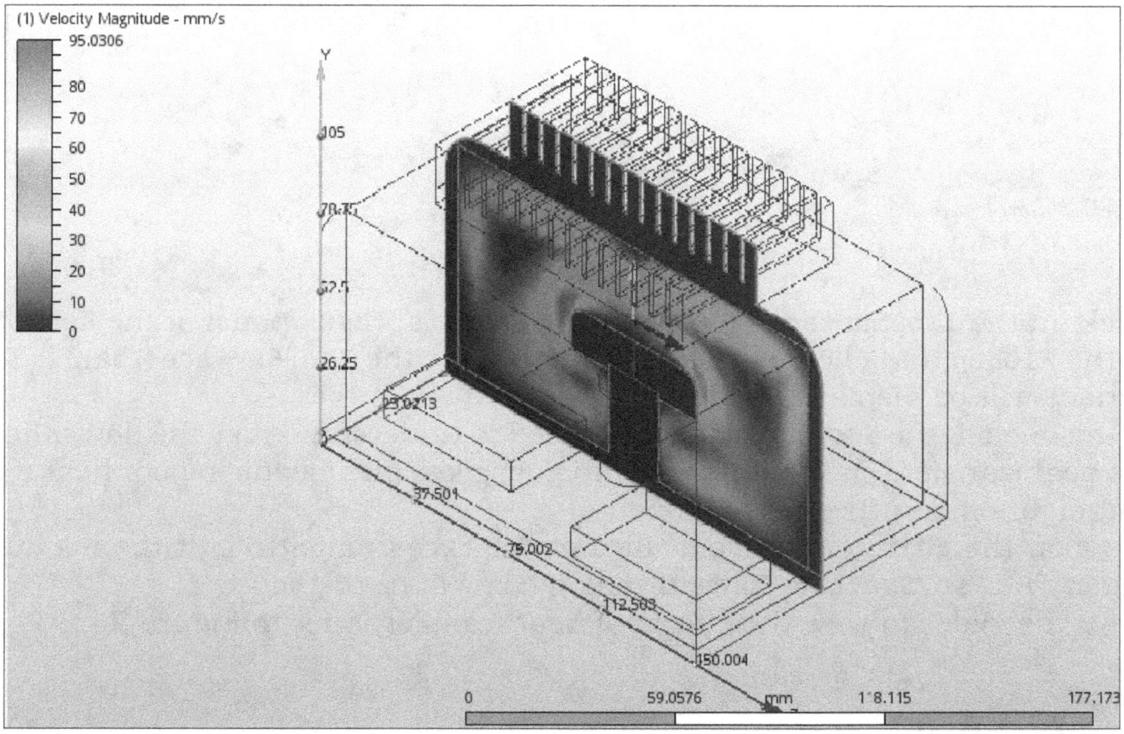

Figure-76. Added velocity plane

- Click on the **Vector** drop-down from the **Planes** contextual panel and select the **Velocity Vector** option to view vectors on plane.
- Click on **Edit** button from the **Planes** contextual panel. The **Plane Control** dialog box will be displayed.
- Move the **Grid spacing** slider of **Plane Control** dialog box towards **Fine**, or directly specify the value as **2.5** in edit box (located in middle of **Grid Spacing** option).
- Change the visual style of added plane from **Shaded** to **Outline** to clearly view the vectors.
- Now, click on **Vector settings** tab of **Plane Control** dialog box and select the **Length Range** radio button.
- Move the **Min** slider towards right, or enter the value as **0.04**. Press enter to apply results.
- Move the **Max** slider towards right, or enter the value as **0.15** and press enter to apply.
- After specifying the parameters for vectors, close the dialog box. The vectors of this model should look like Figure-77.

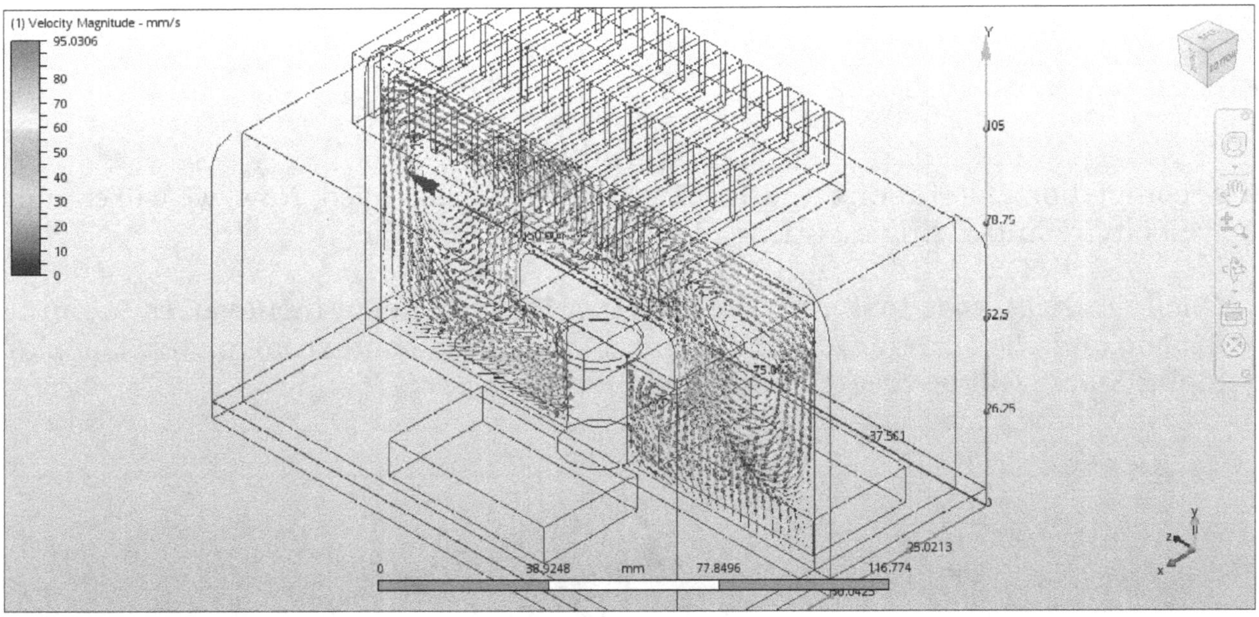

Figure-77. Vectors Practical 3

Iso Surface

- Click on the **Iso Surfaces** tool from the **Results Tasks** panel of the **Results** tab in the **Ribbon** and click on the **Add** button from the **Iso Surfaces** panel. The iso surface will be displayed on model.
- In this model, the **Iso Surface** tool is used to understand how the flow influences the heat transfer. The regions with little air movement leads to poor heat transfer and high temperature of components.
- Click on the **Edit** button from the **Iso Surfaces** panel to edit the iso quantity value. The **Iso Surface Control** dialog box will be displayed.
- Move the slider to view the effects of heat transfer; refer to Figure-78.

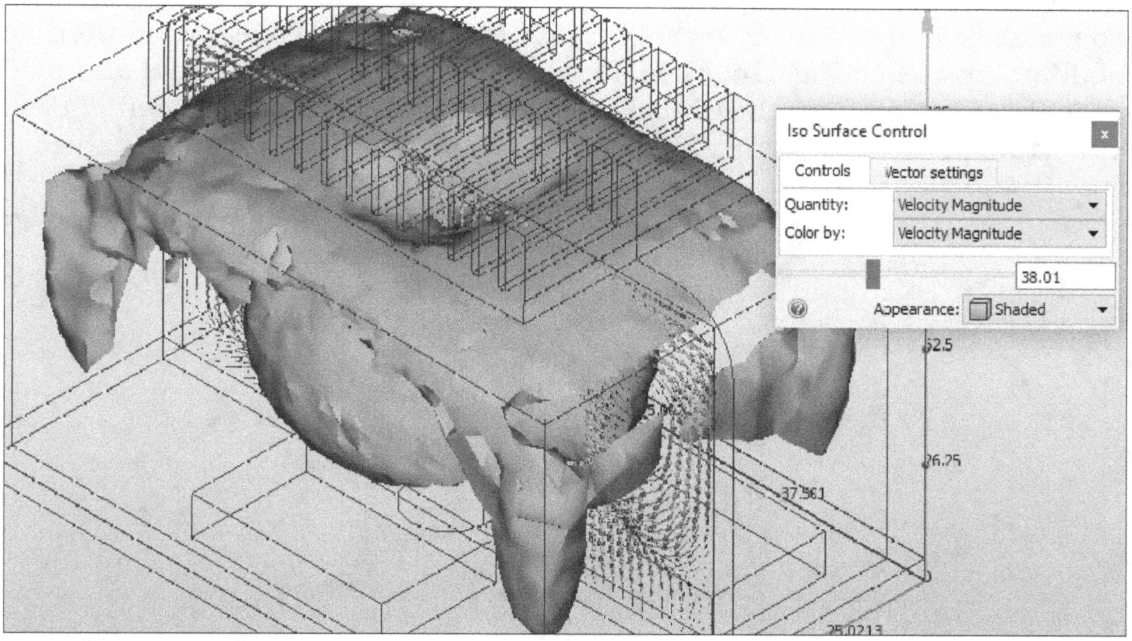

Figure-78. Iso Surface of Practical 3

- Remove/hide the iso surface to see results of next step.

Results based on Temperature

- Activate the **Planes** task and select **None** from **Vector** drop-down to remove the added vectors.
- Change the visual style of previously added plane to **Shaded** and select the **Temperature** option from the **Result** drop-down of the **Planes** contextual panel in the **Ribbon**. The temperature will be displayed on plane; refer to Figure-79.

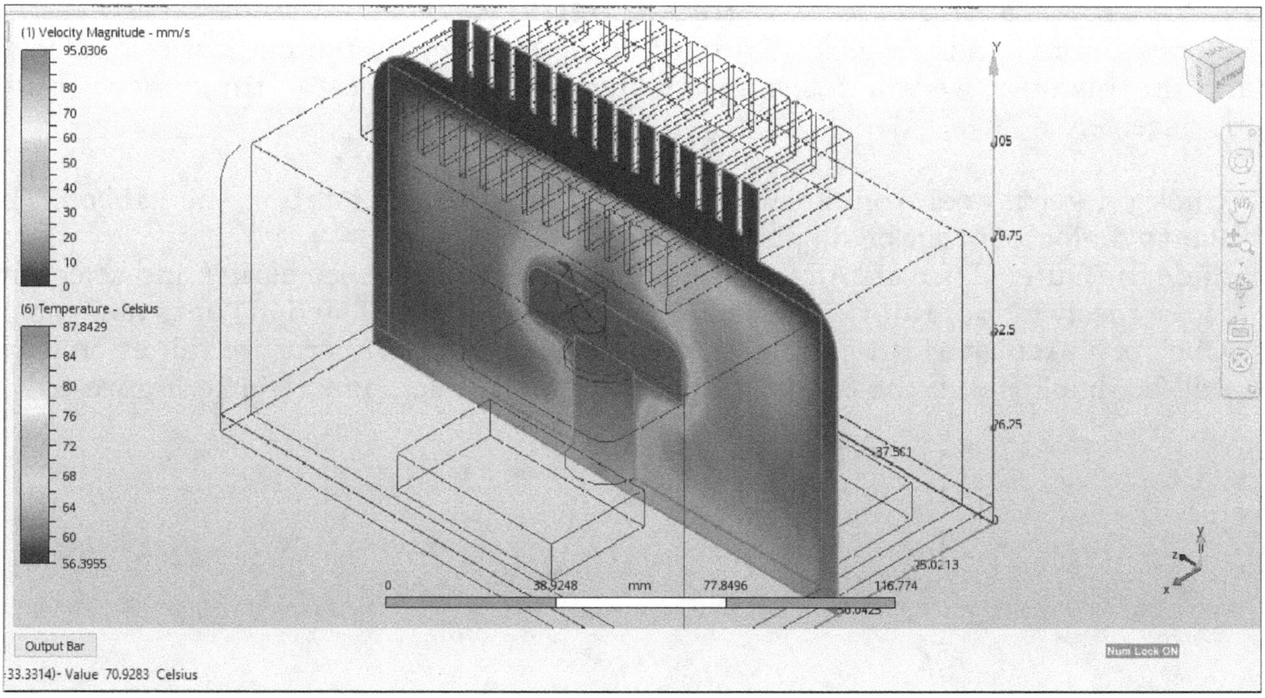

Figure-79. Added Temperature plane

- In the above image, you can see two legends available, i.e. **Velocity Magnitude** and **Temperature**. If you want to remove the **Velocity Magnitude** legend then activate Global task by selecting **Global** tool from the **Results Tasks** panel and select the **Temperature** option from the **Global Result** drop-down of **Global** contextual panel in the **Ribbon**; refer to Figure-80.

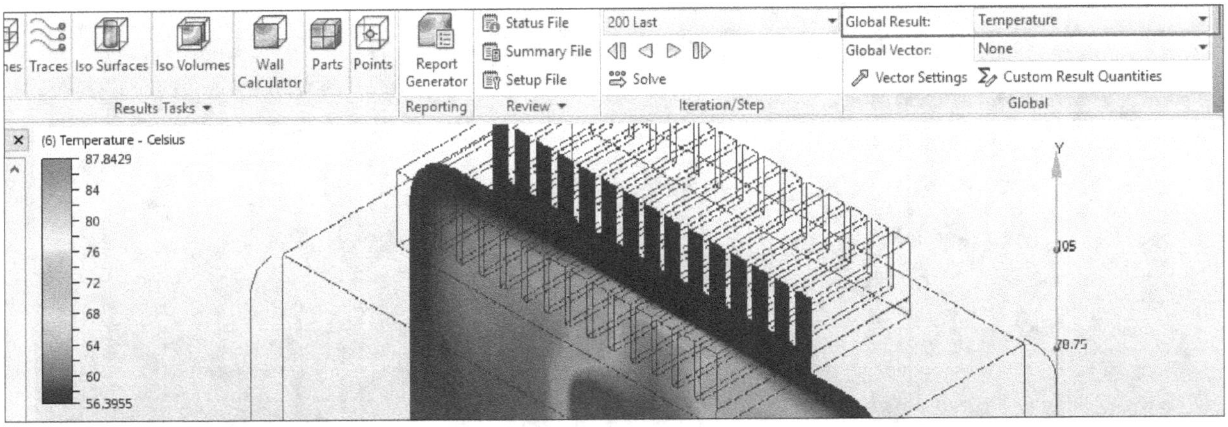

Figure-80. Removed legend

- Click again on the **Planes** tool and set the visual style of plane to **Outline**.
- Click on the **Iso Surfaces** tool from **Results Tasks** panel of **Results** tab and click on **Add** button. The iso surface will be displayed.
- Click in the **Quantity** drop-down from the **Iso Surface** panel and select **Temperature** option. Similarly, select the **Temperature** in **Color By** drop-down to view temperature in iso surface. This iso surface is used to determine the lowest and highest temperature in model. Now, remove the iso surface after checking results.

Result Parts

The **Parts** result task is generally used to determine the temperature of selected parts. In this step, we will determine the temperature values on three receiver and a transceiver.

- Click on **Parts** tool from **Result Tasks** panel of **Results** tab in the **Ribbon**. The **Parts** dialog box will be displayed.
- Hide the Outer Case and Air volume from model as discussed earlier and select the three receiver and transceiver. The selected parts will be listed in **Parts** dialog box.
- Click on **Calculate** button from **Parts** dialog box. The temperature values on parts will be displayed in the **Output** tab of the **Parts** dialog box; refer to Figure-81.

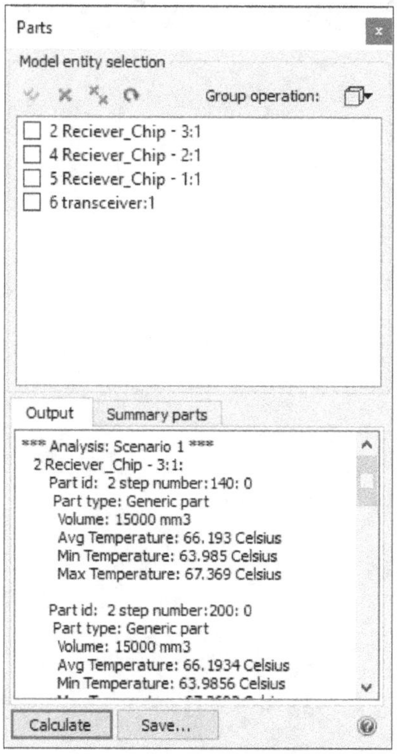

Figure-81. Temperature values in Parts dialog box

FOR STUDENTS NOTES

Chapter 8

Practical and Practice

Topics Covered

The major topics covered in this chapter are:

- ***Practical 4***
- ***Practical 5***
- ***Practice 1***
- ***Practice 2***
- ***Practice 3***

INTRODUCTION

In past chapters, we have learned to use tools for setting up simulation studies. We have also performed analyses using real conditions as per practical in previous chapter. In this chapter, we will continue to work with practical.

PRACTICAL 4

In this practical, we will simulate the flow is centrifugal pump with back - swept blades. The model consists of the volute, inlet pipe, the impeller, and rotating region. The rotating region is a volume that is completely surrounded by the impeller. The working fluid is water and impeller spins at 600 RPM. The pump is operated at the zero head state (maximum flow rate). A head loss can be imposed on the pump by assigning a positive gage pressure boundary condition to the outlet or a negative gage pressure to the inlet. During the analysis, the impeller rotates within the stationary volute. Approximately four complete revolutions are needed for a steady state result. At the beginning of the analysis, we will slowly ramp up the rotational speed to ensure stability and solution accuracy. Once the impeller is rotating at the desired speed, we will use a time step that causes the impeller to rotate through one blade passage per time step.

Opening Model

- Double-click on Autodesk CFD icon from Desktop. The welcome screen of Autodesk CFD will be displayed.
- Click on the **New** button from **Ribbon** and **Browse** the file **Centrifugal Pump Practical 4** from the resource folder downloaded from www.cadcamcaeworks.com.
- Click in the **Name** edit box of **New Design Study** dialog box, specify the name as **Practical 4**, and click on the **Create** button; refer to Figure-1. The model will be displayed along with **Geometry Tools** dialog box. Click on the **Merge** button from the dialog box and click on the **Close** button. The model will be displayed in application as shown in Figure-2.

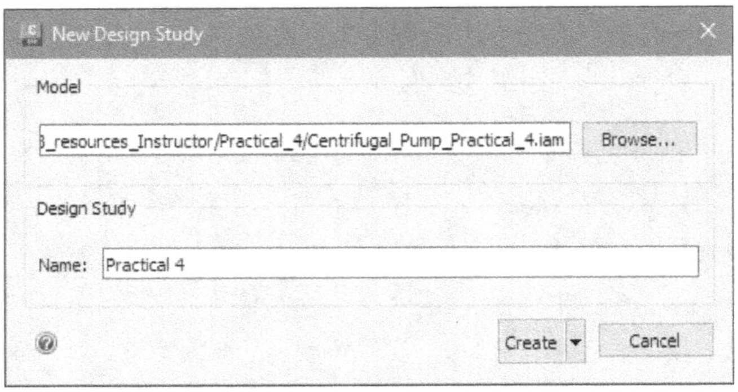

Figure-1. New Desgn Study dialog box of Practical 4

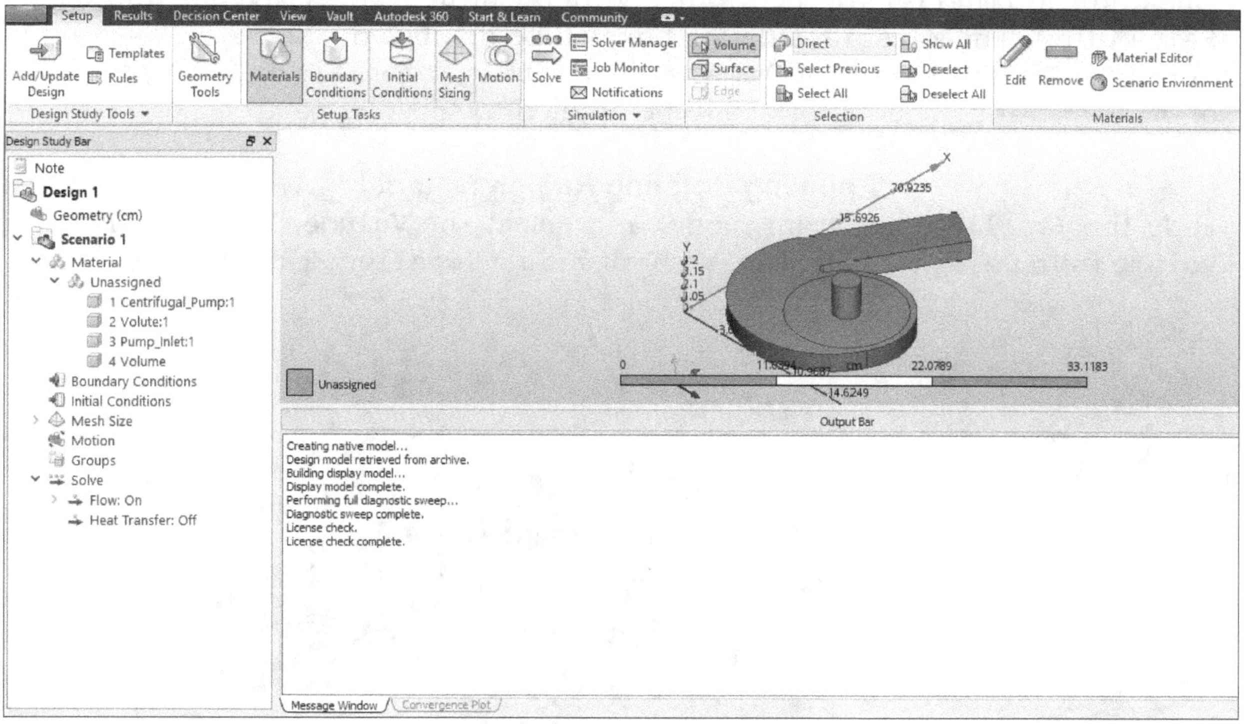

Figure-2. Practical 4

- Change the units of current model from **CM** to **MM**. The procedure to do so has been discussed earlier.

Assigning Materials

In this step, we will assign material to all parts of model.

- Activate the **Materials** tool from **Setup** tab and click on **Edit** button. The **Materials** dialog box will be displayed.
- Select the **Volute**, and **Pump Inlet** from **Design Study Bar**. These components will be highlighted in Graphics Window.
- Select the **Type** as **Fluid**, **Name** as **Water** in the **Materials** dialog box and click on the **Apply** button; refer to Figure-3.

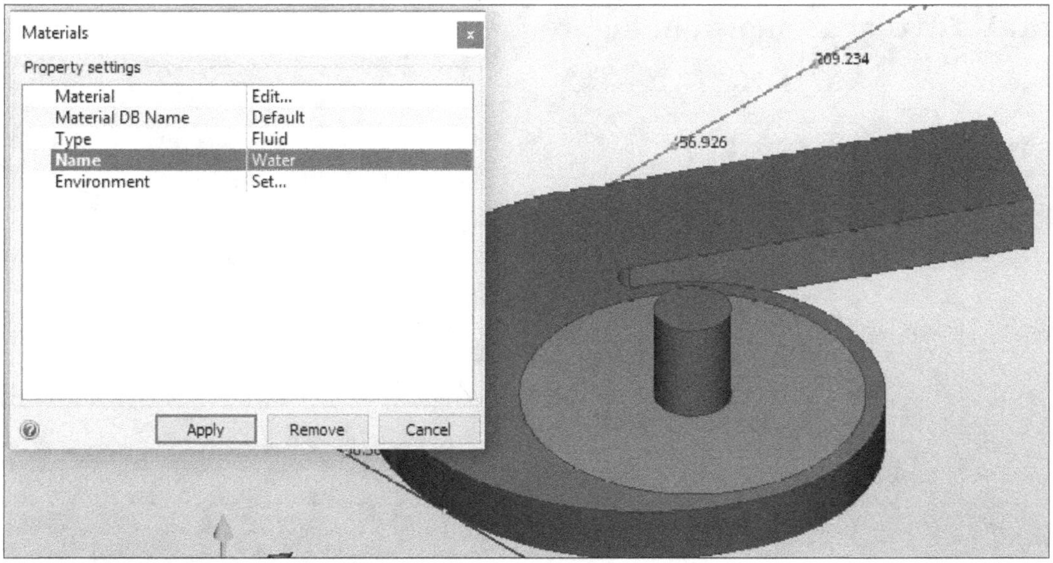

Figure-3. Specifying material to components

- Click on the **Impeller** from Graphics Window or **Design Study Bar** and click on **Edit** button. The **Materials** dialog box will be displayed.
- Select the **Type** as **Solid** and **Name** as **Aluminium** in **Materials** dialog box, and click on **Apply** button. The material will be applied to selected parts.

Applying Rotating Region Material

- Hide the **Impeller** part from model and select the **Volume**. You can also select **Volume** from **Design Study Bar**, without hiding **Impeller**; refer to Figure-4.

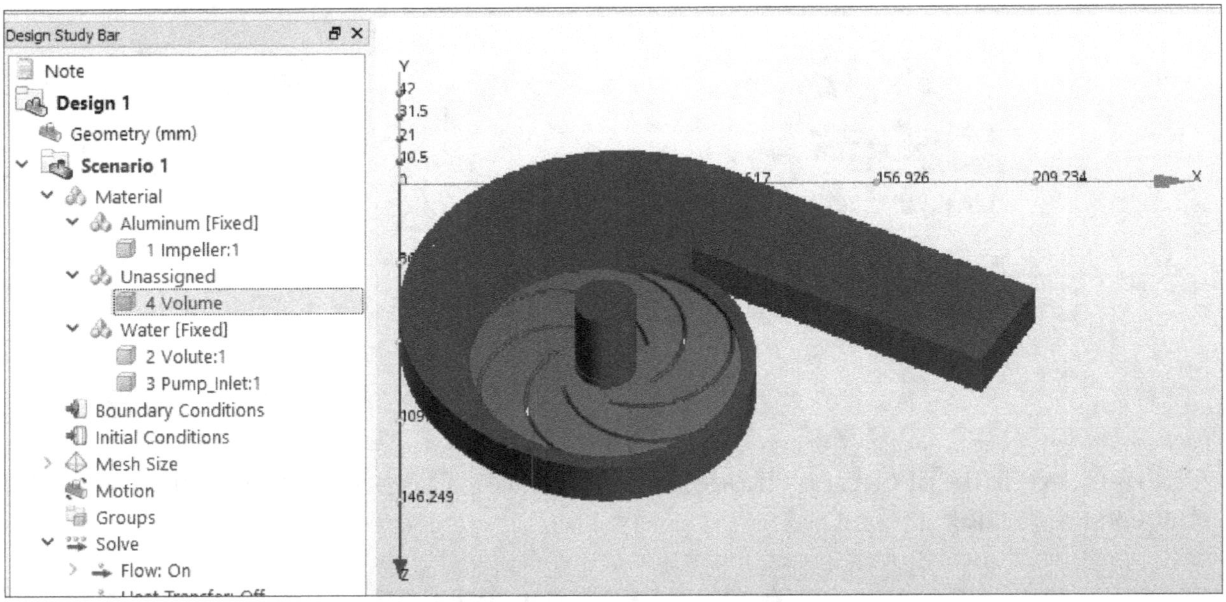

Figure-4. Selecting Volume part

- Click on the **Edit** button from the **Materials** panel and click on **Type** drop-down from **Materials** dialog box and select the **Rotating Region** option to create a rotating region material.
- Click on the **Edit** button from **Material** dialog box; the **Material Editor** dialog box will be displayed.
- Specify the parameters: **Name** as **Rotor**, **Save to database** as **My Materials**, **Scenario Type** as **Known Rotational Speed** option in **Material Editor** dialog box and specify the parameters of **Rotational speed** section (displayed at right of **Material Editor**) as shown in Figure-5.

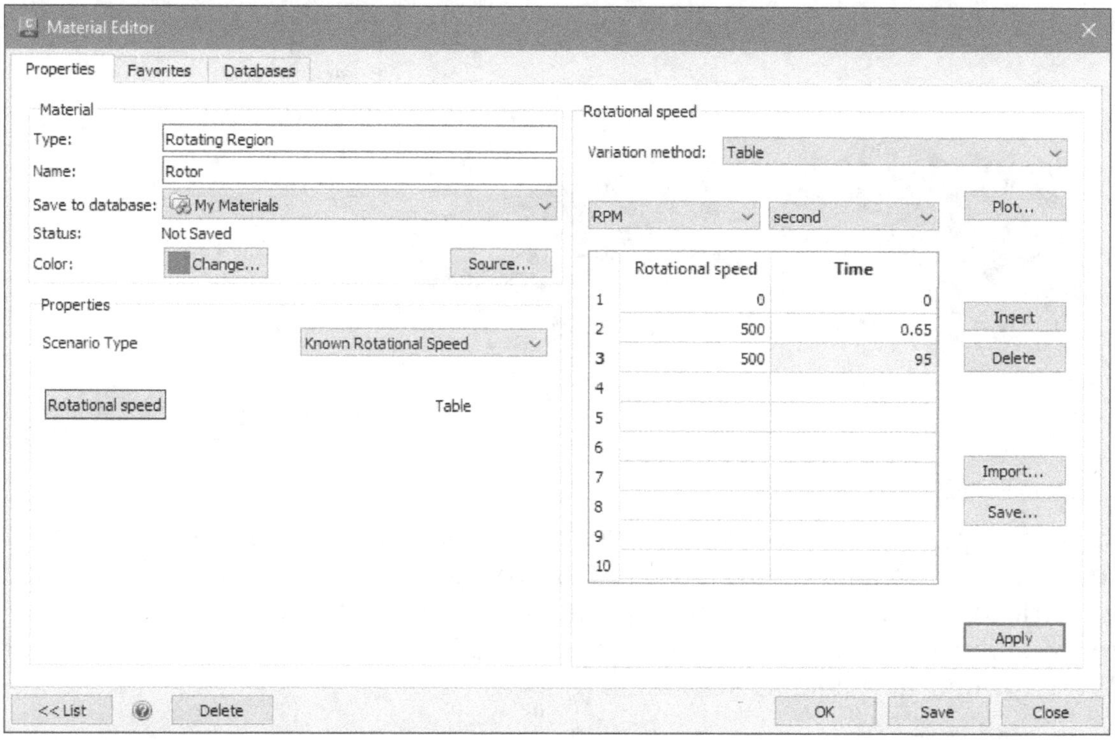

Figure-5. Specifying parameters of Rotational speed

- The values in the table are specified to ramp up the rotational speed of the impeller gradually to avoid impulsive start. This technique often reduces analysis instability, and improves overall accuracy of the solution.
- After specifying the parameters, click on **Apply** button and then the **Save** button to save variation at desired location with specified name. Click on the **OK** button from the **Material Editor** dialog box to save and apply changes in the material. You will be returned to **Materials** dialog box and recently created material will be mentioned there as **Rotor** in the **Name** field.
- Click on the **Axis of Rotation** button and select the **Y** axis from **Axis of Rotation** dialog box. Here, Y axis refers to rotation axis along which impeller rotates.
- After specifying the parameters in **Materials** dialog box, click on **Apply** button. The material will be applied.

Assign Boundary Conditions

We have created and applied necessary materials to all components of model and now we will assign boundary conditions to model.

- Activate the **Boundary Conditions** tool and click on the **Edit** button from the **Boundary Conditions** panel in the **Setup** tab of **Ribbon**. The **Boundary Conditions** dialog box will be displayed.
- Select the **Inlet** and **Outlet** surfaces from the model; refer to Figure-6.

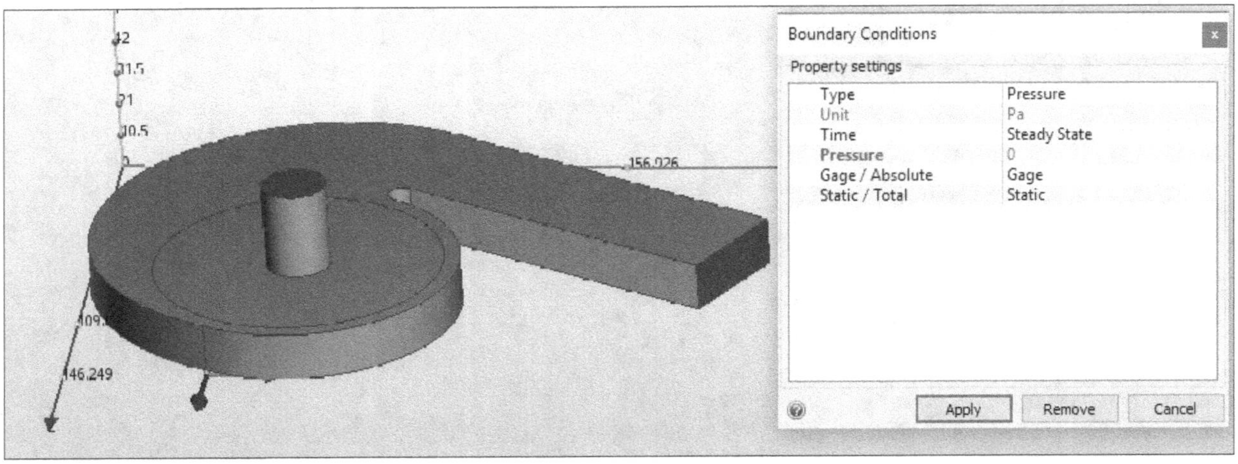

Figure-6. Selecting inlet and outlet surface

- Specify the parameters of **Type** as **Pressure**, **Unit** as **Pa**, and **Pressure** as **0** in the **Boundary conditions** dialog box. We are assigning the zero pressure to both inlet and outlet because fluid is flowing naturally without use of any external force.
- After specifying the parameters, click on **Apply** button. The boundary conditions will be applied to selected surfaces.

Generating Mesh

Generating mesh is kind of an easy task when using auto sizing, but we need to refine the mesh of impeller for creating uniform mesh of whole model.

- Activate the **Mesh Sizing** tool and click on **Autosize** button from **Automatic sizing** panel. The meshing will be created on the model.
- To make the mesh of rotating region uniform for rotating analyses, hide the impeller and right-click on volume. The right-click shortcut menu will be displayed.
- Select the **Edit** option from the right-click shortcut menu. The **Mesh Sizes** dialog box will be displayed.
- Click in the **Size adjustment** edit box and specify the value as **2**, or move the slider to value **2**.
- Click on the **Use Uniform** button for uniform mesh, click on **Apply changes** button and then **Spread Changes** button to apply and spread this setting to whole model.
- Click on **Apply** button to apply the mesh changes; refer to Figure-7.

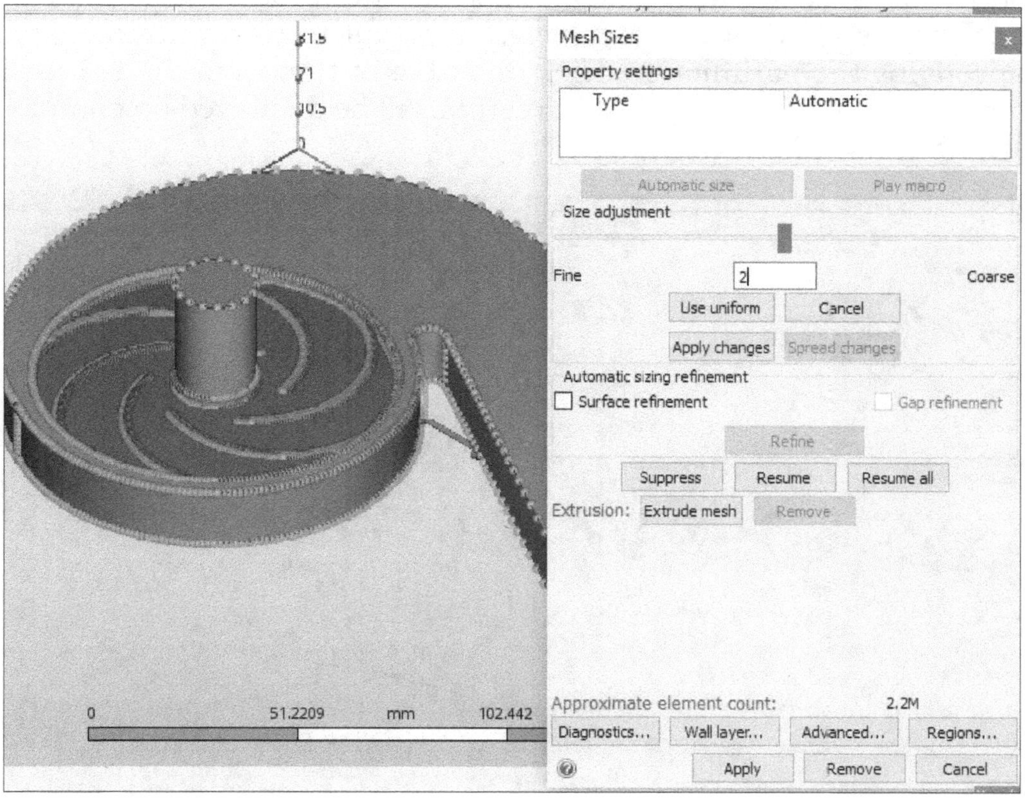

Figure-7. Refining mesh

Solving Analysis

- Click on the **Solve** tool from the **Simulation** panel to solve the analysis. The **Solve** dialog box will be displayed.
- Set the **Solution Mode** to **Transient** option and click in the **Time Step Size** field, the **Time Step Size** dialog box will be displayed. The **Time Step Size** option is used to run several complete rotations quickly. We will use **Time Step Size** such that the impeller rotates a complete blade passage with every time step.
- Select the **Number of blades** radio button from **Time Step Size** dialog box and specify the value as **6** in the edit box of dialog box.
- Click on **Calculate** button. This sets the time step value as **0.02**; refer to Figure-8. Close the **Time Step Size** dialog box.

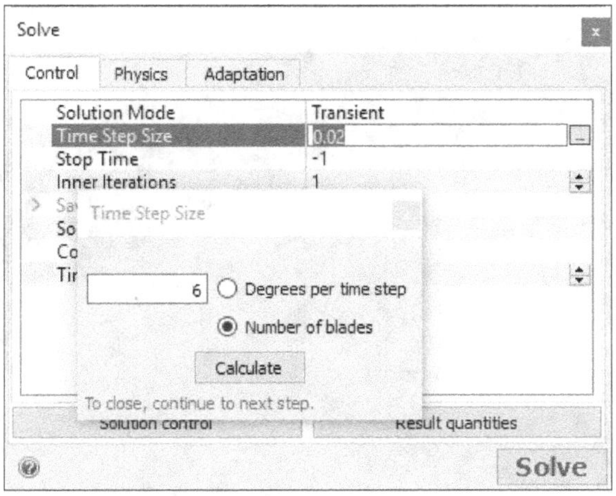

Figure-8. Time Step Size

- Expand the **Save Intervals** node and specify the value of **Results** as **5** and **Time Steps to Run** as **70**. This allows impeller to complete 10 revolutions at full speed.
- After specifying the parameters, click on **Solve** button from the **Solve** dialog box. The software starts the analysis and results will be displayed on completion; refer to Figure-9.

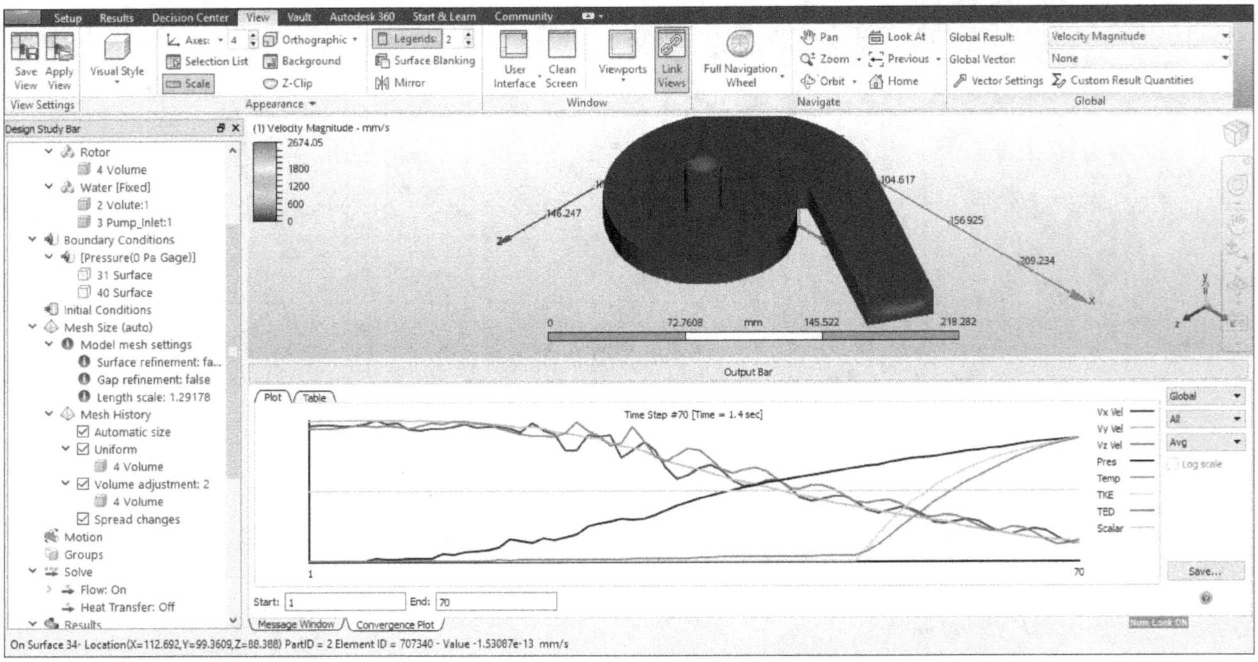

Figure-9. Practical 2 completed analysis

Results

Now, we will examine the velocity results using a cutting plane and vectors.

- Click on the **Planes** tool from **Results Tasks** panel of **Results** tab in the **Ribbon** and click on the **Add** button from the **Planes** panel. The plane will be added along X axis.
- Left-click on plane and set Y axis from displayed menu. Hold the Y triad axis and move the plane downward normal to the model; refer to Figure-10.

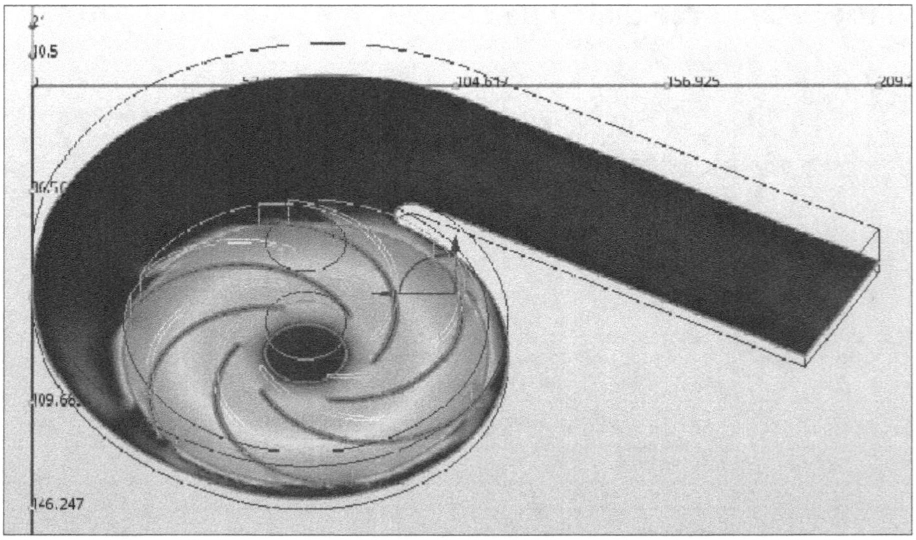

Figure-10. Moving triad axis normal to plane

Animating Velocity Results

Animating the results provide the time history of results. In this model, it is very helpful to understand the flow inside the pump. The animation process helps us to understand how the flow evolves and how long it takes the pump to achieve steady state. The process to view animation is discussed next.

- Right-click on the **Results** node in the **Design Study Bar** and select the **Animation** option from the shortcut menu. The **Animation** dialog box will be displayed; refer to Figure-11.

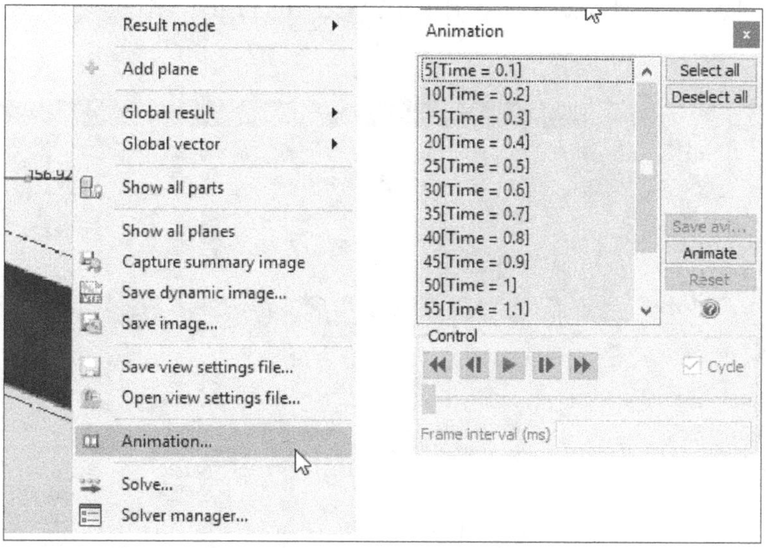

Figure-11. Animation button and Animation dialog box

- Click on **Animate** button from the **Animation** dialog box to activate the animation controls.
- Use the animation control buttons to view the animation.

Note- Due to the animated results, you might not able to see the animation of rotating impeller because the time step was equal to amount of time for single passage to rotate. However, you may see the velocity develop through the impeller and move into volute.

Volume Flow Rate

In this step, we will use Summary Planes and the Critical Values section to access volume flow rate at the current operating point.

- Change the visual style of model to **Outline** and the process to do so has been discussed many times in this book.
- Click on **Make Summary** tool from **Planes** panel to make the plane as summary plane.
- Activate the **Decision Center** tab and update the summary values; refer to Figure-12.

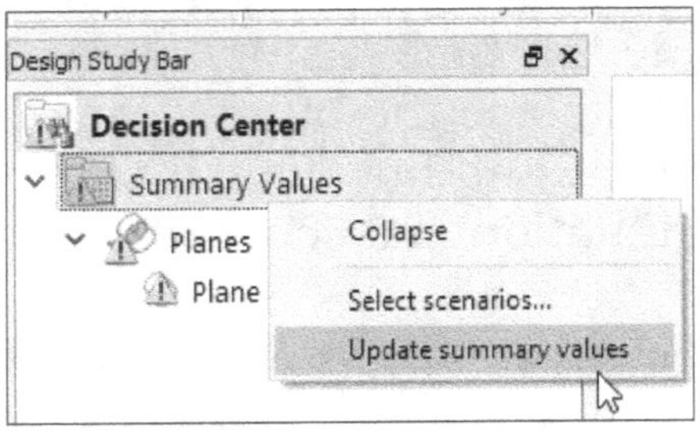

Figure-12. Updating-Summary Values

- The **Summary Plane data** will be displayed at right after updating data; refer to Figure-13.

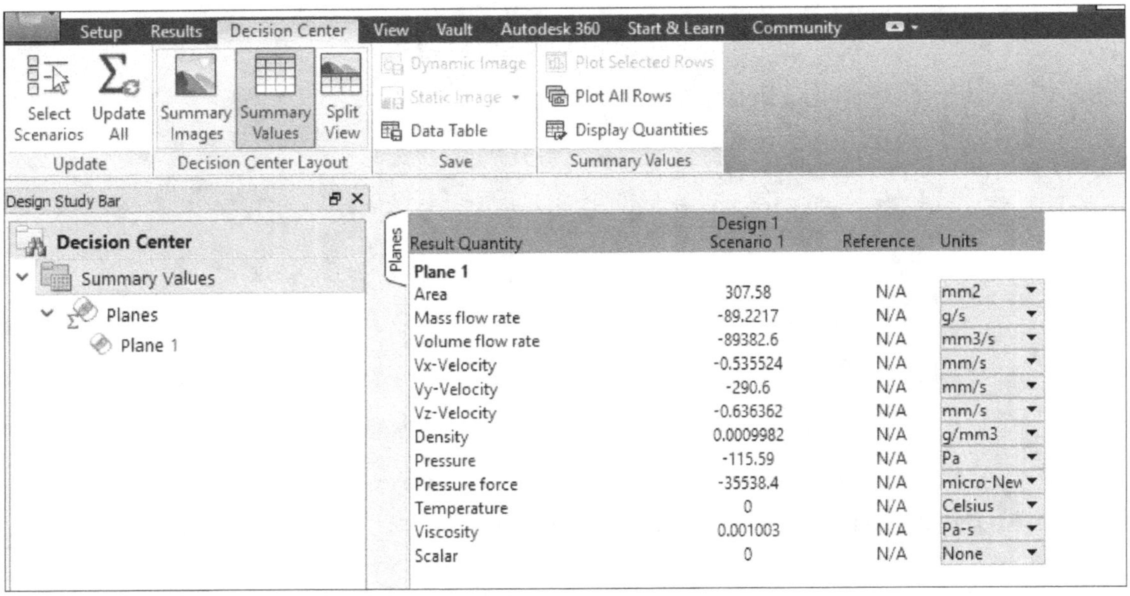

Figure-13. Summary Values data

PRACTICAL 5

In this practical, we will study the external flow aerodynamics around a car. In this model, we need to create an external volume around the model. The air flows around the car at a speed of 90 mph.

Opening the Model

- Double-click on Autodesk CFD icon from Desktop. The welcome screen will be displayed.
- Click on the **New** button from the **Quick Access Toolbar**. The **New Design Study** dialog box will be displayed.
- Browse the **Aerodynamic Model.ipt** file from **Practical 5** folder and specify the **Name** as **Practical 5** in the **New Design Study** dialog box. Click on **Create** button. The model will be displayed; refer to Figure-14. Also, the **Geometry Tools** dialog box will be displayed. Click on the **Merge** button from the dialog box and close it.

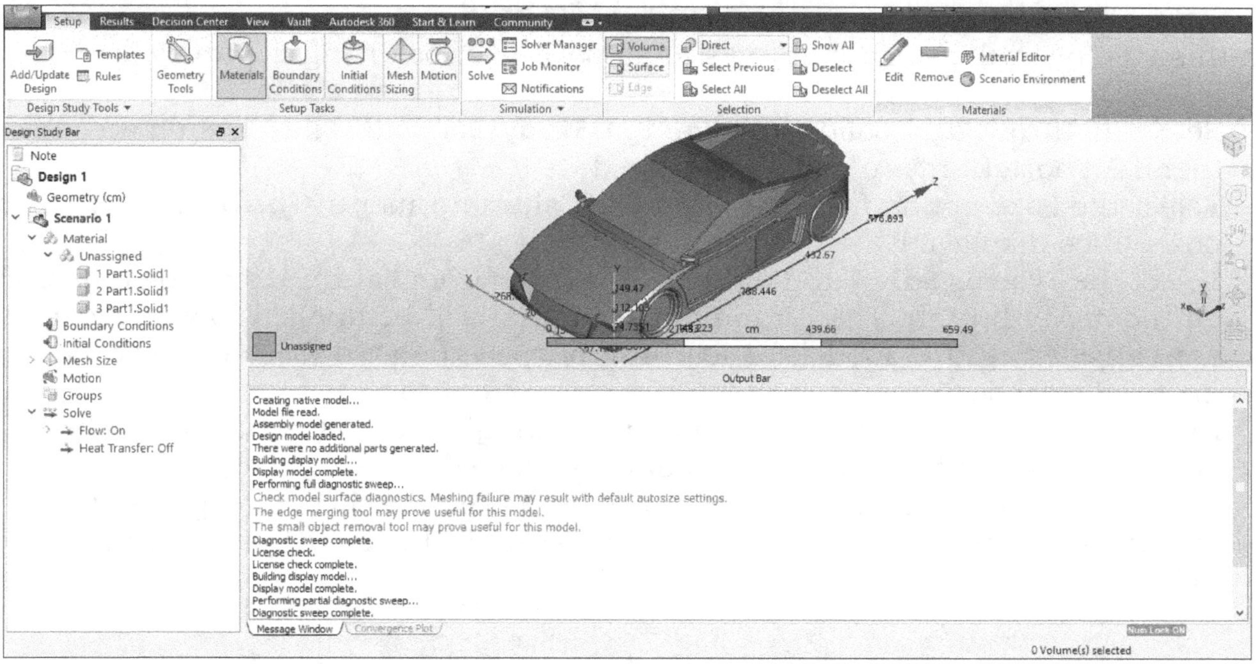

Figure-14. Practical 5

- Change the units from **CM** to **MM** from the **Design Study Bar**.

Creating External Volume

- Click on the **Geometry Tools** button from the **Setup Tasks** tab. The **Geometry Tools** dialog box will be displayed.
- Select the **Ext. Volume** tab from the top in the dialog box. The options to create external volume will displayed.
- Change the parameters of external volume as displayed in Figure-15, and click on **Create** button from **Geometry Tools** dialog box. The volume will be created. Close the **Geometry Tools** dialog box.

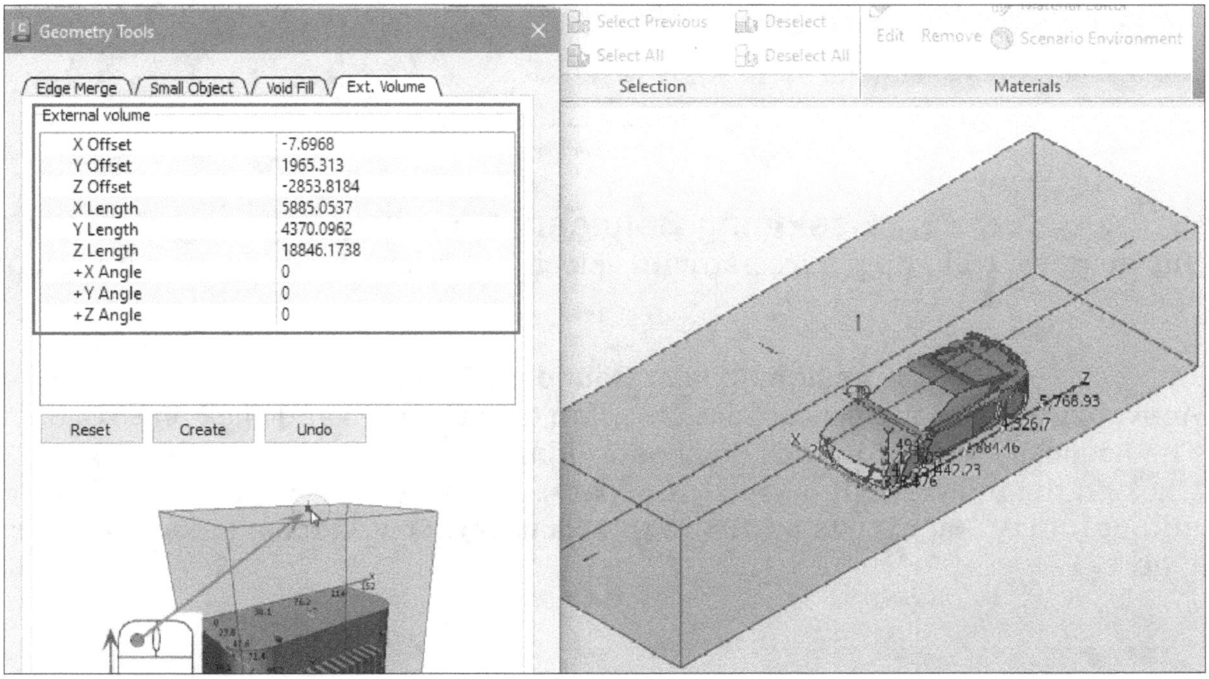

Figure-15. Parameters of external volume

- A new volume named as **CFDCreatedVolume** will be displayed in **Design Study Bar**.

Assigning Material

In this step, we will assign materials to all part before starting the analysis.

- Select all three Part1 solids from **Design Study Bar** and right-click on any one of them. A shortcut menu will be displayed.
- Select the **Edit** option from the right-click shortcut menu. The **Materials** dialog box will be displayed.
- Select the **Type** as **Solid** and **Name** as **Aluminium** from **Materials** dialog box. Click on the **Apply** button. The Aluminium material will be applied to whole car. We are considering this model for learning purpose only so please forgive for this material selection.
- Right-click on the **Unassigned** option from **Design Study Bar** and select the **Edit** option. The **Materials** dialog box will be displayed.
- Select the **Type** as **Fluid** and **Name** as **Air** from the **Materials** dialog box and click on the **Apply** button. The **Air** material will be applied to CFDCreatedVolume; refer to Figure-16.

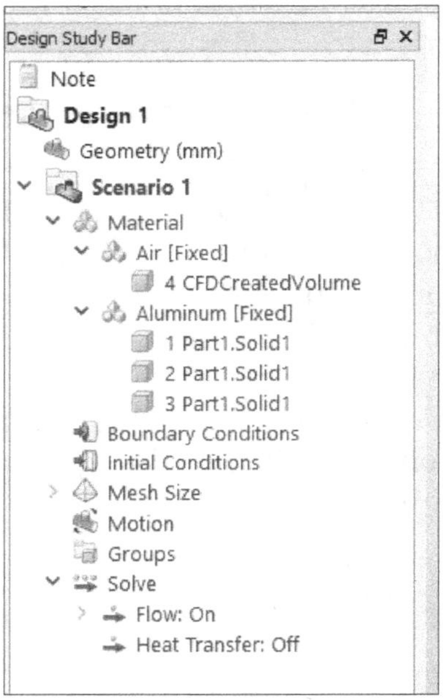

Figure-16. Applied material

Assigning Boundary Condition

In this step, we will apply a free stream velocity to inlet face and pressure to outlet face.

Assigning Inlet Boundary Condition

- Activate the **Boundary Conditions** tool from the **Setup** tab and click on **Edit** button. The **Boundary Conditions** dialog box will be displayed
- Click on the Inlet face and specify the parameters: **Type** as **Velocity**, **Unit** as **mph**, and **Velocity Magnitude** as **100** in the **Boundary Conditions** dialog box; refer to Figure-17.

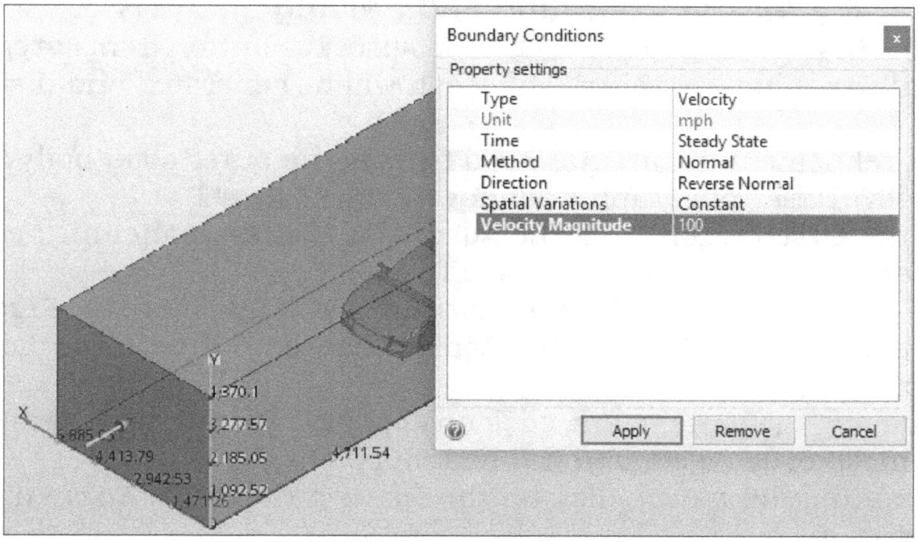

Figure-17. Assigning Inlet boundary condition

- After specifying the parameters, click on **Apply** button. The inlet boundary condition will be applied.

Assigning Outlet Boundary Condition

- Select the outlet face and click on **Edit** button from displayed context menu; the **Boundary Conditions** dialog box will displayed.
- Specify the parameters: **Type** as **Pressure**, **Unit** as **atm**, and **Pressure** as **1** in the **Boundary Conditions** dialog box; refer to Figure-18.

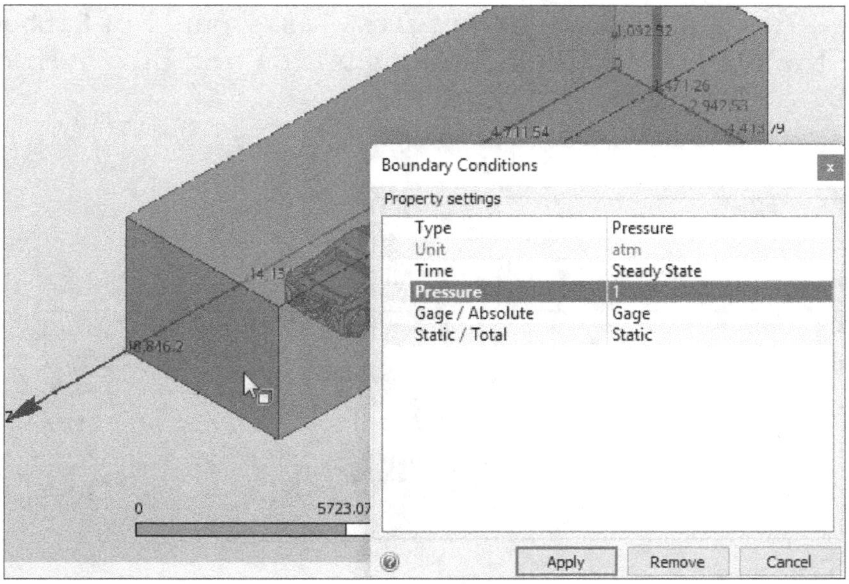

Figure-18. Outlet boundary condition of Practical 5

- After specifying the parameters, click on **Apply** button. The outlet boundary condition will be applied.
- Till now, we have applied materials to all components and boundary condition to inlet as well as outlet faces. Now, it's time to generate the mesh and solve the analysis.

Mesh Generating and Solving analysis

- Activate the **Mesh Sizing** tool and click on **Autosize** button from **Automatic Sizing** contextual panel in the **Ribbon**. The mesh will be generated and displayed in the model.
- For mesh refinement of car, you need to hide the outer solid body. So, hide the **CFDCreatedVolume** from graphic window using **CTRL+MMB**.
- Click on the **Edit** button from the **Automatic Sizing** panel in the **Ribbon**. The **Mesh Sizes** dialog box will be displayed.
- Select the car to activate the **Size adjustment** slider and move the **Size adjustment** slider to make it **0.9**. Click on the **Apply Changes** button from the **Mesh Sizes** dialog box.
- After specifying the parameters, click on **Apply** button from the **Mesh Sizes** dialog box. The mesh of selected area will be refined.
- After generating the mesh, click on the **Solve** button. The **Solve** dialog box will be displayed.
- Set the **Iterations to Run** as **100** and keep other setting of **Solve** dialog box to default.
- After specifying the parameters of **Solve** dialog box, click on **Solve** button. The software will start solving the analysis and results will be displayed on completion of analysis.

Results

In results, we are going to examine the velocity results using plane and vectors.

- Activate the **Planes** tool from the **Results Tasks** panel of **Ribbon** and click on **Add** button; the plane will be added along X axis and displayed on model; refer to Figure-19.

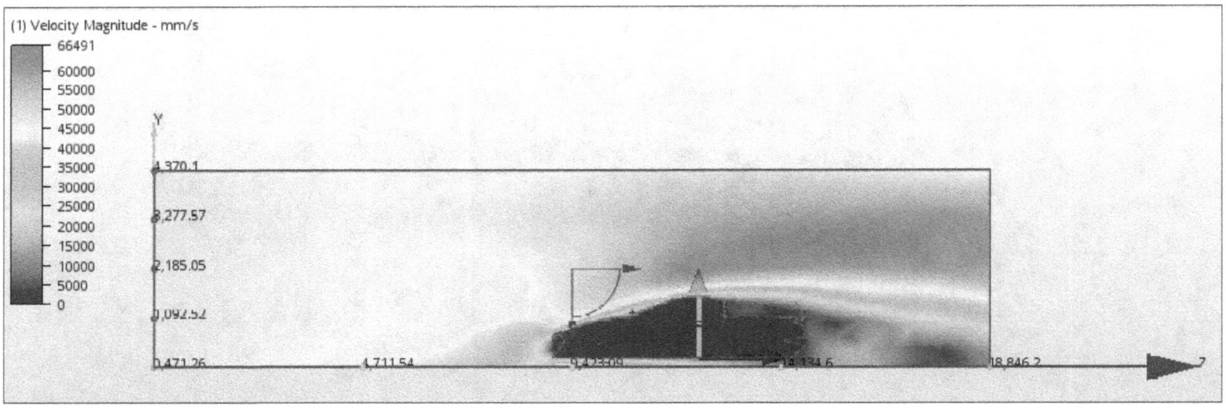

Figure-19. Added plane

- To display velocity vectors, click on the **Vector** drop-down from **Planes** panel and select **Velocity Vector**; the vectors will displayed on model.
- Now, we need to adjust the spacing of the vectors to check the air flow. Click on **Edit** button from the **Planes** contextual tab in **Ribbon**. The **Plane Control** dialog box will be displayed.
- Set the **Visual Style** of plane to **Outline** for clear view of vectors.
- Click on the **Vector settings** tab of the **Plane Control** dialog box.
- Select the **Length range** radio button and move the **Max** slider towards right to adjust the length range of vectors; refer to Figure-20.

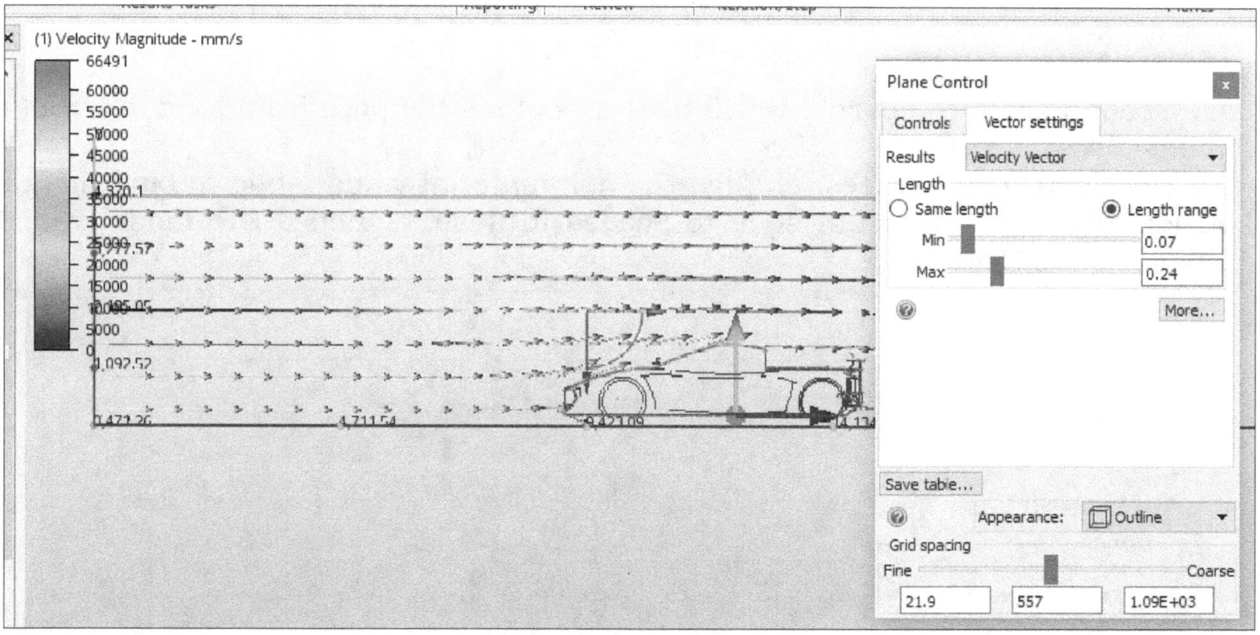

Figure-20. Vector Setting

- After adjusting the vectors, close the **Plane Control** dialog box.
- After analyzing results, remove the plane for particle traces analysis.

Particle Traces

In this step, we examine the velocity results using particle traces. Particle traces show the path of the fluid as it passes around the solid obstructions. We will use these particles to understand the flow path, circulation, and regions of swirl.

- Set the view of model towards inlet because we need to create a particle study and the origin of the particles would be at the inlet of model.
- Activate the **Traces** panel and click on **Add** button. The seeds will be attached with the cursor. The default parameters of traces are good for this study.
- Click on the inlet face to start seed distribution and click again to finalize it. You need to make a rectangle like shape on the half of inlet face; refer to Figure-21.

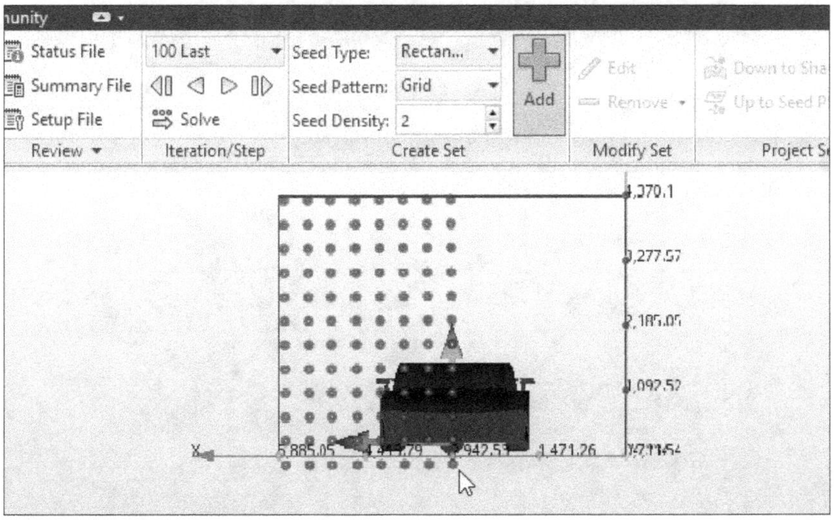

Figure-21. Creating seed distribution for Practical 5

You would know the reason behind apply the seed distribution on only half face later after few steps.

- On second click, the particles will be traces along the path from inlet to outlet of model.
- To clearly view the traces, change the **Air** material visual style to **Outline** and **Aluminium** material visual style to **Shaded** in **Results** node. The model will be displayed as Figure-22.

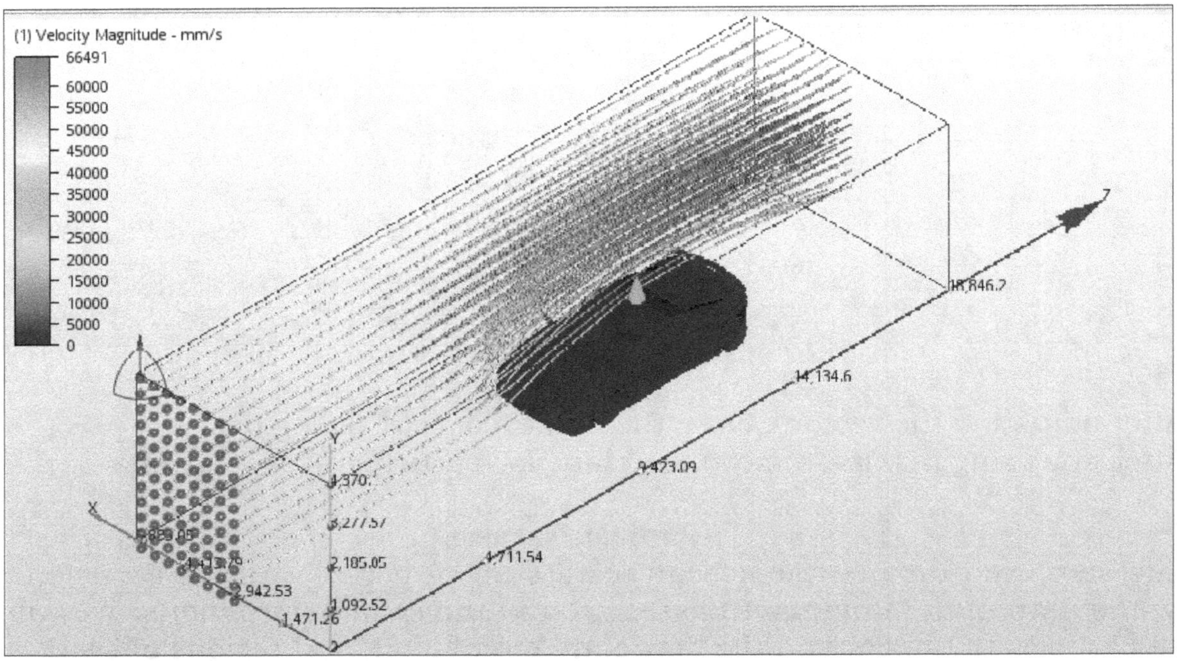

Figure-22. Traces

- With the help of yellow arrow, move the traces on the car to view the effects of traces; refer to Figure-23.

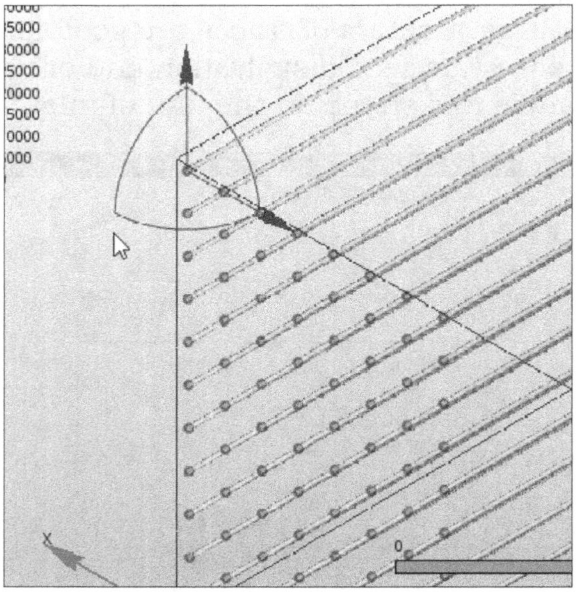

Figure-23. Moving seeds

Animation

- To animate the seeds from inlet to outlet of model, click on **Animate** button from **Process Traces** panel of **Results** tab in the **Ribbon**. The **Animate Traces** dialog box will be displayed.
- Use the animation control button to control the flow of traces; refer to Figure-24.

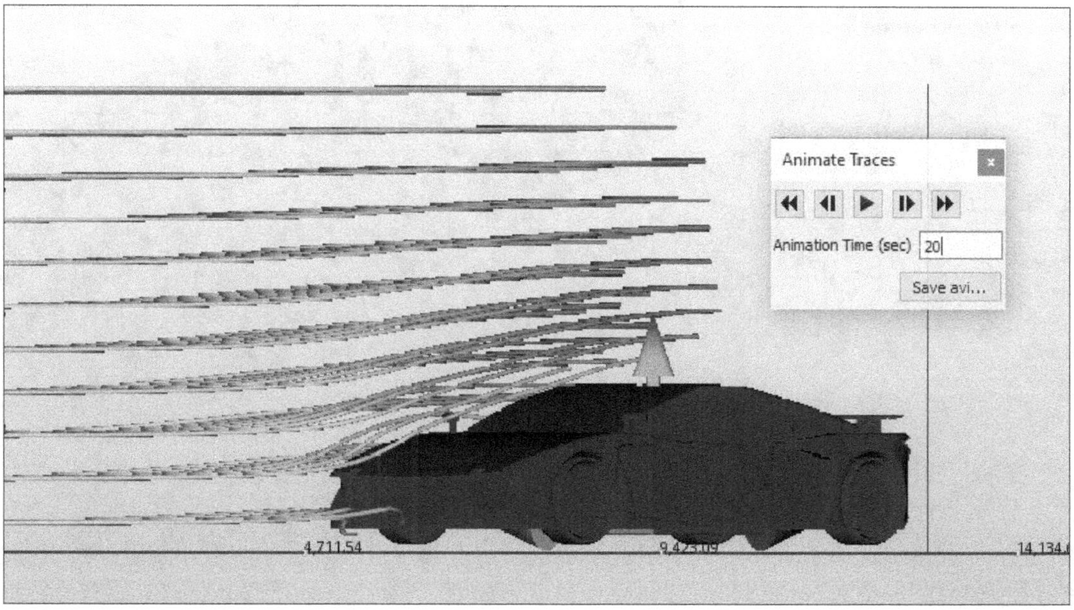

Figure-24. Animating traces

- To save this animation as a video file, click on the **Save avi**. button from the **Animate Traces** dialog box. The **Save AVI File** dialog box will be displayed.
- Set the destination folder and save the animation file.
- Similarly, you can save any type of result in animation mode using **Animate** button.
- Remove the traces for further analysis.

Aerodynamic Force

In this step, we compute the flow induced forces on the car using the **Wall Calculator** tool from **Results** tab.

- Click on the **Wall Calculator** tool from the **Result Tasks** panel of the **Results** tab in the **Ribbon**. The **Wall Results** dialog box will be displayed at the left in graphics area.
- Change the visual style of model from **Outline** to **Shaded** from **View** tab.
- Click on the **Select All** button from the **Wall Results** dialog box. The walls will be selected for analysis but we don't need outer walls, So deselect them using left mouse button; refer to Figure-25. Note that edges of deselected surfaces will not be highlighted.

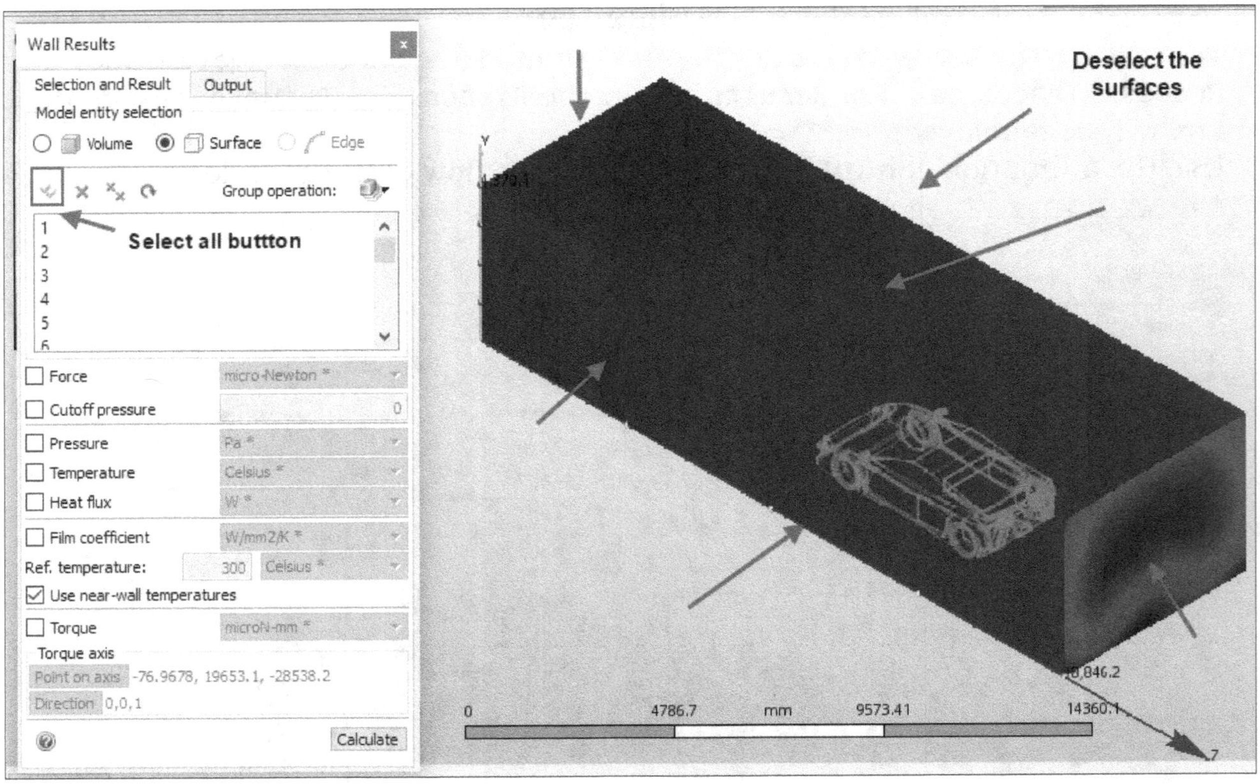

Figure-25. Deselect outer surface

- Select the **Force** radio button and change its unit to **Newton**. Click on the **Calculate** button. The **Output** tab will be displayed with calculated results.
- Scroll this list towards the end because the total force on the car is mentioned in summary section of this **Output** tab which is placed at last of **Output** tab; refer to Figure-26.

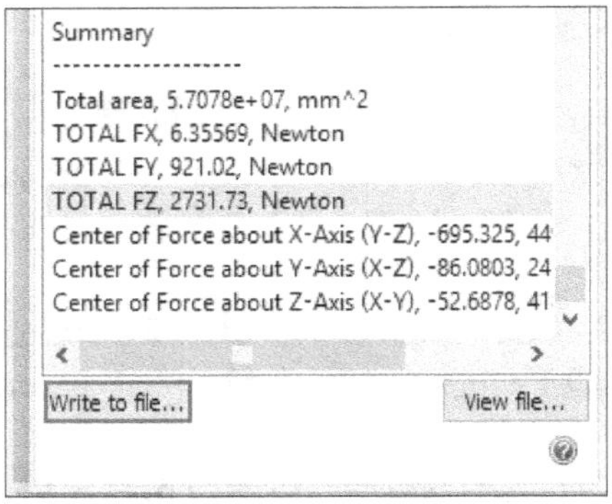

Figure-26. Total force on Car

PRACTICE 1

Below is a centrifugal pump used to mix two types of fluids. The model consists of two fluid inlet and a outlet. Oxygen and Hydrogen are the working fluid, and the centrifugal pump runs at 3000 RPM. The model is available in Practice 1 folder. The model is shown in Figure-27.

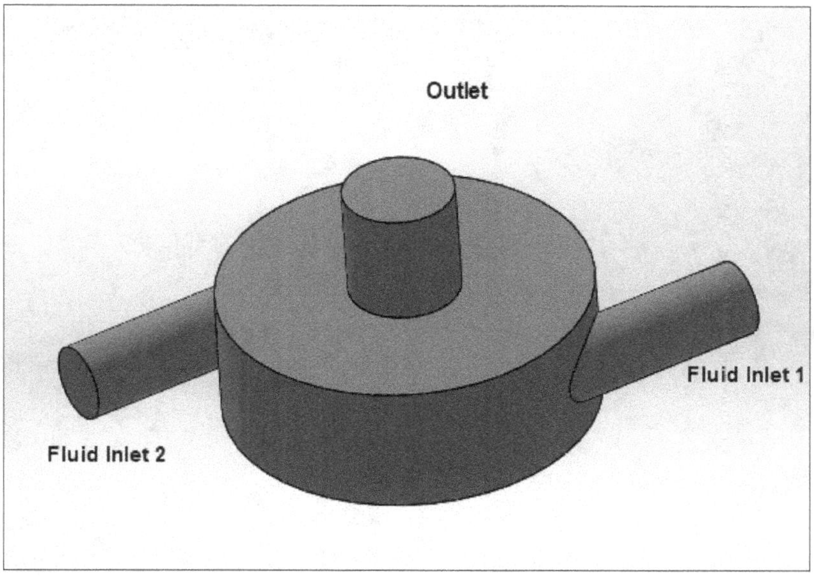

Figure-27. Practice 1

What you need to find is:

- Identify the flow distribution inside the pump due to mixing of two fluid.
- Animate development of flow through the pumps
- Determine the flow rate at outlet.

PRACTICE 2

In this model, there are two trees and two house. We need to assess just how hot the houses are going to get and how much shade they and the tree provide to each other. While creating analysis remember the below points:

- Create an external volume of height 20,000 MM like a square box above the ground level.
- Apply Air material to external volume, Brick material to House, Hardwood material to Tree.
- Assign temperature boundary condition to Environment and Ground.
- Refine the mesh size of 2 houses and trees.
- Create and assign a Grass material for ground; refer to Figure-28.

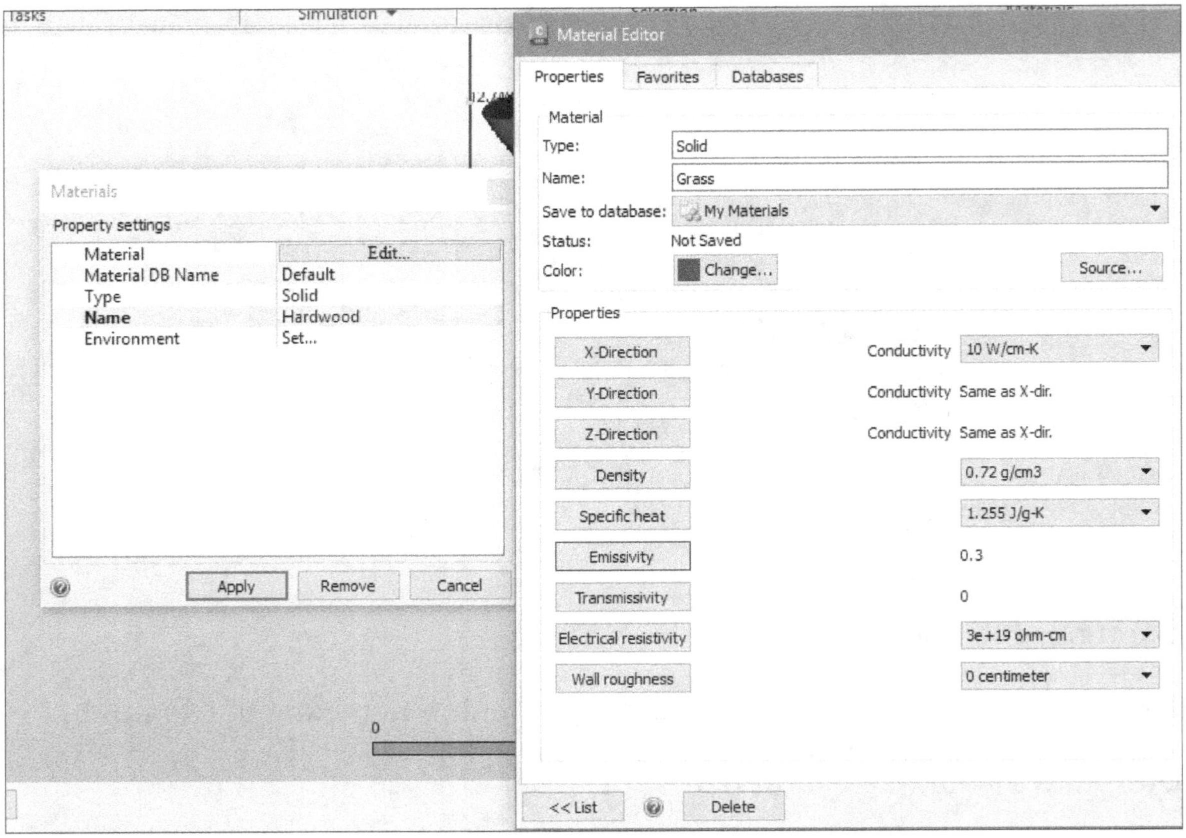

Figure-28. Grass Material

- The model of Practice 2 looks like Figure-29. This is an inventor file and air material should be created in Autodesk CFD.

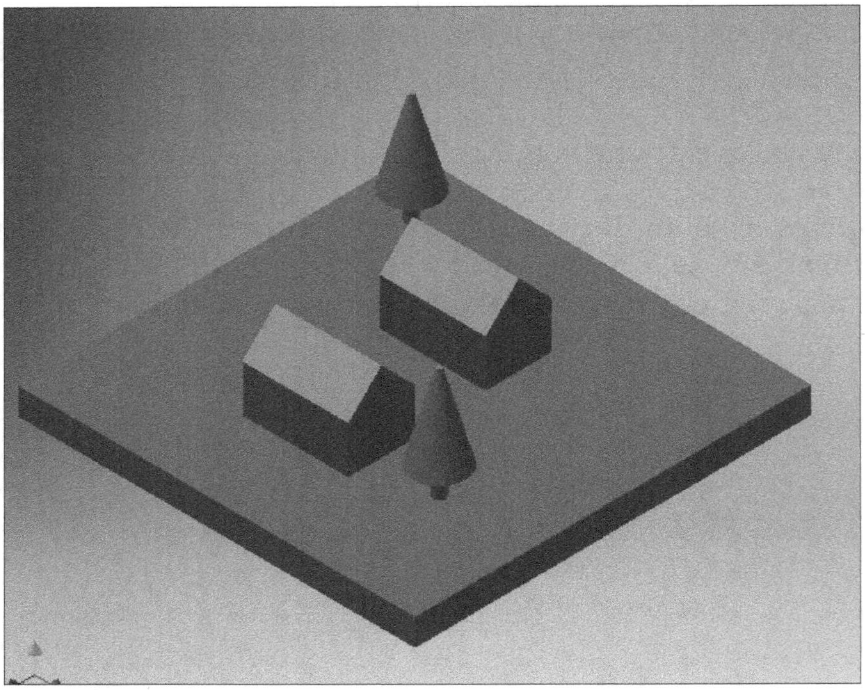

Figure-29. Model Practice 2

What you need to find is:

- Determine the temperature on surfaces of two houses.

PRACTICE 3

In this practice, we will study the compressible flow in a converging diverging nozzle. The geometry of this model is pretty simple; refer to Figure-30.

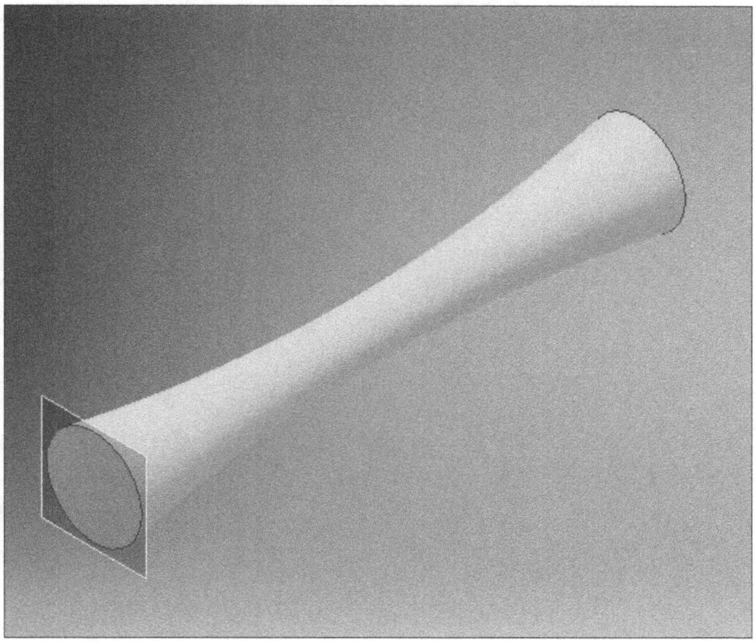

Figure-30. Practice 3

The converging-diverging nozzle has an exit area of 0.014 m^2 and a throat area of 0.008 m^2 resulting in an area ratio of 2. The inlet stagnation temperature is 600 K and the mass flow rate is known to be 4.2 kg/s. Use this information to determine the Mach number and pressure at inlet & outlet. In this practice, you need to :

- Visualize the flow within the nozzle and determine the outlet Mach number.
- Determine the pressure drop inside the model.

FOR STUDENTS NOTES

Index

D

E

F

G

H

I

www.ingramcontent.com/pod-product-compliance
Lightning Source LLC
LaVergne TN
LVHW080025210926
848481LV00011B/3105
* 9 7 8 1 7 7 4 5 9 2 1 2 0 *